MW01715968

THOMSON REUTERS

WESTLAW™

CHOOSE THE **TEXAS CODES** YOU NEED IN A CONVENIENT SOFTBOUND FORMAT!

West's® Texas Statutes and Codes

- Texas Business & Commerce Code
- Texas Civil Practice & Remedies Code
- Texas Corporation & Partnership Laws
- Texas Criminal & Motor Vehicle Code
- Texas Criminal Procedure – Code & Rules
- Texas Environmental Laws
- Texas Family Code
- Texas Finance Code
- Texas Insurance Code
- Texas Local Government Code
- Texas Penal Code
- Texas Probate Code
- Texas Property Code

Texas Annotated Codes Series

- Anderson, Bartlett & East's Texas Uniform Commercial Code Annotated
- Beyer's Texas Property Code Annotated
- Carlson's Texas Employment Laws Annotated
- Cooper, Hensley & Marshall's Texas Rules of Civil Procedure Annotated
- Elliott & Morris' Texas Tax Code Annotated
- Gaba's Texas Environmental Laws Annotated
- Hanby's Texas Rules of Appellate Procedure Annotated
- Johanson's Texas Probate Code Annotated
- Kinkeade & McColloch's Texas Penal Code Annotated
- McGehee's Texas Civil Practice and Remedies Code Annotated
- Roach's Texas Rules of Evidence Annotated
- Sampson & Tindall's Texas Family Code Annotated
- Texas Business Statutes Annotated
- Texas Civil Practice Statutes and Rules Annotated

For more information or to order:
Go to **legalsolutions.thomsonreuters.com**
or call **1-800-344-5009**

THOMSON REUTERS™

© 2013 Thomson Reuters **TX-1**

ROACH'S

TEXAS RULES OF EVIDENCE ANNOTATED

WITH FEDERAL RULES OF EVIDENCE APPENDIX

ANNOTATIONS BY

JOHN R. ROACH, JUSTICE (ret.), 5TH DISTRICT
COURT OF APPEALS OF TEXAS

MICHAEL J. MCCORMICK, PRESIDING JUDGE (ret.),
TEXAS COURT OF CRIMINAL APPEALS

2013 EDITION

THOMSON REUTERS™

Mat #: 41273966

© 2013 Thomson Reuters

ISBN: 978–0–314–65824–1

This publication was created to provide you with accurate and authoritative information concerning the subject matter covered; however, this publication was not necessarily prepared by persons licensed to practice law in a particular jurisdiction. The publisher is not engaged in rendering legal or other professional advice and this publication is not a substitute for the advice of an attorney. If you require legal or other expert advice, you should seek the services of a competent attorney or other professional.

West's and Westlaw are registered in the U.S. Patent and Trademark Office.

About the Authors

John R. Roach

John R. Roach served as a justice on the Fifth District Court of Appeals of Texas at Dallas until his retirement on June 30, 2001. Before his appointment to that position in 1997, he had served as the presiding judge of the 199th Judicial District Court in Collin County. He was first elected to that office in 1980 after defeating opposition in both primary and general elections of that year. He was reelected without opposition in 1984, 1988, 1992, and 1996. He was also reelected without opposition to the Court of Appeals in 1998 and 2000. For almost seventeen years Roach served as the local administrative judge of the district courts in Collin County and as Chairman of the Board of District Judges, performed additional service as the designated juvenile judge in Collin County, and served as Chairman of the Juvenile Board and as Chairman of the Collin County Purchasing Board. The new juvenile detention facility in Collin County is named the "John R. Roach Juvenile Detention Center."

Mr. Roach has been certified by the Texas Board of Legal Specialization as a specialist in Criminal Law from 1984-2011, in Civil Trial Law from 1987-2007, and in Family Law from 1984–1999.

Mr. Roach graduated from Auburn University at Montgomery, Alabama in May 1971, and received his B.A. in History. He worked full-time during the day and attended college at night. He completed all course requirements for graduation in two and one-half years. In 2009, Mr. Roach was named the Outstanding Graduate of the School of Liberal Arts at Auburn University at Montgomery, and he presented a lecture as a Distinguished Speaker. In January, 2010, Mr. Roach was also named one of the "Top 40" graduates of Auburn University at Montgomery in celebration of the 40 years since its establishment. Mr. Roach graduated from the University of Alabama School of Law in January, 1974. He worked full-time in the evenings and weekends and attended classes during the day. He completed law school in two and one-half years.

Mr. Roach was licensed to practice law in Texas in April 1974, and began his legal career as an assistant district attorney in the Dallas County District Attorney's Office. In 1975, he was assigned to the Specialized Crime Division and prosecuted complex "white collar" crime cases. He was in the general practice of law from 1979 until elected to the district court.

Until his appointment to the Texas Court of Appeals, Roach's legal career had been devoted exclusively to the trial of cases as a lawyer and as a judge. As a judge, Roach was recognized for his extensive and varied trial experience in civil, family and criminal law cases, including death penalty cases, his innovations in the trial of cases and docket management, and his keen observations on the practical aspects of litigation. He frequently speaks before professional organizations and citizen's groups on a variety of legal subjects related to the courts and to trials, and he often serves as a panelist or moderator at legal seminars. Mr. Roach retired on December 31, 2010, after eight years as Criminal District Attorney in Collin County, Texas. Mr. Roach was named the 2008 Lone Star Prosecutor by the Texas and District Attorneys Association on behalf of Texas prosecutors.

Roach is the author of *Roach's Texas Rules of Civil Evidence Annotated,* 1997 edition.

Judge Roach and his wife, Mery, live in Plano, Texas. They have four children: Kelli, Karin, John, and Brian; and eight grandchildren.

Michael J. McCormick

Michael J. McCormick retired as Presiding Judge of the Texas Court of Criminal Appeals on December 31, 2000. He was first elected to that post in a statewide election in 1988 after serving seven years as judge of that court. He was reelected as Presiding Judge in 1994.

As Presiding Judge, McCormick has served as a member of the Texas Judicial Council, the Judicial Redistricting Commission, and the State Law Library Board.

Judge McCormick received his Doctor of Jurisprudence from St. Mary's University School of Law at San Antonio in 1970. His undergraduate B.A. degree was received from the University of Texas at Austin with a major in history and a minor in chemistry and zoology. After being admitted to the Texas Bar in 1970, Judge McCormick began his legal career by serving as a Briefing Attorney to Judge Leon Douglas of the Texas Court of Criminal Appeals. He served as Assistant District Attorney in Travis County, Texas, as Chief Felony Prosecutor in the 167th Judicial District Court and as Chief of the Appellate Division of the Travis County District Attorney's Office in 1971 and 1972. Presiding Judge McCormick was Assistant Director of the Texas District and County Attorneys Association for four years before serving as the Executive Director of the Association through 1980.

Judge McCormick lectures at criminal law seminars and is the author of numerous criminal law manuals, articles and books, including Branch's Annotated Penal Code, 3rd edition and the Texas Justice Court Deskbook. He is the co-author of The Texas Practice Criminal Forms and Trial Manual. In addition, he has been an instructor in the Law Enforcement Department of Southwest Texas State University. He has served as vice chairman of the Commission on Sentencing, director of the Texas Center for the Judiciary, a member of the Judicial Budget Board, a director of the State Bar of Texas, and as a member of numerous State Bar committees.

Judge McCormick was named recipient of the Rosewood Gavel Award from St. Mary's Law School in 1984. In 1992, he was named the Distinguished Law Graduate by St. Mary's University School of Law.

Judge McCormick and his wife, Kathy, have two children, Kelley and Karen.

Publisher's Preface

This publication is designed to provide a compact and authoritative presentation of the recently adopted Texas Rules of Evidence. The publication is intended to combine the most salient features of an unannotated code—compactness and portability—and those of a fully annotated code—interpretive materials—into a single publication incorporating the essential features of both. Thus, the publication contains the text of the Texas Rules of Evidence, accompanied by interpretive aids which have been constructed by the authors and publisher's editorial staff to provide materials which are highly focused, concise, practical, and authoritative. As an additional interpretive and practice aid, the Federal Rules of Evidence, accompanied by the Advisory Committee Notes, are included in an Appendix.

The Commentary, Leading Cases and Leading CLE/Law Review materials have been prepared by the authors. The remainder of the editorial components have been prepared by the editorial staff of the publisher. These components include references to Texas Jurisprudence, Texas Practice, American Jurisprudence (Am Jur) Trials, American Jurisprudence (Am Jur) Proof of Facts through the 3d, American Law Reports (ALR) 3rd through 6th, and ALR Federal through the 2d.

This publication contains the text of the Texas Rules of Evidence, as amended and effective September 1, 2008, which represents the current version as of February 1, 2013. The text of the Federal Rules of Evidence reflects amendments received through January 1, 2013. References to other rules reflect the current versions of those rules and any amendments received through February 1, 2013: Texas Rules of Civil Evidence (1996); Texas Rules of Criminal Evidence (1996); Texas Rules of Civil Procedure; Texas Rules of Appellate Procedure (as amended and effective September 1, 2008). Reference to the Texas Code of Criminal Procedure and to statutes reflect those rules and statutes as amended through the Regular and First Called Sessions of the 82nd Texas Legislature (2011).

The Commentary and Leading Cases cover decisions published through 383 S.W.3d 814 (January 8, 2013).

The Leading CLE/Law Review materials cover course materials, articles, and notes published through January 1, 2013, with particular emphasis upon the following CLE materials:

Advanced Civil Trial Course, State Bar of Texas 2000–2012

Advanced Family Law Course, State Bar of Texas 2000–2012

Advanced Criminal Law Course, State Bar of Texas 2000–2012

Advanced Personal Injury Law Course, State Bar of Texas 2000–2012

To order additional copies of Roach's Texas Rules of Evidence Annotated, call 1–800–344–5009.

*

Authors' Preface

In our experience, there are few, if any, legal subjects more important than the law of evidence. The pervasiveness of evidentiary issues affects the work of all attorneys, including those who have never been in a courtroom. Any attorney's work may one day be challenged in court or relied on as a defense. It is litigation that drives the legal profession. Victory or defeat often turns on a rule of evidence and its correct application. Knowing how to prove the facts essential to a claim or defense, or to prevent an opponent from doing so, lies at the core of what trial lawyers do.

This book is intended to be actually useful in the heat of trial, as well as in the relative calm of trial preparation or in the preparation of an appeal. For the lawyer who never appears in court, this book can provide the context within which he can view his work, which may become the subject of future litigation. For the judge, this book should provide the answers to most of those pesky questions about evidence and about the obligations and the authority of the court in determining the admissibility of evidence that arise in every trial. It will also provide valuable insight to those really tough questions that appear in cases from time to time.

While the Texas Rules of Evidence favor the admissibility of relevant evidence, there are other rules of evidence in Texas with which to be concerned. (The legislature has its own view of the rules of evidence and when, whether and how they should apply in certain contexts, the Constitutions of the State of Texas and of the United States occasionally have some bearing on evidentiary matters, and case law creates still other rules.) Very few of the rules stand alone and outside the context of the other rules. A thorough understanding of the Texas Rules of Evidence requires an understanding of their relationships to one another and to the rules of procedure in civil and criminal cases, as well as how they are affected by constitutional law, statutes and case law. We intended, among other things, that this book be a practical and useful source from which many of those relationships could be recognized and practically applied.

We have again included an appendix containing the Federal Rules of Evidence along with extensive Notes. Texas courts give great weight to federal court interpretation of the Federal Rules of Evidence where the language in the federal rule is identical to that of the Texas rule. Where we are aware of them, we have also included in the commentaries to the state rules the recent changes to the similar Federal Rules of Evidence. We have done so in order to apprise our readers of possible future changes in some of the Texas rules. Presumably, the Advisory Committee on the Rules of the Judicial Conference of the United States considers the recent changes in the Federal Rules of Evidence to be improvements which reduce problems with the rules that have arisen in practice.

Again, we have included cites to some websites to assist in keeping up with rapid changes in the law of evidence arising from significant appellate decisions by Texas and other state and federal courts.

The law of evidence changes frequently and occasionally significantly, so there will be future editions of this book. We invite readers who wish to comment on this book to do so, particularly those who have suggestions on its improvement or of cases that should be cited.

John R. Roach
Plano, Texas

Michael J. McCormick
Austin, Texas

*

Acknowledgment by John Roach

Very little that is truly worthwhile is accomplished alone. This book is no exception. My thanks to Terrie Jenevein for urging me to undertake the original of this project, and to our original and former editor, Jim Watson, who did good work and whose ideas and suggestions greatly improved the usefulness of this book. My thanks, too, to the co-author of this book, Judge Michael McCormick.

I also want to acknowledge the occasional assistance of one of my daughters, Kelli Roach, a Texas lawyer, and one of my sons, John R. Roach, Jr., a Texas judge.

*

Dedication by John Roach

This book is dedicated to my wife, Mery, to whom I have been married for more than 47 years, to our now grown children, Kelli, Karin, John, and Brian, to our daughter in law, Laura Bohlman Roach, and to our eight grandchildren, Jared, Nathan, Danielle, Austin, Michael, John, Jacob, and Jack.

*

Table of Contents

TEXAS RULES OF EVIDENCE

ARTICLE I. GENERAL PROVISIONS

Rule		Page
101.	Title and Scope	2
102.	Purpose and Construction	4
103.	Rulings on Evidence	5
104.	Preliminary Questions	11
105.	Limited Admissibility	15
106.	Remainder of or Related Writings or Recorded Statements	16
107.	Rule of Optional Completeness	18

ARTICLE II. JUDICIAL NOTICE

201.	Judicial Notice of Adjudicative Facts	20
202.	Determination of Law of Other States	24
203.	Determination of the Laws of Foreign Countries	26
204.	Determination of Texas City and County Ordinances, the Contents of the Texas Register, and the Rules of Agencies Published in the Administrative Code	27

ARTICLE III. PRESUMPTIONS

[Reserved]

ARTICLE IV. RELEVANCY AND ITS LIMITS

401.	Definition of "Relevant Evidence"	31
402.	Relevant Evidence Generally Admissible; Irrelevant Evidence Inadmissible	31
403.	Exclusion of Relevant Evidence on Special Grounds	37
404.	Character Evidence Not Admissible to Prove Conduct; Exceptions; Other Crimes	40
405.	Methods of Proving Character	45
406.	Habit; Routine Practice	46
407.	Subsequent Remedial Measures; Notification of Defect	47
408.	Compromise and Offers to Compromise	49
409.	Payment of Medical and Similar Expenses	51
410.	Inadmissibility of Pleas, Plea Discussions and Related Statements	52
411.	Liability Insurance	53
412.	Evidence of Previous Sexual Conduct in Criminal Cases	54

ARTICLE V. PRIVILEGES

Rule		Page
501.	Privileges Recognized Only as Provided	57
502.	Required Reports Privileged by Statute	65
503.	Lawyer–Client Privilege	65
504.	Husband–Wife Privileges	72
505.	Communications to Members of the Clergy	76
506.	Political Vote	77
507.	Trade Secrets	78
508.	Identity of Informer	80
509.	Physician–Patient Privilege	82
510.	Confidentiality of Mental Health Information in Civil Cases	87
511.	Waiver of Privilege by Voluntary Disclosure	91
512.	Privileged Matter Disclosed Under Compulsion or Without Opportunity to Claim Privilege	92
513.	Comment Upon or Inference From Claim of Privilege; Instruction	92

ARTICLE VI. WITNESSES

601.	Competency and Incompetency of Witnesses	95
602.	Lack of Personal Knowledge	98
603.	Oath or Affirmation	99
604.	Interpreters	100
605.	Competency of Judge as a Witness	101
606.	Competency of Juror as a Witness	106
607.	Who May Impeach	105
608.	Evidence of Character and Conduct of a Witness	105
609.	Impeachment by Evidence of Conviction of Crime	108
610.	Religious Beliefs or Opinions	114
611.	Mode and Order of Interrogation and Presentation	115
612.	Writing Used to Refresh Memory	116
613.	Prior Statements of Witnesses: Impeachment and Support	118
614.	Exclusion of Witnesses	121
615.	Production of Statements of Witnesses in Criminal Cases	122

ARTICLE VII. OPINIONS AND EXPERT TESTIMONY

701.	Opinion Testimony by Lay Witnesses	125
702.	Testimony by Experts	128
703.	Bases of Opinion Testimony by Experts	143
704.	Opinion on Ultimate Issue	146
705.	Disclosure of Facts or Data Underlying Expert Opinion	147
706.	Audit in Civil Cases	149

ARTICLE VIII. HEARSAY

Rule		Page
801.	Definitions	151
802.	Hearsay Rule	156
803.	Hearsay Exceptions: Availability of Declarant Immaterial	157
804.	Hearsay Exceptions; Declarant Unavailable	172
805.	Hearsay Within Hearsay	176
806.	Attacking and Supporting Credibility of Declarant	176

ARTICLE IX. AUTHENTICATION AND IDENTIFICATION

901.	Requirement of Authentication or Identification	179
902.	Self–Authentication	182
903.	Subscribing Witness' Testimony Unnecessary	187

ARTICLE X. CONTENTS OF WRITINGS, RECORDINGS, AND PHOTOGRAPHS

1001.	Definitions	189
1002.	Requirement of Originals	190
1003.	Admissibility of Duplicates	190
1004.	Admissibility of Other Evidence of Contents	192
1005.	Public Records	193
1006.	Summaries	194
1007.	Testimony or Written Admission of Party	195
1008.	Functions of Court and Jury	195
1009.	Translation of Foreign Language Documents	196

APPENDIX: FEDERAL RULES OF EVIDENCE

ARTICLE I. GENERAL PROVISIONS

101.	Scope; Definitions	200
102.	Purpose	202
103.	Rulings on Evidence	203
104.	Preliminary Questions	207
105.	Limiting Evidence That Is Not Admissible Against Other Parties or for Other Purposes	211
106.	Remainder of or Related Writings or Recorded Statements	211

ARTICLE II. JUDICIAL NOTICE

201.	Judicial Notice of Adjudicative Facts	212

ARTICLE III. PRESUMPTIONS IN CIVIL CASES

Rule		Page
301.	Presumptions in Civil Cases Generally	218
302.	Applying State Law to Presumptions in Civil Cases	223

ARTICLE IV. RELEVANCY AND ITS LIMITS

401.	Test for Relevant Evidence	224
402.	General Admissibility of Relevant Evidence	225
403.	Excluding Relevant Evidence for Prejudice, Confusion, Waste of Time, or Other Reasons	227
404.	Character Evidence; Crimes or Other Acts	228
405.	Methods of Proving Character	234
406.	Habit; Routine Practice	236
407.	Subsequent Remedial Measures	237
408.	Compromise Offers and Negotiations	239
409.	Offers to Pay Medical and Similar Expenses	244
410.	Pleas, Plea Discussions, and Related Statements	245
411.	Liability Insurance	248
412.	Sex-Offense Cases: The Victim's Sexual Behavior or Predisposition	249
413.	Similar Crimes in Sexual-Assault Cases	257
414.	Similar Crimes in Child-Molestation Cases	266
415.	Similar Acts in Civil Cases Involving Sexual Assault or Child Molestation	267

ARTICLE V. PRIVILEGES

501.	Privilege in General	268
502.	Attorney–Client Privilege and Work Product; Limitations on Waiver	272

ARTICLE VI. WITNESSES

601.	Competency to Testify in General	283
602.	Need for Personal Knowledge	285
603.	Oath or Affirmation to Testify Truthfully	286
604.	Interpreter	286
605.	Judge's Competency as a Witness	287
606.	Juror's Competency as a Witness	288
607.	Who May Impeach a Witness	292
608.	A Witness's Character for Truthfulness or Untruthfulness	293
609.	Impeachment by Evidence of a Criminal Conviction	297
610.	Religious Beliefs or Opinions	306
611.	Mode and Order of Examining Witnesses and Presenting Evidence	307
612.	Writing Used to Refresh a Witness's Memory	312
613.	Witness's Prior Statement	314
614.	Court's Calling or Examining a Witness	315
615.	Excluding Witnesses	316

ARTICLE VII. OPINIONS AND EXPERT TESTIMONY

Rule		Page
701.	Opinion Testimony by Lay Witnesses	318
702.	Testimony by Expert Witnesses	320
703.	Bases of an Expert's Opinion Testimony	327
704.	Opinion on an Ultimate Issue	330
705.	Disclosing the Facts or Data Underlying an Expert's Opinion	331
706.	Court-Appointed Expert Witnesses	333

ARTICLE VIII. HEARSAY

801.	Definitions That Apply to This Article; Exclusions from Hearsay	339
802.	The Rule Against Hearsay	348
803.	Exceptions to the Rule Against Hearsay—Regardless of Whether the Declarant Is Available as a Witness	349
804.	Exceptions to the Rule Against Hearsay—When the Declarant Is Unavailable as a Witness	372
805.	Hearsay Within Hearsay	384
806.	Attacking and Supporting the Declarant's Credibility	385
807.	Residual Exception	388

ARTICLE IX. AUTHENTICATION AND IDENTIFICATION

901.	Authenticating or Identifying Evidence	388
902.	Evidence That Is Self-Authenticating	393
903.	Subscribing Witness's Testimony	397

ARTICLE X. CONTENTS OF WRITINGS, RECORDINGS, AND PHOTOGRAPHS

1001.	Definitions That Apply to This Article	398
1002.	Requirement of the Original	400
1003.	Admissibility of Duplicates	401
1004.	Admissibility of Other Evidence of Content	402
1005.	Copies of Public Records to Prove Content	403
1006.	Summaries to Prove Content	404
1007.	Testimony or Statement of a Party to Prove Content	404
1008.	Functions of Court and Jury	405

ARTICLE XI. MISCELLANEOUS RULES

1101.	Applicability of Rules	406
1102.	Amendments	412
1103.	Title	412

Table of Cases T–1
Index I–1

*

TEXAS RULES OF EVIDENCE

Effective March 1, 1998

ARTICLE I. GENERAL PROVISIONS

Rule
101. Title and Scope.
102. Purpose and Construction.
103. Rulings on Evidence.
104. Preliminary Questions.
105. Limited Admissibility.
106. Remainder of or Related Writings or Recorded Statements.
107. Rule of Optional Completeness.

Cross References

Evidence in Civil Actions Generally, V.T.C.A., Civil Practice & Remedies Code § 18.001 et seq.

Proof of Lost Records, V.T.C.A., Civil Practice & Remedies Code § 19.001 et seq.

Depositions, Civil Actions, V.T.C.A., Civil Practice & Remedies Code § 20.001 et seq.

Interpreters, Civil Actions, V.T.C.A., Civil Practice & Remedies Code § 21.001 et seq.

Witnesses, Civil Actions, V.T.C.A., Civil Practice & Remedies Code § 22.001 et seq.

Evidence in Criminal Actions Generally, Vernon's Ann.C.C.P. Art. 38.01 et seq.

Use of Depositions as Evidence, Vernon's Ann.C.C.P. Art. 39.12.

Use of Depositions for Impeachment, Vernon's Ann.C.C.P. Art. 39.13.

Victim Impact Statement, Vernon's Ann.C.C.P. Art. 56.03.

Rules of Appellate Procedure in Criminal Cases, V.T.C.A., Government Code § 22.108.

Rules of Evidence in Criminal Cases, V.T.C.A., Government Code § 22.109.

Small Claims Courts, V.T.C.A., Government Code § 28.001 et seq.

Burden of Proof Beyond Reasonable Doubt, V.T.C.A., Penal Code § 2.01.

Burden of Proof as to Exceptions to Offenses, V.T.C.A., Penal Code § 2.02.

Burden of Proof as to Defenses to Prosecution, V.T.C.A., Penal Code § 2.03.

Burden of Proof as to Affirmative Offenses, V.T.C.A., Penal Code § 2.04.

Presumptions, V.T.C.A., Penal Code § 2.05.

Testimonial Immunity as to Organized Crime Offenses, V.T.C.A., Penal Code § 71.04.

Party as Witness, Vernon's Ann.Rules Civ.Proc., Rule 181.

Depositions, Civil Proceedings, Vernon's Ann.Rules Civ.Proc., Rule 187 et seq.

Integrated Legal Research System References

Texas Jur 3d

24 Texas Jur 3d, Criminal Law §§ 3358 et seq.

35 Texas Jur 3d, Evidence §§ 1 et seq., 7 et seq., 17 et seq., 154.

Rule 101. Title and Scope

(a) Title. These rules shall be known and cited as the Texas Rules of Evidence.

(b) Scope. Except as otherwise provided by statute, these rules govern civil and criminal proceedings (including examining trials before magistrates) in all courts of Texas, except small claims courts.

(c) Hierarchical Governance in Criminal Proceedings. Hierarchical governance shall be in the following order: the Constitution of the United States, those federal statutes that control states under the supremacy clause, the Constitution of Texas, the Code of Criminal Procedure and the Penal Code, civil statutes, these rules, and the common law. Where possible, inconsistency is to be removed by reasonable construction.

(d) Special Rules of Applicability in Criminal Proceedings.

(1) *Rules not applicable in certain proceedings.* These rules, except with respect to privileges, do not apply in the following situations:

(A) the determination of questions of fact preliminary to admissibility of evidence when the issue is to be determined by the court under Rule 104;

(B) proceedings before grand juries;

(C) proceedings in an application for habeas corpus in extradition, rendition, or interstate detainer;

(D) a hearing under Code of Criminal Procedure article 46.02, by the court out of the presence of a jury, to determine whether there is sufficient evidence of incompetency to require a jury determination of the question of incompetency;

(E) proceedings regarding bail except hearings to deny, revoke or increase bail;

(F) a hearing on justification for pretrial detention not involving bail;

(G) proceedings for the issuance of a search or arrest warrant; or

(H) proceedings in a direct contempt determination.

(2) *Applicability of privileges.* These rules with respect to privileges apply at all stages of all actions, cases, and proceedings.

(3) *Military justice hearings.* Evidence in hearings under the Texas Code of Military Justice, TEX. GOV'T CODE § 432.001–432.195, shall be governed by that Code.

Eff. March 1, 1998.

Commentary

In general

These rules, as they apply in civil cases, were first promulgated and adopted by the Supreme Court of Texas by its order of November 23, 1982, to be effective on September 1, 1983. The court's authority was derived from Vernon's Ann.Civ.St. art. 1731(a) (since repealed and replaced by V.T.C.A., Government Code §§ 22.003, 22.004). Both the present and the former statutes granting the Supreme Court rule-making power specifically reserve the supremacy of statutory enactments, as does Vernon's Ann.Rules Evid., Rule 101(b), when referring to "[E]xcept as otherwise provided by statute," and Vernon's Ann.Rules Evid., Rule 402, which provides, in part, that "[A]ll relevant evidence is admissible, except as otherwise provided by Constitution, by statute . . . ".

The Texas Rules of Criminal Evidence were first approved by the Texas Court of Criminal Appeals effective September 1, 1986, pursuant to the authority granted to it by V.T.C.A., Government Code § 22.109. The grant of authority to promulgate rules of evidence in criminal cases did not specifically recognize the supremacy of statutory enactments, but the Texas Rules of Criminal Evidence, as promulgated, did. The rules of evidence in criminal cases were made subject to the Constitutions of the United States and of Texas, "federal statutes that control states under the supremacy clause [of the U.S. Constitution], . . . the Code of Criminal Procedure and the Penal Code, [and] civil statutes . . . " V.T.C.A., Government Code § 22.109 specifically reserves to the legislature the right to disapprove any of the rules of evidence promulgated in criminal cases. (TEX. R. [CRIM.] EVID. 412(e) [now Vernon's Ann.Rules Evid., Rule 412(e)] has been disapproved by the legislature. Acts 1193, 73rd Leg., ch. 900, § 1.17, eff. Sept. 1, 1994; and V.T.C.A., Penal Code § 22.011 was amended in 1993 to eliminate the promiscuity defense to the offense of sexual assault). In other words, the Texas Rules of Evidence are not the only applicable rules of evidence in Texas cases.

The Texas Rules of Evidence are rules of procedure governing the admissibility of evidence, and, as such, the evidentiary rules existing at the time of the trial will apply at the trial. *Willard v. State, 719 S.W.2d 595 (Tex. Crim. App. 1986); Freeman v. State, 786 S.W.2d 56 (Tex. App.—Houston [1st Dist.] 1990, no pet.); Medrano v. State, 768 S.W.2d 502 (Tex. App.—El Paso 1989, pet. ref'd).* However, a careful attorney might consider whether the Texas Rules of Evidence involve substantive law issues when privileges are claimed. See *Carmell v. Texas, 527 U.S. 1002, 119 S.Ct. 2336 (2000)* (a statutory rule of evidence determined to be a substantive law matter [an *ex post facto* law] where it affects the sufficiency of the evidence to meet the burden of proof in a criminal case).

Administrative proceedings

It should be noted that these rules also apply in contested cases before state administrative agencies. V.T.C.A., Government Code § 2001.081. There are exceptions, however, depending on which state agency is involved and the purpose of the contested hearing.

Certain criminal proceedings

These rules are not applicable in certain criminal matters, but evidentiary privileges that apply in criminal cases always apply in all criminal proceedings. Vernon's Ann.Rules Evid., Rules 101(d)(1), 101(d)(2). See *Granados v. State, 85 S.W.3d 217, 227 (Tex. Crim. App. 2002)* ("The rules of evidence, except with respect to privileges, do not apply in suppression hearings; the rules are inapplicable to the determination of questions of fact preliminary to admissibility of evidence when the issue is to be determined by the court."). See *Ford v. State, 305 S.W.3d 530, (Tex. Crim. App. 2009)* (at a pre-trial motion to suppress hearing in criminal case, the trial court may rely on any relevant, reliable, and credible information, even if unsworn hearsay). See also *Hall v. State, 297 S.W.3d 294 (Tex. Crim. App. 2009)* (Rule 702 does not apply in suppression hearings; however, where scientific evidence [such as new technology] offered to establish probable case to arrest is not reliable, the evidence obtained as a result of that arrest is inadmissible and subject to the granting of a motion to suppress).

Uniform Rules of Evidence

For text of corresponding provisions of Uniform Rules of Evidence and notes of decisions relating thereto, which may provide guidance in interpreting the Texas Rule, see Rule 101, 13A Uniform Laws Annotated, and Rules 1101, 1102, 13B Uniform Laws Annotated.

Federal Rules of Evidence

The corresponding provisions of the Federal Rules of Evidence are Rules 101, 1101 and 1103. For the text of the Rule and Advisory Committee Notes, which may provide guidance in interpreting the Texas Rule, see the Appendix to this volume.

Integrated Legal Research System References

West's Texas Digest Key Numbers

Courts ⚷85.

Texas Practice

Addison, Texas Practice Guide, Evidence § 1:1 et seq.

Texas Jur 3d

35 Texas Jur 3d, Evidence § 4.

Annotations

Federal Rules of Evidence or state evidentiary rules as applicable in diversity cases, 84 ALR Fed 283.

Rule 102. Purpose and Construction

These rules shall be construed to secure fairness in administration, elimination of unjustifiable expense and delay, and promotion of growth and development of the law of evidence to the end that the truth may be ascertained and proceedings justly determined.

Eff. March 1, 1998.

Commentary

Uniform Rules of Evidence

For text of corresponding provisions of Uniform Rules of Evidence and notes of decisions relating thereto, which may provide guidance in interpreting the Texas Rule, see Rule 102, 13A Uniform Laws Annotated.

Federal Rules of Evidence

The corresponding provision of the Federal Rules of Evidence is Rule 102. For the text of the Rule and Advisory Committee Notes, which may provide guidance in interpreting the Texas Rule, see the Appendix to this volume.

Integrated Legal Research System References

West's Texas Digest Key Numbers

Courts ⚷85.

Texas Practice

Addison, Texas Practice Guide, Evidence § 1:14 et seq.

Texas Jur 3d

35 Texas Jur 3d, Evidence § 4.

Rule 103. Rulings on Evidence

(a) Effect of Erroneous Ruling. Error may not be predicated upon a ruling which admits or excludes evidence unless a substantial right of the party is affected, and

(1) *Objection.* In case the ruling is one admitting evidence, a timely objection or motion to strike appears of record, stating the specific ground of objection, if the specific ground was not apparent from the context. When the court hears objections to offered evidence out of the presence of the jury and rules that such evidence be admitted, such objections shall be deemed to apply to such evidence when it is admitted before the jury without the necessity of repeating those objections.

(2) *Offer of proof.* In case the ruling is one excluding evidence, the substance of the evidence was made known to the court by offer, or was apparent from the context within which questions were asked.

(b) Record of Offer and Ruling. The offering party shall, as soon as practicable, but before the court's charge is read to the jury, be allowed to make, in the absence of the jury, its offer of proof. The court may add any other or further statement which shows the character of the evidence, the form in which it was offered, the objection made, and the ruling thereon. The court may, or at the request of a party shall, direct the making of an offer in question and answer form.

(c) Hearing of Jury. In jury cases, proceedings shall be conducted, to the extent practicable, so as to prevent inadmissible evidence from being suggested to the jury by any means, such as making statements or offers of proof or asking questions in the hearing of the jury.

(d) Fundamental Error in Criminal Cases. In a criminal case, nothing in these rules precludes taking notice of fundamental errors affecting substantial rights although they were not brought to the attention of the court.

Eff. March 1, 1998.

Commentary

In general

This rule should be read in conjunction with Vernon's Ann.Rules App.Proc., Rule 33. Trial tactics aside, a perfect objection, timely made and stating on the record the correct, specific ground of objection, and upon which a ruling, also on the record, is obtained from the trial court excluding or admitting evidence, is of no consequence unless the ruling affects a substantial right of a party. *ESIS, Inc., Servicing Contractor v. Johnson, 908 S.W.2d 554 (Tex. App.—Fort Worth 1995, writ denied); North Dallas Diagnostic Ctr. v. Dewberry, 900 S.W.2d 90 (Tex. App.—Dallas 1995, writ denied)*; Vernon's Ann.Rules App.Proc., Rules 44.1 and 61.1 (no judgment to be reversed for an error of law by the trial court, unless it probably caused the rendition of an improper judgment, or probably prevented the appellant from making a proper presentation of the case to the appellate court). See *Gee v. Liberty Mut. Fire Ins. Co., 765 S.W.2d 394 (Tex. 1989); McCraw v. Maris, 828 S.W.2d 756 (Tex. 1992).* The trial court can be wrong some of the time without committing reversible error. See *Knisley v. State, 81 S.W.3d 478 (Tex. App.—Dallas 2002, no pet. h.)* (when a trial court's decision to admit or exclude evidence is correct on any theory of law applicable to the case, there is no error, even if the trial judge has given a legally incorrect reason).

When a witness provides a response, a portion of which is responsive and another portion which is non-responsive, the opposing party is required to specify which portion of the response is inadmissible, in order to preserve error for appellate review. See *Jackson v. State, 889 S.W.2d 615, 617 (Tex. App.—Houston [14th Dist.] 1994, pet. ref'd).* However, neither the rules of evidence nor appellate procedure require this level of specificity where the subject of the nonresponsive answer is apparent. *Heidelberg v. State, 36 S.W.3d 668 (Tex. App.—Houston [14th Dist.] 2001, no pet. h.). Whittaker v. State, 286 S.W.3d 355 (Tex. Crim. App. 2009)* (if offered evidence that is objected to contains both admissible and inadmissible evidence, the trial court may safely admit or exclude it all; the trial court is not required to sift through such offered and objected-to evidence in order to segregate the admissible from the inadmissible; the party making an insufficiently specific offer or objection has no complaint on appeal).

Failure to object preserves nothing for review, but fundamental errors affecting substantial rights of the defendant will be reviewed in criminal cases even in the absence of proper objection. Vernon's Ann.Rules Evid., Rule 103(d).

Offers of proof and formal bills of exception

This rule provides that if the court's ruling excludes evidence, the proponent of the evidence must make the substance of the evidence known to the court in order to complain on appeal about the evidence offered being excluded. While this rule does not draw a distinction between proof which would bear on the credibility of a witness for bias or prejudice, and that which would bear on the credibility of the substance of the testimony, there is such a distinction. An offer of proof of excluded evidence regarding the credibility of the substance of the testimony requires a specific offer of proof containing the content of the challenge to the exclusion of such evidence. This permits a reviewing court to properly assess the admissibility of the excluded evidence. When a party seeks to show bias or prejudice of a witness by establishing the characteristics of the witness bearing on that issue, the proponent of the excluded evidence need only show that he was prevented from asking specific questions stated in the offer of proof, not what the answers would or might have been. *Holmes v. State, 323 S.W.3d 163 (Tex.Crim.App. 2009).* See also *In re Estate of Miller, 243 S.W.3d 831 (Tex. App.—Dallas, 2008, no pet. h.)* (reiterates the requirements for preservation of error on appeal for evidence excluded at trial; defines and distinguishes offers of proof and formal bills of exception and the requirements of each), cited below. See also, *In re Commitment of Day, 342 S.W.3d 193 (Tex. App.—Beaumont 2011, pet. denied),* cited below.

The requirement of an adverse ruling

If an objection is sustained and the objecting party wants more relief, that party should ask for more in the form of a request that the jury be instructed to disregard the offending evidence, and if so instructed, a motion for a mistrial, if truly desired. Until the court overrules an objection or motion (that is, until an adverse ruling is obtained from the trial court), there is nothing to complain about on appeal. *Chavis v. Director, State Worker's Compensation Div., 924 S.W.2d 439 (Tex. App.—Beaumont 1996, n.w.h.).* It has been suggested that this case law rule be made a part of either Tex. R. [Civ.] Evid. 103 or Vernon's Ann.Rules App.Proc., Rule 52 (now Vernon's Ann.Rules App.Proc., Rule 33). (Bridges & Moss, *Evidence Update,* in State Bar Litigation Section Report, *The Advocate*, Spring 1996, at Vol. 15, No. 1, comment, at 172). See *Cockrell v. State, 933 S.W.2d 73, 89 (Tex. Crim. App. 1996)* (Vernon's Ann.Rules App.Proc., Rule 52(a) [now in Vernon's Ann.Rules App.Proc., Rule 33] requires that a defendant in a criminal case pursue an objection to a jury argument to an adverse ruling, or the defendant waives the complaint on appeal). *Geuder v. State, 115 S.W.3d 11 (Tex. Crim. App. 2003)* (even if outside the jury's presence, adverse ruling on an objection preserves appellate review of the admission of evidence).

Running objections

It is the practice in Texas that a party making a proper objection to the introduction of testimony of a witness may assume, when the objection is overruled, that the judge will make a similar ruling as to other offers of similar evidence and is not required to repeat the objection. *Commerce, Crowdus & Canton, Ltd. v. DKS Constr., Inc., 776 S.W.2d 615 (Tex. App.—Dallas 1989, no writ).* This is referred to as having a running objection, and is primarily limited to those instances where the similar evidence is elicited from the same witness. *City of Fort Worth v. Holland, 748 S.W.2d 112 (Tex. App.—Fort Worth 1988, writ denied); Leaird's, Inc. v. Wrangler, Inc., 31 S.W.3d 688 (Tex. App.—Waco 2000, pet. denied)* (a running objection is limited to similar evidence elicited from the same witness; where a different witness testifies to the same evidence without objection, any error in overruling the running objection as to the first witness is harmless). Running objections are an exception to the rule that objections must be made contemporaneously with the offer of the objectionable evidence. *Ethington v. State, 819 S.W.2d 854 (Tex. Crim. App. 1991).* In all other respects, the requirements to preserve error in the admission or exclusion of evidence remain. The trial court's permission to use a running objection must be timely obtained and appear on the record. *City of Fort Worth v. Holland, supra.* Relying on a running objection is very risky.

Uniform Rules of Evidence

For text of corresponding provisions of Uniform Rules of Evidence and notes of decisions relating thereto, which may provide guidance in interpreting the Texas Rule, see Rule 103, 13A Uniform Laws Annotated.

Federal Rules of Evidence

The corresponding provision of the Federal Rules of Evidence is Rule 103. For the text of the Rule and Advisory Committee Notes, which may provide guidance in interpreting the Texas Rule, see the Appendix to this volume.

Leading Cases

Allen v. St. Paul Fire and Marine Ins. Co., 960 S.W.2d 909 (Tex. App.—Texarkana 1998, no pet. h.) (failure to object to summary judgment evidence waives error). See also *Direct Communications, Inc. v. Lunsford, 906 S.W.2d 537 (Tex. App.—Dallas 1995, no writ)*, cited below.

Atlantic Richfield Co. v. Misty Products, Inc., 820 S.W.2d 414, 421 (Tex. App.—Houston [14th Dist.] 1991, writ denied), (to preserve a complaint for appeal, a party must present to the trial court a timely request, objection, or motion, state the specific grounds for it, and obtain a ruling before the evidence is admitted). See also *Rendleman v. Clarke, 909 S.W.2d 56 (Tex. App.—Houston [14th Dist.] 1995, dism'd as moot)* and *Goff v. State, 931 S.W.2d 537 (Tex. Crim. App. 1996)*, cited below.

Banda v. Garcia, 41 Tex.S.Ct.J. 79, 955 S.W.2d 270 (Tex. 1997) (failure to object will waive requirement that testimony of opposing attorney must be under oath in order to be considered when opponent knows or should know that objection is necessary). See also *In re Estate of Arndt, 187 S.W.3d 84, 87 (Tex. App.—Beaumont 2005, no pet. h.)*

Bay Area Health Group, Ltd. v. McShane, 239 S.W.3d 231 (Tex. 2007) (to preserve error for appellate review, the complaining party must timely and specifically object to the evidence complained of and obtain a ruling on that objection, each and every time that evidence is offered, unless a timely requested running objection is allowed to that evidence by the trial court.). See *Running objections*, in the *Commentary, supra.*

Beall v. Ditmore, 867 S.W.2d 791, 795 (Tex. App.—El Paso 1993, writ denied) ("... in order to be considered timely, [the objection] must be specific enough to enable the trial court to understand the precise nature of the error alleged and interposed at such a point in the proceedings so as to enable the trial court the opportunity to cure the error alleged, if any. 'Timeliness' defies definition and generally the question of what is timely or otherwise must be left to the sound discretion of the trial judge, but such objection need not be immediate").

Beavers on Behalf of Beavers v. Northrop Worldwide Aircraft Servs., Inc., 821 S.W.2d 669 (Tex. App.—Amarillo 1991, writ denied) (an objection is not waived when parts of objected to evidence are offered by the opponent to rebut, explain, or demonstrate the *untruthfulness* of the evidence admitted over objection).

Blue v. State, 41 S.W.3d 129 (Tex. Crim. App. 2000) (failure to object preserves nothing for review). See *Williams v. State, 937 S.W.2d 479 (Tex. Crim. App. 1996)*, cited below.

Burks v. State, 876 S.W.2d 877 (Tex. Crim. App. 1994) (any error in failing to exclude evidence over proper objection harmless where same evidence admitted without objection; "[A]s regards specificity [of an objection or motion], all a party has to do to avoid forfeiture of a complaint on appeal is to let the trial judge know what he wants, why he thinks himself entitled to it, and to do so clearly enough for the judge to understand him at a time when the trial court is in a proper position to do something about it"). See also *Benavides v. Cushman, Inc., 189 S.W.3d 875, 885 (Tex. App.—Houston [1st Dist.] 2006, no pet. h.)*

In re Commitment of Day, 342 S.W.3d 193, 199-201, 206 (Tex. App.—Beaumont 2011, pet. denied) (to preserve error when a ruling excludes evidence, the substance of the evidence must have been made known to the trial court through an offer of proof, unless the substance of the evidence was apparent from the context within which the evidence was offered).

Direct Communications v. Lunsford, 906 S.W.2d 537 (Tex. App.—Dallas 1995, no writ) (failure to object to summary judgment evidence waives error). See also *Allen v. St. Paul Fire and Marine Ins. Co., 960 S.W.2d 909 (Tex. App.—Texarkana 1998, no pet. h.)*, cited above.

General Motors Corp. v. Iracheta, 161 S.W.3d 462, 471 (Tex. 2005) (an objection must be timely made; that is, when ground for objection becomes apparent, but the objection need not anticipate a deficiency before it exists).

Geuder v. State, 115 S.W.3d 11 (Tex. Crim. App. 2003) (even if outside the jury's presence, adverse ruling on an objection preserves appellate review of the admission of evidence).

Goff v. State, 931 S.W.2d 537 (Tex. Crim. App. 1996) (trial objections which do not comport with arguments on appeal do not preserve error). Also see *Atlantic Richfield Co. v. Misty Products, Inc., 820 S.W.2d 414, 421 (Tex. App.—Houston [14th Dist.] 1991, writ denied)*, cited above, and *Rendleman v. Clarke, 909 S.W.2d 56 (Tex. App.—Houston [14th Dist.] 1995)*, cited below.

Greenberg Traurig of New York, P.C. v. Moody, 161 S.W.3d 56, 90 (Tex. App.—Houston [14th Dist.] 2005, no pet. h.) (a pretrial motion to strike designation of experts not a motion *in limine* in this case; there is a distinction between a motion *in limine* and a pretrial hearing on admissibility under rule 166 of the Texas Rules of Civil Procedure; while a ruling on a motion *in limine* presents nothing for review, a ruling on a pretrial motion regarding the admissibility of evidence does).

Guidry v. State, 9 S.W.3d 133, 153 (Tex. Crim. App. 1999) (unless excluded evidence is apparent from the context of the record, the offering party must present a timely offer of proof or bill of exceptions, nothing is presented for review "[A]bsent a showing of what such evidence would have been, or an offer of a statement concerning what the excluded evidence would show").

Huckaby v. A.G. Perry & Son, Inc., 20 S.W.3d 194 (Tex. App.—Texarkana 2000, pet. denied) (pretrial motion which sought to exclude evidence of prior and subsequent accidents for lack of similarity to the subject accident was not a motion in limine; obtaining a ruling on the motion during pretrial hearing preserved error, even though evidence not objected to during trial). See also *Clark v. Trailways, Inc., 774 S.W.2d 644 (Tex. 1989)*, cited above. Compare Rule 103(a)(2) of the Federal Rules of Evidence to these cases. See Appendix.

Marin Real Estate Partners, L.P. v. Vogt, 373 S.W.3d 57 (Tex. App.—San Antonio 2011, no pet.) (contention that expert witness' testimony was "pure speculation" did not require a more specific objection because the face of the record was sufficient for the court to determine the reliability of an expert's opinion).

Martinez v. State, 98 S.W.3d 189 (Tex. Crim. App. 2003) (to preserve error to the admission of evidence, opponent must make a proper objection each time the evidence is offered unless the opponent has the court's permission to make a running objection, or has requested a hearing outside the presence of the jury; a motion in limine does not preserve error). See also, *Schindler Elevator Corp. v. Anderson, 78 S.W.3d 392, 403–404 (Tex. App.—Houston [14th Dist.] 2001, no pet. h.)*, cited below.

Melendez v. Exxon Corp., 998 S.W.2d 266 (Tex. App.—Houston [14th Dist.] 1999, no pet.) (if substance of the evidence is apparent from the context of the questions asked, an offer of proof is not required in order to preserve error). See also *Raw Hide Oil & Gas, Inc. v. Maxus Exploration Co., 766 S.W.2d 264, 274 (Tex. App.—Amarillo 1988, writ denied)*, cited below.

In re Estate of Miller (Tex. App.—Dallas 2008 no pet. h) (reiterates the requirements for preservation of error on appeal for evidence excluded at trial; defines and distinguishes offers of proof and formal bills of exception and the requirements of each).

Raw Hide Oil & Gas, Inc. v. Maxus Exploration Co., 766 S.W.2d 264, 274 (Tex. App.—Amarillo 1988, writ denied) ("To preserve error concerning the exclusion of evidence by offer of proof, the appellate record must show that (1) the substance of the evidence sought to be admitted was made known to the court, and (2) the court either ruled adversely to its admission or, after timely request, affirmatively refused to rule. An offer of proof or objection to the refusal to rule on the offer must be made prior to the court's charge being read to the jury"). See also *Melendez v. Exxon Corp., 998 S.W.2d 266 (Tex. App.—Houston [14th Dist.] 1999, no pet.)*, cited above. See also *Hooper v. Chittaluru, 222 S.W.3d 103 (Tex. App.—Houston [14th Dist.] 2006, pet. denied); Langley v. Commission on Lawyer Discipline, 191 S.W.3d 913, 915 (Tex. App.—Dallas 2006, no pet. h.).*

Rendleman v. Clarke, 909 S.W.2d 56 (Tex. App.—Houston [14th Dist.] 1995, dism'd as moot) (to preserve a complaint for appeal, a party must present to the trial court a timely request, objection, or motion, state the specific grounds for it, and obtain a ruling before the evidence is admitted). See also *Atlantic Richfield Co. v. Misty Products, Inc., 820 S.W.2d 414, 421 (Tex. App.—Houston [14th Dist.] 1991, writ denied)*, and *Goff v. State, 931 S.W.2d 537 (Tex. Crim. App. 1996)*, cited above.

Richardson v. Green, 677 S.W.2d 497 (Tex. 1984) (if evidence is admitted over objection, the objection must be reurged if the same evidence is offered again or the objection is waived).

Rotella v. State, 2004 WL 1682885 (Tex. Crim. App. 2004) (per curiam) (unpublished) (overruled objection on the record at pretrial hearing to admissibility of evidence to be offered at trial sufficient to preserve error; reference offered to meet, destroy, or explain the evidence at trial not a waiver of the overruled pretrial objection to that evidence).

Schindler Elevator Corp. v. Anderson, 78 S.W.3d 392, 403–404 (Tex. App.—Houston [14th Dist.] 2001, no pet. h.) (to preserve error to the admission of evidence, opponent must make a proper objection each time the evidence is offered unless the opponent has the court's permission to make a running objection, or has requested a hearing outside the presence of the jury; a motion in limine does not preserve error). See also *Martinez v. State, 98 S.W.3d 189 (Tex. Crim. App. 2003)*, cited above.

Sciarrilla v. Osborne, 946 S.W.2d 919 (Tex. App.—Beaumont 1997, writ denied) (where specific ground for objection is not stated, general objection amounts to no objection at all).

Service Corp. Intern. v. Guerra, 348 S.W. 3d 221, 234 (Tex. 2011) (the failure to object to an attorney's statements during voir dire of the jury panel, *without more*, does not waive a later objection to evidence offered during trial, because statements by lawyers during the jury selection process are not evidence [emphasis added]).

Southwest Country Enters. v. Lucky Lady Oil, 991 S.W.2d 490 (Tex. App.—Fort Worth 1999, pet. denied) (granting a motion in limine not a ruling on the admissibility of evidence and does not preserve error in exclusion of evidence).

Terrell v. State, 949 S.W.2d 49 (Tex. App.—Texarkana 1997, no pet.) (defendant failed to preserve for review claim trial court erred in excluding evidence where neither a formal or informal bill of exception nor an offer of proof made regarding substance of evidence excluded).

United Blood Servs. v. Longoria, 938 S.W.2d 29 (Tex. 1997) (there is no difference between standards for evidence that would be admissible in summary judgment proceeding and those applicable in a trial).

Wilford v. State, 739 S.W.2d 854, 865 (Tex. Crim. App. 1987) (failure to object to subsequently elicited testimony waives error).

Williams v. State, 937 S.W.2d 479 (Tex. Crim. App. 1996) (failure to object preserves nothing for review). But see Vernon's Ann.Rules Evid., Rule 103(d) (fundamental errors affecting substantial rights of the defendant will be reviewed in criminal cases even in the absence of proper objection). See also *Blue v. State, 41 S.W.3d 129 (Tex. Crim. App. 2000).*

Wood Oil Distributing Co., Inc., State v., 751 S.W.2d 863 (Tex. 1988) (rulings on motions in limine preserve nothing for review. See *Dallas County v. Crestview Corners Car Wash, 370 S.W.3d 25 (Tex. App.—Dallas 2012, pet. denied)* (nothing is preserved for appeal by a trial court's ruling on a motion in limine, citing *Wood Oil Distributing Co., Inc.*)).

Leading CLE/Law Review Publications

King and Miskel, *Comprehensive Guide to Evidence,* 37th Annual Advanced Family Law Course, State Bar of Texas (2011).

Wise, *Preservation of Error,* 37th Annual Advanced Criminal Law Course, State Bar of Texas (2011).

Integrated Legal Research System References

West's Texas Digest Key Numbers

Criminal Law ⚷670–672, 1036.1.

Texas Practice

Addison, Texas Practice Guide, Evidence § 1:24 et seq.

Texas Jur 3d

24 Texas Jur 3d, Criminal Law § 3369.

26 Texas Jur 3d, Criminal Law §§ 4534 et seq.

35 Texas Jur 3d, Evidence §§ 7 et seq., 17 et seq.

Annotations

Admissibility, in civil proceeding, of evidence obtained through unlawful search and seizure, 105 ALR5th 1.

Construction of provision of Rule 43(c) of the Federal Rules of Civil Procedure, and similar state provisions, providing for entry into record of evidence excluded by trial court, 9 ALR3d 508.

Error in evidentiary ruling in federal civil case as harmless or prejudicial under Rule 103(a), Federal Rules of Evidence, 84 ALR Fed 28.

Rule 104. Preliminary Questions

(a) Questions of Admissibility Generally. Preliminary questions concerning the qualification of a person to be a witness, the existence of a privilege, or the admissibility of evidence shall be determined by the court, subject to the provisions of subdivision (b). In making its determination the court is not bound by the rules of evidence except those with respect to privileges.

(b) Relevancy Conditioned on Fact. When the relevancy of evidence depends upon the fulfillment of a condition of fact, the court shall admit it upon, or subject to the introduction of evidence sufficient to support a finding of the fulfillment of the condition.

(c) Hearing of Jury. In a criminal case, a hearing on the admissibility of a confession shall be conducted out of the hearing of the jury. All other civil or criminal hearings on preliminary matters shall be conducted out of the hearing of the jury when the interests of justice so require or in a criminal case when an accused is a witness and so requests.

(d) Testimony by Accused Out of the Hearing of the Jury. The accused in a criminal case does not, by testifying upon a preliminary matter out of the hearing of the jury, become subject to cross-examination as to other issues in the case.

(e) Weight and Credibility. This rule does not limit the right of a party to introduce before the jury evidence relevant to weight or credibility.

Eff. March 1, 1998.

Cross References

Functions of Court and Jury, Vernon's Ann.Rules of Evid., Rule 1008.

Commentary

Preliminary questions of admissibility

In the usual course of a trial, the preliminary issues of admissibility are easily handled: if a proper objection is made that the evidence offered lacks the threshold predicate for admissibility, the judge sustains the objection if he agrees and overrules the objection if he does not. At times, an opponent of the offered evidence may, with the permission of the trial judge, take the witness on "voir dire," that is, question the proponent's witness on his qualifications, the existence of a privilege, or the predicate for admissibility of the offered evidence, and then make his objections to the evidence at the close of the "voir dire." This is often accomplished simply and in the presence of the jury.

At other times during a trial, the opponent of the evidence may obtain permission of the court to "voir dire" the proponent's witness outside the presence of the jury, and even offer his own witnesses and evidence in opposition to the offered evidence, also outside the presence of the jury, and then make his objections at the conclusion of the hearing. In the appropriate case, the opponent of the evidence might move for, or the court on its own motion may order, a pretrial hearing that includes a "mini-trial" to resolve preliminary issues concerning the admissibility of evidence, the qualifications of a witness or the existence of a privilege, as may be applicable. This pretrial hearing technique on the motion of the opponent to offered scientific evidence was used to good effect by the trial judge in *E.I. du Pont de Nemours and Co., Inc. v. Robinson, 923 S.W.2d 549 (Tex. 1995)*. See Commentary to Rule 702, *infra*.

When given the opportunity to examine a witness on a preliminary matter, whether in the presence of the jury or not, an opponent of the evidence is in a position to take control of the proponent's witness if the proponent of the evidence and the trial court let him. The court can prevent this by not allowing the opponent of the evidence to "voir dire" the witness when ordinary cross-examination will serve as well. The proponent of the evidence can do his part by making timely objections to the excesses of the opponent. When the trial court does allow the questioning of the witness on "voir dire" by the opponent, the trial court can strictly limit the scope of the inquiry to the issue for which the right to question the witness out of turn was granted, whether the proponent objects or not. The trial court has the authority to control the presentation of the evidence. Vernon's Ann.Rules Evid., Rules 611(a) and 403; Vernon's Ann.Rules Civ.Proc., Rule 265. Note that Rule 103(a)(1) provides that "[W]hen the court hears objections to offered evidence out of the presence of the jury and rules that such evidence be admitted, such objections shall be deemed to apply to such evidence when it is admitted before the jury without the necessity of repeating those objections."

Conditional admission of evidence

Offers of evidence conditioned on later proof of a fact to establish its relevancy should be avoided, because failure to fulfill the condition will often result in unnecessary confusion, and sometimes even a mistrial or reversal on appeal. See *Owens–Corning Fiberglas Corp. v. Keeton, 922 S.W.2d 658 (Tex. App.—Austin 1996, writ denied)*; Vernon's Ann.Rules Evid., Rule, 103(a)(1). See also *Harrell v. State, 884 S.W.2d 154 (Tex. Crim. App. 1994).* The trial court can avoid these potential problems by not accepting such conditional offers, unless the fulfillment of the condition is a question of fact to be resolved by the trier of fact. See *Harrell, supra.* While Vernon's Ann.Rules Evid., Rule 104(b) allows a conditional admission of evidence, it does not require it.

Admission of evidence before the jury

After a preliminary hearing on the question of the admissibility of evidence, the court must admit the evidence for the jury's consideration when the evidence is sufficient to raise an issue of fact for the jury to resolve in determining its answers to the questions submitted to it. *Mathis v. State, 930 S.W.2d 203 (Tex. App.—Houston [14th Dist.] 1996, n.w.h.)*; *Steenbergen v. Ford Motor Co., 814 S.W.2d 755 (Tex. App.—Dallas 1991, writ denied)* (preliminary questions concerning admissibility of evidence are determined by the trial court and this determination will not be disturbed absent an abuse of discretion). See *E.I. du Pont de Nemours and Co., Inc. v. Robinson, 923 S.W.2d 549 (Tex. 1995).*

With respect to the admissibility of an extraneous offense in a criminal jury trial, the trial court must make a preliminary determination that a jury could reasonably find beyond a reasonable doubt that the defendant committed the extraneous offense. *Harrell v. State, supra.* The court must also make the determination required by Vernon's Ann.Rules Evid., Rule 403, that the probative value of the evidence outweighs the danger of unfair prejudice. The trial court in a criminal case must often make preliminary determinations as to the voluntariness of confessions, consent to search, and similar matters for which the burden of proof may vary, depending on the nature of the preliminary question to be resolved. Once the trial court determines such preliminary matters to be admissible, they may then be submitted to a jury for determination from the evidence beyond a reasonable doubt, if in issue. See *Mitchell v. State, 931 S.W.2d 950 (Tex. Crim. App. 1996).*

Uniform Rules of Evidence

For text of corresponding provisions of Uniform Rules of Evidence and notes of decisions relating thereto, which may provide guidance in interpreting the Texas Rule, see Rule 104, 13A Uniform Laws Annotated.

Federal Rules of Evidence

The corresponding provision of the Federal Rules of Evidence is Rule 104. For the text of the Rule and Advisory Committee Notes, which may provide guidance in interpreting the Texas Rule, see the Appendix to this volume.

Leading Cases

DuBose v. State, 915 S.W.2d 493 (Tex. Crim. App. 1996), citing *State v. Montgomery, 810 S.W.2d 372 (Tex. Crim. App. 1990)* (the trial judge determines the facts, their legal significance, the credibility of witnesses and the weight to be given their testimony at a hearing on a motion to suppress; these determinations will not be disturbed on appeal if the trial court's rulings are at least within the "zone of reasonable disagreement"). See *Guzman v. State, 955 S.W.2d 85, 89 (Tex. Crim. App. 1990)*, cited below.

E.I. du Pont de Nemours and Co., Inc. v. Robinson, 923 S.W.2d 549 (Tex. 1995) (the trial judge determines the relevancy of offered evidence and, in the case of offered scientific evidence, the judge determines its reliability, where the issue is raised by the opponent's proper and timely objection; the opponent need only object to reliability of expert testimony, and need not present controverting evidence).

Guzman v. State, 955 S.W.2d 85, 89 (Tex. Crim. App. 1990) (the trial court should give almost total deference to a trial court's determination of historical facts that are supported by the record, especially when trial court's fact findings are based on evaluation of credibility and demeanor of witnesses). See *DuBose v. State, 915 S.W.2d 493 (Tex. Crim. App. 1996)*, cited above.

Harrell v. State, 884 S.W.2d 154 (Tex. Crim. App. 1994) (the admissibility of an extraneous offense is determined by the trial court, but must be submitted to the jury if the trial court finds that jury could reasonably conclude that the defendant committed the extraneous offense beyond a reasonable doubt).

Nelson v. State, 765 S.W.2d 401 (Tex. Crim. App. 1989) (defendant testifying before a jury on the issue of guilt or punishment may prevent admission of testimony given by him in a hearing on a preliminary matter conducted by the trial judge outside the presence of the jury that the State offers against him).

North Dallas Diagnostic Ctr. v. Dewberry, 900 S.W.2d 90 (Tex. App.—Dallas 1995, writ denied) (upon proper objection, the burden is on the proponent of the evidence to establish the threshold predicate for admissibility).

St. Paul Med. Ctr. v. Cecil, 842 S.W.2d 808 (Tex. App.—Dallas 1992, no writ) (whether experts in a particular field reasonably rely on particular data in formulating their opinions is a matter for preliminary determination by the trial court).

Steenbergen v. Ford Motor Co., 814 S.W.2d 755 (Tex. App.—Dallas 1991, writ denied) (when authenticity of evidence is challenged, the trial court first determines preliminary questions about its admissibility).

Integrated Legal Research System References

West's Texas Digest Key Numbers

Criminal Law ⚷667–671.
Witnesses ⚷277.

Texas Practice

Addison, Texas Practice Guide, Evidence § 1:68 et seq.

Texas Jur 3d

24 Texas Jur 3d, Criminal Law § 3367.
35 Texas Jur 3d, Evidence §§ 7 et seq., 17 et seq.

Annotations

Admissibility of hearsay evidence for court's determination, under Rule 104(a) of the Federal Rules of Evidence, of preliminary questions of fact, 39 ALR Fed 720.

Right of accused to be present at suppression hearing or at other hearing or conference between court and attorneys concerning evidentiary questions, 23 ALR4th 955.

Rule 105. Limited Admissibility

(a) Limiting Instruction. When evidence which is admissible as to one party or for one purpose but not admissible as to another party or for another purpose is admitted, the court, upon request, shall restrict the evidence to its proper scope and instruct the jury accordingly; but, in the absence of such request the court's action in admitting such evidence without limitation shall not be a ground for complaint on appeal.

(b) Offering Evidence for Limited Purpose. When evidence referred to in paragraph (a) is excluded, such exclusion shall not be a ground for complaint on appeal unless the proponent expressly offers the evidence for its limited, admissible purpose or limits its offer to the party against whom it is admissible.

Eff. March 1, 1998.

Commentary

In general

A court may admit evidence over proper objection if there is any other basis for the admissibility of the evidence; upon proper objection, a court may exclude evidence even if there is another ground upon which the evidence may be admissible. *Owens–Corning Fiberglas Corp. v. Malone, 972 S.W.2d 35, 43 (Tex. 1998)*; *Perry v. Texas Municipal Power Agency, 667 S.W.2d 259 (Tex. App.—Houston [1st. Dist.] 1984, writ ref'd n.r.e.)*; *Pennington v. Brock, 841 S.W.2d 127 (Tex. App.—Houston [14th Dist.] 1992, no writ)*. In the latter instance, the proponent of the evidence must "expressly" offer the evidence on a ground or for a purpose for which it is admissible. This has long been the rule in Texas. It is not difficult to see why judges like this rule: they can rule either way in these situations and not err, and they don't have to read anyone's mind about what is meant or intended. *Whittaker v. State, 286 S.W.3d 355 (Tex. Crim. App. 2009)*.

Where evidence is admitted for a limited purpose, the opponent of the evidence has the burden of objecting and requesting a limiting instruction at the time of the introduction of the evidence. Waiting to object and to request a limiting instruction until the time the charge is prepared is waiting too long. *Wesbrook v. State, 29 S.W.3d 103 (Tex. Crim. App. 2000); Delgado v. State, 235 S.W.3d 244 (Tex. Crim. App. 2007)*.

Uniform Rules of Evidence

For text of corresponding provisions of Uniform Rules of Evidence and notes of decisions relating thereto, which may provide guidance in interpreting the Texas Rule, see Rule 105, 13A Uniform Laws Annotated.

Federal Rules of Evidence

The corresponding provision of the Federal Rules of Evidence is Rule 105. For the text of the Rule and Advisory Committee Notes, which may provide guidance in interpreting the Texas Rule, see the Appendix to this volume.

Leading Cases

Azar Nut Co. v. Caille, 720 S.W.2d 685 (Tex. App.—El Paso 1986), aff'd, 734 S.W.2d 667 (Tex. 1987) (even otherwise inadmissible evidence may be admitted to rebut a false impression, unless such evidence is irrelevant or prejudicial). See also *Gabriel v. Lovewell, 164 S.W.3d 835 (Tex. App.—Texarkana 2005, no pet. h.)* ("[O]pening the door or inviting testimony that would otherwise pertain to an inadmissible subject matter does not mean that such testimony is necessarily invited into evidence in any form, including hearsay; however, where such testimony pertains to the same subject matter and is directly contrary to earlier testimony, it is admissible, including hearsay").

Horizon/CMS Healthcare Corp. v. Auld, 985 S.W.2d 216 (Tex. App.—Fort Worth 1999, rev'd on other grounds, 34 S.W.3d 887 (Tex. 2000) (evidence admitted as to one party or for one purpose but not admissible as to another party or for another purpose is subject to a Rule 105 limiting instruction, if requested; if no request, admission of evidence without limitation is not a basis for complaint on appeal).

Larson v. Cactus Util. Co., 730 S.W.2d 640 (Tex. 1987) (where offered evidence should be considered for a limited purpose, it is the opponent's burden to secure a limiting instruction).

Porter v. Nemir, 900 S.W.2d 376 (Tex. App.—Austin 1995, no writ) (failure to request a limiting instruction precludes consideration of whether the trial court abused its discretion in refusing to admit the evidence).

Puente v. State, 888 S.W.2d 521 (Tex. App.—San Antonio 1994, no pet.) (when the trial court admits evidence for a limited purpose, the court should instruct the jury, if requested to do so, that the evidence is to be considered only for the limited purpose; the requested instruction must inform the trial court as to what specific limitation should be placed upon the evidence for its admissibility).

Wesbrook v. State, 29 S.W.3d 103 (Tex. Crim. App. 2000) (when evidence is received without a proper limiting instruction, it becomes part of the general evidence in the case and may be used as proof to the full extent of its rational persuasive power). See also *Garcia v. State, 887 S.W.2d 862 (Tex. Crim. App. 1994)*, cited above.

Wolfe v. Wolfe, 918 S.W.2d 533 (Tex. App.—El Paso 1996, writ denied) (if other competent evidence of a fact in question appears in the record, the improper admission of other evidence of that fact will not constitute reversible error).

Integrated Legal Research System References

West's Texas Digest Key Numbers

Criminal Law ⚷783.

Texas Practice

Addison, Texas Practice Guide, Evidence § 1:88 et seq.

Texas Jur 3d

24 Texas Jur 3d, Criminal Law § 3207.
26 Texas Jur 3d, Criminal Law § 4923.
35 Texas Jur 3d, Evidence §§ 13, 22.

Rule 106. Remainder of or Related Writings or Recorded Statements

When a writing or recorded statement or part thereof is introduced by a party, an adverse party may at that time introduce any other part or any other writing or recorded statement which ought in fairness to be considered contemporaneously with it. "Writing or recorded statement" includes depositions.

Eff. March 1, 1998.

Commentary

In general

This rule is sometimes referred to as the "rule of optional completeness," but it is not. Vernon's Ann.Rules Evid., Rule 106 applies only to writings and recorded statements that are offered during the trial, and those writings and recorded statements that should be considered at the same time in the interest of showing fairly the full meaning or the context of the writing or recording offered. Merely because part of a writing or recording has been offered is not a basis for the admission of the whole writing or recording, or the whole of some other writing or recording, but only that part "which ought in fairness to be considered contemporaneously with it." The common law rule of optional completeness is not limited by Rule 106 and is not limited to writings and recorded statements but is meant to allow the supplementation of incomplete evidence. The essential difference between this rule and the common law rule of optional completeness is the reference in this rule to contemporaneous consideration of the evidence and the limitation to writings and recorded statements. It is the rule of optional completeness that allows a party to "walk through" a door opened by an opponent during trial by offering evidence that otherwise might be inadmissible. See Vernon's Ann.Rules Evid., Rule 107 (Rule of Optional Completeness). The two are frequently confused and often mistakenly applied interchangeably. See Leading Cases, below.

There is a risk to the trial lawyer that one's opponent will seize the opportunity to take over the witness and the case under the guise of this rule. The judge, however, has the authority to exercise control over the presentation of the evidence, and that authority is not subverted by this rule. See Vernon's Ann.Rules Evid., Rules 611(a), 403; Vernon's Ann.Rules Civ.Proc., Rule 265. The trial judge should be reminded of this when necessary to limit an opponent's improper use of this rule. See Richardson, *Offering and Excluding Evidence,* cited below.

Official Comment to former Rule 106

The comment to former Rule 106 of the Rules of Civil Evidence and the Rules of Criminal Evidence provided in pertinent part as follows: "This is the federal rule with one modification. Under the federal rule, a party may require his opponent to introduce evidence contrary to the latter's own case. The Committee believes the better practice is to permit the party himself to introduce such evidence contemporaneously with the introduction of the incomplete evidence. This rule does not in any way circumscribe the right of a party to develop fully the matter on cross-examination or as part of his own case. Nor does it alter the common law doctrine that the rule of optional completeness, as to writings, oral conversations, or other matters, may take precedence over exclusionary doctrines such as the hearsay or best evidence rule or the first-hand knowledge requirement."

Uniform Rules of Evidence

For text of corresponding provisions of Uniform Rules of Evidence and notes of decisions relating thereto, which may provide guidance in interpreting the Texas Rule, see Rule 106, 13A Uniform Laws Annotated.

Federal Rules of Evidence

The corresponding provision of the Federal Rules of Evidence is Rule 106. For the text of the Rule and Advisory Committee Notes, which may provide guidance in interpreting the Texas Rule, see the Appendix to this volume.

Leading Cases

Jones v. Colley, 820 S.W.2d 863 (Tex. App.—Texarkana 1991, writ denied) (an edited video tape deposition is permissible, especially when the other side is allowed to immediately introduce its own edited video tape deposition or the entire deposition of the same witness; no requirement that either party in this instance present their respective video tape depositions in chronological order).

Meuth v. Hartgrove, 811 S.W.2d 626 (Tex. App.—Austin 1990, writ denied) (TEX. R. [CIV.] EVID. 106 does not require that a writing or recording be excluded if it evidences only a part of an occurrence, such as a tape recording that recorded only a part of a conversation).

Texas Dep't of Human Servs. v. Green, 855 S.W.2d 136 (Tex. App.—Austin 1993, writ denied) (an edited video tape deposition is permissible, especially when the other side is allowed to immediately afterwards present the entire deposition).

Leading CLE/Law Review Publications

Richardson, *Offering and Excluding Evidence,* Adv. Civ. Trial Course, State Bar of Texas (1996) (contains suggestions on arguments to make to the trial court in an effort to limit an opponent's use of TEX. R. [CIV.] EVID. 106).

Integrated Legal Research System References

West's Texas Digest Key Numbers

Criminal Law ⚷396.

Evidence ⚷155.

Texas Practice

Addison, Texas Practice Guide, Evidence § 1:100 et seq.

Texas Jur 3d

24 Texas Jur 3d, Criminal Law § 3429.

35 Texas Jur 3d, Evidence § 154.

Annotations

Requirement, under Rule 106 of Federal Rules of Evidence, that when writing or recorded statement or part thereof is introduced in evidence, another part or another writing or recorded statement must also be introduced in evidence, 75 ALR Fed 892.

Rule 107. Rule of Optional Completeness

When part of an act, declaration, conversation, writing or recorded statement is given in evidence by one party, the whole on the same subject may be inquired into by the other, and any other act, declaration, writing or recorded statement which is necessary to make it fully understood or to explain the same may also be given in evidence, as when a letter is read, all letters on the same subject between the same parties may be given. "Writing or recorded statement" includes depositions.

Eff. March 1, 1998.

Commentary

In general

This rule does not permit, as Rule 106 does, the contemporaneous offer of the remainder of a writing or recorded statement. See Commentary to Rule 106, *supra*. Depositions in criminal cases are governed by the Texas Code of Criminal Procedure. See Vernon's Ann.C.C.P. Art. 39.01 et seq. Admission of evidence under Rule 107 is limited to omitted information necessary to prevent confusion or false impressions that may be raised by the presentation of only a selected part of the material. Where Rule 107 justifies admission of evidence, the material is still subject to a Rule 403 balancing test. *Sauceda v. State, 162 S.W.3d 591 (Tex. App.—Houston [14th Dist.] 2005, pet. ref'd).*

Uniform Rules of Evidence

There is no corresponding provision in the Uniform Rules of Evidence.

Federal Rules of Evidence

There is no corresponding provision in the Federal Rules of Evidence.

Leading Cases

Credille v. State, 925 S.W.2d 112 (Tex. App.—Houston [14th Dist.] 1996, pet. ref'd) (rule is one of admissibility and permits the introduction of otherwise inadmissible evidence when that evidence is necessary to fully and fairly explain a matter "opened up" by the adverse party).

Holifield v. State, 856 S.W.2d 575 (Tex. App.—Beaumont 1993, pet. ref'd) (evidence which is used to fully explain a matter opened up by the opposing party need not necessarily be admissible).

Livingston v. State, 739 S.W.2d 311 (Tex. Crim. App. 1987) (after reference by defense counsel to a witness' statement by reading from it, State could offer other portions of that statement which contradicted it or placed it in proper context).

Pena v. State, 353 S.W.3d 797, 814 (Tex. Crim. App. 2011) (the rule of optional completeness (Rule 107) is an exception to the hearsay rule to the extent that the evidence offered is within the ambit of Rule 107; [T]his evidentiary rule "is designed to reduce the possibility of the jury receiving a false impression from hearing only a part of some act, conversation, or writing.," quoting *Walters v. State, 247 S.W.3d 204, 218 (Tex. Crim. App. 2007)).*

Integrated Legal Research System References

West's Texas Digest Key Numbers

Criminal Law ⚷396.

Evidence ⚷155.

Texas Jur 3d

24A Texas Jur 3d, Criminal Law § 3654.

ARTICLE II. JUDICIAL NOTICE

Rule
201. Judicial Notice of Adjudicative Facts.
202. Determination of Law of Other States.
203. Determination of the Laws of Foreign Countries.
204. Determination of Texas City and County Ordinances, the Contents of the Texas Register, and the Rules of Agencies Published in the Administrative Code.

Integrated Legal Research System References

West's Texas Digest Key Numbers

Evidence ⚷1–52.

Texas Jur 3d

24 Texas Jur 3d, Criminal Law § 3388 et seq.

35 Texas Jur 3d, Evidence §§ 49–68.

Texas Forms

7 Texas Pl & Pr Forms, Evidence & Witnesses §§ 111:3–111.14.

Rule 201. Judicial Notice of Adjudicative Facts

(a) Scope of Rule. This rule governs only judicial notice of adjudicative facts.

(b) Kinds of Facts. A judicially noticed fact must be one not subject to reasonable dispute in that it is either (1) generally known within the territorial jurisdiction of the trial court or (2) capable of accurate and ready determination by resort to sources whose accuracy cannot reasonably be questioned.

(c) When Discretionary. A court may take judicial notice, whether requested or not.

(d) When Mandatory. A court shall take judicial notice if requested by a party and supplied with the necessary information.

(e) Opportunity to Be Heard. A party is entitled upon timely request to an opportunity to be heard as to the propriety of taking judicial notice and the tenor of the matter noticed. In the absence of prior notification, the request may be made after judicial notice has been taken.

(f) Time of Taking Notice. Judicial notice may be taken at any stage of the proceeding.

(g) Instructing Jury. In civil cases, the court shall instruct the jury to accept as conclusive any fact judicially noticed. In criminal cases, the court shall instruct the jury that it may, but is not required to, accept as conclusive any fact judicially noticed.

Eff. March 1, 1998.

Commentary

In general

Judicial notice is a means whereby a fact relevant to the case can be conclusively established without the necessity of formal proof. Judicial notice is not evidence but is a substitute for evidence. Vernon's Ann.Rules Evid., Rule 201(b) describes generally the kinds of facts that can be judicially noticed, but, as usual, the devil is in the details.

A great deal of confusion exists regarding the matter of a court taking *notice* of its own files, as distinguished from taking *judicial notice* of its files. It is one thing for a court to notice the contents of its files as to what papers have or have not been filed, the allegations they contain, who the parties and the attorneys are, what notations have been placed on the docket sheet, what the historical facts are regarding the procedural history of the particular case, and the like. It is quite another to purport to judicially notice the allegations contained in the papers filed with the court as being true, something the court cannot do. The confusion is the result of using the term "judicial notice" in a generic sense rather than as the term of art it is. The distinction is often unrecognized and sometimes ignored. *Guyton v. Monteau, 332 S.W.3d 687 (Tex. App.—Houston [14th Dist.] 2011, no pet).* [See Leading Cases, below.]

Adjudicative facts

Adjudicative facts are those facts which are relevant and concern the immediate parties: who did what, where, when, how, and with what motive or intent. *First Nat'l Bank of Amarillo v. Jarnigan, 794 S.W.2d 54 (Tex. App.—Amarillo 1990, writ denied).* An adjudicative fact cannot be judicially noticed unless it is a fact "not subject to reasonable dispute in that it is either (1) generally known within the jurisdiction of the trial court or (2) capable of accurate and ready determination by resort to sources whose accuracy cannot reasonably be questioned." Vernon's Ann.Rules Evid., Rule 201(b). The adjudicative fact noticed must be relevant to the issues in the case. Vernon's Ann.Rules Evid., Rule 402. See 23 Tx. Dig. 2d § 5(2)–50 (West 2011) (lists matters of which judicial notice has been taken).

Jury instructions

Although Vernon's Ann.Rules Evid., Rule 201(g) appears to make it mandatory that the trial court instruct the jury in civil cases to accept as conclusive any fact judicially noticed, this mandate is not as broad as it seems when considered in light of the provisions of Vernon's Ann.Rules Civ.Proc., Rule 277, which restricts the trial court to giving those instructions to the jury "as shall be proper to enable the jury to render a verdict." If the fact judicially noticed is not necessary to a finding of fact by the jury on a question submitted to it, then there is no reason to instruct the jury to accept the unnecessary fact as conclusive. To do so might lead the trial court into the trap of either commenting on the weight of the evidence or advising the jury of the effect of their answers to the questions submitted, both of which are proscribed by Vernon's Ann.Rules Civ.Proc., Rule 277. For an excellent example of the pitfalls of taking judicial notice, see *First Nat'l Bank of Amarillo v. Jarnigan, supra.* See also *American Bankers Ins. Co. of Florida v. Caruth, 786 S.W.2d 427 (Tex. App.—Dallas 1990, no writ).*

The concerns about taking judicial notice of facts not necessary to the findings the jury is required to make apply with equal force in criminal cases. See Vernon's Ann.C.C.P. Art. 36.14 (Charge of the Court). In criminal cases, however, the jury is not required to accept as conclusive any fact that has been judicially noticed (and of which the jury has been informed), and it must be so instructed. See also, *Watts v. State, 99 S.W.3d 604 (Tex. Crim. App. 2003).*

Uniform Rules of Evidence

For text of corresponding provisions of Uniform Rules of Evidence and notes of decisions relating thereto, which may provide guidance in interpreting the Texas Rule, see Rule 201, 13A Uniform Laws Annotated.

Federal Rules of Evidence

The corresponding provision of the Federal Rules of Evidence is Rule 201. For the text of the Rule and Advisory Committee Notes, which may provide guidance in interpreting the Texas Rule, see the Appendix to this volume.

Leading Cases

Flores, Ex parte, 537 S.W.2d 458 (Tex. Crim. App. 1976) (an appellate court may take judicial notice of its own records in the same or related proceedings involving same or nearly same parties). See *Huffman v. State, 479 S.W.2d 62 (Tex. Crim. App. 1972)* and *Salinas v. State, 542 S.W.2d 864 (Tex. Crim. App. 1976)*, cited below.

Graff v. Whittle, 947 S.W.2d 629 (Tex. App.—Texarkana 1997, pet. denied) (appellate court can take judicial notice of the population of a county for the first time on appeal).

Guyton v. Monteau, 332 S.W.3d 687 (Tex. App.—Houston [14th Dist.] 2011, no pet.) (although a judge may have personal knowledge of a fact, that is not judicial knowledge; a judge may personally know a fact of which he cannot take judicial notice; the trial court may not take judicial notice of the truth of factual statements and allegations contained in the pleadings, affidavits, or other documents in the file; when evidence is the subject of improper judicial notice, it amounts to no evidence).

Hernandez v. Houston Lighting & Power Co., 795 S.W.2d 775 (Tex. App.—Houston [14th Dist.] 1990, no writ) (when requirements of Tex. R. [Civ.] Evid. 201 are met, taking judicial notice is mandatory, if the fact noticed is applicable to the case).

Hernandez v. State, 116 S.W.3d 26 (Tex. Crim. App. 2003) (appellate courts may take judicial notice of other appellate opinions concerning specific scientific theory or methodology in evaluating a trial judge's Rule 702 "gatekeeping" decision; but judicial notice on appeal cannot serve as the sole source of support for a bare trial court record concerning scientific reliability).

Huffman v. State, 479 S.W.2d 62 (Tex. Crim. App. 1972) (an appellate court may take judicial notice of its own records in the same or related proceedings involving same or nearly same parties). See *Ex parte Flores, 537 S.W.2d 458 (Tex. Crim. App. 1976)*, cited above, and *Salinas v. State, 542 S.W.2d 864 (Tex. Crim. App. 1976)*, cited below.

Klein v. Dimock, 705 S.W.2d 408 (Tex. App.—Fort Worth 1986, writ ref'd n.r.e.) (a court may take judicial notice of its own papers on file in the same case). *Cf. Tschirhart v. Tschirhart, 876 S.W.2d 507 (Tex. App.—Austin 1994)*, cited below.

Langdale v. Villamil, 813 S.W.2d 187 (Tex. App.—Houston [14th Dist.] 1991, no writ) (a court may take judicial notice of matters of public record for the first time on appeal).

National County Mut. Fire Ins. Co. v. Hood, 693 S.W.2d 638 (Tex. App.—Houston [14th Dist.] 1985, n.w.h.) (a trial court can take judicial notice of records of its own court in a case concerning the same subject matter and between the same or practically the same parties).

Salinas v. State, 542 S.W.2d 864 (Tex. Crim. App. 1976) (generally, an appellate court cannot go to the record of another case for the purpose of considering testimony found there but not shown in the record case before it). See *Huffman v. State, 479 S.W.2d 62 (Tex. Crim. App. 1972)* and *Ex parte Flores, 537 S.W.2d 458 (Tex. Crim. App. 1976)*, cited above.

Southwestern Elec. Power Co. v. Martin, 844 S.W.2d 229 (Tex. App.—Texarkana 1992, writ denied) (a court cannot judicially notice the records of another court).

Striegler, In Interest of, 915 S.W.2d 629 (Tex. App.—Amarillo 1996, writ denied) (attorney not listed as an expert on the issue of attorney's fees in response to interrogatory can testify as fact witness as to legal services performed and the fee charged; trial court can take judicial notice of the necessity of the services rendered and the reasonableness of the fee for those services, relying, in part, on V.T.C.A., Civil Practice & Remedies Code § 38.001 et seq.).

Tran v. Fiorenza, 934 S.W.2d 740 (Tex. App.—Houston [1st Dist.] 1996, n.w.h.) (appellate court declines to take notice of the canon law of the Catholic Church for the first time on appeal on the ground that such evidence was unavailable to the trial court when it considered the motions for summary judgment in the case).

Traweek v. Larkin, 708 S.W.2d 942 (Tex. App.—Tyler 1986, writ ref'd n.r.e.) (a court cannot take judicial notice of testimony at a previous trial unless the prior testimony is admitted into evidence).

Tschirhart v. Tschirhart, 876 S.W.2d 507 (Tex. App.—Austin 1994) (taking judicial notice of what is on file with the court is not taking judicial notice of the truth of the allegations contained in those papers-something the trial court cannot do). See *Klein v. Dimock, 705 S.W.2d 408 (Tex. App.—Fort Worth 1986, writ ref'd n.r.e.)*, cited above.

Turner v. State, 733 S.W.2d 218 (Tex. Crim. App. 1987) (in a criminal case, a trial court may notice judicially all of its own records, including all judgments and convictions entered by it).

Wilson v. State, 677 S.W.2d 518, 523 (Tex. Crim. App. 1984) ("[A]s a general rule, . . . the courts will not take judicial notice of the proceedings or record in another cause, whether such cause was tried in the same court or in another court . . . " and "[A] trial court generally lacks the power to take judicial notice of the records or documents that might be on file in another trial court").

Integrated Legal Research System References

West's Texas Digest Key Numbers

Criminal Law ⚷304, 777.

Evidence ⚷1–52.

Texas Practice

Addison, Texas Practice Guide, Evidence § 2:3 et seq.

Texas Jur 3d

24 Texas Jur 3d, Criminal Law §§ 3389–3391.

35 Texas Jur 3d, Evidence §§ 66–98.

Texas Forms

7 Texas Pl & Pr Forms, Evidence & Witnesses §§ 111:4–111:8.

Annotations

Judicial notice of attorney customs and practices, 61 ALR5th 707.

Judicial notice as to location of street address within particular political subdivision, 86 ALR3d 484.

Judicial notice as to assessed valuations, 42 ALR3d 1439.

What constitutes "adjudicative facts" within meaning of Rule 201 of Federal Rules of Evidence concerning judicial notice of adjudicative facts, 150 ALR Fed 543.

Effect of Rule 201(g) of the Federal Rules of Evidence, providing for instruction in criminal case that jury need not accept as conclusive fact judicially noticed, on propriety of taking judicial notice on appeal under Rule 201(f), 49 ALR Fed 911.

Rule 202. Determination of Law of Other States

A court upon its own motion may, or upon the motion of a party shall, take judicial notice of the constitutions, public statutes, rules, regulations, ordinances, court decisions, and common law of every other state, territory, or jurisdiction of the United States. A party requesting that judicial notice be taken of such matter shall furnish the court sufficient information to enable it properly to comply with the request, and shall give all parties such notice, if any, as the court may deem necessary, to enable all parties fairly to prepare to meet the request. A party is entitled upon timely request to an opportunity to be heard as to the propriety of taking judicial notice and the tenor of the matter noticed. In the absence of prior notification, the request may be made after judicial notice has been taken. Judicial notice of such matters may be taken at any stage of the proceeding. The court's determination shall be subject to review as a ruling on a question of law.

Eff. March 1, 1998.

Commentary

In general

It has been held that, in the absence of proof to the contrary, the trial court may presume that the law of another state applicable in the case would be the same as in Texas. *Creavin v. Moloney, 773 S.W.2d 698 (Tex. App.—Corpus Christi 1989, writ denied)* (citing *Ogletree v. Crates, 363 S.W.2d 431 (Tex. 1963))*; See also *Ewing v. Ewing, 739 S.W.2d 470 (Tex. App.—Corpus Christi 1987, no writ).* The greater weight of authority, however, indicates that this presumption no longer exists under TEX. R. [CIV.] EVID. 202. *Keene Corp. v. Rogers, 863 S.W.2d 168 (Tex. App.—Texarkana 1993, no writ)* (when a court on its own motion seeks out the law of another state, it is not necessary for a party to provide the court with information concerning the appropriate law; there is no presumption mentioned in Rule 202 that the law of another jurisdiction is the same as Texas law). See also *Knops v. Knops, 763 S.W.2d 864 (Tex. App.—San Antonio 1988, no writ)* (the trial court is not required to take judicial notice of the law of another jurisdiction unless the proponent has properly complied with Rule 202). When a proponent of the law of another state requests the trial court to take judicial notice of it, that party has the burden of showing the law of the other state. If the presumption existed for the proponent of the law of another state that, in the absence of proof to the contrary, the law in the other jurisdiction is the same as in Texas, the burden to show what the law of another state is, if different from Texas law, would be on the party not relying on it. This is contrary to the plain language of the rule.

There is a difference between taking judicial notice of the law of another state that establishes a fact relevant to the case and determining whether the law of another state should apply in the case. This difference causes considerable confusion. The issue of a choice-of-law determination is distinct from the court's power to generally take judicial notice of a foreign state's law. *Pittsburgh Corning Corp. v. Walters, 1 S.W.3d 759, 769 (Tex. App.—Corpus Christi 1999, pet. denied).* In choice of law determinations, the party who relies on the applicability of the law of another state to the issues before the Texas court has the burden to establish what the law of the other state is. If the proponent of the law of another state fails to meet its burden, the trial court may presume that the law of the other state is the same as the law in Texas. *Colvin v. Colvin, 291 S.W.3d 508, 514 (Tex.App.—Tyler 2009)* ("Faced with an untimely motion [under TRE 202] providing inadequate proof of the content of a sister state's law, the trial court did not abuse its discretion by applying the law of Texas.").

It is now mandatory in criminal cases, as it is and has been in civil cases, for the trial court to take judicial notice of the laws of other states and territories and of the United States, provided that the other requirements of this rule are met, and provided the law that is noticed has some legal or factual significance to the case. *Burlington Northern Santa Fe Ry. Co. v. Gunderson, Inc., 235 S.W.3d 287 (Tex. App.—Fort Worth, 2007, no pet. h.).*

Uniform Rules of Evidence

There is no corresponding provision in the Uniform Rules of Evidence.

Federal Rules of Evidence

There is no corresponding provision in the Federal Rules of Evidence. See Rule 44.1, Federal Rules of Civil Procedure, and Rule 26.1, Federal Rules of Criminal Procedure.

Leading Cases

Bartley v. Budget Rent–A–Car Corp., 919 S.W.2d 747 (Tex. App.—Amarillo 1996, writ denied) (if applicable, a trial court may judicially notice the law of another state, provided that the requirements of TEX. R. [CIV.] EVID. 202 are met; judicial notice of the law of another state does not necessarily mandate the application of that law).

Daugherty v. Southern Pacific Transp. Co., 772 S.W.2d 81 (Tex. 1989) (a trial court can judicially notice a statute or regulation of another state that has not been pleaded, but TEX. R. [CIV.] EVID. 202 requires the proponent to furnish the trial court sufficient information from which such law can be determined, to show that it is applicable to the case, and to furnish notice to all parties).

Integrated Legal Research System References

West's Texas Digest Key Numbers

Criminal Law ⚷304, 320, 429 et seq., 468.

Evidence ⚷35.

Texas Practice

Addison, Texas Practice Guide, Evidence § 2:50 et seq.

Texas Jur 3d

24 Texas Jur 3d, Criminal Law §§ 3393, 3394.

35 Texas Jur 3d, Evidence § 48 et seq.

Texas Forms

7 Texas Pl & Pr Forms, Evidence & Witnesses §§ 111:5, 111:10.

Rule 203. Determination of the Laws of Foreign Countries

A party who intends to raise an issue concerning the law of a foreign country shall give notice in the pleadings or other reasonable written notice, and at least 30 days prior to the date of trial such party shall furnish all parties copies of any written materials or sources that the party intends to use as proof of the foreign law. If the materials or sources were originally written in a language other than English, the party intending to rely upon them shall furnish all parties both a copy of the foreign language text and an English translation. The court, in determining the law of a foreign nation, may consider any material or source, whether or not submitted by a party or admissible under the rules of evidence, including but not limited to affidavits, testimony, briefs, and treatises. If the court considers sources other than those submitted by a party, it shall give all parties notice and a reasonable opportunity to comment on the sources and to submit further materials for review by the court. The court, and not a jury, shall determine the laws of foreign countries. The court's determination shall be subject to review as a ruling on a question of law.

Eff. March 1, 1998.

Commentary

In general

Determination of the law of a foreign country must be based on proof after the requisite notice in a proponent's pleadings or otherwise, as provided in this rule. This rule does not refer to judicial notice of the law of the foreign country, but rather to its determination by the trial court. Rule 203 does not allow the trial court to take judicial notice of the law of a foreign country on its own motion, but makes it clear that determination of the law of a foreign country must be supported by proof. The trial court can, on its own, consider legally authoritative sources as evidence of what the law of a foreign country is. *Dubai Petroleum Co. v. Kazi, 12 S.W.3d 71 (Tex. 2000).* The determination by the trial court of that law is, however, reviewable on appeal as a question of law. *Long Distance Int'l, Inc. v. Telefonos de Mexico, 49 S.W.3d 347 (Tex. 2001).* The materials and sources that the trial court considered in determining the law of a foreign country should appear as a part of the appellate record. *Pennwell Corp. v. Ken Assocs., Inc., 123 S.W.3d 756, 761 (Tex. App.–Houston* [14th Dist.] *2003, pet. denied).*

Uniform Rules of Evidence

There is no corresponding provision in the Uniform Rules of Evidence.

Federal Rules of Evidence

There is no corresponding provision in the Federal Rules of Evidence. See Rule 44.1, Federal Rules of Civil Procedure, and Rule 26.1, Federal Rules of Criminal Procedure.

Leading Cases

Exxon Corp. v. Breezevale, Ltd. 82 S.W.3d 429 (Tex. App.—Dallas 2003, pet. filed) (a party cannot rely on foreign law as applying to the issues in a case without notice and proof of the foreign law).

Garcia-Chapa, Matter of Estates of, 33 S.W.3d 859 (Tex. App.—Corpus Christi 2000, no pet. h.) (although the law of Mexico should have been applied, failure to provide proof of that law precludes its application).

Lawrenson v. Global Marine, Inc., 869 S.W.2d 519 (Tex. App.—Texarkana 1993, writ denied) (there is a distinction between taking judicial notice of adjudicative facts and the determination of the law of a foreign country, which requires proof; the determination of the law of a foreign country is not a fact question, but a question of law and reviewable as such).

Ossorio v. Leon, 705 S.W.2d 219 (Tex. App.—San Antonio 1985, no writ) (the court determines the law of foreign countries; that determination is reviewable as a ruling on a question of law).

Reading and Bates Constr. Co. v. Baker Energy Resources Corp., 976 S.W.2d 702 (Tex. App.—Houston [1st Dist.] 1998, pet. denied). (Rule 203 only process by which court may determine the law of a foreign country; determination is one of law to be reviewed on appeal *de novo*).

Integrated Legal Research System References

West's Texas Digest Key Numbers

Criminal Law ⚿304, 320, 429 et seq., 468.
Evidence ⚿37.

Texas Practice

Addison, Texas Practice Guide, Evidence § 2:70 et seq.

Texas Jur 3d

24 Texas Jur 3d, Criminal Law § 3393.
35 Texas Jur 3d, Evidence § 52.

Rule 204. Determination of Texas City and County Ordinances, the Contents of the Texas Register, and the Rules of Agencies Published in the Administrative Code

A court upon its own motion may, or upon the motion of a party shall, take judicial notice of the ordinances of municipalities and counties of Texas, of the contents of the Texas Register, and of the codified rules of the agencies published in the Administrative Code. Any party requesting that judicial notice be taken of such matter shall furnish the court sufficient information to enable it properly to comply with the request, and shall give all parties such notice, if any, as the court may deem necessary, to enable all parties fairly to prepare to meet the request. A party is entitled upon timely request to an opportunity to be heard as to the propriety of taking judicial notice and the tenor of the matter noticed. In the absence of prior notification, the request may be made after judicial notice has been taken. The court's determination shall be subject to review as a ruling on a question of law.

Eff. March 1, 1998.

Commentary

Uniform Rules of Evidence

There is no corresponding provision in the Uniform Rules of Evidence.

Federal Rules of Evidence

There is no corresponding provision in the Federal Rules of Evidence. See Rule 44.1, Federal Rules of Civil Procedure, and Rule 26.1, Federal Rules of Criminal Procedure.

Leading Cases

Eckmann v. Des Rosiers, 940 S.W.2d 394 (Tex. App.—Austin 1997, n.w.h.) (administrative regulations published in the Texas Register and Texas Administrative Code are "legislative facts", not adjudicative facts, and are to be judicially noticed by the trial court, whether requested by a party or not, when such regulations are a part of the body of law to be considered when rendering a decision).

Metro Fuels v. City of Austin, 827 S.W.2d 531 (Tex. App.—Austin 1992, no writ) (for an appellate court to review an ordinance, there must be compliance with Tex. R. [Civ.] Evid. 204, and the ordinance must be made a part of the record (even though an appellate court can take judicial notice of the ordinances of cities and counties in Texas pursuant to Rule 204), because municipal ordinances are difficult to research and verify, unlike state agency rules published in the Texas Register). See *Office of Public Util. Counsel v. Public Util. Comm'n of Tex., 878 S.W.2d 598 (Tex. 1994)*, cited below.

Office of Public Util. Counsel v. Public Util. Comm'n of Tex., 878 S.W.2d 598 (Tex. 1994) (the court of appeals erred by refusing to take judicial notice of a published order of the Public Utility Commission). See *Metro Fuels v. City of Austin, 827 S.W.2d 531 (Tex. App.—Austin 1992, no writ)*, cited above.

Sungrowth VI, California Ltd., State v., 713 S.W.2d 175, 178 fn. 2 (Tex. App.—Austin 1986, writ ref'd n.r.e.) (" ... this provision of the ... Ordinance was not introduced into evidence at trial, we may nevertheless take judicial notice of its provisions. Under Tex.R.Evid.Ann. 204, ... a trial court may now take judicial notice of a municipal ordinance. An appellate court may take judicial notice of facts which may be properly noticed by a trial court even though the trial court was not formally requested to do so and did not formally announce that it had done so"). See *Houston, City of v. First City, 827 S.W.2d 462 (Tex. App.—Houston [1st Dist.] 1992, writ denied)*, cited above.

Volosen v. State, 227 S.W.3d 77 (Tex. Crim. App. 2007) (the burden of production of an ordinance is on the party relying on it; even where the court takes judicial notice of an ordinance on its own motion, over an objection, the party relying on it must present it to the court [thus, making it part of the record]).

Integrated Legal Research System References

West's Texas Digest Key Numbers

Criminal Law ⚷304, 320, 429 et seq., 468.

Evidence ⚷27–33.

Texas Practice

Addison, Texas Practice Guide, Evidence § 2:80 et seq.

Texas Jur 3d

24 Texas Jur 3d, Criminal Law § 3394.

35 Texas Jur 3d, Evidence § 52.

ARTICLE III. PRESUMPTIONS

[No rules adopted at this time.]

Cross References

Presumption as to Foreign Interest Rate, V.T.C.A., Civil Practice & Remedies Code § 18.031.

Traffic Device Presumed Lawful, V.T.C.A., Civil Practice & Remedies Code § 18.032.

Presumption of Innocence, Vernon's Ann.C.C.P. Art. 38.03.

Presumption, V.T.C.A., Penal Code § 2.05.

Presumption for Theft by Check, V.T.C.A., Penal Code § 31.06.

Commentary

Uniform Rules of Evidence

There are three provisions in the Uniform Rules of Evidence relating to presumptions: Rule 301 (Presumptions in General in Civil Actions and Proceedings), Rule 302 (Applicability of Federal Law in Civil Actions and Proceedings) and Rule 303 (Presumptions in Criminal Cases). For the text of the Rules and notes of decisions relating thereto, see 13A Uniform Laws Annotated.

Federal Rules of Evidence

There are two provisions in the Federal Rules of Evidence relating to presumptions: Rule 301 (Presumptions in General in Civil Actions and Proceedings) and Rule 302 (Applicability of State Law in Civil Actions and Proceedings). For the text of the Rules and Advisory Committee Notes, see the Appendix to this volume.

Integrated Legal Research System References

West's Texas Digest Key Numbers

Criminal Law ⚷301–336.

Evidence ⚷53–89.

ARTICLE IV. RELEVANCY AND ITS LIMITS

Rule
401. Definition of "Relevant Evidence".
402. Relevant Evidence Generally Admissible; Irrelevant Evidence Inadmissible.
403. Exclusion of Relevant Evidence on Special Grounds.
404. Character Evidence Not Admissible to Prove Conduct; Exceptions; Other Crimes.
405. Methods of Proving Character.
406. Habit; Routine Practice.
407. Subsequent Remedial Measures; Notification of Defect.
408. Compromise and Offers to Compromise.
409. Payment of Medical and Similar Expenses.
410. Inadmissibility of Pleas, Plea Discussions and Related Statements.
411. Liability Insurance.
412. Evidence of Previous Sexual Conduct in Criminal Cases.

Cross References

Evidence in Prosecutions for Murder, Family Violence, Vernon's Ann.C.C.P. Art. 38.36.

Evidence of Extraneous Offenses or Acts, Vernon's Ann.C.C.P. Art. 38.37.

Integrated Legal Research System References

West's Texas Digest Key Numbers

Evidence ⚷99–117.

Texas Jur 3d

18 Texas Jur 3d, Criminal Law § 363 et seq.

24 Texas Jur 3d, Criminal Law §§ 3417 et seq., 3421 et seq., 3424 et seq., 3448 et seq., 3456 et seq., 3467 et seq.

35 Texas Jur 3d, Evidence §§ 146–194, 243, 244, 249.

Am Jur Trials

Facebook, MySpace, LinkedIn, Twitter, and Other Social Media in Trials, 122 Am Jur Trials 421.

Am Jur Proof of Facts

Admission of Character Evidence and Evidence of Other Acts, 21 Am Jur Proof of Facts 3d 629.

Establishing an Adequate Foundation for Proof of Medical Expenses, 23 Am Jur Proof of Facts 3d 243.

Evidence of Subsequent Remedial Measures in Civil Cases, 30 Am Jur Proof of Facts 3d 307.

Habit of Person, 7 Am Jur Proof of Facts 3d 523.

Proof of Damages for Brain–Damaged Infant, 22 Am Jur Proof of Facts 3d 83.

Routine Business Practice, 35 Am Jur Proof of Facts 2d 589.

Rule 401. Definition of "Relevant Evidence"

"Relevant evidence" means evidence having any tendency to make the existence of any fact that is of consequence to the determination of the action more probable or less probable than it would be without the evidence.

Eff. March 1, 1998.

Commentary

Uniform Rules of Evidence

For text of corresponding provisions of Uniform Rules of Evidence and notes of decisions relating thereto, which may provide guidance in interpreting the Texas Rule, see Rule 401, 13A Uniform Laws Annotated.

Federal Rules of Evidence

The corresponding provision of the Federal Rules of Evidence is Rule 401. For the text of the Rule and Advisory Committee Notes, which may provide guidance in interpreting the Texas Rule, see the Appendix to this volume.

Leading Cases

Erazo v. State, 144 S.W.3d 487 (Tex. Crim. App. 2004) (prejudicial effect of photo outweighs its probative value when it is not relevant).

Miller v. State, 36 S.W.3d 503 (Tex. Crim. App. 2001) (discussing relevancy and admissibility of evidence of an act subsequent to an offense and the affirmative defense of duress to that offense).

Leading CLE/Law Review Publications

Brown, *Eight Gates for Expert Witnesses*, 36 Hous. L. Rev. 743 (1999).

Integrated Legal Research System References

West's Texas Digest Key Numbers

Criminal Law ⚷338.

Evidence ⚷99.

Texas Practice

Addison, Texas Practice Guide, Evidence § 4:1 et seq.

Texas Jur 3d

24 Texas Jur 3d, Criminal Law § 3417.

35 Texas Jur 3d, Evidence §§ 147–151.

Rule 402. Relevant Evidence Generally Admissible; Irrelevant Evidence Inadmissible

All relevant evidence is admissible, except as otherwise provided by Constitution, by statute, by these rules, or by other rules prescribed pursuant to statutory authority. Evidence which is not relevant is inadmissible.

Eff. March 1, 1998.

Commentary

A. In General

This rule warns that some relevant evidence will not be admissible, and that all evidence not relevant is inadmissible. Although some types of relevant evidence are explicitly excluded by these rules, a rule will often provide for the admissibility of the relevant evidence if offered for another specific purpose, that is, a limited purpose, other than the one prohibited. The limitation of the offer to its proper scope is the subject of Rule 105, discussed earlier.

Aside from the rules regarding privileges and other specific provisions of the Texas Rules of Evidence, there are many other statutory restrictions, and a few case law restrictions, on the use and admissibility of relevant evidence. As has previously been noted (see the Commentary to Rule 101), the Texas Rules of Evidence are not all of the rules of evidence in Texas cases.

Uniform Rules of Evidence

For text of corresponding provisions of Uniform Rules of Evidence and notes of decisions relating thereto, which may provide guidance in interpreting the Texas Rule, see Rule 402, 13A Uniform Laws Annotated.

Federal Rules of Evidence

The corresponding provision of the Federal Rules of Evidence is Rule 402. For the text of the Rule and Advisory Committee Notes, which may provide guidance in interpreting the Texas Rule, see the Appendix to this volume.

B. Examples of Statutory Restrictions/Modifications on the Admission of Relevant Evidence

Usage of trade. Evidence of a relevant usage of trade offered by a party is not admissible unless and until he has given the other party notice the court finds sufficient to prevent unfair surprise to that other party. V.T.C.A., Bus. & Com. Code § 1.205(f) (Tex. UCC).

Parol or extrinsic evidence. The terms of an agreement in writing intended by the parties to be a final expression of their agreement with respect to such terms may not be contradicted by evidence of any prior agreement or of a contemporaneous oral agreement but may be explained or supplemented (1) by course of dealing or usage of trade (Tex. UCC § 1.205) or by course of performance (Tex. UCC § 2.208) and (2) by evidence of consistent additional terms unless the court finds the writing to have been intended also as a complete and exclusive statement of the terms of the agreement. V.T.C.A., Bus. & Com. Code § 2.202 (Tex. UCC).

Proof of market price. Evidence of a relevant price prevailing at a time and place other than described [here] offered by one party is not admissible unless and until he has given the other party such notice as the court finds sufficient to prevent unfair surprise. V.T.C.A., Bus. & Com. Code § 2.723(c) (Tex. UCC).

Prevailing price. Where the prevailing rent or value of any goods regularly leased in any established commodity market is in issue, reports in official publications or trade journals or in newspapers or periodicals of general circulation published as the reports of that market are admissible in evidence; circumstances of the preparation of the report may be shown to affect its weight but not its admissibility. V.T.C.A., Bus. & Com. Code § 2.724 (Tex. UCC).

Prevailing rental value of leased goods. Evidence of a relevant rent prevailing at a time or place or for a lease term other than the one described in this chapter offered by one party is not admissible unless and until the party has given the other party notice the court finds sufficient to prevent unfair surprise. V.T.C.A., Bus. & Com. Code § 2A.507(c) (Tex. UCC).

Acknowledgment of justness of claim barred by limitations. Acknowledgment of the justness of a claim that appears to be barred by limitations is not admissible in evidence to defeat the law of limitations if made after the time that the claim is due unless the acknowledgment is in writing and is signed by the party to be charged. V.T.C.A., Civil Practice & Remedies Code § 16.065.

Communications of sympathy. Any communication that "(1) expresses sympathy or a general sense of benevolence relating to the pain, suffering, or death of an individual involved in an accident; (2) is made to the individual or a person related to the individual within the second degree by consanguinity of affinity, as determined under Subchapter B, Chapter 573, Government Code; and (3) is offered to prove liability of the communicator in relation to the individual" is not admissible in a civil trial. However, a communication, including an excited utterance, which also includes a statement concerning negligence or culpable conduct is admissible to prove the liability of the communicator. V.T.C.A., Civil Practice & Remedies Code § 18.061 (applies to proceedings that begin on or after September 1, 1999).

Affidavits concerning costs and necessity of services rendered. An affidavit that the amount a person charged for a service was reasonable at the time and place that the service was provided and that the service was necessary is sufficient evidence to support a finding of fact by judge or jury that the amount charged was reasonable or that the service was necessary. This statute provides a method by which the affidavit may be controverted. By its terms, this provision does not apply to an action on a sworn account. V.T.C.A., Civil Practice & Remedies Code § 18.001.

Plaintiff's sexual history. In an action for sexual exploitation by a mental health services provider, evidence of plaintiff's sexual history and reputation is not admissible unless the plaintiff claims damage to sexual functioning, or the defendant requests a hearing before trial and makes an offer of proof of the relevancy of the history or reputation, and the court finds that the history or reputation is relevant and that the probative value of the evidence outweighs its prejudicial effect; the court may allow the admission only of evidence of the plaintiff's conduct determined by the court to be relevant; no other evidence of plaintiff's sexual history may be introduced. V.T.C.A., Civil Practice & Remedies Code § 81.008.

Exemplary damages. Evidence relevant only to the amount of exemplary damages is not admissible during the first phase of a bifurcated trial. V.T.C.A., Civil Practice & Remedies Code § 41.011(b).

Admissions made in course of conciliation. Evidence of anything said or of an admission made in the course of a conciliation of an international commercial dispute is not admissible in evidence, and its disclosure may not be compelled in any arbitration or civil action in which, under law, testimony may be compelled to be given; unless the document otherwise provides, a document prepared for the purpose of, in the course of, or pursuant to the conciliation is not admissible in evidence, and disclosure of the document may not be compelled in any arbitration or civil action in which, under law, testimony may be compelled. V.T.C.A., Civil Practice & Remedies Code § 172.304.

Testimony of child victim of certain offenses. Recording of an oral statement of the child made before the indictment is returned or the complaint has been filed is not admissible into evidence except as provided. Vernon's Ann. C.C.P. Art. 38.071.

Communications by drug abusers. A communication to any person involved in the treatment or examination of drug abusers by a person being treated voluntarily or being examined for admission to voluntary treatment for drug abuse is not admissible. Vernon's Ann.C.C.P. Art. 38.101.

Statement of accused deaf person. If the accused is a deaf person, the accused's statement is not admissible against the accused unless the required warnings are interpreted to the deaf person by an interpreter who is qualified and sworn as provided in Article 38.31 of this code. Vernon's Ann.C.C.P. Art. 38.22.

Illegally obtained evidence. Evidence obtained in violation of the law not to be admitted in evidence against the accused on the trial in any criminal case. Vernon's Ann.C.C.P. Art. 38.23.

Evidence of retaining attorney. Evidence that a person has contacted or retained an attorney is not admissible on the issue of whether the person committed a criminal offense. In a criminal case, neither the judge nor the attorney representing the state may comment on the fact that the defendant has contacted or retained an attorney in the case. Vernon's Ann.C.C.P. Art. 38.38.

Insanity defense. Unless notice is timely filed as required, evidence on the insanity defense is not admissible unless the court finds that good cause exists for failure to give notice. Vernon's Ann.C.C.P. Art. 46.03.

Statements of juveniles. Certain statements of a juvenile are inadmissible if proceedings involving the juvenile are transferred to district court, or if the state proceeds on a petition approved by a grand jury. V.T.C.A., Family Code § 51.09.

Juvenile adjudication hearings. Illegally obtained evidence is inadmissible in an adjudication hearing. V.T.C.A., Family Code § 54.03.

Statement by child abuse victim. Out of court statement by child abuse victim not inadmissible because of hearsay rule in certain circumstances. V.T.C.A., Family Code § 54.031; V.T.C.A., Government Code § 2001.122 (as applied to administrative hearings). Vernon's Ann.C.C.P. Art. 38.072 (as applied to criminal cases).

Evidence in certain municipal courts. In Wichita Falls, Fort Worth, Garland, and Addison, testimony, exhibits, or evidence given by a witness in the municipal court is solely for that proceeding or its appeal and is privileged *and* inadmissible in any civil proceeding. V.T.C.A., Government Code §§ 30.122, 30.152, 30.460, 30.662. Testimony, exhibits, and evidence given by a witness in a proceeding in a municipal court of record in El Paso are solely for the purposes of that proceeding or an appeal from that proceeding; in any civil proceeding, evidence relating to such testimony, exhibits, evidence, or reproductions of testimony, exhibits, or evidence is privileged and not admissible except for impeachment purposes. V.T.C.A., Government Code § 30.040(c).

Statements made to crime stoppers councils or programs. Evidence of a communication between a person submitting a report of a criminal act to the crime stoppers advisory council or a local crime stoppers program and the person who accepted the report on behalf of the council or local crime stoppers program is not admissible in a court or an administrative proceeding. V.T.C.A., Government Code § 414.008. See *Thomas v. State, 837 S.W.2d 106 (Tex. Crim. App. 1992)* (although crime stopper reports are initially inadmissible, a defendant can request an *in camera* inspection of the report to determine whether there is exculpatory evidence and, if so, it must be revealed to the defendant). See also *In re Hinterlong, 109 S.W.3d 611 (Tex. App.—Fort Worth 2003, orig. proceeding)* (crime stoppers privilege unconstitutional as applied to party because it violates the open courts provision of the Texas Constitution).

Contested administrative hearings. In a contested administrative hearing, the rules of evidence in a nonjury civil case in a district court apply, except that evidence which is inadmissible under those rules is admissible under the conditions set forth in this section. V.T.C.A., Government Code § 2001.081.

Immunization surveys. Information obtained from a physician's medical records by a person conducting an immunization survey for the health department is not admissible as evidence in a suit against the physician that involves an injury relating to the immunization of an individual. V.T.C.A., Health & Safety Code § 161.002.

Statement of owner in animal cruelty hearing. A statement of an owner made at a hearing to determine whether an animal is being cruelly treated is not admissible in a trial of the owner for an offense under V.T.C.A., Penal Code § 42.09, involving animal cruelty. V.T.C.A., Health & Safety Code § 821.023(b).

Information disclosed to State Insurance Board. "Any information, document, record, or statement required to be made or disclosed to the Board under this article [Agent's License: Application, Issuance, Renewal, and Cancellation] is a privileged communication, and is not admissible in evidence in any court action or proceeding except under a subpoena issued by a court of record." V.A.T.S. Insurance Code, art. 9.36 § 3(d).

Suit to recover assets of an impaired insurer. "In any lawsuit brought by a conservator or receiver of an impaired insurer or agent for the purpose of recovering assets of the impaired insurer or agent, the fact that claims against the impaired insurer or agent have been or will be paid under this article is not admissible for any purpose and may not be placed before any jury by evidence, argument, or reference in any manner." V.A.T.S. Insurance Code, art. 9.48 § 19(a).

Administrative class actions in certain insurance cases. In administrative class actions brought by members of the insurance buying public or the attorney general, evidence of compliance or an attempt to comply with Texas Board of Insurance requirements to refund premiums is inadmissible, except that evidence of compliance or attempts to comply with the Board's requirements to refund premiums may be introduced by the defendant for the purpose of establishing good faith or to show compliance with the Board's requirements. V.A.T.S. Insurance Code, art. 21.21, § 14(c).

Private class actions in certain insurance cases. In class action suits, evidence of attempts to comply with the provisions of this section is inadmissible, except that evidence of compliance or attempts to comply with the provisions of this section may be introduced by a defendant for the purpose of establishing good faith or to show compliance with the provisions of this section. V.A.T.S. Insurance Code, art. 21.21 § 19(e).

Extra-hazardous employer. Identification of an employer as an extra-hazardous employer is not admissible in any judicial proceeding unless the conditions of this section are met. V.T.C.A., Labor Code § 411.050.

Injunctive relief against oil and gas conservation law. Before any injunctive relief granted against an oil and gas conservation law, rule, or order of the Texas Railroad Commission becomes effective, plaintiff is required to post a bond; a finding by a court in granting injunctive relief that a party is likely to suffer damage is inadmissible as evidence of damage in a suit on the bond. V.T.C.A., Natural Resources Code § 85.252.

Plugging an oil well. Paying money to plug a well is not an admission that the person paying the money is obligated to plug or replug the well; evidence that a person has paid money to the commission is not admissible against the person in a suit in which the person's obligation to plug a well is an issue, and introducing the evidence is a compulsory ground for mistrial. V.T.C.A., Natural Resources Code § 89.084.

Boating accident reports. Boating accident reports are confidential and inadmissible in court as evidence. V.T.C.A., Parks & Wildlife Code § 31.105.

Shippers declaration of value. Shipper's declaration of value is not admissible evidence in a court action unless the carrier, when accepting the shipment, provides and maintains either insurance or bonds in an amount at least equal to the declared value of the property. V.T.C.A., Transportation Code § 5.003.

Driver's license suspension hearing affidavits. In administrative hearings for the suspension of driver's licenses, an affidavit of a qualified person as to the reliability of a breath test instrument, and the controverting affidavit of an expert, are admissible; affidavit is inadmissible if the affiant's presence was timely requested and he did not appear for hearing. V.T.C.A., Transportation Code § 524.038.

Seat belts and child passenger seats. Use or nonuse of a child passenger safety seat system is not admissible evidence in a civil trial. V.T.C.A., Transportation Code § 545.412. Use or nonuse of a safety belt is not admissible evidence in a civil trial. V.T.C.A., Transportation Code § 545.413. Sections 545.412 and 545.413 of the Texas Transportation Code have been repealed as of September 1, 2003, but still apply to causes of action filed on or before June 30, 2003. See Acts 2003, 78th Leg., R.S., ch. 204, § 8.01, Tex. Gen. Laws 863.

Response of witnesses recorded in accident reports. An individual's response to the information requested on an accident report form as provided by § 550.064(b)(4) is not admissible evidence in a civil trial. V.T.C.A., Transportation Code § 550.066.

C. Examples of Case Law Restrictions/Modifications on the Admission of Relevant Evidence

Collateral source rule. A wrongdoer should not have the benefit of insurance independently procured by an injured party, and to which the wrongdoer was not privy. *Brown v. American Transfer and Storage Co., 601 S.W.2d 931 (Tex. 1980), cert. denied, 449 U.S. 1015, 101 S.Ct. 575.* The collateral source rule precludes a tortfeasor from obtaining the benefit of payment conferred upon the injured parties from sources other than the tortfeasor; evidence of payments from collateral sources is inadmissible. *Jones v. Red Arrow Heavy Hauling, Inc., 816 S.W.2d 134 (Tex. App.—Beaumont 1991, writ denied).* The common-law collateral source rule does not allow recovery as damages of medical expenses a health care provider is not entitled to charge. *Haygood v. De Escabedo, 356 S.W.3d 390, 396 (Tex. 2011).*

Parol evidence rule. In the absence of fraud, accident or mistake, extrinsic evidence is not admissible to vary, add to, or contradict the terms of a written instrument that is facially complete and unambiguous. *Pitman v. Lightfoot, 937 S.W.2d 496 (Tex. App.—San Antonio 1996, writ denied)*, citing, *Martin v. Ford, 853 S.W.2d 680, 681 (Tex. App.—Texarkana 1993, writ denied); Houston Exploration Company v. Wellington Underwriting Agencies, Ltd, 352 S.W.3d 462 (Tex. 2011).*

Communications during a judicial proceeding. Statements, whether by affidavit or otherwise, made during the course of a judicial proceeding, including pretrial hearings, are privileged and cannot serve as the basis for a claim arising from the statements. *Bird v. W.C.W., 868 S.W.2d 767 (Tex. 1994)*; *Laub v. Pesikoff, 979 S.W.2d 686 (Tex. App.—Houston [1st Dist.] 1998, pet. denied).* See also *McIntyre v. Wilson, 50 S.W.3d 674 (Tex. App.—Dallas 2001, pet. denied)* (parties and witnesses have absolute immunity from subsequent liability for their testimony in judicial proceedings).

Leading CLE/Law Review Publications

Blakely & Herasimchuk, *Article IV: Relevancy and Its Limits*, 30 Hous. L. Rev. 281 (1993).

Integrated Legal Research System References

West's Texas Digest Key Numbers

Criminal Law ⚷338.

Evidence ⚷99.

Texas Practice

Addison, Texas Practice Guide, Evidence § 4:19 et seq.

Texas Jur 3d

24 Texas Jur 3d, Criminal Law § 3417.

35 Texas Jur 3d, Evidence §§ 143, 145, 146.

Rule 403. Exclusion of Relevant Evidence on Special Grounds

Although relevant, evidence may be excluded if its probative value is substantially outweighed by the danger of unfair prejudice, confusion of the issues, or misleading the jury, or by considerations of undue delay, or needless presentation of cumulative evidence.

Eff. March 1, 1998.

Commentary

In general

Relevant evidence cannot be excluded merely because it prejudices a party in the mind of a judge or jury. After all, the point of evidence is to do exactly that to the opposing party. A general objection that offered evidence is prejudicial neither preserves error nor implicates this rule.

This is one of the rules that gives the trial court control over the case and the presentation of the evidence by allowing the court to exclude "rabbit trails" and repetition.

Extraneous offense evidence

If a Rule 404(b) objection is made to extraneous offense evidence, the proponent of the evidence must persuade the trial court that the evidence has relevance apart from character conformity, e.g., that it tends to establish some elemental fact, such as identity or intent; that it tends to establish some evidentiary fact, such as motive, opportunity, or preparation leading inferentially to an elemental fact; or that it rebuts a defensive theory by showing the absence of mistake or accident. *Montgomery v. State, 810 S.W.2d 372, 387–88 (Tex. Crim. App. 1990)*; *Powell v. State, 5 S.W.3d 369, 383 (Tex. App.—Texarkana 1999, pet. ref'd), cert. denied, 529 U.S. 1116, 120 S.Ct. 1976, 146 L.Ed.2d 805 (2000).* If the trial court overrules an objection to the admissibility of the evidence under Rule 404(b), the objecting party must also make a Rule 403 objection, explaining that the prejudicial potential substantially outweighs the probative value of the evidence, in order to preserve error under Rule 403. *Montgomery v. State, 810 S.W.2d 372, 387–88 (Tex. Crim. App. 1990); Powell v. State, 5 S.W.3d 369, 383 (Tex. App.—Texarkana 1999, pet. ref'd), cert. denied, 529*

U.S. 1116, 120 S.Ct. 1976, 146 L.Ed.2d 805 (2000); *Casey v. State, 215 S.W.3d 870 (Tex. Crim. App. 2007).*

Uniform Rules of Evidence

For text of corresponding provisions of Uniform Rules of Evidence and notes of decisions relating thereto, which may provide guidance in interpreting the Texas Rule, see Rule 403, 13A Uniform Laws Annotated.

Federal Rules of Evidence

The corresponding provision of the Federal Rules of Evidence is Rule 403. For the text of the Rule and Advisory Committee Notes, which may provide guidance in interpreting the Texas Rule, see the Appendix to this volume.

Leading Cases

Alamo, City of v. Casas, 960 S.W.2d 240 (Tex. App.—Corpus Christi 1997, pet. denied) (an objection that offered evidence is not relevant is not an objection under Rule 403 that probative value of offered evidence is outweighed by the danger of unfair prejudice or other considerations expressed by that rule).

Bean v. Baxter Health Care Corp., 965 S.W.2d 656 (Tex. App.—Houston [14th Dist.] 1998, no pet. h.) (error to overrule Rule 403 objection to videotape without viewing it, but error harmless where contents or videotape is cumulative to other evidence in the case).

In re D.O., 338 S.W.3d 29, 37 (Tex. App.—Eastland 2011, no pet.) (Rule 403 presumes that relevant evidence is more probative than prejudicial, so excluding evidence under the rule is "an extraordinary remedy that must be used sparingly").

Dudley v. Humana Hosp. Corp., 817 S.W.2d 124 (Tex. App.—Houston [14th Dist.] 1991, no writ) (in a medical malpractice case alleging an unsuccessful surgery, evidence that a physician was under stress during the surgery because he was under investigation for illegally dispensing prescription drugs excluded as cumulative).

Haygood v. De Escabedo, 356 S.W.3d 390, 398 (Tex. 2011) (evidence which is not relevant is inadmissible, including evidence of a claim for damages that are not compensable; a claimant is not entitled to recover medical charges that a provider is not entitled to be paid, thus evidence of such charges is irrelevant to the issue of damages).

Johnson v. City of Houston, 928 S.W.2d 251 (Tex. App.—Houston [14th Dist.] 1996, n.w.h.) (relying on the common law rule and asserting that an exception to the common law rule exists for the admissibility of acts that would show a system, scheme or design). See William J. Bridge and Frederick C. Moss, *Evidence Update*, in State Bar Litigation Section Report, *The Advocate*, Vol. 15, No.1, Spring 1996, comment at 175, and *Missouri Pacific R.R. Co. v. Roberts, 849 S.W.2d 367 (Tex. App.—Eastland 1993, writ denied)*, cited below.

LSR Jt. Venture No. 2 v. Callewart, 837 S.W.2d 693 (Tex. App.—Dallas 1992, writ denied) (trial court should balance the probative effect of relevant evidence against the danger of unfair prejudice or confusion; one factor to consider is whether the fact to be proved could be proved by other evidence).

Miller v. State, 36 S.W.3d 503 (Tex. Crim. App. 2001) (discussing relevancy and admissibility of evidence of an act subsequent to an offense and the affirmative defense of duress to that offense).

Missouri Pacific R.R. Co. v. Roberts, 849 S.W.2d 367 (Tex. App.—Eastland 1993, writ denied) (common law rule [*res inter alios acta*] that evidence of prior acts or transactions of a party with non-parties is not relevant evidence that the party acted similarly in the case on trial, does not exist independently of Tex. R. [Civ.] Evid. 403); contra *Johnson v. City of Houston, 928 S.W.2d 251 (Tex. App.—Houston [14th Dist.] 1996, n.w.h.)*, cited above; and see William J. Bridge and Frederick C. Moss, *Evidence Update*, in State Bar Litigation Section Report, *The Advocate*, Vol. 15, No.1, Spring 1996, comment at 175.

Montgomery v. State, 810 S.W.2d 372 (Tex. Crim. App. 1990) (in weighing probative value against substantial risk of prejudice, Vernon's Ann.Rules Evid., Rule 403 favors the admissibility of the evidence). See also *Williams v. State, 958 S.W.2d 186 (Tex. Crim. App. 1997).*

Perry v. New Hampshire, 565 U.S. ___, 132 S.Ct. 716 (2012) ("Due Process clause does not require a preliminary judicial inquiry of the reliability of eye witness identification unless the identification was procured under unnecessarily suggestive circumstances arranged by law enforcement.").

Pittsburgh Corning Corp. v. Walters, 1 S.W.3d 759 (Tex. App.—Corpus Christi 1999, pet. denied) (to be excluded on rule 403 grounds, it must be shown that the evidence is *unfairly* prejudicial to the opponent of the evidence and that the danger of unfair prejudice that would exist if the evidence is admitted would substantially outweigh its probative value).

Poole v. State, 974 S.W.2d 892 (Tex. App.—Austin 1998, pet. ref'd) (record need not affirmatively show that the trial court performed the Rule 403 balancing test).

Republic Waste Services, Ltd. v. Martinez, 335 S.W.3d 401 (Tex. App.—Houston [1st Dist.] 2011, no pet.) (evidence that a decedent in a wrongful death case was an illegal immigrant who might have been deported was properly excluded because the probative value of the evidence was slight due to its speculative nature, while the prejudicial effect of the evidence was high).

Sims v. Brackett, 885 S.W.2d 450 (Tex. App.—Corpus Christi 1994, writ denied) (when exercising its discretion in reaching its decision to admit or exclude evidence under Tex. R. [Civ.] Evid. 403, the court can exercise its discretion by choosing only among legitimate and legal alternatives; the ruling will not be disturbed on appeal unless the trial court abuses that discretion).

Williams v. State, 958 S.W.2d 186 (Tex. Crim. App. 1997) (when objection to prejudice versus probative value is made, the trial judge has no discretion but to engage in the balancing test required by Rule 403, but a trial judge is not required to sua sponte place any findings he makes or conclusions he draws when engaging in this test into the record). See also *Montgomery v. State, 810 S.W.2d 372 (Tex. Crim. App. 1990).*

Leading CLE/Law Review Publications

Brown, *Eight Gates for Expert Witnesses*, 36 Hous. L. Rev. 743 (1999).

Integrated Legal Research System References

West's Texas Digest Key Numbers

Criminal Law ⚷338.

Evidence ⚷99.

Texas Practice

Addison, Texas Practice Guide, Evidence § 4:47 et seq.

Texas Jur 3d

24 Texas Jur 3d, Criminal Law § 3431.

35 Texas Jur 3d, Evidence § 158.

Am Jur Proof of Facts

Establishing Foundation to Admit Computer Generated Evidence as Demonstrative or Substantive Evidence, 57 Am Jur Proof of Facts 3d 455.

Annotations

Evidence offered by defendant at federal criminal trial as inadmissible, under Rule 403 of Federal Rules of Evidence, on ground that probative value is substantially outweighed by danger of unfair prejudice, confusion of issues, or misleading the jury, 76 ALR Fed 700.

Propriety under Rule 403 of the Federal Rules of Evidence, permitting exclusion of relevant evidence on grounds of prejudice, confusion, or waste of time, of attack on credibility of witness for party, 48 ALR Fed 390.

Rule 404. Character Evidence Not Admissible to Prove Conduct; Exceptions; Other Crimes

(a) Character Evidence Generally. Evidence of a person's character or character trait is not admissible for the purpose of proving action in conformity therewith on a particular occasion, except:

(1) *Character of accused.* Evidence of a pertinent character trait offered:

(A) by an accused in a criminal case, or by the prosecution to rebut the same, or

(B) by a party accused in a civil case of conduct involving moral turpitude, or by the accusing party to rebut the same;

(2) *Character of victim.* In a criminal case and subject to Rule 412, evidence of a pertinent character trait of the victim of the crime offered by an accused, or by the prosecution to rebut the same, or evidence of peaceable character of the victim offered by the prosecution in a homicide case to rebut evidence that the victim was the first aggressor; or in a civil case, evidence of character for violence of the alleged victim of assaultive conduct offered on the issue of self-defense by a party accused of the assaultive conduct, or evidence of peaceable character to rebut the same;

(3) *Character of witness.* Evidence of the character of a witness, as provided in rules 607, 608 and 609.

(b) Other Crimes, Wrongs or Acts. Evidence of other crimes, wrongs or acts is not admissible to prove the character of a person in order to show action in conformity therewith. It may, however, be admissible for other purposes, such as proof of motive, opportunity, intent, preparation, plan, knowledge, identity, or absence of mistake or accident, provided that upon timely request by the accused in a criminal case, reasonable notice is given in advance of trial of intent to introduce in the State's case-in-chief such evidence other than that arising in the same transaction.

Eff. March 1, 1998.

Cross References

Evidence in Prosecutions for Murder, Family Violence, Vernon's Ann.C.C.P. Art. 38.36.

Evidence of Extraneous Offenses or Acts, Vernon's Ann.C.C.P. Art. 38.37 §§ 2, 3.

Commentary

It is important to make the distinction between relevant evidence of conduct on a particular occasion and character evidence offered to prove that the conduct probably occurred on that occasion. This distinction is maintained in Rule 404(a).

This rule lists several exceptions to the general rule excluding evidence of *relevant traits of character* offered to prove "action in conformity therewith on a particular occasion". These exceptions in civil cases are: (1) when a party in a civil case is accused of conduct involving moral turpitude, that party may offer evidence of his good character and, if he does, the accusing party may then offer character evidence to rebut it; and (2) where a party in a civil case is accused of assaultive conduct, that party may offer evidence of the character of the victim for violence on the issue of self defense, and, if he does, the victim may offer evidence of his peaceful character to rebut it.

This rule also makes exceptions to the general rule prohibiting character-conformity evidence in criminal cases: (1) the defendant in any criminal case may place his character in issue, and if he does, the state may offer character evidence to rebut it; (2) subject to the special provisions of Rule 412 (evidence of previous sexual conduct), the defendant may present evidence of a *pertinent* character trait of the victim of a crime, and if he does, the state may present evidence of a pertinent character trait to rebut it; and (3) the state may present evidence of the peaceable character of a homicide victim to rebut a claim by the defendant that the victim was the first aggressor.

Character-conformity evidence is admissible under this rule for impeachment of a witness, whether a party or not, in both civil and criminal cases.

Evidence of other crimes, wrongs or acts of a defendant arising from other transactions is not admissible as character-conformity evidence. It may, however, be admissible for other purposes, as provided by the rule; but, in criminal cases, evidence of crimes, wrongs or acts of a person may not be admissible for those other purposes if, on a timely request by the defendant, the state does not give reasonable notice in advance of trial of its intent to use such evidence in the state's case in chief. This request need not be made of the court and no court order instructing the state to give such reasonable notice is required. A careful lawyer, however, will want to be certain that the record reflects that the request was made of the state and that the request was timely. See also Vernon's Ann.Rules Evid., Rule 609(f) (evidence of a prior conviction not admissible for impeachment under certain circumstances) and Commentary to Rule 609.

If a Rule 404(b) objection is made to extraneous offense evidence, the proponent of the evidence must persuade the trial court that the evidence has relevance apart from character conformity, in that it tends to establish some elemental fact, such as identity or intent; that it tends to establish some evidentiary fact, such as motive, opportunity, or preparation leading inferentially to an elemental fact; or that it rebuts a defensive theory by showing the absence of mistake or accident. *Montgomery v. State, 810 S.W.2d 372, 387–88 (Tex. Crim. App. 1990); Powell v. State, 5 S.W.3d 369, 383 (Tex. App.—Texarkana 1999, pet. ref'd); Service Corp. Intern. v. Guerra, 348 S.W. 3d 221 (Tex. 2011).* If the trial court overrules an objection to the admissibility of the evidence under Rule 404(b), the objecting party must also make a Rule 403 objection, explaining the prejudicial potential substantially outweighs the probative value of the evidence, in order to preserve error under Rule 403. *Montgomery* at 387–88.

Evidence in a criminal case which is relevant to sentencing, including but not limited to the prior criminal record of the defendant, his general reputation, his character, an opinion regarding his character, the circumstances of the offense for which he is being tried, and, notwithstanding Rules 404 and 405 of the rules of evidence, any other evidence of an extraneous crime or bad act, is admissible at the punishment stage of the defendant's trial. The evidence must show beyond a reasonable doubt that the conduct was committed by the defendant or was conduct for which he could be held criminally responsible, regardless of whether he has previously been charged with or finally convicted of the crime or act. Vernon's Ann.C.C.P. Art. 37.07 § 3(a). See *Harrell v. State, 884 S.W.2d 154 (Tex. Crim. App. 1994).*

On timely request of the defendant, notice of intent to introduce such evidence at the punishment stage of a defendant's trial is to be given in the same manner required by Rule 404(b) of the Texas Rules of Evidence. If the attorney representing the state intends to introduce an extraneous crime or bad act that has not resulted in a final conviction in a court of record or a probated or suspended sentence, notice of that intent is reasonable only if the notice includes the date on which and the county in which the alleged crime or bad act occurred and the name of the alleged victim of the crime or bad act. Vernon's Ann.C.C.P. Art. 37.07 § 3(g). The requirement that the attorney representing the state give notice applies only if the defendant makes a timely request to the attorney representing the state for the notice. This request need not be made of the court and no court order instructing the state to give such reasonable notice is required.

This rule should not be confused with Vernon's Ann.Rules Evid., Rule 608, which relates only to character evidence used to impeach, or rehabilitate, any witness on the issue of the witness's credibility.

Uniform Rules of Evidence

For text of corresponding provisions of Uniform Rules of Evidence and notes of decisions relating thereto, which may provide guidance in interpreting the Texas Rule, see Rule 404, 13A Uniform Laws Annotated.

Federal Rules of Evidence

The corresponding provision of the Federal Rules of Evidence is Rule 404. For the text of the Rule and Advisory Committee Notes, which may provide guidance in interpreting the Texas Rule, see the Appendix to this volume.

Leading Cases

Casey v. State, 215 S.W.3d 870 (Tex. Crim. App. 2007) (extraneous-offense evidence is not inadmissible if that evidence is relevant to a material fact apart from its tendency to show conduct in conformity with character; nor is extraneous-offense inadmissible when it is offered to rebut an affirmative defense or a defensive issue that negates one of the elements of the crime charged).

Castaldo v. State, 78 S.W.3d 345 (Tex. Crim. App. 2002) (the rule limiting evidence of other crimes, wrongs, or acts applies not only to the accused, but also to third persons).

G.M.P., Matter of, 909 S.W.2d 198 (Tex. App.—Houston [14th Dist.] 1995, no writ) (the rules of civil evidence allow a person accused of conduct involving moral turpitude to present evidence of a pertinent character trait; such evidence may be offered in the form of reputation testimony).

Hayden v. State, 295 S.W.3d 549 (Tex. Crim. App. 2009) (evidence that a murder victim was a registered sex offender not admissible as victim character evidence because it was unfairly prejudicial under Rule 403; and inadmissible as evidence to rebut testimony the victim was a nice man because it was irrelevant under Rule 404).

Hernandez v. State, 176 S.W.3d 821 (Tex. Crim. App. 2005) (otherwise admissible rule 404(b) evidence is inadmissible unless State complies with notice provisions; however, where the notice provisions of the rule have not been followed and the otherwise admissible evidence is nevertheless admitted, the error is harmful only if the lack of notice is a surprise).

Lopez v. State, 928 S.W.2d 528 (Tex. Crim. App. 1996) (Rule 404(b) does not bar the admission of evidence of other crimes, wrongs or acts to correct false impressions made by a witness).

Magro v. Ragsdale Bros., Inc., 721 S.W.2d 832 (Tex. 1986) (in a products liability case, evidence of inattentiveness, unrelated to the plaintiff's ability to perceive or heed warnings or instructions, and which does not rise to the level of habit, is not admissible to prove that plaintiff would have acted in a consistent manner by ignoring adequate warnings or instructions).

McDonald v. State, 179 S.W.3d 571 (Tex. Crim. App. 2005) (rule 404(b) evidence notice is required where uncharged conduct evidence, which did not arise from the same transaction as the case on trial, is admitted).

McLellan v. Benson, 877 S.W.2d 454 (Tex. App.—Houston [1st Dist.] 1994, no writ) (in a civil suit for sexual assault, other acts of sexual misconduct are admissible to rebut the defensive claim of consent; case discusses the admissibility of other wrongs and acts, proper and timely objections, the court's role, limiting instructions, and the similarities of former Tex. R. [Civ.] Evid. 404 to former Tex. R. [Crim.] Evid. 404).

Page v. State, 137 S.W.3d 75 (Tex. Crim. App. 2004) (rule 404(b) permits the introduction of extraneous bad acts for purpose other than showing character conformity, including proving identification where that is an issue in the case; issue of identity can be raised on defense cross-examination, such as when identifying witness is impeached on a material detail of identification).

Pondexter v. State, 942 S.W.2d 577 (Tex. Crim. App. 1996) (Rule 402 requires that for any evidence to be admissible, it must be relevant, and this includes evidence under Rule 404).

Porter v. Nemir, 900 S.W.2d 376 (Tex. App.—Austin 1995, no writ) (evidence of prior criminal activity admitted to rebut a defense raised by the evidence).

Powell v. State, 63 S.W.3d 435 (Tex. Crim. App. 2001) (introduction of specific acts of uncharged misconduct which refute a defensive theory raised by cross-examination of the complainant in a criminal case is permissible).

Service Corp. Intern. v. Guerra, 348 S.W. 3d 221 (Tex. 2011) (evidence of wrongs or bad acts to show character is in conformity with the allegations against a party is not admissible, but may be admissible to show a party's intent where the wrongs or bad acts are sufficiently connected to the allegations at issue that they may be part of a system, scheme, or plan).

State Bar of Tex. v. Evans, 774 S.W.2d 656 (Tex. 1989) (under Tex. R. [Civ.] Evid. 404(a)(1), the issue is whether the evidence is that of a pertinent trait of character being offered by a party accused of conduct involving moral turpitude, and, if it is, the witnesses may be cross examined on the issue and rebuttal testimony offered by the opposing party).

Torres v. State, 117 S.W.3d 891 (Tex. Crim. App. 2003) (defendant in homicide prosecution who raises issue of self-defense may introduce evidence of deceased's violent character, and specific acts of violence may be introduced to demonstrate the reasonableness of the defendant's fear of danger or to demonstrate that the deceased was the first aggressor, provided such specific acts of violence are relevant apart from showing character conformity).

Leading CLE/Law Review Publications

Burnett, *Extraneous Acts,* 37th Annual Advanced Criminal Law Course, State Bar of Texas (2011).

Integrated Legal Research System References

West's Texas Digest Key Numbers

Criminal Law ⚷376–381.

Evidence ⚷106, 152.

Texas Practice

Addison, Texas Practice Guide, Evidence § 4:96 et seq.

Texas Jur 3d

24 Texas Jur 3d, Criminal Law §§ 3467 et seq.

24A Texas Jur 3d, Criminal Law §§ 3477 et seq.

35 Texas Jur 3d, Evidence §§ 185 et seq., 188 et seq.

Am Jur Proof of Facts

Admission of Character Evidence and Evidence of Other Acts, 21 Am Jur Proof of Facts 3d 629.

Annotations

Admissibility of evidence of prior physical acts of spousal abuse committed by defendant accused of murdering spouse or former spouse, 24 ALR5th 465.

Admissibility of evidence of battered child syndrome on issue of self-defense, 22 ALR5th 787.

Admissibility of evidence of pertinent trait under Rule 404(a) of the Uniform Rules of Evidence, 56 ALR4th 402.

Admissibility of evidence of character or reputation of party in civil action for sexual assault on issues other than impeachment, 100 ALR3d 569.

Admissibility of evidence as to other's character or reputation for turbulence on question of self-defense by one charged with assault or homicide, 1 ALR3d 571.

Admissibility, under Rule 404(b) of Federal Rules of Evidence (28 USCA Appx, Federal Rules of Evidence, Rule 404(b)), of evidence of accused's prior use of illegal drugs in prosecution for conspiracy to distribute such drugs, 114 ALR Fed 511.

Admissibility of evidence of other crimes, wrongs, or acts under Rule 404(b) of Federal Rules of Evidence, in civil cases, 171 ALR Fed 483.

Admissibility, under Rule 404(b) of the Federal Rules of Evidence, of evidence of other crimes, wrongs, or acts similar to offense charged to show preparation or plan, 47 ALR Fed 781.

Admissibility, under Rule 404(b) of Federal Rules of Evidence, of evidence of other crimes, wrongs, or acts not similar to offense charged, 41 ALR Fed 497.

Cross-examination of character witness for accused with reference to particular acts or crimes—modern state rules, 13 ALR4th 796.

When evidence of trait of accused's character is "pertinent" for purposes of admissibility under Rule 404(a)(1) of the Federal Rules of Evidence, 49 ALR Fed 478.

Rule 405. Methods of Proving Character

(a) Reputation or Opinion. In all cases in which evidence of a person's character or character trait is admissible, proof may be made by testimony as to reputation or by testimony in the form of an opinion. In a criminal case, to be qualified to testify at the guilt stage of trial concerning the character or character trait of an accused, a witness must have been familiar with the reputation, or with the underlying facts or information upon which the opinion is based, prior to the day of the offense. In all cases where testimony is admitted under this rule, on cross-examination inquiry is allowable into relevant specific instances of conduct.

(b) Specific Instances of Conduct. In cases in which a person's character or character trait is an essential element of a charge, claim or defense, proof may also be made of specific instances of that person's conduct.

Eff. March 1, 1998.

Cross References

Evidence of Extraneous Offenses or Acts, Vernon's Ann.C.C.P. Art. 38.37 § 2.

Commentary

In general

Until the Texas Rules of Evidence were promulgated in their original forms, there was a great deal of confusion on the part of judges and attorneys as to whether evidence of character or a trait of character was to be established through a witness's own opinion of another's character or trait of character, or through the witness's *knowledge* of the reputation of another in the community for that character or trait, without regard to the witness's own opinion. Under Rule 405(a), this confusion has been put to rest by allowing either method to prove character.

In a criminal case, a reputation or opinion witness as to a relevant character trait of the defendant must have acquired his knowledge of the defendant's reputation, or the underlying facts that support his opinion, prior to the date of the offense for which the defendant is on trial.

Uniform Rules of Evidence

For text of corresponding provisions of Uniform Rules of Evidence and notes of decisions relating thereto, which may provide guidance in interpreting the Texas Rule, see Rule 405, 13A Uniform Laws Annotated.

Federal Rules of Evidence

The corresponding provision of the Federal Rules of Evidence is Rule 405. For the text of the Rule and Advisory Committee Notes, which may provide guidance in interpreting the Texas Rule, see the Appendix to this volume.

Leading Cases

Harrison v. State, 241 S.W.3d 23 (Tex. Crim. App. 2007) (evidence of good character, even if presented by a witness by way of a non-responsive answer, may be rebutted by the asking of "were you aware" questions relevant to the good character trait to which the witness testified). See also *Commentary* to Rule 608.

Integrated Legal Research System References

West's Texas Digest Key Numbers

Criminal Law ⚷376–380.

Evidence ⚷106.

Texas Practice

Addison, Texas Practice Guide, Evidence § 4:135 et seq.

Texas Jur 3d

24 Texas Jur 3d, Criminal Law §§ 3472, 3898.

35 Texas Jur 3d, Evidence §§ 186, 187.

Am Jur Proof of Facts

Admission of Character Evidence and Evidence of Other Acts, 21 Am Jur Proof of Facts 3d 629.

Annotations

Admissibility of evidence of prior physical acts of spousal abuse committed by defendant accused of murdering spouse or former spouse, 24 ALR5th 465.

Admissibility of evidence of character or reputation of party in civil action for sexual assault on issues other than impeachment, 100 ALR3d 569.

Admissibility of evidence as to other's character or reputation for turbulence on question of self-defense by one charged with assault or homicide, 1 ALR3d 571.

Cross-examination of character witness for accused with reference to particular acts or crimes—modern state rules, 13 ALR4th 796.

Opinion evidence as to character of accused under Rule 405(a) of Federal Rules of Evidence, 64 ALR Fed 244.

Rule 406. Habit; Routine Practice

Evidence of the habit of a person or of the routine practice of an organization, whether corroborated or not and regardless of the presence of eyewitnesses, is relevant to prove that the conduct of the person or organization on a particular occasion was in conformity with the habit or routine practice.

Eff. March 1, 1998.

Commentary

Uniform Rules of Evidence

For text of corresponding provisions of Uniform Rules of Evidence and notes of decisions relating thereto, which may provide guidance in interpreting the Texas Rule, see Rule 406, 13A Uniform Laws Annotated.

Federal Rules of Evidence

The corresponding provision of the Federal Rules of Evidence is Rule 406. For the text of the Rule and Advisory Committee Notes, which may provide guidance in interpreting the Texas Rule, see the Appendix to this volume.

Leading Cases

A.V.I., Inc. v. Heathington, 842 S.W.2d 712 (Tex. App.—Amarillo 1992, writ denied) (habit or routine practice is not a restriction on the admissibility of relevant evidence; proof of representations made to others tend to make it more probable that the same representations were made to plaintiff, as claimed, and are therefore relevant and admissible, although such repeated representations might not rise to the level of a habit).

Anderson v. State, 15 S.W.3d 177 (Tex. App.—Texarkana 2000, no pet. h.) (to offer evidence of habit, proponent must at least demonstrate a regular practice of meeting a particular kind of situation).

Pacesetter Corp. v. Barrickman, 885 S.W.2d 256 (Tex. App.—Tyler 1994, no writ) (evidence of a regular response to a repeated, specific situation may also be evidence of a regular practice or consistent behavior of a group; in order to be a habit, conduct must be both regular and frequent).

Waldon v. City of Longview, 855 S.W.2d 875 (Tex. App.—Tyler 1993, no writ) (a few unrelated lapses in judgment do not a habit make).

Integrated Legal Research System References

West's Texas Digest Key Numbers

Criminal Law ⚷372.

Evidence ⚷138, 139.

Texas Practice

Addison, Texas Practice Guide, Evidence § 4:153 et seq.

Texas Jur 3d

35 Texas Jur 3d, Evidence §§ 182–184.

Am Jur Proof of Facts

Habit of Person, 7 Am Jur Proof of Facts 3d 523.

Routine Business Practice, 35 Am Jur Proof of Facts 2d 589.

Annotations

Admissibility of evidence of habit or routine practice under Rule 406, Federal Rules of Evidence, 53 ALR Fed 703.

Habit or routine practice evidence under Uniform Evidence Rule 406, 64 ALR4th 567.

Collateral References

PJC 50.1, Texas Pattern Jury Charges—Malpractice, Premises & Products (1998).

Rule 407. Subsequent Remedial Measures; Notification of Defect

(a) Subsequent Remedial Measures. When, after an injury or harm allegedly caused by an event, measures are taken that, if taken previously, would have made the injury or harm less likely to occur, evidence of the subsequent remedial measures is not admissible to prove negligence, culpable conduct, a defect in a product, a defect in a product's design, or a need for a warning or instruction. This rule does not require the exclusion of evidence of subsequent remedial measures when offered for another purpose, such as proving ownership, control, or feasibility of precautionary measures, if controverted, or impeachment.

(b) Notification of Defect. A written notification by a manufacturer of any defect in a product produced by such manufacturer to purchasers thereof is admissible against the manufacturer on the issue of existence of the defect to the extent that it is relevant.

Eff. March 1, 1998; amended by Supreme Court Aug. 29, 2003, eff. July 1, 2003.

Commentary

Amendments to Rule 407

As part of extensive tort reform legislation passed by the Texas Legislature in 2003, the Supreme Court of Texas has been required to modify Rule 407 by ordering that the rule also apply in cases involving product liability claims, rather than in only negligence claims as Rule 407 previously provided. However, the old rule remains in effect for negligence and product liability cases filed "on or before" July 1, 2003. Prior to the amendment, subsection (a) read: "Subsequent Remedial Measures. When, after an event, measures are taken which, if taken previously, would have made the event less likely to occur, evidence of the subsequent remedial measures is not admissible to prove negligence or culpable conduct in connection with the event. This rule does not require the exclusion of evidence of subsequent remedial measures when offered for another purpose, such as proving ownership, control or feasibility of precautionary measures, if controverted, or impeachment. Nothing in this rule shall preclude admissibility in products liability cases based on strict liability."

Uniform Rules of Evidence

For text of corresponding provisions of Uniform Rules of Evidence and notes of decisions relating thereto, which may provide guidance in interpreting the Texas Rule, see Rule 407, 13A Uniform Laws Annotated.

Federal Rules of Evidence

The corresponding provision of the Federal Rules of Evidence is Rule 407. For the text of the Rule and Advisory Committee Notes, which may provide guidance in interpreting the Texas Rule, see the Appendix to this volume.

Leading Cases

Beavers on Behalf of Beavers v. Northrop Worldwide Aircraft Servs., Inc., 821 S.W.2d 669 (Tex. App.—Amarillo 1991, writ denied) (in a negligence action, subsequent remedial measures taken by a third party are admissible to show that a defendant was *not* the cause of the accident or the injuries to plaintiff).

Brookshire Bros., Inc. v. Lewis, 911 S.W.2d 791 (Tex. App.—Tyler 1995, writ denied) (evidence of subsequent remedial measures taken by a non-party or third party are inadmissible if offered only to show the negligence of the defendant, if the defendant does not dispute the feasibility of subsequent remedial measures).

E.V.R. II Assocs., Ltd. v. Brundige, 813 S.W.2d 552 (Tex. App.—Dallas 1991, no writ) (the rule that subsequent remedial measures are not admissible to show negligence or culpable conduct in connection with an event is inapplicable where the evidence would be valid as to other issues which also exist in the case).

Eoff v. Hal & Charlie Peterson Foundation, 811 S.W.2d 187 (Tex. App.—San Antonio 1991, no writ) (evidence of subsequent remedial measures may be admitted to prove ownership, control or feasibility of precautionary measures only if ownership, control or feasibility of precautionary measures is in dispute).

Integrated Legal Research System References

West's Texas Digest Key Numbers

Evidence ⚷219.10–219.20.

Negligence ⚷131.

Texas Practice

Addison, Texas Practice Guide, Evidence § 4:164 et seq.

Am Jur Proof of Facts

Evidence of Subsequent Remedial Measures in Civil Cases, 30 Am Jur Proof of Facts 3d 307.

Annotations

Admissibility of evidence of subsequent repairs or other remedial measures in products liability cases, 74 ALR3d 1001.

Admissibility of evidence of subsequent remedial measures under Rule 407 of Federal Rules of Evidence, 158 ALR Fed 609.

Admissibility of evidence of repairs, change of conditions, or precautions taken after accident—modern state cases, 15 ALR5th 119.

Products liability: Admissibility of evidence of subsequent repairs or other remedial measures by third party other than defendant, 64 ALR5th 119.

Products liability: Admissibility of evidence of postinjury warning measures undertaken by defendant, 38 ALR4th 583.

Products liability: Admissibility, against manufacturer, of product recall letter, 84 ALR3d 1220.

Rule 408. Compromise and Offers to Compromise

Evidence of (1) furnishing or offering or promising to furnish or (2) accepting or offering or promising to accept, a valuable consideration in compromising or attempting to compromise a claim which was disputed as to either validity or amount is not admissible to prove liability for or invalidity of the claim or its amount. Evidence of conduct or statements made in compromise negotiations is likewise not admissible. This rule does not require the exclusion of any evidence otherwise discoverable merely because it is presented in the course of compromise negotiations. This rule also does not require exclusion when the evidence is offered for another purpose, such as proving bias or prejudice or interest of a witness or a party, negativing a contention of undue delay, or proving an effort to obstruct a criminal investigation or prosecution.

Eff. March 1, 1998.

Commentary

In general

This rule recognizes the prejudicial effect of compromise and offers to compromise as virtually or impliedly admitting to either liability for, or the validity of, a claim and requires the exclusion of such evidence on proper objection, unless offered for another purpose, examples of which are listed in the rule. The limitation of an offer to its proper scope is the subject of Vernon's Ann.Rules Evid., Rule 105.

Whether conduct or statements made during the course of negotiations may or may not be admissible at trial in a civil case (depending on the purpose for which offered), they are discoverable in civil cases in accordance with Vernon's Ann.Rules Civ.Proc., Rule 192.3 and this rule.

As part of the tort reform legislation passed by the Texas Legislature in 2003, the Texas Supreme Court has modified Rule 167 of the Texas Rules of Civil Procedure by establishing provisions regarding offers of settlement and payment of litigation costs. By Rule 167.6, the court has provided that evidence relating to an offer under Rule167 is not admissible in evidence except for the purposes of enforcing a settlement or obtaining litigation costs. The provisions of Rule 167.6 cannot be made known to a jury by any means. Amended Rule 167 became effective on January 1, 2004 and applies only in cases filed on or after that date. See *Amendments to the Texas Rules of Civil Procedure*, Supreme Court of Texas, Misc. Docket No. 03–9160, October 9, 2003.

Uniform Rules of Evidence

For text of corresponding provisions of Uniform Rules of Evidence and notes of decisions relating thereto, which may provide guidance in interpreting the Texas Rule, see Rule 408, 13A Uniform Laws Annotated.

Federal Rules of Evidence

The corresponding provision of the Federal Rules of Evidence is Rule 408. For the text of the Rule and Advisory Committee Notes, which may provide guidance in interpreting the Texas Rule, see the Appendix to this volume.

Leading Cases

Elbaor v. Smith, 845 S.W.2d 240 (Tex. 1992) ("Mary Carter" agreements are void as against public policy; when allowed, such agreements were admissible to show bias, interest, or prejudice of a settling party). See *Scurlock Oil Co. v. Smithwick, 724 S.W.2d 1 (Tex. 1986)*, cited below.

Ford Motor Co. v. Leggat, 904 S.W.2d 643 (Tex. 1995) (settlement agreements are not admissible at trial to prove liability).

L.M.W. v. State, 891 S.W.2d 754 (Tex. App.—Fort Worth 1994, no pet.) (settlement negotiations and conduct and statements made in connection with them in a civil case are not excluded by TEX. R. [CIV.] EVID. 408 from being admissible in a criminal case, if relevant).

Pacesetter Corp. v. Barrickman, 885 S.W.2d 256 (Tex. App.—Tyler 1994, no writ) (recent settlement in a worker's compensation case to refute a claim of financial hardship resulting from wrongful discharge is not admissible under collateral source rule, even if permitted under TEX. R. [CIV.] EVID. 408).

Scurlock Oil Co. v. Smithwick, 724 S.W.2d 1 (Tex. 1986) ("Mary Carter" agreements are void as against public policy; when allowed, such agreements were admissible to show bias, interest, or prejudice of a settling party). See *Elbaor v. Smith, 845 S.W.2d 240 (Tex. 1992)*, cited above.

State Farm Mut. Auto Ins. Co. v. Wilborn, 835 S.W.2d 260 (Tex. App.—Houston [14th Dist.] 1992, no writ) (offers of settlement and compromise are excludable under TEX. R. [CIV.] EVID. 408 in order to allow a party to buy his peace; offers to settle are excludable from evidence because an offer does not represent a party's true position, but is an amount that he is willing to pay or accept in order to avoid the expense or annoyance of litigation).

Tarrant County v. English, 989 S.W.2d 368 (Tex. App.—Fort Worth 1998, pet. denied) (evidence of settlement negotiations may be admitted for other purposes, such as establishing that statements made during the negotiations were misrepresentations).

Texas Farmers Ins. Co. v. Stem, 927 S.W.2d 76 (Tex. App.—Waco 1996, orig. proc.) (in a suit for breach of an insurance contract and for bad faith, the defendant, in defending the breach of contract claim, may wish to avoid the appearance of having admitted liability and invoke the authority of TEX. R. [CIV.] EVID. 408 to prevent the disclosure of the settlement offers it tendered to the plaintiffs, while at the same time evidence of the settlement offers, in addition to being essential to the plaintiff's prosecution of its bad faith claim, may be necessary to the defendant's defense against it).

United States Fire Ins. Co. v. Millard, 847 S.W.2d 668 (Tex. App.—Houston [1st Dist.] 1993, no writ) (TEX. R. [CIV.] EVID. 408 does not require exclusion of offers of settlement and negotiations when offered for a purpose other than proof of liability or the amount of a claim).

Integrated Legal Research System References

West's Texas Digest Key Numbers

Criminal Law ⚷408.

Evidence ⚷213.

Texas Practice

Addison, Texas Practice Guide, Evidence § 4:185 et seq.

Texas Jur 3d

24 Texas Jur 3d, Criminal Law § 3609.

35 Texas Jur 3d, Evidence §§ 243, 244.

Annotations

Evidence involving compromise or offer of compromise as inadmissible under Rule 408 of Federal Rules of Evidence, 72 ALR Fed 592.

Rule 409. Payment of Medical and Similar Expenses

Evidence of furnishing or offering or promising to pay medical, hospital, or similar expenses occasioned by an injury is not admissible to prove liability for the injury.

Eff. March 1, 1998.

Commentary

Uniform Rules of Evidence

For text of corresponding provisions of Uniform Rules of Evidence and notes of decisions relating thereto, which may provide guidance in interpreting the Texas Rule, see Rule 409, 13A Uniform Laws Annotated.

Federal Rules of Evidence

The corresponding provision of the Federal Rules of Evidence is Rule 409. For the text of the Rule and Advisory Committee Notes, which may provide guidance in interpreting the Texas Rule, see the Appendix to this volume.

Integrated Legal Research System References

West's Texas Digest Key Numbers

Evidence ⚷213, 219.

Texas Practice

Addison, Texas Practice Guide, Evidence § 4:219 et seq.

Texas Jur 3d

35 Texas Jur 3d, Evidence § 244.

Am Jur Proof of Facts

Establishing an Adequate Foundation for Proof of Medical Expenses, 23 Am Jur Proof of Facts 3d 243.

Rule 410. Inadmissibility of Pleas, Plea Discussions and Related Statements

Except as otherwise provided in this rule, evidence of the following is not admissible against the defendant who made the plea or was a participant in the plea discussions:

(1) a plea of guilty that was later withdrawn;

(2) in civil cases, a plea of *nolo contendere,* and in criminal cases, a plea of *nolo contendere* that was later withdrawn;

(3) any statement made in the course of any proceedings under Rule 11 of the Federal Rules of Criminal Procedure or comparable state procedure regarding, in a civil case, either a plea of guilty that was later withdrawn or a plea of *nolo contendere,* or in a criminal case, either a plea of guilty that was later withdrawn or a plea of *nolo contendere* that was later withdrawn; or

(4) any statement made in the course of plea discussions with an attorney for the prosecuting authority, in a civil case, that do not result in a plea of guilty or that result in a plea of guilty later withdrawn, or in a criminal case, that do not result in a plea of guilty or a plea of *nolo contendere* or that results in a plea, later withdrawn, of guilty or *nolo contendere.*

However, such a statement is admissible in any proceeding wherein another statement made in the course of the same plea or plea discussions has been introduced and the statement ought in fairness be considered contemporaneously with it.

Eff. March 1, 1998.

Commentary

In general

Rule 410 does not affect the admissibility of the *criminal conviction* resulting from a plea of *nolo contendere*, either to impeach a witness to whom the conviction applies, as permitted by Rule 609, or to prove the conduct for which the defendant was convicted where that conduct is a basis of a claim or defense in a civil suit. It is the fact that the defendant in the criminal case pleaded *nolo contendere* that is inadmissible under this rule, not the fact he was convicted. However, Rule 803(22) excludes as hearsay any judgment of a previous *felony* conviction based on a plea of *nolo contendere* to prove any fact in a civil case that is also essential to the judgment of conviction. See Commentary to Rule 803(22), *infra.* The *conduct* for which a conviction resulted on a plea of *nolo contendere* may be used to prove character or a trait of character under the circumstances allowed by Rules 404 and 405.

The *fact* of the plea of *nolo contendere* is inadmissible in a civil trial where the criminal conduct would be relevant; in other words, the defendant's conduct cannot be proved by the words out of his own mouth when he pleads nolo contendere, or if he withdraws his plea of guilty or by statements he made during plea negotiations "that do not result in a plea of guilty or which result in a plea of guilty later withdrawn." See also Vernon's Ann.C.C.P. Art. 27.02(5) (*plea* of *nolo contendere* may not be used against the defendant as an admission in any civil suit based upon or growing out of the act upon which the criminal prosecution is based).

In criminal cases, a conviction based on a plea of *nolo contendere* that was not withdrawn is admissible as are other convictions in criminal cases.

Uniform Rules of Evidence

For text of corresponding provisions of Uniform Rules of Evidence and notes of decisions relating thereto, which may provide guidance in interpreting the Texas Rule, see Rule 410, 13A Uniform Laws Annotated.

Federal Rules of Evidence

The corresponding provision of the Federal Rules of Evidence is Rule 410. For the text of the Rule and Advisory Committee Notes, which may provide guidance in interpreting the Texas Rule, see the Appendix to this volume.

Integrated Legal Research System References

West's Texas Digest Key Numbers

Criminal Law ⚷406(4).

Evidence ⚷207(4).

Texas Practice

Addison, Texas Practice Guide, Evidence § 4:228 et seq.

Texas Jur 3d

35 Texas Jur 3d, Evidence § 249.

Annotations

Admissibility of defense communications made in connection with plea bargaining, 59 ALR3d 441.

When is statement of accused made in connection with plea bargain negotiations so as to render statement inadmissible under Rule 11(e)(6) of the Federal Rules of Criminal Procedure, 60 ALR Fed 854.

Rule 411. Liability Insurance

Evidence that a person was or was not insured against liability is not admissible upon the issue whether the person acted negligently or otherwise wrongfully. This rule does not require the exclusion of evidence of insurance against liability when offered for another issue, such as proof of agency, ownership, or control, if disputed, or bias or prejudice of a witness.

Eff. March 1, 1998.

Commentary

In general

Insurance against liability, or the lack of it, is another example of evidence inadmissible for one purpose (here to prove negligence or other wrongful conduct) but admissible for other purposes where relevant, even if the evidence might tend to prove negligence or other culpability, or tempt a jury to render a judgment that the insured defendant won't have to pay anyway. Limiting the evidence to its proper scope is the subject of Vernon's Ann.Rules Evid., Rule 105.

Uniform Rules of Evidence

For text of corresponding provisions of Uniform Rules of Evidence and notes of decisions relating thereto, which may provide guidance in interpreting the Texas Rule, see Rule 411, 13A Uniform Laws Annotated.

Federal Rules of Evidence

The corresponding provision of the Federal Rules of Evidence is Rule 411. For the text of the Rule and Advisory Committee Notes, which may provide guidance in interpreting the Texas Rule, see the Appendix to this volume.

Leading Cases

Thornhill v. Ronnie's I–45 Truck Stop, Inc., 944 S.W.2d 780 (Tex. App.—Beaumont 1997) (this rule only prohibits the admission of evidence that a person was or was not insured against liability upon the issue of whether he acted negligently or otherwise wrongfully; it does not require the exclusion of evidence of insurance when offered for the purpose of showing agency, ownership, or control).

Wheeler, Ex parte, 203 S.W.3d 317 (Tex. Crim. App. 2006) (response to question by prosecutor as to whether a witness was aware that defendant's insurance carrier had found her at fault violates this rule because the answer was offered to show that the defendant was culpable).

Integrated Legal Research System References

Texas Practice

Addison, Texas Practice Guide, Evidence § 4:238 et seq.

Texas Jur 3d

35 Texas Jur 3d, Evidence § 171.

Annotations

Admissibility, after enactment of Rule 411, Federal Rules of Evidence, of evidence of liability insurance in negligence actions, 40 ALR Fed 541.

Rule 412. Evidence of Previous Sexual Conduct in Criminal Cases

(a) Reputation or Opinion Evidence. In a prosecution for sexual assault or aggravated sexual assault, or attempt to commit sexual assault or aggravated sexual assault, reputation or opinion evidence of the past sexual behavior of an alleged victim of such crime is not admissible.

(b) Evidence of Specific Instances. In a prosecution for sexual assault or aggravated sexual assault, or attempt to commit sexual assault or aggravated sexual assault, evidence of specific instances of an alleged victim's past sexual behavior is also not admissible, unless:

(1) such evidence is admitted in accordance with paragraphs (c) and (d) of this rule;

(2) it is evidence:

(A) that is necessary to rebut or explain scientific or medical evidence offered by the State;

(B) of past sexual behavior with the accused and is offered by the accused upon the issue of whether the alleged victim consented to the sexual behavior which is the basis of the offense charged;

(C) that relates to the motive or bias of the alleged victim;

(D) is admissible under Rule 609; or

(E) that is constitutionally required to be admitted; and

(3) its probative value outweighs the danger of unfair prejudice.

(c) Procedure for Offering Evidence. If the defendant proposes to introduce any documentary evidence or to ask any question, either by direct examination or cross-examination of any witness, concerning specific instances of the alleged victim's past sexual behavior, the defendant must inform the court out of the hearing of the jury prior to introducing any such evidence or asking any such question. After this notice, the court shall conduct an in camera hearing, recorded by the court reporter, to determine whether the proposed evidence is admissible under paragraph (b) of this rule. The court shall determine what evidence is admissible and shall accordingly limit the questioning. The defendant shall not go outside these limits or refer to any evidence ruled inadmissible in camera without prior approval of the court without the presence of the jury.

(d) Record Sealed. The court shall seal the record of the in camera hearing required in paragraph (c) of this rule for delivery to the appellate court in the event of an appeal.

Eff. March 1, 1998. Amended by Court of Criminal Appeals Dec. 13, 2006, eff. Jan. 1, 2007.

Commentary

In general

By its terms, this rule applies only in criminal cases. In cases involving certain sexual offenses, reputation or opinion evidence of the victim's past sexual behavior is not admissible. Evidence of specific instances of the victim's past sexual behavior is admissible if the procedure required by this rule is met and the offer of this type of evidence is for a purpose authorized by this rule, provided the probative value of the evidence outweighs the danger of unfair prejudice. See *Boyle v. State, 820 S.W.2d 122 (Tex. Crim. App. 1989), cert. den. 503 U.S. 921 (1992).* The *in camera* hearing required by Rule 412(c) is adversarial. Both sides may be present and both may present evidence and cross examine witnesses. *State v. LaPointe, 225 S.W.3d 513 (Tex. Crim. App. 2007).*

Uniform Rules of Evidence

For text of corresponding provisions of Uniform Rules of Evidence and notes of decisions relating thereto, which may provide guidance in interpreting the Texas Rule, see Rule 412, 13A Uniform Laws Annotated.

Federal Rules of Evidence

The corresponding provisions of the Federal Rules of Evidence are Rules 412 and 413. For the text of the Rules and Advisory Committee Notes, which may provide guidance in interpreting the Texas Rule, see the Appendix to this volume.

Integrated Legal Research System References

West's Texas Digest Key Numbers

Witnesses ⚷340(3).

Texas Jur 3d

18 Texas Jur 3d, Criminal Law § 363 et seq.

Annotations

Admissibility of evidence that juvenile prosecuting witness in sex offense case had prior sexual experience for purposes of showing alternative source of child's ability to describe sex acts, 83 ALR4th 685.

Admissibility, in incest prosecution, of evidence of alleged victim's prior sexual acts with persons other than accused, 97 ALR3d 967.

Admissibility in sex offense case, under Rule 412 of Federal Rules of Evidence, of evidence of victim's past sexual behavior, 166 ALR Fed 595.

Admissibility in rape case, under Rule 412 of Federal Rules of Evidence, or evidence of victim's past sexual behavior, 166 ALR Fed 639.

ARTICLE V. PRIVILEGES

Rule
501. Privileges Recognized Only as Provided.
502. Required Reports Privileged by Statute.
503. Lawyer–Client Privilege.
504. Husband–Wife Privileges.
505. Communications to Members of the Clergy.
506. Political Vote.
507. Trade Secrets.
508. Identity of Informer.
509. Physician–Patient Privilege.
510. Confidentiality of Mental Health Information in Civil Cases.
511. Waiver of Privilege by Voluntary Disclosure.
512. Privileged Matter Disclosed Under Compulsion or Without Opportunity to Claim Privilege.
513. Comment Upon or Inference From Claim of Privilege; Instruction.

Cross References

Defendant May Testify, Vernon's Ann.C.C.P. Art. 38.08.

Exceptions to Spousal Adverse Testimony Privilege, Vernon's Ann.C.C.P. Art. 38.10.

Communications by Drug Abusers, Vernon's Ann.C.C.P. Art. 38.101.

Integrated Legal Research System References

West's Texas Digest Key Numbers

Witnesses ⚷184–223.

Texas Jur 3d

24A Texas Jur 3d, Criminal Law § 3761 et seq.

36 Texas Jur 3d, Evidence §§ 506–543.

Rule 501. Privileges Recognized Only as Provided

Except as otherwise provided by Constitution, by statute, by these rules, or by other rules prescribed pursuant to statutory authority, no person has a privilege to:

(1) refuse to be a witness;

(2) refuse to disclose any matter;

(3) refuse to produce any object or writing; or

(4) prevent another from being a witness or disclosing any matter or producing any object or writing.

Eff. March 1, 1998.

Commentary

A. *In General*

Introduction

Privileges are limitations on the admissibility of evidence. The Texas Rules of Evidence favor the admissibility of evidence. Privileges are somewhat inimical to that precept, so a claim of the existence of a privilege, and the evidence necessary to support it, are subject to close scrutiny by the courts. Whether a claimed privilege exists is a determination to be made by the trial court. Vernon's Ann.Rules Evid., Rule 104(a).

This rule contains an acknowledgement that not all privileges that are recognized in Texas are contained in the Texas Rules of Evidence. This rule refers to privileges that may be provided by " ... Constitution, by statute ... or by other rules prescribed pursuant to statutory authority ... ".

Asserting and proving a privilege

The claim of any privilege must be timely, that is, made before or at the time the evidence claimed to be privileged is offered or produced. Because the Texas Rules of Evidence generally favor the admissibility of evidence, the exceptions to admissibility must be proven. Vernon's Ann.Rules Evid., Rule 501 provides that privileges are exceptions to the admissibility of evidence. Therefore, any party who claims the protection of a recognized privilege must not only timely assert it, but must also prove the elements of the privilege. *El Centro del Barrio, Inc. v. Barlow, 894 S.W.2d 775 (Tex. App.—San Antonio 1994, orig. proc.).* A claim of privilege must be asserted at every opportunity, or it may be waived. However, most claims of privilege fail in court not because they were not timely asserted, but because they were not proven by competent evidence. See *Turner v. Montgomery, 836 S.W.2d 848 (Tex. App.—Houston [1st Dist.] 1992, no writ).* See also, Addison, *Making a Prima Facie Case of Privilege,* Vol. 68, No. 1 Texas Bar Journal 84, January 2005.

Waiver

Failure to make a timely claim of privilege or failure to establish the elements of the privilege is a waiver of the privilege. A person may also waive a privilege which he is entitled to assert by: (1) disclosing the privileged material or communication; (2) by calling as a character witness a person to whom a privileged communication was made or to whom privileged information was given; (3) by using a claim of privilege offensively in a civil case; (4) by engaging in conduct which constitutes an exception to the application of the privilege; or (5) in the case of a claim of privilege in response to a proper discovery request in a civil case, by failing to comply with the requirements of Vernon's Ann.Rules Civ.Proc., Rules 193.3 and 193.4 (effective January 1, 1999).

At the heart of a privilege is the confidential nature of the information or communication sought to be protected by the claim of privilege. Voluntary actions which breach this confidentiality, including outright disclosure of the protected information or communication by a person for whom the privilege applies, whether disclosed intentionally *or by inadvertence*, is a waiver of the privilege claimed. *Granada Corp. v. Honorable First Court of Appeals, 844 S.W.2d 223 (Tex. 1992)*; *United States v. Massachusetts Institute of Tech., 129 F.3d 681 (1st Cir. 1997)*; Vernon's Ann.Rules Evid., Rule 511(1). See Commentary, Vernon's Ann.Rules Evid., Rules 612 and 615. *Berger v. Lang, 976 S.W.2d 833 (Tex. App.—Houston [1st Dist.] 1998, pet. denied)* (creating a false impression of the outcome of a grievance matter, which is privileged for the respondent attorney, impliedly invites disclosure of it). Under Vernon's Ann.Rules Civ.Proc., Rule 193.3(d), "[A] party who produces material or information without intending to waive a claim of privilege does not waive that claim under these rules or the Rules of Evidence . . . " if prompt action is taken in accordance with that rule. Thus, an inadvertent disclosure of privileged materials or information in response to a discovery request can be remedied in accordance with the requirements of the rule without waiving the privileged claimed.

The Texas Rules of Evidence specifically provide that an applicable privilege may be waived by calling to testify as a character witness a person to whom a privileged communication has been made, to the extent that such communication is relevant to the character or trait of character inquired about on direct examination. Vernon's Ann.Rules Evid., Rule 511(2).

A claim of privilege by a party asserting affirmative relief in a civil case must be upheld and is not waived unless: (1) the party is truly seeking affirmative relief; (2) at least some of the privileged information sought is that which, if believed, would probably determine the outcome of the claim or defense of the party claiming the privilege; and (3) disclosure of the confidential communication is the only means by which the other party may obtain some of the evidence claimed to be protected. If all three of these elements are present, the privilege is waived, if used offensively. *Texas Dep't of Public Safety Officers Ass'n v. Denton, 897 S.W.2d 757 (Tex. 1995)*; *Republic Ins. Co. v. Davis, 856 S.W.2d 158 (Tex. 1993)*. See *Ginsberg v. Fifth Court of Appeals, 686 S.W.2d 105 (Tex. 1985)*; *DeWitt and Rearick, Inc. v. Ferguson, 699 S.W.2d 692 (Tex. App.—El Paso 1985, orig. proc.)*; *Parten v. Brigham, 785 S.W.2d 165 (Tex. App.—Fort Worth 1989, orig. proc.)*; *Westheimer v. Tennant, 831 S.W.2d 880 (Tex. App.—Houston [14th Dist.] 1992, orig. proc.)*. See also Cornell, *Piercing the Iron Curtain of Silence—The Doctrine of Offensive Use Waiver*, 60 Tex. Bar Journal 304 (1997).

When a privilege is used offensively to resist discovery in a civil case, it is waived if the party resisting discovery is asserting a claim or defense for affirmative relief, some of the material sought to be protected is outcome determinative, and there is no other means by which the other party may obtain some of the material claimed to be privileged. However, in a case involving discovery, the trial court may not dismiss the affirmative claim or defense as a sanction for discovery abuse without first considering and determining the factors set out in *TransAmerican Natural Gas Corp. v. Powell, 811 S.W.2d 913 (Tex. 1991)*. See *Texas Dep't of Public Safety Officers Ass'n v. Denton, supra.*

A party which withholds material or information from discovery under a claim of privilege may not use that material or information at any hearing or trial without first timely amending or supplementing that party's response to that discovery. Vernon's Ann.Rules Civ.Proc., Rule 193.4(c).

Many privileges are deemed not to apply in certain circumstances, that is, there are exceptions to their applicability, depending on the provisions of the rule relating to the particular privilege claimed or depending on case law exceptions. Evidence which, if believed, shows that one or more of the applicable exceptions to a privilege exists will defeat the claim of privilege. In the Texas Rules of Evidence, the lawyer-client privilege, the husband-wife communication privilege, the privilege relating to the identity of an informer, the physician/patient privilege, and the confidentiality privilege of mental health information all contain exceptions to their applicability.

Texas privileges in federal court on state law claims

FED. R. EVID. 501 recognizes only those privileges that arise under the common law of the United States, except where a privilege derives from the Constitution of the United States, an act of Congress or present statutory authority. Privileges arising from Texas law have no applicability in federal criminal cases. They also have no applicability in civil cases in federal court that present a federal question that does not rely on the substantive law of Texas for its resolution. However, privileges under Texas law are recognized in federal courts in cases involving state law claims and claims requiring the substantive law of Texas for resolution. It is unsettled as to whether Texas privileges would be recognized in federal civil cases involving mixed questions of federal and state law. See FED. R. EVID. 501, *Notes of Committee on the Judiciary, House Report 93–650,* Appendix. See also FED. R. EVID. 501, *Notes of Committee on the Judiciary, Senate Report 93–1277,* Appendix.

Uniform Rules of Evidence

For text of corresponding provisions of Uniform Rules of Evidence and notes of decisions relating thereto, which may provide guidance in interpreting the Texas Rule, see Rule 501, 13A Uniform Laws Annotated.

Federal Rules of Evidence

The corresponding provision of the Federal Rules of Evidence is Rule 501. For the text of the Rule and Advisory Committee Notes, which may provide guidance in interpreting the Texas Rule, see the Appendix to this volume.

B. Constitutional Privileges

The word "Constitution", as it appears in this rule, is not limited to any particular constitution, but certainly includes the Constitutions of the State of Texas and of the United States. The constitutions of other states and other countries might apply if they establish privileges that would be applicable in a Texas case. See *Volkswagen A.G. v. Valdez, 909 S.W.2d 900 (Tex. 1995)* or *Ford Motor Co. v. Leggat, 904 S.W.2d 643 (Tex. 1995).* See also *Davidson v. Great Nat'l Life Ins. Co., 737 S.W.2d 312 (Tex. 1987).*

Under the Constitution of the United States, the privilege against self-incrimination is the one with which most people are familiar. But other privileges, or rights having some of the characteristics of privileges, have been recognized as arising from constitutional rights or issues regarding religious matters, illegally obtained evidence, privacy, speech and association, the press and others. *Tilton v. Marshall, 925 S.W.2d 672 (Tex. 1996, orig. proc.).* The Texas Constitution contains a Bill of Rights and other provisions which, in some instances, are more expansive than those of the Federal constitution. Vernon's Ann.Const. Art. I. Cases decided by Texas courts in civil cases on privileges of constitutional magnitude usually rely on the provisions of the United States Constitution, and rarely on the provisions of the Texas Constitution. Perhaps this is an overlooked area of the law of privileges in Texas in civil cases. Criminal practitioners, however, have long been aware of the protections afforded their clients by the Texas Constitution.

C. Privileges Promulgated by the Texas Supreme Court Pursuant to Statutory Authority

The Texas Rules of Civil Procedure provide for privileges from pretrial discovery. These are privileges against being required to provide or divulge certain types of information recognized as privileged under those rules, the Texas Rules of Evidence or any other privilege established in law. The rules of civil procedure provide for the assertion of any appropriate claim of privilege in response to discovery requests, and those rules establish a method for obtaining a hearing and a ruling on a claim of privilege in response to a discovery request. An assertion that material or information is the work product of an attorney is an assertion of privilege. See Vernon's Ann.Rules Civ.Proc., Rules 192.5, 193.3 and 193.4. See also, Albright, *The Texas Work Product Rule,* 27 *The Advocate* 10, State Bar Litigation Report, Summer 2004.

In its 2005 amendments to the Texas Rules of Civil Procedure, the Texas Supreme Court has amended Rule 173 to provide that communications between the guardian ad litem and the party represented by a next friend or guardian, the next friend or guardian, or their attorney are privileged as if the guardian ad litem were the attorney for the party. Tex. R. Civ. Proc. 173.5 (effective February 1, 2005 in all pending cases). See Tex. R. Evid. 503. Rule 173 does not, however, apply to an appointment of a guardian ad litem governed by statute or other rules. Tex. R. Civ. Proc. 173.1.

D. Examples of Statutory Privileges

Chiropractor-patient communications. V.T.C.A., Occupations Code § 201.402.

Communications by a deaf person. If a deaf person communicates through an interpreter to a person under circumstances in which the communication would be privileged and the deaf person could not be required to testify about the communication, the privilege applies to the interpreter as well. V.T.C.A., Civil Practice & Remedies Code § 21.008.

Communications by a sexual assault victim. Communications between a sexual assault victim and a "sexual assault advocate" are privileged against disclosure unless the communication is used in a "criminal investigation or proceeding in response to a subpoena issued in accordance with law." This would include grand jury proceedings as well as a trial and matters incident to it. "Sexual assault advocate" is a term of art defined in the statute. V.T.C.A., Health & Safety Code § 44.071.

Communications with emergency medical services personnel. A communication between certified emergency medical personnel or a physician providing medical supervision and a patient made in the course of providing emergency medical services to the patient is confidential and may not be disclosed except as provided by this statute. V.T.C.A., Health & Safety Code § 773.091.

Counselors in suits for divorce. No person who has counseled parties to a suit for divorce is competent to testify in any action involving the parties or their children. See Vernon's Ann.Rules Evid., Rule 601. The files, records, and other work-products of the counselor are privileged and confidential for all purposes and may not be admitted as evidence in any action involving the parties or their children. V.T.C.A., Family Code § 3.54(d).

Crime Stoppers Advisory Council—privileged information. Evidence of a communication between a person submitting a report of a criminal act to the Crime Stoppers Advisory Council or to a local crime stoppers program and the person who accepted the report on behalf of the council or local crime stoppers program is not admissible in a court or an administrative proceeding, except in a criminal case under certain circumstances. V.T.C.A., Government Code § 414.008.

Dentistry peer review committees. V.T.C.A., Occupations Code § 261.051.

Identity of blood donors. The medical and donor records of a blood bank are confidential and may not be disclosed except under certain circumstances. V.T.C.A., Health & Safety Code § 162.003.

Information privileged from discovery by an inmate. Personal identifying information of an individual is privileged from discovery by an individual who is imprisoned or confined in any correctional facility if the individual to whom the information pertains is (1) an employee of any correctional facility or (2) related within the first degree by consanguinity or affinity to an individual who is an employee of any correctional facility. V.T.C.A., Civil Practice & Remedies Code § 30.010.

Inmate grievance reports. A report, investigation, or supporting documents prepared by the Department of Criminal Justice, Institutional Division in response to an inmate grievance is considered to have been prepared in anticipation of litigation and is confidential, privileged, and not subject to discovery by the inmate in a claim arising out of the same operative facts as are alleged in the grievance. V.T.C.A., Government Code § 501.008.

Journalist's Qualified Testimonial Privilege in Criminal Cases. This privilege is new to Texas law. TEX. CODE CRIM. PROC. ANN. art. 38.11 (effective May 13, 2009).

Journalist's Qualified Testimonial Privilege in Civil Proceedings. V.T.C.A., Civil Practice & Remedies Code § 22.023.

Medical peer review committees. V.T.C.A., Occupations Code § 161.007. See *Memorial Hosp.—The Woodlands v. McCown, 927 S.W.2d 1 (Tex. 1996, orig. proc.)* and *Irving Healthcare Sys. v. Brooks, 927 S.W.2d 12 (Tex. 1996, orig. proc.).*

Nursing home reports. Information from nursing homes and any compilations, reports, or analyses produced from that information are not subject to discovery, subpoena, or other means of legal compulsion for release to any person or entity, except under certain circumstances, and is not admissible in any civil, administrative, or criminal proceeding. The privilege established here is required to be recognized by Rules 501 and 502 of the Texas Rules of Evidence. V.T.C.A., Health & Safety Code § 242.049.

Open government—trade secrets or commercial or financial information. A trade secret or commercial or financial information obtained from a person which is privileged or confidential by statute or judicial decision is excepted from the requirements of V.T.C.A., Government Code § 552.0219 (availability of public information). V.T.C.A., Government Code § 552.110.

Patient-emergency medical services personnel communications. A communication between certified emergency medical services personnel, or a physician providing medical supervision for them, and a patient which is made in the course of providing emergency medical services to the patient is confidential and privileged and may not be disclosed except as provided by V.T.C.A., Health & Safety Code § 773.092. Vernon's Ann.Rules Evid., Rule 501 notwithstanding, the privilege of confidentiality may be claimed in any criminal, civil, or administrative proceeding and may be claimed by the patient or the emergency medical services personnel or physician acting on the patient's behalf. V.T.C.A., Health & Safety Code § 773.09.

Physician-patient communications. V.T.C.A., Occupations Code § 159.001 et seq.

Podiatrist-patient communications. V.T.C.A., Occupations Code § 202.401 et seq.

Podiatry peer review committees. V.T.C.A., Occupations Code §§ 202.454, 202.455.

Privileges in contested cases before State administrative agencies. In a contested case, a state agency shall give effect to the rules of privilege recognized by law. V.T.C.A., Government Code § 2001.083.

Records and proceedings of a medical committee. The records and proceedings of a medical committee are confidential and are not subject to court subpoena. V.T.C.A., Health & Safety Code § 161.032. This section and § 5.06, Medical Practices Act (Article 4495b, Vernon's Texas Civil Statutes), do not apply to records made or maintained in the regular course of business by a hospital, health maintenance organization, medical organization, university medical center or health science center, or extended care facility. This privilege is not limited to only certain causes of action. *Memorial Hosp.-The Woodlands v. McCown, 927 S.W.2d 1, 2 (Tex. 1996, orig. proc.)* (privilege applied in defamation case); *Irving Healthcare Sys. v. Brooks, 927 S.W.2d 12, 14–15 (Tex. 1996, orig. proc.)* (privilege applied in defamation/interference with business relations case). *In re Osteopathic Med. Ctr., 16 S.W.3d 881 (Tex. App.—Fort Worth 2000, orig. proc.)* (privileged applied in premises liability case).

Reports and reportable diseases. Reports, records, and information relating to cases or suspected cases of diseases or health conditions are not public information and may not be released or made public on subpoena or otherwise, with some exceptions. If information is required in a court proceeding involving child abuse, the information shall be disclosed in camera. A state or public health district officer or employee, local health department officer or employee, or health authority may not be examined in a civil, criminal, special, or other proceeding as to the existence or contents of pertinent records of, or reports or information about, a person examined or treated for a reportable disease by the public health district, local health department, or health authority without that person's consent. V.T.C.A., Health & Safety Code § 81.046.

Reports of child abuse or neglect. The requirement to report child abuse or neglect applies without exception to an individual whose personal communications may otherwise be privileged, including an attorney, a member of the clergy, a medical practitioner, a social worker, and a mental health professional. The identity of an individual making a report is confidential and may be disclosed only on the order of a court or to a law enforcement officer for the purposes of conducting a criminal investigation of the report. V.T.C.A., Family Code § 261.101. In a proceeding regarding the abuse or neglect of a child, evidence may not be excluded on the ground of privileged communication except in the case of communications between an attorney and client. V.T.C.A., Family Code § 261.202.

Sexual exploitation of a patient by a mental health services provider. If a mental health services provider or the employer of a mental health services provider has reasonable cause to suspect that a patient has been the victim of sexual exploitation by a mental health services provider during the course of treatment, or if a patient alleges sexual exploitation by a mental health services provider during the course of treatment, information in a report of the allegation or the basis for such belief, including the identity of the alleged victim, is privileged information and is for the exclusive use of the prosecuting attorney or state licensing board that receives the information. V.T.C.A., Civil Practice & Remedies Code § 81.006.

Studies of mental disorders and disabilities. In a study to reduce mental disorders and mental disabilities, the identity of a person whose condition or treatment is studied is confidential and may not be revealed under any circumstances. Information provided for the study and any finding or conclusion resulting from the study is privileged information. V.T.C.A., Health & Safety Code § 533.010.

Title IV–D child support information. Except as provided, all communications made by a recipient of financial assistance under Chapter 31, Human Resources Code, or an applicant for or recipient of services in certain circumstances are privileged. V.T.C.A., Family Code § 231.108(b).

E. Examples of Case Law Privileges

Privileges which are provided for by the laws of other states or even of other countries may be the applicable privileges to be applied in a Texas case. See

Volkswagen A.G. v. Valdez, 909 S.W.2d 900 (Tex. 1995) (materials that are protected by the laws of a foreign government may be exempt from discovery in a Texas proceeding); *Ford Motor Co. v. Leggat, 904 S.W.2d 643 (Tex. 1995)* (communications made in reliance on a well-established and recognized evidentiary privilege afforded to the communication by another state are protected in Texas by the evidentiary privilege of that other state which applies to the communication, if the communication was made in that state).

Some Texas courts have determined that a qualified privilege exists in Texas to protect the identity of confidential sources or informants of reporters. *Channel Two Television Co. v. Dickerson, 725 S.W.2d 470 (Tex. App.—Houston [1st Dist.] 1987, orig. proc.); Dallas Morning News v. Garcia, 822 S.W.2d 675 (Tex. App.—San Antonio 1991, orig. proc.).* The authority for this view has been cited as *Branzburg v. Hayes, 408 U.S. 665, 92 S.Ct. 2646 (1972).* However, *Branzburg* does not establish the existence of such a privilege and the assertion by the First Court of Appeals of Texas in *Channel Two Television Co.* that it does was explicitly disavowed by that court in *Dolcefino v. Ray, 902 S.W.2d 163 (Tex. App.—Houston [1st Dist.] 1995, orig. proc.).* Note, however, that there is a qualified *statutory* privilege for journalists in criminal cases. Tex. Code Crim. Proc. Ann. (Vernon 2010) art. 38.11 (effective May 13, 2009). There is also a qualified statutory privilege in civil proceedings. V.T.C.A., Civil Practice & Remedies Code § 22.023.

Leading CLE/Law Review Publications

Askew, *Survey of the Law of Privilege in Texas Courts,* 23rd Annual Civ. Trial Course, State Bar of Texas (2000).

Cochran, *Selected Privilege Issues*, 33rd Annual Adv. Criminal Law Course, State Bar of Texas (July 2007).

Keltner, *Protecting and Piercing Privilege,* 23rd Annual Civ. Trial Course, State Bar of Texas (2000).

White, *Privileges,* 24th Annual Evidence and Discovery Course, State Bar of Texas (2011).

Wren and Gilliland, *Asserting, Proving and Attacking Privileges,* 27 *The Advocate* 16, State Bar Litigation Section Report (Summer 2004).

Integrated Legal Research System References

West's Texas Digest Key Numbers

Witnesses ⚿184–223, 292.

Texas Practice

Addison, Texas Practice Guide, Evidence § 5:1 et seq.

Texas Jur 3d

24A Texas Jur 3d, Criminal Law § 3761.

Annotations

Marital privilege under Rule 501 of Federal Rules of Evidence, 46 ALR Fed 735.

Psychotherapist-patient privilege under federal common law, 72 ALR Fed 395.

Reportorial privilege as to nonconfidential news information, 60 ALR5th 75.

"Scholar's privilege" under Rule 501 of Federal Rules of Evidence, 81 ALR Fed 904.

Situations in which federal courts are governed by state law of privilege under Rule 501 of Federal Rules of Evidence, 48 ALR Fed 259.

Testimonial privilege for confidential communications between relatives other than husband and wife—state cases, 62 ALR5th 629.

Tort or statutory liability for failure or refusal of witness to give testimony, 61 ALR3d 1297.

Rule 502. Required Reports Privileged by Statute

A person, corporation, association, or other organization or entity, either public or private, making a return or report required by law to be made has a privilege to refuse to disclose and to prevent any other person from disclosing the return or report, if the law requiring it to be made so provides. A public officer or agency to whom a return or report is required by law to be made has a privilege to refuse to disclose the return or report if the law requiring it to be made so provides. No privilege exists under this rule in actions involving perjury, false statements, fraud in the return or report, or other failure to comply with the law in question.

Eff. March 1, 1998.

Commentary

In general

Reports required by law to be made are privileged if the law requiring the report so provides. The agency or person to whom the report is made may refuse to disclose it if the law requiring the report so provides. Statements in such required reports which constitute perjury, which are false, which are not required by the applicable law to be in the report, or which constitute fraud, are not protected by this rule.

Uniform Rules of Evidence

There is no corresponding provision in the Uniform Rules of Evidence

Federal Rules of Evidence

There is no corresponding provision in the Federal Rules of Evidence.

Integrated Legal Research System References

West's Texas Digest Key Numbers

Witnesses ⚷185.

Texas Practice

Addison, Texas Practice Guide, Evidence § 5:45 et seq.

Texas Jur 3d

36 Texas Jur 3d, Evidence § 516.

Rule 503. Lawyer–Client Privilege

(a) Definitions. As used in this rule:

(1) A "client" is a person, public officer, or corporation, association, or other organization or entity, either public or private, who is rendered professional

legal services by a lawyer, or who consults a lawyer with a view to obtaining professional legal services from that lawyer.

(2) A "representative of the client" is:

(A) a person having authority to obtain professional legal services, or to act on advice thereby rendered, on behalf of the client, or

(B) any other person who, for the purpose of effectuating legal representation for the client, makes or receives a confidential communication while acting in the scope of employment for the client.

(3) A "lawyer" is a person authorized, or reasonably believed by the client to be authorized, to engage in the practice of law in any state or nation.

(4) A "representative of the lawyer" is:

(A) one employed by the lawyer to assist the lawyer in the rendition of professional legal services; or

(B) an accountant who is reasonably necessary for the lawyer's rendition of professional legal services.

(5) A communication is "confidential" if not intended to be disclosed to third persons other than those to whom disclosure is made in furtherance of the rendition of professional legal services to the client or those reasonably necessary for the transmission of the communication.

(b) Rules of Privilege.

(1) *General rule of privilege.* A client has a privilege to refuse to disclose and to prevent any other person from disclosing confidential communications made for the purpose of facilitating the rendition of professional legal services to the client:

(A) between the client or a representative of the client and the client's lawyer or a representative of the lawyer;

(B) between the lawyer and the lawyer's representative;

(C) by the client or a representative of the client, or the client's lawyer or a representative of the lawyer, to a lawyer or a representative of a lawyer representing another party in a pending action and concerning a matter of common interest therein;

(D) between representatives of the client or between the client and a representative of the client; or

(E) among lawyers and their representatives representing the same client.

(2) *Special rule of privilege in criminal cases.* In criminal cases, a client has a privilege to prevent the lawyer or lawyer's representative from disclosing any other fact which came to the knowledge of the lawyer or the lawyer's representative by reason of the attorney-client relationship.

(c) Who May Claim the Privilege. The privilege may be claimed by the client, the client's guardian or conservator, the personal representative of a deceased client, or the successor, trustee, or similar representative of a corporation, association, or other organization, whether or not in existence. The person who was the lawyer or the lawyer's representative at the time of the communication is presumed to have authority to claim the privilege but only on behalf of the client.

(d) Exceptions. There is no privilege under this rule:

(1) *Furtherance of crime or fraud.* If the services of the lawyer were sought or obtained to enable or aid anyone to commit or plan to commit what the client knew or reasonably should have known to be a crime or fraud;

(2) *Claimants through same deceased client.* As to a communication relevant to an issue between parties who claim through the same deceased client, regardless of whether the claims are by testate or intestate succession or by *inter vivos* transactions;

(3) *Breach of duty by a lawyer or client.* As to a communication relevant to an issue of breach of duty by a lawyer to the client or by a client to the lawyer;

(4) *Document attested by a lawyer.* As to a communication relevant to an issue concerning an attested document to which the lawyer is an attesting witness; or

(5) *Joint clients.* As to a communication relevant to a matter of common interest between or among two or more clients if the communication was made by any of them to a lawyer retained or consulted in common, when offered in an action between or among any of the clients.

Eff. March 1, 1998.

Commentary

In general

A confidential communication made between a client, or the client's representative, and an attorney, or the attorney's representative, "for the purpose of facilitating the rendition of professional legal services" to the client is privileged. A confidential communication by or between the lawyer and his representative, the client and his representative, representatives of the client, and among lawyers and their representatives for the same client is also protected if the communication is made for the purpose of rendering legal services to the client. In order for the privilege to apply there must actually be an attorney-client relationship, or a reasonable attempt to establish one. If the attorney-client privilege does apply, it not only survives the attorney-client relationship, it survives the client. Vernon's Ann. Rules Evid., Rule 503(c). See *Swidler & Berlin v. United States, 524 U.S. 399, 118 S.Ct. 2081, 141 L.Ed.2d 379 (1998)* (attorney's notes of an initial interview with a client shortly before the client's death are protected by the attorney-client privilege from a government subpoena in a criminal investigation).

The privilege to refuse to disclose a communication protected by the attorney-client privilege, or to prevent another from doing so, belongs to the client. The attorney, or a representative of the attorney, may invoke the privilege, but only on behalf of the client. Vernon's Ann.Rules Evid., Rule 503(c).

Client representatives—before March 1, 1998—the "control group test"

In order for a client to prove the client's claim of an attorney-client privilege arising from the action of its representative, the client must establish: (1) that the representative whose communication on behalf of the client is claimed to be protected by the attorney-client privilege had authority to obtain legal services for the client, or to act for the client on advice rendered pursuant to such legal services; and (2) that the communication sought to be protected was a confidential communication made in order to obtain or render legal advice to the client. *El Centro del Barrio, Inc. v. Barlow, 894 S.W.2d 775 (Tex. App.—San Antonio 1994, orig. proc.).* The representative of the corporation having authority to obtain legal services for the corporation under this rule must be someone who has control over the affairs of the corporation, either individually or as part of group controlling the affairs of the corporation. *National Tank Co. v. Brotherton, 851 S.W.2d 193, 197 (Tex. 1993).* This is referred to as the "control group test" of the authority to claim the attorney-client privilege on behalf of another. The authority to claim and protect the attorney-client privilege is significantly broadened by the adoption of the "subject matter test" of the Texas Rules of Evidence that became effective on March 1, 1998.

Client representatives—effective March 1, 1998—the "subject matter test"

The right of the client to claim the attorney-client privilege now also extends to the action of any other person, whether having the specific authority to obtain legal services for the client or not, "who, for the purpose of effectuating legal representation for the client, makes or receives a confidential communication *while acting within the scope of employment for the client.*" (emphasis added).

Joint defenses and joint representation

This rule also provides that a confidential communication made by the client or his representative, or by his lawyer or a representative of his lawyer, to a lawyer, or a representative of a lawyer representing another party in a pending action, and concerning a matter of common interest in the pending action, for the purpose of facilitating the rendition of professional legal services for the client, is privileged. This is the situation where two or more clients sharing some common interest retain separate counsel and then pool information or design a joint defense See *Strong v. State, 773 S.W.2d 543 (Tex. Crim. App. 1989).* Before embarking on a joint defense of a claim, a careful trial lawyer should consider whether the parties to the joint defense thereby become joint clients of the attorneys involved. If so, it is likely that the confidential communications made during the course of the joint defense concerning matters of common interest, will amount to an exception to the attorney-client privilege in an action, even in the same lawsuit, between or among any of the clients. See TEX. R. [CIV.] EVID. 503(b)(3) and 503(d)(5). See also V.T.C.A., Government Code, Rules of Prof. Conduct, Rule 4.02 (1989), reprinted in V.T.C.A., Government Code, tit. 2, subtit. G app. (Vernon Supp. 1996) (STATE BAR RULES art. X, § 9).

The special rule in criminal cases as stated in Rule 503 (b)(2) is rescinded effective September 1, 2008. Texas Court of Criminal Appeals, Misc. Docket No. 08-100, *Order Amending Texas Rules of Evidence and Appellate Procedure*, effective September 1, 2008. By terms of the order, the amendments are subject to further amendment after the opportunity for public comment before September 1, 2008.

Special rule of privilege in criminal cases (if it still applies)

In criminal cases, the client can prevent the lawyer or the lawyer's representative from disclosing any fact that came to either of them by reason of the attorney-client relationship. This includes information that was not the result of a confidential communication. In other words, what the lawyer or the lawyer's representative knows about the client and his case obtained during the lawyer's representation of the client may not be disclosed over the client's objection. There are exceptions. See *Manning v. State, 773 S.W.2d 568 (Tex. Crim. App. 1989)* (the rule permitting client to prevent attorney from disclosing any fact arising from representation cannot be interpreted literally); *Henderson v. State, 962 S.W.2d 544 (Tex. Crim. App. 1997)* ("attorney-client privilege was legitimately required to yield to the strong public policy interest of protecting a child from death or serious bodily injury").

Other exceptions to the applicability of the attorney-client privilege.

Besides the joint client exception to the applicability of the privilege, this rule also lists four other exceptions: (1) services of the attorney sought by the client in furtherance of a crime of fraud; (2) communications relevant to an issue between parties who claim through the same deceased client of the attorney; (3) communications relevant to a breach of duty of the lawyer to the client or the client to the lawyer; and (4) communications relevant to a document to which the attorney is an attesting witness.

Other obligations of the attorney to preserve client confidences.

See V.T.C.A., Government Code, Rules of Prof. Conduct, Rules 1.02 and 1.05.

Official Comment to former Rule 503

The comment to former Rule 503 of the Rules of Civil Evidence and the Rules of Criminal Evidence provided in pertinent part as follows: "This rule governs only the lawyer/client privilege. It does not restrict the scope of the work product doctrine."

Uniform Rules of Evidence

For text of corresponding provisions of Uniform Rules of Evidence and notes of decisions relating thereto, which may provide guidance in interpreting the Texas Rule, see Rule 502, 13A Uniform Laws Annotated.

Federal Rules of Evidence

There is no corresponding provision in the Federal Rules of Evidence.

Leading Cases

Almendarez v. State, 153 S.W.3d 727 (Tex. App.–Dallas 2005) (under the V.T.C.A., Family Code § 261.202 only the attorney-client privilege survives in any proceeding involving abuse or neglect of a child).

Austin v. State, 934 S.W.2d 672 (Tex. Crim. App. 1996) (application of the attorney-client privilege depends on whether the communication sought to be protected is confidential; communication from attorney about a trial date is not protected).

Comegys v. Glassell, 839 F.Supp. 447 (E.D. Tex. 1993) (there is no independent attorney-client privilege existing between a trustee and the trust's attorney to the exclusion of the beneficiaries as to documents which relate to the administration of the trust or its assets). See *Huie v. DeShazo, 922 S.W.2d 920 (Tex. 1996)*

E.I. DuPont de Nemours and Co., Inc., In re, 136 S.W.3d 218 (Tex. 2004) (party seeking discovery must specify its challenges to an asserted privilege after the party asserting the privilege has made a *prima facie* case; any party may ask for hearing on a claim of privilege and party asserting it must present evidence to support the privilege).

El Centro del Barrio, Inc. v. Barlow, 894 S.W.2d 775 (Tex. App.—San Antonio 1994, orig. proc.) (the burden is on the party seeking to protect the communications to prove the elements of an attorney-client privilege; there are no presumptions of an attorney-client privilege or that the person receiving or seeking the legal advice is one to whom the privilege would apply).

Fontenot, In re, 13 S.W.3d 111 (Tex. App.—Fort Worth 2000, orig. proc.) (statement of insured to insurance adjuster not protected because insured not a client, the insured was not a represented by the adjuster and the adjuster did not take the statement to facilitate the rendition of legal services). See *W & G Trucking, Inc., In re, 990 S.W.2d 473 (Tex. App.—Beaumont 1999)*, cited below.

Ginsberg v. Fifth Court of Appeals, 686 S.W.2d 105 (Tex. 1985) (offensive rather than defensive use of a privilege places matters sought be protected, but which are relevant to the claimant's claim or defense, outside the protection of a privilege). *Note:* The holding in *Ginsberg* has been refined. See *Republic Ins. Co. v. Davis, 856 S.W.2d 158 (Tex. 1993)*; *Texas Dep't of Public Safety Officers Ass'n v. Denton, 897 S.W.2d 757 (Tex. 1995)*, cited below.

Granada Corp. v. Honorable First Court of Appeals, 844 S.W.2d 223 (Tex. 1992) (the crime-fraud exception applies only if a prima facie case is made of contemplated fraud, and then there must be a relationship between the document or information for which the crime-fraud exception to the privilege is claimed and the prima facie proof offered).

Harlandale Indep. Sch. Dist. v. Cornyn, 25 S.W.3d 328 (Tex. App.—Austin 2000, pet. denied) (a report of an investigation by an attorney retained by a school district for that purpose and for the purpose of rendering legal services is protected by the attorney-client privilege and excepted from disclosure under the Texas Public Information Act).

Huie v. DeShazo, 922 S.W.2d 920 (Tex. 1996) (a trustee must fully disclose material facts regarding the administration of a trust, but the trustee is not required to divulge confidential communications made between the trustee and his attorney because the trustee who retains an attorney to advise him in administering a trust is the client, not the trust beneficiaries). See *Comegys v. Glassell, 839 F.Supp. 447 (E.D. Tex. 1993).*

Pittsburgh Corning Corp. v. Caldwell, 861 S.W.2d 423 (Tex. App.—Houston [14th Dist.] 1993, no writ) (when a document is determined by the court to contain information which is privileged, the entire document is privileged).

Pope v. State, 207 S.W.3d 352 (Tex. Crim. App. 2006) (work product doctrine belongs to and protects the attorney and his creative efforts by providing a qualified privilege, but none of the underlying facts are protected; the attorney-client privilege belongs to and protects the client against compelled disclosure of confidential communications and is an evidentiary privilege).

Republic Ins. Co. v. Davis, 856 S.W.2d 158 (Tex. 1993) (offensive use of the attorney-client privilege may waive the privilege under the test first formulated in this case). See *Texas Dep't of Public Safety Officers Ass'n v. Denton, 897 S.W.2d 757 (Tex. 1995)*, cited below, and *Ginsberg v. Fifth Court of Appeals, 686 S.W.2d 105 (Tex. 1985)*, cited above.

Texas Dep't of Public Safety Officers Ass'n v. Denton, 897 S.W.2d 757 (Tex. 1995) (the test first formulated in *Republic Ins. Co. v. Davis*, refined and restated). See *Republic Ins. Co. v. Davis, 856 S.W.2d 158 (Tex. 1993)* and *Ginsberg v. Fifth Court of Appeals, 686 S.W.2d 105 (Tex. 1985)*, cited above.

W & G Trucking, Inc., In re, 990 S.W.2d 473 (Tex. App.—Beaumont 1999, orig. proc.) (statement of insured to insurance adjuster not protected because insured not a client, the insured was not a represented by the adjuster and the adjuster did not take the statement to facilitate the rendition of legal services); *Cf. In re Fontenot, 13 S.W.3d 111 (Tex. App.—Fort Worth 2000, orig. proc.)*, cited above.

Leading CLE/Law Review Publications

Askew, *Privileges Update,* 25th Annual Advanced Evidence and Discovery Course, State Bar of Texas (2012).

Keltner, *The Evolving Attorney-Client Privilege: Business Entities,* 25th Annual Advanced Evidence and Discovery Course, State Bar of Texas (2012).

Keltner, *Lawyer-Client Privilege: It's Not the Rule We Learned in Law School,* 27 *The Advocate* 6, State Bar Litigation Section Report (Summer 2004).

Pikowsky, *Privilege and Confidentiality of Attorney–Client Communication via E–Mail*, 51 Baylor L. Rev. 483 (1999).

Saunders, *Texas Rule of Evidence 503: Defining "Scope of Employment" for Corporations*, 30 St. Mary's L.J. 863 (1999).

Integrated Legal Research System References

West's Texas Digest Key Numbers

Witnesses ⚷197–206, 219.

Texas Practice

Addison, Texas Practice Guide, Evidence § 5:54 et seq.

Texas Jur 3d

24A Texas Jur 3d, Criminal Law § 3775 et seq.

36 Texas Jur 3d, Evidence §§ 518–534.

Am Jur Proof of Facts

Proof of Waiver of Attorney–Client Privilege, 32 Am Jur Proof of Facts 3d 189.

Annotations

Applicability of attorney–client privilege to communications made in presence of or solely to or by nonattorney consultants, professionals, and similar contractors, 66 ALR6th 83.

Applicability of attorney–client privilege to communications made in presence of or solely to or by other attorneys, coparties, and their staff, 64 ALR6th 655.

Applicability of attorney–client privilege to communications made in presence of or solely to or by family members or companion, confidant, or friend of attorneys or client or attesting witnesses for client's will, 67 ALR6th 341.

Applicability of attorney-client privilege to communications made in presence of or solely to or by third person, 14 ALR4th 594.

Applicability of attorney-client privilege to communications with respect to contemplated tortious acts, 2 ALR3d 861.

Applicability of attorney-client privilege to evidence or testimony in subsequent action between parties originally represented contemporaneously by same attorney, with reference to communication to or from one party, 4 ALR4th 765.

Attorney-client privilege as affected by its assertion as to communications, or transmission of evidence, relating to crime already committed, 16 ALR3d 1029.

Attorney-client privilege as extending to communications relating to contemplated civil fraud, 31 ALR4th 458.

Attorney-client privilege: who is "representative of the client" within state statute or rule privileging communications between an attorney and the representative of the client, 66 ALR4th 1227.

Construction and application of self-protection or self-defense exception to attorney–client privilege, 71 ALR6th 249.

Determination of whether a communication is from a corporate client for purposes of the attorney-client privilege—modern cases, 26 ALR5th 628.

Views of United States Supreme Court as to attorney-client privilege, 159 ALR Fed 243.

What corporate communications are entitled to attorney-client privilege—modern cases, 27 ALR5th 76.

What persons or entities may assert or waive corporation's attorney-client privilege—modern cases, 28 ALR5th 1.

Rule 504. Husband–Wife Privileges

(a) Confidential Communication Privilege.

(1) *Definition.* A communication is confidential if it is made privately by any person to the person's spouse and it is not intended for disclosure to any other person.

(2) *Rule of privilege.* A person, whether or not a party, or the guardian or representative of an incompetent or deceased person, has a privilege during marriage and afterwards to refuse to disclose and to prevent another from disclosing a confidential communication made to the person's spouse while they were married.

(3) *Who may claim the privilege.* The confidential communication privilege may be claimed by the person or the person's guardian or representative, or by the spouse on the person's behalf. The authority of the spouse to do so is presumed.

(4) *Exceptions.* There is no confidential communication privilege:

(A) *Furtherance of crime or fraud.* If the communication was made, in whole or in part, to enable or aid anyone to commit or plan to commit a crime or fraud.

(B) *Proceeding between spouses in civil cases.* In (A) a proceeding brought by or on behalf of one spouse against the other spouse, or (B) a proceeding between a surviving spouse and a person who claims through the deceased spouse, regardless of whether the claim is by testate or intestate succession or by inter vivos transaction.

(C) *Crime against spouse or minor child.* In a proceeding in which the party is accused of conduct which, if proved, is a crime against the person of the spouse, any minor child, or any member of the household of either spouse, or, in a criminal proceeding, when the offense charged is under Section 25.01, Penal Code (Bigamy).

(D) *Commitment or similar proceeding.* In a proceeding to commit either spouse or otherwise to place that person or that person's property, or both, under the control of another because of an alleged mental or physical condition.

(E) *Proceeding to establish competence.* In a proceeding brought by or on behalf of either spouse to establish competence.

(b) Privilege not to Testify in Criminal Case.

(1) *Rule of privilege.* In a criminal case, the spouse of the accused has a privilege not to be called as a witness for the state. This rule does not prohibit the spouse from testifying voluntarily for the state, even over objection by the accused. A spouse who testifies on behalf of an accused is subject to cross-examination as provided in rule 611(b).

(2) *Failure to call as witness.* Failure by an accused to call the accused's spouse as a witness, where other evidence indicates that the spouse could testify to relevant matters, is a proper subject of comment by counsel.

(3) *Who may claim the privilege.* The privilege not to testify may be claimed by the person or the person's guardian or representative but not by that person's spouse.

(4) *Exceptions.* The privilege of a person's spouse not to be called as a witness for the state does not apply:

(A) *Certain criminal proceedings.* In any proceeding in which the person is charged with a crime against the person's spouse, a member of the household of either spouse, or any minor, or in an offense charged under Section 25.01, Penal Code (Bigamy).

(B) *Matters occurring prior to marriage.* As to matters occurring prior to the marriage.

Eff. March 1, 1998. Amended by Court of Criminal Appeals Dec. 13, 2006, eff. January 1, 2007.

Cross References

Exceptions to Spousal Adverse Testimony Privilege, Vernon's Ann.C.C.P. Art. 38.10.

Commentary

In general

The husband wife communication privilege is very limited, not only by its own terms, but by the exceptions to it.

For the privilege to apply, there must be a confidential communication to a spouse, it must be privately made, it must not be intended for disclosure to any other person, and it must have been made during the existence of the marriage of the two parties to the communication. *Weaver v. State, 855 S.W.2d 116 (Tex. App.—Houston [14th Dist.] 1993, no pet.).* The privilege may be claimed only by the person making the communication, that person's guardian or representative, or by the spouse on behalf of the person making the communication. The spouse to whom the communication is made may not personally claim the privilege. The privilege may be claimed in any action, whether the person making the confidential communication is a party to that action or not. The privilege exists after the marriage, as well as during it.

This rule has been modified to add as an exception to its protections in a criminal case when the offense charged is bigamy under Section 25.01 of the Texas Penal

Code. *Final Approval of Revisions to the Texas Rules of Appellate Procedure and Texas Rules of Evidence*, Misc. Docket No. 06–100, December 13, 2006, *effective* January 1, 2007.

The communication

The privilege only applies to a communication. Conduct, unless intended to be a substitute for words, is not protected by this privilege. *Sterling v. State, 814 S.W.2d 261 (Tex. App.—Austin 1991, pet. ref'd).* The communication must be made only to a spouse and in private, with no other person present, and not intended for disclosure to any other person.

The requirement of a valid marriage

In Texas, parties may be married ceremonially, or informally (a "common law" marriage), or the parties may declare their marriage in accordance with the applicable statutes, or one or both parties may reasonably believe that they are lawfully married, or the marriage may be voidable but not yet annulled. The existence and validity of a marriage in Texas is governed by the provisions of the V.T.C.A., Family Code § 1.01 et seq. The husband-wife communication privilege implies a valid marriage. Every marriage entered into in Texas is considered valid unless it is expressly made void by the provisions of the Texas Family Code, or unless it is expressly declared voidable by statute *and* is annulled, as provided by the Texas Family Code. V.T.C.A., Family Code § 2.01 et seq.

The existence of a common law marriage is a question of fact. *Aguilar v. State, 715 S.W.2d 645 (Tex. Crim. App. 1986).* However, it is a fact to be determined by the trial court in deciding whether the privilege claimed applies at all under TEX. R. [CIV.] EVID. 104(a). *McDuffie v. State, 854 S.W.2d 195 (Tex. App.—Beaumont 1993, pet. ref'd)*; *Reece v. State, 772 S.W.2d 198 (Tex. App.—Houston [14th Dist.] 1989, no pet.).*

Exceptions to the applicability of the privilege

There are five exceptions within this rule to the applicability of the husband-wife communication privilege. In addition, there is the statutory exception found in V.T.C.A., Family Code § 261.202 (in a proceeding regarding the abuse or neglect of a child, evidence may not be excluded on the ground of privileged communication except in the case of communications between an attorney and client).

Privilege of a spouse not to testify in a criminal case

The spouse of a defendant in a criminal case has a privilege not to be *called* as a witness for the state, but the spouse may testify voluntarily, even over the defendant's objection. The spouse of the defendant can be called as a witness for the state in any case where the defendant is charged with an offense against the spouse, a member of the household of either spouse or any minor. The spouse of a defendant can also be called by the state to testify as to matters occurring prior to the marriage, including communications as well as acts. Failure of a defendant in a criminal case to call his spouse as a witness where other evidence shows that the spouse could testify as to relevant matters may be commented on by the attorneys. See Vernon's Ann.Rules Evid., Rule 513.

Practical considerations

Given the exceptions to the husband-wife communication privilege, the privilege probably has no practical application in any divorce case and in few other family law contexts. The privilege is rarely claimed in other civil cases, which probably accounts for there being no reported civil cases regarding the privilege since the promulgation of this rule. However, the cases interpreting the privilege as set out in the former Texas Rules of Criminal Evidence are instructive, and several have been cited in this commentary. The careful trial lawyer will note that there are notable differences between the "civil" privilege and the "criminal" privilege.

Uniform Rules of Evidence

For text of corresponding provisions of Uniform Rules of Evidence and notes of decisions relating thereto, which may provide guidance in interpreting the Texas Rule, see Rule 504, 13A Uniform Laws Annotated.

Federal Rules of Evidence

There is no corresponding provision in the Federal Rules of Evidence.

Integrated Legal Research System References

West's Texas Digest Key Numbers

Witnesses ⚷187–195.

Texas Practice

Addison, Texas Practice Guide, Evidence § 5:134 et seq.

Texas Jur 3d

24A Texas Jur 3d, Criminal Law § 3768 et seq.

36 Texas Jur 3d, Evidence §§ 535–543.

Annotations

Communication between unmarried couple living together as privileged, 4 ALR4th 422.

Competency of one spouse to testify against other in prosecution for offense against third party as affected by fact that offense against spouse was involved in same transaction, 74 ALR4th 277.

Crimes against spouse within exception permitting testimony by one spouse against other in criminal prosecution—modern state cases, 74 ALR4th 223.

Effect, on competency to testify against spouse or on marital communication privilege, of separation or other marital instability short of absolute divorce, 98 ALR3d 1285.

Existence of spousal privilege where marriage was entered into for purpose of barring testimony, 13 ALR4th 1305.

Marital privilege under Rule 501 of Federal Rules of Evidence, 46 ALR Fed 735.

Presence of child at communication between husband and wife as destroying confidentiality of otherwise privileged communication between them, 39 ALR4th 480.

Propriety and prejudicial effect of prosecutor's argument commenting on failure of defendant's spouse to testify, 26 ALR4th 9.

Waiver of evidentiary privilege by inadvertent disclosure—federal law, 159 ALR Fed 153.

Waiver of evidentiary privilege by inadvertent disclosure—state law, 51 ALR5th 603.

Rule 505. Communications to Members of the Clergy

(a) Definitions. As used in this rule:

(1) A "member of the clergy" is a minister, priest, rabbi, accredited Christian Science Practitioner, or other similar functionary of a religious organization or an individual reasonably believed so to be by the person consulting with such individual.

(2) A communication is "confidential" if made privately and not intended for further disclosure except to other persons present in furtherance of the purpose of the communication.

(b) General Rule of Privilege. A person has a privilege to refuse to disclose and to prevent another from disclosing a confidential communication by the person to a member of the clergy in the member's professional character as spiritual adviser.

(c) Who May Claim the Privilege. The privilege may be claimed by the person, by the person's guardian or conservator, or by the personal representative of the person if the person is deceased. The member of the clergy to whom the communication was made is presumed to have authority to claim the privilege but only on behalf of the communicant.

Eff. March 1, 1998.

Commentary

In general

The communication to a clergyman must be privately made and not intended for further disclosure, except that other persons may also be present without loss of the privilege, if those other persons are present "in furtherance of the purpose of the communication". As is common in the scheme of privilege law in Texas, the privilege belongs to the person making the communication, and, as is also typical, the privilege continues after the death of the communicant.

Uniform Rules of Evidence

For text of corresponding provisions of Uniform Rules of Evidence and notes of decisions relating thereto, which may provide guidance in interpreting the Texas Rule, see Rule 505, 13A Uniform Laws Annotated.

Federal Rules of Evidence

There is no corresponding provision in the Federal Rules of Evidence.

Leading Cases

Bordman v. State, 56 S.W.3d 63, 67–68 (Tex. App.—Houston [14th Dist.] 2001, pet. ref'd) (Section 261.202 of the Texas Family Code prohibits the exclusion of a privileged communication to a church elder in a proceeding regarding the abuse or neglect of a child so that a defendant's confession to a church elder was admissible in the defendant's trial for aggravated sexual assault of a child). See also *Rodriguez v. State, 1997 WL 527843, (Tex. App.—Dallas 1997, pet. ref'd) (unpublished)*, cited below.

Easley v. State, 837 S.W.2d 854 (Tex. App.—Austin 1992, no pet.) (the communication need not be that of a penitent in order to qualify for protection, but not every private communication with a clergyman is privileged; the privilege extends only to a communication to a clergyman as a clergyman).

Gonzalez v. State, 45 S.W.3d 101 (Tex. Crim. App. 2001) ("most significant relationship" test controlled whether California or Texas law would be applied in determining admissibility of defendant's inculpatory statement to pastor during counseling session in California; under that test, California had the more significant relationship with statement; applying California law to determine admissibility would not be contrary to strong public policy of Texas).

Nicholson v. Wittig, 832 S.W.2d 681 (Tex. App.—Houston [1st Dist.] 1992, no writ) (when a person makes a communication with a reasonable expectation of confidentiality to a member of the clergy acting in his professional or spiritual capacity, he may claim the protection of the privilege, but it is not required that the communicant be the individual who seeks, summons, or solicits the presence of the clergyman).

Rodriguez v. State, 1997 WL 527843 (Tex. App.—Dallas 1997, pet. ref'd) (unpublished) (explaining why the Texas Family Code § 261.202 exception to all evidentiary privileges, except the attorney-client privilege, applies in criminal cases). See also, *Bordman v. State, 56 S.W.3d 63, 67–68 (Tex. App.—Houston [14th Dist.] 2001, pet. ref'd).*

Simpson v. Tennant, 871 S.W.2d 301 (Tex. App.—Houston [14th Dist.] 1994, no writ) (the identity of the communicant may be protected by the communications-to-clergymen privilege, either because of the fundamental principles of the privilege, or because a communicant's identity may be inextricably intertwined with the content of the communication).

Integrated Legal Research System References

West's Texas Digest Key Numbers

Witnesses ⚷215.

Texas Practice

Addison, Texas Practice Guide, Evidence § 5:158 et seq.

Texas Jur 3d

36 Texas Jur 3d, Evidence § 522.

Annotations

Communications to clergyman as privileged in federal proceedings, 118 ALR Fed 449.

Subject matter and waiver of privilege covering communications to clergy member or spiritual adviser, 93 ALR5th 327.

Who are "clergy" or like within privilege attaching to communications to clergy members or spiritual advisers, 101 ALR5th 619.

Rule 506. Political Vote

Every person has a privilege to refuse to disclose the tenor of the person's vote at a political election conducted by secret ballot unless the vote was cast illegally.

Eff. March 1, 1998.

Commentary

In general

If it is established that the vote was cast illegally, the voter may be required, over a claim of privilege under this rule, to reveal his vote. As a practical matter, however, the voter may still refuse to answer and claim the privilege against self-incrimination.

Uniform Rules of Evidence

For text of corresponding provisions of Uniform Rules of Evidence and notes of decisions relating thereto, which may provide guidance in interpreting the Texas Rule, see Rule 506, 13A Uniform Laws Annotated.

Federal Rules of Evidence

There is no corresponding provision in the Federal Rules of Evidence.

Integrated Legal Research System References

Texas Practice

Addison, Texas Practice Guide, Evidence § 5:181 et seq.

Texas Jur 3d

36 Texas Jur 3d, Evidence § 526.

Rule 507. Trade Secrets

A person has a privilege, which may be claimed by the person or the person's agent or employee, to refuse to disclose and to prevent other persons from disclosing a trade secret owned by the person, if the allowance of the privilege will not tend to conceal fraud or otherwise work injustice. When disclosure is directed, the judge shall take such protective measure as the interests of the holder of the privilege and of the parties and the furtherance of justice may require.

Eff. March 1, 1998.

Commentary

In general

Only the person who owns the trade secret, or his agent or employee, may refuse to disclose it or prevent another from disclosing it, and then only if the claiming of the privilege will not tend to conceal a fraud or otherwise work an injustice. Under Vernon's Ann.Rules Evid., Rule 104(a), the trial judge determines the existence of the privilege and whether any exceptions or qualifications to the privilege have been established. This rule almost invites its abrogation regarding the disclosure of relevant information claimed to be privileged by allowing the trial judge, under fairly broad circumstances, to require disclosure and then directing him to "take such protective measures as the interests of the holder of the privilege and of the parties and the furtherance of justice may require". This situation most commonly arises in the context of discovery in civil cases, and in disputes in discovery about whether the information claimed to be privileged under this rule is a trade secret. The term "trade secret" is not defined in the specific context of this rule by Texas law. However, the Texas Supreme Court has broadly defined "trade secret" in *Hyde Corp. v. Huffines, 314 S.W.2d 763 (Tex. 1958)*. More recently, the Texas Supreme

Court has referred to a trade secret as "any formula, pattern, device or compilation of information which is used in one's business and presents an opportunity to obtain an advantage over competitors who do not know or use it." *Computer Assocs. Int'l, Inc. v. Altai, Inc., 918 S.W.2d 453, 455 (Tex. 1994).* See also *John Paul Mitchell Sys. v. Randalls Food Mkts., Inc., 17 S.W.3d 721 (Tex. App.—Austin 2000, orig. proc.)* (lists six factors to consider in determining whether information is a trade secret); *In re Bass, 113 S.W.3d 735 (Tex. 2003)* (when court is determining whether information is a trade secret that is protected from discovery, the six factors set forth in the Restatement of Torts [Restatement of Torts § 757; Restatement (Third) of Unfair Competition § 39] are to be weighed in the context of the surrounding circumstances; party claiming a trade secret is not required to satisfy all six factors).

In order to invoke the protections of this rule the party resisting the disclosure of the information has the burden to establish that the information is a trade secret. The burden then shifts to the party seeking the information to establish that the information is necessary for a fair adjudication of its claims. If that burden is met, the court should ordinarily compel disclosure, subject to appropriate protective measures under the rule. The trial court is required to "weigh the degree of the requesting party's need for the information with the potential harm of disclosure to the resisting party." *In re Continental General Tire, Inc., 979 S.W.2d 609 (Tex. 1998, orig. proc.).*

Uniform Rules of Evidence

For text of corresponding provisions of Uniform Rules of Evidence and notes of decisions relating thereto, which may provide guidance in interpreting the Texas Rule, see Rule 507, 13A Uniform Laws Annotated.

Federal Rules of Evidence

There is no corresponding provision in the Federal Rules of Evidence.

Leading Cases

Continental General Tire, Inc., In re, 979 S.W.2d 609 (Tex. 1998, orig. proc.) (explains the scope of Rule 507).

Frost, In re, 998 S.W.2d 938 (Tex. App.—Waco 1999, orig. proc.) (customer list protected by Rule 507 privilege).

John Paul Mitchell Sys. v. Randalls Food Mkts., Inc., 17 S.W.3d 721 (Tex. App.—Austin 2000, orig. proc.) (list of suppliers protected by Rule 507).

Leviton Mfg. Co., In re, 1 S.W.3d 898 (Tex. App.—Waco 1999, orig. proc.) (product prototypes protected by Rule 507 privilege).

Integrated Legal Research System References

West's Texas Digest Key Numbers

Witnesses ⚷294.

Texas Practice

Addison, Texas Practice Guide, Evidence § 5:185 et seq.

Texas Jur 3d

36 Texas Jur 3d, Evidence § 527.

Annotations

In camera trial or hearing and other procedures to safeguard trade secret or the like against undue disclosure in course of civil action involving such secret, 62 ALR2d 509.

Rule 508. Identity of Informer

(a) Rule of Privilege. The United States or a state or subdivision thereof has a privilege to refuse to disclose the identity of a person who has furnished information relating to or assisting in an investigation of a possible violation of a law to a law enforcement officer or member of a legislative committee or its staff conducting an investigation.

(b) Who May Claim. The privilege may be claimed by an appropriate representative of the public entity to which the information was furnished, except the privilege shall not be allowed in criminal cases if the state objects.

(c) Exceptions.

(1) *Voluntary disclosure; informer a witness.* No privilege exists under this rule if the identity of the informer or the informer's interest in the subject matter of the communication has been disclosed to those who would have cause to resent the communication by a holder of the privilege or by the informer's own action, or if the informer appears as a witness for the public entity.

(2) *Testimony on merits.* If it appears from the evidence in the case or from other showing by a party that an informer may be able to give testimony necessary to a fair determination of a material issue on the merits in a civil case to which the public entity is a party, or on guilt or innocence in a criminal case, and the public entity invokes the privilege, the court shall give the public entity an opportunity to show in camera facts relevant to determining whether the informer can, in fact, supply that testimony. The showing will ordinarily be in the form of affidavits, but the court may direct that testimony be taken if it finds that the matter cannot be resolved satisfactorily upon affidavit. If the court finds that there is a reasonable probability that the informer can give the testimony, and the public entity elects not to disclose the informer's identity, the court in a civil case may make any order that justice requires, and in a criminal case shall, on motion of the defendant, and may, on the court's own motion, dismiss the charges as to which the testimony would relate. Evidence submitted to the court shall be sealed and preserved to be made available to the appellate court in the event of an appeal, and the contents shall not otherwise be revealed without consent of the public entity. All counsel and parties shall be permitted to be present at every stage of proceedings under this subdivision except a showing in camera, at which no counsel or party shall be permitted to be present.

(3) *Legality of obtaining evidence.* If information from an informer is relied upon to establish the legality of the means by which evidence was obtained and the court is not satisfied that the information was received from an informer reasonably believed to be reliable or credible, it may require the identity of the informer to be disclosed. The court shall, on request of the public entity, direct that the disclosure be made in camera. All counsel and parties concerned with the issue of legality shall be permitted to be present at every stage of proceedings under this subdivision except a disclosure in camera, at which no counsel or party shall be permitted to be present. If disclosure of the identity of the informer is made in camera, the record thereof shall be sealed and preserved to

be made available to the appellate court in the event of an appeal, and the contents shall not otherwise be revealed without consent of the public entity.

Eff. March 1, 1998.

Commentary

In general

It is the identity of the informer, and information that may tend to identify him, that is privileged under this rule, not the communications made by the informer. This privilege is available only to a public entity that is a party to the case, and only the public entity may invoke it. A public entity cannot invoke this privilege in a criminal case if the state (prosecutor) objects.

There are very few reported civil cases relating to this privilege as it presently exists. The rule itself is straightforward and simple. Complications arise when considering the three exceptions to the privilege and the procedures that the attorneys and the trial court must follow when an exception is shown to probably apply. See *State v. Lowry 802 S.W.2d 669 (Tex. 1991).*

Voluntary disclosure

There is no privilege if the informer testifies in the case for the public entity, or if the informer or the public entity compromise the confidentiality of the identity of the informer by disclosing it.

Testimony on the merits

The privilege does not apply if the informer may be able to give testimony necessary to a fair determination of a material issue on the merits of a case to which the public entity is a party. The party opposing the public entity has the threshold burden of demonstrating that identity must be disclosed. Because that party may not actually know the nature of the informer's testimony, the party is only required to make a plausible showing of how the informer's information may be important. That plausible showing, however, requires evidence, not mere conjecture or speculation. Merely filing a motion for the disclosure of the identity of an informant is not sufficient to obtain a hearing or to compel disclosure. *Bodin v. State, 807 S.W.2d 313 (Tex. Crim. App. 1991).*

Any party may request the *in camera* hearing provided for in this rule. If the public entity invokes the privilege, the trial judge must give the public entity an opportunity to show *in camera* whether the informer can, in fact, supply that testimony. The public entity causes the *in camera* hearing by invoking the privilege, but there is no requirement in the rule that only the public entity may request the hearing. It is error for the trial court to fail to hold the *in camera* hearing. *Bodin v. State, supra.* If after the *in camera* hearing, the trial court then finds that there is a reasonable probability that the informer should give the testimony, the public entity can elect to disclose or not disclose the identity of the informer. If at that point the public entity elects not to disclose the identity of the informer, the trial court may make any order that justice requires. See *Edmond v. State, 911 S.W.2d 487 (Tex. App.—Texarkana 1995, no pet.).*

Legality of obtaining evidence

This exception controls whether the identity of an informer must be disclosed to support the means used to obtain evidence. If the judge is not satisfied that the informer was reliable or credible, he may require that the identity of the informer be disclosed. *Washington v. State, 902 S.W.2d 649 (Tex. App.—Houston [14th Dist.]*

1995, pet. ref'd). An *in camera* hearing is required, if requested by the public entity, when information from an informer is used to establish probable cause to lawfully obtain evidence, but the judge is not satisfied that the informant was reasonably believed to be reliable or credible. *Murray v. State, 864 S.W.2d 111 (Tex. App.—Texarkana 1993, pet. ref'd)*; *Musick v. State, 862 S.W.2d 794 (Tex. App.—El Paso 1993, pet. ref'd).*

Uniform Rules of Evidence

For text of corresponding provisions of Uniform Rules of Evidence and notes of decisions relating thereto, which may provide guidance in interpreting the Texas Rule, see Rule 509, 13A Uniform Laws Annotated.

Federal Rules of Evidence

There is no corresponding provision in the Federal Rules of Evidence.

Integrated Legal Research System References

West's Texas Digest Key Numbers

Witnesses ⚷216(4).

Texas Practice

Addison, Texas Practice Guide, Evidence § 5:203 et seq.

Texas Jur 3d

36 Texas Jur 3d, Evidence § 528.

Am Jur Proof of Facts

Criminal Law—Need for Disclosure of Identity of Informant, 33 Am Jur Proof of Facts 2d 549.

Annotations

Accused's right to, and prosecution's privilege against, disclosure of identity of informer, 76 ALR2d 262.

Rule 509. Physician–Patient Privilege

(a) Definitions. As used in this rule:

(1) A "patient" means any person who consults or is seen by a physician to receive medical care.

(2) A "physician" means a person licensed to practice medicine in any state or nation, or reasonably believed by the patient so to be.

(3) A communication is "confidential" if not intended to be disclosed to third persons other than those present to further the interest of the patient in the consultation, examination, or interview, or those reasonably necessary for the transmission of the communication, or those who are participating in the diagnosis and treatment under the direction of the physician, including members of the patient's family.

(b) Limited Privilege in Criminal Proceedings. There is no physician-patient privilege in criminal proceedings. However, a communication to any person involved in the treatment or examination of alcohol or drug abuse by a person being treated voluntarily or being examined for admission to treatment for alcohol or drug abuse is not admissible in a criminal proceeding.

(c) General Rule of Privilege in Civil Proceedings. In a civil proceeding:

(1) Confidential communications between a physician and a patient, relative to or in connection with any professional services rendered by a physician to the patient are privileged and may not be disclosed.

(2) Records of the identity, diagnosis, evaluation, or treatment of a patient by a physician that are created or maintained by a physician are confidential and privileged and may not be disclosed.

(3) The provisions of this rule apply even if the patient received the services of a physician prior to the enactment of the Medical Liability and Insurance Improvement Act, TEX.REV.CIV.STAT. art. 4590i.

(d) Who May Claim the Privilege in a Civil Proceeding. In a civil proceeding:

(1) The privilege of confidentiality may be claimed by the patient or by a representative of the patient acting on the patient's behalf.

(2) The physician may claim the privilege of confidentiality, but only on behalf of the patient. The authority to do so is presumed in the absence of evidence to the contrary.

(e) Exceptions in a Civil Proceeding. Exceptions to confidentiality or privilege in administrative proceedings or in civil proceedings in court exist:

(1) when the proceedings are brought by the patient against a physician, including but not limited to malpractice proceedings, and in any license revocation proceeding in which the patient is a complaining witness and in which disclosure is relevant to the claims or defense of a physician;

(2) when the patient or someone authorized to act on the patient's behalf submits a written consent to the release of any privileged information, as provided in paragraph (f);

(3) when the purpose of the proceedings is to substantiate and collect on a claim for medical services rendered to the patient;

(4) as to a communication or record relevant to an issue of the physical, mental or emotional condition of a patient in any proceeding in which any party relies upon the condition as a part of the party's claim or defense;

(5) in any disciplinary investigation or proceeding of a physician conducted under or pursuant to the Medical Practice Act, TEX.REV.CIV.STAT. art. 4495b, or of a registered nurse under or pursuant to TEX.REV.CIV.STAT. arts. 4525, 4527a, 4527b, and 4527c, provided that the board shall protect the identity of any patient whose medical records are examined, except for those patients covered under subparagraph (e)(1) or those patients who have submitted written consent to the release of their medical records as provided by paragraph (f);

(6) in an involuntary civil commitment proceeding, proceeding for court-ordered treatment, or probable cause hearing under Tex.Health & Safety Code ch. 462; tit. 7, subtit. C; and tit. 7, subtit. D;

(7) in any proceeding regarding the abuse or neglect, or the cause of any abuse or neglect, of the resident of an "institution" as defined in Tex.Health & Safety Code § 242.002.

(f) Consent.

(1) Consent for the release of privileged information must be in writing and signed by the patient, or a parent or legal guardian if the patient is a minor, or a legal guardian if the patient has been adjudicated incompetent to manage personal affairs, or an attorney ad litem appointed for the patient, as authorized by Tex.Health & Safety Code tit. 7, subtits. C and D; Tex. Prob. Code ch. V; and Tex.Fam.Code § 107.011; or a personal representative if the patient is deceased, provided that the written consent specifies the following:

(A) the information or medical records to be covered by the release;

(B) the reasons or purposes for the release; and

(C) the person to whom the information is to be released.

(2) The patient, or other person authorized to consent, has the right to withdraw consent to the release of any information. Withdrawal of consent does not affect any information disclosed prior to the written notice of the withdrawal.

(3) Any person who received information made privileged by this rule may disclose the information to others only to the extent consistent with the authorized purposes for which consent to release the information was obtained.

Eff. March 1, 1998.

Cross References

Communications by Drug Abusers, Vernon's Ann.C.C.P. Art. 38.101.

Nurse Disciplinary Proceedings, V.T.C.A., Occupations Code §§ 301.401 et seq., 302.401 et seq.

Physician Disciplinary Investigations and Proceedings, V.T.C.A., Occupations Code § 164.001 et seq.

Commentary

In general

This privilege does not apply in criminal cases, except in the very limited circumstances stated in the rule. In civil cases, this privilege protects not only confidential communications between a patient and his physician which have to do with the professional services rendered by the physician to the patient, but also the records of that patient's identity, diagnosis, evaluation or treatment which are created or maintained by the physician. The patient or his representative, or the physician acting on behalf of the patient, may claim the privilege. This rule is silent as to whether the privilege survives the patient, but case law holds that it does. *R.K. v. Ramirez, 887 S.W.2d 836 (Tex. 1994)*; *Brochner v. Thomas, 795 S.W.2d 215 (Tex. App.—Eastland 1990, orig. proc.)*. The physician does not have any independent right to claim the privilege. A hospital has no right to claim the privilege either for itself or the patient. *In re Fort Worth Children's Hosp., 100 S.W.3d 582, 588–589 (Tex. App.—Fort Worth 2003, orig. proc.).* Most of the problems with this otherwise straightforward rule stem from the exceptions to its application. This rule lists seven exceptions to the application to the physician-patient privilege.

Judges and trial lawyers should also consider the privilege of confidentiality as to physician patient communications, and the civil cause of action that can result from its breach, in V.T.C.A., Occupations Code § 159.001, *et seq.* This statute applies in criminal and civil cases, and in criminal cases, to victims, witnesses, and, significantly, to defendants. A careful practitioner will always consult both this rule and § 159.001 *et seq.* when dealing with questions of the physician–patient privilege, as well as V.T.C.A., Civil Practice & Remedies Code § 74.001 *et seq.* (medical liability). See, Dunleavy, *Physician Patient Privilege, H.B. 4 and Other Issues,* 27 *The Advocate* 32, State Bar Litigation Section Report, Summer 2004.

Suits by a patient against a physician

Communications or records protected under this rule are not protected from disclosure if the disclosure of a communication or record is relevant to any proceedings in any court or administrative proceeding *in which the patient has brought the action or is a complaining witness*. This includes actions alleging medical liability and actions involving license revocation proceedings. The key issue will often be whether the disclosure is relevant to the claims or defenses of the physician. *McGowan v. O'Neill, 750 S.W.2d 884 (Tex. App.—Houston [14th Dist.] 1988, orig. proc.).* Also not protected from disclosure is the information held by the patient's prior and subsequent treating physicians which are relevant to the patient's medical liability claim against a physician. *In re Lester Collins, M.D., 286 S.W.3d 911 (Tex. 2009) (orig. proceeding).* See TEX. CIV. PRAC. & REM. CODE ANN. § 74.052.

Consent of the patient

When the patient has consented to the release of information otherwise protected by the physician-patient privilege, the privilege does not apply. However, the consent referred to in this rule, in order to be effective, must be in compliance with the provisions of this rule regarding consent. Even if disclosure is consented to, there are limitations on the use of the information released.

Suits to collect charges for medical services rendered

A physician who sues a patient to collect payment for medical services rendered will necessarily, in order state a cause of action, have to name his patient, plead at least the general nature of the medical services rendered, and the charge for those services. It seems that a patient who fails to pay his medical bills thereby waives his physician-patient privilege at least to the extent that it is necessary to enable the physician to plead and prove his claim for medical services rendered.

Patient-litigant exception

Vernon's Ann.Rules Evid., Rule 509(e)(4) sets out an exception to the physician-patient privilege which has come to be known as the "patient-litigant exception." This is arguably the most important provision in Rule 509 because it virtually eliminates the privilege regarding an otherwise protected communication or record if the communication or record is relevant to the physical, mental or emotional condition of a patient in any proceeding in which any party relies upon the condition as a part of the party's claim or defense *whether or not the patient has put his condition in issue or even whether or not the patient is a party to the suit. R.K. v. Ramirez, 887 S.W.2d 836 (Tex. 1994).* See also TEX. R. [CIV.] EVID. 510(e)(5).

The condition in question must be both relevant and relied upon by a party in the case in his claim or defense. A patient's condition can be said to be relied upon only if there is some consequence from the existence or non-existence of that condition. Whether a condition is part of a claim or defense should be determined from the pleadings, without reference to the evidence that is claimed to be privileged. *R.K. v. Ramirez, supra*; *Bristol–Meyers Squibb Co. v. Hancock, 921 S.W.2d 917 (Tex. App.—Houston [14th Dist.] 1996, orig. proc.).* Any part of a confidential communication or record which is not relevant to a condition in issue remains protected, and the trial court should fashion its orders regarding disclosure to protect the privilege as to those parts. *Bristol-Meyers Squibb Co. v. Hancock, Id.* "A routine allegation of mental anguish or emotional distress does not place the party's mental condition in controversy. The plaintiff must assert mental injury that exceeds the common emotional reaction to an injury or loss." *Coates v. Whittington, 758 S.W.2d 749, (Tex. 1988) (orig. proceeding).*

Interesting questions arise when the condition of the patient is both relevant and relied upon by a party, but the patient is not a party to the lawsuit. Who protects the privilege as to those parts of a confidential communication or record that are not relevant? Must the privilege holder be notified? Does any party owe a duty to the privilege holder to protect his privilege or to afford the privilege holder an opportunity to do so? Does the physician to whom a protected communication was made or who has the protected record have a duty to invoke the privilege on behalf of the patient when this rule provides that he is presumed to have the authority to do so? These questions present some practical problems for the practitioner who should be especially aware of any possibility of a duty arising in one of these situations and the consequences of a breach of that duty. V.T.C.A., Occupations Code §§ 159.001–159.009.

Physician or registered nurse disciplinary investigations or proceedings

Unless the patient is the complaining witness in the investigation or proceeding, or unless the patient has consented in writing to the release of the patient's records, as provided by this rule, the board conducting the investigation or proceeding must keep the identity of the patient confidential as to any medical records the board examines.

Involuntary civil commitment proceedings, etc.

The physician-patient privilege simply does not apply in proceedings of involuntary commitment or court-ordered treatment, or probable cause hearings pursuant to any of the statutes cited in this section of this rule.

Proceedings regarding abuse or neglect of residents of certain institutions

In proceedings regarding abuse or neglect, or the cause of abuse or neglect, of a resident of a defined institution, the physician-patient privilege does not apply.

Health Insurance Portability and Accountability Act of 1996 (HIPAA)

It is beyond the scope of this publication to consider the provisions, merits or ramifications associated with HIPAA. A careful practitioner will review the numerous commentaries, articles and publications regarding the Act, because the act is extensive in scope regarding protected health information and provides civil and criminal penalties for its violation. HIPAA was enacted by Congress in 1996, but the deadline for compliance with the new privacy rules regarding protected health information was April 14, 2003 for the majority of the entities it covers.

HIPAA should always be considered when dealing with the assertion of a physician—patient privilege under Rule 509 of the Texas rules of evidence, or when trying to defeat an assertion of the privilege.

Official Comment to former Civil Rule 509

The comment to former Rule 509 of the Rules of Civil Evidence provided in pertinent part as follows: "This rule only governs disclosures of patient-physician communications in judicial or administrative proceedings. Whether a physician may or must disclose such communications in other circumstances is governed by TEX.REV.CIV.STAT.ANN. art. 4495b, Sec. 5.08."

Uniform Rules of Evidence

For text of corresponding provisions of Uniform Rules of Evidence and notes of decisions relating thereto, which may provide guidance in interpreting the Texas Rule, see Rule 503, 13A Uniform Laws Annotated.

Federal Rules of Evidence

There is no corresponding provision in the Federal Rules of Evidence.

Integrated Legal Research System References

West's Texas Digest Key Numbers

Witnesses ⚷207–214.

Texas Practice

Addison, Texas Practice Guide, Evidence § 5:231 et seq.

Texas Jur 3d

36 Texas Jur 3d, Evidence §§ 563–571.

Annotations

Admissibility of physician's testimony as to patient's statements or declarations, other than res gestae, during medical examination, 37 ALR3d 788.

Applicability in criminal proceedings of privilege as to communications between physician and patient, 7 ALR3d 1458.

Commencing action involving physical condition of plaintiff or decedent as waiving physician-patient privilege as to discovery proceedings, 21 ALR3d 912.

Physician-patient privilege as extending to patient's medical or hospital records, 10 ALR4th 552.

Pretrial testimony or disclosure on discovery by party to personal injury action as to nature of injuries or treatment as waiver of physician-patient privilege, 25 ALR3d 1401.

Privilege, in judicial or quasi-judicial proceedings, arising from relationship between psychiatrist or psychologist and patient, 44 ALR3d 24.

Waiver of privilege as regards one physician as a waiver as to other physicians, 5 ALR3d 1244.

Rule 510. Confidentiality of Mental Health Information in Civil Cases

(a) Definitions. As used in this rule:

(1) "Professional" means any person:

(A) authorized to practice medicine in any state or nation;

(B) licensed or certified by the State of Texas in the diagnosis, evaluation or treatment of any mental or emotional disorder;

(C) involved in the treatment or examination of drug abusers; or

(D) reasonably believed by the patient to be included in any of the preceding categories.

(2) "Patient" means any person who:

(A) consults, or is interviewed by, a professional for purposes of diagnosis, evaluation, or treatment of any mental or emotional condition or disorder, including alcoholism and drug addiction; or

(B) is being treated voluntarily or being examined for admission to voluntary treatment for drug abuse.

(3) A representative of the patient is:

(A) any person bearing the written consent of the patient;

(B) a parent if the patient is a minor;

(C) a guardian if the patient has been adjudicated incompetent to manage the patient's personal affairs; or

(D) the patient's personal representative if the patient is deceased.

(4) A communication is "confidential" if not intended to be disclosed to third persons other than those present to further the interest of the patient in the diagnosis, examination, evaluation, or treatment, or those reasonably necessary for the transmission of the communication, or those who are participating in the diagnosis, examination, evaluation, or treatment under the direction of the professional, including members of the patient's family.

(b) General Rule of Privilege.

(1) Communication between a patient and a professional is confidential and shall not be disclosed in civil cases.

(2) Records of the identity, diagnosis, evaluation, or treatment of a patient which are created or maintained by a professional are confidential and shall not be disclosed in civil cases.

(3) Any person who received information from confidential communications or records as defined herein, other than a representative of the patient acting on the patient's behalf, shall not disclose in civil cases the information except to the extent that disclosure is consistent with the authorized purposes for which the information was first obtained.

(4) The provisions of this rule apply even if the patient received the services of a professional prior to the enactment of Tex.Rev.Civ.Stat. art. 5561h (Vernon Supp.1984)(now codified as Tex.Health & Safety Code §§ 611.001–611.008).

(c) Who May Claim the Privilege.

(1) The privilege of confidentiality may be claimed by the patient or by a representative of the patient acting on the patient's behalf.

(2) The professional may claim the privilege of confidentiality but only on behalf of the patient. The authority to do so is presumed in the absence of evidence to the contrary.

(d) Exceptions. Exceptions to the privilege in court or administrative proceedings exist:

(1) when the proceedings are brought by the patient against a professional, including but not limited to malpractice proceedings, and in any license revocation proceedings in which the patient is a complaining witness and in which disclosure is relevant to the claim or defense of a professional;

(2) when the patient waives the right in writing to the privilege of confidentiality of any information, or when a representative of the patient acting on the patient's behalf submits a written waiver to the confidentiality privilege;

(3) when the purpose of the proceeding is to substantiate and collect on a claim for mental or emotional health services rendered to the patient;

(4) when the judge finds that the patient after having been previously informed that communications would not be privileged, has made communications to a professional in the course of a court-ordered examination relating to the patient's mental or emotional condition or disorder, providing that such communications shall not be privileged only with respect to issues involving the patient's mental or emotional health. On granting of the order, the court, in determining the extent to which any disclosure of all or any part of any communication is necessary, shall impose appropriate safeguards against unauthorized disclosure;

(5) as to a communication or record relevant to an issue of the physical, mental or emotional condition of a patient in any proceeding in which any party relies upon the condition as a part of the party's claim or defense;

(6) in any proceeding regarding the abuse or neglect, or the cause of any abuse or neglect, of the resident of an institution as defined in TEX.HEALTH AND SAFETY CODE § 242.002.

Eff. March 1, 1998.

Commentary

In general

This privilege does not apply in criminal cases.

This privilege is very similar to the physician-patient privilege found in Vernon's Ann.Rules Evid., Rule 509. This privilege protects the confidential communications between a "professional" and a patient, as well as the records of the identity, diagnosis, evaluation, or treatment of a patient that are created or maintained by the professional. A "professional" is: (1) a physician licensed anywhere; (2) a person licensed *by the State of Texas* in the diagnosis, evaluation or treatment of any mental or emotional disorder; (3) a person merely "involved" in the treatment or examination of drug abusers; or (4) anyone the patient reasonably believes to be a person who falls within one of those categories.

The patient or his representative, or the professional acting on behalf of the patient, may claim the privilege, and the privilege survives the patient. The professional does not have any independent right to claim the privilege. There are exceptions to the application of the privilege, and they closely parallel the exceptions found in Vernon's Ann.Rules Evid., Rule 509(e), except in two particulars, which are discussed below.

Patient-litigant exception

The patient-litigant exception to the privilege of confidentiality of mental health information is the same as the patient-litigant exception to the physician-patient privilege. The leading case discussing both of those privileges and the patient-litigant exception is *R.K. v. Ramirez, 887 S.W.2d 836 (Tex. 1994).*

Communications in the course of court-ordered examinations

When a patient is warned in advance that his communications to a professional during a court-ordered examination will not be privileged, the communications made that are related to the emotional or mental health of the patient are not privileged. When ordering the examination, the court is required to impose appropriate safeguards to guard against unauthorized disclosure of the communication. If, in the course of a court-ordered examination, the patient is *not warned* that the communication will not be privileged, any communication made during the examination is privileged, regardless of any other exception to the privilege. *Subia v. Texas Dep't of Human Servs., 750 S.W.2d 827 (Tex. App.—El Paso 1988, no writ).*

Waiver of confidentiality

A patient, or a representative of a patient acting on the patient's behalf, may waive the confidentiality of mental health information, if the waiver is in writing. This exception does not require any particular formality or content in the written waiver. Contrast this with the formal requirements of a consent to the release of privileged information under the physician-patient privilege. Vernon's Ann.Rules Evid., Rule 509.

Uniform Rules of Evidence

For text of corresponding provisions of Uniform Rules of Evidence and notes of decisions relating thereto, which may provide guidance in interpreting the Texas Rule, see Rule 503, 13A Uniform Laws Annotated.

Federal Rules of Evidence

There is no corresponding provision in the Federal Rules of Evidence.

Integrated Legal Research System References

West's Texas Digest Key Numbers

Witnesses ⚷214.5.

Texas Practice

Addison, Texas Practice Guide, Evidence § 5:278 et seq.

Texas Jur 3d

36 Texas Jur 3d, Evidence §§ 572–575.

Annotations

Admissibility of physician's testimony as to patient's statements or declarations, other than res gestae, during medical examination, 37 ALR3d 788.

Applicability of attorney-client privilege to communications made in presence of or solely to or by third person, 14 ALR4th 594.

Commencing action involving physical condition of plaintiff or decedent as waiving physician-patient privilege as to discovery proceedings, 21 ALR3d 912.

Physician-patient privilege as extending to patient's medical or hospital records, 10 ALR4th 552.

Pretrial testimony or disclosure on discovery by party to personal injury action as to nature of injuries or treatment as waiver of physician-patient privilege, 25 ALR3d 1401.

Privilege, in judicial or quasi-judicial proceedings, arising from relationship between psychiatrist or psychologist and patient, 44 ALR3d 24.

Validity, construction, and application of statute limiting physician-patient privilege in judicial proceedings relating to child abuse or neglect, 44 ALR4th 649.

Waiver of privilege as regards one physician as a waiver as to other physicians, 5 ALR3d 1244.

Rule 511. Waiver of Privilege by Voluntary Disclosure

A person upon whom these rules confer a privilege against disclosure waives the privilege if:

(1) the person or a predecessor of the person while holder of the privilege voluntarily discloses or consents to disclosure of any significant part of the privileged matter unless such disclosure itself is privileged; or

(2) the person or a representative of the person calls a person to whom privileged communications have been made to testify as to the person's character or character trait insofar as such communications are relevant to such character or character trait.

Eff. March 1, 1998.

Commentary

Uniform Rules of Evidence

For text of corresponding provisions of Uniform Rules of Evidence and notes of decisions relating thereto, which may provide guidance in interpreting the Texas Rule, see Rule 510, 13A Uniform Laws Annotated.

Federal Rules of Evidence

There is no corresponding provision in the Federal Rules of Evidence.

Integrated legal Research System References

West's Texas Digest Key Numbers

Witnesses ⚷219.

Texas Practice

Addison, Texas Practice Guide, Evidence § 5:308 et seq.

Annotations

Waiver of evidentiary privilege by inadvertent disclosure—federal law, 159 ALR Fed 153.

Waiver of evidentiary privilege by inadvertent disclosure—state law, 51 ALR5th 603.

Rule 512. Privileged Matter Disclosed Under Compulsion or Without Opportunity to Claim Privilege

A claim of privilege is not defeated by a disclosure which was (1) compelled erroneously or (2) made without opportunity to claim the privilege.

Eff. March 1, 1998.

Commentary

Uniform Rules of Evidence

For text of corresponding provisions of Uniform Rules of Evidence and notes of decisions relating thereto, which may provide guidance in interpreting the Texas Rule, see Rule 512, 13A Uniform Laws Annotated.

Federal Rules of Evidence

There is no corresponding provision in the Federal Rules of Evidence.

Integrated Legal Research System References

West's Texas Digest Key Numbers

Witnesses ⚷223.

Texas Practice

Addison, Texas Practice Guide, Evidence § 5:323 et seq.

Rule 513. Comment Upon or Inference From Claim of Privilege; Instruction

(a) Comment or Inference Not Permitted. Except as permitted in Rule 504(b)(2), the claim of a privilege, whether in the present proceeding or upon a prior occasion, is not a proper subject of comment by judge or counsel, and no inference may be drawn therefrom.

(b) Claiming Privilege Without Knowledge of Jury. In jury cases, proceedings shall be conducted, to the extent practicable, so as to facilitate the making of claims of privilege without the knowledge of the jury.

(c) Claim of Privilege Against Self–Incrimination in Civil Cases. Paragraphs (a) and (b) shall not apply with respect to a party's claim, in the present civil proceeding, of the privilege against self-incrimination.

(d) Jury Instruction. Except as provided in Rule 504(b)(2) and in paragraph (c) of this Rule, upon request any party against whom the jury might draw an adverse inference from a claim of privilege is entitled to an instruction that no inference may be drawn therefrom.

Eff. March 1, 1998.

Commentary

In general

The invocation of a privilege by a witness may not be commented upon, and no inference may be drawn from a claim of privilege. However, if the privilege claimed is the privilege against self-incrimination made by a party in a civil case, the claim of privilege may be commented on and reasonable inference adverse to that party may be drawn. It is less clear whether a reasonable inference may be drawn against a non-party witness who claims the privilege against self-incrimination, and against whom that adverse inference may be drawn. See *Wil-Roye Inv. Co. II v. Washington Mut. Bank, FA, 142 S.W.3d 393 (Tex. App.—El Paso, 2004, no pet. h)* (in a case of first impression, adverse inference from non-party agents' assertion of privilege against self-incrimination was permissible in a civil fraud action). A witness in a civil case may be called to testify for the purpose of showing the judge *or jury* that he refuses to testify to relevant facts in the case because his answers to the questions would tend to incriminate him. *Smith v. Smith, 720 S.W.2d 586 (Tex. App.—Houston [1st Dist.] 1986, no writ).*

Failure of a defendant in a criminal case to call his spouse as a witness where other evidence shows that the spouse could testify as to relevant matters may be commented on by the attorneys. Vernon's Ann.Rules Evid., Rule 504(b)(2). See *Benetiz v. State, 5 S.W.3d 95 (Tex. App.—Amarillo 1999, pet. ref'd).*

Uniform Rules of Evidence

For text of corresponding provisions of Uniform Rules of Evidence and notes of decisions relating thereto, which may provide guidance in interpreting the Texas Rule, see Rule 512, 13A Uniform Laws Annotated.

Federal Rules of Evidence

There is no corresponding provision in the Federal Rules of Evidence.

Integrated Legal Research System References

Texas Practice

Addison, Texas Practice Guide, Evidence § 5:334 et seq.

ARTICLE VI. WITNESSES

Rule
601. Competency and Incompetency of Witnesses.
602. Lack of Personal Knowledge.
603. Oath or Affirmation.
604. Interpreters.
605. Competency of Judge as a Witness.
606. Competency of Juror as a Witness.
607. Who May Impeach.
608. Evidence of Character and Conduct of a Witness.
609. Impeachment by Evidence of Conviction of Crime.
610. Religious Beliefs or Opinions.
611. Mode and Order of Interrogation and Presentation.
612. Writing Used to Refresh Memory.
613. Prior Statements of Witnesses: Impeachment and Support.
614. Exclusion of Witnesses.
615. Production of Statements of Witnesses in Criminal Cases.

Cross References

Religious Belief, Vernon's Ann.C.C.P. Art. 1.17.

Religious Opinion, Vernon's Ann.C.C.P. Art. 38.12.

Statements of Accused, Vernon's Ann.C.C.P. Art. 38.21, 38.22.

Interpreters, Criminal Proceedings, Vernon's Ann.C.C.P. Art. 38.30, 38.31.

Interpreters, Civil Proceedings, V.T.C.A., Civil Practice & Remedies Code § 21.001 et seq.

Party as Witness, Vernon's Ann.Rules Civ.Proc., Rule 181.

Interpreters, Civil Proceedings, Vernon's Ann.Rules Civ.Proc., Rule 183.

Integrated Legal Research System References

West's Texas Digest Key Numbers

Witnesses ⚷35–183.5.

Texas Jur 3d

23 Texas Jur 3d, Criminal Law § 2566 et seq.

24A Texas Jur 3d, Criminal Law §§ 3731 et seq., 3837 et seq., 3875 et seq.

36 Texas Jur 3d, Evidence §§ 477 et seq.

37 Texas Jur 3d, Evidence §§ 707–871.

Am Jur Trials

Examination of a Witness Based on a Prior Statement, 49 Am Jur Trials 501.

Persuasive Cross–Examination, 59 Am Jur Trials 1.

Am Jur Proof of Facts

Admission of Character Evidence and Evidence of Other Acts, 21 Am Jur Proof of Facts 3d 629.

Contradiction of Expert Witness Through Use of Authoritative Treatise, 31 Am Jur Proof of Facts 2d 443.

Foundation for Offering Deposition or Other Former Testimony in Evidence, 28 Am Jur Proof of Facts 2d 1.

Impeachment of Witness—Prior Inconsistent Statement, 21 Am Jur Proof of Facts 2d 101.

Impeachment of Witness by Prior Criminal Conviction, 36 Am Jur Proof of Facts 2d 747.

Qualifying Child Witness to Testify, 35 Am Jur Proof of Facts 2d 665.

Rule 601. Competency and Incompetency of Witnesses

(a) General Rule. Every person is competent to be a witness except as otherwise provided in these rules. The following witnesses shall be incompetent to testify in any proceeding subject to these rules:

(1) *Insane persons.* Insane persons who, in the opinion of the court, are in an insane condition of mind at the time when they are offered as a witness, or who, in the opinion of the court, were in that condition when the events happened of which they are called to testify.

(2) *Children.* Children or other persons who, after being examined by the court, appear not to possess sufficient intellect to relate transactions with respect to which they are interrogated.

(b) "Dead Man's Rule" in Civil Actions. In civil actions by or against executors, administrators, or guardians, in which judgment may be rendered for or against them as such, neither party shall be allowed to testify against the others as to any oral statement by the testator, intestate or ward, unless that testimony to the oral statement is corroborated or unless the witness is called at the trial to testify thereto by the opposite party; and, the provisions of this article shall extend to and include all actions by or against the heirs or legal representatives of a decedent based in whole or in part on such oral statement. Except for the foregoing, a witness is not precluded from giving evidence of or concerning any transaction with, any conversations with, any admissions of, or statement by, a deceased or insane party or person merely because the witness is a party to the action or a person interested in the event thereof. The trial court shall, in a proper case, where this rule prohibits an interested party or witness from testifying, instruct the jury that such person is not permitted by the law to give evidence relating to any oral statement by the deceased or ward unless the oral statement is corroborated or unless the party or witness is called at the trial by the opposite party.

Eff. March 1, 1998.

Commentary

In general

This rule is concerned with the capacity of persons to testify as witnesses, declaring that certain witnesses shall not be competent to testify, but that all others are deemed competent. Competency is a preliminary matter to be decided by the trial court under Vernon's Ann.Rules Evid., Rule 104(a) if the issue is raised. A determination that a witness is not competent is a determination of a matter of law that will be overturned on appeal only for an abuse of discretion. *Broussard v. State, 910 S.W.2d 952 (Tex. Crim. App. 1995).* Competency of a witness is never a fact issue, while the credibility of a witness always is.

This rule recognizes that persons with particular conditions of the mind or intellect and persons of a certain status cannot be relied on to give sufficiently trustworthy and reliable testimony.

Insane persons

Every witness is presumed to be sane and competent unless the evidence shows otherwise. The burden of going forward with the evidence and showing the trial court that a witness is insane, and therefore incompetent to testify, rests on the objecting party. *Handl v. Long Trusts, 757 S.W.2d 848 (Tex. App.—Texarkana 1988, no writ).* This rule also applies to persons insane "... when the events happened of which they are called to testify."

The term "insanity" is not defined in this rule or anywhere else in the Texas Rules of Evidence. While the term does have myriad legal and medical definitions in many different contexts, it appears that if, because of a mental disease or defect, a witness either did not have the capacity to observe accurately the event, act or transaction about which he is to testify, or the witness does not have a present capacity to recall and testify accurately to the observed event, act or transaction at the trial, the witness is incompetent to testify.

Children or other persons

This rule applies to all persons, whether children or not, who do not appear to the court to have sufficient intellect to relate transactions with respect to which they are interrogated.

There is no minimum age for competency. *Upton v. State, 894 S.W.2d 426 (Tex. App.—Amarillo 1995, pet. ref'd).* Vernon's Ann.Rules Evid., Rule 601(a)(2) does not require the trial court to conduct an examination of a child who will be a witness to determine the child's competency in the absence of an objection or a motion. *Grayson v. State, 786 S.W.2d 504 (Tex. App.—Dallas 1990, no pet.).* The trial court, if called upon to determine whether a child witness possesses sufficient intellect to relate transactions with respect to which he is interrogated, should consider: (1) the ability of the child to observe intelligently events as they occur; (2) the capacity of the child to recollect the events; (3) the capacity of the child to narrate the events; and (4) awareness by the child of the moral obligation to tell the truth. *Dufrene v. State, 853 S.W.2d 86 (Tex. App.—Houston [14th Dist.] 1993, pet. ref'd).*

The "Dead Man's Rule"

Vernon's Ann.Rules Evid., Rule 601(b) is more limited in scope than the Dead Man's Statute it replaced. Vernon's Ann.Civ.St. art. 3716. Under this rule, certain party-witnesses are still considered incompetent to testify to any *oral statement* made by a testator, intestate or ward in cases brought "by or against executors, administrators or guardians, in which judgment may be rendered for or against them as such" or in any suit "by or against the heirs or legal representatives of a decedent based in whole or in part on such oral statement," unless the oral statement is corroborated or unless the party-witness is called as a witness by the opposing party.

This rule does not prohibit testimony or other evidence of an oral statement made by a decedent, testator, or ward, but only testimony about any such oral statement by specified parties to the types of suits referred to in this rule. Further, this rule does not prohibit testimony or other evidence from any source, including a party, about transactions with a decedent, testator, or ward. This rule applies only in civil cases.

Uniform Rules of Evidence

For text of corresponding provisions of Uniform Rules of Evidence and notes of decisions relating thereto, which may provide guidance in interpreting the Texas Rule, see Rule 601, 13A Uniform Laws Annotated.

Federal Rules of Evidence

The corresponding provision of the Federal Rules of Evidence is Rule 601. For the text of the Rule and Advisory Committee Notes, which may provide guidance in interpreting the Texas Rule, see the Appendix to this volume.

Leading Cases

Broussard v. State, 910 S.W.2d 952 (Tex. Crim. App. 1995) (a judge is neither required nor empowered to force a witness to undergo a psychiatric evaluation for the purpose of a competency determination under TEX. R. [CIV.] EVID. 601).

Cain v. Whitlock, 741 S.W.2d 528 (Tex. App.—Houston [14th Dist.] 1987, no writ) (the corroboration required by TEX. R. [CIV.] EVID. 601(b) need not be sufficient on its own to support the verdict, but it should tend to support the truth of the party-witness's testimony, and such corroboration may come from any competent, legal evidence). See also *Powers v. McDaniel, 785 S.W.2d 915 (Tex. App.—San Antonio 1990, writ denied)*, cited below.

Great Global Assurance Co. v. Keltex Props., Inc., 904 S.W.2d 771 (Tex. App.—Corpus Christi 1995, no writ) (under TEX. R. [CIV.] EVID. 601, a person is not incompetent to testify as a witness because the person has been held in contempt and the court has issued an attachment for that person).

Hunter v. NCNB Texas Nat'l Bank, 857 S.W.2d 722 (Tex. App.—Houston [14th Dist.] 1993, writ denied) (a prior judgment of incompetency creates a rebuttable presumption that a witness is incompetent to testify).

Macias v. State, 776 S.W.2d 255 (Tex. App.—San Antonio 1989, pet. ref'd) (the testimony of a child may contain conflicting and sometimes confusing answers, but that alone does not make the child an incompetent witness, although that may be considered in the assessment of the witness's credibility by the trier of fact).

Parrish v. Brooks, 856 S.W.2d 522 (Tex. App.—Texarkana 1993, writ denied) (a convicted felon is a competent witness, if not otherwise incompetent under TEX. R. [CIV.] EVID. 601).

Powers v. McDaniel, 785 S.W.2d 915 (Tex. App.—San Antonio 1990, writ denied) (the corroboration required by TEX. R. [CIV.] EVID. 601(b) need not be sufficient on its own to support the verdict, but it should tend to support the truth of the party-witness's testimony, and such corroboration may come from any competent, legal evidence). See also *Cain v. Whitlock, 741 S.W.2d 528 (Tex. App.—Houston [14th Dist.] 1987, no writ)*, cited above.

Integrated Legal Research System References

West's Texas Digest Key Numbers

Witnesses ⚷35–49.

Texas Practice

Addison, Texas Practice Guide, Evidence § 6:1 et seq.

Texas Jur 3d

24A Texas Jur 3d, Criminal Law §§ 3731 et seq., 3737 et seq.

36 Texas Jur 3d, Evidence § 488 et seq.

Annotations

Dead man's statutes as affected by Rule 601 of the Uniform Rules of Evidence and similar state rules, 50 ALR4th 1238.

Witnesses: child competency statutes, 60 ALR4th 369.

Rule 602. Lack of Personal Knowledge

A witness may not testify to a matter unless evidence is introduced sufficient to support a finding that the witness has personal knowledge of the matter. Evidence to prove personal knowledge may, but need not, consist of the testimony of the witness. This rule is subject to the provisions of Rule 703, relating to opinion testimony by expert witnesses.

Eff. March 1, 1998.

Commentary

In general

Vernon's Ann.Rules Evid., Rule 701 provides that a nonexpert witness may testify to opinions and inferences which are rationally based on the perception of the witness and which are helpful to a clear understanding of the witness's testimony or the determination of a fact in issue. The "perception of the witness" requirement of Vernon's Ann.Rules Evid., Rule 701 satisfies the personal knowledge requirement of Rule 602. *Bigby v. State, 892 S.W.2d 864 (Tex. Crim. App. 1994)*; *Fairow v. State, 943 S.W.2d 895 (Tex. Crim. App. 1997)*. See also *Havner v. E–Z Mart Stores, Inc., 825 S.W.2d 456 (Tex. 1992)*.

"When there is some reason to doubt whether a witness possesses the requisite personal knowledge, it may be appropriate for the court to afford the opposing party a chance to take the witness on voir dire. But it is neither reasonable nor practical to permit such voir dire when there is no apparent reason for doubting that the witness is testifying from personal knowledge." *Shugars v. State, 814 S.W.2d 897 (Tex. App.—Austin 1991, no pet.)*.

Uniform Rules of Evidence

For text of corresponding provisions of Uniform Rules of Evidence and notes of decisions relating thereto, which may provide guidance in interpreting the Texas Rule, see Rule 602, 13A Uniform Laws Annotated.

Federal Rules of Evidence

The corresponding provision of the Federal Rules of Evidence is Rule 602. For the text of the Rule and Advisory Committee Notes, which may provide guidance in interpreting the Texas Rule, see the Appendix to this volume.

Leading Cases

Geiselman v. Cramer Fin. Group, Inc., 965 S.W.2d 532 (Tex. App.—Houston [14th Dist.] 1997, n.w.h.) (in the absence of affirmative statement of personal knowledge by affiant, error to consider his affidavit as evidence for summary judgment over proper objection).

United Way of San Antonio, Inc. v. Helping Hands Lifeline Foundation, Inc., 949 S.W.2d 707 (Tex. App.—San Antonio 1997, writ denied) (witnesses who are not expert witnesses must have personal knowledge of the facts about which they testify under Vernon's Ann.Rules Evid., Rule 602, and they may not testify as to legal conclusions under Vernon's Ann.Rules Evid., Rule 702).

Leading CLE/Law Review Publications

Simpson, *The "Banjo Rule" On Testimony,* State Bar Litigation Section Report, *The Advocate,* Vol. 20, No. 1 (Spring 2001).

Integrated Legal Research System References

West's Texas Digest Key Numbers

Witnesses ⚷37.

Texas Practice

Addison, Texas Practice Guide, Evidence § 6:34 et seq.

Texas Jur 3d

24A Texas Jur 3d, Criminal Law § 3734 et seq.

36 Texas Jur 3d, Evidence § 495 et seq.

Rule 603. Oath or Affirmation

Before testifying, every witness shall be required to declare that the witness will testify truthfully, by oath or affirmation administered in a form calculated to awaken the witness' conscience and impress the witness' mind with the duty to do so.

Eff. March 1, 1998.

Commentary

In general

"No person shall be disqualified to give evidence in any of the Courts of this State on account of his religious opinions, or for the want of any religious belief, but all oaths or affirmations shall be administered in the mode most binding upon the conscience, and shall be taken subject to the pains and penalties of perjury." Vernon's Ann.Const. Art. I, § 5.

Form and administration of oath or affirmation

No particular form of the oath is required. When the trial judge is confronted with a witness who refuses to take an oath or an affirmation for sincerely held religious reasons, he should accommodate the witness but require of him a public commitment to testify truthfully and awaken in him a recognition of the duty to do so. *Bisby v. State, 907 S.W.2d 949 (Tex. App.—Fort Worth 1995, pet. ref'd).* There is no requirement that the oath be administered in the presence of the jury. *Fagbemi v. State, 778 S.W.2d 119 (Tex. App.—Texarkana 1989, pet. ref'd).* When a child does not appear to understand the obligations of an oath, the questions by the judge may be sufficient to impress on the child-witness the duty to testify truthfully, and the child-witness's answers to the judge's questions may be tantamount to an oath or affirmation. *Macias v. State, 776 S.W.2d 255 (Tex. App.—San Antonio 1989, pet. ref'd).*

Practical considerations

The better practice is to swear all of the witnesses in the presence of the jury. If this does not occur, or one or more witnesses have taken the oath, but not in the presence of the jury, the court should state, in the presence of the jury, that "the record will reflect that the witness has been previously sworn" when the witness is called. If the court does not do this, counsel should request that the court to do so. Remember, too, that the record is blind and must be told what is happening. Certainly, the party relying on the witness wants the jury to know that the witness has committed to tell the truth. If it appears to the jury that the witness has not been sworn, the jury may discount the witness's testimony accordingly.

If a witness has refused to take the oath or an affirmation for conscientiously held religious reasons, the commitment of the witness to tell the truth should be done on the record but outside the presence of the jury so as not to call particular attention to the witness. When that witness testifies, the jury and the record can be informed by the court that the witness has been "sworn".

Uniform Rules of Evidence

For text of corresponding provisions of Uniform Rules of Evidence and notes of decisions relating thereto, which may provide guidance in interpreting the Texas Rule, see Rule 603, 13A Uniform Laws Annotated.

Federal Rules of Evidence

The corresponding provision of the Federal Rules of Evidence is Rule 603. For the text of the Rule and Advisory Committee Notes, which may provide guidance in interpreting the Texas Rule, see the Appendix to this volume.

Integrated Legal Research System References

West's Texas Digest Key Numbers

Witnesses ⟹227.

Texas Practice

Addison, Texas Practice Guide, Evidence § 6:49 et seq.

Texas Jur 3d

24A Texas Jur 3d, Criminal Law § 3840.

Annotations

Sufficiency, under Rules 603 and 604 of Federal Rules of Evidence, of wording of oath, affirmation, or other declaration made by witness, or proposed witness or by court, relating to truthfulness of witness' testimony, 127 ALR Fed 207.

Rule 604. Interpreters

An interpreter is subject to the provisions of these rules relating to qualification as an expert and the administration of an oath or affirmation to make a true translation.

Eff. March 1, 1998.

Cross References

Interpreters, Vernon's Ann.C.C.P. Art. 38.30, 38.31.

Commentary

In general

Vernon's Ann.Rules Civ.Proc., Rule 187 provides that "[T]he court may appoint an interpreter of its own selection and may fix the interpreter's reasonable compensation. The compensation shall be paid out of funds provided by law or by one or more of the parties as the court may direct, and may be taxed ultimately as costs, in the discretion of the court." See also Vernon's Ann.C.C.P. Chap. 21 (interpreters in criminal cases). A new rule of evidence regarding the translation of foreign language documents is Vernon's Ann.Rules Evid., Rule 1009.

Uniform Rules of Evidence

For text of corresponding provisions of Uniform Rules of Evidence and notes of decisions relating thereto, which may provide guidance in interpreting the Texas Rule, see Rule 604, 13A Uniform Laws Annotated.

Federal Rules of Evidence

The corresponding provision of the Federal Rules of Evidence is Rule 604. For the text of the Rule and Advisory Committee Notes, which may provide guidance in interpreting the Texas Rule, see the Appendix to this volume.

Integrated Legal Research System References

West's Texas Digest Key Numbers

Criminal Law ⚷642.

Witnesses ⚷230.

Texas Practice

Addison, Texas Practice Guide, Evidence § 6:57 et seq.

Texas Jur 3d

24A Texas Jur 3d, Criminal Law § 3844.

36 Texas Jur 3d, Evidence § 509.

Annotations

Disqualification, for bias, of one offered as interpreter of testimony, 6 ALR4th 158.

Sufficiency, under Rules 603 and 604 of Federal Rules of Evidence, of wording of oath, affirmation, or other declaration made by witness, or proposed witness or by court, relating to truthfulness of witness' testimony, 127 ALR Fed 207.

Rule 605. Competency of Judge as a Witness

The judge presiding at the trial may not testify in that trial as a witness. No objection need be made in order to preserve the point.

Eff. March 1, 1998.

Commentary

In general

A judge is competent to testify in any case in which he is not presiding, but the Code of Judicial Conduct may be used to determine whether a judge should be *allowed* to testify in certain situations. *Joachim v. Chambers, 815 S.W.2d 234 (Tex.*

1991). See also *Orion Enters., Inc. v. Pope, 927 S.W.2d 654 (Tex. App.—San Antonio 1996, orig. proc.).* A judge is prohibited from voluntarily testifying as a character witness in any case. V.T.C.A., Government Code, Jud. Conduct, Canon 2, pt. B (1996). Rule 605 also applies to persons performing judicial functions that conflict with a witness's role in proceedings in which the rules of evidence apply. *Bradley v. State ex rel. White, 990 S.W.2d 245 (Tex. 1999).*

Uniform Rules of Evidence

For text of corresponding provisions of Uniform Rules of Evidence and notes of decisions relating thereto, which may provide guidance in interpreting the Texas Rule, see Rule 605, 13A Uniform Laws Annotated.

Federal Rules of Evidence

The corresponding provision of the Federal Rules of Evidence is Rule 605. For the text of the Rule and Advisory Committee Notes, which may provide guidance in interpreting the Texas Rule, see the Appendix to this volume.

Integrated Legal Research System References

West's Texas Digest Key Numbers

Criminal Law ⚷1036.2.

Witnesses ⚷68.

Texas Practice

Addison, Texas Practice Guide, Evidence § 6:67 et seq.

Texas Jur 3d

24A Texas Jur 3d, Criminal Law § 3749.

36 Texas Jur 3d, Evidence § 510.

Annotations

Disqualification of judge on ground of being a witness in the case, 22 ALR3d 1198.

Judge as witness in cause not on trial before him, 86 ALR3d 633.

Rule 606. Competency of Juror as a Witness

(a) At the Trial. A member of the jury may not testify as a witness before that jury in the trial of the case in which the juror is sitting as a juror. If the juror is called so to testify, the opposing party shall be afforded an opportunity to object out of the presence of the jury.

(b) Inquiry Into Validity of Verdict or Indictment. Upon an inquiry into the validity of a verdict or indictment, a juror may not testify as to any matter or statement occurring during the jury's deliberations, or to the effect of anything on any juror's mind or emotions or mental processes, as influencing any juror's assent to or dissent from the verdict or indictment. Nor may a juror's affidavit or any statement by a juror concerning any matter about which the juror would be precluded from testifying be admitted in evidence for any of these purposes. However, a juror may testify: (1) whether any outside influence was improperly brought to bear upon any juror; or (2) to rebut a claim that the juror was not qualified to serve.

Eff. March 1, 1998.

Commentary

In general

This rule closely follows the former rule in civil cases. However, the provision in the former criminal rule "that a juror may testify as to any matter relevant to the validity of the verdict or indictment" has been eliminated. This change may have a significant effect on the applicability of prior case law involving proof of allegations of jury misconduct in motions for new trial filed in criminal cases. See *Buentello v. State, 826 S.W.2d 610 (Tex. Crim. App. 1992).*

The Texas Supreme Court has held that: (1) this and other rules prohibiting juror testimony as to any matter or statement during deliberations, but permitting it with regard to outside influences, are constitutional; (2) juror testimony about statements made during deliberations and offered to show a juror's erroneous or incorrect answer on voir dire examination is inadmissible under rule 606; (3) evidence of jurors' alleged act of trading answers on issues and juror speculation as to whether alcohol was involved in an accident and whether the user received a settlement was not evidence of outside influences, and was, therefore, inadmissible under rule 606; and (4) evidence of a juror bias during deliberations is not admissible under rule 606. However, an alleged conversation between jurors during a trial break is not part of deliberations and is admissible under this rule. *Golden Eagle Archery, Inc. v. Jackson, 24 S.W.3d 362 (Tex. 2000).*

Uniform Rules of Evidence

For text of corresponding provisions of Uniform Rules of Evidence and notes of decisions relating thereto, which may provide guidance in interpreting the Texas Rule, see Rule 606, 13A Uniform Laws Annotated.

Federal Rules of Evidence

The corresponding provision of the Federal Rules of Evidence is Rule 606. For the text of the Rule and Advisory Committee Notes, which may provide guidance in interpreting the Texas Rule, see the Appendix to this volume.

Leading Cases

American Motorists Ins. Co. v. Sells, 747 S.W.2d 27 (Tex. App.—Texarkana 1988, writ denied) (see *Kendall v. Whataburger, Inc., 759 S.W.2d 751 (Tex. App.—Houston [1st Dist.] 1988, no writ)*, cited below.

Clancy v. Zale Corp., 705 S.W.2d 820 (Tex. App.—Dallas 1986, writ ref'd n.r.e.) ("outside influence" must involve matters not in evidence and which come from outside the jury and its deliberations).

Crowson v. Kansas City Southern Railway Co., 11 S.W.3d 300 (Tex. App.—Eastland 1999, no pet.) (textbook not in evidence about discounting cash flow brought into the jury room by a juror and used to compute damages not an outside influence).

Editorial Caballero S.A de C.V. v. Playboy Enterprises, Inc., 359 S.W.3d 318 (Tex. App.—Corpus Christi 2012, pet. denied) (where information from outside the jury and its deliberation comes from a juror or jurors, that information is not an outside influence, even where that information is intended by the juror or jurors to prejudice the vote; thus, evidence of such information and its source is not admissible on the issue of jury misconduct).

Glover v. State, 110 S.W.3d 549 (Tex. App.—Waco 2003, no pet. h.) (juror cannot be called to testify to impeach his own verdict).

Golden v. First City Nat'l Bank in Grand Prairie, 751 S.W.2d 639 (Tex. App.—Dallas 1988, no writ) (testimony or affidavits by any juror regarding his mental processes or statements or matters occurring during jury deliberations are inadmissible).

Golden Eagle Archery, Inc. v. Jackson, 24 S.W.3d 362 (Tex. 2000) (preclusion of post-verdict testimony about matters and statements occurring during deliberations to prove juror misconduct or bias under Vernon's Ann.Rules Evid., Rule 606 or Vernon's Ann.Rules Civ.Proc., Rule 327(b) does not violate the Texas Constitution).

Kendall v. Whataburger, Inc., 759 S.W.2d 751 (Tex. App.—Houston [1st Dist.] 1988, no writ) (testimony, affidavits or other evidence by a juror as to matters or statements occurring during jury deliberations may not be considered by the court when an issue of jury misconduct is raised unless it bears on whether any outside influence was improperly brought to bear upon any juror; comments by a juror to other jurors during deliberations are not an outside influence). See also *Kiefer v. Continental Airlines, Inc., 10 S.W.3d 34 (Tex. App.—Houston [14th Dist.] 1999, pet. denied)*; *Soliz v. Saenz, 779 S.W.2d 929 (Tex. App.—Corpus Christi 1989, writ denied)*; *Texaco, Inc. v. Pennzoil, Co., 729 S.W.2d 768 (Tex. App.—Houston [1st Dist.] 1987, writ ref'd n.r.e.)*, cited below; *American Motorists Ins. Co. v. Sells, 747 S.W.2d 27 (Tex. App.—Texarkana 1988, writ denied)*, cited above; and Vernon's Ann.Rules Civ.Proc., Rule 327(b).

Kiefer v. Continental Airlines, Inc., 10 S.W.3d 34 (Tex. App.—Houston [14th Dist.] 1999, pet. denied) (see *Kendall v. Whataburger, 759 S.W.2d 751 (Tex. App.—Houston [1st Dist.] 1988, no writ)*, cited above.

Soliz v. Saenz, 779 S.W.2d 929 (Tex. App.—Corpus Christi 1989, writ denied) (see *Kendall v. Whataburger, Inc., 759 S.W.2d 751 (Tex. App.—Houston [1st Dist.] 1988, no writ)*, cited above.

Texaco, Inc. v. Pennzoil, Co., 729 S.W.2d 768 (Tex. App.—Houston [1st Dist.] 1987, writ ref'd n.r.e.) (see *Kendall v. Whataburger, Inc., 759 S.W.2d 751 (Tex. App.—Houston [1st Dist.] 1988, no writ)*, cited above.

Integrated Legal Research System References

West's Texas Digest Key Numbers

Criminal Law ⚷957.

Witnesses ⚷68.

Texas Practice

Addison, Texas Practice Guide, Evidence § 6:83 et seq.

Texas Jur 3d

24A Texas Jur 3d, Criminal Law § 3752.

36 Texas Jur 3d, Evidence § 511.

Annotations

Admissibility, in civil case, of juror's affidavit or testimony relating to juror's misconduct outside jury room, 32 ALR3d 1356.

Competency of juror as witness, under Rule 606(b) of Federal Rules of Evidence, upon inquiry into validity of verdict or indictment, 65 ALR Fed 835.

Trial jurors as witnesses in same state court or related case, 86 ALR3d 781.

Rule 607. Who May Impeach

The credibility of a witness may be attacked by any party, including the party calling the witness.

Eff. March 1, 1998.

Commentary

In general

The general rule is that a party is not entitled to impeach a witness on a collateral matter. *Penwell v. Barrett, 724 S.W.2d 902 (Tex. App.—San Antonio 1987, no writ).* An exception has been recognized at common law when a witness leaves a false impression. In that instance, the opposing party is allowed to correct that false impression on cross-examination or on rebuttal, even with specific instances of conduct. See *Ramirez v. State, 802 S.W.2d 674 (Tex. Crim. App. 1990)* (as long as a party is correcting a false impression made by a witness, specific instances of conduct of the witness may used pursuant to TEX. R. [CRIM.] EVID. 607). *Ramirez* is helpful authority to judges and attorneys in civil cases because the former TEX. R. [CIV.] EVID. 607, the former TEX. R. [CRIM.] EVID. 607, and this rule are substantively identical.

Uniform Rules of Evidence

For text of corresponding provisions of Uniform Rules of Evidence and notes of decisions relating thereto, which may provide guidance in interpreting the Texas Rule, see Rule 607, 13A Uniform Laws Annotated.

Federal Rules of Evidence

The corresponding provision of the Federal Rules of Evidence is Rule 607. For the text of the Rule and Advisory Committee Notes, which may provide guidance in interpreting the Texas Rule, see the Appendix to this volume.

Integrated Legal Research System References

West's Texas Digest Key Numbers

Witnesses ⚷319, 321.

Texas Practice

Addison, Texas Practice Guide, Evidence § 6:127 et seq.

Texas Jur 3d

37 Texas Jur 3d, Evidence § 788 et seq.

Annotations

Impeachment of federal trial witness with respect to intoxication, 106 ALR Fed 371.

Propriety, under Federal Rule of Evidence 607, of impeachment of party's own witness, 89 ALR Fed 13.

Rule 608. Evidence of Character and Conduct of a Witness

(a) Opinion and Reputation Evidence of Character. The credibility of a witness may be attacked or supported by evidence in the form of opinion or reputation, but subject to these limitations:

(1) the evidence may refer only to character for truthfulness or untruthfulness; and

(2) evidence of truthful character is admissible only after the character of the witness for truthfulness has been attacked by opinion or reputation evidence or otherwise.

(b) Specific Instances of Conduct. Specific instances of the conduct of a witness, for the purpose of attacking or supporting the witness' credibility, other than conviction of crime as provided in Rule 609, may not be inquired into on cross-examination of the witness nor proved by extrinsic evidence.

Eff. March 1, 1998.

Commentary

In general

A clear distinction should be made between the witnesses who testify to the facts in a case and the reputation witnesses who are called to attack or support the credibility of those fact witnesses. The distinction is critical to understanding the rules relating to impeaching fact witnesses and impeaching reputation witness.

Every witness who testifies puts his credibility in issue. Vernon's Ann.Rules Evid., Rule 611(b). There are many ways to impeach the credibility of a witness, but if one is going to do it by way of opinion or reputation evidence, then this rule is going to apply. See also Vernon's Ann.Rules Evid., Rule 404(a)(3) and Vernon's Ann.Rules Evid., Rules 607. Vernon's Ann.Rules Evid., Rule 405 allows proof of character or a trait of character, and inquiry on cross-examination of relevant specific instances of conduct in certain circumstances. But, if the trait of character is for truthfulness or untruthfulness of a fact witness, specific instances of conduct for the purpose of attacking or supporting the credibility of the fact witness, other than conviction of a crime under Vernon's Ann.Rules Evid., Rule 609, are not admissible under this rule. *Service Lloyds Ins. Co. v. Martin, 855 S.W.2d 816 (Tex. App.—Dallas 1993, no writ).*

In criminal cases, a reputation witness who offers his knowledge or opinion of a defendant's reputation for a particular trait of character, including truthfulness, must be shown to have either knowledge of the defendant's reputation for the character trait in issue or to have knowledge of facts to support his opinion of that character trait. That knowledge of the *defendant's* reputation or of the facts supporting the witness's opinion of that reputation must have been acquired before the date of the offense for which the defendant in a criminal case is on trial. Vernon's Ann.Rules Evid., Rule 405.

Impeaching a reputation witness

When a fact witness's reputation for truthfulness is attacked, a party may then present evidence of his truthful character by, among other means, reputation witnesses. When a reputation witness testifies as to the character of a fact witness for truthfulness, Vernon's Ann.Rules Evid., Rule 405(a) allows "do you know" or "have you heard" questions to be asked of the reputation witness to test the basis for his personal knowledge or opinion. These questions are aimed at impeaching the reputation witness, not by specific instances of *his* conduct, but by specific instances of conduct of the fact witness for whom the reputation witness is testifying and whose reputation for truthfulness he purports to know. There are, however, limitations on the right to cross-examine a character witness about specific instances of a fact witness's conduct: (1) there must be some factual basis for the incidents inquired about, (2) those instances must be relevant to the character trait at issue (truthfulness, in this instance), and (3) upon proper objection, the proponent of the evidence must expressly offer it for its limited, admissible purpose, or there is no error in excluding it. *Matter of G.M.P., 909 S.W.2d 198 (Tex. App.—Houston [14th Dist.] 1995, no writ)*; Vernon's Ann.Rules Evid., Rule 105(b).

The factual basis for the incidents inquired about must be presented outside the presence of the jury and must establish a basis from which the trial court can test the good faith of the proponent of the evidence in asking the questions. *In re G.M.P., supra.* The party about whom the evidence of specific instances of his own conduct is being offered to impeach his reputation witness should request an instruction in the jury charge to limit the jury's consideration of the evidence of specific instances of conduct to the purpose for which it was admitted, namely, to aid the jury in assessing the credibility of the *reputation witness*, if it does so aid the jury, and for no other purpose. If the trial court excludes the evidence after a proper objection, the offering party has the obligation under Vernon's Ann.Rules Evid., Rule 105 to expressly offer the evidence for its limited purpose of testing the credibility of the reputation witness in order to establish a basis for a complaint about the exclusion of that evidence. If the evidence is admitted for that limited purpose, the trial court in its charge should so inform the jury on the request of any party.

This technique can be used against a reputation witness regarding any trait of character of another about which he is testifying.

Discovery of reputation witnesses

A character witness is a fact witness whose identity should be revealed in response to a proper interrogatory. Vernon's Ann.Rules Civ.Proc., Rule 215(5) is applicable to all witnesses in civil cases whose identity is discoverable. A character witness who is not named in response to an interrogatory inquiring of fact witnesses should be excluded from testifying, upon proper objection. *Clayton v. First State Bank of Gainesville, 777 S.W.2d 577 (Tex. App.—Fort Worth 1989, writ denied).* There is no general right of discovery of the identity of purely reputation witnesses in criminal cases. However, the prosecution has an affirmative duty to produce material, exculpatory evidence. *Brady v. Maryland, 373 U.S. 83, 83 S.Ct. 1194, 10 L.Ed.2d 215 (1963).* See *United States v. Bagley, 473 U.S. 667, 676, 105 S.Ct. 3375, 3380, 87 L.Ed.2d 481 (1985)* (impeachment evidence included within the scope of the term "exculpatory evidence").

Objections and preservation of error

Rule 608(b) and Rule 613(b) serve distinct and different purposes regarding the impeachment of witnesses; therefore, any trial objection based on either of those rules does not preserve error for review under the other. *Dixon v. State, 2 S.W.3d 263 (Tex. Crim. App. 1998).*

Uniform Rules of Evidence

For text of corresponding provisions of Uniform Rules of Evidence and notes of decisions relating thereto, which may provide guidance in interpreting the Texas Rule, see Rule 608, 13A Uniform Laws Annotated.

Federal Rules of Evidence

The corresponding provision of the Federal Rules of Evidence is Rule 608. For the text of the Rule and Advisory Committee Notes, which may provide guidance in interpreting the Texas Rule, see the Appendix to this volume.

Integrated Legal Research System References

West's Texas Digest Key Numbers

Witnesses ⚷333–341.

Texas Practice

Addison, Texas Practice Guide, Evidence § 6:133 et seq.

Texas Jur 3d

25 Texas Jur 3d, Criminal Law § 3944 et seq.

37 Texas Jur 3d, Evidence § 814 et seq.

Annotations

Attacking or supporting credibility of witness by evidence in form of opinion or reputation, under Rule 608(a) of Federal Rules of Evidence, 52 ALR Fed 440.

Construction and application of Rule 608(b) of Federal Rules of Evidence dealing with use of specific instances of conduct to attack or support credibility, 36 ALR Fed 564.

Impeachment of federal trial witness with respect to intoxication, 106 ALR Fed 371.

Rule 609. Impeachment by Evidence of Conviction of Crime

(a) General Rule. For the purpose of attacking the credibility of a witness, evidence that the witness has been convicted of a crime shall be admitted if elicited from the witness or established by public record but only if the crime was a felony or involved moral turpitude, regardless of punishment, and the court determines that the probative value of admitting this evidence outweighs its prejudicial effect to a party.

(b) Time Limit. Evidence of a conviction under this rule is not admissible if a period of more than ten years has elapsed since the date of the conviction or of the release of the witness from the confinement imposed for that conviction, whichever is the later date, unless the court determines, in the interests of justice, that the probative value of the conviction supported by specific facts and circumstances substantially outweighs its prejudicial effect.

(c) Effect of Pardon, Annulment, or Certificate of Rehabilitation. Evidence of a conviction is not admissible under this rule if:

(1) based on the finding of the rehabilitation of the person convicted, the conviction has been the subject of a pardon, annulment, certificate of rehabilitation, or other equivalent procedure, and that person has not been convicted of a subsequent crime which was classified as a felony or involved moral turpitude, regardless of punishment;

(2) probation has been satisfactorily completed for the crime for which the person was convicted, and that person has not been convicted of a subsequent

crime which was classified as a felony or involved moral turpitude, regardless of punishment; or

(3) based on a finding of innocence, the conviction has been the subject of a pardon, annulment, or other equivalent procedure.

(d) Juvenile Adjudications. Evidence of juvenile adjudications is not admissible, except for proceedings conducted pursuant to Title III, Family Code, in which the witness is a party, under this rule unless required to be admitted by the Constitution of the United States or Texas.

(e) Pendency of Appeal. Pendency of an appeal renders evidence of a conviction inadmissible.

(f) Notice. Evidence of a conviction is not admissible if after timely written request by the adverse party specifying the witness or witnesses, the proponent fails to give to the adverse party sufficient advance written notice of intent to use such evidence to provide the adverse party with a fair opportunity to contest the use of such evidence.

Eff. March 1, 1998.

Commentary

A. In General

Generally

A prior felony conviction, or a conviction for an offense involving moral turpitude, whether a felony or not, is admissible to impeach the credibility of a witness to whom the conviction applies. A person who has committed such an offense has thereby demonstrated that he has a defect of character such that his word is suspect or not worthy of belief. However, there are limitations to the admissibility of prior convictions to impeach. These limitations are to account for the rehabilitation, pardon, or reform of the offender, the passage of time, or the lack of finality of the judgment of conviction because the case is on appeal. These factors lessen the impact, importance or probative value of the prior convictions on the issue of the witness's credibility. It is not necessary that the prior conviction be somehow relevant to the issues in the lawsuit. The concept of relevancy expressed in Vernon's Ann.Rules Evid., Rule 401 is not involved in this context. See *Theus v. State, 845 S.W.2d 874 (Tex. Crim. App. 1992).*

Preliminary determination

Under this rule, the trial court must make a preliminary determination as to whether the probative value of admitting the evidence of the prior conviction outweighs its prejudicial effect to a party.

Nolo contendre pleas

Vernon's Ann.Rules Evid., Rule 410 provides that, except as that rule permits, evidence of a *plea* of *nolo contendere* is not admissible in a civil case against the defendant who made the plea. However, neither Rule 410, nor Rule 609 prohibit the use of the *fact of conviction*, whether after a plea of *nolo contendere* or not, for the purpose of impeachment. See Commentary to Rule 410, *supra*.

Uniform Rules of Evidence

For text of corresponding provisions of Uniform Rules of Evidence and notes of decisions relating thereto, which may provide guidance in interpreting the Texas Rule, see Rule 609, 13A Uniform Laws Annotated.

Federal Rules of Evidence

The corresponding provision of the Federal Rules of Evidence is Rule 609. For the text of the Rule and Advisory Committee Notes, which may provide guidance in interpreting the Texas Rule, see the Appendix to this volume.

B. Limitations on the Use of Prior Convictions to Impeach a Witness

The issue of credibility

This rule allows the use of prior convictions to impeach the credibility of a witness, whether a party or not. The prior conviction used for that purpose must be for a felony offense or an offense involving moral turpitude, regardless of the punishment involved.

A felony offense is any offense for which the sentence *could* include confinement in a penitentiary or a state jail facility. A crime involving moral turpitude is a crime that involves dishonesty, fraud, deceit, misrepresentation, or deliberate violence. *Duncan v. Board of Disciplinary Appeals, 898 S.W.2d 759 (Tex. 1995).* Whether a particular offense involves moral turpitude is a question of law. *Id.*

Completion of probation

A prior felony conviction or a conviction for an offense involving moral turpitude resulting in a probated sentence for the offender can be used to impeach the witness to whom the conviction applies if the period for which the sentence was probated has not been completed. However, if the period of probation has been completed, the prior conviction cannot be used unless it can be shown that the witness has been subsequently convicted of a felony or a crime involving moral turpitude, regardless of the punishment, within the past ten years.

Vernon's Ann.Rules Evid., Rule 609(c)(2) refers to probation being "satisfactorily completed" for the crime for which the witness was convicted as an impediment to the use of a prior conviction where probation had been granted. The probation need only be completed: that is, served out, whether satisfactorily or not. *Ex parte Menchaca, 854 S.W.2d 128 (Tex. Crim. App. 1993).* If the offender received probation for a felony or for an offense involving moral turpitude, and that probation was later revoked, probation has not been completed. Instead, the offender then has a final conviction as of the date of the revocation of his probation. The ten year period for remoteness begins to run from the date of the revocation of probation (the date of conviction) or the date of the release of the offender from confinement imposed for the conviction, whichever is later, and not from the date of the granting of probation.

Remoteness

If more that ten years have elapsed since the date of conviction or release of the defendant from confinement, whichever is later, the conviction is deemed to be too remote in time to be of any value to the determination of the credibility of the witness to whom the conviction applies. However, if it can be shown that because of other specific facts and circumstances the probative value of even a remote conviction would substantially outweigh its prejudicial effect, the trial court may admit the evidence of the remote prior conviction in the interests of justice.

Other evidence of specific facts and circumstances regarding the probative value of the remote prior conviction may include other convictions for felony offenses or crimes involving moral turpitude that are not remote, subsequent convictions for the same or a similar offenses as the offense involved in the remote prior conviction, or evidence that the witness is an habitual offender, or is an habitual offender as defined in the Texas Penal Code. See V.T.C.A., Penal Code § 12.42.

Request for notice of intent to use prior convictions

In every case, a trial lawyer should consider making a written request of his opponent to state, in writing, whether he intends to offer evidence of prior convictions as to any specified witnesses. If the party of whom the request is made fails to respond in writing in sufficient time, the prior convictions will not be admissible against those specified witnesses for the purpose of impeaching their credibility. Vernon's Ann.Rules Evid., Rule 609(f) does not require a motion to the court, or a court order. A request of intent to use prior convictions to impeach the credibility of a witness (served pursuant to Vernon's Ann.Rules Civ.Proc., Rule 21(a) in a civil case) may lie quietly and forgotten in an opponent's file, and at trial the opponent will find that he cannot impeach the specified witnesses with their prior convictions. On the other hand, if the opponent does respond to the request, the trial lawyer can take the appropriate actions in an attempt to forestall the use of the prior convictions or to lessen their impact on the trier of fact.

C. Practical Considerations

Proving a prior conviction by the witness's own testimony

A fact witness may be asked if he has been convicted of a felony or a crime involving moral turpitude in the past. If the witness's answer is "no," his answer must be taken, unless the answer is incorrect or false, in which case the prior conviction can be proved by extrinsic evidence. If the witness answers affirmatively that he has before been convicted of a felony or a crime involving moral turpitude, the answer still leaves the remainder of the predicate unestablished. Further evidence may show that the conviction is not admissible because it is remote, the conviction is not for a felony, or is not for a crime involving moral turpitude, the witness received probation which has been completed, the case in which the conviction was obtained is on appeal, or the probative value of admitting the evidence is outweighed by its prejudicial effect to a party. For this reason, the jury should never be given the opportunity to hear the answer to the question, without there first being a hearing outside the presence of the jury to determine if the entire predicate can be shown, and to give the trial court the opportunity to compare the probative value of the evidence with its prejudicial effect, if the entire predicate is established.

Keeping the matter away from the jury before a hearing is held can be the subject of a motion in limine filed, and ruled on by the trial court, prior to trial. Whether a motion in limine is filed or not, a proper and timely objection will bring the matter to the attention of the trial court before the jury hears the answer to the question. If, after a hearing, the court admits the affirmative answer, the witness has been impeached, and no extrinsic evidence of the conviction is permitted.

As a practical matter, most witnesses who have been convicted of crimes don't know whether the conviction was for a felony, and most have no idea whether the conviction was for an offense involving moral turpitude, or whether they received probation, or many other of the finer points of their criminal histories. The likelihood of getting an erroneous answer about prior convictions involved is very high when the witness is asked directly and the interrogator does not know the answer before he asks the question. This phenomenon alone is more than adequate reason to assure that a hearing outside the presence of the jury is held before the question is answered.

Failure to timely respond in writing to a Rule 609(f) request may preclude even asking the witness if he has been convicted of a felony or a crime involving moral turpitude within the past ten years.

Proving a prior conviction by public record

The public record referred to in the Rule 609(a) is the judgment in the underlying criminal case. This document will contain the date of conviction, whether the defendant received probation or a jail or penitentiary sentence, the name of the offense, the name of the defendant, the required formal recitations, and usually will contain the date of the offense and a fingerprint of the defendant. Documents obtained from the penitentiary, referred to by criminal law practitioners as "pen packets," will include an official copy of the judgment, a photograph and a full set of fingerprints. A judgment should provide most, if not all, of the information that the trial lawyer needs to know to determine whether he can establish the predicate required by this rule. If the judgment is not sufficient to meet the required predicate, the lawyer will have to find other evidence to establish it.

The most difficult fact to establish when using an official record of a prior conviction will often be the identity of the person shown in the documents. Before a judgment of conviction can be admitted into evidence in any context, including to impeach a witness, it must be shown that the person named in the judgment is the same person against whom it is to be used at trial. The fact that the person named in the judgment and the person against whom it is to be used have exactly the same name is not sufficient. Proof that the judgment pertains to the person against whom it is to be used can be established by fingerprints, photographs, or the testimony of witnesses such as the prosecutor, the probation officer, or any other person who can testify of their own personal knowledge that the defendant convicted in the criminal case is the same as the person in question.

When a judgment of conviction is available to impeach a witness with a prior conviction, the *simplest* means is to ask the witness if he is the same person who was convicted of the named crime, in the case identified by cause number, in the identified court, and on the date stated in the judgment. The witness may admit it or deny it. If admitted, the witness is impeached and no further extrinsic evidence of the conviction is admissible. If the witness denies the conviction or states that he does not know or cannot remember, he may be impeached by the admission of the judgment, provided that the judgment is shown to pertain to the witness.

When a judgment of conviction is available to impeach a witness with a prior conviction, the *most effective* means is by proving up the prior conviction independently of the witness's testimony, after the witness has testified. If proof can be readily shown that the witness and the person named in the judgment of conviction are the same person, the official record may be admitted into evidence. The record contains much more information than just the name of the crime. It contains the evidence necessary to meet the elements of proof required by this rule, and the members of the jury get to hold it in their hands and read it at their leisure in the jury room.

Weighing the probative value and prejudicial effect of a prior conviction used to impeach

Vernon's Ann.Rules Evid., Rule 609(a) requires the trial court to make a determination that proof of a prior conviction to impeach the credibility of a witness is not outweighed by its prejudicial effect to a party. The trial court should consider, among other factors, whether a limiting instruction given pursuant to Vernon's Ann.Rules Evid., Rule 105 would lessen the prejudicial effect of the prior conviction and serve to restrict the jury to considering the prior conviction only for the purpose for which it was admitted.

Juvenile adjudications

Evidence of juvenile adjudications is not admissible to impeach a witness in a civil case except as provided by this rule. Evidence of juvenile adjudications is admissible in the punishment stage of a criminal case to impeach a witness where the adjudication is for a felony or a misdemeanor punishable by confinement in jail (that is, class A and B misdemeanors). Vernon's Ann.C.C.P. Art. 37.07 § 3(a).

Leading Cases

Allied Chem. Co. v. DeHaven, 824 S.W.2d 257 (Tex. App.—Houston [14th Dist.] 1992, no writ) (a conviction must meet the requirements of Rule 609 or it is inadmissible for the purposes of impeachment).

Dallas County Bail Bond Bd. v. Mason, 773 S.W.2d 586 (Tex. App.—Dallas 1989, no writ) (an offense involving dishonesty or false statement is an offense involving moral turpitude).

Delk v. State, 855 S.W.2d 700 (Tex. Crim. App. 1993) (when a witness leaves a false impression of law abiding conduct, his otherwise irrelevant criminal history is admissible to expose the falsehood). See *Prescott v. State, 744 S.W.2d 128 (Tex. Crim. App. 1988)*, cited below.

Oadra v. Stegall, 871 S.W.2d 882 (Tex. App.—Houston [14th Dist.] 1994, no writ) (trial court's determination that the probative value of evidence of a prior felony conviction for impeachment purposes was outweighed by its prejudicial effect was not an abuse of discretion). See *Porter v. Nemir, 900 S.W.2d 376 (Tex. App.—Austin 1995, no writ)*, cited below.

Porter v. Nemir, 900 S.W.2d 376 (Tex. App.—Austin 1995, no writ) (the trial court's determination that the probative value of a conviction for sexual abuse of a child did not outweigh its prejudicial effect was not an abuse of discretion). See *Oadra v. Stegall, 871 S.W.2d 882 (Tex. App.—Houston [14th Dist.] 1994, no writ)*, cited above.

Prescott v. State, 744 S.W.2d 128 (Tex. Crim. App. 1988) (when a witness leaves a false impression of law abiding conduct, his otherwise irrelevant criminal history is admissible to expose the falsehood). See *Delk v. State, 855 S.W.2d 700 (Tex. Crim. App. 1993)*, cited above.

Integrated Legal Research System References

West's Texas Digest Key Numbers

Witnesses ⚷337, 345.

Texas Practice

Addison, Texas Practice Guide, Evidence § 6:153 et seq.

Texas Jur 3d

25 Texas Jur 3d, Criminal Law § 3935 et seq.

37 Texas Jur 3d, Evidence § 824 et seq.

Annotations

Admissibility of evidence of other offense where record has been expunged or erased, 82 ALR4th 913.

Construction and application of Rule 609(a) of the Federal Rules of Evidence permitting impeachment of witness by evidence of prior conviction of crime, 39 ALR Fed 570.

Construction and application of Rule 609(c) of the Federal Rules of Evidence, providing that evidence of conviction is not admissible to attack credibility of witness if conviction has been subject of pardon, annulment, or other procedure based on finding of rehabilitation or innocence, 42 ALR Fed 942.

Construction and application of Rule 609(b) of Federal Rules of Evidence setting time limit on admissibility of evidence of conviction of crime to attack credibility of witness, 160 ALR Fed 201.

Conviction by court-martial as proper subject of cross-examination for impeachment purposes, 7 ALR4th 468.

Permissibility of impeaching credibility of witness by showing former conviction, as affected by pendency of appeal from conviction or motion for new trial, 16 ALR3d 726.

Privilege of witness to refuse to give answers tending to disgrace or degrade him or his family, 88 ALR3d 374.

Requirement that defendant in state court testify in order to preserve alleged trial error in rulings on admissibility of prior conviction impeachment evidence under Uniform Rule of Evidence 609, or similar provision or holding—post Luce cases, 80 ALR4th 1028.

Right to impeach credibility of accused by showing prior conviction, as affected by remoteness in time of prior offense, 67 ALR3d 824.

Right to impeach witness in criminal case by inquiry or evidence as to witness' criminal activity for which witness was arrested or charged, but not convicted—modern state cases, 28 ALR4th 505.

Use of unrelated misdemeanor conviction (other than for traffic offense) to impeach general credibility of witness in state civil case, 97 ALR3d 1150.

What constitutes crime involving "dishonesty or false statement" under Rule 609(A)(2) of the Uniform Rules of Evidence or similar state rule, 82 ALR5th 359.

What constitutes crime involving "dishonesty or false statement" under Rule 609(A)(2) of Uniform Rules of Evidence or similar state rule—Crimes involving violence or potential for violence, 83 ALR5th 277.

What constitutes crime involving "dishonesty or false statement" under Rule 609(A)(2) of Uniform Rules of Evidence or similar state rule—Nonviolent crimes, 84 ALR5th 487.

Rule 610. Religious Beliefs or Opinions

Evidence of the beliefs or opinions of a witness on matters of religion is not admissible for the purpose of showing that by reason of their nature the witness' credibility is impaired or enhanced.

Eff. March 1, 1998.

Commentary

Official Comment to former Civil Rule 610

The comment to former Rule 610 of the Rules of Civil Evidence provided in pertinent part as follows: "While the rule forecloses inquiry beliefs or opinions of a witness for the purpose of showing that his character for truthfulness is affected by their nature, an inquiry for the purpose of showing interest or bias because of them is not within the prohibition. Thus disclosure of affiliation with a church which is a party to the litigation would be allowable under the rule."

Uniform Rules of Evidence

For text of corresponding provisions of Uniform Rules of Evidence and notes of decisions relating thereto, which may provide guidance in interpreting the Texas Rule, see Rule 610, 13A Uniform Laws Annotated.

Federal Rules of Evidence

The corresponding provision of the Federal Rules of Evidence is Rule 610. For the text of the Rule and Advisory Committee Notes, which may provide guidance in interpreting the Texas Rule, see the Appendix to this volume.

Integrated Legal Research System References

West's Texas Digest Key Numbers

Witnesses ⚷340(2).

Texas Practice

Addison, Texas Practice Guide, Evidence § 6:191 et seq.

Annotations

Propriety and prejudicial effect of impeaching witness by reference to religious belief or lack of it, 76 ALR3d 539.

Propriety and prejudicial effect of questions or comments as to witness' religious beliefs or standards designed to enhance credibility, 27 ALR4th 1167.

Rule 611. Mode and Order of Interrogation and Presentation

(a) Control by Court. The court shall exercise reasonable control over the mode and order of interrogating witnesses and presenting evidence so as to (1) make the interrogation and presentation effective for the ascertainment of the truth, (2) avoid needless consumption of time, and (3) protect witnesses from harassment or undue embarrassment.

(b) Scope of Cross–Examination. A witness may be cross-examined on any matter relevant to any issue in the case, including credibility.

(c) Leading Questions. Leading questions should not be used on the direct examination of a witness except as may be necessary to develop the testimony of the witness. Ordinarily leading questions should be permitted on cross-examination. When a party calls a hostile witness, an adverse party, or a witness identified with an adverse party, interrogation may be by leading questions.

Eff. March 1, 1998.

Commentary

Official Comment to former Civil Evidence Rule 611

The comment to former Rule 611 of the Rules of Civil Evidence provided in pertinent part as follows: "The purpose of the amendment [1988 amendment altering language of former rule to permit leading testimony in order to develop the testimony of a witness] is to permit, in the court's discretion, the use of leading questions on preliminary or introductory matters, refreshing memory, questions to ignorant or illiterate persons or children, all as permitted by prior Texas practice and the common law.

"The rule also conforms to tradition in making the use of leading questions on cross-examination a matter of right. The purpose of the qualification 'ordinarily' is to furnish a basis for denying the use of leading questions when the cross-examination is cross-examination in form only and not in fact, as for example, the 'cross-examination' of a party by his own counsel after being called by the opponent (savoring more of re-direct) or of an insured defendant who proves to be friendly to the plaintiff."

Uniform Rules of Evidence

For text of corresponding provisions of Uniform Rules of Evidence and notes of decisions relating thereto, which may provide guidance in interpreting the Texas Rule, see Rule 611, 13A Uniform Laws Annotated.

Federal Rules of Evidence

The corresponding provision of the Federal Rules of Evidence is Rule 611. For the text of the Rule and Advisory Committee Notes, which may provide guidance in interpreting the Texas Rule, see the Appendix to this volume.

Integrated Legal Research System References

West's Texas Digest Key Numbers

Witnesses ⚷224, 240–244, 268.

Texas Practice

Addison, Texas Practice Guide, Evidence § 6:197 et seq.

Texas Jur 3d

24A Texas Jur 3d, Criminal Law §§ 3838, 3851 et seq., 3884 et seq.

37 Texas Jur 3d, Evidence § 707 et seq.

Annotations

Construction and application of provision of Rule 611(b) of Federal Rules of Evidence that cross-examination should be limited to subject matter of direct examination, 45 ALR Fed 639.

Cross-examination by leading questions of witness friendly to or biased in favor of cross-examiner, 38 ALR2d 952.

Cross-examination of character witness for accused with reference to particular acts or crimes—modern state rules, 13 ALR4th 796.

Permissibility of testimony by telephone in state trial, 85 ALR4th 476.

Rule 612. Writing Used to Refresh Memory

If a witness uses a writing to refresh memory for the purpose of testifying either

(1) while testifying;

(2) before testifying, in civil cases, if the court in its discretion determines it is necessary in the interests of justice; or

(3) before testifying, in criminal cases;

an adverse party is entitled to have the writing produced at the hearing, to inspect it, to cross-examine the witness thereon, and to introduce in evidence those portions which relate to the testimony of the witness. If it is claimed that the writing contains matters not related to the subject matter of the testimony the court shall examine the writing in camera, excise any portion not so related, and order delivery of the remainder to the party entitled thereto. Any portion withheld over objections shall be preserved and made available to the appellate court in the event of an appeal. If a writing is not produced or delivered pursuant to order under this rule, the court shall make any order justice requires, except that in criminal cases when the prosecution elects not to comply, the order shall be one striking the testimony or, if the court in its discretion determines that the interests of justice so require, declaring a mistrial.

Eff. March 1, 1998.

Commentary

In general

This rule does not require that the writing referred to be a writing made by the witness or adopted by the witness as his own. It may be any writing the witness uses to refresh his memory for the purpose of testifying, either before testifying or while testifying.

Examination of writing by opponent

When a witness uses any writing to refresh his memory *while testifying*, he thereby waives any claim of attorney-client privilege or work product protection regarding that writing, and the writing must be produced to the adverse party at the hearing in which the witness testifies. *Goode v. Shoukfeh, 943 S.W.2d 441 (Tex. 1997)*; *City of Denison v. Grisham, 716 S.W.2d 121 (Tex. App.—Dallas 1986, no writ)*. When a witness refreshes his memory from a writing *before testifying*, the trial court has the discretion whether to require the writing to be produced to the adverse party at the hearing in which the witness testifies. This discretion does not extend to writings that were used by the witness to refresh his memory before testifying in a civil case and which are shown to be privileged. *Goode v. Shoukfeh, supra*. The difference seems to be that if the writing is used at a hearing by the witness to refresh his memory while testifying, the writing is being used in the presence of the trier of fact (or will be, in the case of a deposition), thus placing the contents of the writing in issue. Further, it would seem that the attorney-client privilege and any work product protection regarding a writing used by a witness to refresh his memory before he testified, would remain intact, if claimed and properly proved, because the writing was not used in the presence of the trier of fact, so its contents are not an issue. See *Skinner v. State, 956 S.W.2d 532 (Tex. Crim. App. 1997)* (document "used before the jury" waives work product privilege and the other side is entitled to inspect the document where such use puts the contents of the document in issue).

In criminal cases, a writing *used* by a witness to refresh his memory, either before or while testifying, must be produced to the opponent for examination and for use in cross-examining the witness, regardless of whether the writing is claimed to be privileged. The writing need not be produced until the witness is passed for cross-examination. However, the writing may be discoverable. Vernon's Ann.C.C.P. Art.

39.14. Or, it may be required to be produced before trial pursuant to *Brady v. Maryland*, *supra* (prosecutors have an affirmative duty to disclose all material, exculpatory evidence to the defense). If the writing was *made* by a witness in a criminal case and it relates to the subject matter concerning which the witness has testified, whether the witness used the writing to refresh his memory or not, the writing must be produced for examination and use on the motion of the party that did not call the witness. Vernon's Ann.Rules Evid., Rule 615.

Testimony of the witness

The hearing referred to in the rule refers to testimony at a deposition, at a hearing before the court or at trial. See *City of Denison*, *supra*. When a witness uses a writing to refresh his memory, his subsequent testimony must be from his memory thus refreshed, not from the writing. Of course, that refreshed memory must be of matters about which the witness has personal knowledge. TEX. R. [CIV.] EVID. 602.

Uniform Rules of Evidence

For text of corresponding provisions of Uniform Rules of Evidence and notes of decisions relating thereto, which may provide guidance in interpreting the Texas Rule, see Rule 612, 13A Uniform Laws Annotated.

Federal Rules of Evidence

The corresponding provision of the Federal Rules of Evidence is Rule 612. For the text of the Rule and Advisory Committee Notes, which may provide guidance in interpreting the Texas Rule, see the Appendix to this volume.

Integrated Legal Research System References

West's Texas Digest Key Numbers

Witnesses ⚷253–257.

Texas Practice

Addison, Texas Practice Guide, Evidence § 6:232 et seq.

Texas Jur 3d

24A Texas Jur 3d, Criminal Law § 3875 et seq.

37 Texas Jur 3d, Evidence § 749 et seq.

Am Jur Trials

Examination of a Witness Based on a Prior Statement, 49 Am Jur Trials 501.

Annotations

Use of writing to refresh witness' memory, as governed by Rule 612 of Federal Rules of Evidence, 73 ALR Fed 423.

Rule 613. Prior Statements of Witnesses: Impeachment and Support

(a) Examining Witness Concerning Prior Inconsistent Statement. In examining a witness concerning a prior inconsistent statement made by the witness, whether oral or written, and before further cross-examination concerning, or extrinsic evidence of, such statement may be allowed, the witness must be told the contents of such statement and the time and place and the person to whom it was made, and must be afforded an opportunity to explain or deny such statement. If written, the writing need not be shown to the witness at that time, but on request the same shall be shown to opposing counsel. If the witness unequivocally admits having made such statement, extrinsic evidence of same shall not be admitted. This provision does not apply to admissions of a party-opponent as defined in Rule 801(e)(2).

(b) Examining Witness Concerning Bias or Interest. In impeaching a witness by proof of circumstances or statements showing bias or interest on the part of such witness, and before further cross-examination concerning, or extrinsic evidence of, such bias or interest may be allowed, the circumstances supporting such claim or the details of such statement, including the contents and where, when and to whom made, must be made known to the witness, and the witness must be given an opportunity to explain or to deny such circumstances or statement. If written, the writing need not be shown to the witness at that time, but on request the same shall be shown to opposing counsel. If the witness unequivocally admits such bias or interest, extrinsic evidence of same shall not be admitted. A party shall be permitted to present evidence rebutting any evidence impeaching one of said party's witnesses on grounds of bias or interest.

(c) Prior Consistent Statements of Witnesses. A prior statement of a witness which is consistent with the testimony of the witness is inadmissible except as provided in Rule 801(e)(1)(B).

Eff. March 1, 1998.

Commentary

In general

This rule sets out the particulars required to impeach a witness with his prior inconsistent statement and with proof of bias or motive. This rule also provides a path for the rehabilitation of a witness impeached by his prior statements under this rule.

Impeachment by a prior inconsistent statement of a witness

The statement intended to be used to impeach a witness must actually be inconsistent with his testimony on a matter relevant to the case and not merely on a collateral matter. *McGary v. State, 750 S.W.2d 782 (Tex. Crim. App. 1988).* See Commentary to Rule 607, *supra*. The prior inconsistent statement may be written or oral, but if the statement contains matters which are not inconsistent with the witness's testimony, only those portions which are inconsistent are admissible for the purposes of impeachment. See Vernon's Ann.Rules Evid., Rule 106 (remainder of or related writings or recorded statements).

The witness must be told of the time, place and circumstances of the making of the statement, as well as the contents of the statement, and then be given an opportunity to explain or deny the statement. *Ramsey v. Lucky Stores, Inc., 853 S.W.2d 623 (Tex. App.—Houston [1st Dist.] 1993, writ denied).* If the witness unequivocally admits to having made the statement, impeachment is complete, and neither the statement nor any other evidence of its contents is admissible. *Id.*; *Downen v. Texas Gulf Shrimp Co., 846 S.W.2d 506 (Tex. App.—Corpus Christi 1993, writ denied).* If the statement is in writing, the witness has no right to see it, although the opposing attorney does have that right.

If the impeachment evidence is admitted before the jury, the opposing attorney should consider asking the trial court to instruct the jury to limit its consideration of the evidence to the purpose for which it was offered, namely, to aid the jury, if it does, in judging the credibility of the witness against whom the evidence was offered. If the impeachment evidence is excluded, the proponent of the evidence must offer the evidence for its limited purpose pursuant to Vernon's Ann.Rules Evid., Rule 105 in order to complain of its exclusion on appeal.

Impeachment with a prior inconsistent statement in the manner prescribed by this rule does not apply to an admission of a party.

Impeachment by showing bias or interest of a witness

Bias or interest of a witness can be shown by proof of circumstances or statements which show the bias or interest. The same considerations of fairness to the witness are involved in showing the bias or interest as are involved in proving a prior inconsistent statement. A party who offered the witness is permitted to attempt to rehabilitate the witness impeached by evidence of the witness's bias or interest.

Admissibility of a prior consistent statement of a witness

A prior *consistent* statement of a witness is not admissible except as provided in Vernon's Ann.Rules Evid., Rule 801(e)(1)(B) ("A statement is not hearsay if . . . [T]he declarant testifies at the trial or hearing and is subject to cross-examination concerning the statement, and the statement is . . . consistent with his testimony and is offered to rebut an express or implied charge against him of recent fabrication or improper influence or motive . . . "). See *Rivas v. State, 275 S.W.3d 880 (Tex. Crim. App. 2009)* (Except as provided by Rule 801(e)(1)(B), a prior statement of a witness consistent with his testimony is inadmissible.).

Objections and preservation of error

Rule 608(b) and Rule 613(b) serve distinct and different purposes regarding the impeachment of witnesses; therefore, any trial objection based on either of those rules does not preserve error for review under the other. *Dixon v. State, 2 S.W.3d 263 (Tex. Crim. App. 1998).*

Uniform Rules of Evidence

For text of corresponding provisions of Uniform Rules of Evidence and notes of decisions relating thereto, which may provide guidance in interpreting the Texas Rule, see Rule 613, 13A Uniform Laws Annotated.

Federal Rules of Evidence

The corresponding provision of the Federal Rules of Evidence is Rule 613. For the text of the Rule and Advisory Committee Notes, which may provide guidance in interpreting the Texas Rule, see the Appendix to this volume.

Integrated Legal Research System References

West's Texas Digest Key Numbers

Witnesses ⚷379–397.

Texas Practice

Addison, Texas Practice Guide, Evidence § 6:246 et seq.

Texas Jur 3d

25 Texas Jur 3d, Criminal Law § 3950 et seq.

37 Texas Jur 3d, Evidence § 788 et seq.

Annotations

Admissibility of impeached witness' prior consistent statement—modern state civil cases, 59 ALR4th 1000.

Admissibility of impeached witness' prior consistent statement—modern state criminal cases, 58 ALR4th 1014.

Use of prior inconsistent statements for impeachment of testimony of witnesses under Rule 613, Federal Rules of Evidence, 152 ALR Fed 375.

Rule 614. Exclusion of Witnesses

At the request of a party the court shall order witnesses excluded so that they cannot hear the testimony of other witnesses, and it may make the order of its own motion. This rule does not authorize exclusion of:

(1) a party who is a natural person or in civil cases the spouse of such natural person;

(2) an officer or employee of a party in a civil case or a defendant in a criminal case that is not a natural person designated as its representative by its attorney;

(3) a person whose presence is shown by a party to be essential to the presentation of the party's cause; or

(4) the victim in a criminal case, unless the victim is to testify and the court determines that the victim's testimony would be materially affected if the victim hears other testimony at the trial.

Eff. March 1, 1998.

Commentary

In general

This is "the rule." The rule is mandatory when invoked by a party, although the court on its own motion may make the order to exclude the witnesses from hearing the testimony of other witnesses. Certain witnesses may not be excluded, with some exceptions.

In criminal cases, and notwithstanding this rule, the court may not exclude a witness who for the purposes of the prosecution is a victim, a close relative of a deceased victim, or a guardian of a victim unless the court determines that the testimony of the witness would be materially affected by other testimony the witness would hear at trial. TEX. CODE CRIM. PROC. ANN. art. 36.03 (Vernon 2005).

Uniform Rules of Evidence

For text of corresponding provisions of Uniform Rules of Evidence and notes of decisions relating thereto, which may provide guidance in interpreting the Texas Rule, see Rule 615, 13A Uniform Laws Annotated.

Federal Rules of Evidence

The corresponding provision of the Federal Rules of Evidence is Rule 615. For the text of the Rule and Advisory Committee Notes, which may provide guidance in interpreting the Texas Rule, see the Appendix to this volume.

Leading Cases

Drilex Sys., Inc., v. Flores, 1 S.W.3d 112 (Tex. 1999) (expert witnesses are not automatically exempt from the rule).

Integrated Legal Research System References

West's Texas Digest Key Numbers

Witnesses ⚷246(2).

Texas Practice

Addison, Texas Practice Guide, Evidence § 6:267 et seq.

Texas Jur 3d

23 Texas Jur 3d, Criminal Law § 2958 et seq.

Annotations

Exclusion from courtroom of expert witnesses during taking of testimony in civil case, 85 ALR2d 478.

Exclusion of witnesses under Rule 615 of Federal Rules of Evidence, 181 ALR Fed 549.

Prejudicial effect of improper failure to exclude from courtroom or to sequester or separate state's witnesses in criminal case, 74 ALR4th 705.

Rule 615. Production of Statements of Witnesses in Criminal Cases

(a) Motion for Production. After a witness other than the defendant has testified on direct examination, the court, on motion of a party who did not call the witness, shall order the attorney for the state or the defendant and defendant's attorney, as the case may be, to produce, for the examination and use of the moving party, any statement of the witness that is in their possession and that relates to the subject matter concerning which the witness has testified.

(b) Production of Entire Statement. If the entire contents of the statement relate to the subject matter concerning which the witness has testified, the court shall order that the statement be delivered to the moving party.

(c) Production of Excised Statement. If the other party claims that the statement contains matter that does not relate to the subject matter concerning which the witness has testified, the court shall order that it be delivered to the court in camera. Upon inspection, the court shall excise the portions of the statement that do not relate to the subject matter concerning which the witness has testified, and shall order that the statement, with such material excised, be delivered to the moving party. Any portion withheld over objection shall be preserved and made available to the appellate court in the event of appeal.

(d) Recess for Examination of Statement. Upon delivery of the statement to the moving party, the court, upon application of that party, shall recess proceedings in the trial for a reasonable examination of such statement and for preparation for its use in the trial.

(e) Sanction for Failure to Produce Statement. If the other party elects not to comply with an order to deliver a statement to the moving party, the court shall order that the testimony of the witness be stricken from the record and that the trial proceed, or, if it is the attorney for the state who elects not to comply, shall declare a mistrial if required by the interest of justice.

(f) Definition. As used in this rule, a "statement" of a witness means:

(1) a written statement made by the witness that is signed or otherwise adopted or approved by the witness:

(2) a substantially verbatim recital of an oral statement made by the witness that is recorded contemporaneously with the making of the oral statement and that is contained in a stenographic, mechanical, electrical, or other recording or a transcription thereof; or

(3) a statement, however taken or recorded, or a transcription thereof, made by the witness to a grand jury.

Eff. March 1, 1998.

Commentary

In general

This rule applies to a written or recorded statement of a witness in a criminal case that relates to the matter about which he has testified, whether the witness has used the statement to refresh his memory or not. See Vernon's Ann.Rules Evid., Rule 612. After a witness in a criminal case testifies on direct examination, the other party is entitled to the production of the statement for examination and for use in cross-examination of the witness. It must be a statement that is actually in possession of the party calling the witness. This rule applies only to a witness who is not the defendant. See *Pondexter v. State, 942 S.W.2d 577 (Tex. Crim. App. 1996)*; *Jenkins v. State, 912 S.W.2d 793 (Tex. Crim. App. 1993, with opinion on grant of reconsideration, October 11, 1995)* (contains a good discussion of former Tex. R. [Crim.] Evid. 614 [now Vernon's Ann.Rules Evid., Rule 615]).

If the statement is a statement with which the witness has refreshed his memory, but was not a statement made or adopted by the witness as his own, it must be produced pursuant to Vernon's Ann.Rules Evid., Rule 612. See Commentary to Vernon's Ann.Rules Evid., Rule 612.

Uniform Rules of Evidence

There is no corresponding provision in the Uniform Rules of Evidence

Federal Rules of Evidence

There is no corresponding provision in the Federal Rules of Evidence.

Integrated Legal Research System References

West's Texas Digest Key Numbers

Criminal Law ⚷665.

ARTICLE VII. OPINIONS AND EXPERT TESTIMONY

Rule
701. Opinion Testimony by Lay Witnesses.
702. Testimony by Experts.
703. Bases of Opinion Testimony by Experts.
704. Opinion on Ultimate Issue.
705. Disclosure of Facts or Data Underlying Expert Opinion.
706. Audit in Civil Cases.

Cross References

Forensic Analysis of Evidence, Vernon's Ann.C.C.P. Art. 38.35.

Integrated Legal Research System References

West's Texas Digest Key Numbers

Witnesses ⚷470–574.

Texas Jur 3d

24A Texas Jur 3d, Criminal Law § 3785 et seq.

36 Texas Jur 3d, Evidence §§ 576–706.

Texas Forms

7 Texas Pl & Pr Forms, Evidence & Witnesses § 111:19.

Am Jur Trials

Audio Recordings: Evidence, Experts, and Technology, 48 Am Jur Trials 1.

The Business Appraiser as an Expert Witness, 59 Am Jur Trials 155.

The Daubert Challenge to the Admissibility of Scientific Evidence, 60 Am Jur Trials 1.

Locating Medical Experts, 2 Am Jur Trials 357.

Presenting Plaintiff's Medical Proof—Common Injuries and Conditions, 6 Am Jur Trials 1.

Selecting and Preparing Expert Witnesses, 2 Am Jur Trials 585.

Toxic Experts, 52 Am Jur Trials 473.

Use of Engineers as Experts, 6 Am Jur Trials 555.

Use of Medical Consultants, 4 Am Jur Trials 253.

Using Hypothetical Questions, 5 Am Jur Trials 675.

Using the Human Factors Expert in Civil Litigation, 40 Am Jur Trials 629.

Am Jur Proof of Facts

Admissibility and Reliability of Laboratory Analysis of Soil, Water, and Air Samples in Environmental Litigation, 24 Am Jur Proof of Facts 3d 609.

Challenge to Eyewitness Identification Through Expert Testimony, 35 Am Jur Proof of Facts 3d 1.

Contradiction of Expert Witness Through Use of Authoritative Treatise, 31 Am Jur Proof of Facts 2d 443.

Corroboration of a Child's Sexual Abuse Allegation with Behavioral Evidence, 25 Am Jur Proof of Facts 3d 189.

Expert Testimony at Sentencing, 21 Am Jur Proof of Facts 645.

Expert Testimony at Sentencing, 103 Am Jur Proof of Facts 3d 81.

Proof of Contamination in Toxic Tort Cases Through Expert Testimony, 39 Am Jur Proof of Facts 3d 539.

Proof of Criminal Identity or Paternity Through Polymerase Chain Reaction (PCR) Testing, 36 Am Jur Proof of Facts 3d 1.

Proof of Malpractice by Chiropractor, 55 Am Jur Proof of Facts 3d 1.

Qualification of Medical Expert Witness, 33 Am Jur Proof of Facts 2d 179.

Qualifying Historians as Expert Witnesses, 130 Am Jur Proof of Facts 3d 89.

Collateral References

Berger, *The Supreme Court's Trilogy on the Admissibility of Expert Testimony*, Federal Judicial Center Reference Manual on Scientific Evidence, Second Edition, at 9 (2000).

Diamond, *Reference Guide on Survey Research*, Federal Judicial Center Reference Manual on Scientific Evidence, Second Edition, at 229 (2000).

Goldstein & Henifin, *Reference Guide on Toxicology*, Federal Judicial Center Reference Manual on Scientific Evidence, Second Edition, at 401 (2000).

Green, Freedman & Gordis, *Reference Guide on Epidemiology*, Federal Judicial Center Reference Manual on Scientific Evidence, Second Edition, at 333 (2000).

Hall & Lazear, *Reference Guide on Estimation of Economic Losses in Damages Awards*, Federal Judicial Center Reference Manual on Scientific Evidence, Second Edition, at 277 (2000).

Henifin, Kipen & Poulter, *Reference Guide on Medical Testimony*, Federal Judicial Center Reference Manual on Scientific Evidence, Second Edition, at 439 (2000).

Kaye & Freedman, *Reference Guide on Statistics*, Federal Judicial Center Reference Manual on Scientific Evidence, Second Edition, at 83 (2000).

Kaye & Sensabaugh, *Reference Guide on DNA Evidence*, Federal Judicial Center Reference Manual on Scientific Evidence, Second Edition, at 485 (2000).

Petroski, *Reference Guide on Engineering Practice and Methods*, Federal Judicial Center Reference Manual on Scientific Evidence, Second Edition, at 577 (2000).

Rubinfeld, *Reference Guide on Multiple Regression*, Federal Judicial Center Reference Manual on Scientific Evidence, Second Edition, at 179 (2000).

Schwarzer & Cecil, *Management of Expert Evidence*, Federal Judicial Center Reference Manual on Scientific Evidence, Second Edition, at 39 (2000).

For text of Management of Expert Evidence and other related publications, see the Federal Judicial Center website at http://www.fjc.gov.

Rule 701. Opinion Testimony by Lay Witnesses

If the witness is not testifying as an expert, the witness' testimony in the form of opinions or inferences is limited to those opinions or inferences which are (a) rationally based on the perception of the witness and (b) helpful to a clear understanding of the witness' testimony or the determination of a fact in issue.

Eff. March 1, 1998.

Commentary

In general

A nonexpert witness (a "fact witness") can only testify as to facts within his personal knowledge, except as permitted by this rule. Vernon's Ann.Rules Evid., Rule 602. The "perception of the witness" requirement of Vernon's Ann.Rules Evid., Rule 701 satisfies the personal knowledge requirement of Rule 602. *Bigby v. State, 892 S.W.2d 864 (Tex. Crim. App. 1994)*; *Fairow v. State, 943 S.W.2d 895 (Tex. Crim. App. 1997). Board of Trustees of Fire and Police Retiree Health Fund v. Towers, Perrin, Forster & Crosby, Inc., 191 S.W.3d 185, 193 (Tex. App.—San Antonio 2005, pet. denied).* See also *Havner v. E–Z Mart Stores, Inc., 825 S.W.2d 456 (Tex. 1992).* This rule, it should be noted, requires more than that an opinion by a nonexpert witness be rationally based on that witness's perception. It also requires that the opinion or inference of the witness be helpful either to an understanding of the witness's testimony or the determination of a fact in issue.

Uniform Rules of Evidence

For text of corresponding provisions of Uniform Rules of Evidence and notes of decisions relating thereto, which may provide guidance in interpreting the Texas Rule, see Rule 701, 13B Uniform Laws Annotated.

Federal Rules of Evidence

The corresponding provision of the Federal Rules of Evidence is Rule 701. For the text of the Rule and Advisory Committee Notes, which may provide guidance in interpreting the Texas Rule, see the Appendix to this volume.

Leading Cases

Coker v. Burghardt, 833 S.W.2d 306 (Tex. App.—Dallas 1992, writ denied) (an owner of a motor vehicle may testify to the cost of repairing it).

Ethicon, Inc. v. Martinez, 835 S.W.2d 826 (Tex. App.—Austin 1992, writ denied) (opinion or inference testimony about another's state of mind which is rationally based on the witness's perception is admissible under Tex. R. [Civ.] Evid. 701). See also *Solomon v. State, 49 S.W.3d 356 (Tex. Crim. App. 2001)*, cited below.

Fairow v. State, 943 S.W.2d 895 (Tex. Crim. App. 1997) (non-expert witnesses may testify to their opinions or inferences provided the opinion or inference is rationally based on the objective perception of the witness; the proponent of the testimony must establish that the witness has personal knowledge of events upon which his opinion is based and that it is an opinion that a reasonable person could draw under the circumstances).

Hinojosa v. Columbia St. David's Healthcare Sys., 106 S.W.3d 380 (Tex. App.—Austin 2003, no pet. h.) (lay testimony is insufficient to refute an expert's testimony; however, lay persons in medical malpractice cases may testify about their observations of another's physical condition even when that testimony contradicts a medical expert's testimony).

J.C., In re, 892 S.W.2d 87 (Tex. App.—El Paso 1995, no writ) (witness not qualified to testify as an expert on the age of bruises, but he could testify to the age of bruises based on his perception of his personal experiences with his own bruises).

Jelinek v. Casas, 328 S.W.3d 526, 532-533 (Tex. 2010) (lay testimony may be used as evidence of causation in some circumstances in medical malpractice actions, but when expert testimony is required, lay testimony is insufficient; general rule in medical malpractice actions is expert testimony is required to establish causation as to medical conditions outside the common knowledge and experience of jurors; when lay testimony is credited as evidence of causation, it usually highlights a connection between two events that is apparent to a casual observer; non-expert evidence alone is sufficient in a medical malpractice action to support a finding of causation in limited circumstances where both the occurrence and conditions complained of are such that the general experience and common sense of laypersons are sufficient to evaluate the conditions and whether they were probably caused by the occurrence).

Osbourn v. State, 92 S.W.3d 531 (Tex. Crim. App. 2002) (lay witness's testimony can include opinions, beliefs, or inferences as long as they are drawn from the witness's own experiences or observations).

Porras v. Craig, 675 S.W.2d 503 (Tex. 1984) (an owner of property may testify as to the market value of the property, but not to its intrinsic or sentimental value).

Redman Homes, Inc. v. Ivy, 920 S.W.2d 664 (Tex. 1996) (property owner can testify as to value of his property if based on owner's estimate of market value and not intrinsic or other value such as replacement cost, citing *Porras v. Craig, Id.*).

Reid Road Mun. Utility Dist. No. 2 v. Speedy Stop Food Stores, Ltd., 337 S.W.3d 846, 849-850 (Tex. 2011) (the " 'Property Owner Rule' falls within the ambit of Texas Rule of Evidence 701" and therefore the owner must establish the predicate that a witness "is personally familiar with the property and its fair market value, but the Property Owner Rule creates a presumption as to both. An expert need not necessarily testify as an expert witness since he may have special knowledge, skill, experience, training, or education in a particular subject, but testify only to matters based on personal perception and opinions." If so, the witness's testimony is not expert testimony for purposes of Rule 702 and the witness need not be so designated or identified).

Solomon v. State, 49 S.W.3d 356 (Tex. Crim. App. 2001) (opinion or inference testimony about another's state of mind which is rationally based on the witness's perception is admissible under Tex. R. [Civ.] Evid. 701). See also *Ethicon, Inc. v. Martinez, 835 S.W.2d 826 (Tex. App.—Austin 1992, writ denied)*, cited above.

Star Houston, Inc. v. Kundak, 843 S.W.2d 294 (Tex. App.—Houston [14th Dist.] 1992, no writ) (an automobile owner may testify as to his opinion of the value of the use of his vehicle, as well as to the market value of it).

Straitway Transport, Inc. v. Mundorf, 6 S.W.3d 734 (Tex. App.—Corpus Christi 1999, pet. denied) ("To require a party to qualify as an expert witness, and to be identified as such in discovery, in order to explain why his decision [regarding his choice among various methods to pen cattle] was not negligent, is to elevate form over substance").

Integrated Legal Research System References

West's Texas Digest Key Numbers

Criminal Law ⚷448–463.

Evidence ⚷470–503.

Texas Practice

Addison, Texas Practice Guide, Evidence § 7:1 et seq.

Texas Jur 3d

24A Texas Jur 3d, Criminal Law § 3789 et seq.

36 Texas Jur 3d, Evidence § 582 et seq.

Annotations

Ability to see, hear, smell, or otherwise sense, as proper subject of opinion by lay witness, 10 ALR3d 258.

Admissibility of expert or opinion evidence—Supreme Court cases, 177 ALR Fed 77.

Construction and application of Rule 701 of Federal Rules of Evidence, providing for opinion testimony by lay witnesses under certain circumstances, 44 ALR Fed 919.

Rule 702. Testimony by Experts

If scientific, technical, or other specialized knowledge will assist the trier of fact to understand the evidence or to determine a fact in issue, a witness qualified as an expert by knowledge, skill, experience, training, or education may testify thereto in the form of an opinion or otherwise.

Eff. March 1, 1998.

Commentary

In general

There are special rules for the qualification of and challenge to an expert witness on the standard of care issue in medical liability cases. V.T.C.A., Civil Practice & Remedies Code § 74.001 *et seq.* See *Larson v. Downing, 197 S.W.3d 303 (Tex. 2006).*

It should be kept in mind that Vernon's Ann.Rules Evid., Rule 702 also applies to expert opinion or testimony about technical and other matters involving specialized knowledge, not just matters of science. The standards governing the admissibility of expert opinion or testimony have changed significantly.

Fundamental decisions and important trends

The federal courts have for many years judged the admissibility of scientific evidence pursuant to the test first stated in *Frye v. United States, 293 F. 1013 (D.C. Cir. 1923).* Neither the Texas Supreme Court nor the Texas Court of Criminal Appeals has ever adopted the *Frye* test, and the United States Supreme Court has now specifically rejected the *Frye* test in the light of FED. R. EVID. 702. *Daubert v. Merrell Dow Pharmaceuticals, Inc., 509 U.S. 579, 113 S.Ct. 2786, 125 L.Ed.2d 469 (1993).* Because FED. R. EVID. 702 is identical to Vernon's Ann.Rules Evid., Rule 702, the Texas Supreme Court and the Texas Court of Criminal Appeals have given great weight to the reasoning in *Daubert*.

Decisions of the Texas Supreme Court and the Texas Court of Criminal Appeals since 1992 have fundamentally and significantly changed the law of evidence in Texas relating to expert opinions and testimony. The significance of these cases can hardly be exaggerated. These and other cases which are part of the evolving law in this area are discussed below in generally chronological order. Each of these cases make it clear that the trial judge has "gatekeeping" responsibilities on preliminary issues regarding the relevancy of the expert's opinion or testimony, its reliability, the qualifications of the expert in the area in which he renders an opinion or gives his testimony, and whether the probative value of the testimony or opinion "is substantially outweighed by the danger of unfair prejudice, confusion of the issues, or misleading the jury, or by considerations of undue delay, or needless presentation of cumulative evidence." Vernon's Ann.Rules Evid., Rule 403. These cases also provide, where the issue was considered, that, after a proper objection, it is the proponent of the evidence who has the burden to persuade the trial court of the relevancy and reliability of the expert testimony or opinion, the qualifications of the expert and the probative value of the expert testimony or opinion. If the offered expert opinion or testimony meets the legal threshold as determined by the trial court in accordance with the standards established in these cases, the jury will hear the evidence and will be the "sole judges of the credibility of the witnesses and the weight to be given their testimony ... " Vernon's Ann.Rules Civ.Proc., Rule 226a. See Vernon's Ann.C.C.P. Art 38.04.

There has been some question as to whether the *Daubert* application of Rule 702 applies only in the cases of expert testimony or opinion in matters of science, or whether it should apply in all cases involving the offer of expert opinion or testimony. The issue in criminal cases in Texas has been resolved in favor of applying the *Daubert* construct to all such cases whether involving matters of science or not. The Texas Court of Criminal Appeals has held that its view of Rule 702 is not restricted to novel scientific evidence, which it considered in *Kelly v. State. Kelly v. State, 824 S.W.2d 568 (Tex. Crim. App. 1992).* See *Hartman v. State, 946 S.W.2d 60 (Tex. Crim. App. 1997)* and the commentary below. The court has stated that the general principles of the *Kelly* and *Daubert* decisions governing the admissibility of scientific evidence also *generally* govern the admission of non-scientific expert evidence and opinions. The Texas Supreme Court has adopted a similar view. See *Gammill v. Jack Williams Chevrolet, Inc., 972 S.W.2d 713 (Tex. 1998)* and the commentary below. The United States Supreme Court has determined that the *Daubert* construct should be applied in a flexible manner to all issues regarding the admissibility of any expert opinion or testimony. See *Kumho Tire Co., Ltd. v. Carmichael, 526 U.S. 137, 119 S.Ct. 1167, 143 L. Ed.2d 238 (1999),* and the commentary below.

Kelly v. State, 824 S.W.2d 568 (Tex. Crim. App. 1992).

This prescient case deals with the admissibility of scientific evidence, specifically DNA evidence, in criminal cases. The court stated that while it had sometimes nodded in the direction of the *Frye* test to determine the admissibility of scientific evidence, it had never adopted that test, and, in any event, the test was no longer viable in light of TEX. R. [CRIM.] EVID. 702 (which was identical to TEX. R. [CIV.] EVID. 702, both of which are now Vernon's Ann.Rules Evid., Rule 702). The court determined that TEX. R. [CRIM.] EVID. 104(a), 104(c), 402, 403, and 702 were to be applied in determining the admissibility of expert testimony. In questions involving scientific evidence in a criminal case, the burden is on the proponent of that evidence to persuade the trial court *by clear and convincing evidence*, outside the presence of the jury, that the offered evidence is both reliable and relevant, and that the person rendering the expert testimony or opinion is qualified to do so. *Kelly,* at 573.

To be considered reliable, evidence based on scientific theory must satisfy three criteria: (1) the underlying scientific theory must be valid; (2) the technique applying the theory must be valid; and (3) the technique must have been properly applied on occasion in question. *Kelly,* at 573.

The Court of Criminal Appeals also set out seven *non-exclusive* factors that a trial court could consider in determining the reliability of scientific evidence: (1) the extent to which the underlying scientific theory and technique are accepted as valid by the relevant scientific community, if such a community can be ascertained; (2) the qualifications of the expert(s) testifying; (3) the existence of literature supporting or rejecting the underlying scientific theory and technique; (4) the potential rate of error of the technique; (5) the availability of other experts to test and evaluate the technique; (6) the clarity with which the underlying scientific theory and technique can be explained to the court; and (7) the experience and skill of the person(s) who applied the technique on the occasion in question. *Kelly*, at 573.

Kelly is also significant for the civil practitioner because the appellate court's approach to the issues of the relevance and reliability of expert testimony or opinions, and the obligations of the trial court, foreshadowed the coming changes in civil cases, and because it has been relied on by the Texas Supreme Court in formulating its view of Vernon's Ann.Rules Evid., Rule 702.

Daubert v. Merrell Dow Pharmaceuticals, Inc., 509 U.S. 579, 113 S.Ct. 2786, 125 L.Ed.2d 469 (1993).

In this case the United States Supreme Court rejected the *Frye* test for expert scientific testimony or opinions in federal cases in light of FED. R. EVID. 702.

Daubert sets out four *non-exclusive* factors that a trial court may consider in determining the reliability of scientific expert testimony or opinion: (1) whether the theory or technique can be and has been tested; (2) whether the theory or technique has been subjected to peer review and publication; (3) the known or potential rate of error and the standards controlling a technique's operation; and (4) general acceptance in the scientific community.

E.I. du Pont de Nemours and Co., Inc. v. Robinson, 923 S.W.2d 549 (Tex. 1995).

This case represents the first time that the Texas Supreme Court considered the proper standard for the admission of expert testimony regarding matters of science under TEX. R. [CIV.] EVID. 702. The court held that before an expert witness will be permitted to state his opinion or give expert testimony, over proper objection, the proponent of the evidence must establish that the witness is not only qualified to testify or render his opinion as an expert, but also that the testimony or the opinion is both relevant and based on a reliable foundation. These are preliminary determinations to be made by the trial court pursuant to TEX. R. [CIV.] EVID. 104, 401, 402, 403 and 702. In making these determinations, the trial courts should focus solely on the validity of principles and methodology underlying the testimony, not the conclusions generated, which are a matter for the jury. However, it is not enough under TEX. R. [CIV.] EVID. 702 to just allow the trier of fact to determine the credibility of the expert witness and the weight to be given his testimony without the trial court making the required preliminary determinations.

Robinson lists six *non-exclusive* factors that the trial court may consider in determining the reliability of expert testimony or opinion in matters of science: (1) the extent to which the theory has been or can be tested; (2) the extent to which the technique relies upon the subjective interpretation of the expert; (3) whether the theory has been subjected to peer review and/or publication; (4) the technique's potential rate of error; (5) whether the underlying theory or technique has been generally accepted as valid by the relevant scientific community; and (6) the non-judicial uses which have been made of the theory or technique. If the witness is determined by the trial court to be qualified to render an expert opinion or give expert testimony, and the expert opinion or testimony is determined by the trial court to be both relevant and reliable, then the trial court must determine if the evidence is sufficiently probative to avoid being excluded under TEX. R. [CIV.] EVID. 403.

Heise v. Presbyterian Hosp. of Dallas, 888 S.W.2d 264 (Tex. App.—Eastland 1994), rev'd sub nom. Broders v. Heise, 924 S.W.2d 148 (Tex. 1996).

This significant case is a good example of how the Texas Supreme Court views TEX. R. [CIV.] EVID. 702 in light of its decision in *Robinson*. In this medical liability case involving failure to timely diagnose and treat a head injury, the plaintiff offered as an expert a physician trained in the area of emergency medicine who testified that, in reasonable medical probability, the patient in question would have survived with earlier diagnosis and treatment. The court reiterated that once the testimony is objected to, the proponent of the expert testimony or opinion has the burden to prove the qualifications of the witness to testify as an expert. Further, the expert witness must be qualified by knowledge, skill, experience, training or education in the very area in which he gives expert testimony or opinions.

The court specifically rejected the contention that any physician could always testify as to a medical causation issue against any other physician in a medical liability case. If the expert is not qualified to testify on the matter about which he proposes to render an opinion, his opinion would not be relevant, and, therefore, it would not be of assistance to the trier of fact.

Burroughs Wellcome Co. v. Crye, 907 S.W.2d 497 (Tex. 1995).

In this products liability case, the court held that where an expert witness expresses an opinion as to causation based on assumed facts that vary materially from the actual, undisputed facts, the opinion is without probative value and cannot support a verdict or a judgment. The concurring opinion discusses *Robinson* and scientific studies not based on scientifically reliable methodology.

S.V. v. R.V., 933 S.W.2d 1 (Tex. 1996).

The majority held that expert testimony was not an issue in this case, but a concurring opinion by Justice Gonzalez gave a good idea of where the court would go, given the opportunity. That concurring opinion discusses the testimony of the experts in this case regarding repressed memories of past sexual abuse, and concludes that the evidence did not meet the standards for admissibility expressed in *E.I. du Pont de Nemours and Co., Inc. v. Robinson*.

The Texas Supreme Court overruled the motion for rehearing in this case. In a concurring opinion on the decision to overrule the motion for rehearing, Justice Gonzalez, the author of the majority opinion in *Robinson,* makes it clear that *Robinson* is to provide the exclusive standard for evaluating the reliability of expert testimony about anything characterized as science, and he suggests that "trial courts apply *Robinson* (meaning *E.I. du Pont de Nemours and Co., Inc. v. Robinson*) across the board in determining the admissibility of scientific evidence." *S.V. v. R.V.* at 43.

Hartman v. State, 946 S.W.2d 60 (Tex. Crim. App. 1997).

Any confusion about whether the holding in *Kelly v. State* applied only in cases involving novel scientific evidence was dispelled by the holding in this case. Specifically, the court held that the *Kelly* test for determining admissibility of scientific evidence, requiring that scientific evidence be sufficiently reliable and relevant to help a jury in reaching accurate results, is not limited to novel scientific evidence but, rather, applies to all scientific evidence. Scientific evidence must meet a three-pronged test in order to be determined to be reliable and, if relevant, to be admissible: (1) the underlying scientific theory must be valid; (2) the technique applying the theory must be valid; and (3) the technique must have been properly applied on the occasion in question. To determine whether this test is met, the trial court should consider the non-exclusive list of factors in *Kelly v. State* and *Daubert v. Merrell Dow Pharmaceuticals, Inc.*

In a concurring and dissenting opinion in which Judge McCormick joined, Judge Keller stated that in many instances parts (1) and (2) of the test can be decided by appellate courts as matters of law, and that the validity of a particular scientific theory or technique may be so well established that parties should not be required to relitigate its admissibility.

Merrell Dow Pharmaceuticals, Inc. v. Havner, 953 S.W.2d 706 (Tex. 1997).

The question in this case was whether the scientific evidence presented by plaintiffs was sufficiently reliable and relevant on the issue of whether the drug Bendectin caused the birth defects that were the subject of this products liability case. The court held that the scientific evidence presented by plaintiffs was not reliable, and therefore, not relevant, and no evidence of causation in this case. Thus, the evidence was legally insufficient to support the verdict.

The issue of the scientific reliability of plaintiff's evidence was raised by motions in limine which sought to exclude the testimony of experts and other causation evidence. The trial court denied each of the motions after a lengthy hearing. As required by *Robinson,* objections to the evidence required the proponent of the evidence in this case to establish that a witness is not only qualified to testify or render his opinion as an expert as to causation, but also that the testimony or the opinion is both relevant and based on a reliable foundation. These are preliminary determinations to be made by the trial court pursuant to TEX. R. [CIV.] EVID. 104, 401, 402, 403 and 702.

The bare opinion of an expert is not enough to support a finding of fact. *Havner* at 711, citing, *Burroughs Wellcome Co. v. Crye,* at 499. If the data upon which the expert relies are unreliable, then the expert's opinion is unreliable; and even if the underlying data are reliable, the expert's testimony remains unreliable if the expert draws conclusions from that data by way of flawed methodology or reasoning. A scientific expert's testimony which is unreliable is *no evidence*. The court reiterated the non-exclusive factors of *Robinson* that the trial court should consider in determining whether an expert's testimony is reliable: (1) the extent to which theory has been or can be tested; (2) the extent to which technique relies upon subjective interpretation of expert; (3) whether the theory has been subjected to peer review and publication; (4) the technique's potential rate of error; (5) whether the underlying theory or technique has been generally accepted as valid by relevant scientific community; and (6) nonjudicial uses that have been made of theory or technique. The court discusses several of these factors as they bear on its determination that the scientific evidence in this case on the issue of causation was unreliable.

The court specifically held that properly designed and executed epidemiological studies which indicate that exposure to a toxic substance more than doubled the risk of injury may be a part of all of the evidence supporting a finding of causation in a toxic tort case, but other factors *must* be considered, and the plaintiff *must, in addition, offer evidence excluding other possible causes of disease or injury with reasonable certainty*. Even if a statistically significant association is found in a properly designed and executed epidemiological study, that association does not equate to causation. (The court gave the example that there is a demonstrable association between summertime and death by drowning, but summertime does not cause drowning). See *Merck & Co., Inc. v. Garza, 347 S.W.3d 256 (Tex. 2011)* (a party attempting to prove general causation using epidemiological evidence must satisfy the *Havner* requirements for reliability).

The court stated that the trial courts must make a determination of reliability from all the evidence. Trial courts should allow a party to present the best available evidence that meets the *Robinson* criteria; and only then should a trial court determine from a totality of the evidence, including all factors affecting the reliability of particular studies, whether there is legally sufficient evidence to support a judgment.

Gammill v. Jack Williams Chevrolet, Inc., 972 S.W.2d 713 (Tex. 1998).

In this case, the court emphasized that: (1) whether an expert is qualified is a preliminary question to be decided by the trial court; (2) a party offering the expert's testimony bears the burden to prove that the witness is qualified, and must demonstrate that the witness possesses special knowledge as to the very matter on which he proposes to give an opinion; (3) the trial court's acceptance of a witness's qualifications as an expert is reviewable for an abuse of discretion; (4) the proponent of scientific expert testimony has burden to demonstrate that such evidence is relevant and reliable before it can be admitted; (5) scientific evidence that has no relationship to any of the issues in the case is irrelevant and does not satisfy requirement that the testimony be of assistance to the jury, and is therefore inadmissible; (6) scientific evidence not grounded in the methods and procedures of science is no more than subjective belief or unsupported speculation; unreliable evidence is of no assistance to the trier of fact, and is, therefore, inadmissible; (7) factors a trial court will find helpful in determining whether the underlying theories and techniques of the proffered evidence are scientifically reliable will differ with each particular case; (8) the reliability standard for expert testimony applies to all scientific expert testimony, not just novel or unconventional scientific evidence; (9) scientific opinion based on a witness's individual skill, experience, or training must still meet reliability and relevance requirements, but need not necessarily meet specific factors in assessing reliability, such as peer review or assessment of rate of error of technique expert relied on; (10) the court in discharging its duty as gatekeeper must determine how the reliability of particular scientific expert testimony is to be assessed; (11) the trial court does not have to admit opinion evidence which is connected to existing data just because the expert says it is; and (12) in exercising its gatekeeper function, trial court does not determine whether an expert's conclusions are correct, but only whether the analysis used to reach them is reliable.

It should be noted that this opinion discusses Rule 702 as it relates to scientific evidence and scientific reliability. The experts involved in this case were engineers, but the evidence they presented to the trial court was referred to by the Texas Supreme Court as scientific evidence. The court did not specifically state that *Robinson* would apply to what it would characterize as non-scientific evidence except to say that even non-scientific evidence is subject to the relevancy and reliability requirements of *Robinson*. More recent Texas Supreme Court and Texas Court of Criminal Appeals cases, however, clearly indicate that the principles stated in *Kelly* and *Robinsion* will apply in all cases involving expert testimony (although with less rigor in some cases than in others), not just in cases involving scientific evidence. *Kumho Tire Co., Ltd, infra,* makes it clear that in the federal courts *Daubert* will apply to all expert witnesses, and Rule 702 of the Federal Rules of Evidence have been amended to that effect.

Kumho Tire Co., Ltd. v. Carmichael, 526 U.S. 137, 119 S.Ct. 1197 (1999).

When a tire on a vehicle failed and the vehicle overturned, one passenger died and the others were injured. The tire's maker and distributor were sued on the plaintiff's claim that the tire was defective. Plaintiff's expert was offered to prove that a defect in the tire's manufacture or design caused the blow-out. The trial court determined that it should flexibly apply the *Daubert* standards to Rule 702 to determine if the expert's opinion was not only relevant, but also reliable. After doing so, and concluding that the expert's testimony was not reliable, the trial court excluded the expert's testimony. The U.S. Court of Appeals for the Eleventh Circuit reversed, concluding that as a matter of law the *Daubert* standards applied only to scientific evidence, and that, therefore, the standards did not apply to the expert's testimony. The United States Supreme Court reversed the appellate court and held that: (1) the *Daubert* factors apply to the testimony of engineers and other experts who are not scientists; (2) the *Daubert* factors are illustrative and non-exclusive and do not constitute a definitive checklist or test; and (3) the court of appeals must apply an abuse of discretion standard when it reviews a trial court's decision to admit or exclude evidence.

Practical considerations

In cases involving expert testimony, a party opposing that evidence should consider filing a pretrial motion with the trial court setting forth its objections to the evidence and to the experts to be offered by the other side and requesting a pretrial hearing. If the court consents, the issues can be tried by the court long before a jury panel comes to the courthouse. This procedure was used in *Robinson, Kelly* and *Havner*. A motion for summary judgment can also be effectively used to contest expert evidence before trial. *Robinson* and *Kelly* require only a proper legal objection to the evidence in order to put the proponent of the expert evidence to his proof. No controverting evidence is required to be produced by the opponent of that evidence. An objection that the expert evidence is not reliable must be timely made, that is, before the trial or when the evidence is offered. An objection to the reliability of expert evidence after a jury verdict is not timely. *Maritime Overseas Corp. v. Ellis, 971 S.W.2d 402 (Tex. 1998).* Thus, objectively unreliable expert evidence which is not objected to as unreliable will support a verdict. Thus, when a trial court must evaluate underlying methodology, technique, or basis used by an expert, an objection must be timely made to allow the court to make the analysis. "However, when the challenge is restricted to the face of the record, for example, when expert testimony is speculative or conclusory on its face, then a party may challenge the legal sufficiency of the evidence even in the absence of any objection to its admissibility." *Coastal Transport Co., Inc. v. Crown Central Petroleum Corp., 136 S.W.3d 227, 233 (Tex. 2004); Duncan–Hubert v. Mitchell, 310 S.W.3d 92 (Tex. App.—Dallas 2010, pet. denied); Marin Real Estate Partners, L.P. v. Vogt, 373 S.W.3d 57 (Tex. App.—San Antonio 2011, no pet.).*

Matters involving the qualifications of expert witnesses and the reliability and relevancy of their opinions may be reached on summary judgment. See *United Blood Servs. v. Longoria, 938 S.W.2d 29 (Tex. 1997).* Summary judgment was used in *Gammill v. Jack Williams Chevrolet, Inc., supra.*

A trial court could, by pre-trial order, require the proponent of scientific evidence to disclose to all parties in advance of trial the "science" or "expertise" he relies on and the experts he will call to testify to it at the trial. The trial court could then require the opponent of that evidence to make any objections to the expert evidence and the expert opinions or testimony to be offered at trial, in advance, and, if there are any proper objections, to order the parties to try the "science" or "expertise" questions in a pretrial hearing, even in the absence of a request by a party to do so. If the proponent fails to disclose the expert evidence he will offer at trial, the trial court could exclude it. If the opponent of the evidence fails to make a proper objection, the evidence could be admitted at trial. Vernon's Ann.Rules Evid., Rule 104 specifically provides that preliminary questions concerning the admissibility of evidence are to be determined by the trial court. The exclusion of evidence not revealed in response to a proper discovery request is a permissible and frequent sanction, upon proper objection. Vernon's Ann.Rules Civ.Proc., Rule 215. *Gee v. Liberty Mut. Fire Ins. Co., 765 S.W.2d 394 (Tex. 1989)*; *E.F. Hutton & Co., Inc. v. Youngblood, 741 S.W.2d 363 (Tex. 1987)*; *Morrow v. H.E.B., Inc., 714 S.W.2d 297 (Tex. 1986)*; *Gutierrez v. Dallas Indep. Sch. Dist., 729 S.W.2d 691 (Tex. 1987).* The trial court has the authority to exercise control over the presentation of the evidence. Vernon's Ann.Rules Evid., Rule 611(a). The trial court may assist in the disposition of the case. Vernon's Ann.Rules Civ.Proc., Rule 166. If the issues are joined, the trial court may conduct a pretrial hearing on the preliminary question involving the admissibility of the offered scientific evidence, as in *Robinson.* Vernon's Ann.C.C.P. Art. 28.01 (pretrial hearings) allows the court to hear motions to suppress filed by the defendant. It was at a motion to suppress hearing that the trial court determined the question of admissibility of the scientific evidence in *Kelly.* Vernon's Ann.C.C.P. Art. 28.01 does not authorize the State to make a pretrial challenge to the admission of the defendant's expert evidence, but, barring a constitutional challenge, such as denial of due process as in *Ake v. Oklahoma, 470 U.S. 68, 105 S.Ct. 1087, 84 L.Ed.2d 53 (1985)*, a preliminary hearing on the admissibility of evidence is authorized by Vernon's Ann.Rules Evid., Rule 104 and on the admissibility of expert testimony or opinion by Vernon's Ann.Rules Evid., Rule 705(b) and (c).

If, after a hearing, the trial court decides to exclude the evidence, the case may be disposed of in some manner other than by a jury trial. In any event, a record will have been created that can be used on appeal. If the trial court decides to admit the evidence, no further hearing outside the presence of the jury should be required when the same evidence is offered at trial, but the party against whom such evidence is offered at trial should remember to timely object to its admission on a proper ground to avoid any risk of waiving the objection, the provisions of Vernon's Ann.Rules Evid., Rule 103(a)(1) notwithstanding. These pretrial techniques on the court's own motion or on the appropriate motion of a party are especially suited for any complex issues concerning the admissibility of evidence that the trial court must determine under Vernon's Ann.Rules Evid., Rule 104. See Commentary to Vernon's Ann.Rules Evid., Rule 104, *supra.*

Although an attack on an opponent's expert may be successful at a pretrial hearing or on motion for summary judgment, some trial courts are allowing the proponent of the expert an opportunity to find another expert that might be more successful in withstanding an objection. However regrettable this may be, it alerts the opponent of an expert to make his objection and to attempt to defeat the expert at a point in the proceedings where neither the proponent of the expert nor the judge can do anything about it, if successful. That point is during trial. Be aware, however, an objection to the *qualifications* of a medical expert in a medical tort case must be made no later than 21 days after the date the objecting party receives a copy of the expert's curriculum vitae or the date of the witness's deposition. *Ocomen v. Rubio, 24 S.W.3d 461 (Tex. App.—Houston [1st Dist.] 2000, no pet. h.)*; V.T.C.A., Civil Practice & Remedies Code § 74.351.

Problems with court-appointed expert witnesses for indigent defendants in criminal cases.

An indigent defendant in a criminal case is usually entitled to the appointment of expert witnesses necessary to assist in his defense. See *Ake v. Oklahoma, 470 U.S. 68, 105 S.Ct. 1087, 84 L.Ed.2d 53 (1985).* Presumably, the defendant is entitled to a *qualified* expert appointed by the court. While a criminal defendant is not entitled to the appointment of an expert whose opinions snugly fit the defendant's defensive theories, what if the appointed expert is successfully challenged in the trial court, whether for lack of qualifications, poor methodology or unreliability of his expert opinions? Must the trial court then appoint another expert until one is found who is qualified, who does use proper methodology, and whose opinion is reliable? What if the challenge to the defendant's appointed expert is successful *at trial*? Is the indigent defendant entitled to a mistrial? A new trial? Will it matter if the trial court determines that the expert is qualified but has not used the proper methodology or reached a reliable conclusion?

Uniform Rules of Evidence

For text of corresponding provisions of Uniform Rules of Evidence and notes of decisions relating thereto, which may provide guidance in interpreting the Texas Rule, see Rule 702, 13B Uniform Laws Annotated.

Federal Rules of Evidence

The corresponding provision of the Federal Rules of Evidence is Rule 702. For the text of the Rule and Advisory Committee Notes, which may provide guidance in interpreting the Texas Rule, see the Appendix to this volume.

Other Leading Cases

America West Airlines, Inc. v. Tope, 935 S.W.2d 908 (Tex. App.—El Paso 1996, n.w.h.) (a clinical social worker for seventeen years with a B.S. degree in mathematics and chemistry, a master's degree in psychology, a M.S.W. degree, and licensed as a psychologist in the state of New Mexico, and as a social worker in Texas, qualified as an expert witness, but exclusion of his testimony was not an abuse of discretion because the testimony failed on other indicia of reliability factors of *Robinson*).

Burrow v. Arce, 997 S.W.2d 229 (Tex. 1999) (in a summary judgment proceeding, affidavit of qualified expert not sufficient to show entitlement to judgment as a matter of law where the opinion of the expert is expressed without a showing of a sufficient basis for the opinion which the expert, because of his knowledge, skill, experience training or education, is qualified to give).

Cooper Tire & Rubber v. Mendez, 204 S.W.3d 797 (Tex. 2006) (where a witness called as an expert assumes a fact not in evidence necessary to the reliability of his opinion, his opinion cannot supply it; where opinion evidence is unsupported by objective evidence, the expert's opinion is not evidence).

Damian v. Bell Helicopter Textron, Inc., 352 S.W.3d 124 (Tex. App.—Ft. Worth 2010, no pet.) (to preserve a complaint that an expert's testimony is unreliable a party must object to the testimony before trial or when it is offered; pretrial challenge by motion to strike, or the like, to the reliability or speculative nature of an expert's testimony sufficient to preserve error; no objection required to preserve error when expert's testimony is speculative and conclusory on its face).

Dico Tire, Inc. v. Cisneros, 953 S.W.2d 776 (Tex. App.—Corpus Christi 1997, writ denied) (expert testimony derived from specialized knowledge or technical experience had to establish the "reasonable probability" of causal connection between product and injury; expert not providing scientific evidence, so testimony was not required to be scientifically reliable).

Duncan–Hubert v. Mitchell, 310 S.W.3d 92 (Tex. App.—Dallas 2010, pet. denied) (objections to the reliability of an expert's testimony [methodology, technique, qualifications, relevancy, and the like] must be made at a time the trial court can do something about it, or on appeal if the lack of reliability is apparent from the record). See also, *Marin Real Estate Partners, L.P. v. Vogt, 373 S.W.3d 57 (Tex. App.—San Antonio 2011, no pet.)* (contention that expert witness' testimony was "pure speculation" did not require a more specific objection because the face of the record was sufficient for the court to determine the reliability of an expert's opinion).

Fletcher v. State, 39 S.W.3d 274 (Tex. App.—Texarkana 2001, no pet. h.) (expert testimony as to weight of controlled substance).

General Elec. Co. v. Joiner, 522 U.S. 136, 118 S.Ct. 512 (1997) (the question of the admissibility of expert scientific evidence is not a fact question, but a question of whether the trial court's decision admitting or excluding such evidence is an abuse of discretion; *Daubert v. Merrell Dow Pharmaceuticals, Inc.* did not change the standard of appellate review).

General Motors Corp. v. Iracheta, 161 S.W.3d 462, 470–471, (Tex. 2005) ("___the naked and unsupported opinion or conclusion of a witness does not constitute evidence of probative force and will not support a jury finding even when admitted without objection").

GTE Southwest, Inc. v. Bruce, 998 S.W.2d 605 (Tex. 1999) (*not* excluding expert testimony on a matter within the common knowledge of jurors not error where the expert testimony is "merely cumulative"). See also *K–Mart Corp. v. Honeycutt, 24 S.W.3d 357 (Tex. 2000)*, cited below.

Guadalupe-Blanco River Auth. v. Kraft, 77 S.W.3d 805 (Tex. 2002) (expert's "bald assurance" that he used a widely accepted appraisal method in a condemnation case is not sufficient to demonstrate that his opinion is reliable).

Guevara v. Ferrar, 247 S.W.3d 662 (Tex. 2007) (in a personal injury case, expert medical evidence is required to prove causation of the injury and the necessity of particular medical treatments for the injury, unless that evidence is within the common knowledge and experience of laypersons).

Hamal v. State, 352 S.W.3d 835 (Tex. App.—Dallas 2011, no pet.) (proponent of scientific evidence must show by clear and convincing evidence the evidence offered is both relevant and reliable).

Hernandez v. State, 116 S.W.3d 26 (Tex. Crim. App. 2003) (once a particular type of scientific evidence is established as reliable, or a particular methodology is established as reliable, a court may take judicial notice of that reliability to the extent it is relevant to the issues in the case and thereby relieve the proponent of the evidence the burden of producing evidence supporting the fact). See also *Weatherred v. State, 15 S.W.3d 540, 542 n.4 (Tex. Crim. App. 2000).*

Holland v. Lovelace, 352 S.W.3d 777 (Tex. App.—Dallas 2011, no pet.) (jury may accept or reject all or any portion of the testimony of an expert it does not find credible).

IHS Cedars Treatment Ctr. of DeSoto, Texas, Inc. v. Mason, 143 S.W.3d 794 (Tex. 2003) (testimony by expert witness in a medical liability case on issue of breach and causation without an explanation of how the conduct of the defendants was the cause in fact of the injuries suffered by the plaintiff is no evidence of causation).

Jelinek v. Casas, 328 S.W.3d 526, 532-533 (Tex. 2010) ("[I]t is not enough for an expert to simply opine that the defendant's negligence caused the plaintiff's injury. The expert must also, to a reasonable degree of medical probability, explain how and why the negligence caused the injury." If the opinion is merely conclusory it is not evidence, regardless of whether an objection to the offer of the opinion is made. "When the circumstances are equally consistent with either of two facts, neither fact may be inferred.").

Jordan v. State, 928 S.W.2d 550 (Tex. Crim. App. 1996) (where eyewitness identification of appellant as a robber is disputed issue, expert testimony about factors affecting reliability of eyewitness identification is relevant because it would assist the jury to determine a fact in issue; issue of reliability of the expert opinion was not raised in this case, so reliability analysis of *Daubert, Kelly* and *Robinson* not implicated).

K–Mart Corp. v. Honeycutt, 24 S.W.3d 357 (Tex. 2000) (it is not error to exclude expert testimony about a matter that is within the common knowledge of jurors because such testimony is of no assistance to the jury); See also *GTE Southwest, Inc. v. Bruce, 998 S.W.2d 605 (Tex. 1999)*, cited above.

Leitch v. Hornsby, 935 S.W.2d 114 (Tex. 1996) (where there is no medical testimony linking alleged negligence to an injury, some competent evidence making that connection required; incompetent opinion testimony is not evidence, and a finding supported only by such testimony is no evidence).

Mack Trucks, Inc. v. Tamez, 206 S.W.3d 572, 577 (Tex. 2006) ("The reliability inquiry as to expert testimony does not ask whether the expert's conclusions appear to be correct; it asks whether the methodology and analysis used to reach those conclusions is reliable . . .").

Menefee v. Ohman, 323 S.W.3d 509, 514 (Tex. App.—Fort Worth 2010, no pet.) ("To be an 'expert' on the departure from a physician's standard of care, a person must be a physician who (1) is practicing medicine at the time such testimony is given or was practicing medicine at the time the claim arose; (2) has knowledge of accepted standards of medical care for the diagnosis, care, or treatment of the illness, injury, or condition involved in the claim; and (3) is qualified on the basis of training or experience to offer an expert opinion regarding those accepted standards of medical care.").

Merck & Co., Inc. v. Garza, 347 S.W.3d 256 (Tex. 2011) (a party attempting to prove general causation using epidemiological evidence must satisfy the *Havner* requirements for reliability).

Minnesota Mining & Mfg. Co. v. Atterbury, 978 S.W.2d 183 (Tex. App.—Texarkana 1998, pet. denied) (studies relied on by expert not shown to be reliable either by the expert or from any other source; examination of patient and medical history as a basis of expert opinion only an isolated case, not proof of causation). *Note*: This is a lengthy case, but contains an exhaustive review of cases applying *Daubert* and *Robinson*, and is very instructive on the application of those cases and their progeny to the issues of causation in this breast implant case.

Morton Int'l v. Gillespie, 39 S.W.3d 651 (Tex. App.—Texarkana 2001, no pet. h.) (expert testimony regarding airbag operation).

Osbourn v. State, 92 S.W.3d 531, 536 (Tex. Crim. App. 2002) (witness capable of being qualified as an expert may testify as a lay witness regarding events the witness personally perceived and render opinions on those perceptions under Rule 701; that same person who may qualify as an expert may also testify about theories, facts and data used in the witness's area of expertise under Rule 702).

Pediatrix Medical Group, Inc., v. Robinson, 352 S.W.3d 879 (Tex. App.—Dallas 2011, no pet.) (physician not of the same school of medicine as medical defendant competent to testify if he has practical knowledge of what is usually done by a practitioner under circumstances similar to those confronting the defendant).

Schutz v. State, 957 S.W.2d 52 (Tex. Crim. App. 1997) (expert testimony must aid, not supplant, the jury's decision; it does not assist the jury if it constitutes "a direct opinion on the truthfulness" of a child complainant's allegations).

Sciarrilla v. Osborne, 946 S.W.2d 919 (Tex. App.—Beaumont 1997, writ denied) (state trooper qualified to testify as an accident reconstruction expert based on training and experience).

Spin Doctor Golf, Inc. v. Paymentech, L.P., 296 S.W.3d 354 (Tex. App.—Dallas 2009, pet. stricken) (only general experience in a specialized field does not qualify a witness as an expert).

Taylor v. Texas Dept. Of Protective and Regulatory Services, 160 S.W.3d 641, 650 (Tex. App.—Austin 2005, pet. denied) (the court of criminal appeals makes a distinction between areas of expert testimony involving scientific analysis and those which do not—the distinction between "hard" sciences and "soft" sciences—while the Texas Supreme Court has not yet adopted that approach. *See* Comment, *Gammill v. Jack Williams Chevrolet, Inc.* cited on page 130.

Texas Dep't of Public Safety v. Struve, 79 S.W.3d 796 (Tex. App.—Corpus Christi 2002, no pet. h.) (police officer need not be an expert to testify that a person he observed was intoxicated; if he bases his opinion on his observations and his training and experience, then his qualifications must be established as an expert).

Transcontinental Ins. Co. v. Crump, 330 S.W.3d 211, 216-217 (Tex. 2010) ("[T]he relevance and reliability requirements of Rule 702 [apply] to all expert evidence offered under that rule, even though the criteria for assessing relevance and reliability must vary, depending on the nature of the evidence." Conclusory statements by an expert that do not tend to make the existence of a material fact more probable or less probable cannot support a judgment even when no objection was made to the expert's statements at trial).

United Blood Servs. v. Longoria, 938 S.W.2d 29 (Tex. 1997) (there is no difference between the standards for evidence that would be admissible in a summary judgment proceeding and those applicable at trial, including the burden of establishing an expert's qualifications). *Note:* It requires only a little reflection to see the extraordinary ramifications of this case as it relates to summary judgment practice and the applicability of *Robinson*.

State v. Vela, 209 S.W.3d 128 (Tex. Crim. App. 2006) (three separate conditions regarding the admissibility of expert testimony: qualification, reliability, and evidence).

Wal-Mart Stores, Inc. v. Merrell, 313 S.W. 3d 837, 840 (Tex. 2010) (an expert's failure to explain or adequately disprove alternative theories of causation makes his theory speculative and conclusory).

Waring v. Wommack, 945 S.W.2d 889 (Tex. App.—Austin 1997, n.w.h.) (applying the factors indicated in *Robinson*, engineer, with degree in mechanical engineering and later training in accident reconstruction, testified to his conclusions based on tests performed, physical evidence from accident, and application of laws of physics; testimony reliable and relevant and, therefore, admissible on the issue of whether parties had time to avoid the accident).

Yard v. DaimlerChrysler Corp., 44 S.W.3d 238 (Tex. App.—Fort Worth 2001, no pet. h.) (a qualified physician may testify about injuries, but not about the cause of them unless he has personal knowledge of the cause or demonstrated expertise regarding the causal mechanism, in this case whether an airbag caused the injuries to plaintiff).

Websites

http://www.fjc.gov

www.daubertontheweb.com

www.junkscience.com

Leading CLE/Law Review Publications

Adrogue & Ratliff, *Kicking the Tires after Kumho: The Bottom Line on Admitting Financial Expert Testimony*, 37 Hous. L. Rev. 431 (2000).

Adrogue & Ratliff, *Preparation & Admission of Experts: Daubert Factors, Caveats & Considerations,* 33 *The Advocate* 17, State Bar of Texas Litigation Report, *Expert Witnesses* (Winter 2005).

Brown, *Daubert/Expert Witness Update,* Litigation Update Institute, State Bar of Texas (2011).

Brown, *Eight Gates for Expert Witnesses*, 36 Houston L. Rev. 743 (1999).

Brown, *Procedural Issues Under Daubert*, 36 Houston L. Rev. 1133 (1999).

Daniel, *Expert Testimony*, 32nd Annual Advanced Criminal Law Course, State Bar of Texas (2005).

Daniel, *Expert Witnesses*, 33rd Annual Adv. Criminal Law Course, State Bar of Texas (July 2007).

Dawson, *Expert Witnesses,* 24th Annual Advanced Evidence and Discovery Course, State Bar of Texas (2011).

Fitzgerald and Foxman, *Criminal Law: Experts and Expertise—An Update*, 69 Tex. Bar Journal 746 (September 2006).

Gardner, *Expert Testimony in Capacity and Commitment Proceedings*, 69 Texas Bar Journal 760 (September 2006).

Goldstein and Keasler, *Bad Science, Bad Law—Judging Science on Appeal and Related Ethical Issues, Vol. 74, No. 7* Tex. Bar J. 568 (July 2011).

Hanks and Polinger–Hyman, *Redefining the Battlefield, Expert Reports in Medical Malpractice Litigation After H.B. 4,* Vol. 67, No. 11 Tex. Bar J. 936 (December 2004).

Hirsch and Donald, *Living in a World of Expertise, The Perils of Innocence–Guidelines for Trial Counsel Careful Handling of Expert Witnesses, 26 The Advocate* 61, State Bar of Texas Litigation Section Report (Spring 2004).

Hon, *Claims of Mental Retardation in Capital Litigation*, 69 Tex. Bar J. 742 (September 2006).

Jordan, Fletcher, and Horan, *Current Expert Issues,* 34th Annual Advanced Civil Trial Course, State Bar of Texas (2011).

Keller, *Bridging the Analytical Gap: The Gammill Alternative to Overcoming Robinson & Havner Challenges to Expert Testimony*, 33 St. Mary's L.J. 277 (2002).

McCurley, McCurley, and Eyck, *Shrinking the Shrinks Down to Size: Excluding Mental Health Experts and Effective Cross Examination Strategies*, 25th Annual Adv. Fam. Law Course, State Bar of Texas (1999).

Merillat, *The Question of Future Dangerousness of Capital Defendants*, 69 Tex. Bar J. 738 (September 2006).

Morris, *Experts and Daubert,* Adv. Crim. Law Course, State Bar of Texas (2001).

Orsinger, *Daubert with Emphasis on Commercial Litigation, Damages, and the Nonscientific Expert,* 23rd Annual Adv. Civ. Trial Course, State Bar of Texas (2000).

Orsinger, *Reliability of Expert Witnesses in State and Federal Court,* 25th Annual Adv. Fam. Law Course, State Bar of Texas (1999).

Shadwick and Hachem, *Expert Witnesses in Child Abuse and Neglect Cases Involving Termination of Parental Rights*, 69 Texas Bar J. 756 (September 2006)

Stilwell, *Kumho Tire: The Battle of the Experts Continues*, 19 Rev. Litig. 193 (2000).

Temple and Hollabaugh, *Expert Witness Issues On Appeal In State and Federal Court: Securing the Record from Adverse Robinson/Havner Rulings and the Standards of Review,* 33 *The Advocate* 28, State Bar of Texas Litigation Report, *Expert Witnesses* (Winter 2005).

Tottenham and Matson, *Daubert/Robinson: When You Should Request a Hearing and How to Do It,* The Ultimate Trial Notebook, State Bar of Texas Annual Meeting (June 2000).

Watts, *Daubert, Robinson, and Kumho Tire–What's the Rule Now in Texas?,* Adv. Personal Injury Law Course, State Bar of Texas (1999).

Integrated Legal Research System References

West's Texas Digest Key Numbers

Criminal Law ⚷469–481.

Evidence ⚷547–560.

Texas Practice

Addison, Texas Practice Guide, Evidence § 7:44 et seq.

Texas Jur 3d

24A Texas Jur 3d, Criminal Law § 3815 et seq.

36 Texas Jur 3d, Evidence § 653 et seq.

Am Jur Trials

Audio Recordings: Evidence, Experts, and Technology, 48 Am Jur Trials 1.

Expert Witnesses—Defense Perspective, 82 Am Jur Trials 97.

Presenting Plaintiff's Medical Proof—Common Injuries and Conditions, 6 Am Jur Trials 1.

Selecting and Using Expert Witnesses, 2 Am Jur Trials 585.

Use of Engineers as Experts, 6 Am Jur Trials 555.

Using Hypothetical Questions, 5 Am Jur Trials 675.

Using the Human Factors Expert in Civil Litigation, 40 Am Jur Trials 629.

Am Jur Proof of Facts

Admissibility and Reliability of Hair Sample Testing to Prove Illegal Drug Use, 47 Am Jur Proof of Facts 3d 203.

Admissibility and Reliability of Laboratory Analysis of Soil, Water, and Air Samples in Environmental Litigation, 24 Am Jur Proof of Facts 3d 609.

Establishing Foundation to Admit Computer Generated Evidence as Demonstrative or Substantive Evidence, 57 Am Jur Proof of Facts 3d 455.

Proof of Malpractice by Chiropractor, 55 Am Jur Proof of Facts 3d 1.

Qualification of Medical Expert Witness, 33 Am Jur Proof of Facts 2d 179.

Qualifying Historians as Expert Witnesses, 130 Am Jur Proof of Facts 3d 89.

Annotations

Admissibility of drug courier profile testimony in criminal prosecution, 69 ALR5th 425.

Admissibility of expert and opinion evidence as to cause or origin of fire, 84 ALR5th 69.

Admissibility of expert or opinion evidence—Supreme Court cases, 177 ALR Fed 77.

Admissibility of expert and opinion evidence as cause or origin of fire in criminal prosecution for arson or related offense-modern cases, 85 ALR5th 187.

Admissibility of expert or opinion evidence of battered-woman syndrome on issue of self-defense, 58 ALR5th 749.

Admissibility of expert testimony concerning domestic-violence syndromes to assist jury in evaluating victim's testimony or behavior, 57 ALR5th 315.

Admissibility of expert testimony as to susceptibility of defendant to inducement for purpose of establishing entrapment defense, 70 ALR5th 491.

Admissibility of expert testimony on child sexual abuse accommodation (CSAAS) in criminal case, 85 ALR5th 595.

Admissibility of expert testimony regarding reliability of accused's confession where accused allegedly suffered from mental disorder or defect at time of confession, 82 ALR5th 591.

Admissibility of lay witness interpretation of surveillance photograph or videotape, 74 ALR5th 643.

Admissibility of results of presumptive tests indicating presence of blood on object, 82 ALR5th 67.

Admissibility in federal criminal case of results of polygraph (lie detector) test—post Daubert cases, 140 ALR Fed 525.

Qualification as expert to testify as to findings or results of scientific test to determine alcoholic content of blood, 77 ALR2d 971.

Testing qualifications of expert witness, other than handwriting expert, by objective tests or experiments, 78 ALR2d 1281.

When will expert testimony "assist trier of fact" so as to be admissible at federal trial under Rule 702 of Federal Rules of Evidence, 75 ALR Fed 461.

Collateral References

Berger, *The Supreme Court's Trilogy on the Admissibility of Expert Testimony*, Federal Judicial Center Reference Manual on Scientific Evidence, Second Edition, at 9 (2000).

Diamond, *Reference Guide on Survey Research*, Federal Judicial Center Reference Manual on Scientific Evidence, Second Edition, at 229 (2000).

Goldstein & Henifin, *Reference Guide on Toxicology*, Federal Judicial Center Reference Manual on Scientific Evidence, Second Edition, at 401 (2000).

Green, Freedman & Gordis, *Reference Guide on Epidemiology*, Federal Judicial Center Reference Manual on Scientific Evidence, Second Edition, at 333 (2000).

Hall & Lazear, *Reference Guide on Estimation of Economic Losses in Damages Awards*, Federal Judicial Center Reference Manual on Scientific Evidence, Second Edition, at 277 (2000).

Henifin, Kipen & Poulter, *Reference Guide on Medical Testimony*, Federal Judicial Center Reference Manual on Scientific Evidence, Second Edition, at 439 (2000).

Kaye & Freedman, *Reference Guide on Statistics*, Federal Judicial Center Reference Manual on Scientific Evidence, Second Edition, at 83 (2000).

Kaye & Sensabaugh, *Reference Guide on DNA Evidence*, Federal Judicial Center Reference Manual on Scientific Evidence, Second Edition, at 485 (2000).

Petroski, *Reference Guide on Engineering Practice and Methods*, Federal Judicial Center Reference Manual on Scientific Evidence, Second Edition, at 577 (2000).

Rubinfeld, *Reference Guide on Multiple Regression*, Federal Judicial Center Reference Manual on Scientific Evidence, Second Edition, at 179 (2000).

Schwarzer & Cecil, *Management of Expert Evidence*, Federal Judicial Center Reference Manual on Scientific Evidence, Second Edition, at 39 (2000).

For text of Management of Expert Evidence and other related publications, see the Federal Judicial Center website at http://www.fjc.gov.

Rule 703. Bases of Opinion Testimony by Experts

The facts or data in the particular case upon which an expert bases an opinion or inference may be those perceived by, reviewed by, or made known to the expert at or before the hearing. If of a type reasonably relied upon by experts in the particular field in forming opinions or inferences upon the subject, the facts or data need not be admissible in evidence.

Eff. March 1, 1998.

Commentary

In general

Before the adoption of the Texas Rules of Civil Evidence, expert opinions were not admissible in evidence if based solely on hearsay not in evidence. *Moore v. Grantham, 599 S.W.2d 287 (Tex. 1980).* Today, expert opinions or inferences are admissible even if based on facts or data not admissible in evidence, including hearsay, if those otherwise inadmissible facts or data are "of a type reasonably relied upon by experts in the particular field" in forming the opinion expressed or drawing the inference stated. See *St. Paul Med. Ctr. v. Cecil, 842 S.W.2d 808 (Tex. App.—Dallas 1992, no writ).* The question of whether the facts or data relied upon by the testifying expert are of the type relied upon by experts in the particular field in forming their opinions about the subject, is a preliminary matter for the trial court under TEX. R. [CIV.] EVID. 104(a). *Id.*

Interestingly, the cases of *Robinson* and *Havner* imply that whether the facts or data relied upon by a testifying scientific expert actually are of a type reasonably relied upon by other experts in the particular field in forming *their* opinions or inferences on the subject must be established by evidence other than the testifying expert's bald statement that they are. But see *Robinson, dissent at 567* and Leading Cases, *infra*. See also *Burrow v. Arce, 997 S.W.2d 229 (Tex. 1999)* (a claim will not stand or fall on the mere statement of a qualified expert that his conclusions are correct). *Guadalupe-Blanco River Auth. v. Kraft, 77 S.W.3d 805, 809–810 (Tex. 2002)* (an expert's "bald assurance" that he is using the correct methodology is not sufficient to show that his opinion is reliable; the underlying data on which an expert relies should be independently evaluated in determining if the expert's opinion is reliable). See also *Dallas County v. Crestview Corners Car Wash, 370 S.W.3d 25 (Tex. App.—Dallas 2012, pet. denied).*

If an expert witness renders an opinion on the type of facts or data reasonably relied upon by other experts in that field in forming their opinions on the subject, must those underlying facts or data be disclosed on cross examination if privileged? This question was raised, but not answered, in *Skinner v. State, 956 S.W.2d 532 (Tex. Crim. App. 1997).*

In federal court civil cases the answer is "yes" to all information that has been considered by the expert witness in forming his opinions. FED. RULE CIV. P. 26(a)(2)(B); and the answer is "yes" to all documents that have been provided to, reviewed by, or prepared by or for the testifying expert in civil cases in Texas Courts. TEX. R. CIV. P. 192.3(e)(6). See *In re Christus Spohn Hospital Kleberg, 222 S.W.3d 434 (Tex. 2007).*

Texas Rule of Evidence 705 provides for the disclosure of facts or data underlying expert opinions, and 705 (d) refers to facts or data that are inadmissible, with no mention of whether privileged facts or data are inadmissible facts or data within the meaning of that rule.

Uniform Rules of Evidence

For text of corresponding provisions of Uniform Rules of Evidence and notes of decisions relating thereto, which may provide guidance in interpreting the Texas Rule, see Rule 703, 13B Uniform Laws Annotated.

Federal Rules of Evidence

The corresponding provision of the Federal Rules of Evidence is Rule 703. For the text of the Rule and Advisory Committee Notes, which may provide guidance in interpreting the Texas Rule, see the Appendix to this volume.

Leading Cases

Boswell v. Brazos Elec. Power Co–op., Inc., 910 S.W.2d 593 (Tex. App.—Fort Worth 1995, writ denied) (under TEX. R. [CIV.] EVID. 703, the facts or data upon which an expert relies need not be admissible in evidence if of a type reasonably relied upon by experts).

E.I. du Pont de Nemours and Co., Inc. v. Robinson, 923 S.W.2d 549, 567 (Tex. 1995) (". . . the expert's own testimony is sufficient to demonstrate the permissibility of the bases for the proffered opinions"). See *Moore v. Polish Power, Inc., 720 S.W.2d 183 (Tex. App.—Dallas 1986, writ ref'd n.r.e.)*, cited below.

Havner v. E–Z Mart Stores, Inc., 825 S.W.2d 456, dissent at 465 (Tex. 1992) (an expert's opinion must be based on facts or data arising from: (1) firsthand knowledge of the expert; (2) hypothetical questions to the expert based on facts in evidence; and (3) other data or facts reviewed by the expert "which are reasonably relied upon by experts in the particular field in forming opinions or inferences upon the subject").

Lipsey v. Texas Dep't of Health, 727 S.W.2d 61, 72 (Tex. App.—Austin 1987, writ ref'd n.r.e.) (whether facts or data are reasonably relied upon in a particular field by other experts in forming their opinions on the matter involved may be established by the testimony of the testifying expert). But see *Merrell Dow Pharmaceuticals, Inc. v. Havner, 907 S.W.2d 535 (Tex. App.—Corpus Christi 1994), rev'd on other grounds, 953 S.W.2d 706 (Tex. 1997)*, cited below.

Merrell Dow Pharmaceuticals, Inc. v. Havner, 907 S.W.2d 535 (Tex. App.—Corpus Christi 1994), rev'd on other grounds, 953 S.W.2d 706 (Tex. 1997) (whether facts or data are reasonably relied upon in a particular field by other experts in forming their opinions on the matter involved may be established by the testimony of the testifying expert). See *Moore v. Polish Power, Inc., 720 S.W.2d 183 (Tex. App.—Dallas 1986)*, cited below, and *Lipsey v. Texas Dep't of Health, 727 S.W.2d 61, 72 (Tex. App.—Austin 1987, writ ref'd n.r.e.)*, cited above.

Moore v. Polish Power, Inc., 720 S.W.2d 183 (Tex. App.—Dallas 1986, writ ref'd n.r.e) (an expert stating his opinion is competent to testify that what he bases his opinion on are facts and data reasonably relied upon by other experts in the field formulating such opinions; the reasonableness of such reliance need not be independently established). See also dissent *E.I. du Pont de Nemours and Co., Inc. v. Robinson, 923 S.W.2d 549, 567 (Tex. 1995)*, cited above. But see also *Merrell Dow Pharmaceuticals, Inc. v. Havner, 907 S.W.2d 535 (Tex. App.—Corpus Christi 1994)*, cited above.

Onwuteaka v. Gill, 908 S.W.2d 276 (Tex. App.—Houston [1st Dist.] 1995, no writ) (weakness of facts or data to support an expert's opinion or testimony goes to the weight of the evidence rather than its admissibility; expert opinion based solely on speculation and surmise is no evidence at all).

Welder v. Welder, 794 S.W.2d 420 (Tex. App.—Corpus Christi 1990, no writ), citing *Liptak v. Pensabene, 736 S.W.2d 953 (Tex. App.—Tyler 1987, no writ)*; *Sharpe v. Safway Scaffolds Co. of Houston, Inc., 687 S.W.2d 386 (Tex. App.—Houston [14th Dist.] 1985, no writ)*; *Seaside Indus., Inc. v. Cooper, 766 S.W.2d 566 (Tex. App.—Dallas 1989, no writ)* (even if the summaries or data relied on by an expert are hearsay, the expert testimony is admissible if the summaries or data are of a type reasonably relied upon by experts in the field in forming such opinions).

Leading CLE/Law Review Publications

Blend, *Using Expert Witnesses in Employment Litigation*, 17 Rev. Litig. 27 (1998).

Brown, *Eight Gates for Expert Witnesses*, 36 Hous. L. Rev. 743 (1999).

Brown, *Procedural Issues Under Daubert*, 36 Hous. L. Rev. 1133 (1999).

Integrated Legal Research System References

West's Texas Digest Key Numbers

Criminal Law ⚷478.

Evidence ⚷505–534.

Texas Practice

Addison, Texas Practice Guide, Evidence § 7:172 et seq.

Texas Jur 3d

24A Texas Jur 3d, Criminal Law § 3826 et seq.

36 Texas Jur 3d, Evidence §§ 669—672.

Am Jur Trials

Presenting Plaintiff's Medical Proof—Common Injuries and Conditions, 6 Am Jur Trials 1.

Using Hypothetical Questions at the Trial, 5 Am Jur Trials 675.

Am Jur Proof of Facts

Establishing Foundation to Admit Computer Generated Evidence as Demonstrative or Substantive Evidence, 57 Am Jur Proof of Facts 3d 455.

Qualifying Historians as Expert Witnesses, 130 Am Jur Proof of Facts 3d 89.

Annotations

Admissibility of expert testimony regarding credibility of confession, 73 ALR5th 581.

Admissibility of testimony of expert, as to basis of his opinion, to matters otherwise excludible as hearsay—state cases, 89 ALR4th 456.

Qualifications of nonmedical psychologist to testify as to mental condition or competency, 72 ALR5th 529.

What information is of type "reasonably relied upon by experts" within Rule 703, Federal Rules of Evidence, permitting expert opinion based on information not admissible in evidence, 49 ALR Fed 363.

Rule 704. Opinion on Ultimate Issue

Testimony in the form of an opinion or inference otherwise admissible is not objectionable because it embraces an ultimate issue to be decided by the trier of fact.

Eff. March 1, 1998.

Commentary

Uniform Rules of Evidence

For text of corresponding provisions of Uniform Rules of Evidence and notes of decisions relating thereto, which may provide guidance in interpreting the Texas Rule, see Rule 704, 13B Uniform Laws Annotated.

Federal Rules of Evidence

The corresponding provision of the Federal Rules of Evidence is Rule 704. For the text of the Rule and Advisory Committee Notes, which may provide guidance in interpreting the Texas Rule, see the Appendix to this volume.

Leading Cases

Birchfield v. Texarkana Mem'l Hosp., 747 S.W.2d 361 (Tex. 1987) (an expert may testify on mixed question of fact and law, provided his opinion is based on proper legal concepts made known to him; opinions that acts were negligent, grossly negligent, or the proximate cause of an occurrence must be based on the proper legal definitions of those concepts).

Fairow v. State, 920 S.W.2d 357 (Tex. App.—Houston [1st Dist.] 1996), aff'd, 943 S.W.2d 895 (Tex. Crim. App. 1997) (an opinion of an expert which embraces an ultimate issue to be decided by the trier of fact must be "otherwise admissible"; it is not otherwise admissible if based on mere speculation). *Note:* Expert opinion on an ultimate issue also would not be "otherwise admissible" if it is not reliable, or it did not meet the requirements of Vernon's Ann.Rules Evid., Rules 702 or 703, or is excludable on special grounds under Vernon's Ann.Rules Evid., Rule 403. See Commentary to Rule 702, *supra.* Evidence is not "otherwise admissible" if it is subject to any other valid legal objection actually made.

Louder v. De Leon, 754 S.W.2d 148 (Tex. 1988) (expert testimony on proximate cause, as an ultimate fact to be decided by the trier of fact, is admissible as long as it is based on proper legal concepts).

Pittsburgh Corning Corp. v. Walters, 1 S.W.3d 759 (Tex. App.—Corpus Christi 1999, pet. denied.) (an expert may give his opinion on an ultimate issue, such as negligence or gross negligence, as long as the expert is provided with the proper legal standard as a predicate).

Integrated Legal Research System References

West's Texas Digest Key Numbers

Criminal Law ⚷486.

Evidence ⚷474.5, 569.

Texas Practice

Addison, Texas Practice Guide, Evidence § 7:204 et seq.

Texas Jur 3d

24A Texas Jur 3d, Criminal Law § 3815.

36 Texas Jur 3d, Evidence § 579.

Rule 705. Disclosure of Facts or Data Underlying Expert Opinion

(a) Disclosure of Facts or Data. The expert may testify in terms of opinion or inference and give the expert's reasons therefor without prior disclosure of the underlying facts or data, unless the court requires otherwise. The expert may in any event disclose on direct examination, or be required to disclose on cross-examination, the underlying facts or data.

(b) Voir dire. Prior to the expert giving the expert's opinion or disclosing the underlying facts or data, a party against whom the opinion is offered upon request in a criminal case shall, or in a civil case may, be permitted to conduct a *voir dire* examination directed to the underlying facts or data upon which the opinion is based. This examination shall be conducted out of the hearing of the jury.

(c) Admissibility of opinion. If the court determines that the underlying facts or data do not provide a sufficient basis for the expert's opinion under Rule 702 or 703, the opinion is inadmissible.

(d) Balancing test; limiting instructions. When the underlying facts or data would be inadmissible in evidence, the court shall exclude the underlying facts or data if the danger that they will be used for a purpose other than as explanation or support for the expert's opinion outweighs their value as explanation or support or are unfairly prejudicial. If otherwise inadmissible facts or data are disclosed before the jury, a limiting instruction by the court shall be given upon request.

Eff. March 1, 1998.

Commentary

In general

This rule is based on the former Rule 705 in criminal cases. As such, it adds several new provisions for the civil practitioner.

Part (a) of the rule (which was common to both the civil and criminal versions of the rule) allows "letting the cat out of the bag" when it comes to the disclosure on direct examination of the underlying facts or data supporting the opinion of an expert witness, regardless of whether the facts or data would be otherwise be admissible, although these facts or data must be "of a type reasonably relied upon by experts in the particular field in forming their opinions upon the subject." Recognizing that this part of the rule allows the admission on direct examination of otherwise inadmissible evidence under the guise of expert testimony, some appellate courts determined that it was up to the sound discretion of the trial court as to whether to allow testimony on direct examination as to the underlying facts or data supporting the expert testimony or opinion. See Leading Cases, *infra.* For a different view, see *Sosa By and Through Grant v. Koshy, 961 S.W.2d 420 (Tex. App.—Houston [1st Dist.] 1997, writ denied).* This problem is considerably ameliorated for the opponent of the evidence by parts (b), (c) and (d) of this rule.

Before an expert is allowed to give his opinion or disclose the underlying facts or data supporting it, the trial court in a criminal case must allow the opponent of the evidence to *voir dire* the witness regarding those underlying facts or data outside the presence of the jury in a criminal case. But see *Alba v. State, 905 S.W.2d 581 (Tex. Crim. App. 1995)* (where the underlying facts relied on by the expert are contained within a hypothetical question that assumes facts already in evidence, it is not error for the trial court to refuse *voir dire*). Whether to allow *voir dire* of the expert witness in a civil case is within the sound discretion of the trial court. The trial court must not admit testimony of the underlying facts or data if the expert is not qualified to render the opinion, or the opinion is not reliable. See Recent Decisions and Trends in Commentary to Rule 702.

The underlying facts or data the expert witness relies on as a basis for his testimony or opinion need not be admissible into evidence, but they must otherwise meet the requirements of Rule 703. If the underlying and relied-upon facts or data are *inadmissible* but meet the requirements of Rule 703, they must not be disclosed to the jury on direct examination of the witness if the court determines that the danger of their misuse by the jury outweighs their value as support for or explanation of the expert's testimony or opinion, or if they are unfairly prejudicial. If, after weighing those factors, the trial court allows the disclosure of the facts and data underlying the expert's testimony or opinion, the court must give a limiting instruction to the jury upon the request of any party. Of course, if the underlying facts or data are *admissible* and are of a type reasonably relied upon by experts in the particular field in forming their opinions or inferences on the subject, they may be fully disclosed to the jury on direct examination of the expert witness.

Uniform Rules of Evidence

For text of corresponding provisions of Uniform Rules of Evidence and notes of decisions relating thereto, which may provide guidance in interpreting the Texas Rule, see Rule 705, 13B Uniform Laws Annotated.

Federal Rules of Evidence

The corresponding provision of the Federal Rules of Evidence is Rule 705. For the text of the Rule and Advisory Committee Notes, which may provide guidance in interpreting the Texas Rule, see the Appendix to this volume.

Leading Cases

Boswell v. Brazos Elec. Power Co-op., Inc., 910 S.W.2d 593 (Tex. App.—Fort Worth 1995, writ denied), citing *Beavers on Behalf of Beavers v. Northrop Worldwide Aircraft Servs., Inc., 821 S.W.2d 669 (Tex. App.—Amarillo 1991, writ denied)* (while expert testimony or opinion may be admissible, the underlying facts or data may not be; TEX. R. [CIV.] EVID. 705 does not provide for an absolute right of the expert to disclose all of the facts and underlying data that supports his opinion or testimony on direct examination; the trial court has discretion to exclude such evidence on direct, but the trial court is required to allow disclosure of evidence to discredit an expert on cross-examination).

First Southwest Lloyds Ins. Co. v. MacDowell, 769 S.W.2d 954 (Tex. App.—Texarkana 1989, writ denied) ("... the use of the permissive word 'may' in indicating that the expert 'may in any event disclose ... the underlying facts or data' does not indicate an absolute right of the expert to disclose all of the facts and underlying data under all circumstances; ... the better judicial position is to not allow the affirmative admission of otherwise inadmissible matters merely because such matters happen to be underlying data upon which an expert relies").

Jenkins v. State, 912 S.W.2d 793 (Tex. Crim. App. 1993) (defendant's objections to psychologist's qualifications and request for *voir dire* outside presence of jury to prove his qualifications is not a request for hearing to test underlying facts or data of opinion under TEX. R. [CRIM.] EVID. 705(b)).

Welder v. Welder, 794 S.W.2d 420 (Tex. App.—Corpus Christi 1990, no writ) (TEX. R. [CIV.] EVID. 705 provides that an expert may be required to disclose, *on cross-examination*, the underlying facts or data).

Leading CLE/Law Review Publications

Brown, *Eight Gates for Expert Witnesses*, 36 Hous. L. Rev. 743 (1999).

Brown, *Procedural Issues Under Daubert*, 36 Hous. L. Rev. 1133 (1999).

Tottenham, *Basis of Expert Opinion Evidence as (Impermissible?) Conduit to Circumvent Hearsay Rules*, State Bar of Texas, Adv. Fam. Law Course (1994).

Integrated Legal Research System References

West's Texas Digest Key Numbers

Criminal Law ⚷486.

Evidence ⚷555–555.10.

Texas Practice

Addison, Texas Practice Guide, Evidence § 7:230 et seq.

Am Jur Trials

Using Hypothetical Questions at the Trial, 5 Am Jur Trials 675.

Rule 706. Audit in Civil Cases

Despite any other evidence rule to the contrary, verified reports of auditors prepared pursuant to Rule of Civil Procedure 172, whether in the form of summaries, opinions, or otherwise, shall be admitted in evidence when offered by any party whether or not the facts or data in the reports are otherwise admissible and whether or not the reports embrace the ultimate issues to be decided by the trier of fact. Where exceptions to the reports have been filed, a party may contradict the reports by evidence supporting the exceptions.

Eff. March 1, 1998.

Commentary

In general

The report of an auditor appointed under Vernon's Ann.Rules Civ.Proc., Rule 172 must be taken as true as to an account between the parties in the case unless exceptions to the report are filed within 30 days of the time the report is filed with the court. If an exception is timely filed, the party excepting will be permitted to offer evidence contradicting the report to the extent of the exceptions made to it.

Vernon's Ann.Rules Civ.Proc., Rule 172 provides that "[W]hen an investigation of accounts or examination of vouchers appears necessary for the purpose of justice between the parties to any suit, the court shall appoint an auditor or auditors to state the accounts between the parties and to make report thereof to the court as soon as possible. The auditor shall verify his report by his affidavit stating that he has carefully examined the state of the account between the parties, and that his report contains a true statement thereof, so far as the same has come within his knowledge. Exceptions to such report or of any item thereof must be filed within 30 days of the filing of such report. The court shall award reasonable compensation to such auditor to be taxed as costs of suit."

Uniform Rules of Evidence

There is no corresponding provisions in the Uniform Rules of Evidence.

Federal Rules of Evidence

There is no corresponding provision in the Federal Rules of Evidence.

Leading Cases

Sanchez v. Jary, 768 S.W.2d 933 (Tex. App.—San Antonio 1989, no writ) (if neither side excepts to the report, it is admitted in evidence and is conclusive as to the matters covered by the report).

Simpson v. Canales, 806 S.W.2d 802 (Tex. 1991) (Vernon's Ann.Rules Civ.Proc., Rule 172 requires appointment of an auditor only when "an investigation of accounts or examination of vouchers appears necessary for the purpose of justice between the parties").

West's Texas Digest Key Numbers

Witnesses ⚷4.

Texas Practice

Addison, Texas Practice Guide, Evidence § 7:244 et seq.

ARTICLE VIII. HEARSAY

Rule
801. Definitions.
802. Hearsay Rule.
803. Hearsay Exceptions: Availability of Declarant Immaterial.
804. Hearsay Exceptions; Declarant Unavailable.
805. Hearsay Within Hearsay.
806. Attacking and Supporting Credibility of Declarant.

Cross References

Testimony of Child Who is Victim of Offense, Vernon's Ann.C.C.P. Art. 38.071.

Hearsay Statement of Child Abuse Victim, Vernon's Ann.C.C.P. Art. 38.072.

Integrated Legal Research System References

West's Texas Digest Key Numbers

Evidence ⚷314–324.

Texas Jur 3d

24 Texas Jur 3d, Criminal Law §§ 3519–3551.

35 Texas Jur 3d, Evidence §§ 206–277.

Am Jur Trials

Examination of a Witness Based on a Prior Statement, 49 Am Jur Trials 501.

Facebook, MySpace, LinkedIn, Twitter, and Other Social Media in Trials, 122 Am Jur Trials 421.

Am Jur Proof of Facts

Foundation for Offering Deposition or Other Former Testimony in Evidence, 28 Am Jur Proof of Facts 2d 1.

Rule 801. Definitions

The following definitions apply under this article:

(a) Statement. A "statement" is (1) an oral or written verbal expression or (2) nonverbal conduct of a person, if it is intended by the person as a substitute for verbal expression.

(b) Declarant. A "declarant" is a person who makes a statement.

(c) Matter Asserted. "Matter asserted" includes any matter explicitly asserted, and any matter implied by a statement, if the probative value of the statement as offered flows from declarant's belief as to the matter.

(d) Hearsay. "Hearsay" is a statement, other than one made by the declarant while testifying at the trial or hearing, offered in evidence to prove the truth of the matter asserted.

(e) Statements Which Are Not Hearsay. A statement is not hearsay if:

(1) *Prior statement by witness.* The declarant testifies at the trial or hearing and is subject to cross-examination concerning the statement, and the statement is:

(A) inconsistent with the declarant's testimony, and was given under oath subject to the penalty of perjury at a trial, hearing, or other proceeding except a grand jury proceeding in a criminal case, or in a deposition;

(B) consistent with the declarant's testimony and is offered to rebut an express or implied charge against the declarant of recent fabrication or improper influence or motive;

(C) one of identification of a person made after perceiving the person; or

(D) taken and offered in a criminal case in accordance with Code of Criminal Procedure article 38.071.

(2) *Admission by party-opponent.* The statement is offered against a party and is:

(A) the party's own statement in either an individual or representative capacity;

(B) a statement of which the party has manifested an adoption or belief in its truth;

(C) a statement by a person authorized by the party to make a statement concerning the subject;

(D) a statement by the party's agent or servant concerning a matter within the scope of the agency or employment, made during the existence of the relationship; or

(E) a statement by a co-conspirator of a party during the course and in furtherance of the conspiracy.

(3) *Depositions.* In a civil case, it is a deposition taken in the same proceeding, as same proceeding is defined in Rule of Civil Procedure 203.6(b). Unavailability of deponent is not a requirement for admissibility.

Adopted eff. March 1, 1998. Amended eff. Jan. 1, 1999.

Commentary

In general

This rule defines hearsay and the words of art that make up its constituent elements and declares that certain statements as described in the rule are not hearsay.

Definition of hearsay

To get a good idea of what the elements of hearsay are, it may help to define the word in terms of the meanings of those words of art, so that hearsay is described as (1) an oral or written expression (2) made by a person (3) in words, or by conduct, if the conduct is intended by the person to a be a substitute for words, (4) made outside of court (5) but offered at the trial or hearing (6) to prove the truth of such words or conduct, or to prove the truth of any matter implied by such words or conduct, the probative value of which flows from declarant's belief as to truth of the words or conduct.

Statements which are not hearsay and exceptions to the hearsay rule

The rules regarding hearsay draw three main distinctions: (1) certain statements are declared not to be hearsay (Rule 801(e)); (2) other statements are declared to be exceptions to the hearsay rule, whether the declarant is available or not (Rule 803); and (3) still other statements are declared to be exceptions to the hearsay rule if the declarant is not available (Rule 804).

Prior statement by a witness-declarant

A prior out-of-court statement of a witness is not hearsay if the statement meets one of the four criteria of Rule 801(e)(1), provided the declarant testifies at the trial or hearing and is subject to cross-examination.

Burden of proof for admission of hearsay evidence

The trial court is not required to discern an exception to the inadmissibility of hearsay evidence when an objection is made to it. The proponent of the evidence offered as an exception to the hearsay rule has the burden of showing that the offer is within an exception. *Butler v. Commission for Lawyer Discipline, 928 S.W.2d 659 (Tex. App.—Corpus Christi 1996, n.w.h.).*

Official Comment to former Rule 801

The comment to former Rule 801 of the Rules of Civil Evidence and the Rules of Criminal Evidence provided in pertinent part as follows:

"The definitions in Rule 801(a), (b), (c) and (d) combined bring within the hearsay rule four categories of conduct. These are described and illustrated below.

"(1) A verbal (oral or written) explicit assertion. Illustration. Witness testifies that declarant said 'A shot B.' Declarant's conduct is a statement because it is an oral expression. Because it is an explicit assertion, the matter asserted is that A shot B. Finally, the statement is hearsay because it was not made while testifying at the trial and is offered to prove the truth of the matter asserted.

"(2) A verbal (oral or written) explicit assertion, not offered to prove the matter explicitly asserted, but offered for the truth of a matter implied by the statement, the probative value of the statement flowing from declarant's belief as to the matter. Illustration. The only known remedy for X disease is medicine Y and the only known use of medicine Y is to cure X disease. To prove that Oglethorpe had X disease, witness testifies that declarant, a doctor, stated, 'The best medicine for Oglethorpe is Y.' The testimony is to a statement because it was a verbal expression. The matter asserted was that Oglethorpe had X disease because that matter is implied from the statement, the probative value of the statement as offered flowing from declarant's belief as to the matter. Finally, the statement is hearsay because it was not made while testifying at the trial and is offered to prove the truth of the matter asserted.

"(3) Non-assertive verbal conduct offered for the truth of a matter implied by the statement, the probative value of the statement flowing from declarant's belief as to the matter. Illustration. In a rape prosecution to prove that Richard, the defendant, was in the room at the time of the rape, W testifies that declarant knocked on the door to the room and shouted, 'Open the door, Richard.' The testimony is to a statement because it was a verbal expression. The matter asserted was that Richard was in the room because that matter is implied from the statement, the probative value of the statement as offered flowing from declarant's belief as to the matter. Finally, the statement is hearsay because it was not made while testifying at the trial and is offered to prove the truth of the matter asserted.

"(4) Nonverbal assertive conduct intended as a substitute for verbal expression. Illustration. W testifies that A asked declarant 'Which way did X go?' and declarant pointed north. This nonverbal conduct of declarant was intended by him as a substitute for verbal expression and so is a statement. The matter asserted is that X went north because that is implied from the statement and the probative value of the statement as offered flows from declarant's belief that X went north. Finally, the statement is hearsay because it was not made at trial and is offered to prove the truth of the matter asserted."

Uniform Rules of Evidence

For text of corresponding provisions of Uniform Rules of Evidence and notes of decisions relating thereto, which may provide guidance in interpreting the Texas Rule, see Rule 801, 13B Uniform Laws Annotated.

Federal Rules of Evidence

The corresponding provision of the Federal Rules of Evidence is Rule 801. For the text of the Rule and Advisory Committee Notes, which may provide guidance in interpreting the Texas Rule, see the Appendix to this volume.

Leading Cases

Dorado v. State, 843 S.W.2d 37 (Tex. Crim. App. 1992) ("outcry testimony" of child abuse victim, offered for the truth of the matters asserted, is hearsay and is objectionable as such unless testimony is permitted by prescribed exception to hearsay rule; Vernon's Ann.C.C.P. Art. 38.072 creates such an exception when requisite statutory conditions are met). See also *Duncan v. State, 95 S.W.3d 669 (Tex. App.—Houston [1st Dist.] 2003, pet. ref'd).*

Hammons v. State, 239 S.W.3d 798 (Tex. Crim. App. 2007) (under Rule 801(e)(1)(B), a charge of recent fabrication or improper motive regarding a declarant's testimony may be implied through tone, tenor, and demeanor during the entirety of cross-examination. Where this occurs, the prior *consistent* out-of-court statements of the declarant [which are consistent with his trial testimony on direct examination] are not objectionable as hearsay).

Hartman v. Trio Transp., Inc., 937 S.W.2d 575 (Tex. App.—Texarkana 1996, writ denied) (a statement by an agent or servant concerning a matter within the scope of his agency or employment made during the existence of the relationship is not hearsay).

Kansas City Southern Railway Co. v. Carter, 778 S.W.2d 911 (Tex. App.—Texarkana 1989, writ denied) (a stipulation by a party in a lawsuit is admissible as an admission against that same party in another lawsuit).

McCraw v. Maris, 828 S.W.2d 756 (Tex. 1992) (out-of-court statements are not hearsay if offered for a purpose other than to prove the truth of the matter asserted).

Norsul Oil & Mining Ltd. v. Commercial Equipment Leasing Co., 703 S.W.2d 345 (Tex. App.—San Antonio 1985, no writ) (Tex. R. [Civ.] Evid. 801(e)(3) and Vernon's Ann.Rules Civ.Proc., Rule 207 permit depositions to be used in lieu of "live" testimony without any requirement that the deponent be unavailable to testify at trial).

Perkins v. State, 902 S.W.2d 88 (Tex. App.—El Paso 1995, pet. ref'd) (an out of court statement is not hearsay if the statement is offered against a party, and it is his own statement).

Saavedra v. State, 297 S.W.3d 342 (Tex. Crim. App. 2009) (where a party is shown to have authorized a language interpreter to speak for that party on the particular occasion, or otherwise adopted the interpreter as his agent for the purposes of translating a particular statement, the out-of-court interpretation is admissible under Rule 801(e)(2)(C) or (D) of these rules).

Texaco, Inc. v. Pennzoil Co., 729 S.W.2d 768 (Tex. App.—Houston [1st Dist.] 1987, writ ref'd n.r.e.) (a party's pleadings in other actions that contain statements inconsistent with the party's present position are receivable as admissions).

Waldon v. City of Longview, 855 S.W.2d 875 (Tex. App.—Tyler 1993, no writ) (when an event is of such significance that a declarant-party would ordinarily be expected to tell of it, the failure of a declarant-party to mention the event in a prior statement may constitute an admission against that party that the event did not occur).

Williams v. State, 790 S.W.2d 643 (Tex. Crim. App. 1990) (co-conspirator's out-of-court statement must be "in furtherance of the conspiracy," and not merely somehow "related to," the conspiracy in order to be admissible over a hearsay objection).

Leading CLE/Law Review Publications

Indelicato and Stewart, *Hearsay,* 37th Annual Advanced Family Law Course, State Bar of Texas (2011).

Integrated Legal Research System References

West's Texas Digest Key Numbers

Criminal Law ⚷419.

Evidence ⚷314.

Texas Practice

Addison, Texas Practice Guide, Evidence § 8:1 et seq.

Texas Jur 3d

24 Texas Jur 3d, Criminal Law § 3519 et seq.

35 Texas Jur 3d, Evidence § 209 et seq.

Am Jur Trials

Examination of a Witness Based on a Prior Statement, 49 Am Jur Trials 501.

Am Jur Proof of Facts

Establishing Foundation to Admit Computer Generated Evidence as Demonstrative or Substantive Evidence, 57 Am Jur Proof of Facts 3d 455.

Annotations

Admissibility as "not hearsay" of statement by party's attorney under Federal Rules of Evidence 801(d)(2)(C) or 801(d)(2)(D), 117 ALR Fed 599.

Admissibility of depositions under Federal Evidence Rule 804(b)(1), 84 ALR Fed 668.

Admissibility of impeached witness' prior consistent statement—modern state criminal cases, 58 ALR4th 1014.

Admissibility of party's own statement under Rule 801(d)(2)(A) of the Federal Rules of Evidence, 191 ALR Fed 27.

Admissibility of statement by coconspirator under Rule 801(d)(2)(E) of Federal Rules of Evidence, 44 ALR Fed 627.

Admissibility of statement under Rule 801(d)(2)(B) of Federal Rules of Evidence, providing that statement is not hearsay if party-opponent has manifested adoption or belief in its truth, 156 ALR Fed 217.

Admissibility of testimony of expert, as to basis of his opinion, to matters otherwise excludible as hearsay—state cases, 89 ALR4th 456.

Effect of Rule 801(d)(1)(B) of the Federal Rules of Evidence upon the admissibility of a witness' prior consistent statement, 47 ALR Fed 639.

Nonverbal reaction to accusation, other than silence alone, as constituting adoptive admission under hearsay rule, 87 ALR3d 706.

Interpreter or translator as party's agent for purposes of "admission by party opponent" exception to hearsay rule (Federal Rules of Evidence, Rules 801(d)(2)(C), 801(d)(2)(D)), 121 ALR Fed 611.

Validity, construction, and application of child hearsay statutes, 71 ALR5th 637.

What is "other proceeding" under Rule 801(d)(1)(A) of Federal Rules of Evidence, excepting from hearsay rule prior inconsistent statement given "at a trial, hearing, or other proceeding," 37 ALR Fed 855.

When is hearsay statement an "excited utterance" admissible under Rule 803(2) of the Federal Rules of Evidence, 155 ALR Fed 583.

Written recitals or statements as within rule excluding hearsay, 10 ALR2d 1035.

Rule 802. Hearsay Rule

Hearsay is not admissible except as provided by statute or these rules or by other rules prescribed pursuant to statutory authority. Inadmissible hearsay admitted without objection shall not be denied probative value merely because it is hearsay.

Eff. March 1, 1998.

Commentary

In general

Before the promulgation of the Texas Rules of Civil Evidence, hearsay evidence had no probative value and would not support a judgment even when admitted without objection. *Richardson v. Green, 677 S.W.2d 497 (Tex. 1984)*. Now, under this rule, hearsay evidence which is not objected to does have probative value. *Texas Commerce Bank Nat'l Ass'n v. New, 3 S.W.3d 515 (Tex. 1999)*. This is consistent with one of the fundamental precepts of the Rules that, in general, all offered evidence is to be admitted and have probative value in the absence of a proper and timely objection. Just how much probative value evidence has is a matter for the trier of fact. Vernon's Ann.Rules Civ.Proc., Rule 226a III.

Uniform Rules of Evidence

For text of corresponding provisions of Uniform Rules of Evidence and notes of decisions relating thereto, which may provide guidance in interpreting the Texas Rule, see Rule 802, 13B Uniform Laws Annotated.

Federal Rules of Evidence

The corresponding provision of the Federal Rules of Evidence is Rule 802. For the text of the Rule and Advisory Committee Notes, which may provide guidance in interpreting the Texas Rule, see the Appendix to this volume.

Integrated Legal Research System References

West's Texas Digest Key Numbers

Criminal Law ⚷419.

Evidence ⚷314.

Texas Practice

Addison, Texas Practice Guide, Evidence § 8:107 et seq.

Texas Jur 3d

24 Texas Jur 3d, Criminal Law § 3519 et seq.

35 Texas Jur 3d, Evidence § 206 et seq.

Annotations

Consideration, in determining facts, of inadmissible hearsay evidence introduced without objection, 79 ALR2d 890.

Rule 803. Hearsay Exceptions: Availability of Declarant Immaterial

The following are not excluded by the hearsay rule, even though the declarant is available as a witness:

(1) Present Sense Impression. A statement describing or explaining an event or condition made while the declarant was perceiving the event or condition, or immediately thereafter.

(2) Excited Utterance. A statement relating to a startling event or condition made while the declarant was under the stress of excitement caused by the event or condition.

(3) Then Existing Mental, Emotional, or Physical Condition. A statement of the declarant's then existing state of mind, emotion, sensation, or physical condition (such as intent, plan, motive, design, mental feeling, pain, or bodily health), but not including a statement of memory or belief to prove the fact remembered or believed unless it relates to the execution, revocation, identification, or terms of declarant's will.

(4) Statements for Purposes of Medical Diagnosis or Treatment. Statements made for purposes of medical diagnosis or treatment and describing medical history, or past or present symptoms, pain, or sensations, or the inception or general character of the cause or external source thereof insofar as reasonably pertinent to diagnosis or treatment.

(5) Recorded Recollection. A memorandum or record concerning a matter about which a witness once had personal knowledge but now has insufficient recollection to enable the witness to testify fully and accurately, shown to have been made or adopted by the witness when the matter was fresh in the witness' memory and to reflect that knowledge correctly, unless the circumstances of preparation cast doubt on the document's trustworthiness. If admitted, the memorandum or record may be read into evidence but may not itself be received as an exhibit unless offered by an adverse party.

(6) Records of Regularly Conducted Activity. A memorandum, report, record, or data compilation, in any form, of acts, events, conditions, opinions, or diagnoses, made at or near the time by, or from information transmitted by, a person with knowledge, if kept in the course of a regularly conducted business activity, and if it was the regular practice of that business activity to make the memorandum, report, record, or data compilation, all as shown by the testimony of the custodian or other qualified witness, or by affidavit that complies with Rule 902(10), unless the source of information or the method or circumstances of preparation indicate lack of trustworthiness. "Business" as used in this paragraph includes any and every kind of regular organized activity whether conducted for profit or not.

(7) Absence of Entry in Records Kept in Accordance With the Provisions of Paragraph (6). Evidence that a matter is not included in the memoranda, reports, records, or data compilations, in any form, kept in accordance with the provisions of paragraph (6), to prove the nonoccurrence or nonexistence of the matter, if the matter was of a kind of which a memorandum, report, record, or data compilation was regularly made and preserved, unless the sources of information or other circumstances indicate lack of trustworthiness.

(8) Public Records and Reports. Records, reports, statements, or data compilations, in any form, of public offices or agencies setting forth:

(A) the activities of the office or agency;

(B) matters observed pursuant to duty imposed by law as to which matters there was a duty to report, excluding in criminal cases matters observed by police officers and other law enforcement personnel; or

(C) in civil cases as to any party and in criminal cases as against the state, factual findings resulting from an investigation made pursuant to authority granted by law;

unless the sources of information or other circumstances indicate lack of trustworthiness.

(9) Records of Vital Statistics. Records or data compilations, in any form, of births, fetal deaths, deaths, or marriages, if the report thereof was made to a public office pursuant to requirements of law.

(10) Absence of Public Record or Entry. To prove the absence of a record, report, statement, or data compilation, in any form, or the nonoccurrence or nonexistence of a matter of which a record, report, statement, or data compilation, in any form, was regularly made and preserved by a public office or agency, evidence in the form of a certification in accordance with Rule 902, or testimony, that diligent search failed to disclose the record, report statement, or data compilation, or entry.

(11) Records of Religious Organizations. Statements of births, marriages, divorces, deaths, legitimacy, ancestry, relationship by blood or marriage, or other similar facts of personal or family history, contained in a regularly kept record of a religious organization.

(12) Marriage, Baptismal, and Similar Certificates. Statements of fact contained in a certificate that the maker performed a marriage or other ceremony or administered a sacrament, made by a member of the clergy, public official, or other person authorized by the rules or practices of a religious organization or by law to perform the act certified, and purporting to have been issued at the time of the act or within a reasonable time thereafter.

(13) Family Records. Statements of fact concerning personal or family history contained in family Bibles, genealogies, charts, engravings on rings, inscriptions on family portraits, engravings on urns, crypts, or tombstones, or the like.

(14) Records of Documents Affecting an Interest in Property. The record of a document purporting to establish or affect an interest in property, as proof of the content of the original recorded document and its execution and delivery by each person by whom it purports to have been executed, if the record is a record of a public office and an applicable statute authorizes the recording of documents of that kind in that office.

(15) Statements in Documents Affecting an Interest in Property. A statement contained in a document purporting to establish or affect an interest in property if the matter stated was relevant to the purpose of the document, unless dealings with the property since the document was made have been inconsistent with the truth of the statement or the purport of the document.

(16) Statements in Ancient Documents. Statements in a document in existence twenty years or more the authenticity of which is established.

(17) Market Reports, Commercial Publications. Market quotations, tabulations, lists, directories, or other published compilations, generally used and relied upon by the public or by persons in particular occupations.

(18) Learned Treatises. To the extent called to the attention of an expert witness upon cross-examination or relied upon by the expert in direct examination, statements contained in published treatises, periodicals, or pamphlets on a subject of history, medicine, or other science or art established as a reliable authority by the testimony or admission of the witness or by other expert testimony or by judicial notice. If admitted, the statements may be read into evidence but may not be received as exhibits.

(19) Reputation Concerning Personal or Family History. Reputation among members of a person's family by blood, adoption, or marriage, or among a person's associates, or in the community, concerning a person's birth, adoption, marriage, divorce, death, legitimacy, relationship by blood, adoption, or marriage, ancestry, or other similar fact of personal or family history.

(20) Reputation Concerning Boundaries or General History. Reputation in a community, arising before the controversy, as to boundaries of or customs affecting lands in the community, and reputation as to events of general history important to the community or state or nation in which located.

(21) Reputation as to Character. Reputation of a person's character among associates or in the community.

(22) Judgment of Previous Conviction. In civil cases, evidence of a judgment, entered after a trial or upon a plea of guilty (but not upon a plea of *nolo contendere*), judging a person guilty of a felony, to prove any fact essential to sustain the judgment of conviction. In criminal cases, evidence of a judgment, entered after a trial or upon a plea of guilty or *nolo contendere*, adjudging a person guilty of a criminal offense, to prove any fact essential to sustain the judgment of conviction, but not including, when offered by the state for purposes other than impeachment, judgments against persons other than the accused. In all cases, the pendency of an appeal renders such evidence inadmissible.

(23) Judgment as to Personal, Family, or General History, or Boundaries. Judgments as proof of matters of personal, family or general history, or boundaries, essential to the judgment, if the same would be provable by evidence of reputation.

(24) Statement Against Interest. A statement which was at the time of its making so far contrary to the declarant's pecuniary or proprietary interest, or so far tended to subject the declarant to civil or criminal liability, or to render invalid a claim by the declarant against another, or to make the declarant an object of hatred, ridicule, or disgrace, that a reasonable person in declarant's position would not have made the statement unless believing it to be true. In criminal cases, a statement tending to expose the declarant to criminal liability is not admissible unless corroborating circumstances clearly indicate the trustworthiness of the statement.

Eff. March 1, 1998.

Cross References

Admissibility of Communications of Sympathy, V.T.C.A., Civil Practice & Remedies Code § 18.061.

Hearsay Statement of Child Abuse Victim, Vernon's Ann.C.C.P. Art. 38.072.

Commentary

In general

Hearsay statements are intrinsically untrustworthy and unreliable, because they are subject to falsehood, calculation, error and being self-serving, without being readily subject to testing or refutation. The exceptions to the hearsay rule are predicated on certain indicia of reliability and trustworthiness, which, if present, render the statements admissible if there is no other evidence that the statements are untrustworthy or unreliable. These indicia of reliability and trustworthiness are the elements of proof that are required to establish the hearsay exception relied upon. All hearsay exceptions require a showing of trustworthiness.

However, an out-of-court statement that is "testimonial" in nature of a witness in a criminal case who is not available for cross-examination at the proceeding in which the statement is offered against the defendant, violates the Confrontation Clause of the 6th Amendment to the U.S. Constitution, assuming the defendant had no prior opportunity, such as in a pretrial hearing, to examine the witness regarding the statement. *Crawford v. Washington, 541 U.S. 36, 124 S.Ct. 1354 (2004).* All of the ramifications of this significant case are as yet unclear and call into question the admissibility of other Rule 803 exceptions such as excited utterances, statements made for the purpose of medical diagnosis, and others when the declarant is not available for cross-examination in a criminal case. This case may even impact the admissibility of a dying declaration in a criminal case offered against the accused under Rule 804(b)(2). See Mallin, *What Does Crawford v. Washington Mean for*

Future Prosecution, Vol. 34, No. 3, *The Texas Prosecutor* 1 May/June 2004. See also www.tdcaa.com (Crawford Watch). See also, Wilson and Cochran, *Crawford, the Hearsay Rule and the Future,* 32nd Annual Advanced Criminal Law Course, State Bar of Texas, 2005. See also *Davis v. Washington & Indiana v. Hammon, 126 S.Ct. 2266, 547 U.S. 813 (2006)*; *Whorton v. Bockting, 549 U.S. 406 (2007).*

There are twenty-four hearsay exceptions listed in this rule, but some exceptions seem to present more difficulties and problems for attorneys and judges than do others.

Present sense impression (1)

A comment describing or explaining an event or condition made by a declarant at or immediately after perceiving the event is admissible under the rationale that the contemporaneous nature of the statement makes it reliable because there is little time for the declarant to suffer a defect of memory or to calculate misstatements. The farther away the statement is made from the perception by the declarant of the event or condition, the less reliable the statement is, because the declarant has had time to reflect upon the event or condition observed and the facts learned after the event. Thus the statement is no longer "immediately" after the event or condition. See *Rabbani v. State, 847 S.W.2d 555 (Tex. Crim. App. 1992)*; *Kubin v. State, 868 S.W.2d 394, 396–97 (Tex. App.—Houston [1st Dist.] 1993, pet. ref'd)*; *First Southwest Lloyds Ins. Co. v. MacDowell, 769 S.W.2d 954 (Tex. App.—Texarkana 1989, writ denied).*

Excited utterance (2)

The "excited utterance" exception to the hearsay rule is closely related to the "present sense impression" exception. In the case of the "excited utterance," however, the time that has elapsed between the event or condition and the statement made by the declarant is more critical. The critical factor in determining when a statement is an excited utterance "is whether the declarant was still dominated by the emotions, excitement, fear, or pain of the event." *McFarland v. State, 845 S.W.2d 824, 846 (Tex. Crim. App. 1992).* See *Lawton v. State, 913 S.W.2d 542 (Tex. Crim. App. 1995).* See also *Salazar v. State, 38 S.W.3d 141 (Tex. Crim. App. 2001).* A statement that is only a narrative of a past event or condition is not an excited utterance regardless of how soon after the event it is made. "The circumstances must show that it was the event speaking through the person and not the person speaking about the event." *First Southwest Lloyds Ins. Co. v. MacDowell, 769 S.W.2d 954 (Tex. App.—Texarkana 1989, writ denied). Zuliani v. State, 97 S.W.3d 589, slip op. at 11–12 (Tex. Crim. App. 2003)* (statements made by a declarant either in response to questioning or after some time had elapsed, 24 hours in this case, are only two factors in determining whether a statement is an excited utterance; neither factor alone is dispositive). See also *Felix v. Gonzalez, 87 S.W.3d 574, 578 (Tex. App.—San Antonio 2002, no pet. h.).* Excited utterances are not confined to statements describing or explaining the startling event itself. *City of Dallas v. Donovan, 768 S.W.2d 905 (Tex. App.—Dallas 1989, no writ).* The event about which an excited utterance is made need not be the event that produced the excited utterance. *McCarty v. State, 257 S.W.3d 238 (Tex. Crim. App. 2008).* Note: it is difficult to see how this interpretation of Rule 803(2) is going to apply except in the very narrow confines of facts similar to those in this case.

An excited utterance is sometimes referred to as a *res gestae* statement, but that term is incorrect and imprecise because it is often used to define more than an excited utterance within the meaning of Vernon's Ann.Rules Evid., Rule 803(2). *First Southwest Lloyds Ins. Co v. MacDowell, supra.* One of the most common questions that arises in trial about the "excited utterance" exception to the hearsay rule is whether there must be independent proof of the occurrence about which the statement made under its influence relates. "To be admissible as [an excited utterance] a statement must be shown to have been a spontaneous reaction to an exciting event, and there must be independent proof of the occurrence to which the statements relate; the statements themselves cannot be used to prove the exciting event." *Richardson v. Green, 677 S.W.2d 497 (Tex. 1984).* See also *Malone v. Foster, 956 S.W.2d 573 (Tex. App.—Dallas 1997), aff'd 977 S.W.2d 562 (Tex. 1998).*

Statement of then existing mental, emotional, or physical condition (3)

When a person testifies about his mental, emotional or physical condition as it existed at some prior time, he is merely testifying about matters within his personal knowledge, and his testimony is not hearsay. When the witness testifies about what someone else said about their mental, emotional or physical condition at the very time the statement was made, and the statement is offered to prove the then existing condition of the *declarant*, that evidence is admissible as an exception to the hearsay rule.

Testimony about why a person who is *presently testifying* acted or believed as he did on a prior occasion, or whether he acted prudently, wisely or in good faith, is original evidence and not hearsay, even if the witness's reasons are based on what others said. Communications received by a person will often be relevant, not as evidence that the facts are as stated in the communication, but as tending to show the knowledge or belief of the person who received the statement. *Chandler v. Chandler, 842 S.W.2d 829 (Tex. App.—El Paso 1992, writ denied).* See the "perception of the witness" requirement of Vernon's Ann.Rules Evid., Rule 701.

"State of mind" is often cited in trial as an argument for the admissibility of what is actually a statement of memory or belief to the fact remembered or believed. See *Gibbs v. State, 819 S.W.2d 821 (Tex. Crim. App. 1991).* A statement of memory or belief is not admissible for the purpose of proving the fact remembered or believed "unless it relates to the execution, revocation, identification, or terms of declarant's will."

Statements for purposes of medical diagnosis or treatment (4)

If reasonably pertinent to diagnosis or treatment, statements of the type described in this rule are admissible if made by the declarant for the purpose of medical diagnosis or treatment. The statements need not be made to a physician. See *Syndex Corp. v. Dean, 820 S.W.2d 869 (Tex. App.—Austin 1991, writ denied)* (the statement need not have been made to a physician, so long as it is made for the purpose of medical treatment, citing the Advisory Committee's Notes to FED. R. EVID. 803(4)); *Moyer v. State, 948 S.W.2d 525 (Tex. App.—Fort Worth 1997, writ ref'd)* (patient's subjective statements to paramedic as recorded in paramedic's incident report admissible under medical diagnosis exception to hearsay rule).

In the case of a child abuse victim, where the cause of the injury is pertinent to physical or psychological treatment or diagnosis, the statements of the child as to the identity of the abuser are admissible as an exception to the hearsay rule, provided the declarant child understood that the statements were made for the purpose of diagnosis or treatment. *Taylor v. State, 268 S.W.3d 261 (Tex. Crim. App. 2008).* This case provides a good discussion of this rule, including issues of qualification of the person to whom the statements are made, the purposes of diagnosis and treatment, when and to what extent the statements given may be pertinent to diagnosis or treatment, and the identity of the perpetrator.

Recorded recollection (5)

There is a great deal of confusion about the applicability of this rule regarding a past recollection recorded and the use of a writing to refresh a witness's present memory under Vernon's Ann.Rules Evid., Rule 612. See Commentary at Rule 612, *supra*. The contents of a past recollection recorded may be read into evidence if the memorandum or record was made or adopted by the witness *when the matter was still fresh in his memory* concerning matters about which he then had personal knowledge but about which he now has no memory or insufficient memory. If, however, a review of the writing or memorandum refreshes the witness's present memory, he will testify from his memory thus refreshed, and the past recollection recorded would not then be admissible as to the matters about which he now has a present, refreshed memory.

The record or memorandum of a past recollection recorded is itself not admissible into evidence, unless offered by the adverse party.

Records of regularly conducted activity (6) and (7)

Both of these rules encompass what has come to be referred to as the "business records exception" to the hearsay rule.

The most common error made by a proponent of business records evidence is to omit one or more of the elements of proof for admissibility. When that occurs, the opponent of the evidence need only object on hearsay grounds, without pointing out the deficiency in the predicate, or, as is most commonly done, object on the grounds of a lack of a proper predicate. In the latter case, the court may require, on its own or at the request of the proponent, that the opponent state how it is that the predicate is lacking or incomplete. In the former case, the court may sustain the objection, with the proponent left on his own to discern the defect in his offer.

Often, the sponsoring witness for the business records sought to be admitted into evidence became the custodian of the records, or other qualified witness, after the recording of the act, event, condition, opinion, or diagnosis was made in that business record. This is not an impediment to the admission of those records if all the elements of the business record exception are met. The custodian or other qualified witness need not have personal knowledge of the matters recorded. An employee of the business need not have personal knowledge of the matter recorded. The rule only requires, in addition to the remaining elements of the business records exception, that the record be made by, or from information transmitted by, a person who does have personal knowledge of the matter recorded. *Webb v. State, 840 S.W.2d 543 (Tex. App.—Dallas 1992, no pet.)*; *Slaton v. Slaton, 987 S.W.2d 180 (Tex. App.—Houston [14th Dist.] 1999, pet. denied)*.

Documents sent from one business to another business may become the business records of the other business, if that other business takes steps, in the course of its own regularly conducted business activity, to assure itself of the accuracy of the information sent or originating from the first business. *Cockrell v. Republic Mortg. Ins. Co., 817 S.W.2d 106 (Tex. App.—Dallas 1991, no writ)*; *Duncan Dev., Inc. v. Haney, 634 S.W.2d 811 (Tex. 1982)*; *Seaside Indus., Inc. v. Cooper, 766 S.W.2d 566 (Tex. App.—Dallas 1989, no writ)*; *Texon Energy Corp. v. Dow Chem. Co., 733 S.W.2d 328 (Tex. App.—Houston [14th Dist.] 1987, writ ref'd n.r.e.)*; *GT & MC, Inc. v. Texas City Refining, Inc., 822 S.W.2d 252 (Tex. App.—Houston [1st Dist.] 1991, writ denied)*. These cases are narrowly decided and do not establish *carte blanche* admissibility for every entry or document in a business record regardless of its source, the method or circumstances of its preparation, or the mere fact that the entry or document exists in business records. See *Associated Indemnity Corp. v. Dixon, 632 S.W.2d 833 (Tex. App.—Dallas 1982, writ ref'd n.r.e.)*; *Texas Employer's*

Ins. Ass'n v. Sauceda, 636 S.W.2d 494 (Tex. App.—San Antonio 1982, no writ); *Hooper v. Torres, 790 S.W.2d 757 (Tex. App.—El Paso 1990, writ denied)*. See also *Garcia v. State, 126 S.W.3d 921 (Tex. Crim. App. 2004)* (while business records may be admissible, it does not follow that all information, from whatever source or of whatever reliability, contained within those business records is therefore admissible unless that information is independently admissible as shown by the establishment of a proper predicate for its admission). See also *Riddle v. Unifund CCR Partners, 298 S.W.3d 780 (Tex. App.—El Paso 2009)*.

In the case of medical diagnoses, there is no requirement that the diagnoses stated in the record be based on reasonable medical probability. See Comment to this rule, citing *Loper v. Andrews, 404 S.W.2d 300 (Tex. 1966)*. However, if the diagnoses are offered as evidence of causation (e.g., a diagnosed condition of frostbite was caused by a spray medication), an expert opinion must be based on reasonable medical probability, whether the opinion is expressed in testimony or in a medical record. *Burroughs Wellcome Co. v. Crye, 907 S.W.2d 497 (Tex. 1995)*. Note, too, that a diagnosis is an expert medical opinion and is, therefore, subject to the requirements of *Kelly, Robinson, Hartman, and Merrell Dow*. See Commentary to Rule 702. See also *Burroughs Wellcome Co. v. Crye, supra*. There is a clear distinction between the diagnosis of a medical condition and the cause in fact of that condition. Diagnosis and causation are not the same thing.

The requirements of Vernon's Ann.Rules Evid., Rule 803(6) must be satisfied before evidence that a matter is not included in a business record is admissible to prove the nonoccurrence or nonexistence of the matter. The matter referred to must be of the kind that would have been in the business record had the matter existed or occurred. *Coleman v. United Savs. Ass'n of Tex., 846 S.W.2d 128 (Tex. App.—Fort Worth 1993, no writ)*. See Shainberg, *Objecting to Computer Generated Business Records*, 25th Annual Advanced Family Law Course, State Bar of Texas 1999.

Public records and reports (8)

The records and reports referred to must be those of a public office or agency. They must refer to the activities of the office or agency, to matters recorded which were both observed pursuant to a duty imposed by law and which observations were required to be reported, or to matters recorded that resulted from an investigation made pursuant to authority granted by law. Observations by law enforcement personnel and recorded in the records or reports of a public office or agency are excluded in *criminal cases*.

Even in criminal cases, the observations made by law enforcement personnel and recorded in the records or reports of a public office or agency may be admissible when the matters recorded are routine business matters as opposed to observations at the scene of a crime. *Pondexter v. State, 942 S.W.2d 577 (Tex. Crim. App. 1996)* (police officer was performing his ordinary, routine duties recording the property taken in and out of the property room; his observations and notations were presumed reliable). *Garcia v. State, 868 S.W.2d 337 (Tex. Crim. App. 1993)* (medical examiners not considered "other law enforcement personnel" for purposes of exclusion under public records hearsay exception; thus, autopsy reports are admissible under hearsay exception for public records). Documents not admissible under rule 803(8)(B) are not admissible under rule 803(6) (business records). *Cole v. State, 839 S.W.2d 798 (Tex. Crim. App. 1990)*.

Ordinarily, a proper predicate for the admissibility of otherwise hearsay evidence includes the indicia of reliability and trustworthiness necessary for admissibility. However, any offer of evidence may attacked as not being reliable or trustworthy despite the existence of a proper predicate. Trustworthiness and reliability are preliminary matters for the trial court to consider when those issues are timely raised. Vernon's Ann.Rules Evid., Rule 104(a). If the evidence is admitted, issues of reliability and trustworthiness are for the trier of fact to resolve. Rule 803(8) states the obvious when providing that public records and reports are an exception to the hearsay rule, and thus admissible "unless the sources of information or other circumstances indicate lack of trustworthiness."

Records of vital statistics (9)

The term "vital statistics" is limited by the rule to records and data compilations of births, fetal deaths, deaths, or marriages. The rule requires as a predicate that the records be made from reports made to a public office pursuant to the requirements of law.

Absence of a public record or entry (10)

The requirements of this rule must be satisfied before evidence that a matter is not included in a public record or entry is admissible to prove the nonoccurrence or nonexistence of the matter. That is, it must be established that the record or entry was regularly made and was also preserved by a public office. The rule does not require that the making of the record or its preservation be pursuant to or required by law. The matter referred to must be of the kind that would have been in the public record had the matter existed or occurred. See *Coleman v. United Savs. Ass'n of Tex., 846 S.W.2d 128 (Tex. App.—Fort Worth 1993, no writ)* (relating to the absence of an entry in a business record under Rule 803(7)).

Records of religious organizations (11)

The records referred to must have been regularly kept, presumably in the regular course of business of a religious organization. This rule does not require all of the predicate elements required for the records of an organized business activity as provided in rule 803(6), but their absence could establish questions of trustworthiness and reliability, if raised. This rule makes no provision for proof of the absence of a record of a religious organization.

Marriage, baptismal and similar certificates (12)

A certification by a person made at or a reasonable time after he performed a marriage or other ceremony, or administered a sacrament, such as a baptism, is proof that the person did perform the ceremony or administered the sacrament as certified. The certificate must be made by a member of the clergy, a public official, or other person "authorized by the rules or practices of a religious organization or by law to perform the act certified." Presumably, a public official must be authorized by law to perform the act certified.

Family records (13)

The major problem that will confront the proponent of this kind of evidence is establishing the authenticity of the record. This rule has no requirement that the person who purportedly recorded the statement of fact, or who made the statement of fact to another who recorded it, and which is offered into evidence, had personal knowledge of the fact stated. The statement of fact refers only to matters of family or personal history.

Records of documents affecting an interest in property (14)

This rule pertains only to the record of a public office of a document actually recorded in a public office which is authorized by statute to record documents of that kind. Thus, the record is proof of the contents of the original document. It is also proof of the execution and the delivery of the original document. See Vernon's Ann.Rules Evid., Rule 1003 and Commentary to Rule 1003, *infra.*

Statements in documents affecting an interest in property (15)

If any statement in a document purports to establish or affect an interest in property, and that statement of interest is relevant to the purpose of the document, that statement is admissible over a hearsay objection, if the property has not been subsequently dealt with in a manner inconsistent with the statement or the "purport of the document." Of course, neither this rule, nor any other of the rules regarding the admissibility of hearsay evidence, abrogates the requirements of relevancy, competency, or materiality of the hearsay statements. See *Madden v. State, 799 S.W.2d 683 (Tex. Crim. App. 1990)* (handwritten list of murder victim's weapons and corresponding serial numbers, which was identified has having been written by the victim and found after the murder in a box among victim's personal papers was admissible as statement affecting interest in property, even though it was not legally executed document such as mortgage). *Note:* It is unclear from the opinion in *Madden* if the list was even signed by the victim, much less executed in the manner of a mortgage. See also *Harris v. State, 846 S.W.2d 960 (Tex. App.—Houston [1st Dist.] 1993, writ ref'd)* (manufacturer's certificate of origin of motor vehicle was admissible as statement in document affecting interest in car dealership's property where certificate established car dealer's interest in vehicle and certificate proved vehicle's identification number).

Statements in ancient documents (16)

The document must have been in existence twenty years or more and it must shown that the document is what it purports to be. *Kamel v. Kamel, 760 S.W.2d 677 (Tex. App.—Tyler 1988, writ denied)* (will 23 years old at time of trial and which was properly authenticated was admissible under ancient documents exception to hearsay rule). The age of the document must be proved from a source other than the document itself. *Graff v. Whittle, 947 S.W.2d 629 (Tex. App.—Texarkana 1997, pet. denied)* (the document cannot proved by accepting the date on the document as its actual age; age should be established by proper predicate outside the document).

Market reports and commercial publications (17)

This rule permits the admission of certain objective data. It does not pertain to subjective matters such as the results of surveys or polls. See *New Braunfels Market Outlet Ctr. v. IHOP Realty Corp., 872 S.W.2d 303 (Tex. App.—Austin 1994, n.w.h.).*

Learned treatises (18)

An expert may be supported in his direct testimony by statements contained in published treatises, periodicals, scientific journals and the like that are called to his attention or that were relied upon by him in rendering his opinion, if those statements are recognized by him as reliable authority, or are established as reliable authority by other expert testimony or by judicial notice. See Vernon's Ann.Rules Evid., Rule 705. An expert may be impeached by asking him whether he agrees or disagrees with particular statements brought to the witness's attention that are contained in treatises, scientific journals or other publications. Such cross-examination, however, is limited to publications which the witness recognizes as authoritative or which have been established as authoritative by other evidence or by judicial notice. *Carter v. Steere Tank Lines, Inc., 835 S.W.2d 176 (Tex. App.—Amarillo 1992, writ denied).* Note that the rule requires that the material actually be published. Even if all the elements of this rule are established, the publication itself is not admissible into evidence, although the statements may be read into evidence. The same kind of treatment is given to depositions and for the same reason: the testimony is to be recalled by the jury, not taken into the jury room. See Vernon's Ann.Rules Civ.Proc., Rule 281.

Statements from the kinds of publications to which this rule refers are admissible only in conjunction with testimony by an expert witness and only for the purposes to which the rule refers. The statements are not independently admissible. *Carlisle v. Philip Morris, Inc., 805 S.W.2d 498 (Tex. App.—Austin 1991, writ denied).*

Reputation concerning personal or family history (19)

The reputed history of a family or any of its members, may be established by a family member, a close associate of a family or any of its members, or by a member of the community, as that reputation relates to the family matters set out in the rule. See *Jones v. State, 950 S.W.2d 386 (Tex. App.—Fort Worth 1997, pet. ref'd)* (witness qualified to give hearsay testimony that capital murder victim was four years old at time of his death, where witness had lived with victim from two to three years, victim was close friend of victim's family for three years, witness testified that he had known victim for three of four years victim was alive, and victim was unavailable as witness). *Note:* The fact that the victim was unavailable as a witness is not a proper factor in the analysis of any section of Rule 803. The rule states in its title that the availability of the declarant is immaterial, and it further provides that the exceptions apply even though the declarant is available as a witness.

Reputation concerning boundaries or general history (20)

The reputation sought to be established in reliance on this rule must be shown to have been in existence before the dispute at trial arose. That reputation must concern only boundaries, customs which affect land in the community and events of general history important to the community, state or nation in which the community is located. See *Roberts v. Allison, 836 S.W.2d 185 (Tex. App.—Tyler 1992, writ denied)* (neighbor's testimony of claimed oral agreement between his grandfather and landowner's predecessor in title granting easement to neighbor's family over road located on landowner's property does not fall "within exception to hearsay rule for evidence of reputation in community concerning boundaries of land in community; there was no contention of community's interest in or knowledge of claim, no contention of existence of general reputation in community concerning alleged right of access, and no proof of recognized vehicles of reputation concerning alleged easement").

Reputation as to character (21)

Although reputation as to character is an exception to the rule against hearsay, the admissibility of character reputation evidence is governed by Vernon's Ann. Rules Evid., Rules 404, 405 and 608.

Judgment of previous conviction (22)

A judgment of conviction for a *felony* on a plea of *nolo contendere* is inadmissible, as hearsay, to prove any fact in a civil case that was essential to sustain the judgment of conviction in a criminal case. In criminal cases the judgment of conviction of a defendant is admissible to prove a fact against that defendant in the present case which was essential to sustain the judgment of conviction in the prior case, whether on a plea of *nolo contendere* or not. The use of judgments of prior convictions for the purpose of impeaching any witness is governed by Vernon's Ann.Rules Evid., Rule 609. A judgment of conviction that is on appeal is inadmissible for either purpose.

Judgment as to personal, family, or general history, or boundaries (23)

Judgments of a court are admissible for many purposes, including proving the existence of the facts necessary to support the judgment. This rule provides that findings essential to support the judgment which relate matters of personal, family or general history, or boundaries are admissible as an exception to the hearsay rule if those same facts could be proved by reputation evidence.

Statement against interest (24)

A statement which is so against one's pecuniary, social or penal interests that he would not have made the statement if were not true is sufficiently trustworthy for admission into evidence as an exception to the hearsay rule. *Robinson v. Harkins & Co., 711 S.W.2d 619 (Tex. 1986).* Such a statement against interest is admissible against the *declarant*, of course, and may be admissible against a party who is not the declarant. See *Holder v. Mellon Mortg. Co., 954 S.W.2d 786 (Tex. App.—Houston [14th Dist.] 1997, rev'd on other grounds, 5 S.W.3d 654 (Tex. 1999).* When admitted against the declarant in a civil case, the statement need not be corroborated by other evidence or corroborating circumstances outside the statement, but if the statement is admitted against a party not the declarant, it would appear that corroboration is required. See *Holder, Id.*

In criminal cases, the criteria for admissibility of a statement against interest against a defendant who is *not* the declarant are: (1) the inculpatory parts of the statement as to the defendant also inculpate the declarant; (2) there is a high degree of independent corroboration of the statement as it relates to both the declarant and the defendant; and (3) the statement is not being offered at the joint trial of the declarant and another as defendants. See *Bingham v. State, 987 S.W.2d 54 (Tex. Crim. App. 1999).* See also *Cofield v. State, 891 S.W.2d 952 (Tex. Crim. App. 1994)*; *Williamson v. United States, 512 U.S. 594, 114 S.Ct. 2431, 129 L.Ed.2d 476 (1994)*; *Lee v. Illinois, 476 U.S. 530, 545, 106 S.Ct. 2056, 90 L.Ed.2d 514 (1986)*; *Bruton v. United States, 391 U.S. 123, 88 S.Ct.1620, 20 L.Ed.2d 476 (1968)*; *Gray v. Maryland, 523 U.S. 185, 118 S.Ct. 1151, 140 L.Ed.2d 294 (1998).* This is an area of evidence law that deals with very complex concepts of constitutional magnitude. See *Lilly v. Virginia, 527 U.S. 116, 119 S.Ct. 1887, 144 L.Ed.2d 117 (1999).* Only statements that are directly against a speaker's penal interest (including "blame-sharing" statements) are admissible under this rule; self-exculpatory statements that merely shift blame to another are not sufficiently against the speaker's interest to qualify for admission against a non-declarant co-defendant at his trial. *Walter v. State, 267 S.W.3d 883 (Tex. Crim. App. 2008).*

The rule provides that, in criminal cases, the statement is not admissible against the declarant as proof of the matters contained in the statement "unless corroborating circumstances clearly indicate the trustworthiness of the statement."

Official Comment to former Rule 803(6)

The comment to former Rule 803(6) of the Rules of Civil Evidence and the Rules of Criminal Evidence provided in pertinent part as follows: "This provision rejects the doctrine of Loper v. Andrews, 404 S.W.2d 300, 305 (Tex. 1966), which required that an entry of a medical opinion or diagnosis meet a test of 'reasonable medical certainty.' "

Uniform Rules of Evidence

For text of corresponding provisions of Uniform Rules of Evidence and notes of decisions relating thereto, which may provide guidance in interpreting the Texas Rule, see Rule 803, 13B Uniform Laws Annotated.

Federal Rules of Evidence

The corresponding provision of the Federal Rules of Evidence is Rule 803. For the text of the Rule and Advisory Committee Notes, which may provide guidance in interpreting the Texas Rule, see the Appendix to this volume.

Websites

www.tdcaa.com

Leading Cases

Crawford v. Washington, 541 U.S. 36, 124 S.Ct. 1354 (2004) (out-of-court statements of a declarant other than a defendant and which are testimonial in nature are inadmissible against the defendant at his trial, unless the declarant is unavailable to testify and the accused had a prior opportunity to cross-exam the declarant regarding those out-of-court statements).

Davis v. Washington & Indiana v. Hammon, 547 U.S. 813 (2006) (answers to questions by law enforcement agents [911 operator] to ascertain the nature of an emergency not testimonial (*Davis v. Washington*); answers to questions by law enforcement agents [a police officer] to ascertain the facts of an event implicating a defendant are testimonial and implicate *Washington v. Crawford, 541 U.S. 36, 124 S.Ct. 1354 (2004).* Note: *Davis* and *Hammon* were decided in the same opinion and are cited as one opinion.

De La Paz v. State, 273 S.W.3d 671(Tex. Crim. App. 2008) ("Generally speaking a hearsay statement is 'testimonial' when the surrounding circumstances objectively indicate that the primary purpose of the interview or interrogation is to establish or prove past events potentially relevant to later criminal prosecution"; after an objection to the admission of such hearsay evidence on confrontation grounds, the State has the burden of establishing the unavailability of the declarant and the defendant's prior opportunity to cross-exam the declarant regarding the declarant's hearsay statements.).

Melendez-Diaz v. Massachusetts, 557 U.S. 305 (2009) (affidavits of laboratory technicians were testimonial in that they served the function of in-court testimony, were made for the purpose of establishing a fact relevant to the case against the defendant, and were made under circumstance indicating that the affiant-declarants would believe that their affidavits would be available for use at a future trial; the laboratory technicians were not unavailable for trial and there was no showing that the defendant had a prior opportunity to cross-exam them on the statements they made in their affidavits; whether records of a regularly conducted activity or records of a government entity, the affidavits admitted were not an exception to the confrontation rights of the defendant over his objection on that ground; a defendant can forfeit his confrontation rights before trial). See TEX. CODE CRIM. PROC. ANN. (Vernon 2009) art. 38.41, § 4, and Rule 902(10) of the Texas Rules of Evidence; See also *Cuadros-Fernandez v. State, 316 S.W.3d 645 (Tex. App.—Dallas 2009, no pet h.) (August 28, 2009)*(cites and discusses *Melendez-Diaz* to reverse on confrontation grounds the admission of DNA laboratory results offered by the State as a business record). *Bullcoming v. New Mexico, 564 U.S. ___, 131 S.Ct. 2705, 180 L.Ed. 2d 610 (2011).*

Michigan v. Bryant, 562 U.S. ___, 131 S.Ct. 1143 (2011) (statements by officers identifying a deceased victim and the victim's description and location of his shooter are not testimonial when their primary purpose is to enable police to meet an ongoing emergency).

State v. Sanchez, 354 S.W.3d 476 (Tex. Crim. App. 2011) (pretrial hearing pursuant to Code of Criminal Procedure article 38.072 § 2(b)(2) is to determine reliability of complainant's out-of-court statement (commonly referred to as "outcry"), and therefore the defendant's opportunity cross examination of the outcry witness at the hearing is inadequate to allow the admission of the hearing testimony at trial).

Wall v. State, 184 S.W.3d 730 (Tex. Crim. App. 2006) (broadest definition of "testimonial" under *Crawford* [Washington v. Crawford, 541 U.S. 36, 124 S.Ct. 1354 (2004)] adopted in Texas criminal jurisprudence, rejecting the notion that all excited utterances under evidence rule 803(2) are non-testimonial).

Leading CLE/Law Review Publications

Morales, *Social Media Evidence: "What You Post or Tweet Can and Will Be Used Against You in a Court of Law"*, 60 *The Advocate* 32, State Bar of Texas Litigation Section Report (Fall 2012).

Paddock, *Utilizing E–Mail as Business Records Under the Texas Rules of Evidence*, 19 Rev. Litig. 61 (2000).

Phillips, *Health Care Providers' Roles after Crawford, Davis, and Hammon*, The Prosecutor, Vol. 40, No. 5 (September/October 2006).

Integrated Legal Research System References

West's Texas Digest Key Numbers

Criminal Law ⚷419.

Evidence ⚷317–337.

Texas Practice

Addison, Texas Practice Guide, Evidence § 8:122 et seq.

Texas Jur 3d

24 Texas Jur 3d, Criminal Law § 3104 et seq.

35 Texas Jur 3d, Evidence § 219 et seq.

Am Jur Trials

Facebook, MySpace, LinkedIn, Twitter, and Other Social Media in Trials, 122 Am Jur Trials 421.

Am Jur Proof of Facts

Establishing Foundation to Admit Computer Generated Evidence as Demonstrative or Substantive Evidence, 57 Am Jur Proof of Facts 3d 455.

Annotations

Admissibility, as against hearsay objection, of report of tests or experiments carried out by independent third party, 19 ALR3d 1008.

Admissibility, as against interest, in criminal case of declaration of commission of criminal act, 92 ALR3d 1164.

Admissibility, as against interest, in civil case of declaration of commission of criminal act, 90 ALR3d 1173.

Admissibility, as res gestae, of accusatory utterances made by homicide victim before the act, 74 ALR3d 963.

Admissibility, as part of res gestae, of spontaneous utterances of unidentified bystander testified to by an interested party, 50 ALR3d 716.

Admissibility in evidence of composite picture or sketch produced by police to identify offender, 23 ALR5th 672.

Admissibility in evidence of professional directories, 7 ALR4th 638.

Admissibility in state court proceedings of police reports under official record exception to hearsay rule, 112 ALR5th 62.

Admissibility of ancient documents as hearsay exception under Rule 803(16) of the Uniform Rules of Evidence, 63 ALR5th 331.

Admissibility of evidence of declarant's then existing mental, emotional, or physical condition under Rule 803(3) of the Uniform Rules of Evidence and similar formulations, 57 ALR5th 141.

Admissibility of evidence of reputation as to land boundaries or customs affecting land, under Rule 803(20) of Uniform Rules of Evidence and similar formulations, 79 ALR4th 1044.

Admissibility of school records under hearsay exceptions, 57 ALR4th 1111.

Admissibility of statements made for purposes of medical diagnosis or treatment as hearsay exception under Rule 803(4) of the Uniform Rules of Evidence, 38 ALR5th 433.

Admissibility of testimony regarding spontaneous declarations made by one incompetent to testify at trial, 15 ALR4th 1043.

Admissibility, under public records exception to hearsay rule, of record kept by public official without express statutory direction or authorization, 80 ALR3d 414.

Admissibility under business entry statutes of hospital records in criminal case, 69 ALR3d 22.

Admissibility of physician's testimony as to patient's statements or declarations, other than res gestae, during medical examination, 37 ALR3d 778.

Admissibility in civil action of electroencephalogram, electrocardiogram, or other record made by instrument used in medical test, or of report based upon such test, 66 ALR2d 536.

Admissibility, on issue of child's legitimacy or parentage, of declarations of parents, relatives, or the child, deceased or unavailable, 31 ALR2d 989.

Admissibility, under Rule 803(8)(C) of Federal Rules of Evidence, of "factual findings resulting from investigation made pursuant to authority granted by law," 180 ALR Fed 61.

Admissibility under Rules 804(b)(1) and 807 of Federal Rules of Evidence (Fed. Rules Evid. Rules 804(b)(1) and 807, 28 U.S.C.A.) of Grand Jury Testimony of Unavailable Witness, 149 ALR Fed 231.

Admissibility and weight of consumer survey in litigation under trademark opposition, trademark infringement, and false designation of origin provisions of Lanham Act, 98 ALR Fed 20.

Admissibility of depositions under Federal Rule of Evidence 804(b)(1), 84 ALR Fed 668.

Admissibility, under Rule 803(10) of Federal Rules of Evidence, of evidence of absence of public record or entry, 70 ALR Fed 198.

Admissibility of records other than police reports, under Rule 803(6), Federal Rules of Evidence, providing for business records exception to hearsay rule, 61 ALR Fed 359.

Admissibility, over hearsay objection, of police observations and investigative findings offered by government in criminal prosecution, excluded from public records exception to hearsay rule under Rule 803(8)(B) or (C), Federal Rules of Evidence, 56 ALR Fed 168.

Admissibility of statements made for purposes of medical diagnosis or treatment as hearsay exception under Rule 803(4) of the Federal Rules of Evidence, 55 ALR Fed 689.

Admissibility of statement under Rule 803(5) of Federal Rules of Evidence, providing for recorded-recollection exception to hearsay rule, 35 ALR Fed 605.

Business records: authentication and verification of bills and invoices under Rule 803(6) of the Uniform Rules of Evidence, 1 ALR4th 316.

Construction and application of Uniform Rule of Evidence 803(17), providing hearsay exception for market reports, and commercial publications, 54 ALR6th 593.

Construction and application of provision of Rule 803(8)(B), Federal Rules of Evidence, excluding from exception to hearsay rule in criminal cases matters observed by law enforcement officers, 37 ALR Fed 831.

Evidence: admissibility of memorandum of telephone conversation, 94 ALR3d 975.

Exception to hearsay rule, under Rule 803(11) or Rule 803(12) of Federal Rules of Evidence, with respect to information contained in records of religious organization, 78 ALR Fed 361.

Exception to hearsay rule, under Rule 803(3) of Federal Rules of Evidence, with respect to statement of declarant's mental, emotional, or physical condition, 75 ALR Fed 170.

Letters to or from customers or suppliers as business records under statutes authorizing reception of business records in evidence, 68 ALR3d 1069.

Necessity, in criminal prosecution, of independent evidence of principal act to allow admission, under res gestae or excited utterance exception to hearsay rule, of statement made at time of, or subsequent to, principal act, 38 ALR4th 1237.

Treatises, periodicals, or pamphlets as exception to hearsay rule under Rule 803 (18) of the Federal Rules of Evidence, 64 ALR Fed 971.

What constitutes statement against interest admissible under Rule 804(b)(3) of Federal Rules of Evidence, 34 ALR Fed 412.

When do corroborating circumstances clearly indicate trustworthiness of hearsay statement tending to expose declarant to criminal liability and offered to exculpate accused, so as to permit admission of statement under Rule 804(b)(3) of Federal Rules of Evidence, 125 ALR Fed 477.

When is hearsay statement "present sense impression" admissible under Rule 803(1) of Federal Rules of Evidence, 165 ALR Fed 491.

When is hearsay statement "excited utterance" admissible under Rule 803(2) of Federal Rules of Evidence, 155 ALR Fed 583.

Rule 804. Hearsay Exceptions; Declarant Unavailable

(a) Definition of Unavailability. "Unavailability as a witness" includes situations in which the declarant:

(1) is exempted by ruling of the court on the ground of privilege from testifying concerning the subject matter of the declarant's statement;

(2) persists in refusing to testify concerning the subject matter of the declarant's statement despite an order of the court to do so;

(3) testifies to a lack of memory of the subject matter of the declarant's statement;

(4) is unable to be present or to testify at the hearing because of death or then existing physical or mental illness or infirmity; or

(5) is absent from the hearing and the proponent of the declarant's statement has been unable to procure the declarant's attendance or testimony by process or other reasonable means.

A declarant is not unavailable as a witness if the declarant's exemption, refusal, claim of lack of memory, inability, or absence is due to the procurement or wrong-doing of the proponent of the declarant's statement for the purpose of preventing the witness from attending or testifying.

(b) Hearsay Exceptions. The following are not excluded if the declarant is unavailable as a witness:

(1) *Former testimony.* In civil cases, testimony given as a witness at another hearing of the same or a different proceeding, or in a deposition taken in the course of another proceeding, if the party against whom the testimony is now offered, or a person with a similar interest, had an opportunity and similar motive to develop the testimony by direct, cross, or redirect examination. In criminal cases, testimony given as a witness at another hearing of the same or a different proceeding, if the party against whom the testimony is now offered had an opportunity and similar motive to develop the testimony by direct, cross, or redirect examination. In criminal cases the use of depositions is controlled by Chapter 39 of the Code of Criminal Procedure.

(2) *Dying declarations.* A statement made by a declarant while believing that the declarant's death was imminent, concerning the cause or circumstances of what the declarant believed to be impending death.

(3) *Statement of personal or family history.*

(A) A statement concerning the declarant's own birth, adoption, marriage, divorce, legitimacy, relationship by blood, adoption, or marriage, ancestry, or other similar fact of personal or family history even though declarant had no means of acquiring personal knowledge of the matter stated; or

(B) A statement concerning the foregoing matters, and death also, of another person, if the declarant was related to the other by blood, adoption, or marriage or was so intimately associated with the other's family as to be likely to have accurate information concerning the matter declared.

Eff. March 1, 1998.

Cross References

Testimony of Child Who is Victim of Offense, Vernon's Ann.C.C.P. Art. 38.071.

Commentary

In general

In order for any of the three hearsay exceptions listed in this rule to apply, the declarant must be unavailable to testify in the present trial or hearing for one or more of the reasons listed in this rule. "Unavailability" is a matter of proof for the proponent of the former testimony, dying declaration, or statement of personal or family history.

Former testimony

The party against whom the former testimony of a presently unavailable witness is now offered, or a person of similar interest as that party, must have had an opportunity to question the witness at the time of the prior testimony, and for the same or similar reason as he does now, before the former testimony is admissible against that party.

Dying declarations

There is no requirement that the declarant actually be dead when his statement concerning the cause or circumstances of what he believes to be his impending death is offered as a dying declaration, only that when he made the statement he believed his death to be imminent. But if not dead, the declarant must be otherwise unavailable.

Statement of personal or family history

Even in the absence of personal knowledge of the matter, a declarant's statement as to his own family history, or the family history of another to whom he is either related by blood, marriage or adoption or with whom he is intimately associated, is admissible as evidence of the matter declared, if the declarant is shown by the proponent of the evidence to be unavailable to testify at the trial or hearing for one or more of the reasons listed in this rule.

Official Comment to former Civil Rule 804

The comment to former Rule 804 of the Rules of Civil Evidence provided in pertinent part as follows: "A deposition in some circumstances may be admissible without regard to unavailability of the deponent. See Rule 801(e)(3) ... and Vernon's Ann.Rules Civ.Proc., Rule 207."

Uniform Rules of Evidence

For text of corresponding provisions of Uniform Rules of Evidence and notes of decisions relating thereto, which may provide guidance in interpreting the Texas Rule, see Rule 804, 13B Uniform Laws Annotated.

Federal Rules of Evidence

The corresponding provision of the Federal Rules of Evidence is Rule 804. For the text of the Rule and Advisory Committee Notes, which may provide guidance in interpreting the Texas Rule, see the Appendix to this volume.

Leading Cases

Coffin v. State, 885 S.W.2d 140 (Tex. Crim. App. 1994) (there is no requirement that, in order for prior testimony to be admitted as an exception to the hearsay rule, the opponent of the evidence had to have an identical motive to challenge the testimony at the prior proceeding as he now has at trial, but only a similar motive).

Keene Corp. v. Rogers, 863 S.W.2d 168 (Tex. App.—Texarkana 1993, no writ) (to use former testimony, the proponent must show (1) that the party against whom the testimony is offered, or a person with a similar interest, had an opportunity and similar motive to cross-examine the witness and (2) that the declarant is unavailable to testify in the case in which a party attempts to offer his testimony; mere comments by an attorney are not sufficient proof of a declarant's unavailability).

Owens–Corning Fiberglas Corp. v. Wasiak, 917 S.W.2d 883 (Tex. App.—Austin 1996, writ granted) affd. 972 S.W.2d 35 (Tex. 1998) (in order for transcribed testimony from another proceeding to be admissible, the proponent of the evidence must show that the declarant is unavailable).

Valle v. State, 109 S.W.3d 500 (Tex. Crim. App. 2003) (testimony of an unavailable witness regarding another's problems while incarcerated, history of abuse, prior good behavior and the like is not admissible as a statement of personal or family history).

Integrated Legal Research System References

West's Texas Digest Key Numbers

Criminal Law ⚷419.

Evidence ⚷272, 285–297, 317, 575–583.

Texas Practice

Addison, Texas Practice Guide, Evidence § 8:250 et seq.

Texas Jur 3d

24A Texas Jur 3d, Criminal Law §§ 3541 et seq.

35 Texas Jur 3d, Evidence §§ 221, 228, 245 et seq., 272 et seq.

Annotations

Admissibility of depositions under Federal Evidence Rule 804(b)(1), 84 ALR Fed 668.

Admissibility of dying declaration in civil case, 47 ALR2d 526.

Admissibility of statement made to government agent by unavailable witness, under Rule 804(b)(5) of Federal Rules of Evidence, providing for admissibility of hearsay statement not covered by any specific exception but having equivalent circumstantial guaranties of trustworthiness, 61 ALR Fed 915.

Admissibility of tape recording or transcript of "911" emergency telephone call, 3 ALR5th 784.

Admissibility under Rules 804(b)(1) and 807 of Federal Rules of Evidence (FED. RULES EVID. 804(b)(1) and 807, 28 U.S.C.A.) of grand jury testimony of unavailable witness, 149 ALR Fed 231.

Denial of recollection as inconsistent with prior statement so as to render statement admissible, 99 ALR3d 934.

Opinion of doctor or other attendant as to declarant's consciousness of imminent death so as to qualify his statement as dying declaration, 48 ALR2d 733.

Statements of declarant as sufficiently showing consciousness of impending death to justify admission of dying declaration, 53 ALR3d 785.

Sufficiency of showing of consciousness of impending death, by circumstances other than statements of declarant, to justify admission of dying declaration, 53 ALR3d 1196.

What constitutes similar motive for purposes of Rule 804(b)(1) of Federal Rules of Evidence, excepting such testimony from hearsay rule if party against whom evidence is offered had opportunity and "similar motive" to develop testimony, 138 ALR Fed 367.

What constitutes statement against interest admissible under Rule 804(b)(3) of Federal Rules of Evidence, 34 ALR Fed 412.

When do corroborating circumstances clearly indicate trustworthiness of hearsay statement tending to expose declarant to criminal liability and offered to exculpate accused, so as to permit admission of statement under Rule 804(b)(3) of Federal Rules of Evidence (28 USCA Appx), 125 ALR Fed 477.

Who is "predecessor in interest" for purposes of Rule 804(b)(1) of Federal Rules of Evidence, 47 ALR Fed 895.

Witness' refusal to testify on ground of self-incrimination as justifying reception of evidence of prior statements or admissions, 43 ALR3d 1413.

Rule 805. Hearsay Within Hearsay

Hearsay included within hearsay is not excluded under the hearsay rule if each part of the combined statements conforms with an exception to the hearsay rule provided in these rules.

Eff. March 1, 1998.

Commentary

Uniform Rules of Evidence

For text of corresponding provisions of Uniform Rules of Evidence and notes of decisions relating thereto, which may provide guidance in interpreting the Texas Rule, see Rule 805, 13B Uniform Laws Annotated.

Federal Rules of Evidence

The corresponding provision of the Federal Rules of Evidence is Rule 805. For the text of the Rule and Advisory Committee Notes, which may provide guidance in interpreting the Texas Rule, see the Appendix to this volume.

Integrated Legal Research System References

West's Texas Digest Key Numbers

Criminal Law ⚷419.

Evidence ⚷314.

Texas Practice

Addison, Texas Practice Guide, Evidence § 8:285 et seq.

Texas Jur 3d

35 Texas Jur 3d, Evidence § 219.

Rule 806. Attacking and Supporting Credibility of Declarant

When a hearsay statement, or a statement defined in Rule 801(e)(2)(C), (D), or (E), or in civil cases a statement defined in Rule 801(e)(3), has been admitted in evidence, the credibility of the declarant may be attacked, and if attacked may be supported by any evidence which would be admissible for those purposes if declarant had testified as a witness. Evidence of a statement or conduct by the declarant at any time, offered to impeach the declarant, is not subject to any requirement that the declarant may have been afforded an opportunity to deny or explain. If the party against whom a hearsay statement has been admitted calls the declarant as a witness, the party is entitled to examine the declarant on the statement as if under cross-examination.

Eff. March 1, 1998.

Commentary

In general

The declarant of any hearsay statement, or of any out of court statement made by another and attributable to a party as an admission, may be impeached (and if impeached, rehabilitated) as any witness may be under these rules. The declarant may be called as a witness for the purpose of cross-examination by the party against whom the statement was admitted. See *Appling v. State, 904 S.W.2d 912 (Tex. App.—Corpus Christi 1995, writ ref'd).*

Uniform Rules of Evidence

For text of corresponding provisions of Uniform Rules of Evidence and notes of decisions relating thereto, which may provide guidance in interpreting the Texas Rule, see Rule 806, 13B Uniform Laws Annotated.

Federal Rules of Evidence

The corresponding provision of the Federal Rules of Evidence is Rule 806. For the text of the Rule and Advisory Committee Notes, which may provide guidance in interpreting the Texas Rule, see the Appendix to this volume.

Integrated Legal Research System References

West's Texas Digest Key Numbers

Witnesses ⚷333, 363, 380, 398.

Texas Practice

Addison, Texas Practice Guide, Evidence § 8:293 et seq.

Texas Jur 3d

35 Texas Jur 3d, Evidence § 219.

ARTICLE IX. AUTHENTICATION AND IDENTIFICATION

Rule
901. Requirement of Authentication or Identification.
902. Self–Authentication.
903. Subscribing Witness' Testimony Unnecessary.

Cross References

Evidence of Handwriting, Vernon's Ann.C.C.P. Art. 38.27.

Integrated Legal Research System References

West's Texas Digest Key Numbers

Evidence ⚷35–183.5.

Texas Jur 3d

24A Texas Jur 3d, Criminal Law § 3655 et seq.

36 Texas Jur 3d, Evidence §§ 362–370, 371 et seq.

Texas Forms

7 Texas Pl & Pr Forms, Evidence & Witnesses §§ 111:28–111:30, 111:37–111:38.

Am Jur Trials

Audio Recordings: Evidence, Experts, and Technology, 48 Am Jur Trials 1.

Facebook, MySpace, LinkedIn, Twitter, and Other Social Media in Trials, 122 Am Jur Trials 421.

Preparing and Using Photographs in Civil Cases, 3 Am Jur Trials 1.

Voicegram Identification Evidence, 54 Am Jur Trials 1.

Am Jur Proof of Facts

Admissibility of Computerized Business Records, 14 Am Jur Proof of Facts 2d 173.

Ancient Documents, 50 Am Jur Proof of Facts 2d 321.

Criminal Pretrial Involving Text Messaging Evidence, 116 Am Jur Proof of Facts 3d 345.

The Dating of Handwriting Through Ink Analysis, 35 Am Jur Proof of Facts 3d 567.

The Effects of Alterations to Documents, 29 Am Jur Proof of Facts 3d 549.

Examination and Identification of Photocopies and Photocopiers, 23 Am Jur Proof of Facts 3d 621.

Foundation for Admissibility of Hospital Records and X–Rays, 38 Am Jur Proof of Facts 2d 145.

Foundation for Admission of Secondary Evidence, 35 Am Jur Proof of Facts 2d 147.

Foundation for Audio Recordings as Evidence, 23 Am Jur Proof of Facts 3d 315.

Foundation for Offering Business Records in Evidence, 34 Am Jur Proof of Facts 2d 509.

Identification of Handprinting and Numerals, 24 Am Jur Proof of Facts 3d 667.

Rule 901. Requirement of Authentication or Identification

(a) General Provision. The requirement of authentication or identification as a condition precedent to admissibility is satisfied by evidence sufficient to support a finding that the matter in question is what its proponent claims.

(b) Illustrations. By way of illustration only, and not by way of limitation, the following are examples of authentication or identification conforming with the requirements of this rule:

(1) *Testimony of witness with knowledge.* Testimony that a matter is what it is claimed to be.

(2) *Nonexpert opinion on handwriting.* Nonexpert opinion as to the genuineness of handwriting, based upon familiarity not acquired for purposes of the litigation.

(3) *Comparison by trier or expert witness.* Comparison by the trier of fact or by expert witness with specimens which have been found by the court to be genuine.

(4) *Distinctive characteristics and the like.* Appearance, contents, substance, internal patterns, or other distinctive characteristics, taken in conjunction with circumstances.

(5) *Voice identification.* Identification of a voice, whether heard firsthand or through mechanical or electronic transmission or recording, by opinion based upon hearing the voice at anytime under circumstances connecting it with the alleged speaker.

(6) *Telephone conversations.* Telephone conversations, by evidence that a call was made to the number assigned at the time by the telephone company to a particular person or business, if:

(A) in the case of a person, circumstances, including self-identification, show the person answering to be the one called; or

(B) in the case of a business, the call was made to a place of business and the conversation related to business reasonably transacted over the telephone.

(7) *Public records or reports.* Evidence that a writing authorized by law to be recorded or filed and in fact recorded or filed in a public office, or a purported public record, report, statement, or data compilation, in any form, is from the public office where items of this nature are kept.

(8) *Ancient documents or data compilation.* Evidence that a document or data compilation, in any form, (A) is in such condition as to create no suspicion concerning its authenticity, (B) was in a place where it, if authentic, would likely be, and (C) has been in existence twenty years or more at the time it is offered.

(9) *Process or system.* Evidence describing a process or system used to produce a result and showing that the process or system produces an accurate result.

(10) *Methods provided by statute or rule.* Any method of authentication or identification provided by statute or by other rule prescribed pursuant to statutory authority.

Eff. March 1, 1998.

Cross References

Evidence of Handwriting, Vernon's Ann.C.C.P. Art. 38.27.

Commentary

In general

This rule eases the degree of proof necessary to show the authenticity of a matter offered by its proponent. If the evidence is sufficient to support a finding that a matter is what it purports to be, and it is otherwise admissible (that is, there is no other valid legal objection to it), it should be admitted under this rule. The trial court has the responsibility to make this preliminary determination of authenticity. Whether something actually is what it purports to be is a matter for the trier of fact. See Vernon's Ann.Rules Evid., Rule 1008 and Commentary, *infra.* Evidence of matters stated in the examples contained within the rule, and which are a part of it, will support a finding by the trial court that those matters are what their proponent says they are. See *Massimo v. State, 144 S.W.3d 210 (Tex. App.–Fort Worth 2004, no pet. h.)* (characteristic evidence [see Rule 901 (b)(4)] of an email sufficient to support a finding that the emails in question are what the proponent of the evidence claims they are).

Even if the trial court determines that evidence is sufficient to support a finding that something is what its proponent says it is, it is still subject to any other valid legal objection.

Uniform Rules of Evidence

For text of corresponding provisions of Uniform Rules of Evidence and notes of decisions relating thereto, which may provide guidance in interpreting the Texas Rule, see Rule 901, 13B Uniform Laws Annotated.

Federal Rules of Evidence

The corresponding provision of the Federal Rules of Evidence is Rule 901. For the text of the Rule and Advisory Committee Notes, which may provide guidance in interpreting the Texas Rule, see the Appendix to this volume.

Leading Cases

Druery v. State, 225 S.W.3d 491 (Tex. Crim. App. 2007), cert. denied, 128 S.Ct. 627 (2007) (the authentication requirement can be satisfied by showing distinctive characteristics like appearance, contents, substance, and internal patterns, taken in conjunction with the circumstances of the preparation of the document; the chain of custody problems do not affect the admissibility of the document, but merely the weight to be given to the evidence, in the absence of evidence of tampering or other fraud.

E.P. Operating Co. v. Sonora Exploration Corp., 862 S.W.2d 149 (Tex. App.—Houston [1st Dist.] 1993, writ denied) (requirement of authentication or identification as a condition precedent to admissibility is satisfied by evidence sufficient to support a finding that the matter in question is what its proponent claims; Rule 901(b) is a nonexclusive list of methods for authenticating or identifying evidence).

G.F.O., Matter of, 874 S.W.2d 729 (Tex. App.—Houston [1st Dist.] 1994, no writ) (a document is considered authentic if a sponsoring witness vouches for its authenticity or if the document meets the requirements of self-authentication). See *Herzig v. Metropolitan Life Ins. Co., 907 S.W.2d 574 (Tex. App.—Corpus Christi 1995, n.w.h.)*, cited below.

Herzig v. Metropolitan Life Ins. Co., 907 S.W.2d 574 (Tex. App.—Corpus Christi 1995, n.w.h.) (whether the testimony is trustworthy is a fact question to be determined by the trier of fact; the trial court's function in a jury trail is to determine admissibility, not the creditability of the sponsoring witness's testimony). See *G.F.O., Matter of, 874 S.W.2d 729 (Tex. App.—Houston [1st Dist.] 1994, no writ)* cited above.

Keene Corp. v. Rogers, 863 S.W.2d 168 (Tex. App.—Texarkana 1993, no writ) (TEX. R. [CIV.] EVID. 901(b)(1) allows for authentication by a witness with knowledge that the exhibit is what it purports to be).

Kephart v. State, 875 S.W.2d 319, 320–321 (Tex. Crim. App. 1994) (when authentication or identification of evidence is necessary, the requirement of authentication "is satisfied by evidence sufficient to support a finding that the matter in question is what its proponent claims"; the problem of authentication "arises whenever the relevance of any evidence depends upon its identity, source, or connection with a particular person, place, thing, or events").

Steenbergen v. Ford Motor Co., 814 S.W.2d 755 (Tex. App.—Dallas 1991, writ denied) (when authenticity of evidence is challenged by proper objection, the trial court determines preliminary questions about its admissibility; when the preliminary proof is sufficient to raise an issue of fact on the genuineness of the evidence, the court must admit it and allow the jury to determine the weight it is to be given; a finding that evidence lacks the predicate for admissibility is within the sound discretion of the trial court).

Leading CLE/Law Review Publications

Morales, *Social Media Evidence: "What You Post or Tweet Can and Will Be Used Against You in a Court of Law"*, 60 *The Advocate* 32, State Bar of Texas Litigation Section Report (Fall 2012).

Orsinger, *Discovery and Authentication,* 37th Annual Advanced Family Law Course, State Bar of Texas (2011).

Integrated Legal Research System References

West's Texas Digest Key Numbers

Criminal Law ⚷339, 386, 404, 429–447.

Evidence ⚷102, 148, 188 et seq., 325–383.

Texas Practice

Addison, Texas Practice Guide, Evidence § 9:1 et seq.

Texas Jur 3d

24A Texas Jur 3d, Criminal Law § 3655 et seq.

36 Texas Jur 3d, Evidence § 362 et seq.

Texas Forms

7 Texas Pl & Pr Forms, Evidence & Witnesses §§ 111:28–111:30.

Am Jur Trials

Audio Recordings: Evidence, Experts, and Technology, 48 Am Jur Trials 1.

Preparing and Using Photographs in Civil Cases, 3 Am Jur Trials 1.

Am Jur Proof of Facts

Admissibility of Computerized Business Records, 14 Am Jur Proof of Facts 2d 173.

Ancient Documents, 50 Am Jur Proof of Facts 2d 321.

Establishing Foundation to Admit Computer Generated Evidence as Demonstrative or Substantive Evidence, 57 Am Jur Proof of Facts 3d 455.

Examination and Identification of Photocopies and Photocopiers, 23 Am Jur Proof of Facts 3d 621.

Foundation for Audio Recordings as Evidence, 23 Am Jur Proof of Facts 3d 315.

Identification of Handprinting and Numerals, 24 Am Jur Proof of Facts 3d 667.

Annotations

Admissibility and Weight of Voice Spectrographic Analysis Evidence, 95 ALR5th 471.

Authentication of blood sample taken from human body for purposes other than determining blood alcohol content, 77 ALR5th 201.

Authentication of blood sample taken from human body for purposes of determining blood alcohol content, 76 ALR5th 1.

Authentication of bullets and other inorganic substances removed from human body for purposes of analysis, 79 ALR5th 237.

Authentication of organic nonblood specimen taken from human body for purposes of analysis, 78 ALR5th 1.

Sufficiency of identification of participants as prerequisite to admissibility of telephone conversation in evidence, 79 ALR3d 79.

Rule 902. Self–Authentication

Extrinsic evidence of authenticity as a condition precedent to admissibility is not required with respect to the following:

(1) Domestic Public Documents Under Seal. A document bearing a seal purporting to be that of the United States, or of any State, district, Commonwealth, territory, or insular possession thereof, or the Panama Canal Zone, or the Trust Territory of the Pacific Islands, or of a political subdivision, department, officer, or agency thereof, and a signature purporting to be an attestation or execution.

(2) Domestic Public Documents Not Under Seal. A document purporting to bear the signature in the official capacity of an officer or employee of any entity included in paragraph (1) hereof, having no seal, if a public officer having a seal and having official duties in the district or political subdivision of the officer or employee certifies under seal that the signer has the official capacity and that the signature is genuine.

(3) Foreign Public Documents. A document purporting to be executed or attested in an official capacity by a person, authorized by the laws of a foreign country to make the execution or attestation, and accompanied by a final certification as to the genuineness of the signature and official position (A) of the executing or attesting person, or (B) of any foreign official whose certificate of genuineness of signature and official position relates to the execution or attestation or is in a chain of certificates of genuineness of signature and official position relating to the execution or attestation. A final certification may be made by a secretary of embassy or legation, consul general, consul, vice consul, or consular agent of the United States, or a diplomatic or consular official of the foreign country assigned or accredited to the United States. If reasonable opportunity has been given to all parties to investigate the authenticity and accuracy of official documents, the court may, for good cause shown, order that they be treated as presumptively authentic without final certification or permit them to be evidenced by an attested summary with or without final certification. The final certification shall be dispensed with whenever both the United States and the foreign country in which the official record is located are parties to a treaty or convention that abolishes or displaces such requirement, in which case the record and the attestation shall be certified by the means provided in the treaty or convention.

(4) Certified Copies of Public Records. A copy of an official record or report or entry therein, or of a document authorized by law to be recorded or filed and actually recorded or filed in a public office, including data compilations in any form certified as correct by the custodian or other person authorized to make the certification, by certificate complying with paragraph (1), (2) or (3) of this rule or complying with any statute or other rule prescribed pursuant to statutory authority.

(5) Official Publications. Books, pamphlets, or other publications purporting to be issued by public authority.

(6) Newspapers and Periodicals. Printed materials purporting to be newspapers or periodicals.

(7) Trade Inscriptions and the Like. Inscriptions, signs, tags, or labels purporting to have been affixed in the course of business and indicating ownership, control, or origin.

(8) Acknowledged Documents. Documents accompanied by a certificate of acknowledgment executed in the manner provided by law by a notary public or other officer authorized by law to take acknowledgments.

(9) Commercial Paper and Related Documents. Commercial paper, signatures thereon, and documents relating thereto to the extent provided by general commercial law.

(10) Business Records Accompanied by Affidavit.

(a) *Records or photocopies; admissibility; affidavit; filing.* Any record or set of records or photographically reproduced copies of such records, which would be admissible under Rule 803(6) or (7) shall be admissible in evidence in any court in this state upon the affidavit of the person who would otherwise provide the prerequisites of Rule 803(6) or (7), that such records attached to such affidavit were in fact so kept as required by Rule 803(6) or (7), provided further, that such record or records along with such affidavit are filed with the clerk of the court for inclusion with the papers in the cause in which the record or records are sought to be used as evidence at least fourteen days prior to the day upon which trial of said cause commences, and provided the other parties to said cause are given prompt notice by the party filing same of the filing of such record or records and affidavit, which notice shall identify the name and employer, if any, of the person making the affidavit and such records shall be made available to the counsel for other parties to the action or litigation for inspection and copying. The expense for copying shall be borne by the party, parties or persons who desire copies and not by the party or parties who file the records and serve notice of said filing, in compliance with this rule. Notice shall be deemed to have been promptly given if it is served in the manner contemplated by Rule of Civil Procedure 21a fourteen days prior to commencement of trial in said cause.

(b) *Form of affidavit.* A form for the affidavit of such person as shall make such affidavit as is permitted in paragraph (a) above shall be sufficient if it follows this form though this form shall not be exclusive, and an affidavit which substantially complies with the provisions of this rule shall suffice, to-wit:

No __________

John Doe	)	IN THE __________
(Name of Plaintiff)	)	
	)	COURT IN AND FOR
v.	)	
	)	
John Roe	)	__________ COUNTY,
(Name of Defendant)	)	TEXAS

AFFIDAVIT

Before me, the undersigned authority, personally appeared _____, who, being by me duly sworn, deposed as follows:

My name is _____, I am of sound mind, capable of making this affidavit, and personally acquainted with the facts herein stated:

I am the custodian of the records of _____. Attached hereto are _____ pages of records from _____. These said _____ pages of records are kept by _____ in the regular course of business, and it was the regular course of business of _____ for an employee or representative of _____, with knowledge of the act, event, condition, opinion, or diagnosis, recorded to make the record or to transmit information thereof to be included in such record; and the record was made at or near the time or reasonably soon thereafter. The records attached hereto are the original or exact duplicates of the original.

____

Affiant

SWORN TO AND SUBSCRIBED before me on the _____ day of _____, 19___.

____

Notary Public, State of Texas
Notary's printed name:

____

My commission expires:

____

(c) *Medical expenses affidavit.* A party may make prima facie proof of medical expenses by affidavit that substantially complies with the following form:

Affidavit of Records Custodian of

____

STATE OF TEXAS §
§
COUNTY OF __________ §

Before me, the undersigned authority, personally appeared _________, who, being by me duly sworn, deposed as follows:

My name is _________. I am of sound mind and capable of making this affidavit, and personally acquainted with the facts herein stated.

I am a custodian of records for _________. Attached to this affidavit are records that provide an itemized statement of the service and the charge for the service that _________ provided to _________ on _________. The attached records are a part of this affidavit.

The attached records are kept by _________ in the regular course of business, and it was the regular course of business of _________ for an employee or representative of _________, with knowledge of the service provided, to make the record or to transmit information to be included in the record. The records were made in the regular course of business at or near the time or reasonably soon after the time the service was provided. The records are the original or a duplicate of the original.

The services provided were necessary and the amount charged for the services was reasonable at the time and place that the services were provided.

The total amount paid for the services was $ ___ and the amount currently unpaid but which _________ has a right to be paid after any adjustments or credits is $ ___.

____
Affiant

SWORN TO AND SUBSCRIBED before me on the ___ day of _________, ___.

____
Notary Public, State of Texas

Notary's printed name: ______________ My commission expires: ______________

(11) Presumptions Under Statutes or Other Rules. Any signature, document, or other matter declared by statute or by other rules prescribed pursuant to statutory authority to be presumptively or prima facie genuine or authentic.

Eff. March 1, 1998. Amended by order of Nov. 13, 2012, eff. March 1, 2013.

Commentary

In general

Documents and writings described in this rule "prove themselves" and no other evidence of their authenticity is required. Business records admissible under Vernon's Ann.Rules Evid., Rules 803(6) and 803(7) can be proven up by affidavit rather than by the custodian of the records or other qualified witness, if offered in compliance with this rule, thus establishing both authenticity and an exception to the hearsay rule. Although a document or writing described in this rule may be shown to be authentic, it is still subject to any valid legal objection. Authenticity and admissibility are not the same thing.

Use of business records accompanied by affidavit as provided in Vernon's Ann. Rules Evid., Rule 903(10) requires filing of the affidavit and the records with the clerk of the court at least fourteen days before the day the trial begins with prompt notice to the other parties of the filing of the affidavit and the records. Notice is considered promptly given if it is served at least fourteen (14) days before trial and in accordance with Vernon's Ann.Rules Civ.Proc., Rule 21a, *even in a criminal case.* See V.T.C.A., Civil Practice & Remedies Code § 18.001 (affidavits concerning costs and necessity of services rendered).

Uniform Rules of Evidence

For text of corresponding provisions of Uniform Rules of Evidence and notes of decisions relating thereto, which may provide guidance in interpreting the Texas Rule, see Rule 902, 13B Uniform Laws Annotated.

Federal Rules of Evidence

The corresponding provision of the Federal Rules of Evidence is Rule 902. For the text of the Rule and Advisory Committee Notes, which may provide guidance in interpreting the Texas Rule, see the Appendix to this volume.

Leading Cases

Director, State Employees Workers' Compensation Div., State of Tex. v. Lara, 901 S.W.2d 635 (Tex. App.—El Paso 1995, writ denied) (a document shown to be authentic is not thereby admissible; it is subject to any proper objection).

Fullick v. City of Baytown, 820 S.W.2d 943 (Tex. App.—Houston [1st Dist.] 1991, no writ) (the form of the affidavit to be used to establish the authenticity of business records under Tex. R. [Civ.] Evid. 902(10) is not exclusive; whatever the form of the affidavit, it must substantially comply with the requirements of that rule).

Leading CLE/Law Review Publications

Paddock, *Utilizing E–Mail as Business Records Under the Texas Rules of Evidence*, 19 Rev. Litig. 61 (2000).

Integrated Legal Research System References

West's Texas Digest Key Numbers

Criminal Law ⚷429, 430.

Evidence ⚷325–383.

Texas Practice

Addison, Texas Practice Guide, Evidence § 9:59 et seq.

Texas Jur 3d

24A Texas Jur 3d, Criminal Law § 3659 et seq.

36 Texas Jur 3d, Evidence § 371 et seq.

Texas Forms

7 Texas Pl & Pr Forms, Evidence & Witnesses §§ 111:37–111:38; 111:41–111:43.

Annotations

Verification and authentication of slips, tickets, bills, invoices, etc., made in regular course of business under the Uniform Business Records as Evidence Act, or similar "Model Acts", 21 ALR2d 773.

Rule 903. Subscribing Witness' Testimony Unnecessary

The testimony of a subscribing witness is not necessary to authenticate a writing unless required by the laws of the jurisdiction whose laws govern the validity of the writing.

Eff. March 1, 1998.

Commentary

Uniform Rules of Evidence

For text of corresponding provisions of Uniform Rules of Evidence and notes of decisions relating thereto, which may provide guidance in interpreting the Texas Rule, see Rule 903, 13B Uniform Laws Annotated.

Federal Rules of Evidence

The corresponding provision of the Federal Rules of Evidence is Rule 903. For the text of the Rule and Advisory Committee Notes, which may provide guidance in interpreting the Texas Rule, see the Appendix to this volume.

Integrated Legal Research System References

West's Texas Digest Key Numbers

Criminal Law ⚷442.

Evidence ⚷374.

Texas Practice

Addison, Texas Practice Guide, Evidence § 9:115 et seq.

ARTICLE X. CONTENTS OF WRITINGS, RECORDINGS, AND PHOTOGRAPHS

Rule
1001. Definitions.
1002. Requirement of Originals.
1003. Admissibility of Duplicates.
1004. Admissibility of Other Evidence of Contents.
1005. Public Records.
1006. Summaries.
1007. Testimony or Written Admission of Party.
1008. Functions of Court and Jury.
1009. Translation of Foreign Language Documents.

Cross References

Proof of Lost Records in Civil Proceedings, V.T.C.A., Civil Practice & Remedies Code § 19.001 et seq.

Written Part of Instrument Controls, Vernon's Ann.C.C.P. Art. 38.25.

Photographic Evidence in Theft Cases, Vernon's Ann.C.C.P. Art. 38.34.

Integrated Legal Research System References

West's Texas Digest Key Numbers

Evidence ⚷161–170, 325–367.

Texas Jur 3d

24A Texas Jur 3d, Criminal Law § 3639 et seq.

35 Texas Jur 3d, Evidence § 287 et seq.

36 Texas Jur 3d, Evidence § 456 et seq.

Am Jur Trials

Preparing and Using Photographs in Criminal Cases, 3 Am Jur Trials 335.

Video Technology, 58 Am Jur Trials 481.

Am Jur Proof of Facts

Admissibility of Computerized Business Records, 14 Am Jur Proof of Facts 2d 173.

Ancient Documents, 50 Am Jur Proof of Facts 2d 321.

The Dating of Handwriting Through Ink Analysis, 35 Am Jur Proof of Facts 3d 567.

The Effects of Alterations to Documents, 29 Am Jur Proof of Facts 3d 549.

Examination and Identification of Photocopies and Photocopiers, 23 Am Jur Proof of Facts 3d 621.

Foundation for Admissibility of Hospital Records and X–Rays, 38 Am Jur Proof of Facts 2d 145.

Foundation for Admission of Secondary Evidence, 35 Am Jur Proof of Facts 2d 147.

Foundation for Offering Business Records in Evidence, 34 Am Jur Proof of Facts 2d 509.

Rule 1001. Definitions

For purposes of this article the following definitions are applicable:

(a) Writings and Recordings. "Writings" and "recordings" consist of letters, words, or numbers or their equivalent, set down by handwriting, typewriting, printing, photostating, photographing, magnetic impulse, mechanical or electronic recording, or other form of data compilation.

(b) Photographs. "Photographs" include still photographs, X-ray films, video tapes, and motion pictures.

(c) Original. An "original" of a writing or recording is the writing or recording itself or any counterpart intended to have the same effect by a person executing or issuing it. An "original" of a photograph includes the negative or any print therefrom. If data are stored in a computer or similar device, any printout or other output readable by sight, shown to reflect the data accurately, is an "original."

(d) Duplicate. A "duplicate" is a counterpart produced by the same impression as the original, or from the same matrix, or by means of photography, including enlargements and miniatures, or by mechanical or electronic re-recording, or by chemical reproduction, or by other equivalent techniques which accurately reproduce the original.

Eff. March 1, 1998.

Commentary

Uniform Rules of Evidence

For text of corresponding provisions of Uniform Rules of Evidence and notes of decisions relating thereto, which may provide guidance in interpreting the Texas Rule, see Rule 1001, 13B Uniform Laws Annotated.

Federal Rules of Evidence

The corresponding provision of the Federal Rules of Evidence is Rule 1001. For the text of the Rule and Advisory Committee Notes, which may provide guidance in interpreting the Texas Rule, see the Appendix to this volume.

Integrated Legal Research System References

West's Texas Digest Key Numbers

Criminal Law ⚷430, 445, 447.

Evidence ⚷161–170.

Texas Practice

Addison, Texas Practice Guide, Evidence § 10:1 et seq.

Am Jur Proof of Facts

Examination and Identification of Photocopies and Photocopiers, 23 Am Jur Proof of Facts 3d 621.

Annotations

Admissibility of duplicates under Rules 1001(4) and 1003 of Federal Rules of Evidence, 72 ALR Fed 732.

Rule 1002. Requirement of Originals

To prove the content of a writing, recording, or photograph, the original writing, recording, or photograph is required except as otherwise provided in these rules or by law.

Eff. March 1, 1998.

Commentary

In general

This is the "best evidence rule." This rule applies only to writings, recordings and photographs. Thus, the best evidence of the *contents* of a writing, recording or photograph is the original of the writing, recording or photograph in question.

Uniform Rules of Evidence

For text of corresponding provisions of Uniform Rules of Evidence and notes of decisions relating thereto, which may provide guidance in interpreting the Texas Rule, see Rule 1002, 13B Uniform Laws Annotated.

Federal Rules of Evidence

The corresponding provision of the Federal Rules of Evidence is Rule 1002. For the text of the Rule and Advisory Committee Notes, which may provide guidance in interpreting the Texas Rule, see the Appendix to this volume.

Integrated Legal Research System References

West's Texas Digest Key Numbers

Criminal Law ⚷430, 445, 447.

Evidence ⚷161–170.

Texas Practice

Addison, Texas Practice Guide, Evidence § 10:17 et seq.

Texas Jur 3d

24A Texas Jur 3d, Criminal Law § 3642 et seq.

35 Texas Jur 3d, Evidence § 287 et seq.

Annotations

Admissibility in evidence of aerial photographs, 85 ALR5th 671.

Rule 1003. Admissibility of Duplicates

A duplicate is admissible to the same extent as an original unless (1) a question is raised as to the authenticity of the original or (2) in the circumstances it would be unfair to admit the duplicate in lieu of the original.

Eff. March 1, 1998.

Commentary

In general

This rule and Vernon's Ann.Rules Evid., Rules 1004, 1005 and 1006 create exceptions to the requirement of "the best evidence rule" that the original writing, recording or photograph is required to prove its contents.

One of the most common mistakes trial lawyers make in offering evidence is to miss an element of the predicate. This is not a problem if the opponent does not object, but no careful trial lawyer should rely on that happening. An exception to a rule excluding evidence is a part of the predicate for admissibility. In the case of an offer of a duplicate of an original writing, recording or photograph, the predicate would include a showing that the duplicate offered is a counterpart to the original, as that term is defined in Vernon's Ann.Rules Evid., Rule 1001(3), produced in a manner required by Vernon's Ann.Rules Evid., Rule 1001(4).

With a complete predicate, the duplicate should be admitted unless the opponent raises a question as to the authenticity of the *original* writing, recording or photograph or demonstrates that "in the circumstances it would be unfair to admit the duplicate in lieu of the original." In that event, the trial court will have the responsibility to determine preliminary issues of admissibility pursuant to Vernon's Ann.Rules Evid., Rule 104. An explanation or accounting for the original is not required as the predicate for the admissibility of a duplicate under Tex. R. [Civ.] Evid. 1003. *Rodriquez v. Ed Hicks Imports, 767 S.W.2d 187 (Tex. App.—Corpus Christi 1989, no writ).*

Uniform Rules of Evidence

For text of corresponding provisions of Uniform Rules of Evidence and notes of decisions relating thereto, which may provide guidance in interpreting the Texas Rule, see Rule 1003, 13B Uniform Laws Annotated.

Federal Rules of Evidence

The corresponding provision of the Federal Rules of Evidence is Rule 1003. For the text of the Rule and Advisory Committee Notes, which may provide guidance in interpreting the Texas Rule, see the Appendix to this volume.

Integrated Legal Research System References

West's Texas Digest Key Numbers

Criminal Law ⚷430, 445.

Evidence ⚷338, 366–383.

Texas Practice

Addison, Texas Practice Guide, Evidence § 10:34 et seq.

Texas Jur 3d

24A Texas Jur 3d, Criminal Law § 3645 et seq.

35 Texas Jur 3d, Evidence § 297 et seq.

Am Jur Proof of Facts

Foundation for Admission of Secondary Evidence, 35 Am Jur Proof of Facts 2d 147.

Foundation for Offering Business Records in Evidence, 34 Am Jur Proof of Facts 2d 509.

Annotations

Admissibility of duplicates under Rules 1001(4) and 1003 of Federal Rules of Evidence, 72 ALR Fed 732.

Carbon copies of letters or other written instruments as evidence, 65 ALR2d 342.

Photographic representation or photostat of writing as primary or secondary evidence within best evidence rule, 76 ALR2d 1356.

Rule 1004. Admissibility of Other Evidence of Contents

The original is not required, and other evidence of the contents of a writing, recording, or photograph is admissible if:

(a) Originals Lost or Destroyed. All originals are lost or have been destroyed, unless the proponent lost or destroyed them in bad faith;

(b) Original Not Obtainable. No original can be obtained by any available judicial process or procedure;

(c) Original Outside the State. No original is located in Texas;

(d) Original in Possession of Opponent. At a time when an original was under the control of the party against whom offered, that party was put on notice, by the pleadings or otherwise, that the content would be a subject of proof at the hearing, and that party does not produce the original at the hearing; or

(e) Collateral Matters. The writing, recording or photograph is not closely related to a controlling issue.

Eff. March 1, 1998.

Commentary

In general

The contents of a writing, recording or photograph can be proved by evidence other than the original if the original is unavailable to the proponent of the evidence for one or more of the reasons listed in this rule, or if the contents of the original pertains to a collateral matter.

Uniform Rules of Evidence

For text of corresponding provisions of Uniform Rules of Evidence and notes of decisions relating thereto, which may provide guidance in interpreting the Texas Rule, see Rule 1004, 13B Uniform Laws Annotated.

Federal Rules of Evidence

The corresponding provision of the Federal Rules of Evidence is Rule 1004. For the text of the Rule and Advisory Committee Notes, which may provide guidance in interpreting the Texas Rule, see the Appendix to this volume.

Integrated Legal Research System References

West's Texas Digest Key Numbers

Criminal Law ⚷447.

Evidence ⚷158–179.

Texas Practice

Addison, Texas Practice Guide, Evidence § 10:42 et seq.

Texas Jur 3d

24A Texas Jur 3d, Criminal Law § 3649.

36 Texas Jur 3d, Evidence § 297 et seq.

Annotations

Admissibility of duplicates under Rules 1001(4) and 1003 of Federal Rules of Evidence, 72 ALR Fed 732.

Federal Rules of Evidence: Admissibility, pursuant to Rule 1004(1), of other evidence of contents of writing, recording, or photograph, where originals were allegedly lost or destroyed, 83 ALR Fed 554.

Photographic representation or photostat of writing as primary or secondary evidence within best evidence rule, 76 ALR2d 1356.

Rule 1005. Public Records

The contents of an official record or of a document authorized to be recorded or filed and actually recorded or filed, including data compilations in any form, if otherwise admissible, may be proved by copy, certified as correct in accordance with Rule 902 or testified to be correct by a witness who has compared it with the original. If a copy which complies with the foregoing cannot be obtained by the exercise of reasonable diligence, then other evidence of the contents may be given.

Eff. March 1, 1998.

Commentary

In general

This rule contains one of those parenthetical traps for the unwary: the contents of an official record referred to in this rule must be "otherwise admissible." It is not enough that the official record is both authorized to be filed or recorded and actually filed or recorded.

Uniform Rules of Evidence

For text of corresponding provisions of Uniform Rules of Evidence and notes of decisions relating thereto, which may provide guidance in interpreting the Texas Rule, see Rule 1005, 13B Uniform Laws Annotated.

Federal Rules of Evidence

The corresponding provision of the Federal Rules of Evidence is Rule 1005. For the text of the Rule and Advisory Committee Notes, which may provide guidance in interpreting the Texas Rule, see the Appendix to this volume.

Integrated Legal Research System References

West's Texas Digest Key Numbers

Criminal Law ⚷429.

Evidence ⚷325–337.

Texas Practice

Addison, Texas Practice Guide, Evidence § 10:58 et seq.

Texas Jur 3d

24A Texas Jur 3d, Criminal Law § 3675 et seq.

35 Texas Jur 3d, Evidence § 302.

Rule 1006. Summaries

The contents of voluminous writings, recordings, or photographs, otherwise admissible, which cannot conveniently be examined in court may be presented in the form of a chart, summary, or calculation. The originals, or duplicates, shall be made available for examination or copying, or both, by other parties at a reasonable time and place. The court may order that they be produced in court.

Eff. March 1, 1998.

Commentary

In general

Summaries of the contents of writings, recordings or photographs can be admitted into evidence if the underlying writings, recordings or photographs are voluminous *and* admissible into evidence. This is another exception to the requirement of an original writing, recording or photograph to prove its contents.

Uniform Rules of Evidence

For text of corresponding provisions of Uniform Rules of Evidence and notes of decisions relating thereto, which may provide guidance in interpreting the Texas Rule, see Rule 1006, 13B Uniform Laws Annotated.

Federal Rules of Evidence

The corresponding provision of the Federal Rules of Evidence is Rule 1006. For the text of the Rule and Advisory Committee Notes, which may provide guidance in interpreting the Texas Rule, see the Appendix to this volume.

Leading Cases

Aquamarine Assocs. v. Burton Shipyard, Inc., 659 S.W.2d 820 (Tex. 1983) (a summary is inadmissible hearsay if the underlying business records upon which it was based are not shown to be admissible).

Uniroyal Goodrich Tire Co. v. Martinez, 977 S.W.2d 328 (Tex. 1998) (charts and diagrams that summarize testimony admissible if underlying information in evidence).

Welder v. Welder, 794 S.W.2d 420 (Tex. App.—Corpus Christi 1990, no writ) (the proponent of the summary must lay the proper predicate for its admission by demonstrating that the underlying records are voluminous, were made available to the opposing party for inspection and use in cross examination, and are themselves admissible).

Integrated Legal Research System References

West's Texas Digest Key Numbers

Criminal Law ⚷432.

Evidence ⚷366–383.

Texas Practice

Addison, Texas Practice Guide, Evidence § 10:67 et seq.

Texas Jur 3d

35 Texas Jur 3d, Evidence § 302.

Annotations

Admissibility of evidence summaries under Uniform Evidence Rule 1006, 59 ALR4th 971.

Admissibility of summaries or charts of writings, recordings, or photographs under Rule 1006 of Federal Rules of Evidence, 198 ALR Fed 427.

Requirement of notice as condition for admission in evidence of summary of voluminous records, 80 ALR3d 405.

Rule 1007. Testimony or Written Admission of Party

Contents of writings, recordings, or photographs may be proved by the testimony or deposition of the party against whom offered or by that party's written admission, without accounting for the nonproduction of the original.

Eff. March 1, 1998.

Commentary

Uniform Rules of Evidence

For text of corresponding provisions of Uniform Rules of Evidence and notes of decisions relating thereto, which may provide guidance in interpreting the Texas Rule, see Rule 1007, 13B Uniform Laws Annotated.

Federal Rules of Evidence

The corresponding provision of the Federal Rules of Evidence is Rule 1007. For the text of the Rule and Advisory Committee Notes, which may provide guidance in interpreting the Texas Rule, see the Appendix to this volume.

Integrated Legal Research System References

West's Texas Digest Key Numbers

Criminal Law ⚷447.

Evidence ⚷183.

Texas Practice

Addison, Texas Practice Guide, Evidence § 10:79 et seq.

Texas Jur 3d

35 Texas Jur 3d, Evidence § 302.

Rule 1008. Functions of Court and Jury

When the admissibility of other evidence of contents of writings, recordings, or photographs under these rules depends upon the fulfillment of a condition of fact, the question whether the condition has been fulfilled is ordinarily for the court to determine in accordance with the provisions of Rule 104. However, when an issue is raised (a) whether the asserted writing ever existed, or (b) whether another writing, recording, or photograph produced at the trial is the original, or (c) whether other evidence of contents correctly reflects the contents, the issue is for the trier of fact to determine as in the case of other issues of fact.

Eff. March 1, 1998.

Commentary

In general

The authenticity of a document, when challenged by proper objection, is a preliminary determination to be made by the trial court. *Steenburgen v. Ford Motor Co., 814 S.W.2d 755 (Tex. App.—Dallas 1991, writ denied).* However, when the "issue is raised (a) whether the asserted writing ever existed, or (b) whether another writing, recording, or photograph produced at the trial is the original, or (c) whether other evidence of contents correctly reflects the contents, the issue is for the trier of fact to determine as in the case of other issues of fact." Vernon's Ann.Rules Evid., Rule 1008. Where the evidence of authenticity of a document which is presented to the trial court by the proponent is sufficient to raise a fact issue, the trial court must admit it and allow the trier of fact to resolve that issue. *Mathis v. State, 930 S.W.2d 203 (Tex. App.—Houston [14th Dist.] 1996, n.w.h.).*

Uniform Rules of Evidence

For text of corresponding provisions of Uniform Rules of Evidence and notes of decisions relating thereto, which may provide guidance in interpreting the Texas Rule, see Rule 1008, 13B Uniform Laws Annotated.

Federal Rules of Evidence

The corresponding provision of the Federal Rules of Evidence is Rule 1008. For the text of the Rule and Advisory Committee Notes, which may provide guidance in interpreting the Texas Rule, see the Appendix to this volume.

Integrated Legal Research System References

Texas Practice

Addison, Texas Practice Guide, Evidence § 10:83 et seq.

Rule 1009. Translation of Foreign Language Documents

(a) Translations. A translation of foreign language documents shall be admissible upon the affidavit of a qualified translator setting forth the qualifications of the translator and certifying that the translation is fair and accurate. Such affidavit, along with the translation and the underlying foreign language documents, shall be served upon all parties at least 45 days prior to the date of trial.

(b) Objections. Any party may object to the accuracy of another party's translation by pointing out the specific inaccuracies of the translation and by stating with specificity what the objecting party contends is a fair and accurate translation. Such objection shall be served upon all parties at least 15 days prior to the date of trial.

(c) Effect of Failure to Object or Offer Conflicting Translation. If no conflicting translation or objection is timely served, the court shall admit a translation submitted under paragraph (a) without need of proof, provided however that the underlying foreign language documents are otherwise admissible under the Texas Rules of Evidence. Failure to serve a conflicting translation under paragraph (a) or failure to timely and properly object to the accuracy of a translation under paragraph (b) shall preclude a party from attacking or offering evidence contradicting the accuracy of such translation at trial.

(d) Effect of Objections or Conflicting Translations. In the event of conflicting translations under paragraph (a) or if objections to another party's translation are served under paragraph (b), the court shall determine whether there is a genuine issue as to the accuracy of a material part of the translation to be resolved by the trier of fact.

(e) Expert Testimony of Translator. Except as provided in paragraph (c), this Rule does not preclude the admission of a translation of foreign language documents at trial either by live testimony or by deposition testimony of a qualified expert translator.

(f) Varying of Time Limits. The court, upon motion of any party and for good cause shown, may enlarge or shorten the time limits set forth in this Rule.

(g) Court Appointment. The court, if necessary, may appoint a qualified translator, the reasonable value of whose services shall be taxed as court costs.

Eff. March 1, 1998.

Commentary

In general

There was no comparable rule in the Texas Rules of Civil Evidence or in the Texas Rules of Criminal Evidence.

This rule accounts for the likelihood of more frequent use of foreign language documents in trials in Texas, and it sets out a procedure whereby those documents and the translations of them can be shown to have the indicia of authenticity, trustworthiness and accuracy suitable for admission into evidence. This rule also assures that the opponent of the evidence will have a means and procedure for challenging the evidence when offered. However, even though all of the requirements of this rule are met, the evidence is still subject to any other valid legal objection.

Uniform Rules of Evidence

There is no corresponding provision in the Uniform Rules of Evidence.

Federal Rules of Evidence

There is no corresponding provision in the Federal Rules of Evidence.

APPENDIX: FEDERAL RULES OF EVIDENCE

HISTORICAL NOTES

Revision Notes and Legislative Reports

For legislative history and purpose of Pub.L. 93–595, see House, Senate and Conference Reports, set out following the text of these rules.

Effective Date and Application of Rules

The Federal Rules of Evidence were adopted by order of the Supreme Court on Nov. 20, 1972, transmitted to Congress by the Chief Justice on Feb. 5, 1973, and to have become effective on July 1, 1973. Pub.L. 93–12, Mar. 30, 1973, 87 Stat. 9, provided that the proposed rules "shall have no force or effect except to the extent, and with such amendments, as they may be expressly approved by Act of Congress". Pub.L. 93–595, Jan. 2, 1975, 88 Stat. 1926, enacted the Federal Rules of Evidence proposed by the Supreme Court, with amendments made by Congress, to take effect on July 1, 1975.

The Rules have been amended Oct. 16, 1975, Pub.L. 94–113, § 1, 89 Stat. 576, eff. Oct. 31, 1975; Dec. 12, 1975, Pub.L. 94–149, § 1, 89 Stat. 805; Oct. 28, 1978, Pub.L. 95–540, § 2, 92 Stat. 2046; Nov. 6, 1978, Pub.L. 95–598, Title II, § 251, 92 Stat. 2673, eff. Oct. 1, 1979; Apr. 30, 1979, eff. Dec. 1, 1980; Apr. 2, 1982, Pub.L. 97–164, Title I, § 142, Title IV, § 402, 96 Stat. 45, 57, eff. Oct. 1, 1982; Oct. 12, 1984, Pub.L. 98–473, Title IV, § 406, 98 Stat. 2067; Mar. 2, 1987, eff. Oct. 1, 1987; Apr. 25, 1988, eff. Nov. 1, 1988; Nov. 18, 1988, Pub.L. 100–690, Title VII, §§ 7046, 7075, 102 Stat. 4400, 4405; Jan. 26, 1990, eff. Dec. 1, 1990; Apr. 30, 1991, eff. Dec. 1, 1991; Apr. 22, 1993, eff. Dec. 1, 1993; Apr. 29, 1994, eff. Dec. 1, 1994; Apr. 11, 1997, eff. Dec. 1, 1997; Apr. 24, 1998, eff. Dec. 1, 1998; Apr. 17, 2000, eff. Dec. 1, 2000; Mar. 27, 2003, eff. Dec. 1, 2003; Apr. 12, 2006, eff. Dec. 1, 2006; Apr. 28, 2010, eff. Dec. 1, 2010; Apr. 26, 2011, eff. Dec. 1, 2011.

ARTICLE I. GENERAL PROVISIONS

Rule

101. Scope; Definitions.
102. Purpose.
103. Rulings on Evidence.
104. Preliminary Questions.
105. Limiting Evidence That Is Not Admissible Against Other Parties or for Other Purposes.
106. Remainder of or Related Writings or Recorded Statements.

HISTORICAL NOTES

Change of Name

United States magistrate appointed under section 631 of Title 28, Judiciary and Judicial Procedure, to be known as United States magistrate judge after Dec. 1, 1990, with any reference to United States magistrate or magistrate in Title 28, in any other Federal statute, etc., deemed a reference to United States magistrate judge appointed under section 631 of Title 28, see section 321 of Pub.L. 101–650, set out as a note under section 631 of Title 28.

Rule 101. Scope; Definitions

(a) Scope. These rules apply to proceedings in United States courts. The specific courts and proceedings to which the rules apply, along with exceptions, are set out in Rule 1101.

(b) Definitions. In these rules:

(1) "civil case" means a civil action or proceeding;

(2) "criminal case" includes a criminal proceeding;

(3) "public office" includes a public agency;

(4) "record" includes a memorandum, report, or data compilation;

(5) a "rule prescribed by the Supreme Court" means a rule adopted by the Supreme Court under statutory authority; and

(6) a reference to any kind of written material or any other medium includes electronically stored information.

(Pub.L. 93–595, § 1, Jan. 2, 1975, 88 Stat. 1929; Mar. 2, 1987, eff. Oct. 1, 1987; Apr. 25, 1988, eff. Nov. 1, 1988; Apr. 22, 1993, eff. Dec. 1, 1993; Apr. 26, 2011, eff. Dec. 1, 2011.)

ADVISORY COMMITTEE NOTES

1972 Proposed Rules

Rule 1101 specifies in detail the courts, proceedings, questions, and stages of proceedings to which the rules apply in whole or in part.

1987 Amendments

United States bankruptcy judges are added to conform this rule with Rule 1101(b) and Bankruptcy Rule 9017.

1988 Amendments

The amendment is technical. No substantive change is intended.

1993 Amendments

This revision is made to conform the rule to changes made by the Judicial Improvements Act of 1990.

2011 Amendments

The language of Rule 101 has been amended, and definitions have been added, as part of the general restyling of the Evidence Rules to make them more easily understood and to make style and terminology consistent throughout the rules. These changes are intended to be stylistic only. There is no intent to change any result in any ruling on evidence admissibility.

The reference to electronically stored information is intended to track the language of Fed. R. Civ. P. 34.

The Style Project

The Evidence Rules are the fourth set of national procedural rules to be restyled. The restyled Rules of Appellate Procedure took effect in 1998. The restyled Rules of Criminal Procedure took effect in 2002. The restyled Rules of Civil Procedure took effect in 2007. The restyled Rules of Evidence apply the same general drafting guidelines and principles used in restyling the Appellate, Criminal, and Civil Rules.

1. General Guidelines.

Guidance in drafting, usage, and style was provided by Bryan Garner, *Guidelines for Drafting and Editing Court Rules*, Administrative Office of the United States Courts (1969) and Bryan Garner, *Dictionary of Modern Legal Usage* (2d ed. 1995). *See also* Joseph Kimble, *Guiding Principles for Restyling the Civil Rules*, in *Preliminary Draft of Proposed Style Revision of the Federal Rules of Civil Procedure*, at page x (Feb. 2005) (available at http://www.uscourts.gov/RulesAndPolicies/rules/Prelim_draft_proposed _ptl.pdf); Joseph Kimble, *Lessons in Drafting from the New Federal Rules of Civil Procedure*, 12 Scribes J. Legal Writing 25 (2008–2009). For specific commentary on the Evidence restyling project, see Joseph Kimble, *Drafting Examples from the Proposed New Federal Rules of Evidence*, 88 Mich. B.J. 52 (Aug. 2009); 88 Mich. B.J. 46 (Sept. 2009); 88 Mich. B.J. 54 (Oct. 2009); 88 Mich. B.J. 50 (Nov. 2009).

2. *Formatting Changes.*

Many of the changes in the restyled Evidence Rules result from using format to achieve clearer presentations. The rules are broken down into constituent parts, using progressively indented subparagraphs with headings and substituting vertical for horizontal lists. "Hanging indents" are used throughout. These formatting changes make the structure of the rules graphic and make the restyled rules easier to read and understand even when the words are not changed. Rules 103, 404(b), 606(b), and 612 illustrate the benefits of formatting changes.

3. Changes to Reduce Inconsistent, Ambiguous, Redundant, Repetitive, or Archaic Words.

The restyled rules reduce the use of inconsistent terms that say the same thing in different ways. Because different words are presumed to have different meanings, such inconsistencies can result in confusion. The restyled rules reduce inconsistencies by using the same words to express the same meaning. For example, consistent expression is achieved by not switching between "accused" and "defendant" or between "party opponent" and "opposing party" or between the various formulations of civil and criminal action/case/proceeding.

The restyled rules minimize the use of inherently ambiguous words. For example, the word "shall" can mean "must," "may," or something else, depending on context. The potential for confusion is exacerbated by the fact the word "shall" is no longer generally used in spoken or clearly written English. The restyled rules replace "shall" with "must," "may," or "should," depending on which one the context and established interpretation make correct in each rule.

The restyled rules minimize the use of redundant "intensifiers." These are expressions that attempt to add emphasis, but instead state the obvious and create negative implications for other rules. The absence of intensifiers in the restyled rules does not change their substantive meaning. *See, e.g.*, Rule 104(c) (omitting "in all cases"); Rule 602 (omitting "but need not"); Rule 611(b) (omitting "in the exercise of discretion").

The restyled rules also remove words and concepts that are outdated or redundant.

4. Rule Numbers.

The restyled rules keep the same numbers to minimize the effect on research. Subdivisions have been rearranged within some rules to achieve greater clarity and simplicity.

5. No Substantive Change.

The Committee made special efforts to reject any purported style improvement that might result in a substantive change in the application of a rule. The

Committee considered a change to be "substantive" if any of the following conditions were met:

a. Under the existing practice in any circuit, the change could lead to a different result on a question of admissibility (e.g., a change that requires a court to provide either a less or more stringent standard in evaluating the admissibility of particular evidence);

b. Under the existing practice in any circuit, it could lead to a change in the procedure by which an admissibility decision is made (e.g., a change in the time in which an objection must be made, or a change in whether a court must hold a hearing on an admissibility question);

c. The change would restructure a rule in a way that would alter the approach that courts and litigants have used to think about, and argue about, questions of admissibility (e.g., merging Rules 104(a) and 104(b) into a single subdivision); or

d. It changes a "sacred phrase"—one that has become so familiar in practice that to alter it would be unduly disruptive to practice and expectations. Examples in the Evidence Rules include "unfair prejudice" and "truth of the matter asserted."

HISTORICAL NOTES

Change of Name

United States magistrate appointed under section 631 of Title 28, Judiciary and Judicial Procedure, to be known as United States magistrate judge after Dec. 1, 1990, with any reference to United States magistrate or magistrate in Title 28, in any other Federal statute, etc., deemed a reference to United States magistrate judge appointed under section 631 of Title 28, see section 321 of Pub.L. 101–650, set out as a note under section 631 of Title 28.

Rule 102. Purpose

These rules should be construed so as to administer every proceeding fairly, eliminate unjustifiable expense and delay, and promote the development of evidence law, to the end of ascertaining the truth and securing a just determination.

(Pub.L. 93–595, § 1, Jan. 2, 1975, 88 Stat.1929; Apr. 26, 2011, eff. Dec. 1, 2011.)

ADVISORY COMMITTEE NOTES

1972 Proposed Rules

For similar provisions see Rule 2 of the Federal Rules of Criminal Procedure, Rule 1 of the Federal Rules of Civil Procedure, California Evidence Code § 2, and New Jersey Evidence Rule 5.

2011 Amendments

The language of Rule 102 has been amended as part of the restyling of the Evidence Rules to make them more easily understood and to make style and terminology consistent throughout the rules. These changes are intended to be stylistic only. There is no intent to change any result in any ruling on evidence admissibility.

Rule 103. Rulings on Evidence

(a) Preserving a Claim of Error. A party may claim error in a ruling to admit or exclude evidence only if the error affects a substantial right of the party and:

(1) if the ruling admits evidence, a party, on the record:

(A) timely objects or moves to strike; and

(B) states the specific ground, unless it was apparent from the context; or

(2) if the ruling excludes evidence, a party informs the court of its substance by an offer of proof, unless the substance was apparent from the context.

(b) Not Needing to Renew an Objection or Offer of Proof. Once the court rules definitively on the record—either before or at trial—a party need not renew an objection or offer of proof to preserve a claim of error for appeal.

(c) Court's Statement About the Ruling; Directing an Offer of Proof. The court may make any statement about the character or form of the evidence, the objection made, and the ruling. The court may direct that an offer of proof be made in question-and-answer form.

(d) Preventing the Jury from Hearing Inadmissible Evidence. To the extent practicable, the court must conduct a jury trial so that inadmissible evidence is not suggested to the jury by any means.

(e) Taking Notice of Plain Error. A court may take notice of a plain error affecting a substantial right, even if the claim of error was not properly preserved.

(Pub.L. 93–595, § 1, Jan. 2, 1975, 88 Stat. 1929; Apr. 17, 2000, eff. Dec. 1, 2000; Apr. 26, 2011, eff. Dec. 1, 2011.)

ADVISORY COMMITTEE NOTES

1972 Proposed Rules

Note to Subdivision (a). Subdivision (a) states the law as generally accepted today. Rulings on evidence cannot be assigned as error unless (1) a substantial right is affected, and (2) the nature of the error was called to the attention of the judge, so as to alert him to the proper course of action and enable opposing counsel to take proper corrective measures. The objection and the offer of proof are the techniques for accomplishing these objectives. For similar provisions see Uniform Rules 4 and 5; California Evidence Code §§ 353 and 354; Kansas Code of Civil Procedure §§ 60–404 and 60–405. The rule does not purport to change the law with respect to harmless error. See 28 USC § 2111, F.R.Civ.P. 61, F.R.Crim.P. 52, and decisions construing them. The status of constitutional error as harmless or not is treated in Chapman v. California, 386 U.S. 18, 87 S.Ct. 824, 17 L.Ed.2d 705 (1967), reh. denied id. 987, 87 S.Ct. 1283, 18 L.Ed.2d 241.

Note to Subdivision (b). The first sentence is the third sentence of Rule 43(c) of the Federal Rules of Civil Procedure virtually verbatim. Its purpose is to reproduce for an appellate court, insofar as possible, a true reflection of what occurred in the trial court. The second sentence is in part derived from the final sentence of Rule 43(c). It is designed to resolve doubts as to what testimony the witness would have in fact given, and, in nonjury cases, to provide the appellate court with material for a possible final disposition of the case in the event of reversal of a ruling which excluded evidence. See 5 Moore's Federal Practice § 43.11 (2d ed. 1968). Application is made discretionary in view of the practical impossibility of formulating a satisfactory rule in mandatory terms.

Note to Subdivision (c). This subdivision proceeds on the supposition that a ruling which excludes evidence in a jury case is likely to be a pointless procedure if the excluded evidence nevertheless comes to the attention of the jury. *Bruton v. United States,* 389 U.S. 818, 88 S.Ct. 126, 19 L.Ed.2d 70 (1968). Rule 43(c) of the Federal Rules of Civil Procedure provides: "The court may require the offer to be made out of the hearing of the jury." *In re McConnell,* 370 U.S. 230, 82 S.Ct. 1288, 8 L.Ed.2d 434 (1962), left some doubt whether questions on which an offer is based must first be asked in the presence of the jury. The subdivision answers in the negative. The judge can foreclose a particular line of testimony and counsel can protect his record without a series of questions before the jury, designed at best to waste time and at worst "to waft into the jury box" the very matter sought to be excluded.

Note to Subdivision (d). This wording of the plain error principle is from Rule 52(b) of the Federal Rules of Criminal Procedure. While judicial unwillingness to be constructed by mechanical breakdowns of the adversary system has been more pronounced in criminal cases, there is no scarcity of decisions to the same effect in civil cases. In general, see Campbell, Extent to Which Courts of Review Will Consider Questions Not Properly Raised and Preserved, 7 Wis.L.Rev. 91, 160 (1932); Vestal, Sua Sponte Consideration in Appellate Review, 27 Fordham L.Rev. 477 (1958–59); 64 Harv.L.Rev. 652 (1951). In the nature of things the application of the plain error rule will be more likely with respect to the admission of evidence than to exclusion, since failure to comply with normal requirements of offers of proof is likely to produce a record which simply does not disclose the error.

2000 Amendment

The amendment applies to all rulings on evidence whether they occur at or before trial, including so-called "*in limine*" rulings. One of the most difficult questions arising from *in limine* and other evidentiary rulings is whether a losing party must renew an objection or offer of proof when the evidence is or would be offered at trial, in order to preserve a claim of error on appeal. Courts have taken differing approaches to this question. Some courts have held that a renewal at the time the evidence is to be offered at trial is always required. *See, e.g., Collins v. Wayne Corp.*, 621 F.2d 777 (5th Cir. 1980). Some courts have taken a more flexible approach, holding that renewal is not required if the issue decided is one that (1) was fairly presented to the trial court for an initial ruling, (2) may be decided as a final matter before the evidence is actually offered, and (3) was ruled on definitively by the trial judge, *See, e.g., Rosenfeld v. Basquiat*, 78 F.3d 84 (2d Cir. 1996) (admissibility of former testimony under the Dead Man's Statute; renewal not required). Other courts have distinguished between objections to evidence, which must be renewed when evidence is offered, and offers of proof, which need not be renewed after a definitive determination is made that the evidence is inadmissible. *See, e.g., Fusco v. General Motors Corp.*, 11 F.3d 259 (1st Cir. 1993). Another court, aware of this Committee's proposed amendment, has adopted its approach. *Wilson v. Williams*, 182 F. 3d 562 (7th Cir.1999) (en banc). Differing views on this question create uncertainty for litigants and unnecessary work for the appellate courts.

The amendment provides that a claim of error with respect to a definitive ruling is preserved for review when the party has otherwise satisfied the objection or offer of proof requirements of Rule 103(a). When the ruling is definitive, a renewed objection or offer of proof at the time the evidence is to be offered is more a formalism than a necessity. *See* Fed.R.Civ.P. 46 (formal exceptions unnecessary); Fed.R.Cr.P. 51 (same); *United States v. Mejia–Alarcon*, 995 F.2d 982, 986 (10th Cir. 1993) ("Requiring a party to renew an objection when the district court has issued a definitive ruling on a matter that can be fairly decided before trial would be in the nature of a formal exception and therefore unnecessary."). On the other hand, when the trial court appears to have reserved its ruling or to have indicated that the ruling is provisional, it makes sense to require the party to bring the issue to the court's attention subsequently. *See, e.g., United States v. Vest*, 116 F.3d 1179, 1188 (7th Cir. 1997) (where the trial court ruled *n limine* that testimony from defense witnesses could not be admitted, but allowed the defendant to seek leave at trial to call the witnesses should their testimony turn out to be relevant, the defendant's failure to seek such leave at trial meant that it was "too late to reopen the issue now on appeal"); *United States v. Valenti*, 60 F.3d 941 (2d Cir. 1995) (failure to proffer evidence at trial waives any claim of error where the trial judge had stated that he would reserve judgment on the *in limine* motion until he had heard the trial evidence).

The amendment imposes the obligation on counsel to clarify whether an *in limine* or other evidentiary ruling is definitive when there is doubt on that point. *See, e.g., Walden v. Georgia–Pacific Corp.*, 126 F.3d 506, 520 (3d Cir. 1997) (although "the district court told plaintiffs' counsel not to reargue every ruling, it did not countermand its clear opening statement that all of its rulings were tentative, and counsel never requested clarification, as he might have done.").

Even where the court's ruling is definitive, nothing in the amendment prohibits the court from revisiting its decision when the evidence is to be offered. If the court changes its initial ruling, or if the opposing party violates the terms of the initial ruling, objection must be made when the evidence is offered to preserve the claim of error for appeal. The error, if any, in such a situation occurs only when the evidence is offered and admitted. *United States Aviation Underwriters, Inc. v. Olympia Wings, Inc.*, 896 F.2d 949, 956 (5th Cir. 1990) ("objection is required to preserve error when an opponent, or the court itself, violates a motion *in limine* that was granted"); *United States v. Roenigk*, 810 F.2d 809 (8th Cir. 1987) (claim of error was not preserved where the defendant failed to object at trial to secure the benefit of a favorable advance ruling).

A definitive advance ruling is reviewed in light of the facts and circumstances before the trial court at the time of the ruling. If the relevant facts and circumstances change materially after the advance ruling has been made, those facts and circumstances cannot be relied upon on appeal unless they have been brought to the attention of the trial court by way of a renewed, and timely, objection, offer of proof, or motion to strike. *See Old Chief v. United States*, 519 U.S. 172, 182, n.6 (1997) ("It is important that a reviewing court evaluate the trial court's decision from its perspective when it had to rule and not indulge in review by hindsight."). Similarly, if the court decides in an advance ruling that proffered evidence is admissible subject to the eventual introduction by the proponent of a foundation for the evidence, and that foundation is never provided, the opponent cannot claim error based on the failure to establish the foundation unless the opponent calls that failure to the court's attention by a timely motion to strike or other suitable motion. *See Huddleston v. United States*, 485 U.S. 681, 690, n.7 (1988) ("It is, of course, not the responsibility of the judge *sua sponte* to ensure that the foundation evidence is offered; the objector must move to strike the evidence if at the close of the trial the offeror has failed to satisfy the condition.").

Nothing in the amendment is intended to affect the provisions of Fed.R.Civ.P. 72(a) or 28 U.S.C. § 636(b)(1) pertaining to nondispositive pretrial rulings by magistrate judges in proceedings that are not before a magistrate judge by consent of the parties. Fed.R.Civ.P. 72(a) provides that a party who fails to file a written objection to a magistrate judge's nondispositive order within ten days of receiving a copy "may not thereafter assign as error a defect" in the order. 28 U.S.C. § 636(b)(1) provides that any party "may serve and file written objections to such proposed findings and recommendations as provided by rules of court" within ten days of receiving a copy of the order. Several courts have held that a party must comply with this statutory provision in order to preserve a claim of error. *See, e.g., Wells v. Shriners Hospital*, 109 F.3d 198, 200 (4th Cir. 1997)("[i]n this circuit, as in others, a party 'may' file objections within ten days or he may not, as he chooses, but he 'shall' do so if he wishes further consideration."). When Fed.R.Civ.P. 72(a) or 28 U.S.C. § 636(b)(1) is operative, its requirement must be satisfied in order for a party to preserve a claim of error on appeal, even where Evidence Rule 103(a) would not require a subsequent objection or offer of proof.

Nothing in the amendment is intended to affect the rule set forth in *Luce v. United States*, 469 U.S. 38 (1984), and its progeny. The amendment provides that an objection or offer of proof need not be renewed to preserve a claim of error with respect to a definitive pretrial ruling. *Luce* answers affirmatively a separate question: whether a criminal defendant must testify at trial in order to preserve a claim of error predicated upon a trial court's decision to admit the defendant's prior convictions for impeachment. The *Luce* principle has been extended by many lower courts to other situations. *See United States v. DiMatteo*, 759 F.2d 831 (11th Cir. 1985) (applying *Luce* where the defendant's witness would be impeached with evidence offered under Rule 608). *See also United States v. Goldman*, 41 F.3d 785, 788 (1st Cir. 1994) ("Although *Luce* involved impeachment by conviction under Rule 609, the reasons given by the Supreme Court for requiring the defendant to testify apply with full force to the kind of Rule 403 and 404 objections that are advanced by Goldman in this case."); *Palmieri v. DeFaria*, 88 F.3d 136 (2d Cir. 1996) (where the plaintiff decided to take an adverse judgment rather than challenge an advance ruling by putting on evidence at trial, the *in limine* ruling would not be reviewed on appeal); *United States v. Ortiz*, 857 F.2d 900 (2d Cir. 1988) (where uncharged misconduct is ruled admissible if the defendant pursues a certain defense, the defendant must actually pursue that defense at trial in order to preserve a claim of error on appeal); *United States v. Bond*, 87 F.3d 695 (5th Cir. 1996) (where the trial court rules *in limine* that the defendant would waive his fifth amendment privilege were he to testify, the defendant must take the stand and testify in order to challenge that ruling on appeal).

The amendment does not purport to answer whether a party who objects to evidence that the court finds admissible in a definitive ruling, and who then offers the evidence to "remove the sting" of its anticipated prejudicial effect, thereby waives the right to appeal the trial court's ruling. *See, e.g., United States v. Fisher*, 106 F.3d 622 (5th Cir. 1997) (where the trial judge ruled *in limine* that the government could use a prior conviction to impeach the defendant if he testified, the defendant did not waive his right to appeal by introducing the conviction on direct examination); *Judd v. Rodman*, 105 F.3d 1339 (11th Cir. 1997) (an objection made *in limine* is sufficient to preserve a claim of error when the movant, as a matter of trial strategy, presents the objectionable evidence herself on direct examination to minimize its prejudicial effect); *Gill v. Thomas*, 83 F.3d 537, 540 (1st Cir. 1996) ("by offering the misdemeanor evidence himself, Gill waived his opportunity to object and thus did not preserve the issue for appeal"); *United States v. Williams*, 939 F.2d 721

(9th Cir. 1991) (objection to impeachment evidence was waived where the defendant was impeached on direct examination).

GAP Report—Proposed Amendment to Rule 103(a)

The Committee made the following changes to the published draft of the proposed amendment to Evidence Rule 103(a):

1. A minor stylistic change was made in the text, in accordance with the suggestion of the Style Subcommittee of the Standing Committee on Rules of Practice and Procedure.

2. The second sentence of the amended portion of the published draft was deleted, and the Committee Note was amended to reflect the fact that nothing in the amendment is intended to affect the rule of *Luce v. United States*.

3. The Committee Note was updated to include cases decided after the proposed amendment was issued for public comment.

4. The Committee Note was amended to include a reference to a Civil Rule and a statute requiring objections to certain Magistrate Judge rulings to be made to the District Court.

5. The Committee Note was revised to clarify that an advance ruling does not encompass subsequent developments at trial that might be the subject of an appeal.

2011 Amendments

The language of Rule 103 has been amended as part of the restyling of the Evidence Rules to make them more easily understood and to make style and terminology consistent throughout the rules. These changes are intended to be stylistic only. There is no intent to change any result in any ruling on evidence admissibility.

HISTORICAL NOTES

Conference Committee Notes, House Report No. 93–1597

The House bill contains the word "judge". The Senate amendment substitutes the word "court" in order to conform with usage elsewhere in the House bill.

The Conference adopts the Senate amendment.

Rule 104. Preliminary Questions

(a) In General. The court must decide any preliminary question about whether a witness is qualified, a privilege exists, or evidence is admissible. In so deciding, the court is not bound by evidence rules, except those on privilege.

(b) Relevance That Depends on a Fact. When the relevance of evidence depends on whether a fact exists, proof must be introduced sufficient to support a finding that the fact does exist. The court may admit the proposed evidence on the condition that the proof be introduced later.

(c) Conducting a Hearing So That the Jury Cannot Hear It. The court must conduct any hearing on a preliminary question so that the jury cannot hear it if:

(1) the hearing involves the admissibility of a confession;

(2) a defendant in a criminal case is a witness and so requests; or

(3) justice so requires.

(d) Cross–Examining a Defendant in a Criminal Case. By testifying on a preliminary question, a defendant in a criminal case does not become subject to cross-examination on other issues in the case.

(e) Evidence Relevant to Weight and Credibility. This rule does not limit a party's right to introduce before the jury evidence that is relevant to the weight or credibility of other evidence.

(Pub.L. 93–595, § 1, Jan. 2, 1975, 88 Stat.1930; Mar. 2, 1987, eff. Oct. 1, 1987; Apr. 26, 2011, eff. Dec. 1, 2011.)

ADVISORY COMMITTEE NOTES

1972 Proposed Rule

Note to Subdivision (a). The applicability of a particular rule of evidence often depends upon the existence of a condition. Is the alleged expert a qualified physician? Is a witness whose former testimony is offered unavailable? Was a stranger present during a conversation between attorney and client? In each instance the admissibility of evidence will turn upon the answer to the question of the existence of the condition. Accepted practice, incorporated in the rule, places on the judge the responsibility for these determinations. McCormick § 53; Morgan, Basic Problems of Evidence 45–50 (1962).

To the extent that these inquiries are factual, the judge acts as a trier of fact. Often, however, rulings on evidence call for an evaluation in terms of a legally set standard. Thus when a hearsay statement is offered as a declaration against interest, a decision must be made whether it possesses the required against-interest characteristics. These decisions, too, are made by the judge.

In view of these considerations, this subdivision refers to preliminary requirements generally by the broad term "questions," without attempt at specification.

This subdivision is of general application. It must, however, be read as subject to the special provisions for "conditional relevancy" in subdivision (b) and those for confessions in subdivision (d).

If the question is factual in nature, the judge will of necessity receive evidence pro and con on the issue. The rule provides that the rules of evidence in general do not apply to this process. McCormick § 53, p. 123, n. 8, points out that the authorities are "scattered and inconclusive," and observes:

"Should the exclusionary law of evidence, 'the child of the jury system' in Thayer's phrase, be applied to this hearing before the judge? Sound sense backs the view that it should not, and that the judge should be empowered to hear any relevant evidence, such as affidavits or other reliable hearsay."

This view is reinforced by practical necessity in certain situations. An item, offered and objected to, may itself be considered in ruling on admissibility, though not yet admitted in evidence. Thus, the content of an asserted declaration against interest must be considered in ruling whether it is against interest. Again, common practice calls for considering the testimony of a witness, particularly a child, in determining competency. Another example is the requirement of Rule 602 dealing with personal knowledge. In the case of hearsay, it is enough, if the declarant "so far as appears [has] had an opportunity to observe the fact declared." McCormick, § 10, p. 19.

If concern is felt over the use of affidavits by the judge in preliminary hearings on admissibility, attention is directed to the many important judicial determinations made on the basis of affidavits. Rule 47 of the Federal Rules of Criminal Procedure provides:

"An application to the court for an order shall be by motion. * * * It may be supported by affidavit."

The Rules of Civil Procedure are more detailed. Rule 43(e), dealing with motions generally, provides:

"When a motion is based on facts not appearing of record the court may hear the matter on affidavits presented by the respective parties, but the court may direct that the matter be heard wholly or partly on oral testimony or depositions." Rule 4(g) provides for proof of service by affidavit. Rule 56 provides in detail for the entry of summary judgment based on affidavits. Affidavits may supply the foundation for temporary restraining orders under Rule 65(b).

The study made for the California Law Revision Commission recommended an amendment to Uniform Rule 2 as follows:

"In the determination of the issue aforesaid [preliminary determination], exclusionary rules shall not apply, subject, however, to Rule 45 and any valid claim of privilege." Tentative Recommendation and a Study Relating to the Uniform Rules of Evidence (Article VIII, Hearsay), Cal.Law Revision Comm'n, Rep., Rec. & Studies, 470 (1962). The proposal was not adopted in the California Evidence Code. The Uniform Rules are likewise silent on the subject. However, New Jersey Evidence Rule 8(1), dealing with preliminary inquiry by the judge, provides:

"In his determination the rules of evidence shall not apply except for Rule 4 [exclusion on grounds of confusion, etc.] or a valid claim of privilege."

Note to Subdivision (b). In some situations, the relevancy of an item of evidence, in the large sense, depends upon the existence of a particular preliminary fact. Thus when a spoken statement is relied upon to prove notice to X, it is without probative value unless X heard it. Or if a letter purporting to be from Y is relied upon to establish an admission by him, it has no probative value unless Y wrote or authorized it. Relevance in this sense has been labelled "conditional relevancy." Morgan, Basic Problems of Evidence 45–46 (1962). Problems arising in connection with it are to be distinguished from problems of logical relevancy, e.g., evidence in a murder case that accused on the day before purchased a weapon of the kind used in the killing, treated in Rule 401.

If preliminary questions of conditional relevancy were determined solely by the judge, as provided in subdivision (a), the functioning of the jury as a trier of fact would be greatly restricted and in some cases virtually destroyed. These are appropriate questions for juries. Accepted treatment, as provided in the rule, is consistent with that given fact questions generally. The judge makes a preliminary determination whether the foundation evidence is sufficient to support a finding of fulfillment of the condition. If so, the item is admitted. If after all the evidence on the issue is in, pro and con, the jury could reasonably conclude that fulfillment of the condition is not established, the issue is for them. If the evidence is not such as to allow a finding, the judge withdraws the matter from their consideration. Morgan, *supra;* California Evidence Code § 403; New Jersey Rule 8(2). See also Uniform Rules 19 and 67.

The order of proof here, as generally, is subject to the control of the judge.

Note to Subdivision (c). Preliminary hearings on the admissibility of confessions must be conducted outside the hearing of the jury. See *Jackson v. Denno,* 378 U.S. 368, 84 S.Ct. 1774, 12 L.Ed.2d 908 (1964). Otherwise, detailed treatment of when preliminary matters should be heard outside the hearing of the jury is not feasible. The procedure is time consuming. Not infrequently the same evidence which is relevant to the issue of establishment of fulfillment of a condition precedent to admissibility is also relevant to weight or credibility, and time is saved by taking foundation proof in the presence of the jury. Much evidence on preliminary questions, though not relevant to jury issues, may be heard by the jury with no adverse effect. A great deal must be left to the discretion of the judge who will act as the interests of justice require.

Note to Subdivision (d). The limitation upon cross-examination is designed to encourage participation by the accused in the determination of preliminary matters. He may testify concerning them without exposing himself to cross-examination generally. The provision is necessary because of the breadth of cross-examination under Rule 611(b).

The rule does not address itself to questions of the subsequent use of testimony given by an accused at a hearing on a preliminary matter. See *Walder v. United States,* 347 U.S. 62 (1954); *Simmons v. United States,* 390 U.S. 377 (1968); *Harris v. New York,* 401 U.S. 222 (1971).

Note to Subdivision (e). For similar provisions see Uniform Rule 8; California Evidence Code § 406; Kansas Code of Civil Procedure § 60–408; New Jersey Evidence Rule 8(1).

1974 Enactment

Rule 104(c) as submitted to the Congress provided that hearings on the admissibility of confessions shall be conducted outside the presence of the jury and hearings on all other preliminary matters should be so conducted when the interests of justice require. The Committee amended the Rule to provide that where an accused is a witness as to a preliminary matter, he has the right, upon his request, to be heard outside the jury's presence. Although recognizing that in some cases duplication of evidence would occur and that the procedure could be subject to abuse, the Committee believed that a proper regard for the right of an accused not to testify generally in the case dictates that he be given an option to testify out of the presence of the jury on preliminary matters.

The Committee construes the second sentence of subdivision (c) as applying to civil actions and proceedings as well as to criminal cases, and on this assumption has left the sentence unamended. House Report No. 93–650.

Under rule 104(c) the hearing on a preliminary matter may at times be conducted in front of the jury. Should an accused testify in such a hearing, waiving his privilege against self-incrimination as to the preliminary issue, rule 104(d) provides that he will not generally be subject to cross-examination as to any other issue. This rule is not, however, intended to immunize the accused from cross-examination where, in testifying about a preliminary issue, he injects other issues into the hearing. If he could not be cross-examined about any issues gratuitiously raised by him beyond the scope of the preliminary matters, injustice might result. Accordingly, in order to prevent any such unjust result, the committee intends the rule to be construed to provide that the accused may subject himself to cross-examination as to issues raised by his own testimony upon a preliminary matter before a jury. Senate Report No. 93–1277.

1987 Amendments

The amendments are technical. No substantive change is intended.

2011 Amendments

The language of Rule 104 has been amended as part of the restyling of the Evidence Rules to make them more easily understood and to make style and terminology consistent throughout the rules. These changes are intended to be stylistic only. There is no intent to change any result in any ruling on evidence admissibility.

Rule 105. Limiting Evidence That Is Not Admissible Against Other Parties or for Other Purposes

If the court admits evidence that is admissible against a party or for a purpose—but not against another party or for another purpose—the court, on timely request, must restrict the evidence to its proper scope and instruct the jury accordingly.

(Pub.L. 93–595, § 1, Jan. 2, 1975, 88 Stat. 1930; Apr. 26, 2011, eff. Dec. 1, 2011.)

ADVISORY COMMITTEE NOTES

1972 Proposed Rules

A close relationship exists between this rule and Rule 403 which requires exclusion when "probative value is substantially outweighed by the danger of unfair prejudice, confusion of the issues, or misleading the jury." The present rule recognizes the practice of admitting evidence for a limited purpose and instructing the jury accordingly. The availability and effectiveness of this practice must be taken into consideration in reaching a decision whether to exclude for unfair prejudice under Rule 403. In *Bruton v. United States,* 389 U.S. 818, 88 S.Ct. 126, 19 L.Ed.2d 70 (1968), the Court ruled that a limiting instruction did not effectively protect the accused against the prejudicial effect of admitting in evidence the confession of a codefendant which implicated him. The decision does not, however, bar the use of limited admissibility with an instruction where the risk of prejudice is less serious.

Similar provisions are found in Uniform Rule 6; California Evidence Code § 355; Kansas Code of Civil Procedure § 60–406; New Jersey Evidence Rule 6. The wording of the present rule differs, however, in repelling any implication that limiting or curative instructions are sufficient in all situations.

1974 Enactment

Rule 106 as submitted by the Supreme Court (now Rule 105 in the bill) dealt with the subject of evidence which is admissible as to one party or for one purpose but is not admissible against another party or for another purpose. The Committee adopted this Rule without change on the understanding that it does not affect the authority of a court to order a severance in a multi-defendant case. House Report No. 93–650.

2011 Amendments

The language of Rule 105 has been amended as part of the restyling of the Evidence Rules to make them more easily understood and to make style and terminology consistent throughout the rules. These changes are intended to be stylistic only. There is no intent to change any result in any ruling on evidence admissibility.

Rule 106. Remainder of or Related Writings or Recorded Statements

If a party introduces all or part of a writing or recorded statement, an adverse party may require the introduction, at that time, of any other part—or any other writing or recorded statement—that in fairness ought to be considered at the same time.

(Pub.L. 93–595, § 1, Jan. 2, 1975, 88 Stat. 1930; Mar. 2, 1987, eff. Oct. 1, 1987; Apr. 26, 2011, eff. Dec. 1, 2011.)

ADVISORY COMMITTEE NOTES

1972 Proposed Rules

The rule is an expression of the rule of completeness. McCormick § 56. It is manifested as to depositions in Rule 32(a)(4) of the Federal Rules of Civil Procedure, of which the proposed rule is substantially a restatement.

The rule is based on two considerations. The first is the misleading impression created by taking matters out of context. The second is the inadequacy of repair work when delayed to a point later in the trial. See McCormick § 56; California Evidence Code § 356. The rule does not in any way circumscribe the right of the adversary to develop the matter on cross-examination or as part of his own case.

For practical reasons, the rule is limited to writings and recorded statements and does not apply to conversations.

1987 Amendments

The amendments are technical. No substantive change is intended.

2011 Amendments

The language of Rule 106 has been amended as part of the restyling of the Evidence Rules to make them more easily understood and to make style and terminology consistent throughout the rules. These changes are intended to be stylistic only. There is no intent to change any result in any ruling on evidence admissibility.

ARTICLE II. JUDICIAL NOTICE

Rule
201. Judicial Notice of Adjudicative Facts.

Rule 201. Judicial Notice of Adjudicative Facts

(a) Scope. This rule governs judicial notice of an adjudicative fact only, not a legislative fact.

(b) Kinds of Facts That May Be Judicially Noticed. The court may judicially notice a fact that is not subject to reasonable dispute because it:

(1) is generally known within the trial court's territorial jurisdiction; or

(2) can be accurately and readily determined from sources whose accuracy cannot reasonably be questioned.

(c) Taking Notice. The court:

(1) may take judicial notice on its own; or

(2) must take judicial notice if a party requests it and the court is supplied with the necessary information.

(d) Timing. The court may take judicial notice at any stage of the proceeding.

(e) Opportunity to Be Heard. On timely request, a party is entitled to be heard on the propriety of taking judicial notice and the nature of the fact to be noticed. If the court takes judicial notice before notifying a party, the party, on request, is still entitled to be heard.

(f) Instructing the Jury. In a civil case, the court must instruct the jury to accept the noticed fact as conclusive. In a criminal case, the court must instruct the jury that it may or may not accept the noticed fact as conclusive.

(Pub.L. 93–595, § 1, Jan. 2, 1975, 88 Stat. 1930; Apr. 26, 2011, eff. Dec. 1, 2011.)

ADVISORY COMMITTEE NOTES

1972 Proposed Rules

Note to Subdivision (a). This is the only evidence rule on the subject of judicial notice. It deals only with judicial notice of "adjudicative" facts. No rule deals with judicial notice of "legislative" facts. Judicial notice of matters of foreign law is treated in Rule 44.1 of the Federal Rules of Civil Procedure and Rule 26.1 of the Federal Rules of Criminal Procedure.

The omission of any treatment of legislative facts results from fundamental differences between adjudicative facts and legislative facts. Adjudicative facts are simply the facts of the particular case. Legislative facts, on the other hand, are those which have relevance to legal reasoning and the lawmaking process, whether in the formulation of a legal principle or ruling by a judge or court or in the enactment of a legislative body. The terminology was coined by Professor Kenneth Davis in his article An Approach to Problems of Evidence in the Administrative Process, 55 Harv.L.Rev. 364, 404–407 (1942). The following discussion draws extensively upon his writings. In addition, see the same author's Judicial Notice, 55 Colum.L.Rev. 945 (1955); Administrative Law Treatise, ch. 15 (1958); A System of Judicial Notice Based on Fairness and Convenience, in Perspectives of Law 69 (1964).

The usual method of establishing adjudicative facts is through the introduction of evidence, ordinarily consisting of the testimony of witnesses. If particular facts are outside the area of reasonable controversy, this process is dispensed with as unnecessary. A high degree of indisputability is the essential prerequisite.

Legislative facts are quite different. As Professor Davis says:

"My opinion is that judge-made law would stop growing if judges, in thinking about questions of law and policy, were forbidden to take into account the facts they believe, as distinguished from facts which are 'clearly * * * within the domain of the indisputable.' Facts most needed in thinking about difficult problems of law and policy have a way of being outside the domain of the clearly indisputable." A System of Judicial Notice Based on Fairness and Convenience, *supra*, at 82. An illustration is *Hawkins v. United States,* 358 U.S. 74, 79 S.Ct. 136, 3 L.Ed.2d 125 (1958), in which the Court refused to discard the common law rule that one spouse could not testify against the other, saying, "Adverse testimony given in criminal proceedings would, we think, be likely to destroy almost any marriage." This conclusion has a large intermixture of fact, but the factual aspect is scarcely "indisputable." See Hutchins and Slesinger, Some Observations on the Law of Evidence—Family Relations, 13 Minn.L.Rev. 675 (1929). If the destructive effect of the giving of adverse testimony by a spouse is not indisputable, should the Court have refrained from considering it in the absence of supporting evidence?

"If the Model Code or the Uniform Rules had been applicable, the Court would have been barred from thinking about the essential factual ingredient of the problems before it, and such a result would be obviously intolerable. What the law needs at its growing points is more, not less, judicial thinking about the factual ingredients of problems of what the law ought to be, and the needed facts are seldom 'clearly' indisputable." Davis, *supra,* at 83.

Professor Morgan gave the following description of the methodology of determining domestic law:

"In determining the content or applicability of a rule of domestic law, the judge is unrestricted in his investigation and conclusion. He may reject the propositions of either party or of both parties. He may consult the sources of pertinent data to which they refer, or he may refuse to do so. He may make an independent search for persuasive data or rest content with what he has or what the parties present. * * * [T]he parties do no more than to assist; they control no part of the process." Morgan, Judicial Notice, 57 Harv.L.Rev. 269, 270–271 (1944).

This is the view which should govern judicial access to legislative facts. It renders inappropriate any limitation in the form of indisputability, any formal requirements of notice other than those already inherent in affording opportunity to hear and be heard and exchanging briefs, and any requirement of formal findings at any level. It should, however leave open the possibility of introducing evidence through regular channels in appropriate situations. See *Borden's Farm Products Co. v. Baldwin,* 293 U.S. 194, 55 S.Ct. 187, 79 L.Ed. 281 (1934), where the cause was remanded for the taking of evidence as to the economic conditions and trade practices underlying the New York Milk Control Law.

Similar considerations govern the judicial use of non-adjudicative facts in ways other than formulating laws and rules. Thayer described them as a part of the judicial reasoning process.

"In conducting a process of judicial reasoning, as of other reasoning, not a step can be taken without assuming something which has not been proved; and the capacity to do this with competent judgment and efficiency, is imputed to judges and juries as part of their necessary mental outfit." Thayer, Preliminary Treatise on Evidence 279–280 (1898).

As Professor Davis points out, A System of Judicial Notice Based on Fairness and Convenience, in Perspectives of Law 69, 73 (1964), every case involves the use of hundreds or thousands of non-evidence facts. When a witness in an automobile accident case says "car," everyone, judge and jury included, furnishes, from non-evidence sources within himself, the supplementing information that the "car" is an automobile, not a railroad car, that it is self-propelled, probably by an internal combustion engine, that it may be assumed to have four wheels with pneumatic rubber tires, and so on. The judicial process cannot construct every case from scratch, like Descartes creating a world based on the postulate *Cogito, ergo sum.* These items could not possibly be introduced into evidence, and no one suggests that they be. Nor are they appropriate subjects for any formalized treatment of judicial notice of facts. See Levin and Levy, Persuading the Jury with Facts Not in Evidence: The Fiction–Science Spectrum, 105 U.Pa.L.Rev. 139 (1956).

Another aspect of what Thayer had in mind is the use of non-evidence facts to appraise or assess the adjudicative facts of the case. Pairs of cases from two jurisdictions illustrate this use and also the difference between non-evidence facts thus used and adjudicative facts. In People v. Strook, 347 Ill. 460, 179 N.E. 821 (1932), venue in Cook County had been held not established by testimony that the crime was committed at 7956 South Chicago Avenue, since judicial notice would not be taken that the address was in Chicago. However, the same court subsequently ruled that venue in Cook County was established by testimony that a crime occurred at 8900 South Anthony Avenue, since notice would be taken of the common practice of omitting the name of the city when speaking of local addresses, and the witness was testifying in Chicago. *People v. Pride,* 16 Ill.2d 82, 156 N.E.2d 551 (1951). And in *Hughes v. Vestal,* 264 N.C. 500, 142 S.E.2d 361 (1965), the Supreme Court of

North Carolina disapproved the trial judge's admission in evidence of a state-published table of automobile stopping distances on the basis of judicial notice, though the court itself had referred to the same table in an earlier case in a "rhetorical and illustrative" way in determining that the defendant could not have stopped her car in time to avoid striking a child who suddenly appeared in the highway and that a nonsuit was properly granted. *Ennis v. Dupree,* 262 N.C. 224, 136 S.E.2d 702 (1964). See also *Brown v. Hale,* 263 N.C. 176, 139 S.E.2d 210 (1964); *Clayton v. Rimmer,* 262 N.C. 302, 136 S.E.2d 562 (1964). It is apparent that this use of non-evidence facts in evaluating the adjudicative facts of the case is not an appropriate subject for a formalized judicial notice treatment.

In view of these considerations, the regulation of judicial notice of facts by the present rule extends only to adjudicative facts.

What, then, are "adjudicative" facts? Davis refers to them as those "which relate to the parties," or more fully:

"When a court or an agency finds facts concerning the immediate parties—who did what, where, when, how, and with what motive or intent—the court or agency is performing an adjudicative function, and the facts are conveniently called adjudicative facts. * * *

"Stated in other terms, the adjudicative facts are those to which the law is applied in the process of adjudication. They are the facts that normally go to the jury in a jury case. They relate to the parties, their activities, their properties, their businesses." 2 Administrative Law Treatise 353.

Note to Subdivision (b). With respect to judicial notice of adjudicative facts, the tradition has been one of caution in requiring that the matter be beyond reasonable controversy. This tradition of circumspection appears to be soundly based, and no reason to depart from it is apparent. As Professor Davis says:

"The reason we use trial-type procedure, I think, is that we make the practical judgment, on the basis of experience, that taking evidence, subject to cross-examination and rebuttal, is the best way to resolve controversies involving disputes of adjudicative facts, that is, facts pertaining to the parties. The reason we require a determination on the record is that we think fair procedure in resolving disputes of adjudicative facts calls for giving each party a chance to meet in the appropriate fashion the facts that come to the tribunal's attention, and the appropriate fashion for meeting disputed adjudicative facts includes rebuttal evidence, cross-examination, usually confrontation, and argument (either written or oral or both). The key to a fair trial is opportunity to use the appropriate weapons (rebuttal evidence, cross-examination, and argument) to meet adverse materials that come to the tribunal's attention." A System of Judicial Notice Based on Fairness and Convenience, in Perspectives of Law 69, 93 (1964).

The rule proceeds upon the theory that these considerations call for dispensing with traditional methods of proof only in clear cases. Compare Professor Davis' conclusion that judicial notice should be a matter of convenience, subject to requirements of procedural fairness. *Id.,* 94.

This rule is consistent with Uniform Rule 9(1) and (2) which limit judicial notice of facts to those "so universally known that they cannot reasonably be the subject of dispute," those "so generally known or of such common notoriety within the territorial jurisdiction of the court that they cannot reasonably be the subject of dispute," and those "capable of immediate and accurate determination by resort to easily accessible sources of indisputable accuracy." The traditional textbook treatment has included these general categories (matters of common knowledge, facts capable of verification), McCormick §§ 324, 325, and then has passed on into detailed treatment of such specific topics as facts relating to the personnel and records of the court, *Id.* § 327, and other governmental facts, *Id.* § 328. The California draftsmen, with a background of detailed statutory regulation of judicial notice, followed a somewhat similar pattern. California Evidence Code §§ 451, 452. The Uniform Rules, however, were drafted on the theory that these particular matters are included within the general categories and need no specific mention. This approach is followed in the present rule.

The phrase "propositions of generalized knowledge," found in Uniform Rule 9(1) and (2) is not included in the present rule. It was, it is believed, originally included in Model Code Rules 801 and 802 primarily in order to afford some minimum recognition to the right of the judge in his "legislative" capacity (not acting as the trier of fact) to take judicial notice of very limited categories of generalized knowledge. The limitations thus imposed have been discarded herein as undesirable, unworkable, and contrary to existing practice. What is left, then, to be considered, is the status of a "proposition of generalized knowledge" as an "adjudicative" fact to be noticed judicially and communicated by the judge to the jury. Thus viewed, it is considered to be lacking practical significance. While judges use judicial notice of "propositions of generalized knowledge" in a variety of situations: determining the validity and meaning of statutes, formulating common law rules, deciding whether evidence should be admitted, assessing the sufficiency and effect of evidence, all are essentially nonadjudicative in nature. When judicial notice is seen as a significant vehicle for progress in the law, these are the areas involved, particularly in developing fields of scientific knowledge. See McCormick 712. It is not believed that judges now instruct juries as to "propositions of generalized knowledge" derived from encyclopedias or other sources, or that they are likely to do so, or, indeed, that it is desirable that they do so. There is a vast difference between ruling on the basis of judicial notice that radar evidence of speed is admissible and explaining to the jury its principles and degree of accuracy, or between using a table of stopping distances of automobiles at various speeds in a judicial evaluation of testimony and telling the jury its precise application in the case. For cases raising doubt as to the propriety of the use of medical texts by lay triers of fact in passing on disability claims in administrative proceedings, see *Sayers v. Gardner,* 380 F.2d 940 (6th Cir.1967); *Ross v. Gardner,* 365 F.2d 554 (6th Cir.1966); *Sosna v. Celebrezze,* 234 F.Supp. 289 (E.D.Pa.1964); *Glendenning v. Ribicoff,* 213 F.Supp. 301 (W.D.Mo.1962).

Notes to Subdivisions (c) and (d). Under subdivision (c) the judge has a discretionary authority to take judicial notice, regardless of whether he is so requested by a party. The taking of judicial notice is mandatory, under subdivision (d), only when a party requests it and the necessary information is supplied. This scheme is believed to reflect existing practice. It is simple and workable. It avoids troublesome distinctions in the many situations in which the process of taking judicial notice is not recognized as such.

Compare Uniform Rule 9 making judicial notice of facts universally known mandatory without request, and making judicial notice of facts generally known in the jurisdiction or capable of determination by resort to accurate sources discretionary in the absence of request but mandatory if request is made and the information furnished. But see Uniform Rule 10(3), which directs the judge to decline to take judicial notice if available information fails to convince him that the matter falls clearly within Uniform Rule 9 or is insufficient to enable him to notice it judicially. Substantially the same approach is found in California Evidence Code §§ 451–453 and in New Jersey Evidence Rule 9. In contrast, the present rule treats alike all adjudicative facts which are subject to judicial notice.

Note to Subdivision (e). Basic considerations of procedural fairness demand an opportunity to be heard on the propriety of taking judicial notice and the tenor of the matter noticed. The rule requires the granting of that opportunity upon request. No formal scheme of giving notice is provided. An adversely affected party may learn in advance that judicial notice is in contemplation, either by virtue of being served with a copy of a request by another party under subdivision (d) that judicial notice be taken, or through an advance indication by the judge. Or he may have no advance notice at all. The likelihood of the latter is enhanced by the frequent failure to recognize judicial notice as such. And in the absence of advance notice, a request made after the fact could not in fairness be considered untimely. See the provision for hearing on timely request in the Administrative Procedure Act, 5 U.S.C. § 556(e). See also Revised Model State Administrative Procedure Act (1961), 9C U.L.A. § 10(4) (Supp.1967).

Note to Subdivision (f). In accord with the usual view, judicial notice may be taken at any stage of the proceedings, whether in the trial court or on appeal. Uniform Rule 12; California Evidence Code § 459; Kansas Rules of Evidence § 60–412; New Jersey Evidence Rule 12; McCormick § 330, p. 712.

Note to Subdivision (g). Much of the controversy about judicial notice has centered upon the question whether evidence should be admitted in disproof of facts of which judicial notice is taken.

The writers have been divided. Favoring admissibility are Thayer, Preliminary Treatise on Evidence 308 (1898); 9 Wigmore § 2567; Davis, A System of Judicial Notice Based on Fairness and Convenience, in Perspectives of Law, 69, 76–77 (1964). Opposing admissibility are Keeffe, Landis and Shaad, Sense and Nonsense about Judicial Notice, 2 Stan.L.Rev. 664, 668 (1950); McNaughton, Judicial Notice—Excerpts Relating to the Morgan–Whitmore Controversy, 14 Vand.L.Rev. 779 (1961); Morgan, Judicial Notice, 57 Harv.L.Rev. 269, 279 (1944); McCormick 710–711. The Model Code and the Uniform Rules are predicated upon indisputability of judicially noticed facts.

The proponents of admitting evidence in disproof have concentrated largely upon legislative facts. Since the present rule deals only with judicial notice of adjudicative facts, arguments directed to legislative facts lose their relevancy.

Within its relatively narrow area of adjudicative facts, the rule contemplates there is to be no evidence before the jury in disproof. The judge instructs the jury to take judicially noticed facts as established. This position is justified by the undesirable effects of the opposite rule in limiting the rebutting party, though not his opponent, to admissible evidence, in defeating the reasons for judicial notice, and in affecting the substantive law to an extent and in ways largely unforeseeable. Ample protection and flexibility are afforded by the broad provision for opportunity to be heard on request, set forth in subdivision (e).

Authority upon the propriety of taking judicial notice against an accused in a criminal case with respect to matters other than venue is relatively meager. Proceeding upon the theory that the right of jury trial does not extend to matters which are beyond reasonable dispute, the rule does not distinguish between criminal and civil cases. *People v. Mayes,* 113 Cal. 618, 45 P. 860 (1896); *Ross v. United States,* 374 F.2d 97 (8th Cir.1967). Cf. *State v. Main,* 94 R.I. 338, 180 A.2d 814 (1962); *State v. Lawrence,* 120 Utah 323, 234 P.2d 600 (1951).

Note on Judicial Notice of Law. By rules effective July 1, 1966, the method of invoking the law of a foreign country is covered elsewhere. Rule 44.1 of the Federal Rules of Civil Procedure; Rule 26.1 of the Federal Rules of Criminal Procedure. These two new admirably designed rules are founded upon the assumption that the manner in which law is fed into the judicial process is never a proper concern of the rules of evidence but rather of the rules of procedure. The Advisory Committee on Evidence, believing that this assumption is entirely correct, proposes no evidence rule with respect to judicial notice of law, and suggests that those matters of law which, in addition to foreign-country law, have traditionally been treated as requiring pleading and proof and more recently as the subject of judicial notice be left to the Rules of Civil and Criminal Procedure.

1974 Enactment

Rule 201(g) as received from the Supreme Court provided that when judicial notice of a fact is taken, the court shall instruct the jury to accept that fact as established. Being of the view that mandatory instruction to a jury in a criminal case to accept as conclusive any fact judicially noticed is inappropriate because contrary to the spirit of the Sixth Amendment right to a jury trial, the Committee adopted the 1969 Advisory Committee draft of this subsection, allowing a mandatory instruction in civil actions and proceedings and a discretionary instruction in criminal cases. House Report No. 93–650.

2011 Amendments

The language of Rule 201 has been amended as part of the restyling of the Evidence Rules to make them more easily understood and to make style and terminology consistent throughout the rules. These changes are intended to be stylistic only. There is no intent to change any result in any ruling on evidence admissibility.

ARTICLE III. PRESUMPTIONS IN CIVIL CASES

Rule

301. Presumptions in Civil Cases Generally.
302. Applying State Law to Presumptions in Civil Cases.

Rule 301. Presumptions in Civil Cases Generally

In a civil case, unless a federal statute or these rules provide otherwise, the party against whom a presumption is directed has the burden of producing evidence to rebut the presumption. But this rule does not shift the burden of persuasion, which remains on the party who had it originally.

(Pub.L. 93–595, § 1, Jan. 2, 1975, 88 Stat. 1931; Apr. 26, 2011, eff. Dec. 1, 2011.)

ADVISORY COMMITTEE NOTES

1972 Proposed Rules

This rule governs presumptions generally. See Rule 302 for presumptions controlled by state law and Rule 303 [deleted] for those against an accused in a criminal case.

Presumptions governed by this rule are given the effect of placing upon the opposing party the burden of establishing the nonexistence of the presumed fact, once the party invoking the presumption establishes the basic facts giving rise to it. The same considerations of fairness, policy, and probability which dictate the allocation of the burden of the various elements of a case as between the prima facie case of a plaintiff and affirmative defenses also underlie the creation of presumptions. These considerations are not satisfied by giving a lesser effect to presumptions. Morgan and Maguire, Looking Backward and Forward at Evidence, 50 Harv.L.Rev. 909, 913 (1937); Morgan, Instructing the Jury upon Presumptions and Burden of Proof, 47 Harv.L.Rev. 59, 82 (1933); Cleary, Presuming and Pleading: An Essay on Juristic Immaturity, 12 Stan.L.Rev. 5 (1959).

The so-called "bursting bubble" theory, under which a presumption vanishes upon the introduction of evidence which would support a finding of the nonexistence of the presumed fact, even though not believed, is rejected as according presumptions too "slight and evanescent" an effect. Morgan and Maguire, *supra,* at p. 913.

In the opinion of the Advisory Committee, no constitutional infirmity attends this view of presumptions. In *Mobile, J. & K. C. R. Co. v. Turnipseed,* 219 U.S. 35, 31 S.Ct. 136, 55 L.Ed. 78 (1910), the Court upheld a Mississippi statute which provided that in actions against railroads proof of injury inflicted by the running of trains should be prima facie evidence of negligence by the railroad. The injury in the case had resulted from a derailment. The opinion made the points (1) that the only effect of the statute was to impose on the railroad the duty of producing some evidence to the contrary, (2) that an inference may be supplied by law if there is a rational connection between the fact proved and the fact presumed, as long as the opposite party is not precluded from presenting his evidence to the contrary, and (3) that considerations of public policy arising from the character of the business justified the application in question. Nineteen years later, in *Western & Atlantic R. Co. v. Henderson,* 279 U.S. 639, 49 S.Ct. 445, 73 L.Ed. 884 (1929), the Court overturned a Georgia statute making railroads liable for damages done by trains, unless the railroad made it appear that reasonable care had been used, the presumption being against the railroad. The declaration alleged the death of plaintiff's husband from a grade crossing collision, due to specified acts of negligence by defendant. The jury were instructed that proof of the injury raised a presumption of negligence; the burden shifted to the railroad to prove ordinary care; and unless it did so, they should find for plaintiff. The instruction was held erroneous in an opinion stating (1) that there was no rational connection between the mere fact of collision and negligence on the part of anyone, and (2) that the statute was different from that in *Turnipseed* in imposing a burden upon the railroad. The reader is left in a state of some confusion. Is the difference between a derailment and a grade crossing collision of no significance? Would the *Turnipseed* presumption have been bad if it had imposed a burden of persuasion on defendant, although that would in nowise have impaired its "rational connection"? If *Henderson* forbids imposing a burden of persuasion on defendants, what happens to affirmative defenses?

Two factors serve to explain *Henderson.* The first was that it was common ground that negligence was indispensable to liability. Plaintiff thought so, drafted her complaint accordingly, and relied upon the presumption. But how in logic could the same presumption establish her alternative grounds of negligence that the engineer was so blind he could not see decedent's truck and that he failed to stop after he saw it? Second, take away the basic assumption of no liability without fault, as *Turnipseed* intimated might be done ("considerations of public policy arising out of the character of the business"), and the structure of the decision in *Henderson* fails. No question of logic would have arisen if the statute had simply said: a prima facie case of liability is made by proof of injury by a train; lack of negligence is an affirmative defense, to be pleaded and proved as other affirmative defenses. The problem would be one of economic due process only. While it seems likely that the Supreme Court of 1929 would have voted that due process was denied, that result today would be unlikely. See, for example, the shift in the direction of absolute liability in the consumer cases. Prosser, The Assault upon the Citadel (Strict Liability to the Consumer), 69 Yale L.J. 1099 (1960).

Any doubt as to the constitutional permissibility of a presumption imposing a burden of persuasion of the nonexistence of the presumed fact in civil cases is laid at rest by *Dick v. New York Life Ins. Co.,* 359 U.S. 437, 79 S.Ct. 921, 3 L.Ed.2d 935 (1959). The Court unhesitatingly applied the North Dakota rule that the presumption against suicide imposed on defendant the burden of proving that the death of insured, under an accidental death clause, was due to suicide.

"Proof of coverage and of death by gunshot wound shifts the burden to the insurer to establish that the death of the insured was due to his suicide." 359 U.S. at 443, 79 S.Ct. at 925.

"In a case like this one, North Dakota presumes that death was accidental and places on the insurer the burden of proving that death resulted from suicide." *Id.* at 446, 79 S.Ct. at 927.

The rational connection requirement survives in criminal cases, *Tot v. United States,* 319 U.S. 463, 63 S.Ct. 1241, 87 L.Ed. 1519 (1943), because the Court has been unwilling to extend into that area the greater-includes-the-lesser theory of *Ferry v. Ramsey,* 277 U.S. 88, 48 S.Ct. 443, 72 L.Ed. 796 (1928). In that case the Court sustained a Kansas statute under which bank directors were personally liable for deposits made with their assent and with knowledge of insolvency, and the fact of insolvency was prima facie evidence of assent and knowledge of insolvency. Mr. Justice Holmes pointed out that the state legislature could have made the directors personally liable to depositors in every case. Since the statute imposed a less stringent liability, "the thing to be considered is the result reached, not the possibly inartificial or clumsy way of reaching it." *Id.* at 94, 48 S.Ct. at 444. Mr. Justice Sutherland dissented: though the state could have created an absolute liability, it did not purport to do so; a rational connection was necessary, but lacking, between the liability created and the prima facie evidence of it; the result might be different if the basis of the presumption were being open for business.

The Sutherland view has prevailed in criminal cases by virtue of the higher standard of notice there required. The fiction that everyone is presumed to know the law is applied to the substantive law of crimes as an alternative to complete unenforceability. But the need does not extend to criminal evidence and procedure, and the fiction does not encompass them. "Rational connection" is not fictional or artificial, and so it is reasonable to suppose that Gainey should have known that his presence at the site of an illicit still could convict him of being connected with (carrying on) the business, *United States v. Gainey,* 380 U.S. 63, 85 S.Ct. 754, 13 L.Ed.2d 658 (1965), but not that Romano should have known that his presence at a still could convict him of possessing it, *United States v. Romano,* 382 U.S. 136, 86 S.Ct. 279, 15 L.Ed.2d 210 (1965).

In his dissent in Gainey, Mr. Justice Black put it more artistically:

"It might be argued, although the Court does not so argue or hold, that Congress if it wished could make presence at a still a crime in itself, and so Congress should be free to create crimes which are called 'possession' and 'carrying on an illegal distillery business' but which are defined in such a way that unexplained presence is sufficient and indisputable evidence in all cases to support conviction for those offenses. See *Ferry v. Ramsey,* 277 U.S. 88, 48 S.Ct. 443, 72 L.Ed. 796. Assuming for the sake of argument that Congress could make unexplained presence a criminal act, and ignoring also the refusal of this Court in other cases to uphold a statutory presumption on such a theory, see *Heiner v. Donnan,* 285 U.S. 312, 52 S.Ct. 358, 76 L.Ed. 772, there is no indication here that Congress intended to adopt such a misleading method of draftsmanship, nor in my judgment could the statutory provisions if so construed escape condemnation for vagueness, under the principles applied in *Lanzetta v. New Jersey,* 306 U.S. 451, 59 S.Ct. 618, 83 L.Ed. 888, and many other cases." 380 U.S. at 84, n. 12, 85 S.Ct. at 766.

And the majority opinion in *Romano* agreed with him:

"It may be, of course, that Congress has the power to make presence at an illegal still a punishable crime, but we find no clear indication that it intended to so exercise this power. The crime remains possession, not presence, and with all due deference to the judgment of Congress, the former may not constitutionally be inferred from the latter." 382 U.S. at 144, 86 S.Ct. at 284.

The rule does not spell out the procedural aspects of its application. Questions as to when the evidence warrants submission of a presumption and what instructions are proper under varying states of fact are believed to present no particular difficulties.

1974 Enactment

Rule 301 as submitted by the Supreme Court provided that in all cases a presumption imposes on the party against whom it is directed the burden of proving that the nonexistence of the presumed fact is more probable than its existence. The Committee limited the scope of Rule 301 to "civil actions and proceedings" to effectuate its decision not to deal with the question of presumptions in criminal cases. (See note on [proposed] Rule 303 in discussion of Rules deleted). With respect to the weight to be given a presumption in a civil case, the Committee agreed with the judgment implicit in the Court's version that the so-called "bursting bubble" theory of presumptions, whereby a presumption vanishes upon the appearance of any contradicting evidence by the other party, gives to presumptions too slight an effect. On the other hand, the Committee believed that the Rule proposed by the Court, whereby a presumption permanently alters the burden of persuasion, no matter how much contradicting evidence is introduced—a view shared by only a few courts—lends too great a force to presumptions. Accordingly, the Committee amended the Rule to adopt an intermediate position under which a presumption does not vanish upon the introduction of contradicting evidence, and does not change the burden of persuasion; instead it is merely deemed sufficient evidence of the fact presumed, to be considered by the jury or other finder of fact. House Report No. 93–650.

The rule governs presumptions in civil cases generally. Rule 302 provides for presumptions in cases controlled by State law.

As submitted by the Supreme Court, presumptions governed by this rule were given the effect of placing upon the opposing party the burden of establishing the nonexistence of the presumed fact, once the party invoking the presumption established the basic facts giving rise to it.

Instead of imposing a burden of persuasion on the party against whom the presumption is directed, the House adopted a provision which shifted the burden of going forward with the evidence. They further provided that "even though met with contradicting evidence, a presumption is sufficient evidence of the fact presumed, to be considered by the trier of fact." The effect of the amendment is that presumptions are to be treated as evidence.

The committee feels the House amendment is ill-advised. As the joint committees (the Standing Committee on Practice and Procedure of the Judicial Conference and the Advisory Committee on the Rules of Evidence) stated: "Presumptions are not evidence, but ways of dealing with evidence." This treatment requires juries to perform the task of considering "as evidence" facts upon which they have no direct evidence and which may confuse them in performance of their duties. California had a rule much like that contained in the House amendment. It was sharply criticized by Justice Traynor in *Speck v. Sarver* [20 Cal.2d 585, 128 P.2d 16, 21 (1942)] and was repealed after 93 troublesome years [Cal.Ev.Code 1965 § 600].

Professor McCormick gives a concise and compelling critique of the presumption as evidence rule:

> "Another solution, formerly more popular than now, is to instruct the jury that the presumption is 'evidence', to be weighed and considered with the testimony in the case. This avoids the danger that the jury may infer that the presumption is conclusive, but it probably means little to the jury, and certainly runs counter to accepted theories of the nature of evidence." [McCormick, Evidence, 669 (1954); *Id.* 825 (2d ed. 1972)].

For these reasons the committee has deleted that provision of the House-passed rule that treats presumptions as evidence. The effect of the rule as adopted by the committee is to make clear that while evidence of facts giving rise to a presumption shifts the burden of coming forward with evidence to rebut or meet the presumption, it does not shift the burden of persuasion on the existence of the presumed facts. The burden of persuasion remains on the party to whom it is allocated under the rules governing the allocation in the first instance.

The court may instruct the jury that they may infer the existence of the presumed fact from proof of the basic facts giving rise to the presumption. However, it would be inappropriate under this rule to instruct the jury that the inference they are to draw is conclusive. Senate Report 93–1277.

The House bill provides that a presumption in civil actions and proceedings shifts to the party against whom it is directed the burden of going forward with evidence to meet or rebut it. Even though evidence contradicting the presumption is offered, a presumption is considered sufficient evidence of the presumed fact to be considered by the jury. The Senate amendment provides that a presumption shifts to the party against whom it is directed the burden of going forward with evidence to meet or rebut the presumption, but it does not shift to that party the burden of persuasion on the existence of the presumed fact.

Under the Senate amendment, a presumption is sufficient to get a party past an adverse party's motion to dismiss made at the end of his case-in-chief. If the adverse party offers no evidence contradicting the presumed fact, the court will instruct the jury that if it finds the basic facts, it may presume the existence of the presumed fact. If the adverse party does offer evidence contradicting the presumed fact, the court cannot instruct the jury that it may *presume* the existence of the presumed fact from proof of the basic facts. The court may, however, instruct the jury that it may infer the existence of the presumed fact from proof of the basic facts.

The conference adopts the Senate amendment. House Conference Report No. 93–1597.

2011 Amendments

The language of Rule 301 has been amended as part of the restyling of the Evidence Rules to make them more easily understood and to make style and terminology consistent throughout the rules. These changes are intended to be stylistic only. There is no intent to change any result in any ruling on evidence admissibility.

Rule 302. Applying State Law to Presumptions in Civil Cases

In a civil case, state law governs the effect of a presumption regarding a claim or defense for which state law supplies the rule of decision.

(Pub.L. 93–595, § 1, Jan. 2, 1975, 88 Stat. 1931; Apr. 26, 2011, eff. Dec. 1, 2011.)

ADVISORY COMMITTEE NOTES

1972 Proposed Rules

A series of Supreme Court decisions in diversity cases leaves no doubt of the relevance of *Erie Railroad Co. v. Tompkins,* 304 U.S. 64, 58 S.Ct. 817, 82 L.Ed. 1188 (1938), to questions of burden of proof. These decisions are *Cities Service Oil Co. v. Dunlap,* 308 U.S. 208, 60 S.Ct. 201, 84 L.Ed. 196 (1939), *Palmer v. Hoffman,* 318 U.S. 109, 63 S.Ct. 477, 87 L.Ed. 645 (1943), and *Dick v. New York Life Ins. Co.,* 359 U.S. 437, 79 S.Ct. 921, 3 L.Ed.2d 935 (1959). They involved burden of proof, respectively, as to status as bona fide purchaser, contributory negligence, and nonaccidental death (suicide) of an insured. In each instance the state rule was held to be applicable. It does not follow, however, that all presumptions in diversity cases are governed by state law. In each case cited, the burden of proof question had to do with a substantive element of the claim or defense. Application of the state law is called for only when the presumption operates upon such an element. Accordingly the rule does not apply state law when the presumption operates upon a lesser aspect of the case, i.e. "tactical" presumptions.

The situations in which the state law is applied have been tagged for convenience in the preceding discussion as "diversity cases." The designation is not a completely accurate one since *Erie* applies to any claim or issue having its source in state law, regardless of the basis of federal jurisdiction, and does not apply to a federal claim or issue, even though jurisdiction is based on diversity. *Vestal, Erie R.R. v. Tompkins:* A Projection, 48 Iowa L.Rev. 248, 257 (1963); Hart and Wechsler, The Federal Courts and the Federal System, 697 (1953); 1A Moore, Federal Practice ¶ 0.305[3] (2d ed. 1965); Wright, Federal Courts, 217–218 (1963). Hence the rule employs, as appropriately descriptive, the phrase "as to which state law supplies the rule of decision." See A.L.I. Study of the Division of Jurisdiction Between State and Federal Courts, § 2344(c), p. 40, P.F.D. No. 1 (1965).

2011 Amendments

The language of Rule 302 has been amended as part of the restyling of the Evidence Rules to make them more easily understood and to make style and terminology consistent throughout the rules. These changes are intended to be stylistic only. There is no intent to change any result in any ruling on evidence admissibility.

ARTICLE IV. RELEVANCE AND ITS LIMITS

Rule

401. Test for Relevant Evidence.
402. General Admissibility of Relevant Evidence.
403. Excluding Relevant Evidence for Prejudice, Confusion, Waste of Time, or Other Reasons.
404. Character Evidence; Crimes or Other Acts.
405. Methods of Proving Character.
406. Habit; Routine Practice.
407. Subsequent Remedial Measures.
408. Compromise Offers and Negotiations.

Rule
409. Offers to Pay Medical and Similar Expenses.
410. Pleas, Plea Discussions, and Related Statements.
411. Liability Insurance.
412. Sex–Offense Cases: The Victim's Sexual Behavior or Predisposition.
413. Similar Crimes in Sexual–Assault Cases.
414. Similar Crimes in Child–Molestation Cases.
415. Similar Acts in Civil Cases Involving Sexual Assault or Child Molestation.

Rule 401. Test for Relevant Evidence

Evidence is relevant if:

(a) it has any tendency to make a fact more or less probable than it would be without the evidence; and

(b) the fact is of consequence in determining the action.

(Pub.L. 93–595, § 1, Jan. 2, 1975, 88 Stat.1931; Apr. 26, 2011, eff. Dec. 1, 2011.)

ADVISORY COMMITTEE NOTES

1972 Proposed Rules

Problems of relevancy call for an answer to the question whether an item of evidence, when tested by the processes of legal reasoning, possesses sufficient probative value to justify receiving it in evidence. Thus, assessment of the probative value of evidence that a person purchased a revolver shortly prior to a fatal shooting with which he is charged is a matter of analysis and reasoning.

The variety of relevancy problems is coextensive with the ingenuity of counsel in using circumstantial evidence as a means of proof. An enormous number of cases fall in no set pattern, and this rule is designed as a guide for handling them. On the other hand, some situations recur with sufficient frequency to create patterns susceptible of treatment by specific rules. Rule 404 and those following it are of that variety; they also serve as illustrations of the application of the present rule as limited by the exclusionary principles of Rule 403.

Passing mention should be made of so-called "conditional" relevancy. Morgan, Basic Problems of Evidence 45–46 (1962). In this situation, probative value depends not only upon satisfying the basic requirement of relevancy as described above but also upon the existence of some matter of fact. For example, if evidence of a spoken statement is relied upon to prove notice, probative value is lacking unless the person sought to be charged heard the statement. The problem is one of fact, and the only rules needed are for the purpose of determining the respective functions of judge and jury. See Rules 104(b) and 901. The discussion which follows in the present note is concerned with relevancy generally, not with any particular problem of conditional relevancy.

Relevancy is not an inherent characteristic of any item of evidence but exists only as a relation between an item of evidence and a matter properly provable in the case. Does the item of evidence tend to prove the matter sought to be proved? Whether the relationship exists depends upon principles evolved by experience or science, applied logically to the situation at hand. James, Relevancy, Probability and the Law, 29 Calif.L.Rev. 689, 696, n. 15 (1941), in Selected Writings on Evidence and Trial 610, 615, n. 15 (Fryer ed. 1957). The rule summarizes this relationship as a "tendency to make the existence" of the fact to be proved "more probable or less probable." Compare Uniform Rule 1(2) which states the crux of relevancy as "a tendency in reason," thus perhaps emphasizing unduly the logical

THOMSON REUTERS™

PACKING SLIP

Not a Remittable Document

0GND

412034161

Shipped From:
THOMSON-WEST
545 WESCOTT RD
EAGAN MN 55123-1310

Shipped To:
CONRAD OKECHI
6264 MELODY LN
DALLAS TX 75231-7579
214-290-6899

Ship To Account #	Purchase Order #	Order Date	Order #	Delivery #
1004624575		11/01/2013	200340752	412034161

ISBN	Material #	Product Description	Order Qty	Ship Qty
	14926100	ROACHS TX RULES OF CIVIL EVIDENCE ANNO FULL SET 1 Items in Full Set	1	1

Return Policy - If you are not completely satisfied with the products * you purchased or licensed, you may return them within 45 days of the original invoice (ship date) for a full credit or refund. To ensure accurate processing always enclose with your return a copy of the original delivery or billing document and include a brief explanation of the reason for return.

*This policy does not apply to online services. Subscriber is responsible for any applicable charges associated with online products. Please refer to your subscriber agreement for specific terms and conditions.

Return Information

1. To ensure proper identification, enclose a copy of this form in each box you are returning.
2. A return label is located below. Adhere it to the return package.
3. Securely Pack and return all merchandise. For your security, insure contents for its value. No COD shipments will be accepted.
4. All delivery or postage expense associated with the return of this merchandise is the responsibility of the customer.

Please allow up to 4 weeks for your return to process.

FROM:
CONRAD OKECHI
6264 MELODY LN
DALLAS TX 75231-7579
USA

Place Postage Here

MERCHANDISE RETURN LABEL

WEST
A Thomson Reuters business
Returns - BLDG B
545 WESCOTT RD
EAGAN MN 55123-1310

200340752
412034161
Telesales -
Inbound

Please check a reason for the return:

___ Refused
___ Sub Cancelled
___ Dup acct/order
___ Not Ordered
___ Address Error
___ Quantity damage

Other________________________

Return Label

MANAGE YOUR ACCOUNT ONLINE! For more information, please visit: legalsolutions.thomsonreuters.com/myaccount

Questions? Please contact West Customer Service at 1-800-328-4880.

process and ignoring the need to draw upon experience or science to validate the general principle upon which relevancy in a particular situation depends.

The standard of probability under the rule is "more * * * probable than it would be without the evidence." Any more stringent requirement is unworkable and unrealistic. As McCormick § 152, p. 317, says, "A brick is not a wall," or, as Falknor, Extrinsic Policies Affecting Admissibility, 10 Rutgers L.Rev. 574, 576 (1956), quotes Professor McBaine, "* * * [I]t is not to be supposed that every witness can make a home run." Dealing with probability in the language of the rule has the added virtue of avoiding confusion between questions of admissibility and questions of the sufficiency of the evidence.

The rule uses the phrase "fact that is of consequence to the determination of the action" to describe the kind of fact to which proof may properly be directed. The language is that of California Evidence Code § 210; it has the advantage of avoiding the loosely used and ambiguous word "material." Tentative Recommendation and a Study Relating to the Uniform Rules of Evidence (Art. I. General Provisions), Cal.Law Revision Comm'n, Rep., Rec. & Studies, 10–11 (1964). The fact to be proved may be ultimate, intermediate, or evidentiary; it matters not, so long as it is of consequence in the determination of the action. Cf. Uniform Rule 1(2) which requires that the evidence relate to a "material" fact.

The fact to which the evidence is directed need not be in dispute. While situations will arise which call for the exclusion of evidence offered to prove a point conceded by the opponent, the ruling should be made on the basis of such considerations as waste of time and undue prejudice (see Rule 403), rather than under any general requirement that evidence is admissible only if directed to matters in dispute. Evidence which is essentially background in nature can scarcely be said to involve disputed matter, yet it is universally offered and admitted as an aid to understanding. Charts, photographs, views of real estate, murder weapons, and many other items of evidence fall in this category. A rule limiting admissibility to evidence directed to a controversial point would invite the exclusion of this helpful evidence, or at least the raising of endless questions over its admission. Cf. California Evidence Code § 210, defining relevant evidence in terms of tendency to prove a disputed fact.

2011 Amendments

The language of Rule 401 has been amended as part of the restyling of the Evidence Rules to make them more easily understood and to make style and terminology consistent throughout the rules. These changes are intended to be stylistic only. There is no intent to change any result in any ruling on evidence admissibility.

Rule 402. General Admissibility of Relevant Evidence

Relevant evidence is admissible unless any of the following provides otherwise:

- the United States Constitution;
- a federal statute;
- these rules; or
- other rules prescribed by the Supreme Court.

Irrelevant evidence is not admissible.

(Pub.L. 93–595, § 1, Jan. 2, 1975, 88 Stat. 1931; Apr. 26, 2011, eff. Dec. 1, 2011.)

ADVISORY COMMITTEE NOTES

1972 Proposed Rules

The provisions that all relevant evidence is admissible, with certain exceptions, and that evidence which is not relevant is not admissible are "a presupposition involved in the very conception of a rational system of evidence." Thayer, Preliminary Treatise on Evidence 264 (1898). They constitute the foundation upon which the structure of admission and exclusion rests. For similar provisions see California Evidence Code §§ 350, 351. Provisions that all relevant evidence is admissible are found in Uniform Rule 7(f); Kansas Code of Civil Procedure § 60–407(f); and New Jersey Evidence Rule 7(f); but the exclusion of evidence which is not relevant is left to implication.

Not all relevant evidence is admissible. The exclusion of relevant evidence occurs in a variety of situations and may be called for by these rules, by the Rules of Civil and Criminal Procedure, by Bankruptcy Rules, by Act of Congress, or by constitutional considerations.

Succeeding rules in the present article, in response to the demands of particular policies, require the exclusion of evidence despite its relevancy. In addition, Article V recognizes a number of privileges; Article VI imposes limitations upon witnesses and the manner of dealing with them; Article VII specifies requirements with respect to opinions and expert testimony; Article VIII excludes hearsay not falling within an exception; Article IX spells out the handling of authentication and identification; and Article X restricts the manner of proving the contents of writings and recordings.

The Rules of Civil and Criminal Procedure in some instances require the exclusion of relevant evidence. For example, Rules 30(b) and 32(a)(3) of the Rules of Civil Procedure, by imposing requirements of notice and unavailability of the deponent, place limits on the use of relevant depositions. Similarly, Rule 15 of the Rules of Criminal Procedure restricts the use of depositions in criminal cases, even though relevant. And the effective enforcement of the command, originally statutory and now found in Rule 5(a) of the Rules of Criminal Procedure, that an arrested person be taken without unnecessary delay before a commissioner or other similar officer is held to require the exclusion of statements elicited during detention in violation thereof. *Mallory v. United States,* 354 U.S. 449, 77 S.Ct. 1356, 1 L.Ed.2d 1479 (1957); 18 U.S.C. § 3501(c).

While congressional enactments in the field of evidence have generally tended to expand admissibility beyond the scope of the common law rules, in some particular situations they have restricted the admissibility of relevant evidence. Most of this legislation has consisted of the formulation of a privilege or of a prohibition against disclosure. 8 U.S.C. § 1202(f), records of refusal of visas or permits to enter United States confidential, subject to discretion of Secretary of State to make available to court upon certification of need; 10 U.S.C. § 3693, replacement certificate of honorable discharge from Army not admissible in evidence; 10 U.S.C. § 8693, same as to Air Force; 11 U.S.C. § 25(a)(10), testimony given by bankrupt on his examination not admissible in criminal proceedings against him, except that given in hearing upon objection to discharge; 11 U.S.C. § 205(a), railroad reorganization petition, if dismissed, not admissible in evidence; 11 U.S.C. § 403(a), list of creditors filed with municipal composition plan not an admission; 13 U.S.C. § 9(a), census information confidential, retained copies of reports privileged; 47 U.S.C. § 605, interception and divulgence of wire or radio communications prohibited unless authorized by sender. These statutory provisions would remain undisturbed by the rules.

The rule recognizes but makes no attempt to spell out the constitutional considerations which impose basic limitations upon the admissibility of relevant evidence. Examples are evidence obtained by unlawful search and seizure. *Weeks v. United States,* 232 U.S. 383, 34 S.Ct. 341, 58 L.Ed. 652 (1914); *Katz v. United States,* 389 U.S. 347, 88 S.Ct. 507, 19 L.Ed.2d 576 (1967); incriminating statement elicited from an accused in violation of right to counsel. *Massiah v. United States,* 377 U.S. 201, 84 S.Ct. 1199, 12 L.Ed.2d 246 (1964).

1974 Enactment

Rule 402 as submitted to the Congress contained the phrase "or by other rules adopted by the Supreme Court". To accommodate the view that the Congress should not appear to acquiesce in the Court's judgment that it has authority under the existing Rules Enabling Acts to promulgate Rules of Evidence, the Committee amended the above phrase to read "or by other rules prescribed by the Supreme Court pursuant to statutory authority" in this and other Rules where the reference appears. House Report No. 93–650.

2011 Amendments

The language of Rule 402 has been amended as part of the restyling of the Evidence Rules to make them more easily understood and to make style and terminology consistent throughout the rules. These changes are intended to be stylistic only. There is no intent to change any result in any ruling on evidence admissibility.

Rule 403. Excluding Relevant Evidence for Prejudice, Confusion, Waste of Time, or Other Reasons

The court may exclude relevant evidence if its probative value is substantially outweighed by a danger of one or more of the following: unfair prejudice, confusing the issues, misleading the jury, undue delay, wasting time, or needlessly presenting cumulative evidence.

(Pub.L. 93–595, § 1, Jan. 2, 1975, 88 Stat. 1932; Apr. 26, 2011, eff. Dec. 1, 2011.)

ADVISORY COMMITTEE NOTES

1972 Proposed Rules

The case law recognizes that certain circumstances call for the exclusion of evidence which is of unquestioned relevance. These circumstances entail risks which range all the way from inducing decision on a purely emotional basis, at one extreme, to nothing more harmful than merely wasting time, at the other extreme. Situations in this area call for balancing the probative value of and need for the evidence against the harm likely to result from its admission. Slough, Relevancy Unraveled, 5 Kan.L.Rev. 1, 12–15 (1956); Trautman, Logical or Legal Relevancy—A Conflict in Theory, 5 Van.L.Rev. 385, 392 (1952); McCormick § 152, pp. 319–321. The rules which follow in this Article are concrete applications evolved for particular situations. However, they reflect the policies underlying the present rule, which is designed as a guide for the handling of situations for which no specific rules have been formulated.

Exclusion for risk of unfair prejudice, confusion of issues, misleading the jury, or waste of time, all find ample support in the authorities. "Unfair prejudice" within its context means an undue tendency to suggest decision on an improper basis, commonly, though not necessarily, an emotional one.

The rule does not enumerate surprise as a ground for exclusion, in this respect following Wigmore's view of the common law. 6 Wigmore § 1849. Cf. McCormick § 152, p. 320, n. 29, listing unfair surprise as a ground for exclusion but stating that it is usually "coupled with the danger of prejudice and confusion of issues." While Uniform Rule 45 incorporates surprise as a ground and is followed in Kansas Code of Civil Procedure § 60–445, surprise is not included in California Evidence Code § 352 or New Jersey Rule 4, though both the latter otherwise substantially embody Uniform Rule 45. While it can scarcely be doubted that claims of unfair surprise may still be justified despite procedural requirements of notice and instrumentalities of discovery, the granting of a continuance is a more appropriate remedy than exclusion of the evidence. Tentative Recommendation and a Study Relating to the Uniform Rules of Evidence (Art. VI. Extrinsic Policies Affecting Admissibility), Cal.Law Revision Comm'n, Rep., Rec. & Studies, 612 (1964). Moreover, the impact of a rule excluding evidence on the ground of surprise would be difficult to estimate.

In reaching a decision whether to exclude on grounds of unfair prejudice, consideration should be given to the probable effectiveness or lack of effectiveness of a limiting instruction. See Rule 106 [now 105] and Advisory Committee's Note thereunder. The availability of other means of proof may also be an appropriate factor.

2011 Amendments

The language of Rule 403 has been amended as part of the restyling of the Evidence Rules to make them more easily understood and to make style and terminology consistent throughout the rules. These changes are intended to be stylistic only. There is no intent to change any result in any ruling on evidence admissibility.

Rule 404. Character Evidence; Crimes or Other Acts

(a) Character Evidence.

(1) Prohibited Uses. Evidence of a person's character or character trait is not admissible to prove that on a particular occasion the person acted in accordance with the character or trait.

(2) Exceptions for a Defendant or Victim in a Criminal Case. The following exceptions apply in a criminal case:

(A) a defendant may offer evidence of the defendant's pertinent trait, and if the evidence is admitted, the prosecutor may offer evidence to rebut it;

(B) subject to the limitations in Rule 412, a defendant may offer evidence of an alleged victim's pertinent trait, and if the evidence is admitted, the prosecutor may:

(i) offer evidence to rebut it; and

(ii) offer evidence of the defendant's same trait; and

(C) in a homicide case, the prosecutor may offer evidence of the alleged victim's trait of peacefulness to rebut evidence that the victim was the first aggressor.

(3) Exceptions for a Witness. Evidence of a witness's character may be admitted under Rules 607, 608, and 609.

(b) Crimes, Wrongs, or Other Acts.

(1) Prohibited Uses. Evidence of a crime, wrong, or other act is not admissible to prove a person's character in order to show that on a particular occasion the person acted in accordance with the character.

(2) Permitted Uses; Notice in a Criminal Case. This evidence may be admissible for another purpose, such as proving motive, opportunity, intent, preparation, plan, knowledge, identity, absence of mistake, or lack of accident. On request by a defendant in a criminal case, the prosecutor must:

(A) provide reasonable notice of the general nature of any such evidence that the prosecutor intends to offer at trial; and

(B) do so before trial—or during trial if the court, for good cause, excuses lack of pretrial notice.

(Pub.L. 93–595, § 1, Jan. 2, 1975, 88 Stat.1932; Mar. 2, 1987, eff. Oct. 1, 1987; Apr. 30, 1991, eff. Dec. 1, 1991; Apr. 17, 2000, eff. Dec. 1, 2000; Apr. 12, 2006, eff. Dec. 1, 2006; Apr. 26, 2011, eff. Dec. 1, 2011.)

ADVISORY COMMITTEE NOTES

1972 Proposed Rules

Note to Subdivision (a). This subdivision deals with the basic question whether character evidence should be admitted. Once the admissibility of character evidence in some form is established under this rule, reference must then be made to Rule 405, which follows, in order to determine the appropriate method of proof. If the character is that of a witness, see Rules 608 and 610 for methods of proof.

Character questions arise in two fundamentally different ways. (1) Character may itself be an element of a crime, claim, or defense. A situation of this kind is commonly referred to as "character in issue." Illustrations are: the chastity of the victim under a statute specifying her chastity as an element of the crime of seduction, or the competency of the driver in an action for negligently entrusting a motor vehicle to an incompetent driver. No problem of the general relevancy of character evidence is involved, and the present rule therefore has no provision on the subject. The only question relates to allowable methods of proof, as to which see Rule 405, immediately following. (2) Character evidence is susceptible of being used for the purpose of suggesting an inference that the person acted on the occasion in question consistently with his character. This use of character is often described as "circumstantial." Illustrations are: evidence of a violent disposition to prove that the person was the aggressor in an affray, or evidence of honesty in disproof of a charge of theft. This circumstantial use of character evidence raises questions of relevancy as well as questions of allowable methods of proof.

In most jurisdictions today, the circumstantial use of character is rejected but with important exceptions: (1) an accused may introduce pertinent evidence of good character (often misleadingly described as "putting his character in issue"), in which event the prosecution may rebut with evidence of bad character; (2) an accused may introduce pertinent evidence of the character of the victim, as in support of a claim of self-defense to a charge of homicide or consent in a case of rape, and the prosecution may introduce similar evidence in rebuttal of the character evidence, or, in a homicide case, to rebut a claim that deceased was the first aggressor, however proved; and (3) the character of a witness may be gone into as bearing on his credibility. McCormick §§ 155–161. This pattern is incorporated in the rule. While its basis lies more in history and experience than in logic an underlying justification can fairly be found in terms of the relative presence and absence of prejudice in the various situations. Falknor, Extrinsic Policies Affecting

Admissibility, 10 Rutgers L.Rev. 574, 584 (1956); McCormick § 157. In any event, the criminal rule is so deeply imbedded in our jurisprudence as to assume almost constitutional proportions and to override doubts of the basic relevancy of the evidence.

The limitation to pertinent traits of character, rather than character generally, in paragraphs (1) and (2) is in accordance with the prevailing view. McCormick § 158, p. 334. A similar provision in Rule 608, to which reference is made in paragraph (3), limits character evidence respecting witnesses to the trait of truthfulness or untruthfulness.

The argument is made that circumstantial use of character ought to be allowed in civil cases to the same extent as in criminal cases, i.e. evidence of good (nonprejudicial) character would be admissible in the first instance, subject to rebuttal by evidence of bad character. Falknor, Extrinsic Policies Affecting Admissibility, 10 Rutgers L.Rev. 574, 581–583 (1956); Tentative Recommendation and a Study Relating to the Uniform Rules of Evidence (Art. VI. Extrinsic Policies Affecting Admissibility), Cal.Law Revision Comm'n, Rep., Rec. & Studies, 657–658 (1964). Uniform Rule 47 goes farther, in that it assumes that character evidence in general satisfies the conditions of relevancy, except as provided in Uniform Rule 48. The difficulty with expanding the use of character evidence in civil cases is set forth by the California Law Revision Commission in its ultimate rejection of Uniform Rule 47, *id.,* 615:

"Character evidence is of slight probative value and may be very prejudicial. It tends to distract the trier of fact from the main question of what actually happened on the particular occasion. It subtly permits the trier of fact to reward the good man and to punish the bad man because of their respective characters despite what the evidence in the case shows actually happened."

Much of the force of the position of those favoring greater use of character evidence in civil cases is dissipated by their support of Uniform Rule 48 which excludes the evidence in negligence cases, where it could be expected to achieve its maximum usefulness. Moreover, expanding concepts of "character," which seem of necessity to extend into such areas as psychiatric evaluation and psychological testing, coupled with expanded admissibility, would open up such vistas of mental examinations as caused the Court concern in *Schlagenhauf v. Holder,* 379 U.S. 104, 85 S.Ct. 234, 13 L.Ed.2d 152 (1964). It is believed that those espousing change have not met the burden of persuasion.

Note to Subdivision (b). Subdivision (b) deals with a specialized but important application of the general rule excluding circumstantial use of character evidence. Consistently with that rule, evidence of other crimes, wrongs, or acts is not admissible to prove character as a basis for suggesting the inference that conduct on a particular occasion was in conformity with it. However, the evidence may be offered for another purpose, such as proof of motive, opportunity, and so on, which does not fall within the prohibition. In this situation the rule does not require that the evidence be excluded. No mechanical solution is offered. The determination must be made whether the danger of undue prejudice outweighs the probative value of the evidence in view of the availability of other means of proof and other facts appropriate for making decision of this kind under Rule 403. Slough and Knightly, Other Vices, Other Crimes, 41 Iowa L.Rev. 325 (1956).

1974 Enactment

Note to Subdivision (b). The second sentence of Rule 404(b) as submitted to the Congress began with the words "This subdivision does not exclude the evidence when offered". The Committee amended this language to read "It may, however, be admissible", the words used in the 1971 Advisory Committee draft, on the ground that this formulation properly placed greater emphasis on admissibility than did the final Court version. House Report No. 93–650.

Note to Subdivision (b). This rule provides that evidence of other crimes, wrongs, or acts is not admissible to prove character but may be admissible for other specified purposes such as proof of motive.

Although your committee sees no necessity in amending the rule itself, it anticipates that the use of the discretionary word "may" with respect to the admissibility of evidence of crimes, wrongs, or acts is not intended to confer any arbitrary discretion on the trial judge. Rather, it is anticipated that with respect to permissible uses for such evidence, the trial judge may exclude it only on the basis of those considerations set forth in Rule 403, i.e., prejudice, confusion or waste of time. Senate Report No. 93–1277.

1987 Amendments

The amendments are technical. No substantive change is intended.

1991 Amendments

Rule 404(b) has emerged as one of the most cited Rules in the Rules of Evidence. And in many criminal cases evidence of an accused's extrinsic acts is viewed as an important asset in the prosecution's case against an accused. Although there are a few reported decisions on use of such evidence by the defense, *see, e.g., United States v. McClure,* 546 F.2d 670 (5th Cir.1990) (acts of informant offered in entrapment defense), the overwhelming number of cases involve introduction of that evidence by the prosecution.

The amendment to Rule 404(b) adds a pretrial notice requirement in criminal cases and is intended to reduce surprise and promote early resolution on the issue of admissibility. The notice requirement thus places Rule 404(b) in the mainstream with notice and disclosure provisions in other rules of evidence. *See, e.g.,* Rule 412 (written motion of intent to offer evidence under rule), Rule 609 (written notice of intent to offer conviction older than 10 years), Rule 803(24) and 804(b)(5) (notice of intent to use residual hearsay exceptions).

The Rule expects that counsel for both the defense and the prosecution will submit the necessary request and information in a reasonable and timely fashion. Other than requiring pretrial notice, no specific time limits are stated in recognition that what constitutes a reasonable request or disclosure will depend largely on the circumstances of each case. *Compare* Fla.Stat.Ann. § 90.404(2)(b) (notice must be given at least 10 days before trial) *with* Tex.R.Evid. 404(b) (no time limit).

Likewise, no specific form of notice is required. The Committee considered and rejected a requirement that the notice satisfy the particularity requirements normally required of language used in a charging instrument. *Cf.* Fla.Stat.Ann. § 90.404(2)(b) (written disclosure must describe uncharged misconduct with particularity required of an indictment or information). Instead, the Committee opted for a generalized notice provision which requires the prosecution to apprise the defense of the general nature of the evidence of extrinsic acts. The Committee does not intend that the amendment will supercede other rules of admissibility or disclosure, such as the Jencks Act, 18 U.S.C. § 3500, et. seq. nor require the prosecution to disclose directly or indirectly the names and addresses of its witnesses, something it is currently not required to do under Federal Rule of Criminal Procedure 16.

The amendment requires the prosecution to provide notice, regardless of how it intends to use the extrinsic act evidence at trial, i.e., during its case-in-chief, for impeachment, or for possible rebuttal. The court in its discretion may, under the facts, decide that the particular request or notice was not reasonable, either because of the lack of timeliness or completeness. Because the notice requirement serves as condition precedent to admissibility of 404(b) evidence, the offered evidence is inadmissible if the court decides that the notice requirement has not been met.

Nothing in the amendment precludes the court from requiring the government to provide it with an opportunity to rule *in limine* on 404(b) evidence before it is offered or even mentioned during trial. When ruling *in limine,* the court may require the government to disclose to it the specifics of such evidence which the court must consider in determining admissibility.

The amendment does not extend to evidence of acts which are "intrinsic" to the charged offense, *see United States v. Williams,* 900 F.2d 823 (5th Cir.1990) (noting distinction between 404(b) evidence and intrinsic offense evidence). Nor is the amendment intended to redefine what evidence would otherwise be admissible under Rule 404(b). Finally, the Committee does not intend through the amendment to affect the role of the court and the jury in considering such evidence. *See United States v. Huddleston,* 485 U.S. 681, 108 S.Ct. 1496 (1988).

2000 Amendments

Rule 404(a)(1) has been amended to provide that when the accused attacks the character of an alleged victim under subdivision (a)(2) of this Rule, the door is opened to an attack on the same character trait of the accused. Current law does not allow the government to introduce negative character evidence as to the accused unless the accused introduces evidence of good character. *See, e.g., United States v. Fountain*, 768 F.2d 790 (7th Cir. 1985) (when the accused offers proof of self-defense, this permits proof of the alleged victim's character trait for peacefulness, but it does not permit proof of the accused's character trait for violence).

The amendment makes clear that the accused cannot attack the alleged victim's character and yet remain shielded from the disclosure of equally relevant evidence concerning the same character trait of the accused. For example, in a murder case with a claim of self-defense, the accused, to bolster this defense, might offer evidence of the alleged victim's violent disposition. If the government has evidence that the accused has a violent character, but is not allowed to offer this evidence as part of its rebuttal, the jury has only part of the information it needs for an informed assessment of the probabilities as to who was the initial aggressor. This may be the case even if evidence of the accused's prior violent acts is admitted under Rule 404(b), because such evidence can be admitted only for limited purposes and not to show action in conformity with the accused's character on a specific occasion. Thus, the amendment is designed to permit a more balanced presentation of character evidence when an accused chooses to attack the character of the alleged victim.

The amendment does not affect the admissibility of evidence of specific acts of uncharged misconduct offered for a purpose other than proving character under Rule 404(b). Nor does it affect the standards for proof of character by evidence of other sexual behavior or sexual offenses under Rules 412–415. By its placement in Rule 404(a)(1), the amendment covers only proof of character by way of reputation or opinion.

The amendment does not permit proof of the accused's character if the accused merely uses character evidence for a purpose other than to prove the alleged victim's propensity to act in a certain way. *See United States v. Burks*, 470 F.2d 432, 434–5 (D.C.Cir. 1972) (evidence of the alleged victim's violent character, when known by the accused, was admissible "on the issue of whether or not the defendant reasonably feared he was in danger of imminent great bodily harm"). Finally, the amendment does not permit proof of the accused's character when the accused attacks the alleged victim's character as a witness under Rule 608 or 609.

The term "alleged" is inserted before each reference to "victim" in the Rule, in order to provide consistency with Evidence Rule 412.

GAP Report—Proposed Amendment to Rule 404(a)

The Committee made the following changes to the published draft of the proposed amendment to Evidence Rule 404(a):

1. The term "a pertinent trait of character" was changed to "the same trait of character," in order to limit the scope of the government's rebuttal. The Committee Note was revised to accord with this change in the text.

2. The word "alleged" was added before each reference in the Rule to a "victim" in order to provide consistency with Evidence Rule 412. The Committee Note was amended to accord with this change in the text.

3. The Committee Note was amended to clarify that rebuttal is not permitted under this Rule if the accused proffers evidence of the alleged victim's character for a purpose other than to prove the alleged victim's propensity to act in a certain manner.

2006 Amendments

The Rule has been amended to clarify that in a civil case evidence of a person's character is never admissible to prove that the person acted in conformity with the character trait. The amendment resolves the dispute in the case law over whether the exceptions in subdivisions (a)(1) and (2) permit the circumstantial use of character evidence in civil cases. *Compare Carson v. Polley*, 689 F.2d 562, 576 (5th Cir. 1982) ("when a central issue in a case is close to one of a criminal nature, the exceptions to the Rule 404(a) ban on character evidence may be invoked"), *with SEC v. Towers Financial Corp.*, 966 F.Supp. 203 (S.D.N.Y. 1997) (relying on the terms "accused" and "prosecution" in Rule 404(a) to conclude that the exceptions in subdivisions (a)(1) and (2) are inapplicable in civil cases). The amendment is consistent with the original intent of the Rule, which was to prohibit the circumstantial use of character evidence in civil cases, even where closely related to criminal charges. *See Ginter v. Northwestern Mut. Life Ins. Co.*, 576 F.Supp. 627, 629–30 (D. Ky.1984) ("It seems beyond peradventure of doubt that the drafters of F.R.Evi. 404(a) explicitly intended that all character evidence, except where 'character is at issue' was to be excluded" in civil cases).

The circumstantial use of character evidence is generally discouraged because it carries serious risks of prejudice, confusion and delay. *See Michelson v. United States,* 335 U.S. 469, 476 (1948) ("The overriding policy of excluding such evidence, despite its admitted probative value, is the practical experience that its disallowance tends to prevent confusion of issues, unfair surprise and undue prejudice."). In criminal cases, the so-called "mercy rule" permits a criminal defendant to introduce evidence of pertinent character traits of the defendant and the victim. But that is because the accused, whose liberty is at stake, may need "a counterweight against the strong investigative and prosecutorial resources of the government." C. Mueller & L. Kirkpatrick, *Evidence: Practice Under the Rules*, pp. 264–5 (2d ed. 1999). See also Richard Uviller, *Evidence of Character to Prove Conduct: Illusion, Illogic, and Injustice in the Courtroom*, 130 U.Pa.L.Rev. 845, 855 (1982) (the rule prohibiting circumstantial use of character evidence "was relaxed to allow the criminal defendant with so much at stake and so little available in the way of conventional proof to have special dispensation to tell the factfinder just what sort of person he really is"). Those concerns do not apply to parties in civil cases.

The amendment also clarifies that evidence otherwise admissible under Rule 404(a)(2) may nonetheless be excluded in a criminal case involving sexual misconduct. In such a case, the admissibility of evidence of the victim's sexual behavior and predisposition is governed by the more stringent provisions of Rule 412.

Nothing in the amendment is intended to affect the scope of Rule 404(b). While Rule 404(b) refers to the "accused," the "prosecution," and a "criminal case," it does so only in the context of a notice requirement. The admissibility standards of Rule 404(b) remain fully applicable to both civil and criminal cases.

2011 Amendments

The language of Rule 404 has been amended as part of the restyling of the Evidence Rules to make them more easily understood and to make style and terminology consistent throughout the rules. These changes are intended to be stylistic only. There is no intent to change any result in any ruling on evidence admissibility.

Rule 405. Methods of Proving Character

(a) By Reputation or Opinion. When evidence of a person's character or character trait is admissible, it may be proved by testimony about the person's reputation or by testimony in the form of an opinion. On cross- examination of the character witness, the court may allow an inquiry into relevant specific instances of the person's conduct.

(b) By Specific Instances of Conduct. When a person's character or character trait is an essential element of a charge, claim, or defense, the character or trait may also be proved by relevant specific instances of the person's conduct.

(Pub.L. 93–595, § 1, Jan. 2, 1975, 88 Stat. 1932; Mar. 2, 1987, eff. Oct. 1, 1987; Apr. 26, 2011, eff. Dec. 1, 2011.)

ADVISORY COMMITTEE NOTES

1972 Proposed Rules

The rule deals only with allowable methods of proving character, not with the admissibility of character evidence, which is covered in Rule 404.

Of the three methods of proving character provided by the rule, evidence of specific instances of conduct is the most convincing. At the same time it possesses the greatest capacity to arouse prejudice, to confuse, to surprise, and to consume time. Consequently the rule confines the use of evidence of this kind to cases in which character is, in the strict sense, in issue and hence deserving of a searching inquiry. When character is used circumstantially and hence occupies a lesser status in the case, proof may be only by reputation and opinion. These latter methods are also available when character is in issue. This treatment is, with respect to specific instances of conduct and reputation, conventional contemporary common law doctrine. McCormick § 153.

In recognizing opinion as a means of proving character, the rule departs from usual contemporary practice in favor of that of an earlier day. See 7 Wigmore § 1986, pointing out that the earlier practice permitted opinion and arguing strongly for evidence based on personal knowledge and belief as contrasted with "the secondhand, irresponsible product of multiplied guesses and gossip which we term 'reputation'." It seems likely that the persistence of reputation evidence is due to its largely being opinion in disguise. Traditionally character has been regarded primarily in moral overtones of good and bad: chaste, peaceable, truthful, honest. Nevertheless, on occasion nonmoral considerations crop up, as in the case of the incompetent driver, and this seems bound to happen increasingly. If character is defined as the kind of person one is, then account must be taken of varying ways of arriving at the estimate. These may range from the opinion of the employer who has found the man honest to the opinion of the psychiatrist based upon examination and testing. No effective dividing line exists between character and mental capacity, and the latter traditionally has been provable by opinion.

According to the great majority of cases, on cross-examination inquiry is allowable as to whether the reputation witness has heard of particular instances of conduct pertinent to the trait in question. *Michelson v. United States,* 335 U.S. 469, 69 S.Ct. 213, 93 L.Ed. 168 (1948); Annot., 47 A.L.R.2d 1258. The theory is that, since the reputation witness relates what he has heard, the inquiry tends to shed light on the accuracy of his hearing and reporting. Accordingly, the opinion witness would be asked whether he knew, as well as whether he had heard. The fact is, of course, that these distinctions are of slight if any practical significance, and the second sentence of subdivision (a) eliminates them as a factor in formulating questions. This recognition of the propriety of inquiring into specific instances of conduct does not circumscribe inquiry otherwise into the bases of opinion and reputation testimony.

The express allowance of inquiry into specific instances of conduct on cross-examination in subdivision (a) and the express allowance of it as part of a case in chief when character is actually in issue in subdivision (b) contemplate that testimony of specific instances is not generally permissible on the direct examination of an ordinary opinion witness to character. Similarly as to witnesses to the character of witnesses under Rule 608(b). Opinion testimony on direct in these situations ought in general to correspond to reputation testimony as now given, *i.e.,* be confined to the nature and extent of observation and acquaintance upon which the opinion is based. See Rule 701.

1974 Enactment

Note to Subdivision (a). Rule 405(a) as submitted proposed to change existing law by allowing evidence of character in the form of opinion as well as reputation testimony. Fearing, among other reasons, that wholesale allowance of opinion testimony might tend to turn a trial into a swearing contest between conflicting character witnesses, the Committee decided to delete from this Rule, as well as from Rule 608(a) which involves a related problem, reference to opinion testimony. House Report No. 93–650.

The Senate makes two language changes in the nature of conforming amendments. The Conference adopts the Senate amendments. House Report No. 93–1597.

1987 Amendments

The amendment is technical. No substantive change is intended.

2011 Amendments

The language of Rule 405 has been amended as part of the restyling of the Evidence Rules to make them more easily understood and to make style and terminology consistent throughout the rules. These changes are intended to be stylistic only. There is no intent to change any result in any ruling on evidence admissibility.

Rule 406. Habit; Routine Practice

Evidence of a person's habit or an organization's routine practice may be admitted to prove that on a particular occasion the person or organization acted in accordance with the habit or routine practice. The court may admit this evidence regardless of whether it is corroborated or whether there was an eyewitness.

(Pub.L. 93–595, § 1, Jan. 2, 1975, 88 Stat. 1932; Apr. 26, 2011, eff. Dec. 1, 2011.)

ADVISORY COMMITTEE NOTES

1972 Proposed Rules

An oft-quoted paragraph, McCormick, § 162, p. 340, describes habit in terms effectively contrasting it with character:

"Character and habit are close akin. Character is a generalized description of one's disposition, or of one's disposition in respect to a general trait, such as honesty, temperance, or peacefulness. 'Habit,' in modern usage, both lay and psychological, is more specific. It describes one's regular response to a repeated specific situation. If we speak of character for care, we think of the person's tendency to act prudently in all the varying situations of life, in business, family life, in handling automobiles and in walking across the street. A habit, on the other hand, is the person's regular practice of meeting a particular kind of situation with a specific type of conduct, such as the habit of going down a particular stairway two stairs at a time, or of giving the hand-signal for a left turn, or of alighting from railway cars while they are moving. The doing of the habitual acts may become semi-automatic."

Equivalent behavior on the part of a group is designated "routine practice of an organization" in the rule.

Agreement is general that habit evidence is highly persuasive as proof of conduct on a particular occasion. Again quoting McCormick § 162, p. 341:

"Character may be thought of as the sum of one's habits though doubtless it is more than this. But unquestionably the uniformity of one's response to habit is far greater than the consistency with which one's conduct conforms to character or disposition. Even though character comes in only exceptionally as evidence of an act, surely any sensible man in investigating whether X did a particular act would be greatly helped in his inquiry by evidence as to whether he was in the habit of doing it."

When disagreement has appeared, its focus has been upon the question what constitutes habit, and the reason for this is readily apparent. The extent to which instances must be multiplied and consistency of behavior maintained in order to rise to the status of habit inevitably gives rise to differences of opinion. Lewan, Rationale of Habit Evidence, 16 Syracuse L.Rev. 39, 49 (1964). While adequacy of sampling and uniformity of response are key factors, precise standards for measuring their sufficiency for evidence purposes cannot be formulated.

The rule is consistent with prevailing views. Much evidence is excluded simply because of failure to achieve the status of habit. Thus, evidence of intemperate "habits" is generally excluded when offered as proof of drunkenness in accident cases, Annot., 46 A.L.R.2d 103, and evidence of other assaults is inadmissible to prove the instant one in a civil assault action, Annot., 66 A.L.R.2d 806. In *Levin v. United States,* 119 U.S.App.D.C. 156, 338 F.2d 265 (1964), testimony as to the religious "habits" of the accused, offered as tending to prove that he was at home observing the Sabbath rather than out obtaining money through larceny by trick, was held properly excluded:

"It seems apparent to us that an individual's religious practices would not be the type of activities which would lend themselves to the characterization of 'invariable regularity.' [1 Wigmore 520.] Certainly the very volitional basis of the activity raises serious questions as to its invariable nature, and hence its probative value." *Id.* at 272.

These rulings are not inconsistent with the trend towards admitting evidence of business transactions between one of the parties and a third person as tending to prove that he made the same bargain or proposal in the litigated situation. Slough, Relevancy Unraveled, 6 Kan.L.Rev. 38–41 (1957). Nor are they inconsistent with such cases as *Whittemore v. Lockheed Aircraft Corp.*, 65 Cal.App.2d 737, 151 P.2d 670 (1944), upholding the admission of evidence that plaintiff's intestate had on four other occasions flown planes from defendant's factory for delivery to his employer airline, offered to prove that he was piloting rather than a guest on a plane which crashed and killed all on board while en route for delivery.

A considerable body of authority has required that evidence of the routine practice of an organization be corroborated as a condition precedent to its admission in evidence. Slough, Relevancy Unraveled, 5 Kan.L.Rev. 404, 449 (1957). This requirement is specifically rejected by the rule on the ground that it relates to the sufficiency of the evidence rather than admissibility. A similar position is taken in New Jersey Rule 49. The rule also rejects the requirement of the absence of eyewitnesses, sometimes encountered with respect to admitting habit evidence to prove freedom from contributory negligence in wrongful death cases. For comment critical of the requirements see Frank, J., in *Cereste v. New York,* N.H. & H.R. Co., 231 F.2d 50 (2d Cir.1956), cert. denied 351 U.S. 951, 76 S.Ct. 848, 100 L.Ed. 1475, 10 Vand.L.Rev. 447 (1957); McCormick § 162, p. 342. The omission of the requirement from the California Evidence Code is said to have effected its elimination. Comment, Cal.Ev.Code § 1105.

2011 Amendments

The language of Rule 406 has been amended as part of the restyling of the Evidence Rules to make them more easily understood and to make style and terminology consistent throughout the rules. These changes are intended to be stylistic only. There is no intent to change any result in any ruling on evidence admissibility.

Rule 407. Subsequent Remedial Measures

When measures are taken that would have made an earlier injury or harm less likely to occur, evidence of the subsequent measures is not admissible to prove:

- negligence;
- culpable conduct;
- a defect in a product or its design; or
- a need for a warning or instruction.

But the court may admit this evidence for another purpose, such as impeachment or—if disputed—proving ownership, control, or the feasibility of precautionary measures.

(Pub.L. 93–595, § 1, Jan. 2, 1975, 88 Stat. 1932; Apr. 11, 1997, eff. Dec. 1, 1997; Apr. 26, 2011, eff. Dec. 1, 2011.)

ADVISORY COMMITTEE NOTES

1972 Proposed Rules

The rule incorporates conventional doctrine which excludes evidence of subsequent remedial measures as proof of an admission of fault. The rule rests on two grounds. (1) The conduct is not in fact an admission, since the conduct is equally consistent with injury by mere accident or through contributory negligence. Or, as Baron Bramwell put it, the rule rejects the notion that "because the world gets wiser as it gets older, therefore it was foolish before." *Hart v. Lancashire & Yorkshire Ry. Co.,* 21 L.T.R. N.S. 261, 263 (1869). Under a liberal theory of relevancy this ground alone would not support exclusion as the inference is still a possible one. (2) The other, and more impressive, ground for exclusion rests on a social policy of encouraging people to take, or at least not discouraging them from taking, steps in furtherance of added safety. The courts have applied this principle to exclude evidence of subsequent repairs, installation of safety devices, changes in company rules, and discharge of employees, and the language of the present rule is broad enough to encompass all of them. See Falknor, Extrinsic Policies Affecting Admissibility, 10 Rutgers L.Rev. 574, 590 (1956).

The second sentence of the rule directs attention to the limitations of the rule. Exclusion is called for only when the evidence of subsequent remedial measures is offered as proof of negligence or culpable conduct. In effect it rejects the suggested inference that fault is admitted. Other purposes are, however, allowable, including ownership or control, existence of duty, and feasibility of precautionary measures, if controverted, and impeachment. 2 Wigmore § 283; Annot., 64 A.L.R.2d 1296. Two recent federal cases are illustrative. *Boeing Airplane Co. v. Brown,* 291 F.2d 310 (9th Cir.1961), an action against an airplane manufacturer for using an allegedly defectively designed alternator shaft which caused a plane crash, upheld the admission of evidence of subsequent design modification for the purpose of showing that design changes and safeguards were feasible. And *Powers v. J.B. Michael & Co.,* 329 F.2d 674 (6th Cir.1964), an action against a road contractor for negligent failure to put out warning signs, sustained the admission of evidence that defendant subsequently put out signs to show that the portion of the road in question was under defendant's control. The requirement that the other purpose be controverted calls for automatic exclusion unless a genuine issue be present and allows the opposing party to lay the groundwork for exclusion by making an admission. Otherwise the factors of undue prejudice, confusion of issues, misleading the jury, and waste of time remain for consideration under Rule 403.

For comparable rules, see Uniform Rule 51; California Evidence Code § 1151; Kansas Code of Civil Procedure § 60–451; New Jersey Evidence Rule 51.

1997 Amendments

The amendment to Rule 407 makes two changes in the rule. First, the words "an injury or harm allegedly caused by" were added to clarify that the rule applies only to changes made after the occurrence that produced the damages giving rise to the action. Evidence of measures taken by the defendant prior to the "event" causing "injury or harm" do not fall within the exclusionary scope of Rule 407 even if they occurred after the manufacture or design of the product. See *Chase v. General Motors Corp.,* 856 F.2d 17, 21–22 (4th Cir. 1988).

Second, Rule 407 has been amended to provide that evidence of subsequent remedial measures may not be used to prove "a defect in a product or its design, or that a warning or instruction should have accompanied a product." This amendment adopts the view of a majority of the circuits that have interpreted Rule 407 to apply to products liability actions. See *Raymond v. Raymond Corp., 938 F.2d 1518,*

1522 (1st Cir. 1991); In re Joint Eastern District and Southern District Asbestos Litigation v. Armstrong World industries, Inc., 995 F.2d 343 (2d Cir. 1993); *Cann v. Ford Motor Co.*, 658 F.2d 54, 60 (2d Cir. 1981), *cert. denied*, 456 U.S. 960 (1982); *Kelly v. Crown Equipment Co.*, 970 F.2d 1273, 1275 (3d Cir. 1992); *Werner v. Upjohn, Inc.*, 628 F.2d 848 (4th Cir. 1980); *cert. denied*, 449 U.S. 1080 (1981); *Grenada Steel Industries, Inc. v. Alabama Oxygen Co., Inc.*, 695 F.2d 883 (5th Cir. 1983); *Bauman v. Volkswagenwerk Aktiengesellschaft*, 621 F.2d 230, 232 (6th Cir. 1980); *Flaminio v. Honda Motor Company, Ltd.*, 733 F.2d 463, 469 (7th Cir. 1984); *Gauthier v. AMF, Inc.*, 788 F.2d 634, 636–37 (9th Cir. 1986).

Although this amendment adopts a uniform federal rule, it should be noted that evidence of subsequent remedial measures may be admissible pursuant to the second sentence of Rule 407. Evidence of subsequent measures that is not barred by Rule 407 may still be subject to exclusion on Rule 403 grounds when the dangers of prejudice or confusion substantially outweigh the probative value of the evidence.

GAP Report on Rule 407. The words "injury or harm" were substituted for the word "event " in line 3. The stylization changes in the second sentence of the rule were eliminated. The words "causing 'injury or harm' " were added to the Committee Note.

2011 Amendments

The language of Rule 407 has been amended as part of the general restyling of the Evidence Rules to make them more easily understood and to make style and terminology consistent throughout the rules. These changes are intended to be stylistic only. There is no intent to change any result in any ruling on evidence admissibility.

Rule 407 previously provided that evidence was not excluded if offered for a purpose not explicitly prohibited by the Rule. To improve the language of the Rule, it now provides that the court may admit evidence if offered for a permissible purpose. There is no intent to change the process for admitting evidence covered by the Rule. It remains the case that if offered for an impermissible purpose, it must be excluded, and if offered for a purpose not barred by the Rule, its admissibility remains governed by the general principles of Rules 402, 403, 801, etc.

Rule 408. Compromise Offers and Negotiations

(a) Prohibited Uses. Evidence of the following is not admissible—on behalf of any party—either to prove or disprove the validity or amount of a disputed claim or to impeach by a prior inconsistent statement or a contradiction:

(1) furnishing, promising, or offering—or accepting, promising to accept, or offering to accept—a valuable consideration in compromising or attempting to compromise the claim; and

(2) conduct or a statement made during compromise negotiations about the claim—except when offered in a criminal case and when the negotiations related to a claim by a public office in the exercise of its regulatory, investigative, or enforcement authority.

(b) Exceptions. The court may admit this evidence for another purpose, such as proving a witness's bias or prejudice, negating a contention of undue delay, or proving an effort to obstruct a criminal investigation or prosecution.

(Pub.L. 93–595, § 1, Jan. 2, 1975, 88 Stat. 1933; Apr. 12, 2006, eff. Dec. 1, 2006; Apr. 26, 2011, eff. Dec. 1, 2011.)

ADVISORY COMMITTEE NOTES

1972 Proposed Rules

As a matter of general agreement, evidence of an offer to compromise a claim is not receivable in evidence as an admission of, as the case may be, the validity or invalidity of the claim. As with evidence of subsequent remedial measures, dealt with in Rule 407, exclusion may be based on two grounds. (1) The evidence is irrelevant, since the offer may be motivated by a desire for peace rather than from any concession of weakness of position. The validity of this position will vary as the amount of the offer varies in relation to the size of the claim and may also be influenced by other circumstances. (2) A more consistently impressive ground is promotion of the public policy favoring the compromise and settlement of disputes. McCormick §§ 76, 251. While the rule is ordinarily phrased in terms of offers of compromise, it is apparent that a similar attitude must be taken with respect to completed compromises when offered against a party thereto. This latter situation will not, of course, ordinarily occur except when a party to the present litigation has compromised with a third person.

The same policy underlies the provision of Rule 68 of the Federal Rules of Civil Procedure that evidence of an unaccepted offer of judgment is not admissible except in a proceeding to determine costs.

The practical value of the common law rule has been greatly diminished by its inapplicability to admissions of fact, even though made in the course of compromise negotiations, unless hypothetical, stated to be "without prejudice," or so connected with the offer as to be inseparable from it. McCormick § 251, pp. 540–541. An inevitable effect is to inhibit freedom of communication with respect to compromise, even among lawyers. Another effect is the generation of controversy over whether a given statement falls within or without the protected area. These considerations account for the expansion of the rule herewith to include evidence of conduct or statements made in compromise negotiations, as well as the offer or completed compromise itself. For similar provisions see California Evidence Code §§ 1152, 1154.

The policy considerations which underlie the rule do not come into play when the effort is to induce a creditor to settle an admittedly due amount for a lesser sum. McCormick § 251, p. 540. Hence the rule requires that the claim be disputed as to either validity or amount.

The final sentence of the rule serves to point out some limitations upon its applicability. Since the rule excludes only when the purpose is proving the validity or invalidity of the claim or its amount, an offer for another purpose is not within the rule. The illustrative situations mentioned in the rule are supported by the authorities. As to proving bias or prejudice of a witness, see Annot., 161 A.L.R. 395, *contra, Fenberg v. Rosenthal,* 348 Ill.App. 510, 109 N.E.2d 402 (1952), and negativing a contention of lack of due diligence in presenting a claim, 4 Wigmore § 1061. An effort to "buy off" the prosecution or a prosecuting witness in a criminal case is not within the policy of the rule of exclusion. McCormick § 251, p. 542.

For other rules of similar import, see Uniform Rules 52 and 53; California Evidence Code §§ 1152, 1154; Kansas Code of Civil Procedure §§ 60–452, 60–453; New Jersey Evidence Rules 52 and 53.

1974 Enactment

Under existing federal law evidence of conduct and statements made in compromise negotiations is admissible in subsequent litigation between the parties. The second sentence of Rule 408 as submitted by the Supreme Court proposed to reverse that doctrine in the interest of further promoting non-judicial settlement of disputes. Some agencies of government expressed the view that the Court formulation was likely to impede rather than assist efforts to achieve settlement of disputes. For one thing, it is not always easy to tell when compromise negotiations begin, and informal dealings end. Also, parties dealing with government agencies would be reluctant to furnish factual information at preliminary meetings; they would wait until "compromise negotiations" began and thus hopefully effect an immunity for themselves with respect to the evidence supplied. In light of these considerations, the Committee recast the Rule so that admissions of liability or opinions given during compromise negotiations continue inadmissible, but evidence of unqualified factual assertions is admissible. The latter aspect of the Rule is drafted, however, so as to preserve other possible objections to the introduction of such evidence. The Committee intends no modification of current law whereby a party may protect himself from future use of his statements by couching them in hypothetical conditional form. House Report No. 93–650.

This rule as reported makes evidence of settlement or attempted settlement of a disputed claim inadmissible when offered as an admission of liability or the amount of liability. The purpose of this rule is to encourage settlements which would be discouraged if such evidence were admissible.

Under present law, in most jurisdictions, statements of fact made during settlement negotiations, however, are excepted from this ban and are admissible. The only escape from admissibility of statements of fact made in a settlement negotiation is if the declarant or his representative expressly states that the statement is hypothetical in nature or is made without prejudice. Rule 408 as submitted by the Court reversed the traditional rule. It would have brought statements of fact within the ban and made them, as well as an offer of settlement, inadmissible.

The House amended the rule and would continue to make evidence of facts disclosed during compromise negotiations admissible. It thus reverted to the traditional rule. The House committee report states that the committee intends to preserve current law under which a party may protect himself by couching his statements in hypothetical form [See House Report No. 93–650 above]. The real impact of this amendment, however, is to deprive the rule of much of its salutary effect. The exception for factual admissions was believed by the Advisory Committee to hamper free communication between parties and thus to constitute an unjustifiable restraint upon efforts to negotiate settlements—the encouragement of which is the purpose of the rule. Further, by protecting hypothetically phrased statements, it constituted a preference for the sophisticated, and a trap for the unwary.

Three States which had adopted rules of evidence patterned after the proposed rules prescribed by the Supreme Court opted for versions of rule 408 identical with the Supreme Court draft with respect to the inadmissibility of conduct or statements made in compromise negotiations [Nev.Rev.Stats. § 48.105; N.Mex.Stats.Anno. (1973 Supp.) § 20–4–408; West's Wis.Stats.Anno. (1973 Supp.) § 904.08].

For these reasons, the committee has deleted the House amendment and restored the rule to the version submitted by the Supreme Court with one additional amendment. This amendment adds a sentence to insure that evidence, such as documents, is not rendered inadmissible merely because it is presented in the course of compromise negotiations if the evidence is otherwise discoverable. A party should not be able to immunize from admissibility documents otherwise discoverable merely by offering them in a compromise negotiation. Senate Report No. 93–1277.

The House bill provides that evidence of admissions of liability or opinions given during compromise negotiations is not admissible, but that evidence of facts disclosed during compromise negotiations is not inadmissible by virtue of having been first disclosed in the compromise negotiations. The Senate amendment provides that evidence of conduct or statements made in compromise negotiations is not admissible. The Senate amendment also provides that the rule does not require the exclusion of any evidence otherwise discoverable merely because it is presented in the course of compromise negotiations.

The House bill was drafted to meet the objection of executive agencies that under the rule as proposed by the Supreme Court, a party could present a fact during compromise negotiations and thereby prevent an opposing party from offering evidence of that fact at trial even though such evidence was obtained from independent sources. The Senate amendment expressly precludes this result.

The Conference adopts the Senate amendment. House Report No. 93–1597.

2006 Amendment

Rule 408 has been amended to settle some questions in the courts about the scope of the Rule, and to make it easier to read. First, the amendment provides that Rule 408 does not prohibit the introduction in a criminal case of statements or conduct during compromise negotiations regarding a civil dispute by a government regulatory, investigative, or enforcement agency. *See, e.g., United States v. Prewitt*, 34 F.3d 436, 439 (7th Cir. 1994) (admissions of fault made in compromise of a civil securities enforcement action were admissible against the accused in a subsequent criminal action for mail fraud). Where an individual makes a statement in the presence of government agents, its subsequent admission in a criminal case should not be unexpected. The individual can seek to protect against subsequent disclosure through negotiation and agreement with the civil regulator or an attorney for the government.

Statements made in compromise negotiations of a claim by a government agency may be excluded in criminal cases where the circumstances so warrant under Rule 403. For example, if an individual was unrepresented at the time the statement was made in a civil enforcement proceeding, its probative value in a subsequent criminal case may be minimal. But there is no absolute exclusion imposed by Rule 408.

In contrast, statements made during compromise negotiations of other disputed claims are not admissible in subsequent criminal litigation, when offered to prove liability for, invalidity of, or amount of those claims. When private parties enter into compromise negotiations they cannot protect against the subsequent use of statements in criminal cases by way of private ordering. The inability to guarantee protection against subsequent use could lead to parties refusing to admit fault, even if by doing so they could favorably settle the private matter. Such a chill on settlement negotiations would be contrary to the policy of Rule 408.

The amendment distinguishes statements and conduct (such as a direct admission of fault) made in compromise negotiations of a civil claim by a government agency from an offer or acceptance of a compromise of such a claim. An offer or acceptance of a compromise of any civil claim is excluded under the Rule if offered against the defendant as an admission of fault. In that case, the predicate for the evidence would be that the defendant, by compromising with the government agency, has admitted the validity and amount of the civil claim, and that this admission has sufficient probative value to be considered as evidence of guilt. But unlike a direct statement of fault, an offer or acceptance of a compromise is not very probative of the defendant's guilt. Moreover, admitting such an offer or acceptance could deter a defendant from settling a civil regulatory action, for fear of evidentiary use in a subsequent criminal action. *See, e.g.*, Fishman, *Jones on Evidence, Civil and*

Criminal, § 22:16 at 199, n.83 (7th ed. 2000) ("A target of a potential criminal investigation may be unwilling to settle civil claims against him if by doing so he increases the risk of prosecution and conviction.").

The amendment retains the language of the original rule that bars compromise evidence only when offered as evidence of the "validity," "invalidity," or "amount" of the disputed claim. The intent is to retain the extensive case law finding Rule 408 inapplicable when compromise evidence is offered for a purpose other than to prove the validity, invalidity, or amount of a disputed claim. *See, e.g., Athey v. Farmers Ins. Exchange*, 234 F.3d 357 (8th Cir. 2000) (evidence of settlement offer by insurer was properly admitted to prove insurer's bad faith); *Coakley & Williams v. Structural Concrete Equip.*, 973 F.2d 349 (4th Cir. 1992) (evidence of settlement is not precluded by Rule 408 where offered to prove a party's intent with respect to the scope of a release); *Cates v. Morgan Portable Bldg. Corp.*, 708 F.2d 683 (7th Cir. 1985) (Rule 408 does not bar evidence of a settlement when offered to prove a breach of the settlement agreement, as the purpose of the evidence is to prove the fact of settlement as opposed to the validity or amount of the underlying claim); *Uforma/Shelby Bus. Forms, Inc. v. NLRB*, 111 F.3d 1284 (6th Cir. 1997) (threats made in settlement negotiations were admissible; Rule 408 is inapplicable when the claim is based upon a wrong that is committed during the course of settlement negotiations). So for example, Rule 408 is inapplicable if offered to show that a party made fraudulent statements in order to settle a litigation.

The amendment does not affect the case law providing that Rule 408 is inapplicable when evidence of the compromise is offered to prove notice. *See, e.g., United States v. Austin*, 54 F.3d 394 (7th Cir. 1995) (no error to admit evidence of the defendant's settlement with the FTC, because it was offered to prove that the defendant was on notice that subsequent similar conduct was wrongful); *Spell v. McDaniel*, 824 F.2d 1380 (4th Cir. 1987) (in a civil rights action alleging that an officer used excessive force, a prior settlement by the City of another brutality claim was properly admitted to prove that the City was on notice of aggressive behavior by police officers).

The amendment prohibits the use of statements made in settlement negotiations when offered to impeach by prior inconsistent statement or through contradiction. Such broad impeachment would tend to swallow the exclusionary rule and would impair the public policy of promoting settlements. *See McCormick on Evidence* at 186 (5th ed. 1999) ("Use of statements made in compromise negotiations to impeach the testimony of a party, which is not specifically treated in Rule 408, is fraught with danger of misuse of the statements to prove liability, threatens frank interchange of information during negotiations, and generally should not be permitted."). *See also EEOC v. Gear Petroleum, Inc.*, 948 F.2d 1542 (10th Cir.1991) (letter sent as part of settlement negotiation cannot be used to impeach defense witnesses by way of contradiction or prior inconsistent statement; such broad impeachment would undermine the policy of encouraging uninhibited settlement negotiations).

The amendment makes clear that Rule 408 excludes compromise evidence even when a party seeks to admit its own settlement offer or statements made in settlement negotiations. If a party were to reveal its own statement or offer, this could itself reveal the fact that the adversary entered into settlement negotiations. The protections of Rule 408 cannot be waived unilaterally because the Rule, by definition, protects both parties from having the fact of negotiation disclosed to the jury. Moreover, proof of statements and offers made in settlement would often have to be made through the testimony of attorneys, leading to the risks and costs of disqualification. *See generally Pierce v. F.R. Tripler & Co.*, 955 F.2d 820, 828 (2d Cir. 1992) (settlement offers are excluded under Rule 408 even if it is the offeror who seeks to admit them; noting that the "widespread admissibility of the substance of settlement offers could bring with it a rash of motions for disqualification of a party's chosen counsel who would likely become a witness at trial").

The sentence of the Rule referring to evidence "otherwise discoverable" has been deleted as superfluous. *See, e.g.*, Advisory Committee Note to Maine Rule of Evidence 408 (refusing to include the sentence in the Maine version of Rule 408 and noting that the sentence "seems to state what the law would be if it were omitted"); Advisory Committee Note to Wyoming Rule of Evidence 408 (refusing to include the sentence in Wyoming Rule 408 on the ground that it was "superfluous"). The intent of the sentence was to prevent a party from trying to immunize admissible information, such as a pre-existing document, through the pretense of disclosing it during compromise negotiations. *See Ramada Development Co. v. Rauch*, 644 F.2d 1097 (5th Cir. 1981). But even without the sentence, the Rule cannot be read to protect pre-existing information simply because it was presented to the adversary in compromise negotiations.

2011 Amendments

The language of Rule 408 has been amended as part of the general restyling of the Evidence Rules to make them more easily understood and to make style and terminology consistent throughout the rules. These changes are intended to be stylistic only. There is no intent to change any result in any ruling on evidence admissibility.

Rule 408 previously provided that evidence was not excluded if offered for a purpose not explicitly prohibited by the Rule. To improve the language of the Rule, it now provides that the court may admit evidence if offered for a permissible purpose. There is no intent to change the process for admitting evidence covered by the Rule. It remains the case that if offered for an impermissible purpose, it must be excluded, and if offered for a purpose not barred by the Rule, its admissibility remains governed by the general principles of Rules 402, 403, 801, etc.

The Committee deleted the reference to "liability" on the ground that the deletion makes the Rule flow better and easier to read, and because "liability" is covered by the broader term "validity." Courts have not made substantive decisions on the basis of any distinction between validity and liability. No change in current practice or in the coverage of the Rule is intended.

Rule 409. Offers to Pay Medical and Similar Expenses

Evidence of furnishing, promising to pay, or offering to pay medical, hospital, or similar expenses resulting from an injury is not admissible to prove liability for the injury.

(Pub.L. 93–595, § 1, Jan. 2, 1975, 88 Stat.1933; Apr. 26, 2011, eff. Dec. 1, 2011.)

ADVISORY COMMITTEE NOTES

1972 Proposed Rules

The considerations underlying this rule parallel those underlying Rules 407 and 408, which deal respectively with subsequent remedial measures and offers of compromise. As stated in Annot., 20 A.L.R.2d 291, 293:

"[G]enerally, evidence of payment of medical, hospital, or similar expenses of an injured party by the opposing party, is not admissible, the reason often given being that such payment or offer is usually made from humane impulses and not from an admission of liability, and that to hold otherwise would tend to discourage assistance to the injured person."

Contrary to Rule 408, dealing with offers of compromise, the present rule does not extend to conduct or statements not a part of the act of furnishing or offering or promising to pay. This difference in treatment arises from fundamental differences in nature. Communication is essential if compromises are to be effected, and consequently broad protection of statements is needed. This is not so in cases of payments or offers or promises to pay medical expenses, where factual statements may be expected to be incidental in nature.

For rules on the same subject, but phrased in terms of "humanitarian motives," see Uniform Rule 52; California Evidence Code § 1152; Kansas Code of Civil Procedure § 60–452; New Jersey Evidence Rule 52.

2011 Amendments

The language of Rule 409 has been amended as part of the restyling of the Evidence Rules to make them more easily understood and to make style and terminology consistent throughout the rules. These changes are intended to be stylistic only. There is no intent to change any result in any ruling on evidence admissibility.

Rule 410. Pleas, Plea Discussions, and Related Statements

(a) Prohibited Uses. In a civil or criminal case, evidence of the following is not admissible against the defendant who made the plea or participated in the plea discussions:

(1) a guilty plea that was later withdrawn;

(2) a nolo contendere plea;

(3) a statement made during a proceeding on either of those pleas under Federal Rule of Criminal Procedure 11 or a comparable state procedure; or

(4) a statement made during plea discussions with an attorney for the prosecuting authority if the discussions did not result in a guilty plea or they resulted in a later-withdrawn guilty plea.

(b) Exceptions. The court may admit a statement described in Rule 410(a)(3) or (4):

(1) in any proceeding in which another statement made during the same plea or plea discussions has been introduced, if in fairness the statements ought to be considered together; or

(2) in a criminal proceeding for perjury or false statement, if the defendant made the statement under oath, on the record, and with counsel present.

(Pub.L. 93–595, § 1, Jan. 2, 1975, 88 Stat. 1933; Pub.L. 94–149, § 1(9), Dec. 12, 1975, 89 Stat. 805; Apr. 30, 1979, eff. Dec. 1, 1980; Apr. 26, 2011, eff. Dec. 1, 2011.)

ADVISORY COMMITTEE NOTES

1972 Proposed Rules

Withdrawn pleas of guilty were held inadmissible in federal prosecutions in *Kercheval v. United States,* 274 U.S. 220, 47 S.Ct. 582, 71 L.Ed. 1009 (1927). The Court pointed out that to admit the withdrawn plea would effectively set at naught the allowance of withdrawal and place the accused in a dilemma utterly inconsistent with the decision to award him a trial. The New York Court of Appeals, in *People v. Spitaleri,* 9 N.Y.2d 168, 212 N.Y.S.2d 53, 173 N.E.2d 35 (1961), reexamined and overturned its earlier decisions which had allowed admission. In addition to the reasons set forth in Kercheval, which was quoted at length, the court pointed out that the effect of admitting the plea was to compel defendant to take the stand by way of explanation and to open the way for the prosecution to call the lawyer who had represented him at the time of entering the plea. State court decisions for and against admissibility are collected in Annot., 86 A.L.R.2d 326.

Pleas of *nolo contendere* are recognized by Rule 11 of the Rules of Criminal Procedure, although the law of numerous States is to the contrary. The present rule gives effect to the principal traditional characteristic of the *nolo* plea, i.e. avoiding the admission of guilt which is inherent in pleas of guilty. This position is consistent with the construction of Section 5 of the Clayton Act, 15 U.S.C. § 16(a), recognizing the inconclusive and compromise nature of judgments based on *nolo* pleas. *General Electric Co. v. City of San Antonio,* 334 F.2d 480 (5th Cir.1964); *Commonwealth Edison Co. v. Allis–Chalmers Mfg. Co.,* 323 F.2d 412 (7th Cir.1963), cert. denied 376 U.S. 939, 84 S.Ct. 794, 11 L.Ed.2d 659; *Armco Steel Corp. v. North Dakota,* 376 F.2d 206 (8th Cir.1967); *City of Burbank v. General Electric Co.,* 329 F.2d 825 (9th Cir.1964). See also state court decisions in Annot., 18 A.L.R.2d 1287, 1314.

Exclusion of offers to plead guilty or *nolo* has as its purpose the promotion of disposition of criminal cases by compromise. As pointed out in McCormick § 251, p. 543.

"Effective criminal law administration in many localities would hardly be possible if a large proportion of the charges were not disposed of by such compromises."

See also *People v. Hamilton,* 60 Cal.2d 105, 32 Cal.Rptr. 4, 383 P.2d 412 (1963), discussing legislation designed to achieve this result. As with compromise offers generally, Rule 408, free communication is needed, and security against having an offer of compromise or related statement admitted in evidence effectively encourages it.

Limiting the exclusionary rule to use against the accused is consistent with the purpose of the rule, since the possibility of use for or against other persons will not impair the effectiveness of withdrawing pleas or the freedom of discussion which the rule is designed to foster. See A.B.A. Standards Relating to Pleas of Guilty § 2.2 (1968). See also the narrower provisions of New Jersey Evidence Rule 52(2) and the unlimited exclusion provided in California Evidence Code § 1153.

1974 Enactment

The Committee added the phrase "Except as otherwise provided by Act of Congress" to Rule 410 as submitted by the Court in order to preserve particular congressional policy judgments as to the effect of a plea of guilty or of nolo contendere. See 15 U.S.C. 16(a). The Committee intends that its amendment refers to both present statutes and statutes subsequently enacted. House Report No. 93–650.

As adopted by the House, rule 410 would make inadmissible pleas of guilty or nolo contendere subsequently withdrawn as well as offers to make such pleas. Such a rule is clearly justified as a means of encouraging pleading. However, the House rule would then go on to render inadmissible for any purpose statements made in connection with these pleas or offers as well.

The committee finds this aspect of the House rule unjustified. Of course, in certain circumstances such statements should be excluded. If, for example, a plea is vitiated because of coercion, statements made in connection with the plea may also have been coerced and should be inadmissible on that basis. In other cases, however, voluntary statements of an accused made in court on the record, in connection with a plea, and determined by a court to be reliable should be admissible even though the plea is subsequently withdrawn. This is particularly true in those cases where, if the House rule were in effect, a defendant would be able to contradict his previous statements and thereby lie with impunity [See *Harris v. New York,* 401 U.S. 222 (1971)]. To prevent such an injustice, the rule has been modified to permit the use of such statements for the limited purposes of impeachment and in subsequent perjury or false statement prosecutions. Senate Report No. 93–1277.

The House bill provides that evidence of a guilty or nolo contendere plea, of an offer of either plea, or of statements made in connection with such pleas or offers of such pleas, is inadmissible in any civil or criminal action, case or proceeding against the person making such plea or offer. The Senate amendment makes the rule inapplicable to a voluntary and reliable statement made in court on the record where the statement is offered in a subsequent prosecution of the declarant for perjury or false statement.

The issues raised by Rule 410 are also raised by proposed Rule 11(e)(6) of the Federal Rules of Criminal Procedure presently pending before Congress. This proposed rule, which deals with the admissibility of pleas of guilty or nolo contendere, offers to make such pleas, and statements made in connection with such pleas, was promulgated by the Supreme Court on April 22, 1974, and in the absence of congressional action will become effective on August 1, 1975. The conferees intend to make no change in the presently-existing case law until that date, leaving the courts free to develop rules in this area on a case-by-case basis.

The Conferees further determined that the issues presented by the use of guilty and nolo contendere pleas, offers of such pleas, and statements made in connection with such pleas or offers, can be explored in greater detail during Congressional consideration of Rule 11(e)(6) of the Federal Rules of Criminal Procedure. The Conferees believe, therefore, that it is best to defer its effective date until August 1, 1975. The Conferees intend that Rule 410 would be superseded by any subsequent Federal Rule of Criminal Procedure or act of Congress with which it is inconsistent, if the Federal Rule of Criminal Procedure or Act of Congress takes effect or becomes law after the date of the enactment of the act establishing the rules of evidence.

The conference adopts the Senate amendment with an amendment that expresses the above intentions. House Report No. 93–1597.

1979 Amendments

Present rule 410 conforms to rule 11(e)(6) of the Federal Rules of Criminal Procedure. A proposed amendment to rule 11(e)(6) would clarify the circumstances in which pleas, plea discussions and related statements are inadmissible in evidence: see Advisory Committee Note thereto. The amendment proposed above would make comparable changes in rule 410.

2011 Amendments

The language of Rule 410 has been amended as part of the restyling of the Evidence Rules to make them more easily understood and to make style and terminology consistent throughout the rules. These changes are intended to be stylistic only. There is no intent to change any result in any ruling on evidence admissibility.

HISTORICAL NOTES

Revision Notes and Legislative Reports

1975 Acts

House Report No. 94–599, see 1975 U.S. Code Cong. and Adm. News, p. 1585.

References in Text

Rule 11 of the Federal Rules of Criminal Procedure, referred to in par. (3), is classified to Title 18, Federal Rules of Criminal Procedure.

Rule 411. Liability Insurance

Evidence that a person was or was not insured against liability is not admissible to prove whether the person acted negligently or otherwise wrongfully. But the court may admit this evidence for another purpose, such as proving a witness's bias or prejudice or proving agency, ownership, or control.

(Pub.L. 93–595, § 1, Jan. 2, 1975, 88 Stat.1933; Mar. 2, 1987, eff. Oct. 1, 1987; Apr. 26, 2011, eff. Dec. 1, 2011.)

ADVISORY COMMITTEE NOTES

1972 Proposed Rules

The courts have with substantial unanimity rejected evidence of liability insurance for the purpose of proving fault, and absence of liability insurance as proof of lack of fault. At best the inference of fault from the fact of insurance coverage is a tenuous one, as is its converse. More important, no doubt, has been the feeling that knowledge of the presence or absence of liability insurance would induce juries to decide cases on improper grounds. McCormick § 168; Annot., 4 A.L.R.2d 761. The rule is drafted in broad terms so as to include contributory negligence or other fault of a plaintiff as well as fault of a defendant.

The second sentence points out the limits of the rule, using well established illustrations. *Id.*

For similar rules see Uniform Rule 54; California Evidence Code § 1155; Kansas Code of Civil Procedure § 60–454; New Jersey Evidence Rule 54.

1987 Amendments

The amendment is technical. No substantive change is intended.

2011 Amendments

The language of Rule 411 has been amended as part of the general restyling of the Evidence Rules to make them more easily understood and to make style and terminology consistent throughout the rules. These changes are intended to be stylistic only. There is no intent to change any result in any ruling on evidence admissibility.

Rule 411 previously provided that evidence was not excluded if offered for a purpose not explicitly prohibited by the Rule. To improve the language of the Rule, it now provides that the court may admit evidence if offered for a permissible purpose. There is no intent to change the process for admitting evidence covered by the Rule. It remains the case that if offered for an impermissible purpose, it must be excluded, and if offered for a purpose not barred by the Rule, its admissibility remains governed by the general principles of Rules 402, 403, 801, etc.

Rule 412. Sex–Offense Cases: The Victim's Sexual Behavior or Predisposition

(a) Prohibited Uses. The following evidence is not admissible in a civil or criminal proceeding involving alleged sexual misconduct:

(1) evidence offered to prove that a victim engaged in other sexual behavior; or

(2) evidence offered to prove a victim's sexual predisposition.

(b) Exceptions.

(1) Criminal Cases. The court may admit the following evidence in a criminal case:

(A) evidence of specific instances of a victim's sexual behavior, if offered to prove that someone other than the defendant was the source of semen, injury, or other physical evidence;

(B) evidence of specific instances of a victim's sexual behavior with respect to the person accused of the sexual misconduct, if offered by the defendant to prove consent or if offered by the prosecutor; and

(C) evidence whose exclusion would violate the defendant's constitutional rights.

(2) Civil Cases. In a civil case, the court may admit evidence offered to prove a victim's sexual behavior or sexual predisposition if its probative value substantially outweighs the danger of harm to any victim and of unfair prejudice to any party. The court may admit evidence of a victim's reputation only if the victim has placed it in controversy.

(c) Procedure to Determine Admissibility.

(1) Motion. If a party intends to offer evidence under Rule 412(b), the party must:

(A) file a motion that specifically describes the evidence and states the purpose for which it is to be offered;

(B) do so at least 14 days before trial unless the court, for good cause, sets a different time;

(C) serve the motion on all parties; and

(D) notify the victim or, when appropriate, the victim's guardian or representative.

(2) Hearing. Before admitting evidence under this rule, the court must conduct an in camera hearing and give the victim and parties a right to attend and be heard. Unless the court orders otherwise, the motion, related materials, and the record of the hearing must be and remain sealed.

(d) Definition of "Victim." In this rule, "victim" includes an alleged victim.

(Added Pub.L. 95–540, § 2(a), Oct. 28, 1978, 92 Stat. 2046; amended Pub.L. 100–690, Title VII, § 7046(a), Nov. 18, 1988, 102 Stat. 4400; Apr. 29, 1994, eff. Dec. 1, 1994; Pub.L. 103–322, Title IV, § 40141(b), Sept. 13, 1994, 108 Stat. 1919; Apr. 26, 2011, eff. Dec. 1, 2011.)

ADVISORY COMMITTEE NOTES

1994 Amendments

Rule 412 has been revised to diminish some of the confusion engendered by the original rule and to expand the protection afforded alleged victims of sexual misconduct. Rule 412 applies to both civil and criminal proceedings. The rule aims to safeguard the alleged victim against the invasion of privacy, potential embarrassment and sexual stereotyping that is associated with public disclosure of intimate sexual details and the infusion of sexual innuendo into the factfinding process. By affording victims protection in most instances, the rule also encourages victims of sexual misconduct to institute and to participate in legal proceedings against alleged offenders

Rule 412 seeks to achieve these objectives by barring evidence relating to the alleged victim's sexual behavior or alleged sexual predisposition, whether offered as substantive evidence of for impeachment, except in designated circumstances in which the probative value of the evidence significantly outweighs possible harm to the victim.

The revised rule applies in all cases involving sexual misconduct without regard to whether the alleged victim or person accused is a party to the litigation. Rule 412 extends to "pattern" witnesses in both criminal and civil cases whose testimony about other instances of sexual misconduct by the person accused is otherwise admissible. When the case does not involve alleged sexual misconduct, evidence relating to a third-party witness' alleged sexual activities is not within the ambit of Rule 412. The witness will, however, be protected by other rules such as Rules 404 and 608, as well as Rule 403.

The terminology "alleged victim" is used because there will frequently be a factual dispute as to whether sexual misconduct occurred. It does not connote any requirement that the misconduct be alleged in the pleadings. Rule 412 does not, however, apply unless the person against whom the evidence is offered can reasonably be characterized as a "victim of alleged sexual misconduct." When this is not the case, as for instance in a defamation action involving statements concerning sexual misconduct in which the evidence is offered to show that the alleged defamatory statements were true or did not damage the plaintiff's reputation, neither Rule 404 nor this rule will operate to bar the evidence; Rule 401 and 403 will continue to control. Rule 412 will, however, apply in a Title VII action in which the plaintiff has alleged sexual harassment.

The reference to a person "accused" is also used in a non-technical sense. There is no requirement that there be a criminal charge pending against the person or even that the misconduct would constitute a criminal offense. Evidence offered to prove allegedly false prior claims by the victim is not barred by Rule 412. However, the evidence is subject to the requirements of Rule 404.

Subdivision (a). As amended, Rule 412 bars evidence offered to prove the victim's sexual behavior and alleged sexual predisposition. Evidence, which might otherwise be admissible under Rules 402, 404(b), 405, 607, 608, 609 of some other evidence rule, must be excluded if Rule 412 so requires. The word "other" is used to suggest some flexibility in admitting evidence "intrinsic" to the alleged sexual misconduct. *Cf.* Committee Note to 1991 amendment to Rule 404(b)

Past sexual behavior connotes all activities that involve actual physical conduct, i.e. sexual intercourse or sexual contact. *See, e.g., United States v. Galloway*, 937 F.2d 542 (10th Cir. 1991), *cert. denied*, 113 S.Ct. 418 (1992) (use of contraceptives inadmissible since use implies sexual activity); *United States v. One Feather*, 702 F.2d 736 (8th Cir. 1983) (birth of an illegitimate child inadmissible); *State v.*

Carmichael, 727 P.2d 918, 925 (Kan. 1986) (evidence of venereal disease inadmissible). In addition, the word "behavior" should be construed to include activities of the mind, such as fantasies of dreams. *See* 23 C. Wright and K. Graham, Jr., *Federal Practice and Procedure*, § 5384 at p. 548 (1980) ("While there may be some doubt under statutes that require 'conduct,' it would seem that the language of Rule 412 is broad enough to encompass the behavior of the mind.").

The rule has been amended to also exclude all other evidence relating to an alleged victim of sexual misconduct that is offered to prove a sexual predisposition. This amendment is designed to exclude evidence that does not directly refer to sexual activities or thoughts but that the proponent believes may have a sexual connotation for the factfinder. Admission of such evidence would contravene Rule 412's objectives of shielding the alleged victim from potential embarrassment and safeguarding the victim against stereotypical thinking. Consequently, unless the (b)(2) exception is satisfied, evidence such as that relating to the alleged victim's mode of dress, speech, or life-style will not be admissible.

The introductory phrase in subdivision (a) was deleted because it lacked clarity and contained no explicit reference to the other provisions of the law that were intended to be overridden. The conditional clause, "except as provided in subdivisions (b) and (c)" is intended to make clear that evidence of the types described in subdivision (a) is admissible only under the strictures of those sections.

The reason for extending the rule to all criminal cases is obvious. The strong social policy of protecting a victim's privacy and encouraging victims to come forward to report criminal acts is not confined to cases that involve a charge of sexual assault. The need to protect the victim is equally great when a defendant is charged with kidnapping, and evidence is offered, either to prove motive or as background, that the defendant sexually assaulted the victim.

The reason for extending Rule 412 to civil cases is equally obvious. The need to protect alleged victims against invasions of privacy, potential embarrassment, and unwarranted sexual stereotyping, and the wish to encourage victims to come forward when they have been sexually molested do not disappear because the context has shifted from a criminal prosecution to a claim for damages or injunctive relief. There is a strong social policy in not only punishing those who engage in sexual misconduct, but in also providing relief to the victim. Thus, Rule 412 applies in any civil case in which a person claims to be the victim of sexual misconduct, such as actions for sexual battery or sexual harassment.

Subdivision (b). Subdivision (b) spells out the specific circumstances in which some evidence may be admissible that would otherwise be barred by the general rule expressed in subdivision (a). As amended, Rule 412 will be virtually unchanged in criminal cases, but will provide protection to any person alleged to be a victim of sexual misconduct regardless of the charge actually brought against an accused. A new exception has been added for civil cases.

In a criminal case, evidence may be admitted under subdivision (b)(1) pursuant to three possible exceptions, provided the evidence also satisfies other requirements for admissibility specified in the Federal Rules of Evidence, including Rule 403. Subdivisions (b)(1)(A) and (b)(1)(B) require proof in the form of specific instances of sexual behavior in recognition of the limited probative value and dubious reliability of evidence of reputation or evidence in the form of an opinion.

Under subdivision (b)(1)(A), evidence of specific instances of sexual behavior with persons other than the person whose sexual misconduct is alleged may be admissible if it is offered to prove that another person was the source of semen, injury or other physical evidence. Where the prosecution has directly or indirectly asserted that the physical evidence originated with the accused, the defendant must be afforded an opportunity to prove that another person was responsible. See *United States v. Begay*, 937 F.2d 515, 523 n. 10 (10th Cir. 1991). Evidence offered for the specific purpose identified in this subdivision may still be excluded if it does not satisfy Rules 401 or 403. *See, e.g.*, *United States v. Azure*, 845 F.2d 1503, 1505-06 (8th Cir. 1988) (10 year old victim's injuries indicated recent use of force; court excluded evidence of consensual sexual activities with witness who testified at in camera hearing that he had never hurt victim and failed to establish recent activities).

Under the exception in subdivision (b)(1)(B), evidence of specific instances of sexual behavior with respect to the person whose sexual misconduct is alleged is admissible if offered to prove consent, or offered by the prosecution. Admissible pursuant to this exception might be evidence of prior instances of sexual activities between the alleged victim and the accused, as well as statements in which the alleged victim expresses an intent to engage in sexual intercourse with the accused, or voiced sexual fantasies involving that specific accused. In a prosecution for child sexual abuse, for example, evidence of uncharged sexual activity between the accused and the alleged victim offered by the prosecution may be admissible pursuant to Rule 404(b) to show a pattern of behavior. Evidence relating to the victim's alleged sexual predisposition is not admissible pursuant to this exception.

Under subdivision (b)(1)(C), evidence of specific instances of conduct may not be excluded if the result would be to deny a criminal defendant the protections afforded by the Constitution. For example, statements in which the victim has expressed an intent to have sex with the first person encountered on a particular occasion might not be excluded without violating the due process right of a rape defendant seeking to prove consent. Recognition of this basic principle was expressed on subdivision (b)(1) of the original rule. The United States Supreme Court has recognized that in various circumstances a defendant may have a right to introduce evidence otherwise precluded by an evidence rule under the Confrontation Clause. *See, e.g., Olden v. Kentucky*, 488 U.S. 227 (1988) (defendant in rape cases had right to inquire into alleged victim's cohabitation with another man to show bias).

Subdivision (b)(2) governs the admissibility of otherwise proscribed evidence in civil cases. It employs a balancing test rather than the specific exceptions stated in subdivision (b)(1) in recognition of the difficulty of foreseeing future developments in the law. Greater flexibility is needed to accommodate evolving causes of action such as claims for sexual harassment.

The balancing test requires the proponent of the evidence, whether plaintiff or defendant, to convince the court that the probative value of the proffered evidence "substantially outweighs the danger of harm to any victim and of unfair prejudice of any party." This test for admitting evidence offered to prove sexual behavior or sexual propensity in civil cases differs in three respects from the general rule governing admissibility set forth in Rule 403. First, it Reverses that usual procedure spelled out in Rule 403 by shifting the burden to the proponent to demonstrate admissibility rather than making the opponent justify exclusion of the evidence. Second, the standard expressed in subdivision (b)(2) is more stringent than in the original rule; it raises the threshold for admission by requiring that the probative value of the evidence *substantially* outweigh the specified dangers. Finally, the Rule 412 test puts "harm to the victim" on the scale in addition to prejudice to the parties.

Evidence of reputation may be received in a civil case only if the alleged victim has put his or her reputation into controversy. The victim may do so without making a specific allegation in a pleading. *Cf.* Fed.R.Civ.P. 35(a).

Subdivision (c). Amended subdivision (c) is more concise and understandable than the subdivision it replaces. The requirement of a motion before trial is continued in the amended rule, as is the provision that a late motion may be permitted for good cause shown. In deciding whether to permit late filing, the court may take into account the conditions previously included in the rule: namely whether the evidence is newly discovered and could not have been obtained earlier through the existence of due diligence, and whether the issue to which such evidence relates has newly arisen in the case. The rule recognizes that in some instances the circumstances that justify an application to introduce evidence otherwise barred by Rule 412 will not become apparent until trial.

The amended rule provides that before admitting evidence that falls within that prohibition of Rule 412(a), the court must hold a hearing in camera at which the alleged victim and any party must be afforded the right to be present and an opportunity to be heard. All papers connected with the motion must be kept and remain under seal during the course of trial and appellate proceedings unless otherwise ordered. This is to assure that the privacy of the alleged victim is preserved in all cases in which the court rules that proffered evidence is not admissible, and in which the hearing refers to matters that are not received, or are received in another form.

The procedures set forth in subdivision (c) do not apply to discovery of a victim's past sexual conduct or predisposition in civil cases, which will be continued to be governed by Fed. R. Civ. P. 26. In order not to undermine the rationale of Rule 412, however, courts should enter appropriate orders pursuant to Fed. R. Civ. P. 26 (c) to protect the victim against unwarranted inquiries and to ensure confidentiality. Courts should presumptively issue protective orders barring discovery unless the party seeking discovery makes a showing that the evidence sought to be discovered would be relevant under the facts and theories of the particular case, and cannot be obtained except through discovery. In an action for sexual harassment, for instance, while some evidence of the alleged victim's sexual behavior and/or predisposition in the workplace may perhaps be relevant, non-work place conduct will usually be irrelevant. *Cf. Burns v. McGregor Electronic Industries, Inc.*, 989 F.2d 959, 962-63 (8th Cir. 1993) (posing for a nude magazine outside work hours is irrelevant to issue of unwelcomeness of sexual advances at work). Confidentiality orders should be presumptively granted as well.

One substantive change made in subdivision (c) is the elimination of the following sentence: "Notwithstanding subdivision (b) of Rule 104, if the relevancy of the evidence which the accused seeks to offer in trial depends upon the fulfillment of a condition of fact, the court, at the hearing in chambers or at a subsequent hearing in chambers scheduled for such purpose, shall accept evidence on the issue of whether such condition of fact is fulfilled and shall determine such issue." On its face, this language would appear to authorize a trial judge to exclude evidence of past sexual conduct between alleged victim and an accused or a defendant in a civil case based upon the judge's belief that such past acts did not occur. Such an authorization raises questions of invasion of the right to a jury trial under the Sixth and Seventh Amendments. *See* 1 S. Saltzburg & M. Martin, *Federal Rules of Evidence Manual*, 396-97 (5th ed. 1990).

The Advisory Committee concluded that the amended rule provided adequate protection for all persons claiming to be the victims of sexual misconduct, and that it was inadvisable to continue to include a provision in the rule that has been confusing and that raises substantial constitutional issues.

[Advisory Committee Note adopted by Congressional Conference Report accompanying Pub.L. 103–322. See H.R. Conf. Rep. No. 103–711, 103rd Cong., 2nd Sess., 383 (1994).]

Congressional Discussion

The following discussion in the House of Representatives of October 10, 1978, preceded passage of H.R. 4727, which enacted Rule 412. The discussion appears in 124 Cong.Record, at page H. 11944.

Mr. MANN. Mr. Speaker, I yield myself such time as I may consume.

Mr. Speaker, for many years in this country, evidentiary rules have permitted the introduction of evidence about a rape victim's prior sexual conduct. Defense lawyers were permitted great latitude in bringing out intimate details about a rape victim's life. Such evidence quite often serves no real purpose and only results in embarrassment to the rape victim and unwarranted public intrusion into her private life.

The evidentiary rules that permit such inquiry have in recent years come under question; and the States have taken the lead to change and modernize their evidentiary rules about evidence of a rape victim's prior sexual behavior. The bill before us similarly seeks to modernize the Federal Evidentiary rules.

The present Federal Rules of Evidence reflect the traditional approach. If a defendant in a rape case raises the defense of consent, that defendant may then offer evidence about the victim's prior sexual behavior. Such evidence may be in the form of opinion evidence, evidence of reputation, or evidence of specific instances of behavior. Rule 404(a)(2) of the Federal Rules of Evidence permits the introduction of evidence of a "pertinent character trait." The advisory committee note to that rule cites, as an example of what the rule covers, the character of a rape victim when the issue is consent. Rule 405 of the Federal Rules of Evidence permits the use of opinion or reputation evidence or the use of evidence of specific behavior to show a character trait.

Thus, Federal evidentiary rules permit a wide ranging inquiry into the private conduct of a rape victim, even though that conduct may have at best a tenuous connection to the offense for which the defendant is being tried.

H.R. 4727 amends the Federal Rules of Evidence to add a new rule, applicable only in criminal cases, to spell out when, and under what conditions, evidence of a rape victim's prior sexual behavior can be admitted. The new rule provides that reputation or opinion evidence about a rape victim's prior sexual behavior is not admissible. The new rule also provides that a court cannot admit evidence of specific instances of a rape victim's prior sexual conduct except in three circumstances.

The first circumstance is where the Constitution requires that the evidence be admitted. This exception is intended to cover those infrequent instances where, because of an unusual chain of circumstances, the general rule of inadmissibility, if followed, would result in denying the defendant a constitutional right.

The second circumstance in which the defendant can offer evidence of specific instances of a rape victim's prior sexual behavior is where the defendant raises the issue of consent and the evidence is of sexual behavior with the defendant. To admit such evidence, however, the court must find that the evidence is relevant and that its probative value outweighs the danger of unfair prejudice.

The third circumstance in which a court can admit evidence of specific instances of a rape victim's prior sexual behavior is where the evidence is of behavior with someone other than the defendant and is offered by the defendant on the issue of whether or not he was the source of semen or injury. Again, such evidence will be admitted only if the court finds that the evidence is relevant and that its probative value outweighs the danger of unfair prejudice.

The new rule further provides that before evidence is admitted under any of these exceptions, there must be an in camera hearing—that is, a proceeding that takes place in the judge's chambers out of the presence of the jury and the general public. At this hearing, the defendant will present the evidence he intends to offer and be able to argue why it should be admitted. The prosecution, of course, will be able to argue against that evidence being admitted.

The purpose of the in camera hearing is twofold. It gives the defendant an opportunity to demonstrate to the court why certain evidence is admissible and ought to be presented to the jury. At the same time, it protects the privacy of the rape victim in those instances when the court finds that evidence is inadmissible. Of course, if the court finds the evidence to be admissible, the evidence will be presented to the jury in open court.

The effect of this legislation, therefore, is to preclude the routine use of evidence of specific instances of a rape victim's prior sexual behavior. Such evidence will be admitted only in clearly and narrowly defined circumstances and only after an in camera hearing. In determining the admissibility of such evidence, the court will consider all of the facts and circumstances surrounding the evidence, such as the amount of time that lapsed between the alleged prior act and the rape charged in the prosecution. The greater the lapse of time, of course, the less likely it is that such evidence will be admitted.

Mr. Speaker, the principal purpose of this legislation is to protect rape victims from the degrading and embarrassing disclosure of intimate details about their private lives. It does so by narrowly circumscribing when such evidence may be admitted. It does not do so, however, by sacrificing any constitutional right possessed by the defendant. The bill before us fairly balances the interests involved—the rape victim's interest in protecting her private life from unwarranted public exposure; the defendant's interest in being able adequately to present a defense by offering relevant and probative evidence; and society's interest in a fair trial, one where unduly prejudicial evidence is not permitted to becloud the issues before the jury.

I urge support of the bill.

Mr. WIGGINS. Mr. Speaker, I yield myself such time as I may consume.

(Mr. WIGGINS asked and was given permission to revise and extend his remarks.)

Mr. WIGGINS. Mr. Speaker, this legislation addresses itself to a subject that is certainly a proper one for our consideration. Many of us have been troubled for years about the indiscriminate and prejudicial use of testimony with respect to a victim's prior sexual behavior in rape and similar cases. This bill deals with that problem. It is not, in my opinion, Mr. Speaker, a perfect bill in the manner in which it deals with the problem, but my objections are not so fundamental as would lead me to oppose the bill.

I think, Mr. Speaker, that it is unwise to adopt a per se rule absolutely excluding evidence of reputation and opinion with respect to the victim—and this bill does that—but it is difficult for me to foresee the specific case in which such evidence might be admissible. The trouble is this, Mr. Speaker: None of us can foresee perfectly all of the various circumstances under which the propriety of evidence might be before the court. If this bill has a defect, in my view it is because it adopts a per se rule with respect to opinion and reputation evidence.

Alternatively we might have permitted that evidence to be considered in camera as we do other evidence under the bill.

I should note, however, in fairness, having expressed minor reservations, that the bill before the House at this time does improve significantly upon the bill which was presented to our committee.

I will not detail all of those improvements but simply observe that the bill upon which we shall soon vote is a superior product to that which was initially considered by our subcommittee.

Mr. Speaker, I ask my colleagues to vote for this legislation as being, on balance, worthy of their support, and urge its adoption.

I reserve the balance of my time.

Mr. MANN. Mr. Speaker, this legislation has more than 100 cosponsors, but its principal sponsor, as well as its architect is the gentlewoman from New York (Ms. Holtzman). As the drafter of the legislation she will be able to provide additional information about the probable scope and effect of the legislation.

I yield such time as she may consume to the gentlewoman from New York (Ms. Holtzman).

(Ms. HOLTZMAN asked and was given permission to revise and extend her remarks.)

Ms. HOLTZMAN. Mr. Speaker, I would like to begin first by complimenting the distinguished gentleman from South Carolina (Mr. Mann), the chairman of the subcommittee, for his understanding of the need for corrective legislation in this area and for the fairness with which he has conducted the subcommittee hearings. I would like also to compliment the other members of the subcommittee, including the gentleman from California (Mr. Wiggins).

Too often in this country victims of rape are humiliated and harassed when they report and prosecute the rape. Bullied and cross-examined about their prior sexual experiences, many find the trial almost as degrading as the rape itself. Since rape trials become inquisitions into the victim's morality, not trials of the defendant's innocence or guilt, it is not surprising that it is the least reported crime. It is estimated that as few as one in ten rapes is ever reported.

Mr. Speaker, over 30 States have taken some action to limit the vulnerability of rape victims to such humiliating cross-examination of their past sexual experiences and intimate personal histories. In federal courts, however, it is permissible still to subject rape victims to brutal cross-examination about their past sexual histories. H.R. 4727 would rectify this problem in Federal courts and I hope, also serve as a model to suggest to the remaining states that reform of existing rape laws is important to the equity of our criminal justice system.

H.R. 4727 applies only to criminal rape cases in Federal courts. The bill provides that neither the prosecution nor the defense can introduce any reputation or opinion evidence about the victim's past sexual conduct. It does permit, however, the introduction of specific evidence about the victim's past sexual conduct in three very limited circumstances.

First, this evidence can be introduced if it deals with the victim's past sexual relations with the defendant and is relevant to the issue of whether she consented. Second, when the defendant claims he had no relations with the victim, he can use evidence of the victim's past sexual relations with others if the evidence rebuts the victim's claim that the rape caused certain physical consequences, such as semen or injury. Finally, the evidence can be introduced if it is constitutionally required.

This last exception, added in subcommittee, will insure that the defendant's constitutional rights are protected.

Before any such evidence can be introduced, however, the court must determine at a hearing in chambers that the evidence falls within one of the exceptions.

Furthermore, unless constitutionally required, the evidence of specific instances of prior sexual conduct cannot be introduced at all it if would be more prejudicial and inflammatory that probative.

Mr. Speaker, I urge adoption of this bill. It will protect women from both injustice and indignity.

Mr. MANN. Mr. Speaker, I have no further requests for time, and I yield back the balance of my time.

Mr. WIGGINS. Mr. Speaker, I have no further requests for time, and yield back the balance of my time.

The SPEAKER pro tempore. The question is on the motion offered by the gentleman from South Carolina (Mr. Mann) that the House suspend the rules and pass the bill H.R. 4727, as amended.

The question was taken; and (two-thirds having voted in favor thereof) the rules were suspended and the bill, as amended, was passed.

A motion to reconsider was laid on the table.

2011 Amendments

The language of Rule 412 has been amended as part of the restyling of the Evidence Rules to make them more easily understood and to make style and terminology consistent throughout the rules. These changes are intended to be stylistic only. There is no intent to change any result in any ruling on evidence admissibility.

HISTORICAL NOTES

Revision Notes and Legislative Reports

1988 Acts

For Related Reports, see 1988 U.S. Code Cong. and Adm. News, p. 5937.

Effective and Applicability Provisions

1978 Acts

Section 3 of Pub.L. 95–540 provided that: "The amendments made by this Act [enacting this rule] shall apply to trials which begin more than thirty days after the date of the enactment of this Act [Oct. 28, 1978]."

Rule 413. Similar Crimes in Sexual–Assault Cases

(a) Permitted Uses. In a criminal case in which a defendant is accused of a sexual assault, the court may admit evidence that the defendant committed any other sexual assault. The evidence may be considered on any matter to which it is relevant.

(b) Disclosure to the Defendant. If the prosecutor intends to offer this evidence, the prosecutor must disclose it to the defendant, including witnesses' statements or a summary of the expected testimony. The prosecutor must do so at least 15 days before trial or at a later time that the court allows for good cause.

(c) Effect on Other Rules. This rule does not limit the admission or consideration of evidence under any other rule.

(d) Definition of "Sexual Assault." In this rule and Rule 415, " sexual assault" means a crime under federal law or under state law (as " state" is defined in 18 U.S.C. § 513) involving:

(1) any conduct prohibited by 18 U.S.C. chapter 109A;

(2) contact, without consent, between any part of the defendant's body—or an object—and another person's genitals or anus;

(3) contact, without consent, between the defendant's genitals or anus and any part of another person's body;

(4) deriving sexual pleasure or gratification from inflicting death, bodily injury, or physical pain on another person; or

(5) an attempt or conspiracy to engage in conduct described in subparagraphs (1)–(4).

(Added Pub.L. 103–322, Title XXXII, § 320935(a), Sept. 13, 1994, 108 Stat. 2136; amended Apr. 26, 2011, eff. Dec. 1, 2011.)

ADVISORY COMMITTEE NOTES

2011 Amendments

The language of Rule 413 has been amended as part of the restyling of the Evidence Rules to make them more easily understood and to make style and terminology consistent throughout the rules. These changes are intended to be stylistic only. There is no intent to change any result in any ruling on evidence admissibility.

HISTORICAL NOTES

Effective and Applicability Provisions

Section 320935(b) to (e) of Pub.L. 103–322, as amended Pub.L. 104–208, Div. A, Title I, § 101(a), [Title I, § 120], Sept. 30, 1996, 110 Stat. 3009–25, provided that:

"**(b) Implementation.**—The amendments made by subsection (a) [enacting Federal Rules of Evidence 413, 414, and 415] shall become effective pursuant to subsection (d).

"**(c) Recommendations by Judicial Conference.**—Not later than 150 days after the date of enactment of this Act [Sept. 13, 1994], the Judicial Conference of the United States shall transmit to Congress a report containing recommendations for amending the Federal Rules of Evidence as they affect the admission of evidence of a defendant's prior sexual assault or child molestation crimes in cases involving sexual assault and child molestation. The Rules Enabling Act [28 U.S.C.A. § 2072] shall not apply to the recommendations made by the Judicial Conference pursuant to this section.

"**(d) Congressional action.**—

"**(1)** If the recommendations described in subsection (c) are the same as the amendment made by subsection (a) [enacting Federal Rules of Evidence 413, 414, and 415], then the amendments made by subsection (a) shall become effective 30 days after the transmittal of the recommendations.

"(2) If the recommendations described in subsection (c) are different than the amendments made by subsection (a) [enacting Federal Rules of Evidence 413, 414, and 415], the amendments made by subsection (a) shall become effective 150 days after the transmittal of the recommendations unless otherwise provided by law.

"(3) If the Judicial Conference fails to comply with subsection (c), the amendments made by subsection (a) [enacting Federal of Evidence 413, 414, and 415] shall become effective 150 days after the date the recommendations were due under subsection (c) unless otherwise provided by law.

"(e) Application.—The amendments made by subsection (a) [enacting Federal Rules of Evidence 413, 414, and 415] shall apply to proceedings commenced on or after the effective date of such amendments, including all trials commenced on or after the effective date of such amendments."

[The Judicial Conference transmitted a report to Congress on Feb. 9, 1995, containing recommendations described in subsec. (c) different than the amendments made by section 320935(a) of Pub.L. 103–322. Congress did not follow the recommendations submitted or provide otherwise by law. Accordingly, Rules 413, 414, and 415, as added by section 320935(a) of Pub.L. 103–322, became effective on July 9, 1995.]

Submitted to the Congress in accordance with section 320935 of the Violent Crime Control and Law Enforcement Act of 1994 (Pub.L. No. 103–322)

I. INTRODUCTION

This report is transmitted to Congress in accordance with the Violent Crime Control and Law Enforcement Act of 1994, Pub.L. No. 103–322 (September 13, 1994). Section 320935 of the Act invited the Judicial Conference of the United States within 150 days (February 10, 1995) to submit "a report containing recommendations for amending the Federal Rules of Evidence as they affect the admission of evidence of a defendant's prior sexual assault or child molestation crimes in cases involving sexual assault or child molestation."

Under the Act, new Rules 413, 414, and 415 would be added to the Federal Rules of Evidence. These Rules would admit evidence of a defendant's past similar acts in criminal and civil cases involving a sexual assault or child molestation offense for its bearing on any matter to which it is relevant. The effective date of new Rules 413–415 is contingent in part upon the nature of the recommendations submitted by the Judicial Conference.

After careful study, the Judicial Conference urges Congress to reconsider its decision on the policy questions underlying the new rules for reasons set out in Part III below.

If Congress does not reconsider its decision on the underlying policy questions, the Judicial Conference recommends incorporation of the provisions of new Rules 413–415 as amendments to Rules 404 and 405 of the Federal Rules of Evidence. The amendments would not change the substance of the congressional enactment but would clarify drafting ambiguities and eliminate possible constitutional infirmities.

II. BACKGROUND

Under the Act, the Judicial Conference was provided 150 days within which to make and submit to Congress alternative recommendations to new Evidence Rules 413–415. Consideration of Rules 413–415 by the Judicial Conference was specifically excepted from the exacting review procedures set forth in the Rules Enabling Act (codified at 28 U.S.C. §§ 2071–2077). Although the Conference acted on these new rules on an expedited basis to meet the Act's deadlines, the review process was thorough.

The new rules would apply to both civil and criminal cases. Accordingly, the Judicial Conference's Advisory Committee on Criminal Rules and the Advisory Committee on Civil Rules reviewed the rules at separate meetings in October 1994. At the same time and in preparation for its consideration of the new rules, the Advisory Committee on Evidence Rules sent out a notice soliciting comment on new Evidence Rules 413, 414, and 415. The notice was sent to the courts, including all federal judges, about 900 evidence law professors, 40 women's rights organizations, and 1,000 other individuals and interested organizations.

III. DISCUSSION

On October 17–18, 1994, the Advisory Committee on Evidence Rules met in Washington, D.C. It considered the public responses, which included 84 written comments, representing 112 individuals, 8 local and 8 national legal organizations. The overwhelming majority of judges, lawyers, law professors, and legal organizations who responded opposed new Evidence Rules 413, 414, and 415. The principal objections expressed were that the rules would permit the admission of unfairly prejudicial evidence and contained numerous drafting problems not intended by their authors.

The Advisory Committee on Evidence Rules submitted its report to the Judicial Conference Committee on Rules of Practice and Procedure (Standing Committee) for review at its January 11–13, 1995 meeting. The committee's report was unanimous except for a dissenting vote by the representative of the Department of Justice. The advisory committee believed that the concerns expressed by Congress and embodied in new Evidence Rules 413, 414, and 415 are already adequately addressed in the existing Federal Rules of Evidence. In particular, Evidence Rule 404(b) now allows the admission of evidence against a criminal defendant of the commission of prior crimes, wrongs, or acts for specified purposes, including to show intent, plan, motive, preparation, identity, knowledge, or absence of mistake or accident.

Furthermore, the new rules, which are not supported by empirical evidence, could diminish significantly the protections that have safeguarded persons accused in criminal cases and parties in civil cases against undue prejudice. These protections form a fundamental part of American jurisprudence and have evolved under long-standing rules and case law. A significant concern identified by the committee was the danger of convicting a criminal defendant for past, as opposed to charged, behavior or for being a bad person.

In addition, the advisory committee concluded that, because prior bad acts would be admissible even though not the subject of a conviction, mini-trials within trials concerning those acts would result when a defendant seeks to rebut such evidence. The committee also noticed that many of the comments received had concluded that the Rules, as drafted, were mandatory—that is, such evidence had to be admitted regardless of other rules of evidence such as the hearsay rule or the Rule 403 balancing test. The committee believed that this position was arguable because Rules 413–415 declare without qualification that such evidence "is admissible." In contrast, the new Rule 412, passed as part of the same legislation, provided that certain evidence "is admissible if it is otherwise admissible under these Rules." Fed.R.Evid. 412(b)(2). If the critics are right, Rules 413–415 free the prosecution from rules that apply to the defendant—including the hearsay rule and Rule 403. If so, serious constitutional questions would arise.

The Advisory Committees on Criminal and Civil Rules unanimously, except for representatives of the Department of Justice, also opposed the new rules. Those committees also concluded that the new rules would permit the introduction of unreliable but highly prejudicial evidence and would complicate trials by causing mini-trials of other alleged wrongs. After the advisory committees reported, the Standing Committee unanimously, again except for the representative of the Department of Justice, agreed with the view of the advisory committees.

It is important to note the highly unusual unanimity of the members of the Standing and Advisory Committees, composed of over 40 judges, practicing lawyers, and academicians, in taking the view that Rules 413–415 are undesirable. Indeed, the only supporters of the Rules were representatives of the Department of Justice.

For these reasons, the Standing Committee recommended that Congress reconsider its decision on the policy questions embodied in new Evidence Rules 413, 414, and 415.

However, if Congress will not reconsider its decision on the policy questions, the Standing Committee recommended that Congress consider an alternative draft recommended by the Advisory Committee on Evidence Rules. That Committee drafted proposed amendments to existing Evidence Rules 404 and 405 that would both correct ambiguities and possible constitutional infirmities identified in new Evidence Rules 413, 414, and 415 yet still effectuate Congressional intent. In particular, the proposed amendments:

(1) expressly apply the other rules of evidence to evidence offered under the new rules;

(2) expressly allow the party against whom such evidence is offered to use similar evidence in rebuttal;

(3) expressly enumerate the factors to be weighed by a court in making its Rule 403 determination;

(4) render the notice provisions consistent with the provisions in existing Rule 404 regarding criminal cases;

(5) eliminate the special notice provisions of Rules 413–415 in civil cases so that notice will be required as provided in the Federal Rules of Civil Procedure; and

(6) permit reputation or opinion evidence after such evidence is offered by the accused or defendant.

The Standing Committee reviewed the new rules and the alternative recommendations. It concurred with the views of the Evidence Rules Committee and recommended that the Judicial Conference adopt them.

IV. RECOMMENDATIONS

The Judicial Conference concurs with the views of the Standing Committee and urges that Congress reconsider its policy determinations underlying Evidence Rules 413–415. In the alternative, the attached amendments to Evidence Rules 404 and 405 are recommended, in lieu of new Evidence Rules 413, 414, and 415. The alternative amendments to Evidence Rules 404 and 405 are accompanied by the Advisory Committee Notes, which explain them in detail.

RULE 404. CHARACTER EVIDENCE NOT ADMISSIBLE TO PROVE CONDUCT; EXCEPTIONS; OTHER CRIMES

* * * *

(4) Character in sexual misconduct cases. Evidence of another act of sexual assault or child molestation, or evidence to rebut such proof or an inference therefrom, if that evidence is otherwise admissible under these rules, in a criminal case in which the accused is charged with sexual assault or child molestation, or in a civil case in which a claim is predicated on a party's alleged commission of sexual assault or child molestation.

(A) In weighing the probative value of such evidence, the court may, as part of its rule 403 determination, consider:

(i) proximity in time to the charged or predicate misconduct;

(ii) similarity to the charged or predicate misconduct;

(iii) frequency of the other acts;

(iv) surrounding circumstances;

(v) relevant intervening events; and

(vi) other relevant similarities or differences.

(B) In a criminal case in which the prosecution intends to offer evidence under this subdivision, it must disclose the evidence, including statements of witnesses or a summary of the substance of any testimony, at a reasonable time in advance of trial, or during trial if the court excuses pretrial notice on good cause shown.

(C) For purposes of this subdivision.

(i) "sexual assault" means conduct—or an attempt or conspiracy to engage in conduct—of the type proscribed by chapter 109A of title 18, United States Code, or conduct that involved deriving sexual pleasure or gratification from inflicting death, bodily injury, or physical pain on another person irrespective of the age of the victim—regardless of whether that conduct would have subjected the actor to federal jurisdiction.

(ii) "child molestation" means conduct—or an attempt or conspiracy to engage in conduct—of the type proscribed by chapter 110 of title 18, United States Code, or conduct, committed in relation to a child below the age of 14 years, either of the type proscribed by chapter 109A of title 18, United States Code, or that involved deriving sexual pleasure or gratification from inflicting death, bodily injury, or physical pain on another person—regardless of whether that conduct would have subjected the actor to federal jurisdiction.

(b) Other crimes, wrongs, or acts. Evidence of other crimes, wrongs, or acts is not admissible to prove the character of a person in order to show action in conformity therewith except as provided in subdivision (a)....

Note to Rule 404(a)(4)

The Committee has redrafted Rules 413, 414 and 415 which the Violent Crime Control and Law Enforcement Act of 1994 conditionally added to the Federal Rules of Evidence.[1] These modifications do not change the substance of the congressional enactment. The changes were made in order to integrate the provisions both substantively and stylistically with the existing Rules of Evidence; to illuminate the intent expressed by the principal drafters of the measure; to clarify drafting ambiguities that might necessitate considerable judicial attention if they remained unresolved; and to eliminate possible constitutional infirmities.

The Committee placed the new provisions in Rule 404 because this rule governs the admissibility of character evidence. The congressional enactment constitutes a new exception to the general rule stated in subdivision (a). The Committee also combined the three separate rules proposed by Congress into one subdivision (a)(4) in accordance with the rules' customary practice of treating criminal and civil issues jointly. An amendment to Rule 405 has been added because the authorization of a new form of character evidence in this rule has an impact on methods of proving character that were not explicitly addressed by Congress. The stylistic changes are self-evident. They are particularly noticeable in the definition section in subdivision (a)(4)(C) in which the Committee eliminated, without any change in meaning, graphic details of sexual acts.

The Committee added language that explicitly provides that evidence under this subdivision must satisfy other rules of evidence such as the hearsay rules in Article VIII and the expert testimony rules in Article VII. Although principal sponsors of the legislation had stated that they intended other evidentiary rules to apply, the Committee believes that the opening phrase of the new subdivision 'if otherwise admissible under these rules' is needed to clarify the relationship between subdivision (a)(4) and other evidentiary provisions.

The Committee also expressly made subdivision (a)(4) subject to Rule 403 balancing in accordance with the repeatedly stated objectives of the legislation's sponsors with which representatives of the Justice Department expressed agreement. Many commentators on Rules 413–415 had objected that Rule 403's applicability was obscured by the actual language employed.

In addition to clarifying the drafters' intent, an explicit reference to Rule 403 may be essential to insulate the rule against constitutional challenge. Constitutional concerns also led the Committee to acknowledge specifically the opposing party's right to offer in rebuttal character evidence that the rules would otherwise bar, including evidence of a third person's prior acts of sexual misconduct offered to prove that the third person rather than the party committed the acts in issue.

In order to minimize the need for extensive and time-consuming judicial interpretation, the Committee listed factors that a court may consider in discharging Rule 403 balancing. Proximity in time is taken into account in a related rule. See Rule 609(b). Similarity, frequency and surrounding circumstances have long been considered by courts in handling other crimes evidence pursuant to Rule 404(b). Relevant intervening events, such as extensive medical treatment of the accused between the time of the prior proffered act and the charged act, may affect the strength of the propensity inference for which the evidence is offered. The final factor—'other relevant similarities or differences'—is added in recognition of the endless variety of circumstances that confront a trial court in rulings on admissibility. Although subdivision (4)(A) explicitly refers to factors that bear on probative value, this enumeration does not eliminate a judge's responsibility to take into account the other factors mentioned in Rule 403 itself—'the danger of unfair prejudice, confusion of the issues, ... misleading the jury, ... undue delay, waste of time, or needless presentation of cumulative evidence.' In addition, the Advisory Committee Note to Rule 403 reminds judges that 'The availability of other means of proof may also be an appropriate factor.'

The Committee altered slightly the notice provision in criminal cases. Providing the trial court with some discretion to excuse pretrial notice was thought preferable to the inflexible 15–day rule provided in Rules 414 and 415. Furthermore, the formulation is identical to that contained in the 1991 amendment to Rule 404(b) so that no confusion will result from having two somewhat different notice provisions in the same rule. The Committee eliminated the notice provision for civil cases stated in Rule 415 because it did not believe that Congress intended to alter the usual time table for disclosure and discovery provided by the Federal Rules of Civil Procedure.

The definition section was simplified with no change in meaning. The reference to 'the law of a State' was eliminated as unnecessarily confusing and restrictive. Conduct committed outside the United States ought equally to be eligible for admission. Evidence offered pursuant to subdivision (a)(4) must relate to a form of conduct proscribed by either chapter 109A or 110 of title 18, United States Code, regardless of whether the actor was subject to federal jurisdiction.

RULE 405. METHODS OF PROVING CHARACTER

(a) Reputation or opinion. In all cases in which evidence of character or a trait of character of a person is admissible, proof may be made by testimony as to reputation or by testimony in the form of an opinion except as provided in subdivision (c) of this rule. On cross-examination, inquiry is allowable into relevant specific instances of conduct.

* * * *

(c) Proof in sexual misconduct cases. In a case in which evidence is offered under rule 404(a)(4), proof may be made by specific instances of conduct, testimony as to reputation, or testimony in the form of an opinion, except that the prosecution or claimant may offer reputation or opinion testimony only after the opposing party has offered such testimony.

Note to Rule 405(c)

The addition of a new subdivision (a)(4) to Rule 404 necessitates adding a new subdivision (c) to Rule 405 to govern methods of proof. Congress clearly intended no change in the preexisting law that precludes the prosecution or a claimant from offering reputation or opinion testimony in its case in chief to prove that the opposing party acted in conformity with character. When evidence is admissible pursuant to Rule 404(a)(4), the proponents proof must consist of specific instances of conduct. The opposing party, however, is free to respond with reputation or opinion testimony (including expert testimony if otherwise admissible) as well as evidence of specific instances. In a criminal case, the admissibility of reputation or opinion testimony would, in any event, be authorized by Rule 404(a)(1). The extension to civil cases is essential in order to provide the opponent with an adequate opportunity to refute allegations about a character for sexual misconduct. Once the opposing party offers reputation or opinion testimony, however, the prosecution or claimant may counter using such methods of proof.

[1] Congress provided that the rules would take effect unless within a specified time period the Judicial Conference made recommendations to amend the rules that Congress enacted.

Congressional Discussion

Floor Statement of the Principal House Sponsor, Representative Susan Molinari, Concerning the Prior Crimes Evidence Rules for Sexual Assault and Child Molestation Cases (Cong.Rec. H8991–92, Aug. 21, 1994):

Mr. Speaker, the revised conference bill contains a critical reform that I have long sought to protect the public from crimes of sexual violence—general rules of admissibility in sexual assault and child molestation cases for evidence that the defendant has committed offenses of the same type on other occasions. The enactment of this reform is first and foremost a triumph for the public—for the women who will not be raped and the children who will not be molested because we have strengthened the legal system's tools for bringing the perpetrators of these atrocious crimes to justice.

Senator Dole and I initially proposed this reform in February of 1991 in the Women's Equal Opportunity Act bill, and we later re-introduced it in the Sexual Assault Prevention Act bills of the 102d and 103d Congresses. The proposal also enjoyed the strong support of the Administration in the 102d Congress, and was included in President Bush's violent crime bill of that Congress, S. 635. The Senate passed the proposed rules on Nov. 5, 1993, by a vote of 75 to 19, in a crime bill amendment offered by Senate Dole. This Chamber endorsed the same rules on June 29, 1994, by a vote of 348 to 62, through a motion to instruct conferees that I offered.

The rules in the revised conference bill are substantially identical to our earlier proposals. We have agreed to a temporary deferral of the effective date of the new rules, pending a report by the Judicial Conference, in order to accommodate procedural objections raised by opponents of the reform. However, regardless of what the Judicial Conference may recommend, the new rules will take effect within at most 300 days of the enactment of this legislation, unless repealed or modified by subsequent legislation.

The need for these rules, their precedential support, their interpretation, and the issues and policy questions they raise have been analyzed at length in the legislative history of this proposal. I would direct the Members' attention particularly to two earlier statements:

The first is the portion of the section-by-section analysis accompanying these rules in section 801 of S. 635, which President Bush transmitted to Congress in 1991. That statement appears on pages S 3238 [to] S 3242 of the daily edition of the Congressional Record for March 13, 1991.

The second is the prepared text of an address—entitled "Evidence of Propensity and Probability in Sex Offense Cases and Other Cases"—by Senior Counsel David J. Karp of the Office of Policy Development of the U.S. Department of Justice. Mr. Karp, who is the author of the new evidence rules, presented this statement on behalf of the Justice Department to the Evidence Section of the Association of American Law Schools on January 9, 1993. The statement provided a detailed account of the views of the legislative sponsors and the Administration concerning the proposed reform, and should also be considered an authoritative part of its legislative history.

These earlier statements address the issues raised by this reform in considerable detail. In my present remarks, I will simply emphasize the following essential points:

The new rules will supersede in sex offense cases the restrictive aspects of Federal Rule of Evidence 404(b). In contrast to Rule 404(b)'s general prohibition of evidence of character or propensity, the new rules for sex offense cases authorize admission and consideration of evidence of an uncharged offense for its bearing "on any matter to which it is relevant." This includes the defendant's propensity to commit sexual assault or child molestation offenses, and assessment of the probability or improbability that the defendant has been falsely or mistakenly accused of such an offense.

In other respects, the general standards of the rules of evidence will continue to apply, including the restrictions on hearsay evidence and the court's authority under Evidence Rule 403 to exclude evidence whose probative value is substantially outweighed by its prejudicial effect. Also, the government (or the plaintiff in a civil case) will generally have to disclose to the defendant any evidence that is to be offered under the new rules at least 15 days before trial.

The proposed reform is critical to the protection of the public from rapists and child molesters, and is justified by the distinctive characteristics of the cases it will affect. In child molestation cases, for example, a history of similar acts tends to be exceptionally probative because it shows an unusual disposition of the defendant—a sexual or sadosexual interest in children—that simply does not exist in ordinary people. Moreover, such cases require reliance on child victims whose credibility can readily be attacked in the absence of substantial corroboration. In such cases, there is a compelling public interest in admitting all significant evidence that will illumine the credibility of the charge and any denial by the defense.

Similarly, adult-victim sexual assault cases are distinctive, and often turn on difficult credibility determinations. Alleged consent by the victim is rarely an issue in prosecutions for other violent crimes—the accused mugger does not claim that the victim freely handed over [his] wallet as a gift—but the defendant in a rape case often contends that the victim engaged in consensual sex and then falsely accused him. Knowledge that the defendant has committed rapes on other occasions is frequently critical in assessing the relative plausibility of these claims and accurately deciding cases that would otherwise become unresolvable swearing matches.

The practical effect of the new rules is to put evidence of uncharged offenses in sexual assault and child molestation cases on the same footing as other types of relevant evidence that are not subject to a special exclusionary rule. The presumption is in favor of admission. The underlying legislative judgment is that the evidence admissible pursuant to the proposed rules is typically relevant and probative, and that its probative value is normally not outweighed by any risk of prejudice or other adverse effects.

In line with this judgment, the rules do not impose arbitrary or artificial restrictions on the admissibility of evidence. Evidence of offenses for which the defendant has not previously been prosecuted or convicted will be admissible, as well as evidence of prior convictions. No time limit is imposed on the uncharged offenses for which evidence may be admitted; as a practical matter, evidence of other sex offenses by the defendant is often probative and properly admitted, notwithstanding very substantial lapses of time in relation to the charged offense or offenses. *See, e.g., United States v. Hadley*, 918 F.2d 848, 850–51 (9th Cir. 1990), *cert. dismissed*, 113 S.Ct. 486 (1992) (evidence of offenses occurring up to 15 years earlier admitted); *State v. Plymate*, 345 N.W.2d 327 (Neb.1984) (evidence of defendant's commission of other child molestations more than 20 years earlier admitted).

Finally, the practical efficacy of these rules will depend on faithful execution by judges of the will of Congress in adopting this critical reform. To implement the legislative intent, the courts must liberally construe these rules to provide the basis for a fully informed decision of sexual assault and child molestation cases, including assessment of the defendant's propensities and questions of probability in light of the defendant's past conduct.

Rule 414. Similar Crimes in Child–Molestation Cases

(a) Permitted Uses. In a criminal case in which a defendant is accused of child molestation, the court may admit evidence that the defendant committed any other child molestation. The evidence may be considered on any matter to which it is relevant.

(b) Disclosure to the Defendant. If the prosecutor intends to offer this evidence, the prosecutor must disclose it to the defendant, including witnesses' statements or a summary of the expected testimony. The prosecutor must do so at least 15 days before trial or at a later time that the court allows for good cause.

(c) Effect on Other Rules. This rule does not limit the admission or consideration of evidence under any other rule.

(d) Definition of "Child" and "Child Molestation." In this rule and Rule 415:

(1) "child" means a person below the age of 14; and

(2) "child molestation" means a crime under federal law or under state law (as "state" is defined in 18 U.S.C. § 513) involving:

(A) any conduct prohibited by 18 U.S.C. chapter 109A and committed with a child;

(B) any conduct prohibited by 18 U.S.C. chapter 110;

(C) contact between any part of the defendant's body—or an object—and a child's genitals or anus;

(D) contact between the defendant's genitals or anus and any part of a child's body;

(E) deriving sexual pleasure or gratification from inflicting death, bodily injury, or physical pain on a child; or

(F) an attempt or conspiracy to engage in conduct described in subparagraphs (A)–(E).

(Added Pub.L. 103–322, Title XXXII, § 320935(a), Sept. 13, 1994, 108 Stat. 2135; amended Apr. 26, 2011, eff. Dec. 1, 2011.)

ADVISORY COMMITTEE NOTES

2011 Amendments

The language of Rule 414 has been amended as part of the restyling of the Evidence Rules to make them more easily understood and to make style and terminology consistent throughout the rules. These changes are intended to be stylistic only. There is no intent to change any result in any ruling on evidence admissibility.

HISTORICAL NOTES

Effective and Applicability Provisions

1995 Acts

Rule effective July 9, 1995, see section 320935(b) to (e) of Pub.L. 103–322, set out as a note under rule 413 of these rules.

Congressional Discussion

See Floor Statement following Rule 413.

Rule 415. Similar Acts in Civil Cases Involving Sexual Assault or Child Molestation

(a) Permitted Uses. In a civil case involving a claim for relief based on a party's alleged sexual assault or child molestation, the court may admit evidence that the party committed any other sexual assault or child molestation. The evidence may be considered as provided in Rules 413 and 414.

(b) Disclosure to the Opponent. If a party intends to offer this evidence, the party must disclose it to the party against whom it will be offered, including witnesses' statements or a summary of the expected testimony. The party must do so at least 15 days before trial or at a later time that the court allows for good cause.

(c) Effect on Other Rules. This rule does not limit the admission or consideration of evidence under any other rule.

(Added Pub.L. 103–322, Title XXXII, § 320935(a), Sept. 13, 1994, 108 Stat. 2137; amended Apr. 26, 2011, eff. Dec. 1, 2011.)

ADVISORY COMMITTEE NOTES

2011 Amendments

The language of Rule 415 has been amended as part of the restyling of the Evidence Rules to make them more easily understood and to make style and terminology consistent throughout the rules. These changes are intended to be stylistic only. There is no intent to change any result in any ruling on evidence admissibility.

HISTORICAL NOTES

Effective and Applicability Provisions

1995 Acts

Rule effective July 9, 1995, see section 320935(b) to (e) of Pub.L. 103–322, set out as a note under rule 413 of these rules.

Congressional Discussion

See Floor Statement following Rule 413.

ARTICLE V. PRIVILEGES

Rule
501. Privilege in General.
502. Attorney–Client Privilege and Work Product; Limitations on Waiver.

Rule 501. Privilege in General

The common law—as interpreted by United States courts in the light of reason and experience—governs a claim of privilege unless any of the following provides otherwise:

- the United States Constitution;
- a federal statute; or
- rules prescribed by the Supreme Court.

But in a civil case, state law governs privilege regarding a claim or defense for which state law supplies the rule of decision.

(Pub.L. 93–595, § 1, Jan. 2, 1975, 88 Stat. 1933; Apr. 26, 2011, eff. Dec. 1, 2011.)

ADVISORY COMMITTEE NOTES

1974 Enactment

Article V as submitted to Congress contained thirteen Rules. Nine of those Rules defined specific non-constitutional privileges which the federal courts must recognize (i.e. required reports, lawyer-client, psychotherapist-patient, husband-wife, communications to clergymen, political vote, trade secrets, secrets of state and other official information, and identity of informer.) Another Rule provided that only those privileges set forth in Article V or in some other Act of Congress could be recognized by the federal courts. The three remaining Rules addressed collateral problems as to waiver of privilege by voluntary disclosure, privileged matter disclosed under compulsion or without opportunity to claim privilege, comment upon or inference from a claim of privilege, and jury instruction with regard thereto.

The Committee amended Article V to eliminate all of the Court's specific Rules on privileges. Instead, the Committee, through a single Rule, 501, left the law of privileges in its present state and further provided that privileges shall continue to be developed by the courts of the United States under a uniform standard applicable both in civil and criminal cases. That standard, derived from Rule 26 of the Federal Rules of Criminal Procedure, mandates the application of the principles of the common law as interpreted by the courts of the United States in the light of reason and experience. The words "person, government, State, or political subdivision thereof" were added by the Committee to the lone term "witnesses" used in Rule 26 to make clear that, as under present law, not only witnesses may have privileges. The Committee also included in its amendment a proviso modeled after Rule 302 and similar to language added by the Committee to Rule 601 relating to the competency of witnesses. The proviso is designed to require the application of State privilege law in civil actions and proceedings governed by *Erie R. Co. v. Tompkins,* 304 U.S. 64 (1938), a result in accord with current federal court decisions. See *Republic Gear Co. v. Borg–Warner Corp.,* 381 F.2d 551, 555–556 n. 2 (2nd Cir.1967). The Committee deemed the proviso to be necessary in the light of the Advisory Committee's view (see its note to Court [proposed] Rule 501) that this result is not mandated under *Erie.*

The rationale underlying the proviso is that federal law should not supersede that of the States in substantive areas such as privilege absent a compelling reason. The Committee believes that in civil cases in the federal courts where an element of a claim or defense is not grounded upon a federal question, there is no federal interest strong enough to justify departure from State policy. In addition, the Committee considered that the Court's proposed Article V would have promoted forum shopping in some civil actions, depending upon differences in the privilege law applied as among the State and federal courts. The Committee's proviso, on the other hand, under which the federal courts are bound to apply the State's privilege law in actions founded upon a State-created right or defense, removes the incentive to "shop". House Report No. 93–650.

Article V as submitted to Congress contained 13 rules. Nine of those rules defined specific nonconstitutional privileges which the Federal courts must recognize (i.e., required reports, lawyer-client, psychotherapist-patient, husband-wife, communications to clergymen, political vote, trade secrets, secrets of state and other official information, and identity of informer). Many of these rules contained controversial modifications or restrictions upon common law privileges. As noted supra, the House amended article V to eliminate all of the Court's specific rules on privileges. Through a single rule, 501, the House provided that privileges shall be governed by the principles of the common law as interpreted by the courts of the United States in the light of reason and experience (a standard derived from rule 26 of the Federal Rules of Criminal Procedure) except in the case of an element of a civil claim or defense as to which State law supplies the rule of decision, in which event state privilege law was to govern.

The committee agrees with the main thrust of the House amendment: that a federally developed common law based on modern reason and experience shall apply except where the State nature of the issues renders deference to State privilege law the wiser course, as in the usual diversity case. The committee understands that thrust of the House amendment to require that State privilege law be applied in "diversity" cases (actions on questions of State law between citizens of different States arising under 28 U.S.C. § 1332). The language of the House amendment, however, goes beyond this in some respects, and falls short of it in others: State privilege law applies even in nondiversity, Federal question civil cases, where an issue governed by State substantive law is the object of the evidence (such issues do sometimes arise in such cases); and, in all instances where State privilege law is to be applied, e.g., on proof of a State issue in a diversity case, a close reading reveals that State privilege law is not to be applied unless the matter to be proved is an element of that state claim or defense, as distinguished from a step along the way in the proof of it.

The committee is concerned that the language used in the House amendment could be difficult to apply. It provides that "in civil actions * * * with respect to an element of a claim or defense as to which State law supplies the rule of decision," State law on privilege applies. The question of what is an element of a claim or defense is likely to engender considerable litigation. If the matter in question constitutes an element of a claim, State law supplies the privilege rule; whereas if it is a mere item of proof with respect to a claim, then, even though State law might supply the rule of decision, Federal law on the privilege would apply. Further, disputes will arise as to how the rule should be applied in an antitrust action or in a tax case where the Federal statute is silent as to a particular aspect of the substantive law in question, but Federal cases had incorporated State law by reference to State law. [For a discussion of reference to State substantive law, see note on Federal Incorporation by Reference of State Law, Hart & Wechsler, The Federal Courts and the Federal System, pp. 491–494 (2d ed. 1973).] Is a claim (or defense) based on such a reference a claim or defense as to which federal or State law supplies the rule of decision?

Another problem not entirely avoidable is the complexity or difficulty the rule introduces into the trial of a Federal case containing a combination of Federal and State claims and defenses, e.g. an action involving Federal antitrust and State unfair competition claims. Two different bodies of privilege law would need to be consulted. It may even develop that the same witness-testimony might be relevant on both counts and privileged as to one but not the other. [The problems with the House formulation are discussed in Rothstein, The Proposed Amendments to the Federal Rules of Evidence, 62 Georgetown University Law Journal 125 (1973) at notes 25, 26 and 70–74 and accompanying text.]

The formulation adopted by the House is pregnant with litigious mischief. The committee has, therefore, adopted what we believe will be a clearer and more practical guideline for determining when courts should respect State rules of privilege. Basically, it provides that in criminal and Federal question civil cases, federally evolved rules on privilege should apply since it is Federal policy which is being enforced. [It is also intended that the Federal law of privileges should be applied with respect to pendent State law claims when they arise in a Federal question case.] Conversely, in diversity cases where the litigation in question turns on a substantive question of State law, and is brought in the Federal courts because the parties reside in different States, the committee believes it is clear that State rules of privilege should apply unless the proof is directed at a claim or defense for which Federal law supplies the rule of decision (a situation which would not commonly arise.) [While such a situation might require use of two bodies of privilege law, federal and state, in the same case, nevertheless the occasions on which this would be required are considerably reduced as compared with the House version, and confined to situations where the Federal and State interests are such as to justify application of neither privilege law to the case as a whole. If the rule proposed here results in two conflicting bodies of privilege law applying to the same piece of evidence in the same case, it is contemplated that the rule favoring reception of the evidence should be applied. This policy is based on the present rule 43(a) of the Federal Rules of Civil Procedure which provides: In any case, the statute or rule which favors the reception of the evidence governs and the evidence shall be presented according to the most convenient method prescribed in any of the statutes or rules to which reference is herein made.] It is intended that the State rules of privilege should apply equally in original diversity actions and diversity actions removed under 28 U.S.C. § 1441(b).

Two other comments on the privilege rule should be made. The committee has received a considerable volume of correspondence from psychiatric organizations and psychiatrists concerning the deletion of rule 504 of the rule submitted by the Supreme Court. It should be clearly understood that, in approving this general rule as to privileges, the action of Congress should not be understood as disapproving any recognition of a psychiatrist-patient, or husband-wife, or any other of the enumerated privileges contained in the Supreme Court rules. Rather, our action should be understood as reflecting the view that the recognition of a privilege based on a confidential relationship and other privileges should be determined on a case-by-case basis.

Further, we would understand that the prohibition against spouses testifying against each other is considered a rule of privilege and covered by this rule and not by rule 601 of the competency of witnesses. Senate Report No. 93–1277.

Rule 501 deals with the privilege of a witness not to testify. Both the House and Senate bills provide that federal privilege law applies in criminal cases. In civil actions and proceedings, the House bill provides that state privilege law applies "to an element of a claim or defense as to which State law supplies the rule of decision." The Senate bill provides that "in civil actions and proceedings arising under 28 U.S.C. § 1332 or 28 U.S.C. § 1335, or between citizens of different States and removed under 28 U.S.C. § 1441(b) the privilege of a witness, person, government, State or political subdivision thereof is determined in accordance with State law, unless with respect to the particular claim or defense, Federal law supplies the rule of decision."

The wording of the House and Senate bills differs in the treatment of civil actions and proceedings. The rule in the House bill applies to evidence that relates to "an element of a claim or defense." If an item of proof tends to support or defeat a claim or defense, or an element of a claim or defense, and if state law supplies the rule of decision for that claim or defense, then state privilege law applies to that item of proof.

Under the provision in the House bill, therefore, state privilege law will usually apply in diversity cases. There may be diversity cases, however, where a claim or defense is based upon federal law. In such instances, federal privilege law will apply to evidence relevant to the federal claim or defense. See *Sola Electric Co. v. Jefferson Electric Co.,* 317 U.S. 173 (1942).

In nondiversity jurisdiction civil cases, federal privilege law will generally apply. In those situations where a federal court adopts or incorporates state law to fill interstices or gaps in federal statutory phrases, the court generally will apply federal privilege law. As Justice Jackson has said:

> A federal court sitting in a non-diversity case such as this does not sit as a local tribunal. In some cases it may see fit for special reasons to give the law of a particular state highly persuasive or even controlling effect, but in the last analysis its decision turns upon the law of the United States, not that of any state.

D'Oench, Duhme & Co. v. Federal Deposit Insurance Corp., 315 U.S. 447, 471 (1942) (Jackson, J., concurring). When a federal court chooses to absorb state law, it is applying the state law as a matter of federal common law. Thus, state law does not supply the rule of decision (even though the federal court may apply a rule derived from state decisions), and state privilege law would not apply. See C.A. Wright, Federal Courts 251–252 (2d ed. 1970); *Holmberg v. Armbrecht,* 327 U.S. 392 (1946); *DeSylva v. Ballentine,* 351 U.S. 570, 581 (1956); 9 Wright & Miller, Federal Rules and Procedure § 2408.

In civil actions and proceedings, where the rule of decision as to a claim or defense or as to an element of a claim or defense is supplied by state law, the House provision requires that state privilege law apply.

The Conference adopts the House provision. House Report No. 93–1597.

2011 Amendments

The language of Rule 501 has been amended as part of the restyling of the Evidence Rules to make them more easily understood and to make style and terminology consistent throughout the rules. These changes are intended to be stylistic only. There is no intent to change any result in any ruling on evidence admissibility.

Rule 502. Attorney–Client Privilege and Work Product; Limitations on Waiver

The following provisions apply, in the circumstances set out, to disclosure of a communication or information covered by the attorney-client privilege or work-product protection.

(a) Disclosure Made in a Federal Proceeding or to a Federal Office or Agency; Scope of a Waiver. When the disclosure is made in a federal proceeding or to a federal office or agency and waives the attorney-client privilege or work-product protection, the waiver extends to an undisclosed communication or information in a federal or state proceeding only if:

(1) the waiver is intentional;

(2) the disclosed and undisclosed communications or information concern the same subject matter; and

(3) they ought in fairness to be considered together.

(b) Inadvertent Disclosure. When made in a federal proceeding or to a federal office or agency, the disclosure does not operate as a waiver in a federal or state proceeding if:

(1) the disclosure is inadvertent;

(2) the holder of the privilege or protection took reasonable steps to prevent disclosure; and

(3) the holder promptly took reasonable steps to rectify the error, including (if applicable) following Federal Rule of Civil Procedure 26(b)(5)(B).

(c) Disclosure Made in a State Proceeding. When the disclosure is made in a state proceeding and is not the subject of a state-court order concerning waiver, the disclosure does not operate as a waiver in a federal proceeding if the disclosure:

(1) would not be a waiver under this rule if it had been made in a federal proceeding; or

(2) is not a waiver under the law of the state where the disclosure occurred.

(d) Controlling Effect of a Court Order. A federal court may order that the privilege or protection is not waived by disclosure connected with the litigation pending before the court—in which event the disclosure is also not a waiver in any other federal or state proceeding.

(e) Controlling Effect of a Party Agreement. An agreement on the effect of disclosure in a federal proceeding is binding only on the parties to the agreement, unless it is incorporated into a court order.

(f) Controlling Effect of This Rule. Notwithstanding Rules 101 and 1101, this rule applies to state proceedings and to federal court-annexed and federal court-mandated arbitration proceedings, in the circumstances set out in the rule. And notwithstanding Rule 501, this rule applies even if state law provides the rule of decision.

(g) Definitions. In this rule:

(1) "attorney-client privilege" means the protection that applicable law provides for confidential attorney-client communications; and

(2) "work-product protection" means the protection that applicable law provides for tangible material (or its intangible equivalent) prepared in anticipation of litigation or for trial.

(Pub.L. 110–322, § 1(a), Sept. 19, 2008, 122 Stat. 3537; Apr. 26, 2011, eff. Dec. 1, 2011.)

ADVISORY COMMITTEE NOTES

2011 Amendments

Rule 502 has been amended by changing the initial letter of a few words from uppercase to lowercase as part of the restyling of the Evidence Rules to make style and terminology consistent throughout the rules. There is no intent to change any result in any ruling on evidence admissibility.

ADVISORY COMMITTEE NOTES

Explanatory Note (Revised 11/28/2007)

This new rule has two major purposes:

1) It resolves some longstanding disputes in the courts about the effect of certain disclosures of communications or information protected by the attorney-client privilege or as work product—specifically those disputes involving inadvertent disclosure and subject matter waiver.

2) It responds to the widespread complaint that litigation costs necessary to protect against waiver of attorney-client privilege or work product have become prohibitive due to the concern that any disclosure (however innocent or minimal) will operate as a subject matter waiver of all protected communications or informa-

tion. This concern is especially troubling in cases involving electronic discovery. *See, e.g., Hopson v. City of Baltimore*, 232 F.R.D. 228, 244 (D.Md. 2005) (electronic discovery may encompass "millions of documents" and to insist upon "record-by-record pre-production privilege review, on pain of subject matter waiver, would impose upon parties costs of production that bear no proportionality to what is at stake in the litigation").

The rule seeks to provide a predictable, uniform set of standards under which parties can determine the consequences of a disclosure of a communication or information covered by the attorney-client privilege or work-product protection. Parties to litigation need to know, for example, that if they exchange privileged information pursuant to a confidentiality order, the court's order will be enforceable. Moreover, if a federal court's confidentiality order is not enforceable in a state court then the burdensome costs of privilege review and retention are unlikely to be reduced.

The rule makes no attempt to alter federal or state law on whether a communication or information is protected under the attorney-client privilege or work-product immunity as an initial matter. Moreover, while establishing some exceptions to waiver, the rule does not purport to supplant applicable waiver doctrine generally.

The rule governs only certain waivers by disclosure. Other common-law waiver doctrines may result in a finding of waiver even where there is no disclosure of privileged information or work product. *See, e.g., Nguyen v. Excel Corp.*, 197 F.3d 200 (5th Cir. 1999) (reliance on an advice of counsel defense waives the privilege with respect to attorney-client communications pertinent to that defense); *Ryers v. Burleson*, 100 F.R.D. 436 (D.D.C. 1983) (allegation of lawyer malpractice constituted a waiver of confidential communications under the circumstances). The rule is not intended to displace or modify federal common law concerning waiver of privilege or work product where no disclosure has been made.

Subdivision (a). The rule provides that a voluntary disclosure in a federal proceeding or to a federal office or agency, if a waiver, generally results in a waiver only of the communication or information disclosed; a subject matter waiver (of either privilege or work product) is reserved for those unusual situations in which fairness requires a further disclosure of related, protected information, in order to prevent a selective and misleading presentation of evidence to the disadvantage of the adversary. *See, e.g., In re United Mine Workers of America Employee Benefit Plans Litig.*, 159 F.R.D. 307, 312 (D.D.C. 1994) (waiver of work product limited to materials actually disclosed, because the party did not deliberately disclose documents in an attempt to gain a tactical advantage). Thus, subject matter waiver is limited to situations in which a party intentionally puts protected information into the litigation in a selective, misleading and unfair manner. It follows that an inadvertent disclosure of protected information can never result in a subject matter waiver. *See* Rule 502(b). The rule rejects the result in *In re Sealed Case*, 877 F.2d 976 (D.C.Cir. 1989), which held that inadvertent disclosure of documents during discovery automatically constituted a subject matter waiver.

The language concerning subject matter waiver—"ought in fairness"—is taken from Rule 106, because the animating principle is the same. Under both Rules, a party that makes a selective, misleading presentation that is unfair to the adversary opens itself to a more complete and accurate presentation.

To assure protection and predictability, the rule provides that if a disclosure is made at the federal level, the federal rule on subject matter waiver governs subsequent state court determinations on the scope of the waiver by that disclosure.

Subdivision (b). Courts are in conflict over whether an inadvertent disclosure of a communication or information protected as privileged or work product constitutes a waiver. A few courts find that a disclosure must be intentional to be a waiver. Most courts find a waiver only if the disclosing party acted carelessly in disclosing the communication or information and failed to request its return in a timely manner. And a few courts hold that any inadvertent disclosure of a communication or information protected under the attorney-client privilege or as work product constitutes a waiver without regard to the protections taken to avoid such a disclosure. *See generally Hopson v. City of Baltimore*, 232 F.R.D. 228 (D.Md. 2005), for a discussion of this case law.

The rule opts for the middle ground: inadvertent disclosure of protected communications or information in connection with a federal proceeding or to a federal office or agency does not constitute a waiver if the holder took reasonable steps to prevent disclosure and also promptly took reasonable steps to rectify the error. This position is in accord with the majority view on whether inadvertent disclosure is a waiver.

Cases such as *Lois Sportswear, U.S.A., Inc. v. Levi Strauss & Co.*, 104 F.R.D. 103, 105 (S.D.N.Y. 1985) and *Hartford Fire Ins. Co. v. Garvey*, 109 F.R.D. 323, 332 (N.D.Cal. 1985), set out a multi-factor test for determining whether inadvertent disclosure is a waiver. The stated factors (none of which is dispositive) are the reasonableness of precautions taken, the time taken to rectify the error, the scope of discovery, the extent of disclosure and the overriding issue of fairness. The rule does not explicitly codify that test, because it is really a set of non-determinative guidelines that vary from case to case. The rule is flexible enough to accommodate any of those listed factors. Other considerations bearing on the reasonableness of a producing party's efforts include the number of documents to be reviewed and the time constraints for production. Depending on the circumstances, a party that uses advanced analytical software applications and linguistic tools in screening for privilege and work product may be found to have taken "reasonable steps" to prevent inadvertent disclosure. The implementation of an efficient system of records management before litigation may also be relevant.

The rule does not require the producing party to engage in a post-production review to determine whether any protected communication or information has been produced by mistake. But the rule does require the producing party to follow up on any obvious indications that a protected communication or information has been produced inadvertently.

The rule applies to inadvertent disclosures made to a federal office or agency, including but not limited to an office or agency that is acting in the course of its regulatory, investigative or enforcement authority. The consequences of waiver, and the concomitant costs of pre-production privilege review, can be as great with respect to disclosures to offices and agencies as they are in litigation.

Subdivision (c). Difficult questions can arise when 1) a disclosure of a communication or information protected by the attorney-client privilege or as work product is made in a state proceeding, 2) the communication or information is offered in a subsequent federal proceeding on the ground that the disclosure waived the privilege or protection, and 3) the state and federal laws are in conflict on the question of waiver. The Committee determined that the proper solution for the federal court is to apply the law that is most protective of privilege and work product. If the state law is more protective (such as where the state law is that an inadvertent disclosure can never be a waiver), the holder of the privilege or protection may well have relied on that law when making the disclosure in the state proceeding. Moreover, applying a more restrictive federal law of waiver could impair the state objective of preserving the privilege or work-product protection for disclosures made in state proceedings.

On the other hand, if the federal law is more protective, applying the state law of waiver to determine admissibility in federal court is likely to undermine the federal objective of limiting the costs of production.

The rule does not address the enforceability of a state court confidentiality order in a federal proceeding, as that question is covered both by statutory law and principles of federalism and comity. *See* 28 U.S.C. § 1738 (providing that state judicial proceedings "shall have the same full faith and credit in every court within the United States . . . as they have by law or usage in the courts of such State . . . from which they are taken"). *See also Tucker v. Ohtsu Tire & Rubber Co.*, 191 F.R.D. 495, 499 (D.Md. 2000) (noting that a federal court considering the enforceability of a state confidentiality order is "constrained by principles of comity, courtesy, and . . . federalism"). Thus, a state court order finding no waiver in connection with a disclosure made in a state court proceeding is enforceable under existing law in subsequent federal proceedings.

Subdivision (d). Confidentiality orders are becoming increasingly important in limiting the costs of privilege review and retention, especially in cases involving electronic discovery. But the utility of a confidentiality order in reducing discovery costs is substantially diminished if it provides no protection outside the particular litigation in which the order is entered. Parties are unlikely to be able to reduce the costs of pre-production review for privilege and work product if the consequence of disclosure is that the communications or information could be used by non-parties to the litigation.

There is some dispute on whether a confidentiality order entered in one case is enforceable in other proceedings. *See generally Hopson v. City of Baltimore*, 232 F.R.D. 228 (D.Md. 2005), for a discussion of this case law. The rule provides that when a confidentiality order governing the consequences of disclosure in that case is entered in a federal proceeding, its terms are enforceable against non-parties in any federal or state proceeding. For example, the court order may provide for return of documents without waiver irrespective of the care taken by the disclosing party; the rule contemplates enforcement of "claw-back" and "quick peek" arrangements as a way to avoid the excessive costs of pre-production review for privilege and work product. *See Zubulake v. UBS Warburg LLC*, 216 F.R.D. 280, 290 (S.D.N.Y. 2003) (noting that parties may enter into "so-called 'claw-back' agreements that allow the parties to forego privilege review altogether in favor of an agreement to return inadvertently produced privilege documents"). The rule provides a party with a predictable protection from a court order—predictability that is needed to allow the party to plan in advance to limit the prohibitive costs of privilege and work product review and retention.

Under the rule, a confidentiality order is enforceable whether or not it memorializes an agreement among the parties to the litigation. Party agreement should not be a condition of enforceability of a federal court's order.

Under subdivision (d), a federal court may order that disclosure of privileged or protected information "in connection with" a federal proceeding does not result in waiver. But subdivision (d) does not allow the federal court to enter an order determining the waiver effects of a separate disclosure of the same information in other proceedings, state or federal. If a disclosure has been made in a state proceeding (and is not the subject of a state-court order on waiver), then subdivision (d) is inapplicable. Subdivision (c) would govern the federal court's determination whether the state-court disclosure waived the privilege or protection in the federal proceeding.

Subdivision (e). Subdivision (e) codifies the well-established proposition that parties can enter an agreement to limit the effect of waiver by disclosure between or among them. Of course such an agreement can bind only the parties to the agreement. The rule makes clear that if parties want protection against non-parties from a finding of waiver by disclosure, the agreement must be made part of a court order.

Subdivision (f). The protections against waiver provided by Rule 502 must be applicable when protected communications or information disclosed in federal proceedings are subsequently offered in state proceedings. Otherwise the holders of protected communications and information, and their lawyers, could not rely on the protections provided by the Rule, and the goal of limiting costs in discovery would be substantially undermined. Rule 502(f) is intended to resolve any potential tension between the provisions of Rule 502 that apply to state proceedings and the possible limitations on the applicability of the Federal Rules of Evidence otherwise provided by Rules 101 and 1101.

The rule is intended to apply in all federal court proceedings, including court-annexed and court-ordered arbitrations, without regard to any possible limitations of Rules 101 and 1101. This provision is not intended to raise an inference about the applicability of any other rule of evidence in arbitration proceedings more generally.

The costs of discovery can be equally high for state and federal causes of action, and the rule seeks to limit those costs in all federal proceedings, regardless of whether the claim arises under state or federal law. Accordingly, the rule applies to state law causes of action brought in federal court.

Subdivision (g). The rule's coverage is limited to attorney-client privilege and work product. The operation of waiver by disclosure, as applied to other evidentiary privileges, remains a question of federal common law. Nor does the rule purport to apply to the Fifth Amendment privilege against compelled self-incrimination.

The definition of work product "materials" is intended to include both tangible and intangible information. *See In re Cendant Corp. Sec. Litig.*, 343 F.3d 658, 662 (3d Cir. 2003) ("work product protection extends to both tangible and intangible work product").

Committee Letter

The letter from the Committee on Rules of Practice and Procedure of the Judicial Conference of the United States to the Committee on the Judiciary of the U.S. Senate and House of Representatives, dated September 26, 2007, provided:

On behalf of the Judicial Conference of the United States, I respectfully submit a proposed addition to the Federal Rules of Evidence. The Conference recommends that Congress adopt this proposed rule as Federal Rule of Evidence 502.

The Rule provides for protections against waiver of the attorney-client privilege or work product immunity. The Conference submits this proposal directly to Congress because of the limitations on the rulemaking function of the federal courts in matters dealing with evidentiary privilege. Unlike all other federal rules of procedure prescribed under the Rules Enabling Act, those rules governing evidentiary privilege must by approved by an Act of Congress, 28 U.S.C. § 2074(b).

Description of the Process Leading to the Proposed Rule

The Judicial Conference Rules Committees have long been concerned about the rising costs of litigation, much of which has been caused by the review, required under current law, of every document produced in discovery, in order to determine whether the document contains privileged information. In 2006, the House Judiciary Committee Chair suggested that the Judicial Conference consider proposing a rule dealing with waiver of attorney-client privilege and work product, in order to limit these rising costs. The Judicial Conference was urged to proceed with rulemaking that would:

- protect against the forfeiture of privilege when a disclosure in discovery is the result of an innocent mistake; and
- permit parties, and courts, to protect against the consequences of waiver by permitting disclosures of privileged information between the parties to litigation.

The task of drafting a proposed rule was referred to the Advisory Committee on Evidence Rules (the "Advisory Committee"). The Advisory Committee prepared a draft Rule 502 and invited a select group of judges, lawyers, and academics to testify before the Advisory Committee about the need for the rule, and to suggest any improvements. The Advisory Committee considered all the testimony presented by these experts and redrafted the rule accordingly. At its Spring 2006 meeting, the Advisory Committee approved for release for public comment a proposed Rule 502 that would provide certain exceptions to the federal common law on waiver of privileges and work product. That rule was approved for release for public comment by the Committee on Rules of Practice and Procedure ("the Standing Committee"). The public comment period began in August 2006 and ended February 15, 2007. The Advisory Committee received more that [sic] 70 public comments, and also heard the testimony of more than 20 witnesses at two public hearings. The rule released for public comment was also carefully reviewed by the Standing Committee's Subcommittee on Style. In April 2007, the Advisory Committee issued a revised proposed Rule 502 taking into account the public comment, the views of the Subcommittee on Style, and its own judgment. The revised rule was approved by the Standing Committee and the Judicial Conference. It is enclosed with this letter.

In order to inform Congress of the legal issues involved in this rule, the proposed Rule 502 also includes a proposed Committee Note of the kind that accompanies all rules adopted through the Rules Enabling Act. This Committee Note may be incorporated as all or part of the legislative history of the rule if it is adopted by Congress. *See, e.g.*, House Conference Report 103–711 (stating that the "Conferees intend that the Advisory Committee Note on [Evidence] Rule 412, as transmitted by the Judicial Conference of the United States to the Supreme Court on October 25, 1993, applies to Rule 412 as enacted by this section" of the Violent Crime Control and Law Enforcement Act of 1994).

Problems Addressed by the Proposed Rule

In drafting the proposed Rule, the Advisory Committee concluded that the current law on waiver of privilege and work product is responsible in large part for the rising costs of discovery, especially discovery of electronic information. In complex litigation the lawyers spend significant amounts of time and effort to preserve the privilege and work product. The reason is that if a protected document is produced, there is a risk that a court will find a subject matter waiver that will apply not only to the instant case and document but to other cases and documents as well. Moreover, an enormous amount of expense is put into document production in order to protect against inadvertent disclosure of privileged information, because the producing party risks a ruling that even a mistaken disclosure can result in a subject matter waiver. Advisory Committee members also expressed the view that the fear of waiver leads to extravagant claims of privilege. Members concluded that if there were a way to produce documents in discovery without risking subject matter waiver, the discovery process could be made much less expensive. The Advisory Committee noted that the existing law on the effect of inadvertent disclosures and on the scope of waiver is far from consistent or certain. It also noted that agreements between parties with regard to the effect of disclosure on privilege are common, but are unlikely to decrease the costs of discovery due to the ineffectiveness of such agreements as to persons not party to them.

Proposed Rule 502 does not attempt to deal comprehensively with either attorney-client privilege or work-product protection. It also does not purport to cover all issues concerning waiver or forfeiture of either the attorney-client privilege or work-product protection. Rather, it deals primarily with issues involved in the disclosure of protected information in federal court proceedings or to a federal public office or agency. The rule binds state courts only with regard to disclosures made in federal proceedings. It deals with disclosures made in state proceedings only to the extent that the effect of those disclosures becomes an issue in federal litigation. The Rule covers issues of scope of waiver, inadvertent disclosure, and the controlling effect of court orders and agreements.

Rule 502 provides the following protections against waiver of privilege or work product:

•*Limitations on Scope of Waiver.* Subdivision (a) provides that if a waiver is found, it applies only to the information disclosed, unless a broader waiver is made necessary by the holder's intentional and misleading use of privileged or protected communications or information.

•*Protections Against Inadvertent Disclosure.* Subdivision (b) provides that an inadvertent disclosure of privileged or protected communications or information, when made at the federal level, does not operate as a waiver if the holder took reasonable steps to prevent such a disclosure and employed reasonably prompt measures to retrieve the mistakenly disclosed communications or information.

•*Effect on State Proceedings and Disclosures Made in State Courts.* Subdivision (c) provides that 1) if there is a disclosure of privileged or protected communications or information at the federal level, then state courts must honor Rule 502 in subsequent state proceedings; and 2) if there is a disclosure of privileged or protected communications or information in a state proceeding, then admissibility in a subsequent federal proceeding is determined by the law that is most protective against waiver.

•*Orders Protecting Privileged Communications Binding on Non-Parties.* Subdivision (d) provides that if a federal court enters an order providing that a disclosure of privileged or protected communications or information does not constitute a waiver, that order is enforceable against all persons and entities in any federal or state proceeding. This provision allows parties in an action in which such an order is entered to limit their costs of pre-production privilege review.

•*Agreements Protecting Privileged Communications Binding on Parties.* Subdivision (e) provides that parties in a federal proceeding can enter into a confidentiality agreement providing for mutual protection against waiver in that proceeding. While those agreements bind the signatory parties, they are not binding on non-parties unless incorporated into a court order.

Drafting Choices Made by the Advisory Committee

The Advisory Committee made a number of important drafting choices in Rule 502. This section explains those choices.

1) The effect in state proceedings of disclosures initially made in state proceedings. Rule 502 does not apply to a disclosure made in a state proceeding when the disclosed communication or information is subsequently offered in another state proceeding. The first draft of Rule 502 provided for uniform waiver rules in federal and state proceedings, regardless of where the initial disclosure was made. This draft raised the objections of the Conference of State Chief Justices. State judges argued that the Rule as drafted offended principles of federalism and comity, by superseding state law of privilege waiver, even for disclosures that are made initially in state proceedings—and even when the disclosed material is then offered in a state proceeding (the so-called "state-to-state" problem). In response to these objections, the Advisory Committee voted unanimously to scale back the Rule, so that it would not cover the "state-to-state" problem. Under the current proposal state courts are bound by the Federal Rule only when a disclosure is made at the federal level and the disclosed communication or information is later offered in a state proceeding (the so-called "federal-to-state" problem).

During the public comment period on the scaled-back rule, the Advisory Committee received many requests from lawyers and lawyer groups to return to the original draft and provide a uniform rule of privilege waiver that would bind both state and federal courts, for disclosures made in either state or federal proceedings. These comments expressed the concern that if states were not bound by a uniform federal rule on privilege waiver, the protections afforded by Rule 502 would be undermined; parties and their lawyers might not be able to rely on the protections of the Rule, for fear that a state law would find a waiver even though the Federal Rule would not.

The Advisory Committee determined that these comments raised a legitimate concern, but decided not to extend Rule 502 to govern a state court's determination of waiver with respect to disclosures made in state proceedings. The Committee relied on the following considerations:

- Rule 502 is located in the Federal Rules of Evidence, a body of rules determining the admissibility of evidence in federal proceedings. Parties in a state proceeding determining the effect of a disclosure made in that proceeding or in other state courts would be unlikely to look to the Federal Rules of Evidence for the answer.
- In the Advisory Committee's view, Rule 502, as proposed herein, does fulfill its primary goal of reducing the costs of discovery in *federal* proceedings. Rule 502 by its terms governs state courts with regard to the effect of disclosures initially made in federal proceedings or to federal offices or agencies. Parties and their lawyers in federal proceedings can therefore predict the consequences of disclosure by referring to Rule 502; there is no possibility that a state court could find a waiver when Rule 502 would not, when the disclosure is initially made at the federal level.

The Judicial Conference has no position on the merits of separate legislation to cover the problem of waiver of privilege and work product when the disclosure is made at the state level and the consequence is to be determined in a state court.

2) Other applications of Rule 502 to state court proceedings. Although disclosures made in state court proceedings and later offered in state proceedings would not be covered, Rule 502 would have an effect on state court proceedings where the disclosure is initially made in a federal proceeding or to a federal office or agency. Most importantly, state courts in such circumstances would be bound by federal protection orders. The other protections against waiver in Rule 502—against mistaken disclosure and subject matter waiver—would also bind state courts as to disclosures initially made at the federal level. The Rule, as submitted, specifically provides that it applies to state proceedings under the circumstances set out in the Rule. This protection is needed, otherwise parties could not rely on Rule 502 even as to federal disclosures, for fear that a state court would find waiver even when a federal court would not.

3) Disclosures made in state proceedings and offered in a subsequent federal proceeding. Earlier drafts of proposed Rule 502 did not determine the question of what rule would apply when a disclosure is made in state court and the waiver determination is to be made in a subsequent federal proceeding. Proposed Rule 502 as submitted herein provides that all of the provisions of Rule 502 apply unless the state law of privilege is more protective (less likely to find waiver) than the federal law. The Advisory Committee determined that this solution best preserved federal interests in protecting against waiver, and also provided appropriate respect for state attempts to give greater protection to communications and information covered by the attorney-client privilege or work-product doctrine.

4) Selective waiver. At the suggestion of the House Judiciary Committee Chair, the Advisory Committee considered a rule that would allow persons and entities to cooperate with government agencies without waiving all privileges as to other parties in subsequent litigation. Such a rule is known as a "selective waiver" rule, meaning that disclosure of protected communications or information to the government waives the protection only selectively—to the government—and not to any other person or entity.

The selective waiver provision proved to be very controversial. The Advisory Committee determined that it would not propose adoption of a selective waiver provision; but in light of the request from the House Judiciary Committee, the Advisory Committee did prepare language for a selective waiver provision should Congress decide to proceed. The draft language for a selective waiver provision is available on request.

Conclusion

Proposed Rule 502 is respectfully submitted for consideration by Congress as a rule that will effectively limit the skyrocketing costs of discovery. Members of the Standing Committee, the Advisory Committee, as well as their reporters and consultants, are ready to assist Congress in any way it sees fit.

Sincerely,

Lee H. Rosenthal

Chair, Committee on Rules of Practice and Procedure

Addendum to Advisory Committee Notes

STATEMENT OF CONGRESSIONAL INTENT REGARDING RULE 502 OF THE FEDERAL RULES OF EVIDENCE

During consideration of this rule in Congress, a number of questions were raised about the scope and contours of the effect of the proposed rule on current law regarding attorney-client privilege and work-product protection. These questions were ultimately answered satisfactorily, without need to revise the text of the rule as submitted to Congress by the Judicial Conference.

In general, these questions are answered by keeping in mind the limited though important purpose and focus of the rule. The rule addresses only the effect of disclosure, under specified circumstances, of a communication that is otherwise protected by attorney-client privilege, or of information that is protected by work-product protection, on whether the disclosure itself operates as a waiver of the privilege or protection for purposes of admissibility of evidence in a federal or state judicial or administrative proceeding. The rule does not alter the substantive law regarding attorney-client privilege or work-product protection in any other respect, including the burden on the party invoking the privilege (or protection) to prove that the particular information (or communication) qualifies for it. And it is not intended to alter the rules and practices governing use of information outside this evidentiary context.

Some of these questions are addressed more specifically below, in order to help further avoid uncertainty in the interpretation and application of the rule.

Subdivision (a)—Disclosure vs. Use

This subdivision does not alter the substantive law regarding when a party's strategic use in litigation of otherwise privileged information obliges that party to waive the privilege regarding other information concerning the same subject matter, so that the information being used can be fairly considered in context. One situation in which this issue arises, the assertion as a defense in patent-infringement litigation that a party was relying on advice of counsel, is discussed elsewhere in this Note. In this and similar situations, under subdivision (a)(1) the party using an attorney-client communication to its advantage in the litigation has, in so doing, intentionally waived the privilege as to other communications concerning the same subject matter, regardless of the circumstances in which the communication being so used was initially disclosed.

Subdivision (b)—Fairness Considerations

The standard set forth in this subdivision for determining whether a disclosure operates as a waiver of the privilege or protection is, as explained elsewhere in this Note, the majority rule in the federal courts. The majority rule has simply been distilled here into a standard designed to be predictable in its application. This distillation is not intended to foreclose notions of fairness from continuing to inform application of the standard in all aspects as appropriate in particular cases—for example, as to whether steps taken to rectify an erroneous inadvertent disclosure were sufficiently prompt under subdivision (b)(3) where the receiving party has relied on the information disclosed.

Subdivisions (a) and (b)—Disclosures to Federal Office or Agency

This rule, as a Federal Rule of Evidence, applies to admissibility of evidence. While subdivisions (a) and (b) are written broadly to apply as appropriate to disclosures of information to a federal office or agency, they do not apply to uses of information—such as routine use in government publications—that fall outside the evidentiary context. Nor do these subdivisions relieve the party seeking to protect the information as privileged from the burden of proving that the privilege applies in the first place.

Subdivision (d)—Court Orders

This subdivision authorizes a court to enter orders only in the context of litigation pending before the court. And it does not alter the law regarding waiver of privilege resulting from having acquiesced in the use of otherwise privileged information. Therefore, this subdivision does not provide a basis for a court to enable parties to agree to a selective waiver of the privilege, such as to a federal agency conducting an investigation, while preserving the privilege as against other parties seeking the information. This subdivision is designed to enable a court to enter an order, whether on motion of one or more parties or on its own motion, that will allow the parties to conduct and respond to discovery expeditiously, without the need for exhaustive pre-production privilege reviews, while still preserving each party's right to assert the privilege to preclude use in litigation of information disclosed in such discovery. While the benefits of a court order under this subdivision would be equally available in government enforcement actions as in private actions, acquiescence by the disclosing party in use by the federal agency of information disclosed pursuant to such an order would still be treated as under current law for purposes of determining whether the acquiescence in use of the information, as opposed to its mere disclosure, effects a waiver of the privilege. The same applies to acquiescence in use by another private party.

Moreover, whether the order is entered on motion of one or more parties, or on the court's own motion, the court retains its authority to include the conditions it deems appropriate In the circumstances.

Subdivision (e)—Party Agreements

This subdivision simply makes clear that while parties to a case may agree among themselves regarding the effect of disclosures between each other in a federal proceeding, it is not binding on others unless it is incorporated into a court order. This subdivision does not confer any authority on a court to enter any order regarding the effect of disclosures. That authority must be found in subdivision (d), or elsewhere.

HISTORICAL NOTES

Revision Notes and Legislative Reports

2008 Acts

Senate Report No. 110–264, see 2008 U.S. Code Cong. and Adm. News, p. 1305.

Effective and Applicability Provisions

2008 Acts

Pub.L. 110–322, § 1(c), Sept. 19, 2008, 122 Stat. 3538, provided that: "The amendments made by this Act [enacting this rule] shall apply in all proceedings commenced after the date of enactment of this Act [Sept. 19, 2008] and, insofar as is just and practicable, in all proceedings pending on such date of enactment [Sept. 19, 2008]."

ARTICLE VI. WITNESSES

Rule

601. Competency to Testify in General.
602. Need for Personal Knowledge.
603. Oath or Affirmation to Testify Truthfully.
604. Interpreter.
605. Judge's Competency as a Witness.
606. Juror's Competency as a Witness.
607. Who May Impeach a Witness.
608. A Witness's Character for Truthfulness or Untruthfulness.
609. Impeachment by Evidence of a Criminal Conviction.
610. Religious Beliefs or Opinions.
611. Mode and Order of Examining Witnesses and Presenting Evidence.
612. Writing Used to Refresh a Witness's Memory.
613. Witness's Prior Statement.
614. Court's Calling or Examining a Witness.
615. Excluding Witnesses.

Rule 601. Competency to Testify in General

Every person is competent to be a witness unless these rules provide otherwise. But in a civil case, state law governs the witness's competency regarding a claim or defense for which state law supplies the rule of decision.

(Pub.L. 93–595, § 1, Jan. 2, 1975, 88 Stat.1934; Apr. 26, 2011, eff. Dec. 1, 2011.)

ADVISORY COMMITTEE NOTES

1972 Proposed Rules

This general ground-clearing eliminates all grounds of incompetency not specifically recognized in the succeeding rules of this Article. Included among the grounds thus abolished are religious belief, conviction of crime, and connection with the litigation as a party or interested person or spouse of a party or interested person. With the exception of the so-called Dead Man's Acts, American jurisdictions generally have ceased to recognize these grounds.

The Dead Man's Acts are surviving traces of the common law disqualification of parties and interested persons. They exist in variety too great to convey conviction of their wisdom and effectiveness. These rules contain no provision of this kind. For the reasoning underlying the decision not to give effect to state statutes in diversity cases, see the Advisory Committee's Note to Rule 501.

No mental or moral qualifications for testifying as a witness are specified. Standards of mental capacity have proved elusive in actual application. A leading commentator observes that few witnesses are disqualified on that ground. Weihofen, Testimonial Competence and Credibility, 34 Geo.Wash.L.Rev. 53 (1965). Discretion is regularly exercised in favor of allowing the testimony. A witness wholly without capacity is difficult to imagine. The question is one particularly suited to the jury as one of weight and credibility, subject to judicial authority to review the sufficiency of the evidence. 2 Wigmore §§ 501, 509. Standards of moral qualification in practice consist essentially of evaluating a person's truthfulness in terms of his own answers about it. Their principal utility is in affording an opportunity on voir dire examination to impress upon the witness his moral duty. This result may, however, be accomplished more directly, and without haggling in terms of legal standards, by the manner of administering the oath or affirmation under Rule 603.

Admissibility of religious belief as a ground of impeachment is treated in Rule 610. Conviction of crime as a ground of impeachment is the subject of Rule 609. Marital relationship is the basis for privilege under Rule 505. Interest in the outcome of litigation and mental capacity are, of course, highly relevant to credibility and require no special treatment to render them admissible along with other matters bearing upon the perception, memory, and narration of witnesses.

1974 Enactment

Rule 601 as submitted to the Congress provided that "Every person is competent to be a witness except as otherwise provided in these rules." One effect of the Rule as proposed would have been to abolish age, mental capacity, and other grounds recognized in some State jurisdictions as making a person incompetent as a witness. The greatest controversy centered around the Rule's rendering inapplicable in the federal courts the so-called Dead Man's Statutes which exist in some States. Acknowledging that there is substantial disagreement as to the merit of Dead Man's Statutes, the Committee nevertheless believed that where such statutes have been enacted they represent State policy which should not be overturned in the absence of a compelling federal interest. The Committee therefore amended the Rule to make competency in civil actions determinable in accordance with State law with respect to elements of claims or defenses as to which State law supplies the rule of decision. Cf. *Courtland v. Walston & Co., Inc.*, 340 F.Supp. 1076, 1087–1092 (S.D.N.Y.1972). House Report No. 93–650.

The amendment to rule 601 parallels the treatment accorded Rule 501 discussed immediately above. Senate Report No. 93–1277.

Rule 601 deals with competency of witnesses. Both the House and Senate bills provide that federal competency law applies in criminal cases. In civil actions and proceedings, the House bill provides that state competency law applies "to an element of a claim or defense as to which State law supplies the rule of decision." The Senate bill provides that "in civil actions and proceedings arising under 28 U.S.C. § 1332 or 28 U.S.C. § 1335, or between citizens of different States and removed under 28 U.S.C. § 1441(b) the competency of a witness, person, government, State or political subdivision thereof is determined in accordance with State law, unless with respect to the particular claim or defense, Federal law supplies the rule of decision."

The wording of the House and Senate bills differs in the treatment of civil actions and proceedings. The rule in the House bill applies to evidence that relates to "an element of a claim or defense." If an item of proof tends to support or defeat a claim or defense, or an element of a claim or defense, and if state law supplies the rule of decision for that claim or defense, then state competency law applies to that item of proof.

For reasons similar to those underlying its action on Rule 501, the Conference adopts the House provision. House Report No. 93–1597.

2011 Amendments

The language of Rule 601 has been amended as part of the restyling of the Evidence Rules to make them more easily understood and to make style and terminology consistent throughout the rules. These changes are intended to be stylistic only. There is no intent to change any result in any ruling on evidence admissibility.

Rule 602. Need for Personal Knowledge

A witness may testify to a matter only if evidence is introduced sufficient to support a finding that the witness has personal knowledge of the matter. Evidence to prove personal knowledge may consist of the witness' s own testimony. This rule does not apply to a witness's expert testimony under Rule 703.

(Pub.L. 93–595, § 1, Jan. 2, 1975, 88 Stat. 1934; Mar. 2, 1987, eff. Oct. 1, 1987; Apr. 25, 1988, eff. Nov. 1, 1988; Apr. 26, 2011, eff. Dec. 1, 2011.)

ADVISORY COMMITTEE NOTES

1972 Proposed Rules

" * * * [T]he rule requiring that a witness who testifies to a fact which can be perceived by the senses must have had an opportunity to observe, and must have actually observed the fact" is a "most pervasive manifestation" of the common law insistence upon "the most reliable sources of information." McCormick § 10, p. 19. These foundation requirements may, of course, be furnished by the testimony of the witness himself; hence personal knowledge is not an absolute but may consist of what the witness thinks he knows from personal perception. 2 Wigmore § 650. It will be observed that the rule is in fact a specialized application of the provisions of Rule 104(b) on conditional relevancy.

This rule does not govern the situation of a witness who testifies to a hearsay statement as such, if he has personal knowledge of the making of the statement. Rules 801 and 805 would be applicable. This rule would, however, prevent him from testifying to the subject matter of the hearsay statement, as he has no personal knowledge of it.

The reference to Rule 703 is designed to avoid any question of conflict between the present rule and the provisions of that rule allowing an expert to express opinions based on facts of which he does not have personal knowledge.

1987 Amendments

The amendments are technical. No substantive change is intended.

1988 Amendments

The amendment is technical. No substantive change is intended.

2011 Amendments

The language of Rule 602 has been amended as part of the restyling of the Evidence Rules to make them more easily understood and to make style and terminology consistent throughout the rules. These changes are intended to be stylistic only. There is no intent to change any result in any ruling on evidence admissibility.

Rule 603. Oath or Affirmation to Testify Truthfully

Before testifying, a witness must give an oath or affirmation to testify truthfully. It must be in a form designed to impress that duty on the witness's conscience.

(Pub.L. 93–595, § 1, Jan. 2, 1975, 88 Stat. 1934; Mar. 2, 1987, eff. Oct. 1, 1987; Apr. 26, 2011, eff. Dec. 1, 2011.)

ADVISORY COMMITTEE NOTES

1972 Proposed Rules

The rule is designed to afford the flexibility required in dealing with religious adults, atheists, conscientious objectors, mental defectives, and children. Affirmation is simply a solemn undertaking to tell the truth; no special verbal formula is required. As is true generally, affirmation is recognized by federal law. "Oath" includes affirmation, 1 U.S.C. § 1; judges and clerks may administer oaths and affirmations, 28 U.S.C. §§ 459, 953; and affirmations are acceptable in lieu of oaths under Rule 43(d) of the Federal Rules of Civil Procedure. Perjury by a witness is a crime, 18 U.S.C. § 1621.

1987 Amendments

The amendments are technical. No substantive change is intended.

2011 Amendments

The language of Rule 603 has been amended as part of the restyling of the Evidence Rules to make them more easily understood and to make style and terminology consistent throughout the rules. These changes are intended to be stylistic only. There is no intent to change any result in any ruling on evidence admissibility.

Rule 604. Interpreter

An interpreter must be qualified and must give an oath or affirmation to make a true translation.

(Pub.L. 93–595, § 1, Jan. 2, 1975, 88 Stat. 1934; Mar. 2, 1987, eff. Oct. 1, 1987; Apr. 26, 2011, eff. Dec. 1, 2011.)

ADVISORY COMMITTEE NOTES

1972 Proposed Rules

The rule implements Rule 43(f) of the Federal Rules of Civil Procedure and Rule 28(b) of the Federal Rules of Criminal Procedure, both of which contain provisions for the appointment and compensation of interpreters.

1987 Amendments

The amendment is technical. No substantive change is intended.

2011 Amendments

The language of Rule 604 has been amended as part of the restyling of the Evidence Rules to make them more easily understood and to make style and terminology consistent throughout the rules. These changes are intended to be stylistic only. There is no intent to change any result in any ruling on evidence admissibility.

Rule 605. Judge's Competency as a Witness

The presiding judge may not testify as a witness at the trial. A party need not object to preserve the issue.

(Pub.L. 93–595, § 1, Jan. 2, 1975, 88 Stat. 1934; Apr. 26, 2011, eff. Dec. 1, 2011.)

ADVISORY COMMITTEE NOTES

1972 Proposed Rules

In view of the mandate of 28 U.S.C. § 455 that a judge disqualify himself in "any case in which he * * * is or has been a material witness," the likelihood that the presiding judge in a federal court might be called to testify in the trial over which he is presiding is slight. Nevertheless the possibility is not totally eliminated.

The solution here presented is a broad rule of incompetency, rather than such alternatives as incompetency only as to material matters, leaving the matter to the discretion of the judge, or recognizing no incompetency. The choice is the result of inability to evolve satisfactory answers to questions which arise when the judge abandons the bench for the witness stand. Who rules on objections? Who compels him to answer? Can he rule impartially on the weight and admissibility of his own testimony? Can he be impeached or cross-examined effectively? Can he, in a jury trial, avoid conferring his seal of approval on one side in the eyes of the jury? Can he, in a bench trial, avoid an involvement destructive of impartiality? The rule of general incompetency has substantial support. See Report of the Special Committee on the Propriety of Judges Appearing as Witnesses, 36 A.B.A.J. 630 (1950); cases collected in Annot. 157 A.L.R. 311; McCormick § 68, p. 147; Uniform Rule 42; California Evidence Code § 703; Kansas Code of Civil Procedure § 60–442; New Jersey Evidence Rule 42. Cf. 6 Wigmore § 1909, which advocates leaving the matter to the discretion of the judge, and statutes to that effect collected in Annot. 157 A.L.R. 311.

The rule provides an "automatic" objection. To require an actual objection would confront the opponent with a choice between not objecting, with the result of allowing the testimony, and objecting, with the probable result of excluding the testimony but at the price of continuing the trial before a judge likely to feel that his integrity had been attacked by the objector.

2011 Amendments

The language of Rule 605 has been amended as part of the restyling of the Evidence Rules to make them more easily understood and to make style and terminology consistent throughout the rules. These changes are intended to be stylistic only. There is no intent to change any result in any ruling on evidence admissibility.

Rule 606. Juror's Competency as a Witness

(a) At the Trial. A juror may not testify as a witness before the other jurors at the trial. If a juror is called to testify, the court must give a party an opportunity to object outside the jury's presence.

(b) During an Inquiry Into the Validity of a Verdict or Indictment.

(1) Prohibited Testimony or Other Evidence. During an inquiry into the validity of a verdict or indictment, a juror may not testify about any statement made or incident that occurred during the jury's deliberations; the effect of anything on that juror's or another juror's vote; or any juror's mental processes concerning the verdict or indictment. The court may not receive a juror's affidavit or evidence of a juror's statement on these matters.

(2) Exceptions. A juror may testify about whether:

(A) extraneous prejudicial information was improperly brought to the jury's attention;

(B) an outside influence was improperly brought to bear on any juror; or

(C) a mistake was made in entering the verdict on the verdict form.

(Pub.L. 93–595, § 1, Jan. 2, 1975, 88 Stat. 1934; Pub.L. 94–149, § 1(10), Dec. 12, 1975, 89 Stat. 805; Mar. 2, 1987, eff. Oct. 1, 1987; Apr. 12, 2006, eff. Dec. 1, 2006; Apr. 26, 2011, eff. Dec. 1, 2011.)

ADVISORY COMMITTEE NOTES

1972 Proposed Rules

Note to Subdivision (a). The considerations which bear upon the permissibility of testimony by a juror in the trial in which he is sitting as juror bear an obvious similarity to those evoked when the judge is called as a witness. See Advisory Committee's Note to Rule 605. The judge is not, however in this instance so involved as to call for departure from usual principles requiring objection to be made; hence the only provision on objection is that opportunity be afforded for its making out of the presence of the jury. Compare Rule 605.

Note to Subdivision (b). Whether testimony, affidavits, or statements of jurors should be received for the purpose of invalidating or supporting a verdict or indictment, and if so, under what circumstances, has given rise to substantial differences of opinion. The familiar rubric that a juror may not impeach his own verdict, dating from Lord Mansfield's time, is a gross oversimplification. The values sought to be promoted by excluding the evidence include freedom of deliberation, stability and finality of verdicts, and protection of jurors against annoyance and embarrassment. *McDonald v. Pless,* 238 U.S. 264, 35 S.Ct. 783, 59 L.Ed. 1300 (1915). On the other hand, simply putting verdicts beyond effective reach can only promote irregularity and injustice. The rule offers an accommodation between these competing considerations.

The mental operations and emotional reactions of jurors in arriving at a given result would, if allowed as a subject of inquiry, place every verdict at the mercy of jurors and invite tampering and harassment. See *Grenz v. Werre,* 129 N.W.2d 681 (N.D.1964). The authorities are in virtually complete accord in excluding the evidence. Fryer, Note on Disqualification of Witnesses, Selected Writings on Evidence and Trial 345, 347 (Fryer ed. 1957); Maguire, Weinstein, et al., Cases on Evidence 887 (5th ed. 1965); 8 Wigmore § 2349 (McNaughton Rev.1961). As to matters other than mental operations and emotional reactions of jurors, substantial authority refuses to allow a juror to disclose irregularities which occur in the jury room, but allows his testimony as to irregularities occurring outside and allows outsiders to testify as to occurrences both inside and out. 8 Wigmore § 2354 (McNaughton Rev.1961). However, the door of the jury room is not necessarily a satisfactory dividing point, and the Supreme Court has refused to accept it for every situation. *Mattox v. United States,* 146 U.S. 140, 13 S.Ct. 50, 36 L.Ed. 917 (1892).

Under the federal decisions the central focus has been upon insulation of the manner in which the jury reached its verdict, and this protection extends to each of the components of deliberation, including arguments, statements, discussions, mental and emotional reactions, votes, and any other feature of the process. Thus testimony or affidavits of jurors have been held incompetent to show a compromise verdict. *Hyde v. United States,* 225 U.S. 347, 382 (1912); a quotient verdict, *McDonald v. Pless,* 238 U.S. 264 (1915); speculation as to insurance coverage. *Holden v. Porter,* 405 F.2d 878 (10th Cir.1969); *Farmers Coop. Elev. Ass'n v. Strand,* 382 F.2d 224, 230 (8th Cir.1967), cert. denied 389 U.S. 1014; misinterpretation of instructions, *Farmers Coop. Elev. Ass'n v. Strand,* supra; mistake in returning verdict, *United States v. Chereton,* 309 F.2d 197 (6th Cir.1962); interpretation of guilty plea by one defendant as implicating others, *United States v. Crosby,* 294 F.2d 928, 949 (2d Cir.1961). The policy does not, however, foreclose testimony by jurors as to prejudicial extraneous information or influences injected into or brought to bear upon the deliberative process. Thus a juror is recognized as competent to testify to statements by the bailiff or the introduction of a prejudicial newspaper account into the jury room, *Mattox v. United States,* 146 U.S. 140 (1892). See also *Parker v. Gladden,* 385 U.S. 363 (1966).

This rule does not purport to specify the substantive grounds for setting aside verdicts for irregularity; it deals only with the competency of jurors to testify concerning those grounds. Allowing them to testify as to matters other than their own inner reactions involves no particular hazard to the values sought to be protected. The rule is based upon this conclusion. It makes no attempt to specify the substantive grounds for setting aside verdicts for irregularity.

See also Rule 6(e) of the Federal Rules of Criminal Procedure and 18 U.S.C. § 3500, governing the secrecy of grand jury proceedings. The present rule does not relate to secrecy and disclosure but to the competency of certain witnesses and evidence.

1974 Enactment

Note to Subdivision (b). As proposed by the Court, Rule 606(b) limited testimony by a juror in the course of an inquiry into the validity of a verdict or indictment. He could testify as to the influence of extraneous prejudicial information brought to the jury's attention (e.g. a radio newscast or a newspaper account) or an outside influence which improperly had been brought to bear upon a juror (e.g. a threat to the safety of a member of his family), but he could not testify as to other irregularities which occurred in the jury room. Under this formulation a quotient verdict could not be attacked through the testimony of a juror, nor could a juror testify to the drunken condition of a fellow juror which so disabled him that he could not participate in the jury's deliberations.

The 1969 and 1971 Advisory Committee drafts would have permitted a member of the jury to testify concerning these kinds of irregularities in the jury room. The

Advisory Committee note in the 1971 draft stated that "* * * the door of the jury room is not a satisfactory dividing point, and the Supreme Court has refused to accept it." The Advisory Committee further commented that—

> The trend has been to draw the dividing line between testimony as to mental processes, on the one hand, and as to the existence of conditions or occurrences of events calculated improperly to influence the verdict on the other hand, without regard to whether the happening is within or without the jury room. * * * The jurors are the persons who know what really happened. Allowing them to testify as to matters other than their own reactions involves no particular hazard to the values sought to be protected. The rule is based upon this conclusion. It makes no attempt to specify the substantive grounds for setting aside verdicts for irregularity.

Objective jury misconduct may be testified to in California, Florida, Iowa, Kansas, Nebraska, New Jersey, North Dakota, Ohio, Oregon, Tennessee, Texas, and Washington.

Persuaded that the better practice is that provided for in the earlier drafts, the Committee amended subdivision (b) to read in the text of those drafts. House Report No. 93–650.

Note to Subdivision (b). As adopted by the House, this rule would permit the impeachment of verdicts by inquiry into, not the mental processes of the jurors, but what happened in terms of conduct in the jury room. This extension of the ability to impeach a verdict is felt to be unwarranted and ill-advised.

The rule passed by the House embodies a suggestion by the Advisory Committee of the Judicial Conference that is considerably broader than the final version adopted by the Supreme Court, which embodied long-accepted Federal law. Although forbidding the impeachment of verdicts by inquiry into the jurors' mental processes, it deletes from the Supreme Court version the proscription against testimony "as to any matter or statement occurring during the course of the jury's deliberations." This deletion would have the effect of opening verdicts up to challenge on the basis of what happened during the jury's internal deliberations, for example, where a juror alleged that the jury refused to follow the trial judge's instructions or that some of the jurors did not take part in deliberations.

Permitting an individual to attack a jury verdict based upon the jury's internal deliberations has long been recognized as unwise by the Supreme Court. In *McDonald v. Pless,* the Court stated:

* * * *

> [L]et it once be established that verdicts solemnly made and publicly returned into court can be attacked and set aside on the testimony of those who took part in their publication and all verdicts could be, and many would be, followed by an inquiry in the hope of discovering something which might invalidate the finding. Jurors would be harassed and beset by the defeated party in an effort to secure from them evidence of facts which might establish misconduct sufficient to set aside a verdict. If evidence thus secured could be thus used, the result would be to make what was intended to be a private deliberation, the constant subject of public investigation—to the destruction of all frankness and freedom of discussion and conference [238 U.S. 264, at 267 (1914)].

* * * *

As it stands then, the rule would permit the harassment of former jurors by losing parties as well as the possible exploitation of disgruntled or otherwise badly-motivated ex-jurors.

Public policy requires a finality to litigation. And common fairness requires that absolute privacy be preserved for jurors to engage in the full and free debate necessary to the attainment of just verdicts. Jurors will not be able to function effectively if their deliberations are to be scrutinized in post-trial litigation. In the interest of protecting the jury system and the citizens who make it work, rule 606 should not permit any inquiry into the internal deliberations of the jurors. Senate Report No. 93–1277.

Note to Subdivision (b). Rule 606(b) deals with juror testimony in an inquiry into the validity of a verdict or indictment. The House bill provides that a juror cannot testify about his mental processes or about the effect of anything upon his or another juror's mind as influencing him to assent to or dissent from a verdict or indictment. Thus, the House bill allows a juror to testify about objective matters occurring during the jury's deliberation, such as the misconduct of another juror or the reaching of a quotient verdict. The Senate bill does not permit juror testimony about any matter or statement occurring during the course of the jury's deliberations. The Senate bill does provide, however, that a juror may testify on the question whether extraneous prejudicial information was improperly brought to the jury's attention and on the question whether any outside influence was improperly brought to bear on any juror.

The Conference adopts the Senate amendment. The Conferees believe that jurors should be encouraged to be conscientious in promptly reporting to the court misconduct that occurs during jury deliberations. House Report No. 93–1597.

1987 Amendments

The amendments are technical. No substantive change is intended.

2006 Amendments

Rule 606(b) has been amended to provide that juror testimony may be used to prove that the verdict reported was the result of a mistake in entering the verdict on the verdict form. The amendment responds to a divergence between the text of the Rule and the case law that has established an exception for proof of clerical errors. *See, e.g., Plummer v. Springfield Term. Ry.,* 5 F.3d 1, 3 (1st Cir. 1993) ("A number of circuits hold, and we agree, that juror testimony regarding an alleged clerical error, such as announcing a verdict different than that agreed upon, does not challenge the validity of the verdict or the deliberation of mental processes, and therefore is not subject to Rule 606(b)."); *Teevee Toons, Inc., v. MP3.Com, Inc.,* 148 F.Supp.2d 276, 278 (S.D.N.Y. 2001) (noting that Rule 606(b) has been silent regarding inquiries designed to confirm the accuracy of a verdict).

In adopting the exception for proof of mistakes in entering the verdict on the verdict form, the amendment specifically rejects the broader exception, adopted by some courts, permitting the use of juror testimony to prove that the jurors were operating under a misunderstanding about the consequences of the result that they agreed upon. *See, e.g., Attridge v. Cencorp Div. of Dover Techs. Int'l, Inc.,* 836 F.2d 113, 116 (2d Cir. 1987); *Eastridge Development Co., v. Halpert Associates, Inc.,* 853 F.2d 772 (10th Cir. 1988). The broader exception is rejected because an inquiry into whether the jury misunderstood or misapplied an instruction goes to the jurors' mental processes underlying the verdict, rather than the verdict's accuracy in capturing what the jurors had agreed upon. *See, e.g., Karl v. Burlington Northern R.R.,* 880 F.2d 68, 74 (8th Cir. 1989) (error to receive juror testimony on whether verdict was the result of jurors' misunderstanding of instructions: "The jurors did not state that the figure written by the foreman was different from that which they agreed upon, but indicated that the figure the foreman wrote down was intended to be a net figure, not a gross figure. Receiving such statements violates Rule 606(b) because the testimony relates to how the jury interpreted the court's instructions, and concerns the jurors' 'mental processes,' which is forbidden by the rule."); *Robles v. Exxon Corp.*, 862 F.2d 1201, 1208 (5th Cir. 1989) ("the alleged error here goes to the substance of what the jury was asked to decide, necessarily implicating the jury's mental processes insofar as it questions the jury's understanding of the court's instructions and application of those instructions to the facts of the case"). Thus, the exception established by the amendment is limited to cases such as "where the jury foreperson wrote down, in response to an interrogatory, a number different from that agreed upon by the jury, or mistakenly stated that the defendant was 'guilty' when the jury had actually agreed that the defendant was not guilty." *Id.*

It should be noted that the possibility of errors in the verdict form will be reduced substantially by polling the jury. Rule 606(b) does not, of course, prevent this precaution. *See* 8 C. Wigmore, *Evidence,* § 2350 at 691 (McNaughten ed. 1961) (noting that the reasons for the rule barring juror testimony, "namely, the dangers of uncertainty and of tampering with the jurors to procure testimony, disappear in large part if such investigation as may be desired is *made by the judge* and takes place *before the jurors' discharge* and separation") (emphasis in original). Errors that come to light after polling the jury "may be corrected on the spot, or the jury may be sent out to continue deliberations, or, if necessary, a new trial may be ordered." C. Mueller & L. Kirkpatrick, *Evidence Under the Rules* at 671 (2d ed. 1999) (citing *Sincox v. United States,* 571 F.2d 876, 878–79 (5th Cir. 1978)).

2011 Amendments

The language of Rule 606 has been amended as part of the restyling of the Evidence Rules to make them more easily understood and to make style and terminology consistent throughout the rules. These changes are intended to be stylistic only. There is no intent to change any result in any ruling on evidence admissibility.

HISTORICAL NOTES

Revision Notes and Legislative Reports

1975 Acts

House Report No. 94–599, see 1975 U.S. Code Cong. and Adm. News, p. 1585.

Rule 607. Who May Impeach a Witness

Any party, including the party that called the witness, may attack the witness's credibility.

(Pub.L. 93–595, § 1, Jan. 2, 1975, 88 Stat.1934; Mar. 2, 1987, eff. Oct. 1, 1987; Apr. 26, 2011, eff. Dec. 1, 2011.)

ADVISORY COMMITTEE NOTES

1972 Proposed Rules

The traditional rule against impeaching one's own witness is abandoned as based on false premises. A party does not hold out his witnesses as worthy of belief, since he rarely has a free choice in selecting them. Denial of the right leaves the party at the mercy of the witness and the adversary. If the impeachment is by a prior statement, it is free from hearsay dangers and is excluded from the category of hearsay under Rule 801(d)(1). Ladd, Impeachment of One's Own Witness—New

Developments, 4 U.Chi.L.Rev. 69 (1936); McCormick § 38; 3 Wigmore §§ 896–918. The substantial inroads into the old rule made over the years by decisions, rules, and statutes are evidence of doubts as to its basic soundness and workability. Cases are collected in 3 Wigmore § 905. Revised Rule 32(a)(1) of the Federal Rules of Civil Procedure allows any party to impeach a witness by means of his deposition, and Rule 43(b) has allowed the calling and impeachment of an adverse party or person identified with him. Illustrative statutes allowing a party to impeach his own witness under varying circumstances are Ill.Rev.Stats.1967, c. 110, § 60; Mass.Laws Annot. 1959, c. 233, § 23; 20 N.M.Stats.Annot. 1953, § 20–2–4; N.Y. CPLR § 4514 (McKinney 1963); 12 Vt.Stats.Annot.1959, §§ 1641a, 1642. Complete judicial rejection of the old rule is found in *United States v. Freeman,* 302 F.2d 347 (2d Cir.1962). The same result is reached in Uniform Rule 20; California Evidence Code § 785; Kansas Code of Civil Procedure § 60–420. See also New Jersey Evidence Rule 20.

1987 Amendments

The amendment is technical. No substantive change is intended.

2011 Amendments

The language of Rule 607 has been amended as part of the restyling of the Evidence Rules to make them more easily understood and to make style and terminology consistent throughout the rules. These changes are intended to be stylistic only. There is no intent to change any result in any ruling on evidence admissibility.

Rule 608. A Witness's Character for Truthfulness or Untruthfulness

(a) Reputation or Opinion Evidence. A witness's credibility may be attacked or supported by testimony about the witness's reputation for having a character for truthfulness or untruthfulness, or by testimony in the form of an opinion about that character. But evidence of truthful character is admissible only after the witness's character for truthfulness has been attacked.

(b) Specific Instances of Conduct. Except for a criminal conviction under Rule 609, extrinsic evidence is not admissible to prove specific instances of a witness's conduct in order to attack or support the witness's character for truthfulness. But the court may, on cross-examination, allow them to be inquired into if they are probative of the character for truthfulness or untruthfulness of:

(1) the witness; or

(2) another witness whose character the witness being cross-examined has testified about.

By testifying on another matter, a witness does not waive any privilege against self-incrimination for testimony that relates only to the witness's character for truthfulness.

(Pub.L. 93–595, § 1, Jan. 2, 1975, 88 Stat.1935; Mar. 2, 1987, eff. Oct. 1, 1987; Apr. 25, 1988, eff. Nov. 1, 1988; Mar. 27, 2003, eff. Dec. 1, 2003; Apr. 26, 2011, eff. Dec. 1, 2011.)

ADVISORY COMMITTEE NOTES

1972 Proposed Rules

Note to Subdivision (a). In Rule 404(a) the general position is taken that character evidence is not admissible for the purpose of proving that the person acted in conformity therewith, subject, however, to several exceptions, one of which is character evidence of a witness as bearing upon his credibility. The present rule develops that exception.

In accordance with the bulk of judicial authority, the inquiry is strictly limited to character for veracity, rather than allowing evidence as to character generally. The result is to sharpen relevancy, to reduce surprise, waste of time, and confusion, and to make the lot of the witness somewhat less unattractive. McCormick § 44.

The use of opinion and reputation evidence as means of proving the character of witnesses is consistent with Rule 405(a). While the modern practice has purported to exclude opinion, witnesses who testify to reputation seem in fact often to be giving their opinions, disguised somewhat misleadingly as reputation. See McCormick § 44. And even under the modern practice, a common relaxation has allowed inquiry as to whether the witnesses would believe the principal witness under oath. *United States v. Walker,* 313 F.2d 236 (6th Cir.1963), and cases cited therein; McCormick § 44, pp. 94–95, n. 3.

Character evidence in support of credibility is admissible under the rule only after the witness' character has first been attacked, as has been the case at common law. Maguire, Weinstein, et al., Cases on Evidence 295 (5th ed. 1965); McCormick § 49, p. 105; 4 Wigmore § 1104. The enormous needless consumption of time which a contrary practice would entail justifies the limitation. Opinion or reputation that the witness is untruthful specifically qualifies as an attack under the rule, and evidence of misconduct, including conviction of crime, and of corruption also fall within this category. Evidence of bias or interest does not. McCormick § 49; 4 Wigmore §§ 1106, 1107. Whether evidence in the form of contradiction is an attack upon the character of the witness must depend upon the circumstances. McCormick § 49. Cf. 4 Wigmore §§ 1108, 1109.

As to the use of specific instances on direct by an opinion witness, see the Advisory Committee's Note to Rule 405, *supra.*

Note to Subdivision (b). In conformity with Rule 405, which forecloses use of evidence of specific incidents as proof in chief of character unless character is an issue in the case, the present rule generally bars evidence of specific instances of conduct of a witness for the purpose of attacking or supporting his credibility. There are, however, two exceptions: (1) specific instances are provable when they have been the subject of criminal conviction, and (2) specific instances may be inquired into on cross-examination of the principal witness or of a witness giving an opinion of his character for truthfulness.

(1) Conviction of crime as a technique of impeachment is treated in detail in Rule 609, and here is merely recognized as an exception to the general rule excluding evidence of specific incidents for impeachment purposes.

(2) Particular instances of conduct, though not the subject of criminal conviction, may be inquired into on cross-examination of the principal witness himself or of a witness who testifies concerning his character for truthfulness. Effective cross-examination demands that some allowance be made for going into matters of this kind, but the possibilities of abuse are substantial. Consequently safeguards are erected in the form of specific requirements that the instances inquired into be probative of truthfulness or its opposite and not remote in time. Also, the overriding protection of Rule 403 requires that probative value not be outweighed by danger of unfair prejudice, confusion of issues, or misleading the jury, and that of Rule 611 bars harassment and undue embarrassment.

The final sentence constitutes a rejection of the doctrine of such cases as *People v. Sorge,* 301 N.Y. 198, 93 N.E.2d 637 (1950), that any past criminal act relevant to credibility may be inquired into on cross-examination, in apparent disregard of the privilege against self-incrimination. While it is clear that an ordinary witness cannot make a partial disclosure of incriminating matter and then invoke the privilege on cross-examination, no tenable contention can be made that merely by testifying he waives his right to foreclose inquiry on cross-examination into criminal activities for the purpose of attacking his credibility. So to hold would reduce the privilege to a nullity. While it is true that an accused, unlike an ordinary witness, has an option whether to testify, if the option can be exercised only at the price of opening up inquiry as to any and all criminal acts committed during his lifetime, the right to testify could scarcely be said to possess much vitality. In *Griffin v. California,* 380 U.S. 609, 85 S.Ct. 1229, 14 L.Ed.2d 106 (1965), the Court held that allowing comment on the election of an accused not to testify exacted a constitutionally impermissible price, and so here. While no specific provision in terms confers constitutional status on the right of an accused to take the stand in his own defense, the existence of the right is so completely recognized that a denial of it or substantial infringement upon it would surely be of due process dimensions. See *Ferguson v. Georgia,* 365 U.S. 570, 81 S.Ct. 756, 5 L.Ed.2d 783 (1961); McCormick § 131; 8 Wigmore § 2276 (McNaughton Rev.1961). In any event, wholly aside from constitutional considerations, the provision represents a sound policy.

1974 Enactment

Note to Subdivision (a). Rule 608(a) as submitted by the Court permitted attack to be made upon the character for truthfulness or untruthfulness of a witness either by reputation or opinion testimony. For the same reason underlying its decision to eliminate the admissibility of opinion testimony in Rule 405(a), the Committee amended Rule 608(a) to delete the reference to opinion testimony.

Note to Subdivision (b). The second sentence of Rule 608(b) as submitted by the Court permitted specific instances of misconduct of a witness to be inquired into on cross-examination for the purpose of attacking his credibility, if probative of truthfulness or untruthfulness, "and not remote in time". Such cross-examination could be of the witness himself or of another witness who testifies as to "his" character for truthfulness or untruthfulness.

The Committee amended the Rule to emphasize the discretionary power of the court in permitting such testimony and deleted the reference to remoteness in time as being unnecessary and confusing (remoteness from time of trial or remoteness from the incident involved?). As recast, the Committee amendment also makes clear the antecedent of "his" in the original Court proposal. House Report No. 93–650.

The Senate amendment adds the words "opinion or" to conform the first sentence of the rule with the remainder of the rule.

The Conference adopts the Senate amendment. House Report No. 93–1597.

1987 Amendments

The amendments are technical. No substantive change is intended.

1988 Amendments

The amendment is technical. No substantive change is intended.

2003 Amendments

The Rule has been amended to clarify that the absolute prohibition on extrinsic evidence applies only when the sole reason for proffering that evidence is to attack or support the witness' character for truthfulness. *See United States v. Abel,* 469 U.S. 45 (1984); *United States v. Fusco,* 748 F.2d 996 (5th Cir. 1984) (Rule 608(b) limits the use of evidence "designed to show that the witness has done things, unrelated to the suit being tried, that make him more or less believable per se"); Ohio R.Evid. 608(b). On occasion the Rule's use of the overbroad term "credibility" has been read "to bar extrinsic evidence for bias, competency and contradiction impeachment since they too deal with credibility." American Bar Association Section of Litigation, *Emerging Problems Under the Federal Rules of Evidence* at 161 (3d ed. 1998). The amendment conforms the language of the Rule to its original intent, which was to impose an absolute bar on extrinsic evidence only if the sole purpose for offering the evidence was to prove the witness' character for veracity. *See* Advisory Committee Note to Rule 608(b) (stating that the Rule is "[i]n conformity with Rule 405, which forecloses use of evidence of specific incidents as proof in chief of character unless character is in issue in the case . . . ").

By limiting the application of the Rule to proof of a witness' character for truthfulness, the amendment leaves the admissibility of extrinsic evidence offered for other grounds of impeachment (such as contradiction, prior inconsistent statement, bias and mental capacity) to Rules 402 and 403. *See, e.g., United States v. Winchenbach,* 197 F.3d 548 (1st Cir. 1999) (admissibility of a prior inconsistent statement offered for impeachment is governed by Rules 402 and 403, not Rule 608(b)); *United States v. Tarantino*, 846 F.2d 1384 (D.C. Cir. 1988) (admissibility of extrinsic evidence offered to contradict a witness is governed by Rules 402 and 403); *United States v. Lindemann,* 85 F.3d 1232 (7th Cir. 1996) (admissibility of extrinsic evidence of bias is governed by Rules 402 and 403).

It should be noted that the extrinsic evidence prohibition of Rule 608(b) bars any reference to the consequences that a witness might have suffered as a result of an alleged bad act. For example, Rule 608(b) prohibits counsel from mentioning that a witness was suspended or disciplined for the conduct that is the subject of impeachment, when that conduct is offered only to prove the character of the witness. *See United States v. Davis,* 183 F.3d 231, 257 n.12 (3d Cir. 1999) (emphasizing that in attacking the defendant's character for truthfulness "the government cannot make reference to Davis's forty-four day suspension or that Internal Affairs found that he lied about" an incident because "[s]uch evidence would not only be hearsay to the extent it contains assertion of fact, it would be inadmissible extrinsic evidence under Rule 608(b)"). *See also* Stephen A. Saltzburg, *Impeaching the Witness: Prior Bad Acts and Extrinsic Evidence*, 7 Crim. Just. 28, 31 (Winter 1993) ("counsel should not be permitted to circumvent the no-extrinsic-evidence provision by tucking a third person's opinion about prior acts into a question asked of the witness who has denied the act").

For purposes of consistency the term "credibility" has been replaced by the term "character for truthfulness" in the last sentence of subdivision (b). The term "credibility" is also used in subdivision (a). But the Committee found it unnecessary to substitute "character for truthfulness" for "credibility" in Rule 608(a), because subdivision (a)(1) already serves to limit impeachment to proof of such character.

Rules 609(a) and 610 also use the term "credibility" when the intent of those Rules is to regulate impeachment of a witness' character for truthfulness. No inference should be derived from the fact that the Committee proposed an amendment to Rule 608(b) but not to Rules 609 and 610.

2011 Amendments

The language of Rule 608 has been amended as part of the general restyling of the Evidence Rules to make them more easily understood and to make style and terminology consistent throughout the rules. These changes are intended to be stylistic only. There is no intent to change any result in any ruling on evidence admissibility.

The Committee is aware that the Rule's limitation of bad-act impeachment to "cross-examination" is trumped by Rule 607, which allows a party to impeach witnesses on direct examination. Courts have not relied on the term "on cross-examination" to limit impeachment that would otherwise be permissible under Rules 607 and 608. The Committee therefore concluded that no change to the language of the Rule was necessary in the context of a restyling project.

Rule 609. Impeachment by Evidence of a Criminal Conviction

(a) In General. The following rules apply to attacking a witness's character for truthfulness by evidence of a criminal conviction:

(1) for a crime that, in the convicting jurisdiction, was punishable by death or by imprisonment for more than one year, the evidence:

(A) must be admitted, subject to Rule 403, in a civil case or in a criminal case in which the witness is not a defendant; and

(B) must be admitted in a criminal case in which the witness is a defendant, if the probative value of the evidence outweighs its prejudicial effect to that defendant; and

(2) for any crime regardless of the punishment, the evidence must be admitted if the court can readily determine that establishing the elements of the crime required proving—or the witness's admitting—a dishonest act or false statement.

(b) Limit on Using the Evidence After 10 Years. This subdivision (b) applies if more than 10 years have passed since the witness's conviction or release from confinement for it, whichever is later. Evidence of the conviction is admissible only if:

(1) its probative value, supported by specific facts and circumstances, substantially outweighs its prejudicial effect; and

(2) the proponent gives an adverse party reasonable written notice of the intent to use it so that the party has a fair opportunity to contest its use.

(c) Effect of a Pardon, Annulment, or Certificate of Rehabilitation. Evidence of a conviction is not admissible if:

(1) the conviction has been the subject of a pardon, annulment, certificate of rehabilitation, or other equivalent procedure based on a finding that the person has been rehabilitated, and the person has not been convicted of a later crime punishable by death or by imprisonment for more than one year; or

(2) the conviction has been the subject of a pardon, annulment, or other equivalent procedure based on a finding of innocence.

(d) Juvenile Adjudications. Evidence of a juvenile adjudication is admissible under this rule only if:

(1) it is offered in a criminal case;

(2) the adjudication was of a witness other than the defendant;

(3) an adult's conviction for that offense would be admissible to attack the adult's credibility; and

(4) admitting the evidence is necessary to fairly determine guilt or innocence.

(e) Pendency of an Appeal. A conviction that satisfies this rule is admissible even if an appeal is pending. Evidence of the pendency is also admissible.

(Pub.L. 93–595, § 1, Jan. 2, 1975, 88 Stat.1935; Mar. 2, 1987, eff. Oct. 1, 1987; Jan. 26, 1990, eff. Dec. 1, 1990; Apr. 12, 2006, eff. Dec. 1, 2006; Apr. 26, 2011, eff. Dec. 1, 2011.)

ADVISORY COMMITTEE NOTES

1972 Proposed Rules

As a means of impeachment, evidence of conviction of crime is significant only because it stands as proof of the commission of the underlying criminal act. There is little dissent from the general proposition that at least some crimes are relevant to credibility but much disagreement among the cases and commentators about which crimes are usable for this purpose. See McCormick § 43; 2 Wright, Federal Practice and Procedure: Criminal § 416 (1969). The weight of traditional authority has been to allow use of felonies generally, without regard to the nature of the particular offense, and of *crimen falsi* without regard to the grade of the offense. This is the view accepted by Congress in the 1970 amendment of § 14–305 of the District of Columbia Code, P.L. 91–358, 84 Stat. 473. Uniform Rule 21 and Model Code Rule 106 permit only crimes involving "dishonesty or false statement." Others have thought that the trial judge should have discretion to exclude convictions if the probative value of the evidence of the crime is substantially outweighed by the danger of unfair prejudice. *Luck v. United States,* 121 U.S.App.D.C. 151, 348 F.2d 763 (1965); McGowan, Impeachment of Criminal Defendants by Prior Convictions, 1970 Law & Soc.Order 1. Whatever may be the merits of those views, this rule is drafted to accord with the Congressional policy manifested in the 1970 legislation.

The proposed rule incorporates certain basic safeguards, in terms applicable to all witnesses but of particular significance to an accused who elects to testify. These protections include the imposition of definite time limitations, giving effect to demonstrated rehabilitation, and generally excluding juvenile adjudications.

Note to Subdivision (a). For purposes of impeachment, crimes are divided into two categories by the rule: (1) those of what is generally regarded as felony grade, without particular regard to the nature of the offense, and (2) those involving dishonesty or false statement, without regard to the grade of the offense. Probable convictions are not limited to violations of federal law. By reason of our constitutional structure, the federal catalog of crimes is far from being a complete one, and resort must be had to the laws of the states for the specification of many crimes. For example, simple theft as compared with theft from interstate commerce. Other instances of borrowing are the Assimilative Crimes Act, making the state law of crimes applicable to the special territorial and maritime jurisdiction of the United States, 18 U.S.C. § 13, and the provision of the Judicial Code disqualifying persons as jurors on the grounds of state as well as federal convictions, 28 U.S.C. § 1865. For evaluation of the crime in terms of seriousness, reference is made to the congressional measurement of felony (subject to imprisonment in excess of one year) rather than adopting state definitions which vary considerably. See 28 U.S.C. § 1865, *supra,* disqualifying jurors for conviction in state or federal court of crime punishable by imprisonment for more than one year.

Note to Subdivision (b). Few statutes recognize a time limit on impeachment by evidence of conviction. However, practical considerations of fairness and relevancy demand that some boundary be recognized. See Ladd, Credibility Tests—Current Trends, 89 U.Pa.L.Rev. 166, 176–177 (1940). This portion of the rule is derived from the proposal advanced in Recommendation Proposing in Evidence Code, § 788(5), p. 142, Cal.Law Rev.Comm'n (1965), though not adopted. See California Evidence Code § 788.

Note to Subdivision (c). A pardon or its equivalent granted solely for the purpose of restoring civil rights lost by virtue of a conviction has no relevance to an inquiry into character. If, however, the pardon or other proceeding is hinged upon a showing of rehabilitation the situation is otherwise. The result under the rule is to render the conviction inadmissible. The alternative of allowing in evidence both the conviction and the rehabilitation has not been adopted for reasons of policy, economy of time, and difficulties of evaluation.

A similar provision is contained in California Evidence Code § 788. Cf. A.L.I. Model Penal Code, Proposed Official Draft § 306.6(3)(e) (1962), and discussion in A.L.I. Proceedings 310 (1961).

Pardons based on innocence have the effect, of course, of nullifying the conviction *ab initio.*

Note to Subdivision (d). The prevailing view has been that a juvenile adjudication is not usable for impeachment. *Thomas v. United States,* 74 App.D.C. 167, 121 F.2d 905 (1941); *Cotton v. United States,* 355 F.2d 480 (10th Cir.1966). This conclusion was based upon a variety of circumstances. By virtue of its informality, frequently diminished quantum of required proof, and other departures from accepted standards for criminal trials under the theory of *parens patriae,* the juvenile adjudication was considered to lack the precision and general probative value of the criminal conviction. While *In re Gault,* 387 U.S. 1, 87 S.Ct. 1428, 18 L.Ed.2d 527 (1967), no doubt eliminates these characteristics insofar as objectionable, other obstacles remain. Practical problems of administration are raised by the common provisions in juvenile legislation that records be kept confidential and that they be destroyed after a short time. While *Gault* was skeptical as to the realities of confidentiality of juvenile records, it also saw no constitutional obstacles to improvement. 387 U.S. at 25, 87 S.Ct. 1428. See also Note, Rights and Rehabilitation in the Juvenile Courts, 67 Colum.L.Rev. 281, 289 (1967). In addition, policy considerations much akin to those which dictate exclusion of adult convictions after rehabilitation has been established strongly suggest a rule of excluding juvenile adjudications. Admittedly, however, the rehabilitative process may in a given case be a demonstrated failure, or the strategic importance of a given witness may be so great as to require the overriding of general policy in the interests of particular justice. See *Giles v. Maryland,* 386 U.S. 66, 87 S.Ct. 793, 17 L.Ed.2d 737 (1967). Wigmore was outspoken in his condemnation of the disallowance of juvenile adjudications to impeach, especially when the witness is the complainant in a case of molesting a minor. 1 Wigmore § 196; 3 *Id.* §§ 924a, 980. The rule recognizes discretion in the judge to effect an accommodation among these various factors by departing from the general principle of exclusion. In deference to the general pattern and policy of juvenile statutes, however, no discretion is accorded when the witness is the accused in a criminal case.

Note to Subdivision (e). The presumption of correctness which ought to attend judicial proceedings supports the position that pendency of an appeal does not preclude use of a conviction for impeachment. *United States v. Empire Packing Co.,* 174 F.2d 16 (7th Cir.1949), cert. denied 337 U.S. 959, 69 S.Ct. 1534, 93 L.Ed. 1758; *Bloch v. United States,* 226 F.2d 185 (9th Cir.1955), cert. denied 350 U.S. 948, 76 S.Ct. 323, 100 L.Ed. 826 and 353 U.S. 959, 77 S.Ct. 868, 1 L.Ed.2d 910; and see *Newman v. United States,* 331 F.2d 968 (8th Cir.1964). *Contra, Campbell v. United States,* 85 U.S.App.D.C. 133, 176 F.2d 45 (1949). The pendency of an appeal is, however, a qualifying circumstance properly considerable.

1974 Enactment

Note to Subdivision (a). Rule 609(a) as submitted by the Court was modeled after Section 133(a) of Public Law 91–358, 14 D.C.Code 305(b)(1), enacted in 1970. The Rule provided that:

> For the purpose of attacking the credibility of a witness, evidence that he has been convicted of a crime is admissible but only if the crime (1) was punishable by death or imprisonment in excess of one year under the law under which he was convicted or (2) involved dishonesty or false statement regardless of the punishment.

As reported to the Committee by the Subcommittee, Rule 609(a) was amended to read as follows:

> For the purpose of attacking the credibility of a witness, evidence that he has been convicted of a crime is admissible only if the crime (1) was punishable by death or imprisonment in excess of one year, unless the court determines that the danger of unfair prejudice outweighs the probative value of the evidence of the conviction, or (2) involved dishonesty or false statement.

In full committee, the provision was amended to permit attack upon the credibility of a witness by prior conviction only if the prior crime involved dishonesty or false statement. While recognizing that the prevailing doctrine in the federal courts and in most States allows a witness to be impeached by evidence of prior felony convictions without restriction as to type, the Committee was of the view that, because of the danger of unfair prejudice in such practice and the deterrent effect upon an accused who might wish to testify, and even upon a witness who was not the accused, cross-examination by evidence of prior conviction should be limited to those kinds of convictions bearing directly on credibility, *i.e.,* crimes involving dishonesty or false statement.

Note to Subdivision (b). Rule 609(b) as submitted by the Court was modeled after Section 133(a) of Public Law 91–358, 14 D.C.Code 305(b)(2)(B), enacted in 1970. The Rule provided:

> Evidence of a conviction under this rule is not admissible if a period of more than ten years has elapsed since the date of the release of the witness from confinement imposed for his most recent conviction, or the expiration of the period of his parole, probation, or sentence granted or imposed with respect to his most recent conviction, whichever is the later date.

Under this formulation, a witness' entire past record of criminal convictions could be used for impeachment (provided the conviction met the standard of subdivision (a)), if the witness had been most recently released from confinement, or the period of his parole or probation had expired, within ten years of the conviction.

The Committee amended the Rule to read in the text of the 1971 Advisory Committee version to provide that upon the expiration of ten years from the date of a conviction of a witness, or of his release from confinement for that offense, that conviction may no longer be used for impeachment. The Committee was of the view that after ten years following a person's release from confinement (or from the date of his conviction) the probative value of the conviction with respect to that person's credibility diminished to a point where it should no longer be admissible.

Note to Subdivision (c). Rule 609(c) as submitted by the Court provided in part that evidence of a witness' prior conviction is not admissible to attack his credibility if the conviction was the subject of a pardon, annulment, or other equivalent procedure, based on a showing of rehabilitation, and the witness has not been convicted of a subsequent crime. The Committee amended the Rule to provide that the "subsequent crime" must have been "punishable by death or imprisonment in excess of one year", on the ground that a subsequent conviction of an offense not a felony is insufficient to rebut the finding that the witness has been rehabilitated. The Committee also intends that the words "based on a finding of the rehabilitation of the person convicted" apply not only to "certificate of rehabilitation, or other equivalent procedure", but also to "pardon" and "annulment.". House Report No. 93–650.

Note to Subdivision (a). As proposed by the Supreme Court, the rule would allow the use of prior convictions to impeach if the crime was a felony or a misdemeanor if the misdemeanor involved dishonesty or false statement. As modified by the House, the rule would admit prior convictions for impeachment purposes only if the offense, whether felony or misdemeanor, involved dishonesty or false statement.

The committee has adopted a modified version of the House-passed rule. In your committee's view, the danger of unfair prejudice is far greater when the accused, as opposed to other witnesses, testifies, because the jury may be prejudiced not merely on the question of credibility but also on the ultimate question of guilt or innocence. Therefore, with respect to defendants, the committee agreed with the House limitation that only offenses involved false statement or dishonesty may be used. By that phrase, the committee means crimes such as perjury or subornation of perjury, false statement, criminal fraud, embezzlement or false pretense, or any other offense, in the nature of *crimen falsi* the commission of which involves some element of untruthfulness, deceit or falsification bearing on the accused's propensity to testify truthfully.

With respect to other witnesses, in addition to any prior conviction involving false statement or dishonesty, any other felony may be used to impeach if, and only if, the court finds that the probative value of such evidence outweighs its prejudicial effect against the party offering that witness.

Notwithstanding this provision, proof of any prior offense otherwise admissible under Rule 404 could still be offered for the purposes sanctioned by that rule. Furthermore, the committee intends that notwithstanding this rule, a defendant's misrepresentation regarding the existence or nature of prior convictions may be met by rebuttal evidence, including the record of such prior convictions. Similarly, such records may be offered to rebut representations made by the defendant regarding his attitude toward or willingness to commit a general category of offense, although denials or other representations by the defendant regarding the specific conduct which forms the basis of the charge against him shall not make prior convictions admissible to rebut such statement.

In regard to either type of representation, of course, prior convictions may be offered in rebuttal only if the defendant's statement is made in response to defense counsel's questions or is made gratuitously in the course of cross-examination. Prior convictions may not be offered as rebuttal evidence if the prosecution has sought to circumvent the purpose of this rule by asking questions which elicit such representations from the defendant.

One other clarifying amendment has been added to this subsection, that is, to provide that the admissibility of evidence of a prior conviction is permitted only upon cross-examination of a witness. It is not admissible if a person does not testify. It is to be understood, however, that a court record of a prior conviction is admissible to prove that conviction if the witness has forgotten or denies its existence.

Note to Subdivision (b). Although convictions over ten years old generally do not have much probative value, there may be exceptional circumstances under which the conviction substantially bears on the credibility of the witness. Rather than exclude all convictions over 10 years old, the committee adopted an amendment in the form of a final clause to the section granting the court discretion to admit convictions over 10 years old, but only upon a determination by the court that the probative value of the conviction supported by specific facts and circumstances, substantially outweighs its prejudicial effect.

It is intended that convictions over 10 years old will be admitted very rarely and only in exceptional circumstances. The rules provide that the decision be supported by specific facts and circumstances thus requiring the court to make specific findings on the record as to the particular facts and circumstances it has considered in determining that the probative value of the conviction substantially outweighs its prejudicial impact. It is expected that, in fairness, the court will give the party against whom the conviction is introduced a full and adequate opportunity to contest its admission. Senate Report No. 93–1277.

Rule 609 defines when a party may use evidence of a prior conviction in order to impeach a witness. The Senate amendments make changes in two subsections of Rule 609.

Note to Subdivision (a). The House bill provides that the credibility of a witness can be attacked by proof of prior conviction of a crime only if the crime involves dishonesty or false statement. The Senate amendment provides that a witness' credibility may be attacked if the crime (1) was punishable by death or imprisonment in excess of one year under the law under which he was convicted or (2) involves dishonesty or false statement, regardless of the punishment.

The Conference adopts the Senate amendment with an amendment. The Conference amendment provides that the credibility of a witness, whether a defendant or someone else, may be attacked by proof of a prior conviction but only if the crime: (1) was punishable by death or imprisonment in excess of one year under the law under which he was convicted and the court determines that the probative value of the conviction outweighs its prejudicial effect to the defendant; or (2) involved dishonesty or false statement regardless of the punishment.

By the phrase "dishonesty and false statement" the Conference means crimes such as perjury or subornation of perjury, false statement, criminal fraud, embezzlement, or false pretense, or any other offense in the nature of *crimen falsi,* the commission of which involves some element of deceit, untruthfulness, or falsification bearing on the accused's propensity to testify truthfully.

The admission of prior convictions involving dishonesty and false statement is not within the discretion of the Court. Such convictions are peculiarly probative of credibility and, under this rule, are always to be admitted. Thus, judicial discretion granted with respect to the admissibility of other prior convictions is not applicable to those involving dishonesty or false statement.

With regard to the discretionary standard established by paragraph (1) of Rule 609(a), the Conference determined that the prejudicial effect to be weighed against the probative value of the conviction is specifically the prejudicial effect *to the defendant.* The danger of prejudice to a witness other than the defendant (such as injury to the witness' reputation in his community) was considered and rejected by the Conference as an element to be weighed in determining admissibility. It was the judgment of the Conference that the danger of prejudice to a nondefendant witness is outweighed by the need for the trier of fact to have as much relevant evidence on the issue of credibility as possible. Such evidence should only be excluded where it presents a danger of improperly influencing the outcome of the trial by persuading the trier of fact to convict the defendant on the basis of his prior criminal record.

Note to Subdivision (b). The House bill provides in subsection (b) that evidence of conviction of a crime may not be used for impeachment purposes under subsection (a) if more than ten years have elapsed since the date of the conviction or the date the witness was released from confinement imposed for the conviction, whichever is later. The Senate amendment permits the use of convictions older than ten years, if the court determines, in the interests of justice, that the probative value of the conviction, supported by specific facts and circumstances, substantially outweighs its prejudicial effect.

The Conference adopts the Senate amendment with an amendment requiring notice by a party that he intends to request that the court allow him to use a conviction older than ten years. The Conferees anticipate that a written notice, in order to give the adversary a fair opportunity to contest the use of the evidence, will ordinarily include such information as the date of the conviction, the jurisdiction, and the offense or statute involved. In order to eliminate the possibility that the flexibility of this provision may impair the ability of a party-opponent to prepare for trial, the Conferees intend that the notice provision operate to avoid surprise. House Report No. 93–1597.

1987 Amendments

The amendments are technical. No substantive change is intended.

1990 Amendments

The amendment to Rule 609(a) makes two changes in the rule. The first change removes from the rule the limitation that the conviction may only be elicited during cross-examination, a limitation that virtually every circuit has found to be inapplicable. It is common for witnesses to reveal on direct examination their convictions to "remove the sting" of the impeachment. *See e.g., United States v. Bad Cob,* 560 F.2d 877 (8th Cir.1977). The amendment does not contemplate that a court will necessarily permit proof of prior convictions through testimony, which might be time-consuming and more prejudicial than proof through a written record. Rules 403 and 611(a) provide sufficient authority for the court to protect against unfair or disruptive methods of proof.

The second change effected by the amendment resolves an ambiguity as to the relationship of Rules 609 and 403 with respect to impeachment of witnesses other than the criminal defendant. *See, Green v. Bock Laundry Machine Co.,* 109 S.Ct. 1981, 490 U.S. 504 (1989). The amendment does not disturb the special balancing test for the criminal defendant who chooses to testify. Thus, the rule recognizes that, in virtually every case in which prior convictions are used to impeach the testifying defendant, the defendant faces a unique risk of prejudice—*i.e.,* the danger that convictions that would be excluded under Fed.R.Evid. 404 will be misused by a jury as propensity evidence despite their introduction solely for impeachment purposes. Although the rule does not forbid all use of convictions to impeach a defendant, it requires that the government show that the probative value of convictions as impeachment evidence outweighs their prejudicial effect.

Prior to the amendment, the rule appeared to give the defendant the benefit of the special balancing test when defense witnesses other than the defendant were called to testify. In practice, however, the concern about unfairness to the defendant is most acute when the defendant's own convictions are offered as evidence. Almost all of the decided cases concern this type of impeachment, and the amendment does not deprive the defendant of any meaningful protection, since Rule 403 now clearly protects against unfair impeachment of any defense witness other than the defendant. There are cases in which a defendant might be prejudiced when a defense witness is impeached. Such cases may arise, for example, when the witness bears a special relationship to the defendant such that the defendant is likely to suffer some spill-over effect from impeachment of the witness.

The amendment also protects other litigants from unfair impeachment of their witnesses. The danger of prejudice from the use of prior convictions is not confined to criminal defendants. Although the danger that prior convictions will be misused as character evidence is particularly acute when the defendant is impeached, the danger exists in other situations as well. The amendment reflects the view that it is desirable to protect all litigants from the unfair use of prior convictions, and that the ordinary balancing test of Rule 403, which provides that evidence shall not be excluded unless its prejudicial effect substantially outweighs its probative value, is appropriate for assessing the admissibility of prior convictions for impeachment of any witness other than a criminal defendant.

The amendment reflects a judgment that decisions interpreting Rule 609(a) as requiring a trial court to admit convictions in civil cases that have little, if anything, to do with credibility reach undesirable results. *See, e.g., Diggs v. Lyons,* 741 F.2d 577 (3d Cir.1984), *cert. denied,* 105 S.Ct. 2157 (1985). The amendment provides the same protection against unfair prejudice arising from prior convictions used for impeachment purposes as the rules provide for other evidence. The amendment finds support in decided cases. *See, e.g., Petty v. Ideco,* 761 F.2d 1146 (5th Cir.1985); *Czaka v. Hickman,* 703 F.2d 317 (8th Cir.1983).

Fewer decided cases address the question whether Rule 609(a) provides any protection against unduly prejudicial prior convictions used to impeach government witnesses. Some courts have read Rule 609(a) as giving the government no protection for its witnesses. *See, e.g., United States v. Thorne,* 547 F.2d 56 (8th Cir.1976); *United States v. Nevitt,* 563 F.2d 406 (9th Cir.1977), *cert. denied,* 444 U.S. 847 (1979). This approach also is rejected by the amendment. There are cases in which impeachment of government witnesses with prior convictions that have little, if anything, to do with credibility may result in unfair prejudice to the government's interest in a fair trial and unnecessary embarrassment to a witness. Fed.R.Evid. 412 already recognizes this and excluded certain evidence of past sexual behavior in the context of prosecutions for sexual assaults.

The amendment applies the general balancing test of Rule 403 to protect all litigants against unfair impeachment of witnesses. The balancing test protects civil litigants, the government in criminal cases, and the defendant in a criminal case who calls other witnesses. The amendment addresses prior convictions offered under Rule 609, not for other purposes, and does not run afoul, therefore, of *Davis v. Alaska,* 415 U.S. 308 (1974). *Davis* involved the use of a prior juvenile adjudication not to prove a past law violation, but to prove bias. The defendant in a criminal case has the right to demonstrate the bias of a witness and to be assured a fair trial, but not to unduly prejudice a trier of fact. *See generally* Rule 412. In any case in which the trial court believes that confrontation rights require admission of impeachment evidence, obviously the Constitution would take precedence over the rule.

The probability that prior convictions of an ordinary government witness will be unduly prejudicial is low in most criminal cases. Since the behavior of the witness is not the issue in dispute in most cases, there is little chance that the trier of fact will misuse the convictions offered as impeachment evidence as propensity evidence. Thus, trial courts will be skeptical when the government objects to impeachment of its witnesses with prior convictions. Only when the government is able to point to a real danger of prejudice that is sufficient to outweigh substantially the probative value of the conviction for impeachment purposes will the conviction be excluded.

The amendment continues to divide subdivision (a) into subsections (1) and (2) thus facilitating retrieval under current computerized research programs which distinguish the two provisions. The Committee recommended no substantive change in subdivision (a)(2), even though some cases raise a concern about the proper interpretation of the words "dishonesty or false statement." These words were used but not explained in the original Advisory Committee Note accompanying Rule 609. Congress extensively debated the rule, and the Report of the House and Senate Conference Committee states that "[b]y the phrase 'dishonesty and false statement,' the Conference means crimes such as perjury, subornation of perjury, false statement, criminal fraud, embezzlement, or false pretense, or any other offense in the nature of *crimen falsi,* commission of which involves some element of deceit, untruthfulness, or falsification bearing on the accused's propensity to testify truthfully." The Advisory Committee concluded that the Conference Report provides sufficient guidance to trial courts and that no amendment is necessary, notwithstanding some decisions that take an unduly broad view of "dishonesty," admitting convictions such as for bank robbery or bank larceny. Subsection (a)(2) continues to apply to any witness, including a criminal defendant.

Finally, the Committee determined that it was unnecessary to add to the rule language stating that, when a prior conviction is offered under Rule 609, the trial court is to consider the probative value of the prior conviction *for impeachment,* not for other purposes. The Committee concluded that the title of the rule, its first sentence, and its placement among the impeachment rules clearly establish that evidence offered under Rule 609 is offered only for purposes of impeachment.

2006 Amendments

The amendment provides that Rule 609(a)(2) mandates the admission of evidence of a conviction only when the conviction required the proof of (or in the case of a guilty plea, the admission of) an act of dishonesty or false statement. Evidence of all other convictions is inadmissible under this subsection, irrespective of whether the witness exhibited dishonesty or made a false statement in the process of the commission of the crime of conviction. Thus, evidence that a witness was convicted for a crime of violence, such as murder, is not admissible under Rule 609(a)(2), even if the witness acted deceitfully in the course of committing the crime.

The amendment is meant to give effect to the legislative intent to limit the convictions that are to be automatically admitted under subdivision (a)(2). The Conference Committee provided that by "dishonesty and false statement" it meant "crimes such as perjury, subornation of perjury, false statement, criminal fraud, embezzlement, or false pretense, or any other offense in the nature of *crimen falsi*, the commission of which involves some element of deceit, untruthfulness, or falsification bearing on the [witness's] propensity to testify truthfully." Historically, offenses classified as *crimina falsi* have included only those crimes in which the ultimate criminal act was itself an act of deceit. *See* Green, *Deceit and the Classification of Crimes: Federal Rule of Evidence 609(a)(2) and the Origins of* Crimen Falsi, 90 J. Crim. L. & Criminology 1087 (2000).

Evidence of crimes in the nature of *crimina falsi* must be admitted under Rule 609(a)(2), regardless of how such crimes are specifically charged. For example, evidence that a witness was convicted of making a false claim to a federal agent is admissible under this subdivision regardless of whether the crime was charged under a section that expressly references deceit (e.g., 18 U.S.C. § 1001, Material Misrepresentation to the Federal Government) or a section that does not (*e.g.*, 18 U.S.C. § 1503, Obstruction of Justice).

The amendment requires that the proponent have ready proof that the conviction required the factfinder to find, or the defendant to admit, an act of dishonesty or false statement. Ordinarily, the statutory elements of the crime will indicate whether it is one of dishonesty or false statement. Where the deceitful nature of the crime is not apparent from the statute and the face of the judgment — as, for example, where the conviction simply records a finding of guilt for a statutory offense that does not reference deceit expressly — a proponent may offer information such as an indictment, a statement of admitted facts, or jury instructions to show that the factfinder had to find, or the defendant had to admit, an act of dishonesty or false statement in order for the witness to have been convicted. *Cf. Taylor v. United States*, 495 U.S. 575, 602 (1990) (providing that a trial court may look to a charging instrument or jury instructions to ascertain the nature of a prior offense where the statute is insufficiently clear on its face); *Shepard v. United States,* 125 S.Ct. 1254 (2005) (the inquiry to determine whether a guilty plea to a crime defined by a nongeneric statute necessarily admitted elements of the generic offense was limited to the charging document's terms, the terms of a plea agreement or transcript of colloquy between judge and defendant in which the factual basis for the plea was confirmed by the defendant, or a comparable judicial record). But the amendment does not contemplate a "mini-trial" in which the court plumbs the record of the previous proceeding to determine whether the crime was in the nature of *crimen falsi*.

The amendment also substitutes the term "character for truthfulness" for the term "credibility" in the first sentence of the Rule. The limitations of Rule 609 are not applicable if a conviction is admitted for a purpose other than to prove the witness's character for untruthfulness. *See, e.g., United States v. Lopez*, 979 F.2d 1024 (5th Cir. 1992) (Rule 609 was not applicable where the conviction was offered for purposes of contradiction). The use of the term "credibility" in subdivision (d) is retained, however, as that subdivision is intended to govern the use of a juvenile adjudication for any type of impeachment.

2011 Amendments

The language of Rule 609 has been amended as part of the restyling of the Evidence Rules to make them more easily understood and to make style and terminology consistent throughout the rules. These changes are intended to be stylistic only. There is no intent to change any result in any ruling on evidence admissibility.

Rule 610. Religious Beliefs or Opinions

Evidence of a witness's religious beliefs or opinions is not admissible to attack or support the witness's credibility.

(Pub.L. 93–595, § 1, Jan. 2, 1975, 88 Stat.1936; Mar. 2, 1987, eff. Oct. 1, 1987; Apr. 26, 2011, eff. Dec. 1, 2011.)

ADVISORY COMMITTEE NOTES

1972 Proposed Rules

While the rule forecloses inquiry into the religious beliefs or opinions of a witness for the purpose of showing that his character for truthfulness is affected by their nature, an inquiry for the purpose of showing interest or bias because of them is not within the prohibition. Thus disclosure of affiliation with a church which is a party to the litigation would be allowable under the rule. Cf. Tucker v. Reil, 51 Ariz. 357, 77 P.2d 203 (1938). To the same effect, though less specifically worded, is California Evidence Code § 789. See 3 Wigmore § 936.

1987 Amendments

The amendment is technical. No substantive change is intended.

2011 Amendments

The language of Rule 610 has been amended as part of the restyling of the Evidence Rules to make them more easily understood and to make style and terminology consistent throughout the rules. These changes are intended to be stylistic only. There is no intent to change any result in any ruling on evidence admissibility.

Rule 611. Mode and Order of Examining Witnesses and Presenting Evidence

(a) Control by the Court; Purposes. The court should exercise reasonable control over the mode and order of examining witnesses and presenting evidence so as to:

(1) make those procedures effective for determining the truth;

(2) avoid wasting time; and

(3) protect witnesses from harassment or undue embarrassment.

(b) Scope of Cross–Examination. Cross-examination should not go beyond the subject matter of the direct examination and matters affecting the witness's credibility. The court may allow inquiry into additional matters as if on direct examination.

(c) Leading Questions. Leading questions should not be used on direct examination except as necessary to develop the witness's testimony. Ordinarily, the court should allow leading questions:

(1) on cross-examination; and

(2) when a party calls a hostile witness, an adverse party, or a witness identified with an adverse party.

(Pub.L. 93–595, § 1, Jan. 2, 1975, 88 Stat. 1936; Mar. 2, 1987, eff. Oct. 1, 1987; Apr. 26, 2011, eff. Dec. 1, 2011.)

ADVISORY COMMITTEE NOTES

1972 Proposed Rules

Note to Subdivision (a). Spelling out detailed rules to govern the mode and order of interrogating witnesses and presenting evidence is neither desirable nor feasible. The ultimate responsibility for the effective working of the adversary system rests with the judge. The rule sets forth the objectives which he should seek to attain.

Item (1) restates in broad terms the power and obligation of the judge as developed under common law principles. It covers such concerns as whether testimony shall be in the form of a free narrative or responses to specific questions, McCormick § 5, the order of calling witnesses and presenting evidence, 6 Wigmore § 1867, the use of demonstrative evidence, McCormick § 179, and the many other questions arising during the course of a trial which can be solved only by the judge's common sense and fairness in view of the particular circumstances.

Item (2) is addressed to avoidance of needless consumption of time, a matter of daily concern in the disposition of cases. A companion piece is found in the discretion vested in the judge to exclude evidence as a waste of time in Rule 403(b).

Item (3) calls for a judgment under the particular circumstances whether interrogation tactics entail harassment or undue embarrassment. Pertinent circumstances include the importance of the testimony, the nature of the inquiry, its relevance to credibility, waste of time, and confusion. McCormick § 42. In *Alford v. United States,* 282 U.S. 687, 694, 51 S.Ct. 218, 75 L.Ed. 624 (1931), the Court pointed out that, while the trial judge should protect the witness from questions which "go beyond the bounds of proper cross-examination merely to harass, annoy or humiliate," this protection by no means forecloses efforts to discredit the witness. Reference to the transcript of the prosecutor's cross-examination in *Berger v. United States,* 295 U.S. 78, 55 S.Ct. 629, 79 L.Ed. 1314 (1935), serves to lay at rest any doubts as to the need for judicial control in this area.

The inquiry into specific instances of conduct of a witness allowed under Rule 608(b) is, of course, subject to this rule.

Note to Subdivision (b). The tradition in the federal courts and in numerous state courts has been to limit the scope of cross-examination to matters testified to on direct, plus matters bearing upon the credibility of the witness. Various reasons have been advanced to justify the rule of limited cross-examination. (1) A party vouches for his own witness but only to the extent of matters elicited on direct. *Resurrection Gold Mining Co. v. Fortune Gold Mining Co.,* 129 F. 668, 675 (8th Cir.1904), quoted in Maguire, Weinstein, et al., Cases on Evidence 277, n. 38 (5th ed. 1965). But the concept of vouching is discredited, and Rule 607 rejects it. (2) A party cannot ask his own witness leading questions. This is a problem properly solved in terms of what is necessary for a proper development of the testimony rather than by a mechanistic formula similar to the vouching concept. See discussion under subdivision (c). (3) A practice of limited cross-examination promotes orderly presentation of the case. *Finch v. Weiner,* 109 Conn. 616, 145 A. 31 (1929). While this latter reason has merit, the matter is essentially one of the order of presentation and not one in which involvement at the appellate level is likely to prove fruitful. See, for example, *Moyer v. Aetna Life Ins. Co.,* 126 F.2d 141 (3rd Cir.1942); *Butler v. New York Central R. Co.,* 253 F.2d 281 (7th Cir.1958); *United States v. Johnson,* 285 F.2d 35 (9th Cir.1960); *Union Automobile Indemnity Ass'n v. Capitol Indemnity Ins. Co.,* 310 F.2d 318 (7th Cir.1962). In evaluating these considerations, McCormick says:

"The foregoing considerations favoring the wide-open or restrictive rules may well be thought to be fairly evenly balanced. There is another factor, however, which seems to swing the balance overwhelmingly in favor of the wide-open rule. This is the consideration of economy of time and energy. Obviously, the wide-open rule presents little or no opportunity for dispute in its application. The restrictive practice in all its forms, on the other hand, is productive in many court rooms, of continual bickering over the choice of the numerous variations of the 'scope of the direct' criterion, and of their application to particular cross-questions. These controversies are often reventilated on appeal, and reversals for error in their determination are frequent. Observance of these vague and ambiguous restrictions is a matter of constant and hampering concern to the cross-examiner. If these efforts, delays and misprisions were the necessary incidents to the guarding of substantive rights or the fundamentals of fair trial, they might be worth the cost. As the price of the choice of an obviously debatable regulation of the order of evidence, the sacrifice seems misguided. The American Bar Association's Committee for the Improvement of the Law of Evidence for the year 1937–38 said this:

'The rule limiting cross-examination to the precise subject of the direct examination is probably the most frequent rule (except the Opinion rule) leading in the trial practice today to refined and technical quibbles which obstruct the progress of the trial, confuse the jury, and give rise to appeal on technical grounds only. Some of the instances in which Supreme Courts have ordered new trials for the mere transgression of this rule about the order of evidence have been astounding.

'We recommend that the rule allowing questions upon any part of the issue known to the witness * * * be adopted. * * * ' " McCormick, § 27, p. 51. See also 5 Moore's Federal Practice ¶ 43.10 (2nd ed. 1964).

The provision of the second sentence, that the judge may in the interests of justice limit inquiry into new matters on cross-examination, is designed for those situations in which the result otherwise would be confusion, complication, or protraction of the case, not as a matter of rule but as demonstrable in the actual development of the particular case.

The rule does not purport to determine the extent to which an accused who elects to testify thereby waives his privilege against self-incrimination. The question is a constitutional one, rather than a mere matter of administering the trial. Under *Simmons v. United States,* 390 U.S. 377, 88 S.Ct. 967, 19 L.Ed.2d 1247 (1968), no general waiver occurs when the accused testifies on such preliminary matters as the validity of a search and seizure or the admissibility of a confession. Rule 104(d), *supra.* When he testifies on the merits, however, can he foreclose inquiry into an aspect or element of the crime by avoiding it on direct? The affirmative answer given in *Tucker v. United States,* 5 F.2d 818 (8th Cir.1925), is inconsistent with the description of the waiver as extending to "all other relevant facts" in *Johnson v. United States,* 318 U.S. 189, 195, 63 S.Ct. 549, 87 L.Ed. 704 (1943). See also *Brown v. United States,* 356 U.S. 148, 78 S.Ct. 622, 2 L.Ed.2d 589 (1958). The situation of an accused who desires to testify on some but not all counts of a multiple-count indictment is one to be approached, in the first instance at least, as a problem of severance under Rule 14 of the Federal Rules of Criminal Procedure. *Cross v. United States,* 118 U.S.App.D.C. 324, 335 F.2d 987 (1964). Cf. *United States v. Baker,* 262 F.Supp. 657, 686 (D.D.C.1966). In all events, the extent of the waiver of the privilege against self-incrimination ought not to be determined as a by-product of a rule on scope of cross-examination.

Note to Subdivision (c). The rule continues the traditional view that the suggestive powers of the leading question are as a general proposition undesirable. Within this tradition, however, numerous exceptions have achieved recognition: The witness who is hostile, unwilling, or biased; the child witness or the adult with communication problems; the witness whose recollection is exhausted; and undisputed preliminary matters. 3 Wigmore §§ 774–778. An almost total unwillingness to reverse for infractions has been manifested by appellate courts. See cases cited in 3 Wigmore § 770. The matter clearly falls within the area of control by the judge over the mode and order of interrogation and presentation and accordingly is phrased in words of suggestion rather than command.

The rule also conforms to tradition in making the use of leading questions on cross-examination a matter of right. The purpose of the qualification "ordinarily" is to furnish a basis for denying the use of leading questions when the cross-examination is cross-examination in form only and not in fact, as for example the "cross-examination" of a party by his own counsel after being called by the opponent (savoring more of re-direct) or of an insured defendant who proves to be friendly to the plaintiff.

The final sentence deals with categories of witnesses automatically regarded and treated as hostile. Rule 43(b) of the Federal Rules of Civil Procedure has included only "an adverse party or an officer, director, or managing agent of a public or private corporation or of a partnership or association which is an adverse party." This limitation virtually to persons whose statements would stand as admissions is believed to be an unduly narrow concept of those who may safely be regarded as hostile without further demonstration. See, for example, *Maryland Casualty Co. v. Kador,* 225 F.2d 120 (5th Cir.1955), and *Degelos v. Fidelity and Casualty Co.,* 313 F.2d 809 (5th Cir.1963), holding despite the language of Rule 43(b) that an insured fell within it, though not a party in an action under the Louisiana direct action statute. The phrase of the rule, "witness identified with" an adverse party, is designed to enlarge the category of persons thus callable.

1974 Enactment

Note to Subdivision (b). As submitted by the Court, Rule 611(b) provided:

> A witness may be cross-examined on any matter relevant to any issue in the case, including credibility. In the interests of justice, the judge may limit cross-examination with respect to matters not testified to on direct examination.

The Committee amended this provision to return to the rule which prevails in the federal courts and thirty-nine State jurisdictions. As amended, the Rule is in the text of the 1969 Advisory Committee draft. It limits cross-examination to credibility and to matters testified to on direct examination, unless the judge permits more, in which event the cross-examiner must proceed as if on direct examination. This traditional rule facilitates orderly presentation by each party at trial. Further, in light of existing discovery procedures, there appears to be no need to abandon the traditional rule.

Note to Subdivision (c). The third sentence of Rule 611(c) as submitted by the Court provided that:

> In civil cases, a party is entitled to call an adverse party or witness identified with him and interrogate by leading questions.

The Committee amended this Rule to permit leading questions to be used with respect to any hostile witness, not only an adverse party or person identified with such adverse party. The Committee also substituted the word "When" for the phrase "In civil cases" to reflect the possibility that in criminal cases a defendant may be entitled to call witnesses identified with the government, in which event the Committee believed the defendant should be permitted to inquire with leading questions. House Report No. 93–650.

Note to Subdivision (b). Rule 611(b) as submitted by the Supreme Court permitted a broad scope of cross-examination: "cross-examination on any matter relevant to any issue in the case" unless the judge, in the interests of justice, limited the scope of cross-examination.

The House narrowed the Rule to the more traditional practice of limiting cross-examination to the subject matter of direct examination (and credibility), but with discretion in the judge to permit inquiry into additional matters in situations where that would aid in the development of the evidence or otherwise facilitate the conduct of the trial.

The committee agrees with the House amendment. Although there are good arguments in support of broad cross-examination from perspectives of developing all relevant evidence, we believe the factors of insuring an orderly and predictable development of the evidence weigh in favor of the narrower rule, especially when discretion is given to the trial judge to permit inquiry into additional matters. The committee expressly approves this discretion and believes it will permit sufficient flexibility allowing a broader scope of cross-examination whenever appropriate.

The House amendment providing broader discretionary cross-examination permitted inquiry into additional matters only as if on direct examination. As a general rule, we concur with this limitation, however, we would understand that this limitation would not preclude the utilization of leading questions if the conditions of subsection (c) of this rule were met, bearing in mind the judge's discretion in any case to limit the scope of cross-examination [see McCormick on Evidence, §§ 24–26 (especially 24) (2d ed. 1972)].

Further, the committee has received correspondence from Federal judges commenting on the applicability of this rule to section 1407 of title 28. It is the committee's judgment that this rule as reported by the House is flexible enough to provide sufficiently broad cross-examination in appropriate situations in multidistrict litigation.

Note to Subdivision (c). As submitted by the Supreme Court, the rule provided: "In civil cases, a party is entitled to call an adverse party or witness identified with him and interrogate by leading questions."

The final sentence of subsection (c) was amended by the House for the purpose of clarifying the fact that a "hostile witness"—that is a witness who is hostile in fact—could be subject to interrogation by leading questions. The rule as submitted by the Supreme Court declared certain witnesses hostile as a matter of law and thus subject to interrogation by leading questions without any showing of hostility in fact. These were adverse parties or witnesses identified with adverse parties. However, the wording of the first sentence of subsection (c) while generally prohibiting the use of leading questions on direct examination, also provides "except as may be necessary to develop his testimony." Further, the first paragraph of the Advisory Committee note explaining the subsection makes clear that they intended that leading questions could be asked of a hostile witness or a witness who was unwilling or biased and even though that witness was not associated with an adverse party. Thus, we question whether the House amendment was necessary.

However, concluding that it was not intended to affect the meaning of the first sentence of the subsection and was intended solely to clarify the fact that leading questions are permissible in the interrogation of a witness, who is hostile in fact, the committee accepts that House amendment.

The final sentence of this subsection was also amended by the House to cover criminal as well as civil cases. The committee accepts this amendment, but notes that it may be difficult in criminal cases to determine when a witness is "identified with an adverse party," and thus the rule should be applied with caution. Senate Report No. 93–1277.

1987 Amendments

The amendment is technical. No substantive change is intended.

2011 Amendments

The language of Rule 611 has been amended as part of the restyling of the Evidence Rules to make them more easily understood and to make style and terminology consistent throughout the rules. These changes are intended to be stylistic only. There is no intent to change any result in any ruling on evidence admissibility.

Rule 612. Writing Used to Refresh a Witness's Memory

(a) Scope. This rule gives an adverse party certain options when a witness uses a writing to refresh memory:

(1) while testifying; or

(2) before testifying, if the court decides that justice requires the party to have those options.

(b) Adverse Party's Options; Deleting Unrelated Matter. Unless 18 U.S.C. § 3500 provides otherwise in a criminal case, an adverse party is entitled to have the writing produced at the hearing, to inspect it, to cross-examine the witness about it, and to introduce in evidence any portion that relates to the witness's testimony. If the producing party claims that the writing includes unrelated matter, the court must examine the writing in camera, delete any unrelated portion, and order that the rest be delivered to the adverse party. Any portion deleted over objection must be preserved for the record.

(c) Failure to Produce or Deliver the Writing. If a writing is not produced or is not delivered as ordered, the court may issue any appropriate order. But if the prosecution does not comply in a criminal case, the court must strike the witness's testimony or—if justice so requires—declare a mistrial.

(Pub.L. 93–595, § 1, Jan. 2, 1975, 88 Stat. 1936; Mar. 2, 1987, eff. Oct. 1, 1987; Apr. 26, 2011, eff. Dec. 1, 2011.)

ADVISORY COMMITTEE NOTES

1972 Proposed Rules

The treatment of writings used to refresh recollection while on the stand is in accord with settled doctrine. McCormick § 9, p. 15. The bulk of the case law has, however, denied the existence of any right to access by the opponent when the writing is used prior to taking the stand, though the judge may have discretion in the matter. *Goldman v. United States,* 316 U.S. 129, 62 S.Ct. 993, 86 L.Ed. 1322 (1942); *Needelman v. United States,* 261 F.2d 802 (5th Cir.1958), cert. dismissed 362 U.S. 600, 80 S.Ct. 960, 4 L.Ed.2d 980, rehearing denied 363 U.S. 858, 80 S.Ct. 1606, 4 L.Ed.2d 1739, Annot., 82 A.L.R.2d 473, 562 and 7 A.L.R.3d 181, 247. An increasing group of cases has repudiated the distinction. *People v. Scott,* 29 Ill.2d 97, 193 N.E.2d 814 (1963); *State v. Mucci,* 25 N.J. 423, 136 A.2d 761 (1957); *State v. Hunt,* 25 N.J. 514, 138 A.2d 1 (1958); *State v. Deslovers,* 40 R.I. 89, 100 A. 64 (1917), and this position is believed to be correct. As Wigmore put it, "the risk of imposition and the need of safeguard is just as great" in both situations. 3 Wigmore § 762, p. 111. To the same effect is McCormick, § 9, p. 17.

The purpose of the phrase "for the purpose of testifying" is to safeguard against using the rule as a pretext for wholesale exploration of an opposing party's files and to insure that access is limited only to those writings which may fairly be said in fact to have an impact upon the testimony of the witness.

The purpose of the rule is the same as that of the *Jencks* statute, 18 U.S.C. § 3500: to promote the search of credibility and memory. The same sensitivity to disclosure of government files may be involved; hence the rule is expressly made subject to the statute, subdivision (a) of which provides: "In any criminal prosecution brought by the United States, no statement or report in the possession of the United States which was made by a Government witness or prospective Government witness (other than the defendant) shall be the subject of subpena, discovery, or inspection until said witness has testified on direct examination in the trial of the case." Items falling within the purview of the statute are producible only as provided by its terms, *Palermo v. United States,* 360 U.S. 343, 351 (1959), and disclosure under the rule is limited similarly by the statutory conditions. With this limitation in mind, some differences of application may be noted. The *Jencks* statute applies only to statements of witnesses; the rule is not so limited. The statute applies only to criminal cases; the rule applies to all cases. The statute applies only to government witnesses; the rule applies to all witnesses. The statute contains no requirement that the statement be consulted for purposes of refreshment before or while testifying; the rule so requires. Since many writings would qualify under either statute or rule, a substantial overlap exists, but the identity of procedures makes this of no importance.

The consequences of nonproduction by the government in a criminal case are those of the *Jencks* statute, striking the testimony or in exceptional cases a mistrial. 18 U.S.C. § 3500(d). In other cases these alternatives are unduly limited, and such possibilities as contempt, dismissal, finding issues against the offender, and the like are available. See Rule 16(g) of the Federal Rules of Criminal Procedure and Rule 37(b) of the Federal Rules of Civil Procedure for appropriate sanctions.

1974 Enactment

As submitted to Congress, Rule 612 provided that except as set forth in 18 U.S.C. 3500, if a witness uses a writing to refresh his memory for the purpose of testifying, "either before or while testifying," an adverse party is entitled to have the writing produced at the hearing, to inspect it, to cross-examine the witness on it, and to introduce in evidence those portions relating to the witness' testimony. The Committee amended the Rule so as still to require the production of writings used by a witness while testifying, but to render the production of writings used by a witness to refresh his memory before testifying discretionary with the court in the interests of justice, as is the case under existing federal law. See Goldman v. United States, 316 U.S. 129 (1942). The Committee considered that permitting an adverse party to require the production of writings used before testifying could result in fishing expeditions among a multitude of papers which a witness may have used in preparing for trial.

The Committee intends that nothing in the Rule be construed as barring the assertion of a privilege with respect to writings used by a witness to refresh his memory. House Report No. 93–650.

1987 Amendments

The amendment is technical. No substantive change is intended.

2011 Amendments

The language of Rule 612 has been amended as part of the restyling of the Evidence Rules to make them more easily understood and to make style and terminology consistent throughout the rules. These changes are intended to be stylistic only. There is no intent to change any result in any ruling on evidence admissibility.

Rule 613. Witness's Prior Statement

(a) Showing or Disclosing the Statement During Examination. When examining a witness about the witness's prior statement, a party need not show it or disclose its contents to the witness. But the party must, on request, show it or disclose its contents to an adverse party's attorney.

(b) Extrinsic Evidence of a Prior Inconsistent Statement. Extrinsic evidence of a witness's prior inconsistent statement is admissible only if the witness is given an opportunity to explain or deny the statement and an adverse party is given an opportunity to examine the witness about it, or if justice so requires. This subdivision (b) does not apply to an opposing party's statement under Rule 801(d)(2).

(Pub.L. 93–595, § 1, Jan. 2, 1975, 88 Stat.1936; Mar. 2, 1987, eff. Oct. 1, 1987; Apr. 25, 1988, eff. Nov. 1, 1988; Apr. 26, 2011, eff. Dec. 1, 2011.)

ADVISORY COMMITTEE NOTES

1972 Proposed Rules

Note to Subdivision (a). The Queen's Case, 2 Br. & B. 284, 129 Eng.Rep. 976 (1820), laid down the requirement that a cross-examiner, prior to questioning the witness about his own prior statement in writing, must first show it to the witness. Abolished by statute in the country of its origin, the requirement nevertheless gained currency in the United States. The rule abolishes this useless impediment, to cross-examination. Ladd, Some Observations on Credibility: Impeachment of Witnesses, 52 Cornell L.Q. 239, 246–247 (1967); McCormick § 28; 4 Wigmore §§ 1259–1260. Both oral and written statements are included.

The provision for disclosure to counsel is designed to protect against unwarranted insinuations that a statement has been made when the fact is to the contrary.

The rule does not defeat the application of Rule 1002 relating to production of the original when the contents of a writing are sought to be proved. Nor does it defeat the application of Rule 26(b)(3) of the Rules of Civil Procedure, as revised, entitling a person on request to a copy of his own statement, though the operation of the latter may be suspended temporarily.

Note to Subdivision (b). The familiar foundation requirement that an impeaching statement first be shown to the witness before it can be proved by extrinsic evidence is preserved but with some modifications. See Ladd, Some Observations on Credibility: Impeachment of Witnesses, 52 Cornell L.Q. 239, 247 (1967). The traditional insistence that the attendance of the witness be directed to the statement on cross-examination is relaxed in favor of simply providing the witness an opportunity to explain and the opposite party an opportunity to examine on the statement, with no specification of any particular time or sequence. Under this procedure, several collusive witnesses can be examined before disclosure of a joint prior inconsistent statement. See Comment to California Evidence Code § 770. Also, dangers of oversight are reduced. See McCormick § 37, p. 68.

In order to allow for such eventualities as the witness becoming unavailable by the time the statement is discovered, a measure of discretion is conferred upon the judge. Similar provisions are found in California Evidence Code § 770 and New Jersey Evidence Rule 22(b).

Under principles of *expression unius* the rule does not apply to impeachment by evidence of prior inconsistent conduct. The use of inconsistent statements to impeach a hearsay declaration is treated in Rule 806.

1987 Amendments

The amendments are technical. No substantive change is intended.

1988 Amendments

The amendment is technical. No substantive change is intended.

2011 Amendments

The language of Rule 613 has been amended as part of the restyling of the Evidence Rules to make them more easily understood and to make style and terminology consistent throughout the rules. These changes are intended to be stylistic only. There is no intent to change any result in any ruling on evidence admissibility.

Rule 614. Court's Calling or Examining a Witness

(a) Calling. The court may call a witness on its own or at a party's request. Each party is entitled to cross-examine the witness.

(b) Examining. The court may examine a witness regardless of who calls the witness.

(c) Objections. A party may object to the court's calling or examining a witness either at that time or at the next opportunity when the jury is not present.

(Pub.L. 93–595, § 1, Jan. 2, 1975, 88 Stat.1937; Apr. 26, 2011, eff. Dec. 1, 2011.)

ADVISORY COMMITTEE NOTES

1972 Proposed Rules

Note to Subdivision (a). While exercised more frequently in criminal than in civil cases, the authority of the judge to call witnesses is well established. McCormick § 8, p. 14; Maguire, Weinstein, et al., Cases on Evidence 303–304 (5th ed. 1965); 9 Wigmore § 2484. One reason for the practice, the old rule against impeaching one's own witness, no longer exists by virtue of Rule 607, *supra*. Other reasons remain, however, to justify the continuation of the practice of calling court's witnesses. The right to cross-examine, with all it implies, is assured. The tendency of juries to associate a witness with the party calling him, regardless of technical aspects of vouching, is avoided. And the judge is not imprisoned within the case as made by the parties.

Note to Subdivision (b). The authority of the judge to question witnesses is also well established. McCormick § 8, pp. 12–13; Maguire, Weinstein, et al., Cases on Evidence 737–739 (5th ed. 1965); 3 Wigmore § 784. The authority is, of course, abused when the judge abandons his proper role and assumes that of advocate, but the manner in which interrogation should be conducted and the proper extent of its exercise are not susceptible of formulation in a rule. The omission in no sense precludes courts of review from continuing to reverse for abuse.

Note to Subdivision (c). The provision relating to objections is designed to relieve counsel of the embarrassment attendant upon objecting to questions by the judge in the presence of the jury, while at the same time assuring that objections are made in apt time to afford the opportunity to take possible corrective measures.

Compare the "automatic" objection feature of Rule 605 when the judge is called as a witness.

2011 Amendments

The language of Rule 614 has been amended as part of the restyling of the Evidence Rules to make them more easily understood and to make style and terminology consistent throughout the rules. These changes are intended to be stylistic only. There is no intent to change any result in any ruling on evidence admissibility.

Rule 615. Excluding Witnesses

At a party's request, the court must order witnesses excluded so that they cannot hear other witnesses' testimony. Or the court may do so on its own. But this rule does not authorize excluding:

(a) a party who is a natural person;

(b) an officer or employee of a party that is not a natural person, after being designated as the party's representative by its attorney;

(c) a person whose presence a party shows to be essential to presenting the party's claim or defense; or

(d) a person authorized by statute to be present.

(Pub.L. 93–595, § 1, Jan. 2, 1975, 88 Stat.1937; Mar. 2, 1987, eff. Oct. 1, 1987; Apr. 25, 1988, eff. Nov. 1, 1988; Pub.L. 100–690, Nov. 18, 1988, Title VII, § 7075(a), 102 Stat. 4405; Apr. 24, 1998, eff. Dec. 1, 1998; Apr. 26, 2011, eff. Dec. 1, 2011.)

ADVISORY COMMITTEE NOTES

1972 Proposed Rules

The efficacy of excluding or sequestering witnesses has long been recognized as a means of discouraging and exposing fabrication, inaccuracy, and collusion. 6 Wigmore §§ 1837–1838. The authority of the judge is admitted, the only question being whether the matter is committed to his discretion or one of right. The rule takes the latter position. No time is specified for making the request.

Several categories of persons are excepted. (1) Exclusion of persons who are parties would raise serious problems of confrontation and due process. Under accepted practice they are not subject to exclusion. 6 Wigmore § 1841. (2) As the equivalent of the right of a natural-person party to be present, a party which is not a natural person is entitled to have a representative present. Most of the cases have involved allowing a police officer who has been in charge of an investigation to remain in court despite the fact that he will be a witness. United States v. Infanzon, 235 F.2d 318, (2d Cir.1956); *Portomene v. United States,* 221 F.2d 582 (5th Cir.1955); *Powell v. United States,* 208 F.2d 618 (6th Cir.1953); *Jones v. United States,* 252 F.Supp. 781 (W.D.Okl.1966). Designation of the representative by the attorney rather than by the client may at first glance appear to be an inversion of the attorney-client relationship, but it may be assumed that the attorney will follow the wishes of the client, and the solution is simple and workable. See California Evidence Code § 777. (3) The category contemplates such persons as an agent who handled the transaction being litigated or an expert needed to advise counsel in the management of the litigation. See 6 Wigmore § 1841, n. 4.

1974 Enactment

Many district courts permit government counsel to have an investigative agent at counsel table throughout the trial although the agent is or may be a witness. The practice is permitted as an exception to the rule of exclusion and compares with the situation defense counsel finds himself in—he always has the client with him to consult during the trial. The investigative agent's presence may be extremely important to government counsel, especially when the case is complex or involves some specialized subject matter. The agent, too, having lived with the case for a long time, may be able to assist in meeting trial surprises where the best-prepared counsel would otherwise have difficulty. Yet, it would not seem the Government could often meet the burden under rule 615 of showing that the agent's presence is essential. Furthermore, it could be dangerous to use the agent as a witness as early in the case as possible, so that he might then help counsel as a nonwitness, since the agent's testimony could be needed in rebuttal. Using another, nonwitness agent from the same investigative agency would not generally meet government counsel's needs.

This problem is solved if it is clear that investigative agents are within the group specified under the second exception made in the rule, for "an officer or employee of a party which is not a natural person designated as its representative by its attorney." It is our understanding that this was the intention of the House committee. It is certainly this committee's construction of the rule. Senate Report No. 93–1277.

1987 Amendments

The amendment is technical. No substantive change is intended.

1988 Amendments

The amendment is technical. No substantive change is intended.

1998 Amendments

The amendment is in response to: (1) the Victim's Rights and Restitution Act of 1990, 42 U.S.C. § 10606, which guarantees, within certain limits, the right of a crime victim to attend the trial; and (2) the Victim Rights Clarification Act of 1997 (18 U.S.C. § 3510).

2011 Amendments

The language of Rule 615 has been amended as part of the restyling of the Evidence Rules to make them more easily understood and to make style and terminology consistent throughout the rules. These changes are intended to be stylistic only. There is no intent to change any result in any ruling on evidence admissibility.

HISTORICAL NOTES

Revision Notes and Legislative Reports

1988 Acts

For Related Reports, see 1988 U.S. Code Cong. and Adm. News, p. 5937.

1988 Amendments

Pub.L. 100–690 inserted "a" before "party which is not a natural person".

ARTICLE VII. OPINIONS AND EXPERT TESTIMONY

Rule
701. Opinion Testimony by Lay Witnesses.
702. Testimony by Expert Witnesses.
703. Bases of an Expert's Opinion Testimony.
704. Opinion on an Ultimate Issue.
705. Disclosing the Facts or Data Underlying an Expert's Opinion.
706. Court–Appointed Expert Witnesses.

Rule 701. Opinion Testimony by Lay Witnesses

If a witness is not testifying as an expert, testimony in the form of an opinion is limited to one that is:

(a) rationally based on the witness's perception;

(b) helpful to clearly understanding the witness's testimony or to determining a fact in issue; and

(c) not based on scientific, technical, or other specialized knowledge within the scope of Rule 702.

(Pub.L. 93–595, § 1, Jan. 2, 1975, 88 Stat.1937; Mar. 2, 1987, eff. Oct. 1, 1987; Apr. 17, 2000, eff. Dec. 1, 2000; Apr. 26, 2011, eff. Dec. 1, 2011.)

ADVISORY COMMITTEE NOTES

1972 Proposed Rules

The rule retains the traditional objective of putting the trier of fact in possession of an accurate reproduction of the event.

Limitation (a) is the familiar requirement of first-hand knowledge or observation.

Limitation (b) is phrased in terms of requiring testimony to be helpful in resolving issues. Witnesses often find difficulty in expressing themselves in language which is not that of an opinion or conclusion. While the courts have made concessions in certain recurring situations, necessity as a standard for permitting opinions and conclusions has proved too elusive and too unadaptable to particular situations for purposes of satisfactory judicial administration. McCormick § 11. Moreover, the practical impossibility of determining by rule what is a "fact," demonstrated by a century of litigation of the question of what is a fact for purposes of pleading under the Field Code, extends into evidence also. 7 Wigmore § 1919. The rule assumes that the natural characteristics of the adversary system will generally lead to an acceptable result, since the detailed account carries more conviction than the broad assertion, and a lawyer can be expected to display his witness to the best advantage. If he fails to do so, cross-examination and argument will point up the weakness. See Ladd, Expert Testimony, 5 Vand.L.Rev. 414, 415–417 (1952). If, despite these considerations, attempts are made to introduce meaningless assertions which amount to little more than choosing up sides, exclusion for lack of helpfulness is called for by the rule.

The language of the rule is substantially that of Uniform Rule 56(1). Similar provisions are California Evidence Code § 800; Kansas Code of Civil Procedure § 60–456(a); New Jersey Evidence Rule 56(1).

1987 Amendments

The amendments are technical. No substantive change is intended.

2000 Amendments

Rule 701 has been amended to eliminate the risk that the reliability requirements set forth in Rule 702 will be evaded through the simple expedient of proffering an expert in lay witness clothing. Under the amendment, a witness' testimony must be scrutinized under the rules regulating expert opinion to the extent that the witness is providing testimony based on scientific, technical, or other specialized knowledge within the scope of Rule 702. *See generally Asplundh Mfg. Div. v. Benton Harbor Eng'g*, 57 F.3d 1190 (3d Cir. 1995). By channeling testimony that is actually expert testimony to Rule 702, the amendment also ensures that a party will not evade the expert witness disclosure requirements set forth in Fed.R.Civ.P. 26 and Fed. R.Crim.P. 16 by simply calling an expert witness in the guise of a layperson. *See* Joseph, *Emerging Expert Issues Under the 1993 Disclosure Amendments to the Federal Rules of Civil Procedure*, 164 F.R.D. 97, 108 (1996) (noting that "there is no good reason to allow what is essentially surprise expert testimony." and that "the Court should be vigilant to preclude manipulative conduct designed to thwart the expert disclosure and discovery process"). *See also United States v. Figueroa-Lopez*, 125 F.3d 1241, 1246 (9th Cir. 1997) (law enforcement agents testifying that the defendant's conduct was consistent with that of a drug trafficker could not testify as lay witnesses; to permit such testimony under Rule 701 "subverts the requirements of Federal Rule of Criminal Procedure 16(a)(1)(E)").

The amendment does not distinguish between expert and lay *witnesses*, but rather between expert and lay *testimony*. Certainly it is possible for the same witness to provide both lay and expert testimony in a single case. *See, e.g, United States v. Figueroa-Lopez*, 125 F.3d 1241, 1246 (9th Cir. 1997) (law enforcement agents could testify that the defendant was acting suspiciously, without being qualified as experts; however, the rules on experts were applicable where the agents testified on the basis of extensive experience that the defendant was using code words to refer to drug quantities and prices). The amendment makes clear that any part of a witness' testimony that is based upon scientific, technical, or other specialized knowledge within the scope of Rule 702 is governed by the standards of Rule 702 and the corresponding disclosure requirements of the Civil and Criminal Rules.

The amendment is not intended to affect the "prototypical example[s] of the type of evidence contemplated by the adoption of Rule 701 relat[ing] to the appearance of persons or things, identity, the manner of conduct, competency of a person, degrees of light or darkness, sound, size, weight, distance, and an endless number of items that cannot be described factually in words apart from inferences." *Asplundh Mfg. Div. v. Benton Harbor Eng' g*, 57 F.3d 1190, 1196 (3d Cir. 1995).

For example, most courts have permitted the owner or officer of a business to testify to the value or projected profits of the business, without the necessity of qualifying the witness as an accountant, appraiser, or similar expert. *See, e.g., Lightning Lube, Inc. v. Witco Corp.* 4 F.3d 1153 (3d Cir. 1993) (no abuse of discretion in permitting the plaintiff's owner to give lay opinion testimony as to damages, as it was based on his knowledge and participation in the day-to-day affairs of the business). Such opinion testimony is admitted not because of experience, training or specialized knowledge within the realm of an expert, but because of the particularized knowledge that the witness has by virtue of his or her position in the business. The amendment does not purport to change this analysis. Similarly, courts have permitted lay witnesses to testify that a substance appeared to be a narcotic, so long as a foundation of familiarity with the substance is established. *See, e.g., United States v. Westbrook*, 896 F.2d 330 (8th Cir. 1990) (two lay witnesses who were heavy amphetamine users were properly permitted to testify that a substance was amphetamine; but it was error to permit another witness to make such an identification where she had no experience with amphetamines). Such testimony is not based on specialized knowledge within the scope of Rule 702, but rather is based upon a layperson's personal knowledge. If, however, that witness were to describe how a narcotic was manufactured, or to describe the intricate workings of a narcotic distribution network, then the witness would have to qualify as an expert under Rule 702. *United States v. Figueroa–Lopez, supra.*

The amendment incorporates the distinctions set forth in *State v. Brown*, 836 S.W.2d 530, 549 (1992), a case involving former Tennessee Rule of Evidence 701, a rule that precluded lay witness testimony based on "special knowledge." In *Brown*, the court declared that the distinction between lay and expert witness testimony is that lay testimony "results from a process of reasoning familiar in everyday life," while expert testimony "results from a process of reasoning which can be mastered only by specialists in the field." The court in *Brown* noted that a lay witness with experience could testify that a substance appeared to be blood, but that a witness would have to qualify as an expert before he could testify that bruising around the eyes is indicative of skull trauma. That is the kind of distinction made by the amendment to this Rule.

GAP Report—Proposed Amendment to Rule 701

The Committee made the following changes to the published draft of the proposed amendment to Evidence Rule 701:

1. The words "within the scope of Rule 702" were added at the end of the proposed amendment, to emphasize that the Rule does not require witnesses to qualify as experts unless their testimony is of the type traditionally considered within the purview of Rule 702. The Committee Note was amended to accord with this textual change.

2. The Committee Note was revised to provide further examples of the kind of testimony that could and could not be proffered under the limitation imposed by the proposed amendment.

2011 Amendments

The language of Rule 701 has been amended as part of the general restyling of the Evidence Rules to make them more easily understood and to make style and terminology consistent throughout the rules. These changes are intended to be stylistic only. There is no intent to change any result in any ruling on evidence admissibility.

The Committee deleted all reference to an "inference" on the grounds that the deletion made the Rule flow better and easier to read, and because any "inference" is covered by the broader term "opinion." Courts have not made substantive decisions on the basis of any distinction between an opinion and an inference. No change in current practice is intended.

Rule 702. Testimony by Expert Witnesses

A witness who is qualified as an expert by knowledge, skill, experience, training, or education may testify in the form of an opinion or otherwise if:

(a) the expert's scientific, technical, or other specialized knowledge will help the trier of fact to understand the evidence or to determine a fact in issue;

(b) the testimony is based on sufficient facts or data;

(c) the testimony is the product of reliable principles and methods; and

(d) the expert has reliably applied the principles and methods to the facts of the case.

(Pub.L. 93–595, § 1, Jan. 2, 1975, 88 Stat. 1937; Apr. 17, 2000, eff. Dec. 1, 2000; Apr. 26, 2011, eff. Dec. 1, 2011.)

ADVISORY COMMITTEE NOTES

1972 Proposed Rules

An intelligent evaluation of facts is often difficult or impossible without the application of some scientific, technical, or other specialized knowledge. The most common source of this knowledge is the expert witness, although there are other techniques for supplying it.

Most of the literature assumes that experts testify only in the form of opinions. The assumption is logically unfounded. The rule accordingly recognizes that an expert on the stand may give a dissertation or exposition of scientific or other principles relevant to the case, leaving the trier of fact to apply them to the facts. Since much of the criticism of expert testimony has centered upon the hypothetical question, it seems wise to recognize that opinions are not indispensable and to encourage the use of expert testimony in non-opinion form when counsel believes the trier can itself draw the requisite inference. The use of opinions is not abolished by the rule, however. It will continue to be permissible for the experts to take the further step of suggesting the inference which should be drawn from applying the specialized knowledge to the facts. See Rules 703 to 705.

Whether the situation is a proper one for the use of expert testimony is to be determined on the basis of assisting the trier. "There is no more certain test for determining when experts may be used than the common sense inquiry whether the untrained layman would be qualified to determine intelligently and to the best possible degree the particular issue without enlightenment from those having a specialized understanding of the subject involved in the dispute." Ladd, Expert Testimony, 5 Vand.L.Rev. 414, 418 (1952). When opinions are excluded, it is because they are unhelpful and therefore superfluous and a waste of time. 7 Wigmore § 1918.

The rule is broadly phrased. The fields of knowledge which may be drawn upon are not limited merely to the "scientific" and "technical" but extend to all "specialized" knowledge. Similarly, the expert is viewed, not in a narrow sense, but as a person qualified by "knowledge, skill, experience, training or education." Thus within the scope of the rule are not only experts in the strictest sense of the word, e.g., physicians, physicists, and architects, but also the large group sometimes called "skilled" witnesses, such as bankers or landowners testifying to land values.

2000 Amendments

Rule 702 has been amended in response to *Daubert v. Merrell Dow Pharmaceuticals, Inc.*, 509 U.S. 579 (1993), and to the many cases applying *Daubert*, including *Kumho Tire Co. v. Carmichael*, 119 S.Ct. 1167 (1999). In *Daubert* the Court charged trial judges with the responsibility of acting as gatekeepers to exclude unreliable expert testimony, and the Court in *Kumho* clarified that this gatekeeper function applies to all expert testimony, not just testimony based in science. *See also Kumho*, 119 S.Ct. at 1178 (citing the Committee Note to the proposed amendment to Rule 702, which had been released for public comment before the date of the *Kumho* decision). The amendment affirms the trial court's role as gatekeeper and provides some general standards that the trial court must use to assess the reliability and helpfulness of proffered expert testimony. Consistently with *Kumho*, the Rule as amended provides that all types of expert testimony present questions of admissibility for the trial court in deciding whether the evidence is reliable and helpful. Consequently, the admissibility of all expert testimony is governed by the principles of Rule 104(a). Under that Rule, the proponent has the burden of establishing that the pertinent admissibility requirements are met by a preponderance of the evidence. *See Bourjaily v. United States*, 483 U.S. 171 (1987).

Daubert set forth a non-exclusive checklist for trial courts to use in assessing the reliability of scientific expert testimony. The specific factors explicated by the *Daubert* Court are (1) whether the expert's technique or theory can be or has been tested—that is, whether the expert's theory can be challenged in some objective sense, or whether it is instead simply a subjective, conclusory approach that cannot reasonably be assessed for reliability; (2) whether the technique or theory has been subject to peer review and publication; (3) the known or potential rate of error of the technique or theory when applied; (4) the existence and maintenance of standards and controls; and (5) whether the technique or theory has been generally accepted in the scientific community. The Court in *Kumho* held that these factors might also be applicable in assessing the reliability of non-scientific expert testimony, depending upon "the particular circumstances of the particular case at issue." 119 S.Ct. at 1175.

No attempt has been made to "codify" these specific factors. *Daubert* itself emphasized that the factors were neither exclusive nor dispositive. Other cases have recognized that not all of the specific *Daubert* factors can apply to every type of expert testimony. In addition to *Kumho*, 119 S.Ct. at 1175, *see Tyus v. Urban Search Management*, 102 F.3d 256 (7th Cir. 1996) (noting that the factors mentioned by the Court in *Daubert* do not neatly apply to expert testimony from a sociologist). *See also Kannankeril v. Terminix Int'l, Inc.*, 128 F.3d 802, 809 (3d Cir. 1997) (holding that lack of peer review or publication was not dispositive where the expert's opinion was supported by "widely accepted scientific knowledge"). The standards set forth in the amendment are broad enough to require consideration of any or all of the specific *Daubert* factors where appropriate.

Courts both before and after *Daubert* have found other factors relevant in determining whether expert testimony is sufficiently reliable to be considered by the trier of fact. These factors include:

(1) Whether experts are "proposing to testify about matters growing naturally and directly out of research they have conducted independent of the litigation, or whether they have developed their opinions expressly for purposes of testifying." *Daubert v. Merrell Dow Pharmaceuticals, Inc.*, 43 F.3d 1311, 1317 (9th Cir. 1995).

(2) Whether the expert has unjustifiably extrapolated from an accepted premise to an unfounded conclusion. *See General Elec. Co. v. Joiner*, 522 U.S. 136, 146 (1997) (noting that in some cases a trial court "may conclude that there is simply too great an analytical gap between the data and the opinion proffered").

(3) Whether the expert has adequately accounted for obvious alternative explanations. *See Claar v. Burlington N.R.R.*, 29 F.3d 499 (9th Cir. 1994) (testimony excluded where the expert failed to consider other obvious causes for the plaintiff's condition). *Compare Ambrosini v. Labarraque*, 101 F.3d 129 (D.C. Cir. 1996) (the possibility of some uneliminated causes presents a question of weight, so long as the most obvious causes have been considered and reasonably ruled out by the expert).

(4) Whether the expert "is being as careful as he would be in his regular professional work outside his paid litigation consulting." *Sheehan v. Daily Racing Form, Inc.*, 104 F.3d 940, 942 (7th Cir. 1997). *See Kumho Tire Co. v. Carmichael*,

119 S.Ct. 1167, 1176 (1999) (*Daubert* requires the trial court to assure itself that the expert "employs in the courtroom the same level of intellectual rigor that characterizes the practice of an expert in the relevant field").

(5) Whether the field of expertise claimed by the expert is known to reach reliable results for the type of opinion the expert would give. *See Kumho Tire Co. v. Carmichael*, 119 S.Ct.1167, 1175 (1999) (*Daubert's* general acceptance factor does not "help show that an expert's testimony is reliable where the discipline itself lacks reliability, as for example, do theories grounded in any so-called generally accepted principles of astrology or necromancy."), *Moore v. Ashland Chemical, Inc.*, 151 F.3d 269 (5th Cir. 1998) (en banc) (clinical doctor was properly precluded from testifying to the toxicological cause of the plaintiff's respiratory problem, where the opinion was not sufficiently grounded in scientific methodology); *Sterling v. Velsicol Chem. Corp.*, 855 F.2d 1188 (6th Cir. 1988) (rejecting testimony based on "clinical ecology" as unfounded and unreliable).

All of these factors remain relevant to the determination of the reliability of expert testimony under the Rule as amended. Other factors may also be relevant. *See Kumho*, 119 S.Ct. 1167, 1176 ("[W]e conclude that the trial judge must have considerable leeway in deciding in a particular case how to go about determining whether particular expert testimony is reliable."). Yet no single factor is necessarily dispositive of the reliability of a particular expert's testimony. *See, e.g., Heller v. Shaw Industries, Inc.*, 167 F.3d 146, 155 (3d Cir. 1999) ("not only must each stage of the expert's testimony be reliable, but each stage must be evaluated practically and flexibly without bright-line exclusionary (or inclusionary) rules."); *Daubert v. Merrell Dow Pharmaceuticals, Inc.*, 43 F.3d 1311, 1317, n.5 (9th Cir. 1995) (noting that some expert disciplines "have the courtroom as a principal theatre of operations" and as to these disciplines "the fact that the expert has developed an expertise principally for purposes of litigation will obviously not be a substantial consideration.").

A review of the caselaw after *Daubert* shows that the rejection of expert testimony is the exception rather than the rule. *Daubert* did not work a "seachange over federal evidence law," and "the trial court's role as gatekeeper is not intended to serve as a replacement for the adversary system." *United States v. 14.38 Acres of Land Situated in Leflore County, Mississippi*, 80 F.3d 1074, 1078 (5th Cir. 1996). As the Court in *Daubert* stated: "Vigorous cross-examination, presentation of contrary evidence, and careful instruction on the burden of proof are the traditional and appropriate means of attacking shaky but admissible evidence." 509 U.S. at 595. Likewise, this amendment is not intended to provide an excuse for an automatic challenge to the testimony of every expert. *See Kumho Tire Co. v. Carmichael*, 119 S.Ct.1167, 1176 (1999) (noting that the trial judge has the discretion "both to avoid unnecessary 'reliability' proceedings in ordinary cases where the reliability of an expert's methods is properly taken for granted, and to require appropriate proceedings in the less usual or more complex cases where cause for questioning the expert's reliability arises.").

When a trial court, applying this amendment, rules that an expert's testimony is reliable, this does not necessarily mean that contradictory expert testimony is unreliable. The amendment is broad enough to permit testimony that is the product of competing principles or methods in the same field of expertise. *See, e.g., Heller v. Shaw Industries, Inc.*, 167 F.3d 146, 160 (3d Cir. 1999) (expert testimony cannot be excluded simply because the expert uses one test rather than another, when both tests are accepted in the field and both reach reliable results). As the court stated in *In re Paoli R.R. Yard PCB Litigation*, 35 F.3d 717, 744 (3d Cir. 1994), proponents "do not have to demonstrate to the judge by a preponderance of the evidence that the assessments of their experts are correct, they only have to demonstrate by a preponderance of evidence that their opinions are reliable.... The evidentiary requirement of reliability is lower than the merits standard of correctness." *See also Daubert v. Merrell Dow Pharmaceuticals, Inc.*, 43 F.3d 1311, 1318 (9th Cir. 1995) (scientific experts might be permitted to testify if they could show that the methods they used were also employed by "a recognized minority of scientists in their field."); *Ruiz-Troche v. Pepsi Cola*, 161 F.3d 77, 85 (1st Cir. 1998) ("*Daubert* neither requires nor empowers trial courts to determine which of several competing scientific theories has the best provenance.").

The Court in *Daubert* declared that the "focus, of course, must be solely on principles and methodology, not on the conclusions they generate." 509 U.S. at 595. Yet as the Court later recognized, "conclusions and methodology are not entirely distinct from one another." *General Elec. Co. v. Joiner*, 522 U.S. 136, 146 (1997). Under the amendment, as under *Daubert*, when an expert purports to apply principles and methods in accordance with professional standards, and yet reaches a conclusion that other experts in the field would not reach, the trial court may fairly suspect that the principles and methods have not been faithfully applied. *See Lust v. Merrell Dow Pharmaceuticals, Inc.*, 89 F.3d 594, 598 (9th Cir. 1996). The amendment specifically provides that the trial court must scrutinize not only the principles and methods used by the expert, but also whether those principles and methods have been properly applied to the facts of the case. As the court noted in *In re Paoli R.R. Yard PCB Litig.*, 35 F.3d 717, 745 (3d Cir. 1994), "*any* step that renders the analysis unreliable ... renders the expert's testimony inadmissible. *This is true whether the step completely changes a reliable methodology or merely misapplies that methodology.*"

If the expert purports to apply principles and methods to the facts of the case, it is important that this application be conducted reliably. Yet it might also be important in some cases for an expert to educate the factfinder about general principles, without ever attempting to apply these principles to the specific facts of the case. For example, experts might instruct the factfinder on the principles of thermodynamics, or bloodclotting, or on how financial markets respond to corporate reports, without ever knowing about or trying to tie their testimony into the facts of the case. The amendment does not alter the venerable practice of using expert testimony to educate the factfinder on general principles. For this kind of generalized testimony, Rule 702 simply requires that: (1) the expert be qualified; (2) the testimony address a subject matter on which the factfinder can be assisted by an expert; (3) the testimony be reliable; and (4) the testimony "fit" the facts of the case.

As stated earlier, the amendment does not distinguish between scientific and other forms of expert testimony. The trial court's gatekeeping function applies to testimony by any expert. *See Kumho Tire Co. v. Carmichael*, 119 S.Ct. 1167, 1171 (1999) ("We conclude that *Daubert's* general holding—setting forth the trial judge's general 'gatekeeping' obligation—applies not only to testimony based on 'scientific' knowledge, but also to testimony based on 'technical' and 'other specialized' knowledge."). While the relevant factors for determining reliability will vary from expertise to expertise, the amendment rejects the premise that an expert's testimony should be treated more permissively simply because it is outside the realm of science. An opinion from an expert who is not a scientist should receive the same degree of scrutiny for reliability as an opinion from an expert who purports to be a scientist. *See Watkins v. Telsmith, Inc.*, 121 F.3d 984, 991 (5th Cir. 1997) ("[I]t seems exactly backwards that experts who purport to rely on general engineering principles and practical experience might escape screening by the district court simply by stating that their conclusions were not reached by any particular method or technique."). Some types of expert testimony will be more objectively verifiable, and subject to the expectations of falsifiability, peer review, and publication, than others. Some types of expert testimony will not rely on anything like a scientific method, and so will have to be evaluated by reference to other standard principles attendant to the particular area of expertise. The trial judge in all cases of proffered expert testimony must find that it is properly grounded, well-reasoned, and not speculative before it can be admitted. The expert's testimony must be grounded in an accepted body of learning or experience in the expert's field, and the expert must explain how the conclusion is so grounded. *See, e.g.*, American College of Trial Lawyers, Standards and Procedures for Determining the Admissibility of Expert Testimony after *Daubert*, 157 F.R.D. 571, 579 (1994) ("[W] hether the testimony concerns economic principles, accounting standards, property valuation or other non-scientific subjects, it should be evaluated by reference to the 'knowledge and experience' of that particular field.").

The amendment requires that the testimony must be the product of reliable principles and methods that are reliably applied to the facts of the case. While the terms "principles" and "methods" may convey a certain impression when applied to scientific knowledge, they remain relevant when applied to testimony based on technical or other specialized knowledge. For example, when a law enforcement agent testifies regarding the use of code words in a drug transaction, the principle used by the agent is that participants in such transactions regularly use code words to conceal the nature of their activities. The method used by the agent is the application of extensive experience to analyze the meaning of the conversations. So long as the principles and methods are reliable and applied reliably to the facts of the case, this type of testimony should be admitted.

Nothing in this amendment is intended to suggest that experience alone—or experience in conjunction with other knowledge, skill, training or education—may not provide a sufficient foundation for expert testimony. To the contrary, the text of Rule 702 expressly contemplates that an expert may be qualified on the basis of experience. In certain fields, experience is the predominant, if not sole, basis for a great deal of reliable expert testimony. *See, e.g., United States v. Jones*, 107 F.3d 1147 (6th Cir. 1997) (no abuse of discretion in admitting the testimony of a handwriting examiner who had years of practical experience and extensive training, and who explained his methodology in detail); *Tassin v. Sears Roebuck*, 946 F.Supp. 1241, 1248 (M.D.La. 1996) (design engineer's testimony can be admissible when the expert's opinions "are based on facts, a reasonable investigation, and traditional technical/mechanical expertise, and he provides a reasonable link between the information and procedures he uses and the conclusions he reaches"). *See also Kumho Tire Co. v. Carmichael*, 119 S.Ct. 1167, 1178 (1999) (stating that "no one denies that an expert might draw a conclusion from a set of observations based on extensive and specialized experience.").

If the witness is relying solely or primarily on experience, then the witness must explain how that experience leads to the conclusion reached, why that experience is a sufficient basis for the opinion, and how that experience is reliably applied to the facts. The trial court's gatekeeping function requires more than simply "taking the expert's word for it." *See Daubert v. Merrell Dow Pharmaceuticals, Inc.*, 43 F.3d 1311, 1319 (9th Cir. 1995) ("We've been presented with only the experts' qualifications, their conclusions and their assurances of reliability. Under *Daubert*, that's not enough."). The more subjective and controversial the expert's inquiry, the more likely the testimony should be excluded as unreliable. *See O'Conner v. Commonwealth Edison Co.*, 13 F.3d 1090 (7th Cir. 1994) (expert testimony based on a completely subjective methodology held properly excluded). *See also Kumho Tire Co. v. Carmichael*, 119 S.Ct. 1167, 1176 (1999) ("[I]t will at times be useful to ask even of a witness whose expertise is based purely on experience, say, a perfume tester able to distinguish among 140 odors at a sniff, whether his preparation is of a kind that others in the field would recognize as acceptable.").

Subpart (1) of Rule 702 calls for a quantitative rather than qualitative analysis. The amendment requires that expert testimony be based on sufficient underlying "facts or data." The term "data" is intended to encompass the reliable opinions of other experts. See the original Advisory Committee Note to Rule 703. The language "facts or data" is broad enough to allow an expert to rely on hypothetical facts that are supported by the evidence. *Id.*

When facts are in dispute, experts sometimes reach different conclusions based on competing versions of the facts. The emphasis in the amendment on " sufficient facts or data" is not intended to authorize a trial court to exclude an expert's testimony on the ground that the court believes one version of the facts and not the other.

There has been some confusion over the relationship between Rules 702 and 703. The amendment makes clear that the sufficiency of the basis of an expert' s testimony is to be decided under Rule 702. Rule 702 sets forth the overarching requirement of reliability, and an analysis of the sufficiency of the expert's basis cannot be divorced from the ultimate reliability of the expert's opinion. In contrast, the "reasonable reliance" requirement of Rule 703 is a relatively narrow inquiry. When an expert relies on inadmissible information, Rule 703 requires the trial court to determine whether that information is of a type reasonably relied on by other experts in the field. If so, the expert can rely on the information in reaching an opinion. However, the question whether the expert is relying on a *sufficient* basis of information—whether admissible information or not—is governed by the requirements of Rule 702.

The amendment makes no attempt to set forth procedural requirements for exercising the trial court's gatekeeping function over expert testimony. *See* Daniel J. Capra, *The Daubert Puzzle*, 38 Ga.L.Rev. 699, 766 (1998) ("Trial courts should be allowed substantial discretion in dealing with *Daubert* questions; any attempt to codify procedures will likely give rise to unnecessary changes in practice and create difficult questions for appellate review."). Courts have shown considerable ingenuity and flexibility in considering challenges to expert testimony under *Daubert*, and it is contemplated that this will continue under the amended Rule. *See, e.g., Cortes-Irizarry v. Corporacion Insular*, 111 F.3d 184 (1st Cir. 1997) (discussing the application of *Daubert* in ruling on a motion for summary judgment); *In re Paoli R.R. Yard PCB Litig.*, 35 F.3d 717, 736, 739 (3d Cir. 1994) (discussing the use of *in limine* hearings); *Claar v. Burlington N.R.R.*, 29 F.3d 499, 502–05 (9th Cir. 1994) (discussing the trial court's technique of ordering experts to submit serial affidavits explaining the reasoning and methods underlying their conclusions).

The amendment continues the practice of the original Rule in referring to a qualified witness as an "expert." This was done to provide continuity and to minimize change. The use of the term "expert" in the Rule does not, however, mean that a jury should actually be informed that a qualified witness is testifying as an "expert." Indeed, there is much to be said for a practice that prohibits the use of the term "expert" by both the parties and the court at trial. Such a practice "ensures that trial courts do not inadvertently put their stamp of authority" on a witness's opinion, and protects against the jury's being "overwhelmed by the so-called 'experts'." Hon. Charles Richey, *Proposals to Eliminate the Prejudicial Effect of the Use of the Word "Expert" Under the Federal Rules of Evidence in Criminal and*

Civil Jury Trials, 154 F.R.D. 537, 559 (1994) (setting forth limiting instructions and a standing order employed to prohibit the use of the term " expert" injury trials).

GAP Report—Proposed Amendment to Rule 702

The Committee made the following changes to the published draft of the proposed amendment to Evidence Rule 702:

1. The word "reliable" was deleted from Subpart (1) of the proposed amendment, in order to avoid an overlap with Evidence Rule 703, and to clarify that an expert opinion need not be excluded simply because it is based on hypothetical facts. The Committee Note was amended to accord with this textual change.

2. The Committee Note was amended throughout to include pertinent references to the Supreme Court's decision in *Kumho Tire Co. v. Carmichael*, which was rendered after the proposed amendment was released for public comment. Other citations were updated as well.

3. The Committee Note was revised to emphasize that the amendment is not intended to limit the right to jury trial, nor to permit a challenge to the testimony of every expert, nor to preclude the testimony of experience-based experts, nor to prohibit testimony based on competing methodologies within a field of expertise.

4. Language was added to the Committee Note to clarify that no single factor is necessarily dispositive of the reliability inquiry mandated by Evidence Rule 702.

2011 Amendments

The language of Rule 702 has been amended as part of the restyling of the Evidence Rules to make them more easily understood and to make style and terminology consistent throughout the rules. These changes are intended to be stylistic only. There is no intent to change any result in any ruling on evidence admissibility.

Rule 703. Bases of an Expert's Opinion Testimony

An expert may base an opinion on facts or data in the case that the expert has been made aware of or personally observed. If experts in the particular field would reasonably rely on those kinds of facts or data in forming an opinion on the subject, they need not be admissible for the opinion to be admitted. But if the facts or data would otherwise be inadmissible, the proponent of the opinion may disclose them to the jury only if their probative value in helping the jury evaluate the opinion substantially outweighs their prejudicial effect.

(Pub.L. 93–595, § 1, Jan. 2, 1975, 88 Stat.1937; Mar. 2, 1987, eff. Oct. 1, 1987; Apr. 17, 2000, eff. Dec. 1, 2000; Apr. 26, 2011, eff. Dec. 1, 2011.)

ADVISORY COMMITTEE NOTES

1972 Proposed Rules

Facts or data upon which expert opinions are based may, under the rule, be derived from three possible sources. The first is the firsthand observation of the witness with opinions based thereon traditionally allowed. A treating physician affords an example. Rheingold, The Basis of Medical Testimony, 15 Vand.L.Rev. 473, 489 (1962). Whether he must first relate his observations is treated in Rule 705. The second source, presentation at the trial, also reflects existing practice. The technique may be the familiar hypothetical question or having the expert attend the trial and hear the testimony establishing the facts. Problems of determining what testimony the expert relied upon, when the latter technique is employed and the testimony is in conflict, may be resolved by resort to Rule 705. The third source contemplated by the rule consists of presentation of data to the expert outside of court and other than by his own perception. In this respect the rule is designed to broaden the basis for expert opinions beyond that current in many jurisdictions and to bring the judicial practice into line with the practice of the experts themselves when not in court. Thus a physician in his own practice bases his diagnosis on information from numerous sources and of considerable variety, including statements by patients and relatives, reports and opinions from nurses, technicians and other doctors, hospital records, and X rays. Most of them are admissible in evidence, but only with the expenditure of substantial time in producing and examining various authenticating witnesses. The physician makes life-and-death decisions in reliance upon them. His validation, expertly performed and subject to cross-examination, ought to suffice for judicial purposes. Rheingold, *supra,* at 531; McCormick § 15. A similar provision is California Evidence Code § 801(b).

The rule also offers a more satisfactory basis for ruling upon the admissibility of public opinion poll evidence. Attention is directed to the validity of the techniques employed rather than to relatively fruitless inquiries whether hearsay is involved. See Judge Feinberg's careful analysis in Zippo Mfg. Co. v. Rogers Imports, Inc., 216 F.Supp. 670 (S.D.N.Y.1963). See also Blum et al., The Art of Opinion Research: A Lawyer's Appraisal of an Emerging Service, 24 U.Chi.L.Rev. 1 (1956); Bonynge Trademark Surveys and Techniques and Their Use in Litigation, 48 A.B.A.J. 329 (1962); Zeisel, The Uniqueness of Survey Evidence, 45 Cornell L.Q. 322 (1960); Annot., 76 A.L.R.2d 919.

If it be feared that enlargement of permissible data may tend to break down the rules of exclusion unduly, notice should be taken that the rule requires that the facts or data "be of a type reasonably relied upon by experts in the particular field." The language would not warrant admitting in evidence the opinion of an "accidentologist" as to the point of impact in an automobile collision based on statements of bystanders since this requirement is not satisfied. See Comment, Cal.Law Rev. Comm'n, Recommendation Proposing an Evidence Code 148–150 (1965).

1987 Amendments

The amendment is technical. No substantive change is intended.

2000 Amendments

Rule 703 has been amended to emphasize that when an expert reasonably relies on inadmissible information to form an opinion or inference, the underlying information is not admissible simply because the opinion or inference is admitted. Courts have reached different results on how to treat inadmissible information when it is reasonably relied upon by an expert in forming an opinion or drawing an inference. *Compare United States v. Rollins*, 862 F.2d 1282 (7th Cir. 1988) (admitting, as part of the basis of an FBI agent's expert opinion on the meaning of code language, the hearsay statements of an informant), *with United States v. 0.59 Acres of Land*, 109 F.3d 1493 (9th Cir. 1997) (error to admit hearsay offered as the basis of an expert opinion, without a limiting instruction). Commentators have also taken differing views. *See e.g.*, Ronald Carlson, *Policing the Bases of Modern Expert Testimony*, 39 Vand.L.Rev. 577 (1986) (advocating limits on the jury's consideration of otherwise inadmissible evidence used as the basis for an expert opinion); Paul Rice, *Inadmissible Evidence as a Basis for Expert Testimony: A Response to Professor Carlson*, 40 Vand.L.Rev. 583 (1987) (advocating unrestricted use of information reasonably relied upon by an expert).

When information is reasonably relied upon by an expert and yet is admissible only for the purpose of assisting the jury in evaluating an expert's opinion, a trial court applying this Rule must consider the information's probative value in assisting the jury to weigh the expert's opinion on the one hand, and the risk of prejudice resulting from the jury's potential misuse of the information for substantive purposes on the other. The information may be disclosed to the jury, upon objection, only if the trial court finds that the probative value of the information in assisting the jury to evaluate the expert's opinion substantially outweighs its prejudicial effect. If the otherwise inadmissible information is admitted under this balancing test, the trial judge must give a limiting instruction upon request, informing the jury that the underlying information must not be used for substantive purposes. *See* Rule 105. In determining the appropriate course, the trial court should consider the probable effectiveness or lack of effectiveness of a limiting instruction under the particular circumstances.

The amendment governs only the disclosure to the jury of information that is reasonably relied on by an expert, when that information is not admissible for substantive purposes. It is not intended to affect the admissibility of an expert's testimony. Nor does the amendment prevent an expert from relying on information that is inadmissible for substantive purposes.

Nothing in this Rule restricts the presentation of underlying expert facts or data when offered by an adverse party. *See* Rule 705. Of course, an adversary's attack on an expert's basis will often open the door to a proponent's rebuttal with information that was reasonably relied upon by the expert, even if that information would not have been discloseable initially under the balancing test provided by this amendment. Moreover, in some circumstances the proponent might wish to disclose information that is relied upon by the expert in order to "remove the sting" from the opponent's anticipated attack, and thereby prevent the jury from drawing an unfair negative inference. The trial court should take this consideration into account in applying the balancing test provided by this amendment.

This amendment covers facts or data that cannot be admitted for any purpose other than to assist the jury to evaluate the expert's opinion. The balancing test provided in this amendment is not applicable to facts or data that are admissible for any other purpose but have not yet been offered for such a purpose at the time the expert testifies.

The amendment provides a presumption against disclosure to the jury of information used as the basis of an expert's opinion and not admissible for any substantive purpose, when that information is offered by the proponent of the expert. In a multi-party case, where one party proffers an expert whose testimony is also beneficial to other parties, each such party should be deemed a "proponent" within the meaning of the amendment.

GAP Report—Proposed Amendment to Rule 703

The Committee made the following changes to the published draft of the proposed amendment to Evidence Rule 703:

1. A minor stylistic change was made in the text, in accordance with the suggestion of the Style Subcommittee of the Standing Committee on Rules of Practice and Procedure.

2. The words "in assisting the jury to evaluate the expert's opinion" were added to the text, to specify the proper purpose for offering the otherwise inadmissible information relied on by an expert. The Committee Note was revised to accord with this change in the text.

3. Stylistic changes were made to the Committee Note.

4. The Committee Note was revised to emphasize that the balancing test set forth in the proposal should be used to determine whether an expert's basis may be disclosed to the jury either (1) in rebuttal or (2) on direct examination to "remove the sting" of an opponent's anticipated attack on an expert's basis.

2011 Amendments

The language of Rule 703 has been amended as part of the general restyling of the Evidence Rules to make them more easily understood and to make style and terminology consistent throughout the rules. These changes are intended to be stylistic only. There is no intent to change any result in any ruling on evidence admissibility.

The Committee deleted all reference to an "inference" on the grounds that the deletion made the Rule flow better and easier to read, and because any "inference" is covered by the broader term "opinion." Courts have not made substantive decisions on the basis of any distinction between an opinion and an inference. No change in current practice is intended.

Rule 704. Opinion on an Ultimate Issue

(a) In General—Not Automatically Objectionable. An opinion is not objectionable just because it embraces an ultimate issue.

(b) Exception. In a criminal case, an expert witness must not state an opinion about whether the defendant did or did not have a mental state or condition that constitutes an element of the crime charged or of a defense. Those matters are for the trier of fact alone.

(Pub.L. 93–595, § 1, Jan. 2, 1975, 88 Stat. 1937; Pub.L. 98–473, Title IV, § 406, Oct. 12, 1984, 98 Stat. 2067; Apr. 26, 2011, eff. Dec. 1, 2011.)

ADVISORY COMMITTEE NOTES

1972 Proposed Rules

The basic approach to opinions, lay and expert, in these rules is to admit them when helpful to the trier of fact. In order to render this approach fully effective and to allay any doubt on the subject, the so-called "ultimate issue" rule is specifically abolished by the instant rule.

The older cases often contained strictures against allowing witnesses to express opinions upon ultimate issues, as a particular aspect of the rule against opinions. The rule was unduly restrictive, difficult of application, and generally served only to deprive the trier of fact of useful information. 7 Wigmore §§ 1920, 1921; McCormick § 12. The basis usually assigned for the rule, to prevent the witness from "usurping the province of the jury," is aptly characterized as "empty rhetoric." 7 Wigmore § 1920, p. 17. Efforts to meet the felt needs of particular situations led to odd verbal circumlocutions which were said not to violate the rule. Thus a witness could express his estimate of the criminal responsibility of an accused in terms of sanity or insanity, but not in terms of ability to tell right from wrong or other more modern standard. And in cases of medical causation, witnesses were sometimes required to couch their opinions in cautious phrases of "might or could," rather than "did," though the result was to deprive many opinions of the positiveness to which they were entitled, accompanied by the hazard of a ruling of insufficiency to support a verdict. In other instances the rule was simply disregarded, and, as concessions to need, opinions were allowed upon such matters as intoxication, speed, handwriting, and value, although more precise coincidence with an ultimate issue would scarcely be possible.

Many modern decisions illustrate the trend to abandon the rule completely. People v. Wilson, 25 Cal.2d 341, 153 P.2d 720 (1944), whether abortion necessary to save life of patient; *Clifford–Jacobs Forging Co. v. Industrial Comm.,* 19 Ill.2d 236, 166 N.E.2d 582 (1960), medical causation; *Dowling v. L. H. Shattuck,* Inc., 91 N.H. 234, 17 A.2d 529 (1941), proper method of shoring ditch; *Schweiger v. Solbeck,* 191 Or. 454, 230 P.2d 195 (1951), cause of landslide. In each instance the opinion was allowed.

The abolition of the ultimate issue rule does not lower the bars so as to admit all opinions. Under Rules 701 and 702, opinions must be helpful to the trier of fact, and Rule 403 provides for exclusion of evidence which wastes time. These provisions afford ample assurances against the admission of opinions which would merely tell the jury what result to reach, somewhat in the manner of the oath-helpers of an earlier day. They also stand ready to exclude opinions phrased in terms of inadequately explored legal criteria. Thus the question, "Did T have capacity to make a will?" would be excluded, while the question, "Did T have sufficient mental capacity to know the nature and extent of his property and the natural objects of his bounty and to formulate a rational scheme of distribution?" would be allowed. McCormick § 12.

For similar provisions see Uniform Rule 56(4); California Evidence Code § 805; Kansas Code of Civil Procedure § 60–456(d); New Jersey Evidence Rule 56(3).

2011 Amendments

The language of Rule 704 has been amended as part of the general restyling of the Evidence Rules to make them more easily understood and to make style and terminology consistent throughout the rules. These changes are intended to be stylistic only. There is no intent to change any result in any ruling on evidence admissibility.

The Committee deleted all reference to an "inference" on the grounds that the deletion made the Rule flow better and easier to read, and because any "inference" is covered by the broader term "opinion." Courts have not made substantive decisions on the basis of any distinction between an opinion and an inference. No change in current practice is intended.

HISTORICAL NOTES

Rule 705. Disclosing the Facts or Data Underlying an Expert's Opinion

Unless the court orders otherwise, an expert may state an opinion—and give the reasons for it—without first testifying to the underlying facts or data. But the expert may be required to disclose those facts or data on cross- examination.

(Pub.L. 93–595, § 1, Jan. 2, 1975, 88 Stat. 1938; Mar. 2, 1987, eff. Oct. 1, 1987; Apr. 22, 1993, eff. Dec. 1, 1993; Apr. 26, 2011, eff. Dec. 1, 2011.)

ADVISORY COMMITTEE NOTES

1972 Proposed Rules

The hypothetical question has been the target of a great deal of criticism as encouraging partisan bias, affording an opportunity for summing up in the middle of the case, and as complex and time consuming. Ladd, Expert Testimony, 5 Vand.

L.Rev. 414, 426–427 (1952). While the rule allows counsel to make disclosure of the underlying facts or data as a preliminary to the giving of an expert opinion, if he chooses, the instances in which he is required to do so are reduced. This is true whether the expert bases his opinion on data furnished him at secondhand or observed by him at firsthand.

The elimination of the requirement of preliminary disclosure at the trial of underlying facts or data has a long background of support. In 1937 the Commissioners on Uniform State Laws incorporated a provision to this effect in their Model Expert Testimony Act, which furnished the basis for Uniform Rules 57 and 58. Rule 4515, N.Y. CPLR (McKinney 1963), provides:

"Unless the court orders otherwise, questions calling for the opinion of an expert witness need not be hypothetical in form, and the witness may state his opinion and reasons without first specifying the data upon which it is based. Upon cross-examination, he may be required to specify the data * * *."

See also California Evidence Code § 802; Kansas Code of Civil Procedure §§ 60–456, 60–457; New Jersey Evidence Rules 57, 58.

If the objection is made that leaving it to the cross-examiner to bring out the supporting data is essentially unfair, the answer is that he is under no compulsion to bring out any facts or data except those unfavorable to the opinion. The answer assumes that the cross-examiner has the advance knowledge which is essential for effective cross-examination. This advance knowledge has been afforded, though imperfectly, by the traditional foundation requirement. Rule 26(b)(4) of the Rules of Civil Procedure, as revised, provides for substantial discovery in this area, obviating in large measure the obstacles which have been raised in some instances to discovery of findings, underlying data, and even the identity of the experts. Friedenthal Discovery and Use of an Adverse Party's Expert Information, 14 Stan.L.Rev. 455 (1962).

These safeguards are reinforced by the discretionary power of the judge to require preliminary disclosure in any event.

1987 Amendment

The amendment is technical. No substantive change is intended.

1993 Amendment

This rule, which relates to the manner of presenting testimony at trial, is revised to avoid an arguable conflict with revised Rules 26(a)(2)(B) and 26(e)(1) of the Federal Rules of Civil Procedure or with revised Rule 16 of the Federal Rules of Criminal Procedure, which require disclosure in advance of trial of the basis and reasons for an expert's opinions.

If a serious question is raised under Rule 702 or 703 as to the admissibility of expert testimony, disclosure of the underlying facts or data on which opinions are based may, of course, be needed by the court before deciding whether, and to what extent, the person should be allowed to testify. This rule does not preclude such an inquiry.

2011 Amendments

The language of Rule 705 has been amended as part of the general restyling of the Evidence Rules to make them more easily understood and to make style and terminology consistent throughout the rules. These changes are intended to be stylistic only. There is no intent to change any result in any ruling on evidence admissibility.

The Committee deleted all reference to an "inference" on the grounds that the deletion made the Rule flow better and easier to read, and because any "inference" is covered by the broader term "opinion." Courts have not made substantive decisions on the basis of any distinction between an opinion and an inference. No change in current practice is intended.

Rule 706. Court–Appointed Expert Witnesses

(a) Appointment Process. On a party's motion or on its own, the court may order the parties to show cause why expert witnesses should not be appointed and may ask the parties to submit nominations. The court may appoint any expert that the parties agree on and any of its own choosing. But the court may only appoint someone who consents to act.

(b) Expert's Role. The court must inform the expert of the expert's duties. The court may do so in writing and have a copy filed with the clerk or may do so orally at a conference in which the parties have an opportunity to participate. The expert:

(1) must advise the parties of any findings the expert makes;

(2) may be deposed by any party;

(3) may be called to testify by the court or any party; and

(4) may be cross-examined by any party, including the party that called the expert.

(c) Compensation. The expert is entitled to a reasonable compensation, as set by the court. The compensation is payable as follows:

(1) in a criminal case or in a civil case involving just compensation under the Fifth Amendment, from any funds that are provided by law; and

(2) in any other civil case, by the parties in the proportion and at the time that the court directs—and the compensation is then charged like other costs.

(d) Disclosing the Appointment to the Jury. The court may authorize disclosure to the jury that the court appointed the expert.

(e) Parties' Choice of Their Own Experts. This rule does not limit a party in calling its own experts.

(Pub.L. 93–595, § 1, Jan. 2, 1975, 88 Stat.1938; Mar. 2, 1987, eff. Oct. 1, 1987; Apr. 26, 2011, eff. Dec. 1, 2011.)

ADVISORY COMMITTEE NOTES

1972 Proposed Rules

The practice of shopping for experts, the venality of some experts, and the reluctance of many reputable experts to involve themselves in litigation, have been matters of deep concern. Though the contention is made that court appointed experts acquire an aura of infallibility to which they are not entitled, Levy, Impartial Medical Testimony—Revisited, 34 Temple L.Q. 416 (1961), the trend is increasingly to provide for their use. While experience indicates that actual appointment is a relatively infrequent occurrence, the assumption may be made that the availability of the procedure in itself decreases the need for resorting to it. The ever-present possibility that the judge may appoint an expert in a given case must inevitably exert a sobering effect on the expert witness of a party and upon the person utilizing his services.

The inherent power of a trial judge to appoint an expert of his own choosing is virtually unquestioned. *Scott v. Spanjer Bros., Inc.,* 298 F.2d 928 (2d Cir.1962); *Danville Tobacco Assn. v. Bryant–Buckner Associates,* Inc., 333 F.2d 202 (4th Cir.1964); Sink, The Unused Power of a Federal Judge to Call His Own Expert Witnesses, 29 S.Cal.L.Rev. 195 (1956); 2 Wigmore § 563, 9 *id.* § 2484; Annot., 95 A.L.R.2d 383. Hence the problem becomes largely one of detail.

The New York plan is well known and is described in Report by Special Committee of the Association of the Bar of the City of New York: Impartial Medical Testimony (1956). On recommendation of the Section of Judicial Administration, local adoption of an impartial medical plan was endorsed by the American Bar Association. 82 A.B.A.Rep. 184–185 (1957). Descriptions and analyses of plans in effect in various parts of the country are found in Van Dusen, A United States District Judge's View of the Impartial Medical Expert System, 32 F.R.D. 498 (1963); Wick and Kightlinger, Impartial Medical Testimony Under the Federal Civil Rules: A Tale of Three Doctors, 34 Ins. Counsel J. 115 (1967); and numerous articles collected in Klein, Judicial Administration and the Legal Profession 393 (1963). Statutes and rules include California Evidence Code §§ 730–733; Illinois Supreme Court Rule 215(d), Ill.Rev.Stat.1969, c. 110A, § 215(d); Burns Indiana Stats.1956, § 9–1702; Wisconsin Stats.Annot.1958, § 957.27.

In the federal practice, a comprehensive scheme for court appointed experts was initiated with the adoption of Rule 28 of the Federal Rules of Criminal Procedure in 1946. The Judicial Conference of the United States in 1953 considered court appointed experts in civil cases, but only with respect to whether they should be compensated from public funds, a proposal which was rejected. Report of the Judicial Conference of the United States 23 (1953). The present rule expands the practice to include civil cases.

Note to Subdivision (a). Subdivision (a) is based on Rule 28 of the Federal Rules of Criminal Procedure, with a few changes, mainly in the interest of clarity. Language has been added to provide specifically for the appointment either on motion of a party or on the judge's own motion. A provision subjecting the court appointed expert to deposition procedures has been incorporated. The rule has been revised to make definite the right of any party, including the party calling him, to cross-examine.

Note to Subdivision (b). Subdivision (b) combines the present provision for compensation in criminal cases with what seems to be a fair and feasible handling of civil cases, originally found in the Model Act and carried from there into Uniform Rule 60. See also California Evidence Code §§ 730–731. The special provision for Fifth Amendment compensation cases is designed to guard against reducing constitutionally guaranteed just compensation by requiring the recipient to pay costs. See Rule 71A(*l*) of the Rules of Civil Procedure.

Note to Subdivision (c). Subdivision (c) seems to be essential if the use of court appointed experts is to be fully effective. Uniform Rule 61 so provides.

Note to Subdivision (d). Subdivision (d) is in essence the last sentence of Rule 28(a) of the Federal Rules of Criminal Procedure.

1987 Amendment

The amendments are technical. No substantive change is intended.

2011 Amendments

The language of Rule 706 has been amended as part of the restyling of the Evidence Rules to make them more easily understood and to make style and terminology consistent throughout the rules. These changes are intended to be stylistic only. There is no intent to change any result in any ruling on evidence admissibility.

ARTICLE VIII. HEARSAY

Rule

801. Definitions That Apply to This Article; Exclusions from Hearsay.
802. The Rule Against Hearsay.
803. Exceptions to the Rule Against Hearsay—Regardless of Whether the Declarant Is Available as a Witness.
804. Exceptions to the Rule Against Hearsay—When the Declarant Is Unavailable as a Witness.
805. Hearsay Within Hearsay.
806. Attacking and Supporting the Declarant's Credibility.
807. Residual Exception.

ADVISORY COMMITTEE NOTES

1972 Proposed Rules

Introductory Note; The Hearsay Problem. The factors to be considered in evaluating the testimony of a witness are perception, memory, and narration. Morgan, Hearsay Dangers and the Application of the Hearsay Concept, 62 Harv. L.Rev. 177 (1948), Selected Writings on Evidence and Trial 764, 765 (Fryer ed. 1957); Shientag, Cross–Examination—A Judge's Viewpoint, 3 Record 12 (1948); Strahorn, A Reconsideration of the Hearsay Rule and Admissions, 85 U.Pa.L.Rev. 484, 485 (1937), Selected Writings, *supra,* 756, 757; Weinstein, Probative Force of Hearsay, 46 Iowa L.Rev. 331 (1961). Sometimes a fourth is added, sincerity, but in fact it seems merely to be an aspect of the three already mentioned.

In order to encourage the witness to do his best with respect to each of these factors, and to expose any inaccuracies which may enter in, the Anglo–American tradition has evolved three conditions under which witnesses will ideally be required to testify: (1) under oath, (2) in the personal presence of the trier of fact, (3) subject to cross-examination.

(1) Standard procedure calls for the swearing of witnesses. While the practice is perhaps less effective than in an earlier time, no disposition to relax the requirement is apparent, other than to allow affirmation by persons with scruples against taking oaths.

(2) The demeanor of the witness traditionally has been believed to furnish trier and opponent with valuable clues. *Universal Camera Corp. v. N.L.R.B.,* 340 U.S. 474, 495–496, 71 S.Ct. 456, 95 L.Ed. 456 (1951); Sahm, Demeanor Evidence: Elusive and Intangible Imponderables, 47 A.B.A.J. 580 (1961), quoting numerous authorities. The witness himself will probably be impressed with the solemnity of the occasion and the possibility of public disgrace. Willingness to falsify may reasonably become more difficult in the presence of the person against whom directed. Rules 26 and 43(a) of the Federal Rules of Criminal and Civil Procedure, respectively, include the general requirement that testimony be taken orally in open court. The Sixth Amendment right of confrontation is a manifestation of these beliefs and attitudes.

(3) Emphasis on the basis of the hearsay rule today tends to center upon the condition of cross-examination. All may not agree with Wigmore that cross-examination is "beyond doubt the greatest legal engine ever invented for the discovery of truth," but all will agree with his statement that it has become a "vital feature" of the Anglo–American system. 5 Wigmore § 1367, p. 29. The belief, or perhaps hope, that cross-examination is effective in exposing imperfections of perception, memory, and narration is fundamental. Morgan, Foreword to Model Code of Evidence 37 (1942).

The logic of the preceding discussion might suggest that no testimony be received unless in full compliance with the three ideal conditions. No one advocates this position. Common sense tells that much evidence which is not given under the three conditions may be inherently superior to much that is. Moreover, when the choice is between evidence which is less than best and no evidence at all, only clear folly would dictate an across-the-board policy of doing without. The problem thus resolves itself into effecting a sensible accommodation between these considerations and the desirability of giving testimony under the ideal conditions.

The solution evolved by the common law has been a general rule excluding hearsay but subject to numerous exceptions under circumstances supposed to furnish guarantees of trustworthiness. Criticisms of this scheme are that it is bulky and complex, fails to screen good from bad hearsay realistically, and inhibits the growth of the law of evidence.

Since no one advocates excluding all hearsay, three possible solutions may be considered: (1) abolish the rule against hearsay and admit all hearsay; (2) admit hearsay possessing sufficient probative force, but with procedural safeguards; (3) revise the present system of class exceptions.

(1) Abolition of the hearsay rule would be the simplest solution. The effect would not be automatically to abolish the giving of testimony under ideal conditions. If the declarant were available, compliance with the ideal conditions would be optional with either party. Thus the proponent could call the declarant as a witness as a form of presentation more impressive than his hearsay statement. Or the opponent could call the declarant to be cross-examined upon his statement. This is the tenor of Uniform Rule 63(1), admitting the hearsay declaration of a person "who is present at the hearing and available for cross-examination." Compare the treatment of declarations of available declarants in Rule 801(d)(1) of the instant rules. If the declarant were unavailable, a rule of free admissibility would make no distinctions in terms of degrees of noncompliance with the ideal conditions and would exact no quid pro quo in the form of assurances of trustworthiness. Rule 503 of the Model Code did exactly that, providing for the admissibility of any hearsay declaration by an unavailable declarant, finding support in the Massachusetts act of 1898, enacted at the instance of Thayer, Mass.Gen.L.1932, c. 233, § 65, and in the English act of 1938, St.1938, c. 28, Evidence. Both are limited to civil cases. The draftsmen of the Uniform Rules chose a less advanced and more conventional position. Comment, Uniform Rule 63. The present Advisory Committee has been unconvinced of the wisdom of abandoning the traditional requirement of some particular assurance of credibility as a condition precedent to admitting the hearsay declaration of an unavailable declarant.

In criminal cases, the Sixth Amendment requirement of confrontation would no doubt move into a large part of the area presently occupied by the hearsay rule in the event of the abolition of the latter. The resultant split between civil and criminal evidence is regarded as an undesirable development.

(2) Abandonment of the system of class exceptions in favor of individual treatment in the setting of the particular case, accompanied by procedural safeguards, has been impressively advocated. Weinstein, The Probative Force of Hearsay, 46 Iowa L.Rev. 331 (1961). Admissibility would be determined by weighing the probative force of the evidence against the possibility of prejudice, waste of time, and the availability of more satisfactory evidence. The bases of the traditional hearsay exceptions would be helpful in assessing probative force. Ladd, The Relationship of the Principles of Exclusionary Rules of Evidence to the Problem of Proof, 18 Minn.L.Rev. 506 (1934). Procedural safeguards would consist of notice of intention to use hearsay, free comment by the judge on the weight of the evidence, and a greater measure of authority in both trial and appellate judges to deal with evidence on the basis of weight. The Advisory Committee has rejected this approach to hearsay as involving too great a measure of judicial discretion, minimizing the predictability of rulings, enhancing the difficulties of preparation for trial, adding a further element to the already over-complicated congeries of pretrial procedures, and requiring substantially different rules for civil and criminal cases. The only way in which the probative force of hearsay differs from the probative force of other testimony is in the absence of oath, demeanor, and cross-examination as aids in determining credibility. For a judge to exclude evidence because he does not believe it has been described as "altogether atypical, extraordinary. * * *" Chadbourn, Bentham and the Hearsay Rule—A Benthamic View of Rule 63(4)(c) of the Uniform Rules of Evidence, 75 Harv.L.Rev. 932, 947 (1962).

(3) The approach to hearsay in these rules is that of the common law, i.e., a general rule excluding hearsay, with exceptions under which evidence is not required to be excluded even though hearsay. The traditional hearsay exceptions are drawn upon for the exceptions, collected under two rules, one dealing with situations where availability of the declarant is regarded as immaterial and the other with those where unavailability is made a condition to the admission of the hearsay statement. Each of the two rules concludes with a provision for hearsay statements not within one of the specified exceptions "but having comparable circumstantial guarantees of trustworthiness." Rules 803(24) and 804(b)(6). This plan is submitted as calculated to encourage growth and development in this area of the law, while conserving the values and experience of the past as a guide to the future.

Confrontation and Due Process. Until very recently, decisions invoking the confrontation clause of the Sixth Amendment were surprisingly few, a fact probably explainable by the former inapplicability of the clause to the states and by the hearsay rule's occupancy of much the same ground. The pattern which emerges from the earlier cases invoking the clause is substantially that of the hearsay rule, applied to criminal cases: an accused is entitled to have the witnesses against him testify under oath, in the presence of himself and trier, subject to cross-examination; yet considerations of public policy and necessity require the recognition of such exceptions as dying declarations and former testimony of unavailable witnesses. *Mattox v. United States,* 156 U.S. 237, 15 S.Ct. 337, 39 L.Ed. 409 (1895); *Motes v. United States,* 178 U.S. 458, 20 S.Ct. 993, 44 L.Ed. 1150 (1900); *Delaney v. United States,* 263 U.S. 586, 44 S.Ct. 206, 68 L.Ed. 462 (1924). Beginning with *Snyder v. Massachusetts,* 291 U.S. 97, 54 S.Ct. 330, 78 L.Ed. 674 (1934), the Court began to speak of confrontation as an aspect of procedural due process, thus extending its applicability to state cases and to federal cases other than criminal. The language of *Snyder* was that of an elastic concept of hearsay. The deportation case of *Bridges v. Wixon,* 326 U.S. 135, 65 S.Ct. 1443, 89 L.Ed. 2103 (1945), may be read broadly as imposing a strictly construed right of confrontation in all kinds of cases or narrowly as the product of a failure of the Immigration and Naturalization Service to follow its own rules. *In re Oliver,* 333 U.S. 257, 68 S.Ct. 499, 92 L.Ed. 682 (1948), ruled that cross-examination was essential to due process in a state contempt proceeding, but in *United States v. Nugent,* 346 U.S. 1, 73 S.Ct. 991, 97 L.Ed. 1417 (1953), the court held that it was not an essential aspect of a "hearing" for a conscientious objector under the Selective Service Act. *Stein v. New York,* 346 U.S. 156, 196, 73 S.Ct. 1077, 97 L.Ed. 1522 (1953), disclaimed any purpose to read the hearsay rule into the Fourteenth Amendment, but in *Greene v. McElroy,* 360 U.S. 474, 79 S.Ct. 1400, 3 L.Ed.2d 1377 (1959), revocation of security clearance without confrontation and cross-examination was held unauthorized, and a similar result was reached in *Willner v. Committee on Character,* 373 U.S. 96, 83 S.Ct. 1175, 10 L.Ed.2d 224 (1963). Ascertaining the constitutional dimensions of the confrontation-hearsay aggregate against the background of these cases is a matter of some difficulty, yet the general pattern is at least not inconsistent with that of the hearsay rule.

In 1965 the confrontation clause was held applicable to the states. *Pointer v. Texas,* 380 U.S. 400, 85 S.Ct. 1065, 13 L.Ed.2d 923 (1965). Prosecution use of former testimony given at a preliminary hearing where petitioner was not represented by counsel was a violation of the clause. The same result would have followed under conventional hearsay doctrine read in the light of a constitutional right to counsel, and nothing in the opinion suggests any difference in essential outline between the hearsay rule and the right of confrontation. In the companion case of *Douglas v. Alabama,* 380 U.S. 415, 85 S.Ct. 1074, 13 L.Ed.2d 934 (1965), however, the result reached by applying the confrontation clause is one reached less readily via the hearsay rule. A confession implicating petitioner was put before the jury by reading it to the witness in portions and asking if he made that statement. The witness refused to answer on grounds of self-incrimination. The result, said the Court, was to deny cross-examination, and hence confrontation. True, it could broadly be said that the confession was a hearsay statement which for all practical purposes was put in evidence. Yet a more easily accepted explanation of the opinion is that its real thrust was in the direction of curbing undesirable prosecutorial behavior, rather than merely applying rules of exclusion, and that the confrontation clause was the means selected to achieve this end. Comparable facts and a like result appeared in *Brookhart v. Janis,* 384 U.S. 1, 86 S.Ct. 1245, 16 L.Ed.2d 314 (1966).

The pattern suggested in *Douglas* was developed further and more distinctly in a pair of cases at the end of the 1966 term. *United States v. Wade,* 388 U.S. 218, 87 S.Ct. 1926, 18 L.Ed.2d 1149 (1967), and *Gilbert v. California,* 388 U.S. 263, 87 S.Ct. 1951, 18 L.Ed.2d 1178 (1967), hinged upon practices followed in identifying accused persons before trial. This pretrial identification was said to be so decisive an aspect of the case that accused was entitled to have counsel present; a pretrial identification made in the absence of counsel was not itself receivable in evidence and, in addition, might fatally infect a courtroom identification. The presence of counsel at the earlier identification was described as a necessary prerequisite for "a meaningful confrontation at trial." *United States v. Wade, supra,* 388 U.S. at p. 236, 87 S.Ct. at p. 1937. *Wade* involved no evidence of the fact of a prior identification and hence was not susceptible of being decided on hearsay grounds. In *Gilbert,* witnesses did testify to an earlier identification, readily classifiable as hearsay under a fairly strict view of what constitutes hearsay. The Court, however, carefully avoided basing the decision on the hearsay ground, choosing confrontation instead. 388 U.S. 263, 272, n. 3, 87 S.Ct. 1951. See also *Parker v. Gladden,* 385 U.S. 363, 87 S.Ct. 468, 17 L.Ed.2d 420 (1966), holding that the right of confrontation was violated when the bailiff made prejudicial statements to jurors, and Note, 75 Yale L.J. 1434 (1966).

Under the earlier cases, the confrontation clause may have been little more than a constitutional embodiment of the hearsay rule, even including traditional exceptions but with some room for expanding them along similar lines. But under the recent cases the impact of the clause clearly extends beyond the confines of the hearsay rule. These considerations have led the Advisory Committee to conclude that a hearsay rule can function usefully as an adjunct to the confrontation right in constitutional areas and independently in nonconstitutional areas. In recognition of the separateness of the confrontation clause and the hearsay rule, and to avoid inviting collisions between them or between the hearsay rule and other exclusionary principles, the exceptions set forth in Rules 803 and 804 are stated in terms of exemption from the general exclusionary mandate of the hearsay rule, rather than in positive terms of admissibility. See Uniform Rule 63(1) to (31) and California Evidence Code §§ 1200–1340.

Rule 801. Definitions That Apply to This Article; Exclusions from Hearsay

(a) Statement. "Statement" means a person's oral assertion, written assertion, or nonverbal conduct, if the person intended it as an assertion.

(b) Declarant. "Declarant" means the person who made the statement.

(c) Hearsay. "Hearsay" means a statement that:

(1) the declarant does not make while testifying at the current trial or hearing; and

(2) a party offers in evidence to prove the truth of the matter asserted in the statement.

(d) Statements That Are Not Hearsay. A statement that meets the following conditions is not hearsay:

(1) A Declarant–Witness's Prior Statement. The declarant testifies and is subject to cross-examination about a prior statement, and the statement:

(A) is inconsistent with the declarant's testimony and was given under penalty of perjury at a trial, hearing, or other proceeding or in a deposition;

(B) is consistent with the declarant's testimony and is offered to rebut an express or implied charge that the declarant recently fabricated it or acted from a recent improper influence or motive in so testifying; or

(C) identifies a person as someone the declarant perceived earlier.

(2) An Opposing Party's Statement. The statement is offered against an opposing party and:

(A) was made by the party in an individual or representative capacity;

(B) is one the party manifested that it adopted or believed to be true;

(C) was made by a person whom the party authorized to make a statement on the subject;

(D) was made by the party's agent or employee on a matter within the scope of that relationship and while it existed; or

(E) was made by the party's coconspirator during and in furtherance of the conspiracy.

The statement must be considered but does not by itself establish the declarant's authority under (C); the existence or scope of the relationship under (D); or the existence of the conspiracy or participation in it under (E).

(Pub.L. 93–595, § 1, Jan. 2, 1975, 88 Stat.1938; Pub.L. 94–113, § 1, Oct. 16, 1975, 89 Stat. 576; Mar. 2, 1987, eff. Oct. 1, 1987; Apr. 11, 1997, eff. Dec. 1, 1997; Apr. 26, 2011, eff. Dec. 1, 2011.)

ADVISORY COMMITTEE NOTES

1972 Proposed Rules

Note to Subdivision (a). The definition of "statement" assumes importance because the term is used in the definition of hearsay in subdivision (c). The effect of the definition of "statement" is to exclude from the operation of the hearsay rule all evidence of conduct, verbal or nonverbal, not intended as an assertion. The key to the definition is that nothing is an assertion unless intended to be one.

It can scarcely be doubted that an assertion made in words is intended by the declarant to be an assertion. Hence verbal assertions readily fall into the category of "statement." Whether nonverbal conduct should be regarded as a statement for purposes of defining hearsay requires further consideration. Some nonverbal conduct, such as the act of pointing to identify a suspect in a lineup, is clearly the equivalent of words, assertive in nature, and to be regarded as a statement. Other nonverbal conduct, however, may be offered as evidence that the person acted as he did because of his belief in the existence of the condition sought to be proved, from which belief the existence of the condition may be inferred. This sequence is, arguably, in effect an assertion of the existence of the condition and hence properly includable within the hearsay concept. See Morgan, Hearsay Dangers and the Application of the Hearsay Concept, 62 Harv.L.Rev. 177, 214, 217 (1948), and the elaboration in Finman, Implied Assertions as Hearsay: Some Criticisms of the Uniform Rules of Evidence, 14 Stan.L.Rev. 682 (1962). Admittedly evidence of this character is untested with respect to the perception, memory, and narration (or their equivalents) of the actor, but the Advisory Committee is of the view that these dangers are minimal in the absence of an intent to assert and do not justify the loss of the evidence on hearsay grounds. No class of evidence is free of the possibility of fabrication, but the likelihood is less with nonverbal than with assertive verbal conduct. The situations giving rise to the nonverbal conduct are such as virtually to eliminate questions of sincerity. Motivation, the nature of the conduct, and the presence or absence of reliance will bear heavily upon the weight to be given the evidence. Falknor, The "Hear-Say" Rule as a "See-Do" Rule: Evidence of Conduct, 33 Rocky Mt.L.Rev. 133 (1961). Similar considerations govern nonassertive verbal conduct and verbal conduct which is assertive but offered as a basis for inferring something other than the matter asserted, also excluded from the definition of hearsay by the language of subdivision (c).

When evidence of conduct is offered on the theory that it is not a statement, and hence not hearsay, a preliminary determination will be required to determine whether an assertion is intended. The rule is so worded as to place the burden upon the party claiming that the intention existed; ambiguous and doubtful cases will be resolved against him and in favor of admissibility. The determination involves no greater difficulty than many other preliminary questions of fact. Maguire, The Hearsay System: Around and Through the Thicket, 14 Vand.L.Rev. 741, 765–767 (1961).

For similar approaches, see Uniform Rule 62(1); California Evidence Code §§ 225, 1200; Kansas Code of Civil Procedure § 60–459(a); New Jersey Evidence Rule 62(1).

Note to Subdivision (c). The definition follows along familiar lines in including only statements offered to prove the truth of the matter asserted. McCormick § 225; 5 Wigmore § 1361, 6 *id.* § 1766. If the significance of an offered statement lies solely in the fact that it was made, no issue is raised as to the truth of anything asserted, and the statement is not hearsay. *Emich Motors Corp. v. General Motors Corp.,* 181 F.2d 70 (7th Cir.1950), rev'd on other grounds 340 U.S. 558, 71 S.Ct. 408, 95 L.Ed. 534, letters of complaint from customers offered as a reason for cancellation of dealer's franchise, to rebut contention that franchise was revoked for refusal to finance sales through affiliated finance company. The effect is to exclude from hearsay the entire category of "verbal acts" and "verbal parts of an act," in which the statement itself affects the legal rights of the parties or is a circumstance bearing on conduct affecting their rights.

The definition of hearsay must, of course, be read with reference to the definition of statement set forth in subdivision (a).

Testimony given by a witness in the course of court proceedings is excluded since there is compliance with all the ideal conditions for testifying.

Note to Subdivision (d). Several types of statements which would otherwise literally fall within the definition are expressly excluded from it:

(1) *Prior statement by witness.* Considerable controversy has attended the question whether a prior out-of-court statement by a person now available for cross-examination concerning it, under oath and in the presence of the trier of fact, should be classed as hearsay. If the witness admits on the stand that he made the statement and that it was true, he adopts the statement and there is no hearsay problem. The hearsay problem arises when the witness on the stand denies having made the statement or admits having made it but denies its truth. The argument in favor of treating these latter statements as hearsay is based upon the ground that the conditions of oath, cross-examination, and demeanor observation did not prevail at the time the statement was made and cannot adequately be supplied by the later examination. The logic of the situation is troublesome. So far as concerns the oath, its mere presence has never been regarded as sufficient to remove a statement from the hearsay category, and it receives much less emphasis than cross-examination as a truth-compelling device. While strong expressions are found to the effect that no conviction can be had or important right taken away on the basis of statements not made under fear of prosecution for perjury, *Bridges v. Wixon,* 326 U.S. 135, 65 S.Ct. 1443, 89 L.Ed. 2103 (1945), the fact is that, of the many common law exceptions to the hearsay rule, only that for reported testimony has required the statement to have been made under oath. Nor is it satisfactorily explained why cross-examination cannot be conducted subsequently with success. The decisions contending most vigorously for its inadequacy in fact demonstrate quite thorough exploration of the weaknesses and doubts attending the earlier statement. *State v. Saporen,* 205 Minn. 358, 285 N.W. 898 (1939); *Ruhala v. Roby,* 379 Mich. 102, 150 N.W.2d 146 (1967); *People v. Johnson,* 68 Cal.2d 646, 68 Cal.Rptr. 599, 441 P.2d 111 (1968). In respect to demeanor, as Judge Learned Hand observed in *Di Carlo v. United States,* 6 F.2d 364 (2d Cir.1925), when the jury decides that the truth is not what the witness says now, but what he said before, they are still deciding from what they see and hear in court. The bulk of the case law nevertheless has been against allowing prior statements of witnesses to be used generally as substantive evidence. Most of the writers and Uniform Rule 63(1) have taken the opposite position.

The position taken by the Advisory Committee in formulating this part of the rule is funded upon an unwillingness to countenance the general use of prior prepared statements as substantive evidence, but with a recognition that particular circumstances call for a contrary result. The judgment is one more of experience than of logic. The rule requires in each instance, as a general safeguard, that the declarant actually testify as a witness, and it then enumerates three situations in which the statement is excepted from the category of hearsay. Compare Uniform Rule 63(1) which allows any out-of-court statement of a declarant who is present at the trial and available for cross-examination.

(A) Prior inconsistent statements traditionally have been admissible to impeach but not as substantive evidence. Under the rule they are substantive evidence. As has been said by the California Law Revision Commission with respect to a similar provision:

"Section 1235 admits inconsistent statements of witnesses because the dangers against which the hearsay rule is designed to protect are largely nonexistent. The declarant is in court and may be examined and cross-examined in regard to his statements and their subject matter. In many cases, the inconsistent statement is more likely to be true than the testimony of the witness at the trial because it was made nearer in time to the matter to which it relates and is less likely to be influenced by the controversy that gave rise to the litigation. The trier of fact has the declarant before it and can observe his demeanor and the nature of his testimony as he denies or tries to explain away the inconsistency. Hence, it is in as good a position to determine the truth or falsity of the prior statement as it is to determine the truth or falsity of the inconsistent testimony given in court. Moreover, Section 1235 will provide a party with desirable protection against the 'turncoat' witness who changes his story on the stand and deprives the party calling him of evidence essential to his case." Comment, California Evidence Code § 1235. See also McCormick § 39. The Advisory Committee finds these views more convincing than those expressed in *People v. Johnson,* 68 Cal.2d 646, 68 Cal.Rptr. 599, 441 P.2d 111 (1968). The constitutionality of the Advisory Committee's view was upheld in *California v. Green,* 399 U.S. 149, 90 S.Ct. 1930, 26 L.Ed.2d 489 (1970). Moreover, the requirement that the statement be inconsistent with the testimony given assures a thorough exploration of both versions while the witness is on the stand and bars any general and indiscriminate use of previously prepared statements.

(B) Prior consistent statements traditionally have been admissible to rebut charges of recent fabrication or improper influence or motive but not as substantive evidence. Under the rule they are substantive evidence. The prior statement is consistent with the testimony given on the stand, and, if the opposite party wishes to open the door for its admission in evidence, no sound reason is apparent why it should not be received generally.

(C) The admission of evidence of identification finds substantial support, although it falls beyond a doubt in the category of prior out-of-court statements. Illustrative are *People v. Gould,* 54 Cal.2d 621, 7 Cal.Rptr. 273, 354 P.2d 865 (1960); *Judy v. State,* 218 Md. 168, 146 A.2d 29 (1958); *State v. Simmons,* 63 Wash.2d 17, 385 P.2d 389 (1963); California Evidence Code § 1238; New Jersey Evidence Rule 63(1)(c); N.Y.Code of Criminal Procedure § 393–b. Further cases are found in 4 Wigmore § 1130. The basis is the generally unsatisfactory and inconclusive nature of courtroom identifications as compared with those made at an earlier time under less suggestive conditions. The Supreme Court considered the admissibility of evidence of prior identification in *Gilbert v. California,* 388 U.S. 263, 87 S.Ct. 1951, 18 L.Ed.2d 1178 (1967). Exclusion of lineup identification was held to be required because the accused did not then have the assistance of counsel. Significantly, the Court carefully refrained from placing its decision on the ground that testimony as to the making of a prior out-of-court identification ("That's the man") violated either the hearsay rule or the right of confrontation because not made under oath, subject to immediate cross-examination, in the presence of the trier. Instead the Court observed:

"There is a split among the States concerning the admissibility of prior extra-judicial identifications, as independent evidence of identity, both by the witness and third parties present at the prior identification. See 71 ALR2d 449. It has been held that the prior identification is hearsay, and, when admitted through the testimony of the identifier, is merely a prior consistent statement. The recent trend, however, is to admit the prior identification under the exception that admits as substantive evidence a prior communication by a witness who is available for cross-examination at the trial. See 5 ALR2d Later Case Service 1225–1228. * * * " 388 U.S. at 272, n. 3, 87 S.Ct. at 1956.

(2) *Admissions.* Admissions by a party-opponent are excluded from the category of hearsay on the theory that their admissibility in evidence is the result of the adversary system rather than satisfaction of the conditions of the hearsay rule. Strahorn, A Reconsideration of the Hearsay Rule and Admissions, 85 U.Pa.L.Rev. 484, 564 (1937); Morgan, Basic Problems of Evidence 265 (1962); 4 Wigmore § 1048. No guarantee of trustworthiness is required in the case of an admission. The freedom which admissions have enjoyed from technical demands of searching for an assurance of truthworthiness in some against-interest circumstance, and from the restrictive influences of the opinion rule and the rule requiring firsthand knowledge, when taken with the apparently prevalent satisfaction with the results, calls for generous treatment of this avenue to admissibility.

The rule specifies five categories of statements for which the responsibility of a party is considered sufficient to justify reception in evidence against him:

(A) A party's own statement is the classic example of an admission. If he has a representative capacity and the statement is offered against him in that capacity, no inquiry whether he was acting in the representative capacity in making the statement is required; the statement need only be relevant to represent affairs. To the same effect in California Evidence Code § 1220. Compare Uniform Rule 63(7), requiring a statement to be made in a representative capacity to be admissible against a party in a representative capacity.

(B) Under established principles an admission may be made by adopting or acquiescing in the statement of another. While knowledge of contents would ordinarily be essential, this is not inevitably so: "X is a reliable person and knows what he is talking about." See McCormick § 246, p. 527, n. 15. Adoption or acquiescence may be manifested in any appropriate manner. When silence is relied upon, the theory is that the person would, under the circumstances, protest the statement made in his presence, if untrue. The decision in each case calls for an evaluation in terms of probable human behavior. In civil cases, the results have generally been satisfactory. In criminal cases, however, troublesome questions have been raised by decisions holding that failure to deny is an admission: the inference is a fairly weak one, to begin with; silence may be motivated by advice of counsel or realization that "anything you say may be used against you"; unusual opportunity is afforded to manufacture evidence; and encroachment upon the privilege against self-incrimination seems inescapably to be involved. However, recent decisions of the Supreme Court relating to custodial interrogation and the right to counsel appear to resolve these difficulties. Hence the rule contains no special provisions concerning failure to deny in criminal cases.

(C) No authority is required for the general proposition that a statement authorized by a party to be made should have the status of an admission by the party. However, the question arises whether only statements to third persons should be so regarded, to the exclusion of statements by the agent to the principal. The rule is phrased broadly so as to encompass both. While it may be argued that the agent authorized to make statements to his principal does not speak for him, Morgan, Basic Problems of Evidence 273 (1962), communication to an outsider has not generally been thought to be an essential characteristic of an admission. Thus a party's books or records are usable against him, without regard to any intent to disclose to third persons. 5 Wigmore § 1557. See also McCormick § 78, pp. 159–161. In accord is New Jersey Evidence Rule 63(8)(a). Cf. Uniform Rule 63(8)(a) and California Evidence Code § 1222 which limit status as an admission in this regard to statements authorized by the party to be made "for" him, which is perhaps an ambiguous limitation to statements to third persons. Falknor, Vicarious Admissions and the Uniform Rules, 14 Vand.L.Rev. 855, 860–861 (1961).

(D) The tradition has been to test the admissibility of statements by agents, as admissions, by applying the usual test of agency. Was the admission made by the agent acting in the scope of his employment? Since few principals employ agents for the purpose of making damaging statements, the usual result was exclusion of the statement. Dissatisfaction with this loss of valuable and helpful evidence has been increasing. A substantial trend favors admitting statements related to a matter within the scope of the agency or employment. *Grayson v. Williams,* 256 F.2d 61 (10th Cir.1958); *Koninklijke Luchtvaart Maatschappij N.V. KLM Royal Dutch Airlines v. Tuller,* 110 U.S.App.D.C. 282, 292 F.2d 775, 784 (1961); *Martin v. Savage Truck Lines,* Inc., 121 F.Supp. 417 (D.D.C.1954), and numerous state court decisions collected in 4 Wigmore, 1964 Supp. pp. 66–73, with comments by the editor that the statements should have been excluded as not within scope of agency. For the traditional view see *Northern Oil Co. v. Socony Mobil Oil Co.,* 347 F.2d 81, 85 (2d Cir.1965) and cases cited therein. Similar provisions are found in Uniform Rule 63(9)(a), Kansas Code of Civil Procedure § 60–460(i)(1), and New Jersey Evidence Rule 63(9)(a).

(E) The limitation upon the admissibility of statements of co-conspirators to those made "during the course and in furtherance of the conspiracy" is in the accepted pattern. While the broadened view of agency taken in item (iv) might suggest wider admissibility of statements of co-conspirators, the agency theory of conspiracy is at best a fiction and ought not to serve as a basis for admissibility beyond that already established. See Levie, Hearsay and Conspiracy, 52 Mich. L.Rev. 1159 (1954); Comment, 25 U.Chi.L.Rev. 530 (1958). The rule is consistent with the position of the Supreme Court in denying admissibility to statements made after the objectives of the conspiracy have either failed or been achieved. *Krulewitch v. United States,* 336 U.S. 440, 69 S.Ct. 716, 93 L.Ed. 790 (1949); *Wong Sun v. United States,* 371 U.S. 471, 490, 83 S.Ct. 407, 9 L.Ed.2d 441 (1963). For similarly limited provisions see California Evidence Code § 1223 and New Jersey Rule 63(9)(b). Cf. Uniform Rule 63(9)(b).

1974 Enactment

Note to Subdivision (d)(1). Present federal law, except in the Second Circuit, permits the use of prior inconsistent statements of a witness for impeachment only. Rule 801(d)(1) as proposed by the Court would have permitted all such statements to be admissible as substantive evidence, an approach followed by a small but growing number of State jurisdictions and recently held constitutional in California v. Green, 399 U.S. 149 (1970). Although there was some support expressed for the Court Rule, based largely on the need to counteract the effect of witness intimidation in criminal cases, the Committee decided to adopt a compromise version of the Rule similar to the position of the Second Circuit. The Rule as amended draws a distinction between types of prior inconsistent statements (other than statements of identification of a person made after perceiving him which are currently admissible, see United States v. Anderson, 406 F.2d 719, 720 (4th Cir.), cert. denied, 395 U.S. 967 (1969)) and allows only those made while the declarant was subject to cross-examination at a trial or hearing or in a deposition, to be admissible for their truth. Compare United States v. DeSisto, 329 F.2d 929 (2nd Cir.), cert. denied, 377 U.S. 979 (1964); United States v. Cunningham, 446 F.2d 194 (2nd Cir.1971) (restricting the admissibility of prior inconsistent statements as substantive evidence to those made under oath in a formal proceeding, but not requiring that there have been an opportunity for cross-examination). The rationale for the Committee's decision is that (1) unlike in most other situations involving unsworn or oral statements, there can be no dispute as to whether the prior statement was made; and (2) the context of a formal proceeding, an oath, and the opportunity for cross-examination provide firm additional assurances of the reliability of the prior statement. House Report No. 93–650.

Note to Subdivision (d)(1)(A). Rule 801 defines what is and what is not hearsay for the purpose of admitting a prior statement as substantive evidence. A prior statement of a witness at a trial or hearing which is inconsistent with his testimony is, of course, always admissible for the purpose of impeaching the witness' credibility.

As submitted by the Supreme Court, subdivision (d)(1)(A) made admissible as substantive evidence the prior statement of a witness inconsistent with his present testimony.

The House severely limited the admissibility of prior inconsistent statements by adding a requirement that the prior statement must have been subject to cross-examination, thus precluding even the use of grand jury statements. The requirement that the prior statement must have been subject to cross-examination appears unnecessary since this rule comes into play only when the witness testifies in the present trial. At that time, he is on the stand and can explain an earlier position and be cross-examined as to both.

The requirement that the statement be under oath also appears unnecessary. Notwithstanding the absence of an oath contemporaneous with the statement, the witness, when on the stand, qualifying or denying the prior statement, is under oath. In any event, of all the many recognized exceptions to the hearsay rule, only one (former testimony) requires that the out-of-court statement have been made under oath. With respect to the lack of evidence of the demeanor of the witness at the time of the prior statement, it would be difficult to improve upon Judge Learned Hand's observation that when the jury decides that the truth is not what the witness says now but what he said before, they are still deciding from what they see and hear in court. [*Di Carlo v. U.S.,* 6 F.2d 364 (2d Cir.1925)].

The rule as submitted by the Court has positive advantages. The prior statement was made nearer in time to the events, when memory was fresher and intervening influences had not been brought into play. A realistic method is provided for dealing with the turncoat witness who changes his story on the stand [see Comment, California Evidence Code § 1235; McCormick, Evidence, § 38 (2nd ed. 1972)].

New Jersey, California, and Utah have adopted a rule similar to this one; and Nevada, New Mexico, and Wisconsin have adopted the identical Federal rule.

For all of these reasons, we think the House amendment should be rejected and the rule as submitted by the Supreme Court reinstated. [It would appear that some of the opposition to this Rule is based on a concern that a person could be convicted solely upon evidence admissible under this Rule. The Rule, however, is not addressed to the question of the sufficiency of evidence to send a case to the jury, but merely as to its admissibility. Factual circumstances could well arise where, if this were the sole evidence, dismissal would be appropriate.]

Note to Subdivision (d)(1)(C). As submitted by the Supreme Court and as passed by the House, subdivision (d)(1)(C) of rule 801 made admissible the prior statement identifying a person made after perceiving him. The committee decided to delete this provision because of the concern that a person could be convicted solely upon evidence admissible under this subdivision.

Note to Subdivision 801(d)(2)(E). The House approved the long-accepted rule that "a statement by a coconspirator of a party during the course and in furtherance of the conspiracy" is not hearsay as it was submitted by the Supreme Court. While the rule refers to a coconspirator, it is this committee's understanding that the rule is meant to carry forward the universally accepted doctrine that a joint venturer is considered as a coconspirator for the purposes of this rule even though no conspiracy has been charged. *United States v. Rinaldi,* 393 F.2d 97, 99 (2d Cir.), cert. denied 393 U.S. 913 (1968); *United States v. Spencer,* 415 F.2d 1301, 1304 (7th Cir., 1969). Senate Report No. 93–1277.

Rule 801 supplies some basic definitions for the rules of evidence that deal with hearsay. Rule 801(d)(1) defines certain statements as not hearsay. The Senate amendments make two changes in it.

Note to Subdivision (d)(1)(A). The House bill provides that a statement is not hearsay if the declarant testifies and is subject to cross-examination concerning the statement and if the statement is inconsistent with his testimony and was given under oath subject to cross-examination and subject to the penalty of perjury at a trial or hearing or in a deposition. The Senate amendment drops the requirement that the prior statement be given under oath subject to cross-examination and subject to the penalty of perjury at a trial or hearing or in a deposition.

The Conference adopts the Senate amendment with an amendment, so that the rule now requires that the prior inconsistent statement be given under oath subject to the penalty of perjury at a trial, hearing, or other proceeding, or in a deposition. The rule as adopted covers statements before a grand jury. Prior inconsistent statements may, of course, be used for impeaching the credibility of a witness. When the prior inconsistent statement is one made by a defendant in a criminal case, it is covered by Rule 801(d)(2).

Note to Subdivision (d)(1)(C). The House bill provides that a statement is not hearsay if the declarant testifies and is subject to cross-examination concerning the statement and the statement is one of identification of a person made after perceiving him. The Senate amendment eliminated this provision.

The Conference adopts the Senate amendment. House Report No. 93–1597.

1987 Amendment

The amendments are technical. No substantive change is intended.

1997 Amendment

Rule 801(d)(2) has been amended in order to respond to three issues raised by *Bourjaily v. United States*, 483 U.S. 171 (1987). First, the amendment codifies the holding in *Bourjaily* by stating expressly that a court shall consider the contents of a coconspirator's statement in determining "the existence of the conspiracy and the participation therein of the declarant and the party against whom the statement is offered." According to *Bourjaily*, Rule 104(a) requires these preliminary questions to be established by a preponderance of the evidence.

Second, the amendment resolves an issue on which the Court had reserved decision. It provides that the contents of the declarant's statement do not alone suffice to establish a conspiracy in which the declarant and the defendant participated. The court must consider in addition the circumstances surrounding the statement, such as the identity of the speaker, the context in which the statement was made, or evidence corroborating the contents of the statement in making its determination as to each preliminary question. This amendment is in accordance with existing practice. Every court of appeals that has resolved this issue requires some evidence in addition to the contents of the statement. *See, e.g.*, *United States v. Beckham*, 968 F.2d 47, 51 (D.C.Cir.1992); *United States v. Sepulveda*, 15 F.3d 1161, 1181–82 (1st Cir.1993), *cert. denied*, 114 S.Ct. 2714 (1994); *United States v. Daly*, 842 F.2d 1380, 1386 (2d Cir.), *cert. denied*, 488 U.S. 821 (1988); *United States v. Clark*, 18 F.3d 1337, 1341–42 (6th Cir.), *cert. denied*, 115 S.Ct. 152 (1994); *United States v. Zambrana*, 841 F.2d 1320, 1344–45 (7th Cir.1988); *United States v. Silverman*, 861 F.2d 571, 577 (9th Cir.1988); *United States v. Gordon*, 844 F.2d 1397, 1402 (9th Cir.1988); *United States v. Hernandez*, 829 F.2d 988, 993 (10th Cir.1987), *cert. denied*, 485 U.S. 1013 (1988); *United States v. Byrom*, 910 F.2d 725, 736 (11th Cir.1990).

Third, the amendment extends the reasoning of Bourjaily to statements offered under subdivisions (C) and (D) of Rule 801(d)(2). In Bourjaily, the Court rejected treating foundational facts pursuant to the law of agency in favor of an evidentiary approach governed by Rule 104(a). The Advisory Committee believes it appropriate to treat analogously preliminary questions relating to the declarant's authority under subdivision (C), and the agency or employment relationship and scope thereof under subdivision (D).

GAP Report on Rule 801. The word "shall" was substituted for the word "may" in line 19. The second sentence of the committee note was changed accordingly.

2011 Amendments

The language of Rule 801 has been amended as part of the general restyling of the Evidence Rules to make them more easily understood and to make style and terminology consistent throughout the rules. These changes are intended to be stylistic only. There is no intent to change any result in any ruling on evidence admissibility.

Statements falling under the hearsay exclusion provided by Rule 801(d)(2) are no longer referred to as "admissions" in the title to the subdivision. The term "admissions" is confusing because not all statements covered by the exclusion are admissions in the colloquial sense—a statement can be within the exclusion even if it "admitted" nothing and was not against the party's interest when made. The term "admissions" also raises confusion in comparison with the Rule 804(b)(3) exception for declarations against interest. No change in application of the exclusion is intended.

HISTORICAL NOTES

For legislative history and purpose of Pub.L. 94–113, see 1975 U.S.Code Cong. and Adm.News, p. 1092.

Effective and Applicability Provisions

1975 Acts

Section 2 of Pub.L. 94–113 provided that: "This Act [enacting cl. (c) of subd. (d)] shall become effective on the fifteenth day after the date of the enactment of this Act [Oct. 16, 1975]."

Rule 802. The Rule Against Hearsay

Hearsay is not admissible unless any of the following provides otherwise:

- a federal statute;
- these rules; or
- other rules prescribed by the Supreme Court.

(Pub.L. 93–595, § 1, Jan. 2, 1975, 88 Stat. 1939; Apr. 26, 2011, eff. Dec. 1, 2011.)

ADVISORY COMMITTEE NOTES

1972 Proposed Rules

The provision excepting from the operation of the rule hearsay which is made admissible by other rules adopted by the Supreme Court or by Act of Congress continues the admissibility thereunder of hearsay which would not qualify under these Evidence Rules. The following examples illustrate the working of the exception:

Federal Rules of Civil Procedure

Rule 4(g): proof of service by affidavit.

Rule 32: admissibility of depositions.

Rule 43(e): affidavits when motion based on facts not appearing of record.

Rule 56: affidavits in summary judgment proceedings.

Rule 65(b): showing by affidavit for temporary restraining order.

Federal Rules of Criminal Procedure

Rule 4(a): affidavits to show grounds for issuing warrants.

Rule 12(b)(4): affidavits to determine issues of fact in connection with motions.

Acts of Congress

10 U.S.C. § 7730: affidavits of unavailable witnesses in actions for damages caused by vessel in naval service, or towage or salvage of same, when taking of testimony or bringing of action delayed or stayed on security grounds.

29 U.S.C. § 161(4): affidavit as proof of service in NLRB proceedings.

38 U.S.C. § 5206: affidavit as proof of posting notice of sale of unclaimed property by Veterans Administration.

2011 Amendments

The language of Rule 802 has been amended as part of the restyling of the Evidence Rules to make them more easily understood and to make style and terminology consistent throughout the rules. These changes are intended to be stylistic only. There is no intent to change any result in any ruling on evidence admissibility.

Rule 803. Exceptions to the Rule Against Hearsay—Regardless of Whether the Declarant Is Available as a Witness

The following are not excluded by the rule against hearsay, regardless of whether the declarant is available as a witness:

(1) Present Sense Impression. A statement describing or explaining an event or condition, made while or immediately after the declarant perceived it.

(2) Excited Utterance. A statement relating to a startling event or condition, made while the declarant was under the stress of excitement that it caused.

(3) Then–Existing Mental, Emotional, or Physical Condition. A statement of the declarant's then-existing state of mind (such as motive, intent, or plan) or emotional, sensory, or physical condition (such as mental feeling, pain, or bodily health), but not including a statement of memory or belief to prove the fact remembered or believed unless it relates to the validity or terms of the declarant's will.

(4) Statement Made for Medical Diagnosis or Treatment. A statement that:

(A) is made for—and is reasonably pertinent to—medical diagnosis or treatment; and

(B) describes medical history; past or present symptoms or sensations; their inception; or their general cause.

(5) Recorded Recollection. A record that:

(A) is on a matter the witness once knew about but now cannot recall well enough to testify fully and accurately;

(B) was made or adopted by the witness when the matter was fresh in the witness's memory; and

(C) accurately reflects the witness's knowledge.

If admitted, the record may be read into evidence but may be received as an exhibit only if offered by an adverse party.

(6) Records of a Regularly Conducted Activity. A record of an act, event, condition, opinion, or diagnosis if:

(A) the record was made at or near the time by—or from information transmitted by—someone with knowledge;

(B) the record was kept in the course of a regularly conducted activity of a business, organization, occupation, or calling, whether or not for profit;

(C) making the record was a regular practice of that activity;

(D) all these conditions are shown by the testimony of the custodian or another qualified witness, or by a certification that complies with Rule 902(11) or (12) or with a statute permitting certification; and

(E) neither the source of information nor the method or circumstances of preparation indicate a lack of trustworthiness.

(7) Absence of a Record of a Regularly Conducted Activity. Evidence that a matter is not included in a record described in paragraph (6) if:

(A) the evidence is admitted to prove that the matter did not occur or exist;

(B) a record was regularly kept for a matter of that kind; and

(C) neither the possible source of the information nor other circumstances indicate a lack of trustworthiness.

(8) Public Records. A record or statement of a public office if:

(A) it sets out:

(i) the office's activities;

(ii) a matter observed while under a legal duty to report, but not including, in a criminal case, a matter observed by law-enforcement personnel; or

(iii) in a civil case or against the government in a criminal case, factual findings from a legally authorized investigation; and

(B) neither the source of information nor other circumstances indicate a lack of trustworthiness.

(9) Public Records of Vital Statistics. A record of a birth, death, or marriage, if reported to a public office in accordance with a legal duty.

(10) Absence of a Public Record. Testimony—or a certification under Rule 902—that a diligent search failed to disclose a public record or statement if the testimony or certification is admitted to prove that:

(A) the record or statement does not exist; or

(B) a matter did not occur or exist, if a public office regularly kept a record or statement for a matter of that kind.

(11) Records of Religious Organizations Concerning Personal or Family History. A statement of birth, legitimacy, ancestry, marriage, divorce, death, relationship by blood or marriage, or similar facts of personal or family history, contained in a regularly kept record of a religious organization.

(12) Certificates of Marriage, Baptism, and Similar Ceremonies. A statement of fact contained in a certificate:

(A) made by a person who is authorized by a religious organization or by law to perform the act certified;

(B) attesting that the person performed a marriage or similar ceremony or administered a sacrament; and

(C) purporting to have been issued at the time of the act or within a reasonable time after it.

(13) Family Records. A statement of fact about personal or family history contained in a family record, such as a Bible, genealogy, chart, engraving on a ring, inscription on a portrait, or engraving on an urn or burial marker.

(14) Records of Documents That Affect an Interest in Property. The record of a document that purports to establish or affect an interest in property if:

(A) the record is admitted to prove the content of the original recorded document, along with its signing and its delivery by each person who purports to have signed it;

(B) the record is kept in a public office; and

(C) a statute authorizes recording documents of that kind in that office.

(15) Statements in Documents That Affect an Interest in Property. A statement contained in a document that purports to establish or affect an interest in property if the matter stated was relevant to the document's purpose—unless later dealings with the property are inconsistent with the truth of the statement or the purport of the document.

(16) Statements in Ancient Documents. A statement in a document that is at least 20 years old and whose authenticity is established.

(17) Market Reports and Similar Commercial Publications. Market quotations, lists, directories, or other compilations that are generally relied on by the public or by persons in particular occupations.

(18) Statements in Learned Treatises, Periodicals, or Pamphlets. A statement contained in a treatise, periodical, or pamphlet if:

(A) the statement is called to the attention of an expert witness on cross-examination or relied on by the expert on direct examination; and

(B) the publication is established as a reliable authority by the expert's admission or testimony, by another expert's testimony, or by judicial notice.

If admitted, the statement may be read into evidence but not received as an exhibit.

(19) Reputation Concerning Personal or Family History. A reputation among a person's family by blood, adoption, or marriage—or among a person's associates or in the community—concerning the person's birth, adoption, legitimacy, ancestry, marriage, divorce, death, relationship by blood, adoption, or marriage, or similar facts of personal or family history.

(20) Reputation Concerning Boundaries or General History. A reputation in a community—arising before the controversy—concerning boundaries of land in the community or customs that affect the land, or concerning general historical events important to that community, state, or nation.

(21) Reputation Concerning Character. A reputation among a person's associates or in the community concerning the person's character.

(22) Judgment of a Previous Conviction. Evidence of a final judgment of conviction if:

(A) the judgment was entered after a trial or guilty plea, but not a nolo contendere plea;

(B) the conviction was for a crime punishable by death or by imprisonment for more than a year;

(C) the evidence is admitted to prove any fact essential to the judgment; and

(D) when offered by the prosecutor in a criminal case for a purpose other than impeachment, the judgment was against the defendant.

The pendency of an appeal may be shown but does not affect admissibility.

(23) Judgments Involving Personal, Family, or General History, or a Boundary. A judgment that is admitted to prove a matter of personal, family, or general history, or boundaries, if the matter:

(A) was essential to the judgment; and

(B) could be proved by evidence of reputation.

(24) [Other Exceptions.] [Transferred to Rule 807.]

(Pub.L. 93–595, § 1, Jan. 2, 1975, 88 Stat. 1939; Pub.L. 94–149, § 1(11), Dec. 12, 1975, 89 Stat. 805; Mar. 2, 1987, eff. Oct. 1, 1987; Apr. 11, 1997, eff. Dec. 1, 1997; Apr. 17, 2000, eff. Dec. 1, 2000; Apr. 26, 2011, eff. Dec. 1, 2011.)

ADVISORY COMMITTEE NOTES

1972 Proposed Rules

The exceptions are phrased in terms of nonapplication of the hearsay rule, rather than in positive terms of admissibility, in order to repel any implication that other possible grounds for exclusion are eliminated from consideration.

The present rule proceeds upon the theory that under appropriate circumstances a hearsay statement may possess circumstantial guarantees of trustworthiness sufficient to justify nonproduction of the declarant in person at the trial even though he may be available. The theory finds vast support in the many exceptions to the hearsay rule developed by the common law in which unavailability of the declarant is not a relevant factor. The present rule is a synthesis of them, with revision where modern developments and conditions are believed to make that course appropriate.

In a hearsay situation, the declarant is, of course, a witness, and neither this rule nor Rule 804 dispenses with the requirement of firsthand knowledge. It may appear from his statement or be inferable from circumstances. See Rule 602.

Note to Paragraphs (1) and (2). In considerable measure these two examples overlap, though based on somewhat different theories. The most significant practical difference will lie in the time lapse allowable between event and statement.

The underlying theory of Exception [paragraph] (1) is that substantial contemporaneity of event and statement negate the likelihood of deliberate or conscious misrepresentation. Moreover, if the witness is the declarant, he may be examined on the statement. If the witness is not the declarant, he may be examined as to the circumstances as an aid in evaluating the statement. Morgan, Basic Problems of Evidence 340–341 (1962).

The theory of Exception [paragraph] (2) is simply that circumstances may produce a condition of excitement which temporarily stills the capacity of reflection and produces utterances free of conscious fabrication. 6 Wigmore § 1747, p. 135. Spontaneity is the key factor in each instance, though arrived at by somewhat different routes. Both are needed in order to avoid needless niggling.

While the theory of Exception [paragraph] (2) has been criticized on the ground that excitement impairs accuracy of observation as well as eliminating conscious fabrication, Hutchins and Slesinger, Some Observations on the Law of Evidence: Spontaneous Exclamations, 28 Colum.L.Rev. 432 (1928), it finds support in cases without number. See cases in 6 Wigmore § 1750; Annot. 53 A.L.R.2d 1245 (statements as to cause of or responsibility for motor vehicle accident); Annot., 4 A.L.R.3d 149 (accusatory statements by homicide victims). Since unexciting events are less likely to evoke comment, decisions involving Exception [paragraph] (1) are far less numerous. Illustrative are *Tampa Elec. Co. v. Getrost,* 151 Fla. 558, 10 So.2d 83 (1942); *Houston Oxygen Co. v. Davis,* 139 Tex. 1, 161 S.W.2d 474 (1942); and cases cited in McCormick § 273, p. 585, n. 4.

With respect to the *time element,* Exception [paragraph] (1) recognizes that in many, if not most, instances precise contemporaneity is not possible and hence a slight lapse is allowable. Under Exception [paragraph] (2) the standard of measurement is the duration of the state of excitement. "How long can excitement prevail? Obviously there are no pat answers and the character of the transaction or event will largely determine the significance of the time factor." Slough, Spontaneous Statements and State of Mind, 46 Iowa L.Rev. 224, 243 (1961); McCormick § 272, p. 580.

Participation by the declarant is not required: a non-participant may be moved to describe what he perceives, and one may be startled by an event in which he is not an actor. Slough, *supra;* McCormick, *supra;* 6 Wigmore § 1755; Annot. 78 A.L.R.2d 300.

Whether *proof of the startling event* may be made by the statement itself is largely an academic question, since in most cases there is present at least circumstantial evidence that something of a startling nature must have occurred. For cases in which the evidence consists of the condition of the declarant (injuries, state of shock), see *Insurance Co. v. Mosely,* 75 U.S. (8 Wall.) 397, 19 L.Ed. 437 (1869); *Wheeler v. United States,* 93 U.S. App.D.C. 159, 211 F.2d 19 (1953), cert. denied 347 U.S. 1019, 74 S.Ct. 876, 98 L.Ed. 1140; *Wetherbee v. Safety Casualty Co.,* 219 F.2d 274 (5th Cir.1955); *Lampe v. United States,* 97 U.S.App.D.C. 160, 229 F.2d 43 (1956). Nevertheless, on occasion the only evidence may be the content of the statement itself, and rulings that it may be sufficient are described as "increasing," Slough, *supra* at 246, and as the "prevailing practice," McCormick § 272, p. 579. Illustrative are *Armour & Co. v. Industrial Commission,* 78 Colo. 569, 243 P. 546 (1926); *Young v. Stewart,* 191 N.C. 297, 131 S.E. 735 (1926). Moreover, under Rule 104(a) the judge is not limited by the hearsay rule in passing upon preliminary questions of fact.

Proof of declarant's perception by his statement presents similar considerations when declarant is identified. *People v. Poland,* 22 Ill.2d 175, 174 N.E.2d 804 (1961). However, when declarant is an unidentified bystander, the cases indicate hesitancy in upholding the statement alone as sufficient, *Garrett v. Howden,* 73 N.M. 307, 387 P.2d 874 (1963); *Beck v. Dye,* 200 Wash. 1, 92 P.2d 1113 (1939), a result which would under appropriate circumstances be consistent with the rule.

Permissible *subject matter* of the statement is limited under Exception [paragraph] (1) to description or explanation of the event or condition, the assumption being that spontaneity, in the absence of a startling event, may extend no farther. In Exception [paragraph] (2), however, the statement need only "relate" to the startling event or condition, thus affording a broader scope of subject matter coverage. 6 Wigmore §§ 1750, 1754. See *Sanitary Grocery Co. v. Snead,* 67 App.D.C. 129, 90 F.2d 374 (1937), slip-and-fall case sustaining admissibility of clerk's statement. "That has been on the floor for a couple of hours," and *Murphy Auto Parts Co., Inc. v. Ball,* 101 U.S.App.D.C. 416, 249 F.2d 508 (1957), upholding admission, on issue of driver's agency, of his statement that he had to call on a customer and was in a hurry to get home. Quick, Hearsay, Excitement, Necessity and the Uniform Rules: A Reappraisal of Rule 63(4), 6 Wayne L.Rev. 204, 206–209 (1960).

Similar provisions are found in Uniform Rule 63(4)(a) and (b); California Evidence Code § 1240 (as to Exception (2) only); Kansas Code of Civil Procedure § 60–460(d)(1) and (2); New Jersey Evidence Rule 63(4).

Note to Paragraph (3). Exception [paragraph] (3) is essentially a specialized application of Exception [paragraph] (1), presented separately to enhance its usefulness and accessibility. See McCormick §§ 265, 268.

The exclusion of "statements of memory or belief to prove the fact remembered or believed" is necessary to avoid the virtual destruction of the hearsay rule which would otherwise result from allowing state of mind, provable by a hearsay statement, to serve as the basis for an inference of the happening of the event which produced the state of mind. *Shepard v. United States,* 290 U.S. 96, 54 S.Ct. 22, 78 L.Ed. 196 (1933); Maguire, The Hillmon Case—Thirty-three Years After, 38 Harv. L.Rev. 709, 719–731 (1925); Hinton, States of Mind and the Hearsay Rule, 1 U.Chi.L.Rev. 394, 421–423 (1934). The rule of *Mutual Life Ins. Co. v. Hillmon,* 145 U.S. 285, 12 S.Ct. 909, 36 L.Ed. 706 (1892), allowing evidence of intention as tending to prove the doing of the act intended, is, of course, left undisturbed.

The carving out, from the exclusion mentioned in the preceding paragraph, of declarations relating to the execution, revocation, identification, or terms of declarant's will represents and *ad hoc* judgment which finds ample reinforcement in the decisions, resting on practical grounds of necessity and expediency rather than logic. McCormick § 271, pp. 577–578; Annot. 34 A.L.R.2d 588, 62 A.L.R.2d 855. A similar recognition of the need for and practical value of this kind of evidence is found in California Evidence Code § 1260.

Note to Paragraph (4). Even those few jurisdictions which have shied away from generally admitting statements of present condition have allowed them if made to a physician for purposes of diagnosis and treatment in view of the patient's strong motivation to be truthful. McCormick § 266, p. 563. The same guarantee of trustworthiness extends to statements of past conditions and medical history, made for purposes of diagnosis or treatment. It also extends to statements as to causation, reasonably pertinent to the same purposes, in accord with the current trend. *Shell Oil Co. v. Industrial Commission,* 2 Ill.2d 590, 119 N.E.2d 224 (1954); McCormick § 266, p. 564; New Jersey Evidence Rule 63(12)(c). Statements as to fault would not ordinarily qualify under this latter language. Thus a patient's statement that he was struck by an automobile would qualify but not his statement that the car was driven through a red light. Under the exception the statement need not have been made to a physician. Statements to hospital attendants, ambulance drivers, or even members of the family might be included.

Conventional doctrine has excluded from the hearsay exception, as not within its guarantee of truthfulness, statements to a physician consulted only for the purpose of enabling him to testify. While these statements were not admissible as substantive evidence, the expert was allowed to state the basis of his opinion, including statements of this kind. The distinction thus called for was one most unlikely to be made by juries. The rule accordingly rejects the limitation. This position is consistent with the provision of Rule 703 that the facts on which expert testimony is based need not be admissible in evidence if of a kind ordinarily relied upon by experts in the field.

Note to Paragraph (5). A hearsay exception for recorded recollection is generally recognized and has been described as having "long been favored by the federal and practically all the state courts that have had occasion to decide the question." *United States v. Kelly,* 349 F.2d 720, 770 (2d Cir.1965), citing numerous cases and sustaining the exception against a claimed denial of the right of confrontation. Many additional cases are cited in Annot., 82 A.L.R.2d 473, 520. The guarantee of trustworthiness is found in the reliability inherent in a record made while events were still fresh in mind and accurately reflecting them. *Owens v. State,* 67 Md. 307, 316, 10 A. 210, 212 (1887).

The principal controversy attending the exception has centered, not upon the propriety of the exception itself, but upon the question whether a preliminary requirement of impaired memory on the part of the witness should be imposed. The authorities are divided. If regard be had only to the accuracy of the evidence, admittedly impairment of the memory of the witness adds nothing to it and should not be required. McCormick § 277, p. 593; 3 Wigmore § 738, p. 76; *Jordan v. People,* 151 Colo. 133, 376 P.2d 699 (1962), cert. denied 373 U.S. 944, 83 S.Ct. 1553, 10 L.Ed.2d 699; *Hall v. State,* 223 Md. 158, 162 A.2d 751 (1960); *State v. Bindhammer,* 44 N.J. 372, 209 A.2d 124 (1965). Nevertheless, the absence of the requirement, it is believed, would encourage the use of statements carefully prepared for purposes of litigation under the supervision of attorneys, investigators, or claim adjusters. Hence the example includes a requirement that the witness not have "sufficient recollection to enable him to testify fully and accurately." To the same effect are California Evidence Code § 1237 and New Jersey Rule 63(1)(b), and this has been the position of the federal courts. *Vicksburg & Meridian R.R. v. O'Brien,* 119 U.S. 99, 7 S.Ct. 118, 30 L.Ed. 299 (1886); Ahern v. Webb, 268 F.2d 45 (10th Cir.1959); and see *N.L.R.B. v. Hudson Pulp and Paper Corp.,* 273 F.2d 660, 665 (5th Cir.1960); *N.L.R.B. v. Federal Dairy Co.,* 297 F.2d 487 (1st Cir.1962). But cf. *United States v. Adams,* 385 F.2d 548 (2d Cir.1967).

No attempt is made in the exception to spell out the method of establishing the initial knowledge or the contemporaneity and accuracy of the record, leaving them to be dealt with as the circumstances of the particular case might indicate. Multiple person involvement in the process of observing and recording, as in *Rathbun v. Brancatella,* 93 N.J.L. 222, 107 A. 279 (1919), is entirely consistent with the exception.

Locating the exception at this place in the scheme of the rules is a matter of choice. There were two other possibilities. The first was to regard the statement as one of the group of prior statements of a testifying witness which are excluded entirely from the category of hearsay by Rule 801(d)(1). That category, however, requires that declarant be "subject to cross-examination," as to which the impaired memory aspect of the exception raises doubts. The other possibility was to include the exception among those covered by Rule 804. Since unavailability is required by that rule and lack of memory is listed as a species of unavailability by the definition of the term in Rule 804(a)(3), that treatment at first impression would seem appropriate. The fact is, however, that the unavailability requirement of the exception is of a limited and peculiar nature. Accordingly, the exception is located at this point rather than in the context of a rule where unavailability is conceived of more broadly.

Note to Paragraph (6). Exception [paragraph] (6) represents an area which has received much attention from those seeking to improve the law of evidence. The Commonwealth Fund Act was the result of a study completed in 1927 by a distinguished committee under the chairmanship of Professor Morgan. Morgan et al., The Law of Evidence: Some Proposals for its Reform 63 (1927). With changes too minor to mention, it was adopted by Congress in 1936 as the rule for federal courts. 28 U.S.C. § 1732. A number of states took similar action. The Commissioners on Uniform State Laws in 1936 promulgated the Uniform Business Records as Evidence Act, 9A U.L.A. 506, which has acquired a substantial following in the states. Model Code Rule 514 and Uniform Rule 63(13) also deal with the subject. Difference of varying degrees of importance exist among these various treatments.

These reform efforts were largely within the context of business and commercial records, as the kind usually encountered, and concentrated considerable attention upon relaxing the requirement of producing as witnesses, or accounting for the nonproduction of, all participants in the process of gathering, transmitting, and recording information which the common law had evolved as a burdensome and crippling aspect of using records of this type. In their areas of primary emphasis on witnesses to be called and the general admissibility of ordinary business and commercial records, the Commonwealth Fund Act and the Uniform Act appear to have worked well. The exception seeks to preserve their advantages.

On the subject of what witnesses must be called, the Commonwealth Fund Act eliminated the common law requirement of calling or accounting for all participants by failing to mention it. *United States v. Mortimer,* 118 F.2d 266 (2d Cir.1941); *La Porte v. United States,* 300 F.2d 878 (9th Cir.1962); McCormick § 290, p. 608. Model Code Rule 514 and Uniform Rule 63(13) did likewise. The Uniform Act, however, abolished the common law requirement in express terms, providing that the requisite foundation testimony might be furnished by "the custodian or other qualified witness." Uniform Business Records as Evidence Act, § 2; 9A U.L.A. 506. The exception follows the Uniform Act in this respect.

The element of unusual reliability of business records is said variously to be supplied by systematic checking, by regularity and continuity which produce habits of precision, by actual experience of business in relying upon them, or by a duty to make an accurate record as part of a continuing job or occupation. McCormick §§ 281, 286, 287; Laughlin, Business Entries and the Like, 46 Iowa L.Rev. 276 (1961). The model statutes and rules have sought to capture these factors and to extend their impact by employing the phrase "regular course of business," in conjunction with a definition of "business" far broader than its ordinarily accepted meaning. The result is a tendency unduly to emphasize a requirement of routineness and repetitiveness and an insistence that other types of records be squeezed into the fact patterns which give rise to traditional business records. The rule therefore adopts the phrase "the course of a regularly conducted activity" as capturing the essential basis of the hearsay exception as it has evolved and the essential element which can be abstracted from the various specifications of what is a "business."

Amplification of the kinds of activities producing admissible records has given rise to problems which conventional business records by their nature avoid. They are problems of the source of the recorded information, of entries in opinion form, of motivation, and of involvement as participant in the matters recorded.

Sources of information presented no substantial problem with ordinary business records. All participants, including the observer or participant furnishing the information to be recorded, were acting routinely, under a duty of accuracy, with employer reliance on the result, or in short "in the regular course of business." If, however, the supplier of the information does not act in the regular course, an essential link is broken; the assurance of accuracy does not extend to the information itself, and the fact that it may be recorded with scrupulous accuracy is of no avail. An illustration is the police report incorporating information obtained from a bystander: the officer qualifies as acting in the regular course but the informant does not. The leading case, *Johnson v. Lutz,* 253 N.Y. 124, 170 N.E. 517 (1930), held that a report thus prepared was inadmissible. Most of the authorities have agreed with the decision. Gencarella v. Fyfe, 171 F.2d 419 (1st Cir.1948); *Gordon v. Robinson,* 210 F.2d 192 (3d Cir.1954); *Standard Oil Co. of California v. Moore,* 251 F.2d 188, 214 (9th Cir.1957), cert. denied 356 U.S. 975, 78 S.Ct. 1139, 2 L.Ed.2d 1148; *Yates v. Bair Transport,* Inc., 249 F.Supp. 681 (S.D.N.Y.1965); Annot., 69 A.L.R.2d 1148. Cf. *Hawkins v. Gorea Motor Express, Inc.,* 360 F.2d 933 (2d Cir.1966); *Contra,* 5 Wigmore § 1530a, n. 1, pp. 391–392. The point is not dealt with specifically in the Commonwealth Fund Act, the Uniform Act, or Uniform Rule

63(13). However, Model Code Rule 514 contains the requirement "that it was the regular course of that business for one with personal knowledge * * * to make such a memorandum or record or to transmit information thereof to be included in such a memorandum or record * * *." The rule follows this lead in requiring an informant with knowledge acting in the course of the regularly conducted activity.

Entries in the form of opinions were not encountered in traditional business records in view of the purely factual nature of the items recorded, but they are now commonly encountered with respect to medical diagnoses, prognoses, and test results, as well as occasionally in other areas. The Commonwealth Fund Act provided only for records of an "act, transaction, occurrence, or event," while the Uniform Act, Model Code Rule 514, and Uniform Rule 63(13) merely added the ambiguous term "condition." The limited phrasing of the Commonwealth Fund Act, 28 U.S.C. § 1732, may account for the reluctance of some federal decisions to admit diagnostic entries. *New York Life Ins. Co. v. Taylor,* 79 U.S.App.D.C. 66, 147 F.2d 297 (1945); *Lyles v. United States,* 103 U.S.App.D.C. 22, 254 F.2d 725 (1957), cert. denied 356 U.S. 961, 78 S.Ct. 997, 2 L.Ed.2d 1067; *England v. United States,* 174 F.2d 466 (5th Cir.1949); *Skogen v. Dow Chemical Co.,* 375 F.2d 692 (8th Cir.1967). Other federal decisions, however, experienced no difficulty in freely admitting diagnostic entries. *Reed v. Order of United Commercial Travelers,* 123 F.2d 252 (2d Cir.1941); *Buckminster's Estate v. Commissioner of Internal Revenue,* 147 F.2d 331 (2d Cir.1944); *Medina v. Erickson,* 226 F.2d 475 (9th Cir.1955); *Thomas v. Hogan,* 308 F.2d 355 (4th Cir.1962); *Glawe v. Rulon,* 284 F.2d 495 (8th Cir.1960). In the state courts, the trend favors admissibility. Borucki v. MacKenzie Bros. Co., 125 Conn. 92, 3 A.2d 224 (1938); *Allen v. St. Louis Public Service Co.,* 365 Mo. 677, 285 S.W.2d 663, 55 A.L.R.2d 1022 (1956); *People v. Kohlmeyer,* 284 N.Y. 366, 31 N.E.2d 490 (1940); *Weis v. Weis,* 147 Ohio St. 416, 72 N.E.2d 245 (1947). In order to make clear its adherence to the latter position, the rule specifically includes both diagnoses and opinions, in addition to acts, events, and conditions, as proper subjects of admissible entries.

Problems of the motivation of the informant have been a source of difficulty and disagreement. In *Palmer v. Hoffman,* 318 U.S. 109, 63 S.Ct. 477, 87 L.Ed. 645 (1943), exclusion of an accident report made by the since deceased engineer, offered by defendant railroad trustees in a grade crossing collision case, was upheld. The report was not "in the regular course of business," not a record of the systematic conduct of the business as a business, said the Court. The report was prepared for use in litigating, not railroading. While the opinion mentions the motivation of the engineer only obliquely, the emphasis on records of routine operations is significant only by virtue of impact on motivation to be accurate. Absence of routineness raises lack of motivation to be accurate. The opinion of the Court of Appeals had gone beyond mere lack of motive to be accurate: the engineer's statement was "dripping with motivations to misrepresent." *Hoffman v. Palmer,* 129 F.2d 976, 991 (2d Cir.1942). The direct introduction of motivation is a disturbing factor, since absence of motive to misrepresent has not traditionally been a requirement of the rule; that records might be self-serving has not been a ground for exclusion. Laughlin, Business Records and the Like, 46 Iowa L.Rev. 276, 285 (1961). As Judge Clark said in his dissent, "I submit that there is hardly a grocer's account book which could not be excluded on that basis." 129 F.2d at 1002. A physician's evaluation report of a personal injury litigant would appear to be in the routine of his business. If the report is offered by the party at whose instance it was made, however, it has been held inadmissible, *Yates v. Bair Transport, Inc.,* 249 F.Supp. 681 (S.D.N.Y.1965), otherwise if offered by the opposite party, *Korte v. New York, N.H. & H.R. Co.,* 191 F.2d 86 (2d Cir.1951), cert. denied 342 U.S. 868, 72 S.Ct. 108, 96 L.Ed. 652.

The decisions hinge on motivation and which party is entitled to be concerned about it. Professor McCormick believed that the doctor's report or the accident report were sufficiently routine to justify admissibility. McCormick § 287, p. 604. Yet hesitation must be experienced in admitting everything which is observed and recorded in the course of a regularly conducted activity. Efforts to set a limit are illustrated by *Hartzog v. United States,* 217 F.2d 706 (4th Cir.1954), error to admit worksheets made by since deceased deputy collector in preparation for the instant income tax evasion prosecution, and *United States v. Ware,* 247 F.2d 698 (7th Cir.1957), error to admit narcotics agents' records of purchases. See also Exception [paragraph] (8), *infra,* as to the public record aspects of records of this nature. Some decisions have been satisfied as to motivation of an accident report if made pursuant to statutory duty, United States v. New York Foreign Trade Zone Operators, 304 F.2d 792 (2d Cir.1962); Taylor v. Baltimore & O.R. Co., 344 F.2d 281 (2d Cir.1965), since the report was oriented in a direction other than the litigation which ensued. Cf. Matthews v. United States, 217 F.2d 409 (5th Cir.1954). The formulation of specific terms which would assure satisfactory results in all cases is not possible. Consequently the rule proceeds from the base that records made in the course of a regularly conducted activity will be taken as admissible but subject to authority to exclude if "the sources of information or other circumstances indicate lack of trustworthiness."

Occasional decisions have reached for enhanced accuracy by requiring involvement as a participant in matters reported. *Clainos v. United States,* 82 U.S.App. D.C. 278, 163 F.2d 593 (1947), error to admit police records of convictions; *Standard Oil Co. of California v. Moore,* 251 F.2d 188 (9th Cir.1957), cert. denied 356 U.S. 975, 78 S.Ct. 1139, 2 L.Ed.2d 1148, error to admit employees' records of observed business practices of others. The rule includes no requirement of this nature. Wholly acceptable records may involve matters merely observed, e.g. the weather.

The form which the "record" may assume under the rule is described broadly as a "memorandum, report, record, or data compilation, in any form." The expression "data compilation" is used as broadly descriptive of any means of storing information other than the conventional words and figures in written or documentary form. It includes, but is by no means limited to, electronic computer storage. The term is borrowed from revised Rule 34(a) of the Rules of Civil Procedure.

Note to Paragraph (7). Failure of a record to mention a matter which would ordinarily be mentioned is satisfactory evidence of its nonexistence. Uniform Rule 63(14), Comment. While probably not hearsay as defined in Rule 801, *supra,* decisions may be found which class the evidence not only as hearsay but also as not within any exception. In order to set the question at rest in favor of admissibility, it is specifically treated here. McCormick § 289, p. 609; Morgan, Basic Problems of Evidence 314 (1962); 5 Wigmore § 1531; Uniform Rule 63(14); California Evidence Code § 1272; Kansas Code of Civil Procedure § 60–460(n); New Jersey Evidence Rule 63(14).

Note to Paragraph (8). Public records are a recognized hearsay exception at common law and have been the subject of statutes without number. McCormick § 291. See, for example, 28 U.S.C. § 1733, the relative narrowness of which is illustrated by its nonapplicability to nonfederal public agencies, thus necessitating resort to the less appropriate business record exception to the hearsay rule. *Kay v. United States,* 255 F.2d 476 (4th Cir.1958). The rule makes no distinction between federal and nonfederal offices and agencies.

Justification for the exception is the assumption that a public official will perform his duty properly and the unlikelihood that he will remember details independently of the record. *Wong Wing Foo v. McGrath,* 196 F.2d 120 (9th Cir.1952), and see *Chesapeake & Delaware Canal Co. v. United States,* 250 U.S. 123, 39 S.Ct. 407, 63 L.Ed. 889 (1919). As to items (a) and (b), further support is found in the reliability factors underlying records of regularly conducted activities generally. See Exception [paragraph] (6), supra.

(a) Cases illustrating the admissibility of records of the office's or agency's own activities are numerous. *Chesapeake & Delaware Canal Co. v. United States,* 250 U.S. 123, 39 S.Ct. 407, 63 L.Ed. 889 (1919), Treasury records of miscellaneous receipts and disbursements; *Howard v. Perrin,* 200 U.S. 71, 26 S.Ct. 195, 50 L.Ed. 374 (1906), General Land Office records; *Ballew v. United States,* 160 U.S. 187, 16 S.Ct. 263, 40 L.Ed. 388 (1895). Pension Office records.

(b) Cases sustaining admissibility of records of matters observed are also numerous. *United States v. Van Hook,* 284 F.2d 489 (7th Cir.1960), remanded for resentencing 365 U.S. 609, 81 S.Ct. 823, 5 L.Ed.2d 821, letter from induction officer to District Attorney, pursuant to army regulations, stating fact and circumstances of refusal to be inducted; *T'Kach v. United States,* 242 F.2d 937 (5th Cir.1957), affidavit of White House personnel officer that search of records showed no employment of accused, charged with fraudulently representing himself as an envoy of the President; *Minnehaha County v. Kelley,* 150 F.2d 356 (8th Cir.1945); Weather Bureau records of rainfall; *United States v. Meyer,* 113 F.2d 387 (7th Cir.1940), cert. denied 311 U.S. 706, 61 S.Ct. 174, 85 L.Ed. 459, map prepared by government engineer from information furnished by men working under his supervision.

(c) The more controversial area of public records is that of the so-called "evaluative" report. The disagreement among the decisions has been due in part, no doubt, to the variety of situations encountered, as well as to differences in principle. Sustaining admissibility are such cases as *United States v. Dumas,* 149 U.S. 278, 13 S.Ct. 872, 37 L.Ed. 734 (1893), statement of account certified by Postmaster General in action against postmaster; *McCarty v. United States,* 185 F.2d 520 (5th Cir.1950), reh. denied 187 F.2d 234, Certificate of Settlement of General Accounting Office showing indebtedness and letter from Army official stating Government had performed, in action on contract to purchase and remove waste food from Army camp; *Moran v. Pittsburgh–Des Moines Steel Co.,* 183 F.2d 467 (3d Cir.1950), report of Bureau of Mines as to cause of gas tank explosion; Petition of W___, 164 F.Supp. 659 (E.D.Pa.1958), report by Immigration and Naturalization Service investigator that petitioner was known in community as wife of man to whom she was not married. To the opposite effect and denying admissibility are *Franklin v. Skelly Oil Co.,* 141 F.2d 568 (10th Cir.1944), State Fire Marshal's report of cause of gas explosion; *Lomax Transp. Co. v. United States,* 183 F.2d 331 (9th Cir.1950), Certificate of Settlement from General Accounting Office in action for naval supplies lost in warehouse fire; *Yung Jin Teung v. Dulles,* 229 F.2d 244 (2d Cir.1956), "Status Reports" offered to justify delay in processing passport applications. Police reports have generally been excluded except to the extent to which they incorporate firsthand observations of the officer. Annot., 69 A.L.R.2d 1148. Various kinds of evaluative reports are admissible under federal statutes: 7 U.S.C. § 78, findings of Secretary of Agriculture prima facie evidence of true grade of grain; 7 U.S.C. § 210(f), findings of Secretary of Agriculture prima facie evidence in action for damages against stockyard owner; 7 U.S.C. § 292, order by Secretary of Agriculture prima facie evidence in judicial enforcement proceedings against producers association monopoly; 7 U.S.C. § 1622(h), Department of Agriculture inspection certificates of products shipped in interstate commerce prima facie evidence; 8 U.S.C. § 1440(c), separation of alien from military service on conditions other than honorable provable by certificate from department in proceedings to revoke citizenship;

18 U.S.C. § 4245, certificate of Director of Prisons that convicted person has been examined and found probably incompetent at time of trial prima facie evidence in court hearing on competency; 42 U.S.C. § 269(b), bill of health by appropriate official prima facie evidence of vessel's sanitary history and condition and compliance with regulations; 46 U.S.C. § 679, certificate of consul presumptive evidence of refusal of master to transport destitute seamen to United States. While these statutory exceptions to the hearsay rule are left undisturbed, Rule 802, the willingness of Congress to recognize a substantial measure of admissibility for evaluative reports is a helpful guide.

Factors which may be of assistance in passing upon the admissibility of evaluative reports include: (1) the timeliness of the investigation, McCormick, Can the Courts Make Wider Use of Reports of Official Investigations? 42 Iowa L.Rev. 363 (1957); (2) the special skill or experience of the official, *id.,* (3) whether a hearing was held and the level at which conducted, Franklin v. Skelly Oil Co., 141 F.2d 568 (10th Cir.1944); (4) possible motivation problems suggested by Palmer v. Hoffman, 318 U.S. 109, 63 S.Ct. 477, 87 L.Ed. 645 (1943). Others no doubt could be added.

The formulation of an approach which would give appropriate weight to all possible factors in every situation is an obvious impossibility. Hence the rule, as in Exception [paragraph] (6), assumes admissibility in the first instance but with ample provision for escape if sufficient negative factors are present. In one respect, however, the rule with respect to evaluative reports under item (c) is very specific: they are admissible only in civil cases and against the government in criminal cases in view of the almost certain collision with confrontation rights which would result from their use against the accused in a criminal case.

Note to Paragraph (9). Records of vital statistics are commonly the subject of particular statutes making them admissible in evidence, Uniform Vital Statistics Act, 9C U.L.A. 350 (1957). The rule is in principle narrower than Uniform Rule 63(16) which includes reports required of persons performing functions authorized by statute, yet in practical effect the two are substantially the same. Comment Uniform Rule 63(16). The exception as drafted is in the pattern of California Evidence Code § 1281.

Note to Paragraph (10). The principle of proving nonoccurrence of an event by evidence of the absence of a record which would regularly be made of its occurrence, developed in Exception [paragraph] (7) with respect to regularly conducted activities, is here extended to public records of the kind mentioned in Exceptions [paragraphs] (8) and (9). 5 Wigmore § 1633(6), p. 519. Some harmless duplication no doubt exists with Exception [paragraph] (7). For instances of federal statutes recognizing this method of proof, see 8 U.S.C. § 1284(b), proof of absence of alien crewman's name from outgoing manifest prima facie evidence of failure to detain or deport, and 42 U.S.C. § 405(c)(3), (4)(B), (4)(C), absence of HEW [Department of Health, Education, and Welfare] record prima facie evidence of no wages or self-employment income.

The rule includes situations in which absence of a record may itself be the ultimate focal point of inquiry, e.g. People v. Love, 310 Ill. 558, 142 N.E. 204 (1923), certificate of Secretary of State admitted to show failure to file documents required by Securities Law, as well as cases where the absence of a record is offered as proof of the nonoccurrence of an event ordinarily recorded.

The refusal of the common law to allow proof by certificate of the lack of a record or entry has no apparent justification, 5 Wigmore § 1678(7), p. 752. The rule takes the opposite position, as to Uniform Rule 63(17); California Evidence Code § 1284; Kansas Code of Civil Procedure § 60–460(c); New Jersey Evidence Rule 63(17). Congress has recognized certification as evidence of the lack of a record. 8 U.S.C.

§ 1360(d), certificate of Attorney General or other designated officer that no record of Immigration and Naturalization Service of specified nature or entry therein is found, admissible in alien cases.

Note to Paragraph (11). Records of activities of religious organizations are currently recognized as admissible at least to the extent of the business records exception to the hearsay rule, 5 Wigmore § 1523, p. 371, and Exception [paragraph] (6) would be applicable. However, both the business record doctrine and Exception [paragraph] (6) require that the person furnishing the information be one in the business or activity. The result is such decisions as Daily v. Grand Lodge, 311 Ill. 184, 142 N.E. 478 (1924), holding a church record admissible to prove fact, date, and place of baptism, but not age of child except that he had at least been born at the time. In view of the unlikelihood that false information would be furnished on occasions of this kind, the rule contains no requirement that the informant be in the course of the activity. See California Evidence Code § 1315 and Comment.

Note to Paragraph (12). The principle of proof by certification is recognized as to public officials in Exceptions [paragraphs] (8) and (10), and with respect to authentication in Rule 902. The present exception is a duplication to the extent that it deals with a certificate by a public official, as in the case of a judge who performs a marriage ceremony. The area covered by the rule is, however, substantially larger and extends the certification procedure to clergymen and the like who perform marriages and other ceremonies or administer sacraments. Thus certificates of such matters as baptism or confirmation, as well as marriage, are included. In principle they are as acceptable evidence as certificates of public officers. See 5 Wigmore § 1645, as to marriage certificates. When the person executing the certificate is not a public official, the self-authenticating character of documents purporting to emanate from public officials, see Rule 902, is lacking and proof is required that the person was authorized and did make the certificate. The time element, however, may safely be taken as supplied by the certificate, once authority and authenticity are established, particularly in view of the presumption that a document was executed on the date it bears.

For similar rules, some limited to certificates of marriage, with variations in foundation requirements, see Uniform Rule 63(18); California Evidence Code § 1316; Kansas Code of Civil Procedure § 60–460(p); New Jersey Evidence Rule 63(18).

Note to Paragraph (13). Records of family history kept in family Bibles have by long tradition been received in evidence. 5 Wigmore §§ 1495, 1496, citing numerous statutes and decisions. See also Regulations, Social Security Administration, 20 C.F.R. § 404.703(c), recognizing family Bible entries as proof of age in the absence of public or church records. Opinions in the area also include inscriptions on tombstones, publicly displayed pedigrees, and engravings on rings. Wigmore, *supra*. The rule is substantially identical in coverage with California Evidence Code § 1312.

Note to Paragraph (14). The recording of title documents is a purely statutory development. Under any theory of the admissibility of public records, the records would be receivable as evidence of the contents of the recorded document, else the recording process would be reduced to a nullity. When, however, the record is offered for the further purpose of proving execution and delivery, a problem of lack of firsthand knowledge by the recorder, not present as to contents, is presented. This problem is solved, seemingly in all jurisdictions, by qualifying for recording only those documents shown by a specified procedure, either acknowledgement or a form of probate, to have been executed and delivered. 5 Wigmore §§ 1647–1651. Thus what may appear in the rule, at first glance, as endowing the record with an effect independently of local law and inviting difficulties of an *Erie* nature under *Cities Service Oil Co. v. Dunlap,* 308 U.S. 208, 60 S.Ct. 201, 84 L.Ed. 196 (1939), is not present, since the local law in fact governs under the example.

Note to Paragraph (15). Dispositive documents often contain recitals of fact. Thus a deed purporting to have been executed by an attorney in fact may recite the existence of the power of attorney, or a deed may recite that the grantors are all the heirs of the last record owner. Under the rule, these recitals are exempted from the hearsay rule. The circumstances under which dispositive documents are executed and the requirement that the recital be germane to the purpose of the document are believed to be adequate guarantees of trustworthiness, particularly in view of the nonapplicability of the rule if dealings with the property have been inconsistent with the document. The age of the document is of no significance, though in practical application the document will most often be an ancient one. See Uniform Rule 63(29), Comment.

Similar provisions are contained in Uniform Rule 63(29); California Evidence Code § 1330; Kansas Code of Civil Procedure § 60–460(aa); New Jersey Evidence Rule 63(29).

Note to Paragraph (16). Authenticating a document as ancient, essentially in the pattern of the common law, as provided in Rule 901(b)(8), leaves open as a separate question the admissibility of assertive statements contained therein as against a hearsay objection. 7 Wigmore § 2145a. Wigmore further states that the ancient document technique of authentication is universally conceded to apply to all sorts of documents, including letters, records, contracts, maps, and certificates, in addition to title documents, citing numerous decisions. *Id.* § 2145. Since most of these items are significant evidentially only insofar as they are assertive, their admission in evidence must be as a hearsay exception. But see 5 *id.* § 1573, p. 429, referring to recitals in ancient deeds as a "limited" hearsay exception. The former position is believed to be the correct one in reason and authority. As pointed out in McCormick § 298, danger of mistake is minimized by authentication requirements, and age affords assurance that the writing antedates the present controversy. See *Dallas County v. Commercial Union Assurance Co.,* 286 F.2d 388 (5th Cir.1961), upholding admissibility of 58–year–old newspaper story. Cf. Morgan, Basic Problems of Evidence 364 (1962), but see *id.* 254.

For a similar provision, but with the added requirement that "the statement has since generally been acted upon as true by persons having an interest in the matter," see California Evidence Code § 1331.

Note to Paragraph (17). Ample authority at common law supported the admission in evidence of items falling in this category. While Wigmore's text is narrowly oriented to lists, etc., prepared for the use of a trade or profession, 6 Wigmore § 1702, authorities are cited which include other kinds of publications, for example, newspaper market reports, telephone directories, and city directories. *Id.* §§ 1702–1706. The basis of trustworthiness is general reliance by the public or by a particular segment of it, and the motivation of the compiler to foster reliance by being accurate.

For similar provisions, see Uniform Rule 63(30); California Evidence Code § 1340; Kansas Code of Civil Procedure § 60–460(bb); New Jersey Evidence Rule 63(30). Uniform Commercial Code § 2–724 provides for admissibility in evidence of "reports in official publications or trade journals or in newspapers or periodicals of general circulation published as the reports of such [established commodity] market."

Note to Paragraph (18). The writers have generally favored the admissibility of learned treatises, McCormick § 296, p. 621; Morgan, Basic Problems of Evidence 366 (1962); 6 Wigmore § 1692, with the support of occasional decisions and rules, *City of Dothan v. Hardy,* 237 Ala. 603, 188 So. 264 (1939); *Lewandowski v. Preferred Risk Mut. Ins. Co.,* 33 Wis.2d 69, 146 N.W.2d 505 (1966), 66 Mich.L.Rev. 183 (1967); Uniform Rule 63(31); Kansas Code of Civil Procedure § 60–460(cc), but the great weight of authority has been that learned treatises are not admissible as substantive evidence though usable in the cross-examination of experts. The foundation of the minority view is that the hearsay objection must be regarded as unimpressive when directed against treatises since a high standard of accuracy is engendered by various factors: the treatise is written primarily and impartially for professionals, subject to scrutiny and exposure for inaccuracy, with the reputation of the writer at stake. 6 Wigmore § 1692. Sound as this position may be with respect to trustworthiness, there is, nevertheless, an additional difficulty in the likelihood that the treatise will be misunderstood and misapplied without expert assistance and supervision. This difficulty is recognized in the cases demonstrating unwillingness to sustain findings relative to disability on the basis of judicially noticed medical texts. *Ross v. Gardner,* 365 F.2d 554 (6th Cir.1966); *Sayers v. Gardner,* 380 F.2d 940 (6th Cir.1967); *Colwell v. Gardner,* 386 F.2d 56 (6th Cir.1967); *Glendenning v. Ribicoff,* 213 F.Supp. 301 (W.D.Mo.1962); *Cook v. Celebrezze,* 217 F.Supp. 366 (W.D.Mo. 1963); *Sosna v. Celebrezze,* 234 F.Supp. 289 (E.D.Pa.1964); and see *McDaniel v. Celebrezze,* 331 F.2d 426 (4th Cir.1964). The rule avoids the danger of misunderstanding and misapplication by limiting the use of treatises as substantive evidence to situations in which an expert is on the stand and available to explain and assist in the application of the treatise if desired. The limitation upon receiving the publication itself physically in evidence, contained in the last sentence, is designed, to further this policy.

The relevance of the use of treatises on cross-examination is evident. This use of treatises has been the subject of varied views. The most restrictive position is that the witness must have stated expressly on direct his reliance upon the treatise. A slightly more liberal approach still insists upon reliance but allows it to be developed on cross-examination. Further relaxation dispenses with reliance but requires recognition as an authority by the witness, developable on cross-examination. The greatest liberality is found in decisions allowing use of the treatise on cross-examination when its status as an authority is established by any means. Annot., 60 A.L.R.2d 77. The exception is hinged upon this last position, which is that of the Supreme Court, *Reilly v. Pinkus,* 338 U.S. 269, 70 S.Ct. 110, 94 L.Ed. 63 (1949), and of recent well considered state court decisions, *City of St. Petersburg v. Ferguson,* 193 So.2d 648 (Fla.App.1967), cert. denied Fla., 201 So.2d 556; *Darling v. Charleston Memorial Community Hospital,* 33 Ill.2d 326, 211 N.E.2d 253 (1965); *Dabroe v. Rhodes Co.,* 64 Wash.2d 431, 392 P.2d 317 (1964).

In Reilly v. Pinkus, *supra,* the Court pointed out that testing of professional knowledge was incomplete without exploration of the witness' knowledge of and attitude toward established treatises in the field. The process works equally well in reverse and furnishes the basis of the rule.

The rule does not require that the witness rely upon or recognize the treatise as authoritative, thus avoiding the possibility that the expert may at the outset block cross-examination by refusing to concede reliance or authoritativeness. Dabroe v. Rhodes Co., *supra.* Moreover, the rule avoids the unreality of admitting evidence for the purpose of impeachment only, with an instruction to the jury not to consider it otherwise. The parallel to the treatment of prior inconsistent statements will be apparent. See Rules 613(b) and 801(d)(1).

Note to Paragraphs (19), (20) and (21). Trustworthiness in reputation evidence is found "when the topic is such that the facts are likely to have been inquired about and that persons having personal knowledge have disclosed facts which have thus been discussed in the community; and thus the community's conclusion, if any has been formed, is likely to be a trustworthy one." 5 Wigmore § 1580, p. 444, and see also § 1583. On this common foundation, reputation as to land boundaries, customs, general history, character, and marriage have come to be regarded as admissible. The breadth of the underlying principle suggests the formulation of an equally broad exception, but tradition has in fact been much narrower and more particularized, and this is the pattern of these exceptions in the rule.

Exception [paragraph] (19) is concerned with matters of personal and family history. Marriage is universally conceded to be a proper subject of proof by evidence of reputation in the community. 5 Wigmore § 1602. As to such items as legitimacy, relationship, adoption, birth, and death, the decisions are divided. *Id.* § 1605. All seem to be susceptible to being the subject of well founded repute. The "world" in which the reputation may exist may be family, associates, or community. This world has proved capable of expanding with changing times from the single uncomplicated neighborhood, in which all activities take place, to the multiple and unrelated worlds of work, religious affiliation, and social activity, in each of which a reputation may be generated. *People v. Reeves,* 360 Ill. 55, 195 N.E. 443 (1935); *State v. Axilrod,* 248 Minn. 204, 79 N.W.2d 677 (1956); Mass.Stat.1947, c. 410, M.G.L.A. c. 233 § 21A; 5 Wigmore § 1616. The family has often served as the point of beginning for allowing community reputation. 5 Wigmore § 1488. For comparable provisions see Uniform Rule 63(26), (27)(c); California Evidence Code §§ 1313, 1314; Kansas Code of Civil Procedure § 60–460(x), (y)(3); New Jersey Evidence Rule 63(26), (27)(c).

The first portion of Exception [paragraph] (20) is based upon the general admissibility of evidence of reputation as to land boundaries and land customs, expanded in this country to include private as well as public boundaries. McCormick § 299, p. 625. The reputation is required to antedate the controversy, though not to be ancient. The second portion is likewise supported by authority, *id.,* and is designed to facilitate proof of events when judicial notice is not available. The historical character of the subject matter dispenses with any need that the reputation antedate the controversy with respect to which it is offered. For similar provisions see Uniform Rule 63(27)(a), (b); California Evidence Code §§ 1320–1322; Kansas Code of Civil Procedure § 60–460(y), (1), (2); New Jersey Evidence Rule 63(27)(a), (b).

Exception [paragraph] (21) recognizes the traditional acceptance of reputation evidence as a means of proving human character. McCormick §§ 44, 158. The exception deals only with the hearsay aspect of this kind of evidence. Limitations upon admissibility based on other grounds will be found in Rules 404, relevancy of character evidence generally, and 608, character of witness. The exception is in effect a reiteration, in the context of hearsay, of Rule 405(a). Similar provisions are contained in Uniform Rule 63(28); California Evidence Code § 1324; Kansas Code of Civil Procedure § 60–460(z); New Jersey Evidence Rule 63(28).

Note to Paragraph (22). When the status of a former judgment is under consideration in subsequent litigation, three possibilities must be noted: (1) the former judgment is conclusive under the doctrine of res judicata, either as a bar or a collateral estoppel; or (2) it is admissible in evidence for what it is worth; or (3) it may be of no effect at all. The first situation does not involve any problem of evidence except in the way that principles of substantive law generally bear upon the relevancy and materiality of evidence. The rule does not deal with the substantive effect of the judgment as a bar or collateral estoppel. When, however, the doctrine of res judicata does not apply to make the judgment either a bar or a collateral estoppel, a choice is presented between the second and third alternatives. The rule adopts the second for judgments of criminal conviction of felony grade. This is the direction of the decisions, Annot., 18 A.L.R.2d 1287, 1299, which manifest an increasing reluctance to reject *in toto* the validity of the law's factfinding processes outside the confines of res judicata and collateral estoppel. While this may leave a jury with the evidence of conviction but without means to evaluate it, as suggested by Judge Hinton, Note 27 Ill.L.Rev. 195 (1932), it seems safe to assume that the jury will give it substantial effect unless defendant offers a satisfactory explanation, a possibility not foreclosed by the provision. But see *North River Ins. Co. v. Militello,* 104 Colo. 28, 88 P.2d 567 (1939), in which the jury found for plaintiff on a fire policy despite the introduction of his conviction for arson. For supporting federal decisions see Clark, J., in *New York & Cuba Mail S.S. Co. v. Continental Cas. Co.,* 117 F.2d 404, 411 (2d Cir.1941); *Connecticut Fire Ins. Co. v. Farrara,* 277 F.2d 388 (8th Cir.1960).

Practical considerations require exclusion of convictions of minor offenses, not because the administration of justice in its lower echelons must be inferior, but because motivation to defend at this level is often minimal or nonexistent. *Cope v. Goble,* 39 Cal.App.2d 448, 103 P.2d 598 (1940); *Jones v. Talbot,* 87 Idaho 498, 394 P.2d 316 (1964); *Warren v. Marsh,* 215 Minn. 615, 11 N.W.2d 528 (1943); Annot., 18 A.L.R.2d 1287, 1295–1297; 16 Brooklyn L.Rev. 286 (1950); 50 Colum.L.Rev. 529 (1950); 35 Cornell L.Q. 872 (1950). Hence the rule includes only convictions of felony grade, measured by federal standards.

Judgments of conviction based upon pleas of *nolo contendere* are not included. This position is consistent with the treatment of *nolo* pleas in Rule 410 and the authorities cited in the Advisory Committee's Note in support thereof.

While these rules do not in general purport to resolve constitutional issues, they have in general been drafted with a view to avoiding collision with constitutional principles. Consequently the exception does not include evidence of the conviction of a third person, offered against the accused in a criminal prosecution to prove any fact essential to sustain the judgment of conviction. A contrary position would seem clearly to violate the right of confrontation. *Kirby v. United States,* 174 U.S. 47, 19 S.Ct. 574, 43 L.Ed. 890 (1899), error to convict of possessing stolen postage stamps with the only evidence of theft being the record of conviction of the thieves. The situation is to be distinguished from cases in which conviction of another person is an element of the crime, e.g. 15 U.S.C. § 902(d), interstate shipment of firearms to a known convicted felon, and, as specifically provided, from impeachment.

For comparable provisions see Uniform Rule 63(20); California Evidence Code § 1300; Kansas Code of Civil Procedure § 60–460(r); New Jersey Evidence Rule 63(20).

Note to Paragraph (23). A hearsay exception in this area was originally justified on the ground that verdicts were evidence of reputation. As trial by jury graduated from the category of neighborhood inquests, this theory lost its validity. It was never valid as to chancery decrees. Nevertheless the rule persisted, though the judges and writers shifted ground and began saying that the judgment or decree was as good evidence as reputation. See *City of London v. Clerke,* Carth. 181, 90 Eng.Rep. 710 (K.B. 1691); *Neill v. Duke of Devonshire,* 8 App.Cas. 135 (1882). The shift appears to be correct, since the process of inquiry, sifting, and scrutiny which is relied upon to render reputation reliable is present in perhaps greater measure in the process of litigation. While this might suggest a broader area of application, the affinity to reputation is strong, and paragraph [paragraph] (23) goes no further, not even including character.

The leading case in the *United States, Patterson v. Gaines,* 47 U.S. (6 How.) 550, 599, 12 L.Ed. 553 (1847), follows in the pattern of the English decisions, mentioning as illustrative matters thus provable: manorial rights, public rights of way, immemorial custom, disputed boundary, and pedigree. More recent recognition of the principle is found in *Grant Bros. Construction Co. v. United States,* 232 U.S. 647, 34 S.Ct. 452, 58 L.Ed. 776 (1914), in action for penalties under Alien Contract Labor Law, decision of board of inquiry of Immigration Service admissible to prove alienage of laborers, as a matter of pedigree; *United States v. Mid–Continent Petroleum Corp.,* 67 F.2d 37 (10th Cir.1933), records of commission enrolling Indians admissible on pedigree; *Jung Yen Loy v. Cahill,* 81 F.2d 809 (9th Cir.1936), board decisions as to citizenship of plaintiff's father admissible in proceeding for declaration of citizenship. *Contra,* In re Estate of Cunha, 49 Haw. 273, 414 P.2d 925 (1966).

1974 Enactment

Note to Paragraph (3). Rule 803(3) was approved in the form submitted by the Court to Congress. However, the Committee intends that the Rule be construed to limit the doctrine of *Mutual Life Insurance Co. v. Hillmon,* 145 U.S. 285, 295–300 (1892), so as to render statements of intent by a declarant admissible only to prove his future conduct, not the future conduct of another person.

Note to Paragraph (4). After giving particular attention to the question of physical examination made solely to enable a physician to testify, the Committee approved Rule 803(4) as submitted to Congress, with the understanding that it is not intended in any way to adversely affect present privilege rules or those subsequently adopted.

Note to Paragraph (5). Rule 803(5) as submitted by the Court permitted the reading into evidence of a memorandum or record concerning a matter about which a witness once had knowledge but now has insufficient recollection to enable him to testify accurately and fully, "shown to have been made when the matter was fresh in his memory and to reflect that knowledge correctly." The Committee amended this Rule to add the words "or adopted by the witness" after the phrase "shown to have been made", a treatment consistent with the definition of "statement" in the Jencks Act, 18 U.S.C. 3500. Moreover, it is the Committee's understanding that a memorandum or report, although barred under this Rule, would nonetheless be admissible if it came within another hearsay exception. This last stated principle is deemed applicable to all the hearsay rules.

Note to Paragraph (6). Rule 803(6) as submitted by the Court permitted a record made "in the course of a regularly conducted activity" to be admissible in certain circumstances. The Committee believed there were insufficient guarantees of reliability in records made in the course of activities falling outside the scope of "business" activities as that term is broadly defined in 28 U.S.C. 1732. Moreover, the Committee concluded that the additional requirement of Section 1732 that it must have been the regular practice of a business to make the record is a necessary further assurance of its trustworthiness. The Committee accordingly amended the Rule to incorporate these limitations.

Note to Paragraph (7). Rule 803(7) as submitted by the Court concerned the *absence* of entry in the records of a "regularly conducted activity." The Committee amended this Rule to conform with its action with respect to Rule 803(6).

Note to Paragraph (8). The Committee approved Rule 803(8) without substantive change from the form in which it was submitted by the Court. The Committee intends that the phrase "factual findings" be strictly construed and that evaluations or opinions contained in public reports shall not be admissible under this Rule.

Note to Paragraph (13). The Committee approved this Rule in the form submitted by the Court, intending that the phrase "Statements of fact concerning personal or family history" be read to include the specific types of such statements enumerated in Rule 803(11). House Report No. 93–650.

Note to Paragraph (4). The House approved this rule as it was submitted by the Supreme Court "with the understanding that it is not intended in any way to adversely affect present privilege rules." We also approve this rule, and we would point out with respect to the question of its relation to privileges, it must be read in conjunction with rule 35 of the Federal Rules of Civil Procedure which provides that whenever the physical or mental condition of a party (plaintiff or defendant) is in controversy, the court may require him to submit to an examination by a physician. It is these examinations which will normally be admitted under this exception.

Note to Paragraph (5). Rule 803(5) as submitted by the Court permitted the reading into evidence of a memorandum or record concerning a matter about which a witness once had knowledge but now has insufficient recollection to enable him to testify accurately and fully, "shown to have been made when the matter was fresh in his memory and to reflect that knowledge correctly." The House amended the rule to add the words "or adopted by the witness" after the phrase "shown to have been made," language parallel to the Jencks Act [18 U.S.C. § 3500].

The committee accepts the House amendment with the understanding and belief that it was not intended to narrow the scope of applicability of the rule. In fact, we understand it to clarify the rule's applicability to a memorandum adopted by the witness as well as one made by him. While the rule as submitted by the Court was silent on the question of who made the memorandum, we view the House amendment as a helpful clarification, noting, however, that the Advisory Committee's note to this rule suggests that the important thing is the accuracy of the memorandum rather than who made it.

The committee does not view the House amendment as precluding admissibility in situations in which multiple participants were involved.

When the verifying witness has not prepared the report, but merely examined it and found it accurate, he has adopted the report, and it is therefore admissible. The rule should also be interpreted to cover other situations involving multiple participants, e.g., employer dictating to secretary, secretary making memorandum at direction of employer, or information being passed along a chain of persons, as in *Curtis v. Bradley* [65 Conn. 99, 31 Atl. 591 (1894); see, also, *Rathbun v. Brancatella,* 93 N.J.L. 222, 107 Atl. 279 (1919); see, also, McCormick on Evidence, § 303 (2d ed. 1972)].

The committee also accepts the understanding of the House that a memorandum or report, although barred under this rule, would nonetheless be admissible if it came within another hearsay exception. We consider this principle to be applicable to all the hearsay rules.

Note to Paragraph (6). Rule 803(6) as submitted by the Supreme Court permitted a record made in the course of a regularly conducted activity to be admissible in certain circumstances. This rule constituted a broadening of the traditional business records hearsay exception which has been long advocated by scholars and judges active in the law of evidence.

The House felt there were insufficient guarantees of reliability of records not within a broadly defined business records exception. We disagree. Even under the House definition of "business" including profession, occupation, and "calling of every kind," the records of many regularly conducted activities will, or may be, excluded from evidence. Under the principle of ejusdem generis, the intent of "calling of every kind" would seem to be related to work-related endeavors—e.g., butcher, baker, artist, etc.

Thus, it appears that the records of many institutions or groups might not be admissible under the House amendments. For example, schools, churches, and hospitals will not normally be considered businesses within the definition. Yet, these are groups which keep financial and other records on a regular basis in a manner similar to business enterprises. We believe these records are of equivalent trustworthiness and should be admitted into evidence.

Three states, which have recently codified their evidence rules, have adopted the Supreme Court version of rule 803(6), providing for admission of memoranda of a "regularly conducted activity." None adopted the words "business activity" used in the House amendment. [See Nev.Rev.Stats. § 15.135; N.Mex.Stats. (1973 Supp.) § 20–4–803(6); West's Wis.Stats.Anno. (1973 Supp.) § 908.03(6).]

Therefore, the committee deleted the word "business" as it appears before the word "activity". The last sentence then is unnecessary and was also deleted.

It is the understanding of the committee that the use of the phrase "person with knowledge" is not intended to imply that the party seeking to introduce the memorandum, report, record, or data compilation must be able to produce, or even identify, the specific individual upon whose first-hand knowledge the memorandum, report, record or data compilation was based. A sufficient foundation for the introduction of such evidence will be laid if the party seeking to introduce the evidence is able to show that it was the regular practice of the activity to base such memorandums, reports, records, or data compilations upon a transmission from a person with knowledge, e.g., in the case of the content of a shipment of goods, upon a report from the company's receiving agent or in the case of a computer printout, upon a report from the company's computer programmer or one who has knowledge of the particular record system. In short, the scope of the phrase "person with knowledge" is meant to be coterminous with the custodian of the evidence or other qualified witness. The committee believes this represents the desired rule in light of the complex nature of modern business organizations.

Note to Paragraph (8). The House approved rule 803(8), as submitted by the Supreme Court, with one substantive change. It excluded from the hearsay exception reports containing matters observed by police officers and other law enforcement personnel in criminal cases. Ostensibly, the reason for this exclusion is that observations by police officers at the scene of the crime or the apprehension of the defendant are not as reliable as observations by public officials in other cases because of the adversarial nature of the confrontation between the police and the defendant in criminal cases.

The committee accepts the House's decision to exclude such recorded observations where the police officer is available to testify in court about his observation. However, where he is unavailable as unavailability is defined in rule 804(a)(4) and (a)(5), the report should be admitted as the best available evidence. Accordingly, the committee has amended rule 803(8) to refer to the provision of [proposed] rule 804(b)(5) [deleted], which allows the admission of such reports, records or other statements where the police officer or other law enforcement officer is unavailable because of death, then existing physical or mental illness or infirmity, or not being successfully subject to legal process.

The House Judiciary Committee report contained a statement of intent that "the phrase 'factual findings' in subdivision (c) be strictly construed and that evaluations or opinions contained in public reports shall not be admissible under this rule." The committee takes strong exception to this limiting understanding of the application of the rule. We do not think it reflects an understanding of the intended operation of the rule as explained in the Advisory Committee notes to this subsection. The Advisory Committee notes on subsection (c) of this subdivision point out that various kinds of evaluative reports are now admissible under Federal statutes. 7 U.S.C. § 78, findings of Secretary of Agriculture prima facie evidence of true grade of grain; 42 U.S.C. § 269(b), bill of health by appropriate official prima facie evidence of vessel's sanitary history and condition and compliance with regulations. These statutory exceptions to the hearsay rule are preserved. Rule 802. The willingness of Congress to recognize these and other such evaluative reports provides a helpful guide in determining the kind of reports which are intended to be admissible under this rule. We think the restrictive interpretation of the House overlooks the fact that while the Advisory Committee assumes admissibility in the first instance of evaluative reports, they are not admissible if, as the rule states, "the sources of information or other circumstances indicate lack of trustworthiness."

The Advisory Committee explains the factors to be considered:

* * * *

> Factors which may be assistance in passing upon the admissibility of evaluative reports include: (1) the timeliness of the investigation, McCormick, Can the Courts Make Wider Use of Reports of Official Investigations? 42 Iowa L.Rev. 363 (1957); (2) the special skill or experience of the official, id.; (3) whether a hearing was held and the level at which conducted, *Franklin v. Skelly Oil Co.,* 141 F.2d 568 (19th Cir.1944); (4) possible motivation problems suggested by *Palmer v. Hoffman,* 318 U.S. 109, 63 S.Ct. 477, 87 L.Ed. 645 (1943). Others no doubt could be added.

* * * *

The committee concludes that the language of the rule together with the explanation provided by the Advisory Committee furnish sufficient guidance on the admissibility of evaluative reports.

Note to Paragraph (24). The proposed Rules of Evidence submitted to Congress contained identical provisions in rules 803 and 804 (which set forth the various hearsay exceptions), admitting any hearsay statement not specifically covered by any of the stated exceptions, if the hearsay statement was found to have "comparable circumstantial guarantees of trustworthiness." The House deleted these provisions (proposed rules 803(24) and 804(b)(6)[(5)]) as injecting "too much uncertainty" into the law of evidence and impairing the ability of practitioners to prepare for trial. The House felt that rule 102, which directs the courts to construe the Rules of Evidence so as to promote growth and development, would permit sufficient flexibility to admit hearsay evidence in appropriate cases under various factual situations that might arise.

We disagree with the total rejection of a residual hearsay exception. While we view rule 102 as being intended to provide for a broader construction and interpretation of these rules, we feel that, without a separate residual provision, the specifically enumerated exceptions could become tortured beyond any reasonable circumstances which they were intended to include (even if broadly construed). Moreover, these exceptions, while they reflect the most typical and well recognized exceptions to the hearsay rule, may not encompass every situation in which the reliability and appropriateness of a particular piece of hearsay evidence make clear that it should be heard and considered by the trier of fact.

The committee believes that there are certain exceptional circumstances where evidence which is found by a court to have guarantees of trustworthiness equivalent to or exceeding the guarantees reflected by the presently listed exceptions, and to have a high degree of prolativeness [sic] and necessity could properly be admissible.

The case of *Dallas County v. Commercial Union Assoc. Co., Ltd.,* 286 F.2d 388 (5th Cir.1961) illustrates the point. The issue in that case was whether the tower of the county courthouse collapsed because it was struck by lightning (covered by insurance) or because of structural weakness and deterioration of the structure (not covered). Investigation of the structure revealed the presence of charcoal and charred timbers. In order to show that lightning may not have been the cause of the charring, the insurer offered a copy of a local newspaper published over 50 years earlier containing an unsigned article describing a fire in the courthouse while it was under construction. The court found that the newspaper did not qualify for admission as a business record or an ancient document and did not fit within any other recognized hearsay exception. The court concluded, however, that the article was trustworthy because it was inconceivable that a newspaper reporter in a small town would report a fire in the courthouse if none had occurred. See also *United States v. Barbati,* 284 F.Supp. 409 (E.D.N.Y.1968).

Because exceptional cases like the *Dallas County* case may arise in the future, the committee has decided to reinstate a residual exception for rules 803 and 804(b).

The committee, however, also agrees with those supporters of the House version who felt that an overly broad residual hearsay exception could emasculate the hearsay rule and the recognized exceptions or vitiate the rationale behind codification of the rules.

Therefore, the committee has adopted a residual exception for rules 803 and 804(b) of much narrower scope and applicability than the Supreme Court version. In order to qualify for admission, a hearsay statement not falling within one of the recognized exceptions would have to satisfy at least four conditions. First, it must have "equivalent circumstantial guarantees of trustworthiness." Second, it must be offered as evidence of a material fact. Third, the court must determine that the statement "is more probative on the point for which it is offered than any other evidence which the proponent can procure through reasonable efforts." This requirement is intended to insure that only statements which have high probative value and necessity may qualify for admission under the residual exceptions. Fourth, the court must determine that "the general purposes of these rules and the interests of justice will best be served by admission of the statement into evidence."

It is intended that the residual hearsay exceptions will be used very rarely, and only in exceptional circumstances. The committee does not intend to establish a broad license for trial judges to admit hearsay statements that do not fall within one of the other exceptions contained in rules 803 and 804(b). The residual exceptions are not meant to authorize major judicial revisions of the hearsay rule, including its present exceptions. Such major revisions are best accomplished by legislative action. It is intended that in any case in which evidence is sought to be admitted under these subsections, the trial judge will exercise no less care, reflection and caution than the courts did under the common law in establishing the now-recognized exceptions to the hearsay rule.

In order to establish a well-defined jurisprudence, the special facts and circumstances which, in the court's judgment, indicates that the statement has a sufficiently high degree of trustworthiness and necessity to justify its admission should be stated on the record. It is expected that the court will give the opposing party a full and adequate opportunity to contest the admission of any statement sought to be introduced under these subsections. Senate Report No. 93–1277.

Rule 803 defines when hearsay statements are admissible in evidence even though the declarant is available as a witness. The Senate amendments make three changes in this rule.

Note to Paragraph (6). The House bill provides in subsection (6) that records of a regularly conducted "business" activity qualify for admission into evidence as an exception to the hearsay rule. "Business" is defined as including "business, profession, occupation and calling of every kind." The Senate amendment drops the requirement that the records be those of a "business" activity and eliminates the definition of "business." The Senate amendment provides that records are admissible if they are records of a regularly conducted "activity."

The Conference adopts the House provision that the records must be those of a regularly conducted "business" activity. The Conferees changed the definition of "business" contained in the House provision in order to make it clear that the records of institutions and associations like schools, churches and hospitals are admissible under this provision. The records of public schools and hospitals are also covered by Rule 803(8), which deals with public records and reports.

Note to Paragraph (8). The Senate amendment adds language, not contained in the House bill, that refers to another rule that was added by the Senate in another amendment ([proposed] Rule 804(b)(5)—Criminal law enforcement records and reports [deleted]).

In view of its action on [proposed] Rule 804(b)(5) (Criminal law enforcement records and reports) [deleted], the Conference does not adopt the Senate amendment and restores the bill to the House version.

Note to Paragraph (24). The Senate amendment adds a new subsection, (24), which makes admissible a hearsay statement not specifically covered by any of the previous twenty-three subsections, if the statement has equivalent circumstantial guarantees of trustworthiness and if the court determines that (A) the statement is offered as evidence of a material fact; (B) the statement is more probative on the point for which it is offered than any other evidence the proponent can procure through reasonable efforts; and (C) the general purposes of these rules and the interests of justice will best be served by admission of the statement into evidence.

The House bill eliminated a similar, but broader, provision because of the conviction that such a provision injected too much uncertainty into the law of evidence regarding hearsay and impaired the ability of a litigant to prepare adequately for trial.

The Conference adopts the Senate amendment with an amendment that provides that a party intending to request the court to use a statement under this provision must notify any adverse party of this intention as well as of the particulars of the statement, including the name and address of the declarant. This notice must be given sufficiently in advance of the trial or hearing to provide any adverse party with a fair opportunity to prepare to contest the use of the statement. House Report No. 93–1597.

1987 Amendment

The amendments are technical. No substantive change is intended.

1997 Amendment

The contents of Rule 803(24) and Rule 804(b)(5) have been combined and transferred to a new Rule 807. This was done to facilitate additions to Rules 803 and 804. No change in meaning is intended.

GAP Report on Rule 803. The words "Transferred to Rule 807" were substituted for "Abrogated."

2000 Amendment

The amendment provides that the foundation requirements of Rule 803(6) can be satisfied under certain circumstances without the expense and inconvenience of producing time-consuming foundation witnesses. Under current law, courts have generally required foundation witnesses to testify. *See, e.g., Tongil Co., Ltd. v. Hyundai Merchant Marine Corp.*, 968 F.2d 999 (9th Cir. 1992) (reversing a judgment based on business records where a qualified person filed an affidavit but did not testify). Protections are provided by the authentication requirements of Rule 902(11) for domestic records, Rule 902(12) for foreign records in civil cases, and 18 U.S.C. § 3505 for foreign records in criminal cases.

GAP Report—Proposed Amendment to Rule 803(6)

The Committee made no changes to the published draft of the proposed amendment to Evidence Rule 803(6).

2011 Amendments

The language of Rule 803 has been amended as part of the restyling of the Evidence Rules to make them more easily understood and to make style and terminology consistent throughout the rules. These changes are intended to be stylistic only. There is no intent to change any result in any ruling on evidence admissibility.

HISTORICAL NOTES

Revision Notes and Legislative Reports

1975 Acts

House Report No. 94–599, see 1975 U.S. Code Cong. and Adm. News, p. 1585.

Rule 804. Exceptions to the Rule Against Hearsay—When the Declarant Is Unavailable as a Witness

(a) Criteria for Being Unavailable. A declarant is considered to be unavailable as a witness if the declarant:

(1) is exempted from testifying about the subject matter of the declarant's statement because the court rules that a privilege applies;

(2) refuses to testify about the subject matter despite a court order to do so;

(3) testifies to not remembering the subject matter;

(4) cannot be present or testify at the trial or hearing because of death or a then-existing infirmity, physical illness, or mental illness; or

(5) is absent from the trial or hearing and the statement's proponent has not been able, by process or other reasonable means, to procure:

(A) the declarant's attendance, in the case of a hearsay exception under Rule 804(b)(1) or (6); or

(B) the declarant's attendance or testimony, in the case of a hearsay exception under Rule 804(b)(2), (3), or (4).

But this subdivision (a) does not apply if the statement's proponent procured or wrongfully caused the declarant's unavailability as a witness in order to prevent the declarant from attending or testifying.

(b) The Exceptions. The following are not excluded by the rule against hearsay if the declarant is unavailable as a witness:

(1) Former Testimony. Testimony that:

(A) was given as a witness at a trial, hearing, or lawful deposition, whether given during the current proceeding or a different one; and

(B) is now offered against a party who had—or, in a civil case, whose predecessor in interest had—an opportunity and similar motive to develop it by direct, cross-, or redirect examination.

(2) Statement Under the Belief of Imminent Death. In a prosecution for homicide or in a civil case, a statement that the declarant, while believing the declarant's death to be imminent, made about its cause or circumstances.

(3) Statement Against Interest. A statement that:

(A) a reasonable person in the declarant's position would have made only if the person believed it to be true because, when made, it was so contrary to the declarant's proprietary or pecuniary interest or had so great a tendency to invalidate the declarant's claim against someone else or to expose the declarant to civil or criminal liability; and

(B) is supported by corroborating circumstances that clearly indicate its trustworthiness, if it is offered in a criminal case as one that tends to expose the declarant to criminal liability.

(4) Statement of Personal or Family History. A statement about:

(A) the declarant's own birth, adoption, legitimacy, ancestry, marriage, divorce, relationship by blood, adoption, or marriage, or similar facts of personal or family history, even though the declarant had no way of acquiring personal knowledge about that fact; or

(B) another person concerning any of these facts, as well as death, if the declarant was related to the person by blood, adoption, or marriage or was so intimately associated with the person's family that the declarant's information is likely to be accurate.

(5) [Other Exceptions.] [Transferred to Rule 807.]

(6) Statement Offered Against a Party That Wrongfully Caused the Declarant's Unavailability. A statement offered against a party that wrongfully caused—or acquiesced in wrongfully causing—the declarant's unavailability as a witness, and did so intending that result.

(Pub.L. 93–595, § 1, Jan. 2, 1975, 88 Stat. 1942; Pub.L. 94–149, § 1(12), (13), Dec. 12, 1975, 89 Stat. 806; Mar. 2, 1987, eff. Oct. 1, 1987; Pub.L. 100–690, Title VII, § 7075(b), Nov. 18, 1988, 102 Stat. 4405; Apr. 11, 1997, eff. Dec. 1, 1997; Apr. 28, 2010, eff. Dec. 1, 2010; Apr. 26, 2011, eff. Dec. 1, 2011.)

ADVISORY COMMITTEE NOTES

1972 Proposed Rules

As to firsthand knowledge on the part of hearsay declarants, see the introductory portion of the Advisory Committee's Note to Rule 803.

Note to Subdivision (a). The definition of unavailability implements the division of hearsay exceptions into two categories by Rules 803 and 804(b).

At common law the unavailability requirement was evolved in connection with particular hearsay exceptions rather than along general lines. For example, see the separate explications of unavailability in relation to former testimony, declarations against interest, and statements of pedigree, separately developed in McCormick §§ 234, 257, and 297. However, no reason is apparent for making distinctions as to what satisfies unavailability for the different exceptions. The treatment in the rule is therefore uniform although differences in the range of process for witnesses between civil and criminal cases will lead to a less exacting requirement under item (5). See Rule 45(e) of the Federal Rules of Civil Procedure and Rule 17(e) of the Federal Rules of Criminal Procedure.

Five instances of unavailability are specified:

(1) Substantial authority supports the position that exercise of a claim of privilege by the declarant satisfies the requirement of unavailability (usually in connection with former testimony). *Wyatt v. State,* 35 Ala.App. 147, 46 So.2d 837 (1950); *State v. Stewart,* 85 Kan. 404, 116 P. 489 (1911); Annot., 45 A.L.R.2d 1354; Uniform Rule 62(7)(a); California Evidence Code § 240(a)(1); Kansas Code of Civil Procedure § 60–459(g)(1). A ruling by the judge is required, which clearly implies that an actual claim of privilege must be made.

(2) A witness is rendered unavailable if he simply refuses to testify concerning the subject matter of his statement despite judicial pressures to do so, a position supported by similar considerations of practicality. *Johnson v. People,* 152 Colo. 586, 384 P.2d 454 (1963); *People v. Pickett,* 339 Mich. 294, 63 N.W.2d 681, 45 A.L.R.2d 1341 (1954). *Contra, Pleau v. State,* 255 Wis. 362, 38 N.W.2d 496 (1949).

(3) The position that a claimed lack of memory by the witness of the subject matter of his statement constitutes unavailability likewise finds support in the cases, though not without dissent. McCormick § 234, p. 494. If the claim is successful, the practical effect is to put the testimony beyond reach, as in the other instances. In this instance, however, it will be noted that the lack of memory must be established by the testimony of the witness himself, which clearly contemplates his production and subjection to cross-examination.

(4) Death and infirmity find general recognition as grounds. McCormick §§ 234, 257, 297; Uniform Rule 62(7)(c); California Evidence Code § 240(a)(3); Kansas Code of Civil Procedure § 60–459(g)(3); New Jersey Evidence Rule 62(6)(c). See also the provisions on use of depositions in Rule 32(a)(3) of the Federal Rules of Civil Procedure and Rule 15(e) of the Federal Rules of Criminal Procedure.

(5) Absence from the hearing coupled with inability to compel attendance by process or other reasonable means also satisfies the requirement. McCormick § 234; Uniform Rule 62(7)(d) and (e); California Evidence Code § 240(a)(4) and (5); Kansas Code of Civil Procedure § 60–459(g)(4) and (5); New Jersey Rule 62(6)(b) and (d). See the discussion of procuring attendance of witnesses who are nonresidents or in custody in *Barber v. Page,* 390 U.S. 719, 88 S.Ct. 1318, 20 L.Ed.2d 255 (1968).

If the conditions otherwise constituting unavailability result from the procurement or wrongdoing of the proponent of the statement, the requirement is not satisfied. The rule contains no requirement that an attempt be made to take the deposition of a declarant.

Note to Subdivision (b). Rule 803, *supra,* is based upon the assumption that a hearsay statement falling within one of its exceptions possesses qualities which justify the conclusion that whether the declarant is available or unavailable is not a relevant factor in determining admissibility. The instant rule proceeds upon a different theory: hearsay which admittedly is not equal in quality to testimony of the declarant on the stand may nevertheless be admitted if the declarant is unavailable and if his statement meets a specified standard. The rule expresses preferences: testimony given on the stand in person is preferred over hearsay, and hearsay, if of the specified quality, is preferred over complete loss of the evidence of the declarant. The exceptions evolved at common law with respect to declarations of unavailable declarants furnish the basis for the exceptions enumerated in the proposal. The term "unavailable" is defined in subdivision (a).

Exception (1). Former testimony does not rely upon some set of circumstances to substitute for oath and cross-examination, since both oath and opportunity to cross-examine were present in fact. The only missing one of the ideal conditions for the giving of testimony is the presence of trier and opponent ("demeanor evidence"). This is lacking with all hearsay exceptions. Hence it may be argued that former testimony is the strongest hearsay and should be included under Rule 803, supra. However, opportunity to observe demeanor is what in a large measure confers depth and meaning upon oath and cross-examination. Thus in cases under Rule 803 demeanor lacks the significance which it possesses with respect to testimony. In any event, the tradition, founded in experience, uniformly favors production of the witness if he is available. The exception indicates continuation of the policy. This preference for the presence of the witness is apparent also in rules and statutes on the use of depositions, which deal with substantially the same problem.

Under the exception, the testimony may be offered (1) against the party *against* whom it was previously offered or (2) against the party *by* whom it was previously offered. In each instance the question resolves itself into whether fairness allows imposing, upon the party against whom now offered, the handling of the witness of the earlier occasion. (1) If the party against whom now offered is the one against whom the testimony was offered previously, no unfairness is apparent in requiring him to accept his own prior conduct of cross-examination or decision not to cross-examine. Only demeanor has been lost, and that is inherent in the situation. (2) If the party against whom now offered is the one *by* whom the testimony was offered previously, a satisfactory answer becomes somewhat more difficult. One possibility is to proceed somewhat along the line of an adoptive admission, i.e. by offering the testimony proponent in effect adopts it. However, this theory savors of discarded concepts of witnesses' belonging to a party, of litigants' ability to pick and choose witnesses, and of vouching for one's own witnesses. Cf. McCormick § 246, pp. 526–527; 4 Wigmore § 1075. A more direct and acceptable approach is simply to recognize direct and redirect examination of one's own witness as the equivalent of cross-examining an opponent's witness. Falknor, Former Testimony and the Uniform Rules: A Comment, 38 N.Y.U.L.Rev. 651, n. 1 (1963); McCormick § 231, p. 483. See also 5 Wigmore § 1389. Allowable techniques for dealing with hostile, double-crossing, forgetful, and mentally deficient witnesses leave no substance to a claim that one could not adequately develop his own witness at the former hearing. An even less appealing argument is presented when failure to develop fully was the result of a deliberate choice.

The common law did not limit the admissibility of former testimony to that given in an earlier trial of the same case, although it did require identity of issues as a means of insuring that the former handling of the witness was the equivalent of what would now be done if the opportunity were presented. Modern decisions reduce the requirement to "substantial" identity. McCormick § 233. Since identity of issues is significant only in that it bears on motive and interest in developing fully the testimony of the witness, expressing the matter in the latter terms is preferable. *Id.* Testimony given at a preliminary hearing was held in *California v. Green,* 399 U.S. 149, 90 S.Ct. 1930, 26 L.Ed.2d 489 (1970), to satisfy confrontation requirements in this respect.

As a further assurance of fairness in thrusting upon a party the prior handling of the witness, the common law also insisted upon identity of parties, deviating only to the extent of allowing substitution of successors in a narrowly construed privity. Mutuality as an aspect of identity is now generally discredited, and the requirement of identity of the offering party disappears except as it might affect motive to develop the testimony. Falknor, *supra,* at 652; McCormick § 232, pp. 487–488. The question remains whether strict identity, or privity, should continue as a requirement with respect to the party against whom offered. The rule departs to the extent of allowing substitution of one with the right and opportunity to develop the testimony with similar motive and interest. This position is supported by modern decisions. McCormick § 232, pp. 489–490; 5 Wigmore § 1388.

Provisions of the same tenor will be found in Uniform Rule 63(3)(b); California Evidence Code §§ 1290–1292; Kansas Code of Civil Procedure § 60–460(c)(2); New Jersey Evidence Rule 63(3). Unlike the rule, the latter three provide either that former testimony is not admissible if the right of confrontation is denied or that it is not admissible if the accused was not a party to the prior hearing. The genesis of these limitations is a caveat in Uniform Rule 63(3) Comment that use of former testimony against an accused may violate his right of confrontation. *Mattox v. United States,* 156 U.S. 237, 15 S.Ct. 337, 39 L.Ed. 409 (1895), held that the right was not violated by the Government's use, on a retrial of the same case, of testimony given at the first trial by two witnesses since deceased. The decision leaves open the questions (1) whether direct and redirect are equivalent to cross-examination for purposes of confrontation, (2) whether testimony given in a different proceeding is acceptable, and (3) whether the accused must himself have been a party to the earlier proceeding or whether a similarly situated person will serve the purpose. Professor Falknor concluded that, if a dying declaration untested by cross-examination is constitutionally admissible, former testimony tested by the cross-examination of one similarly situated does not offend against confrontation. Falknor, *supra,* at 659–660. The constitutional acceptability of dying declarations has often been conceded. *Mattox v. United States,* 156 U.S. 237, 243, 15 S.Ct. 337, 39 L.Ed. 409 (1895); *Kirby v. United States,* 174 U.S. 47, 61, 19 S.Ct. 574, 43 L.Ed. 890 (1899); *Pointer v. Texas,* 380 U.S. 400, 407, 85 S.Ct. 1065, 13 L.Ed.2d 923 (1965).

Exception (2). The exception is the familiar dying declaration of the common law, expanded somewhat beyond its traditionally narrow limits. While the original religious justification for the exception may have lost its conviction for some persons over the years, it can scarcely be doubted that powerful psychological pressures are present. See 5 Wigmore § 1443 and the classic statement of Chief Baron Eyre in Rex v. Woodcock, 1 Leach 500, 502, 168 Eng.Rep. 352, 353 (K.B.1789).

The common law required that the statement be that of the victim, offered in a prosecution for criminal homicide. Thus declarations by victims in prosecutions for other crimes, e.g. a declaration by a rape victim who dies in childbirth, and all declarations in civil cases were outside the scope of the exception. An occasional statute has removed these restrictions, as in Colo.R.S. § 52–1–20, or has expanded the area of offenses to include abortions, 5 Wigmore § 1432, p. 224, n. 4. Kansas by decision extended the exception to civil cases. *Thurston v. Fritz,* 91 Kan. 468, 138 P. 625 (1914). While the common law exception no doubt originated as a result of the exceptional need for the evidence in homicide cases, the theory of admissibility applies equally in civil cases and in prosecutions for crimes other than homicide. The same considerations suggest abandonment of the limitation to circumstances attending the event in question, yet when the statement deals with matters other than the supposed death, its influence is believed to be sufficiently attenuated to justify the limitation. Unavailability is not limited to death. See subdivision (a) of this rule. Any problem as to declarations phrased in terms of opinion is laid at rest by Rule 701, and continuation of a requirement of firsthand knowledge is assured by Rule 602.

Comparable provisions are found in Uniform Rule 63(5); California Evidence Code § 1242; Kansas Code of Civil Procedure § 60–460(e); New Jersey Evidence Rule 63(5).

Exception (3). The circumstantial guaranty of reliability for declarations against interest is the assumption that persons do not make statements which are damaging to themselves unless satisfied for good reason that they are true. *Hileman v. Northwest Engineering Co.,* 346 F.2d 668 (6th Cir.1965). If the statement is that of a party, offered by his opponent, it comes in as an admission, Rule 803(d)(2) [sic; probably should be "Rule 801(d)(2)"], and there is no occasion to inquire whether it is against interest, this not being a condition precedent to admissibility of admissions by opponents.

The common law required that the interest declared against be pecuniary or proprietary but within this limitation demonstrated striking ingenuity in discovering an against-interest aspect. Higham v. Ridgway, 10 East 109, 103 Eng.Rep. 717 (K.B.1808); Reg. v. Overseers of Birmingham, 1 B. & S. 763, 121 Eng.Rep. 897 (Q.B.1861); McCormick, § 256, p. 551, nn. 2 and 3.

The exception discards the common law limitation and expands to the full logical limit. One result is to remove doubt as to the admissibility of declarations tending to establish a tort liability against the declarant or to extinguish one which might be asserted by him, in accordance with the trend of the decisions in this country. McCormick § 254, pp. 548–549. Another is to allow statements tending to expose declarant to hatred, ridicule, or disgrace, the motivation here being considered to be as strong as when financial interests are at stake. McCormick § 255, p. 551. And finally, exposure to criminal liability satisfies the against-interest requirement. The refusal of the common law to concede the adequacy of a penal interest was no doubt indefensible in logic, see the dissent of Mr. Justice Holmes in *Donnelly v. United States,* 228 U.S. 243, 33 S.Ct. 449, 57 L.Ed. 820 (1913), but one senses in the decisions a distrust of evidence of confessions by third persons offered to exculpate the accused arising from suspicions of fabrication either of the fact of the making of the confession or in its contents, enhanced in either instance by the required unavailability of the declarant. Nevertheless, an increasing amount of decisional law recognizes exposure to punishment for crime as a sufficient stake. *People v. Spriggs,* 60 Cal.2d 868, 36 Cal.Rptr. 841, 389 P.2d 377 (1964); *Sutter v. Easterly,* 354 Mo. 282, 189 S.W.2d 284 (1945); Band's Refuse Removal, Inc. v. Fairlawn Borough, 62 N.J.Super. 522, 163 A.2d 465 (1960); *Newberry v. Commonwealth,* 191 Va. 445, 61 S.E.2d 318 (1950); Annot., 162 A.L.R. 446. The requirement of corroboration is included in the rule in order to effect an accommodation between these competing considerations. When the statement is offered by the accused by way of exculpation, the resulting situation is not adapted to control by rulings as to the weight of the evidence, and hence the provision is cast in terms of a requirement preliminary to admissibility. Cf. Rule 406(a). The requirement of corroboration should be construed in such a manner as to effectuate its purpose of circumventing fabrication.

Ordinarily the third-party confession is thought of in terms of exculpating the accused, but this is by no means always or necessarily the case: it may include statements implicating him, and under the general theory of declarations against interest they would be admissible as related statements. Douglas v. Alabama, 380 U.S. 415, 85 S.Ct. 1074, 13 L.Ed.2d 934 (1965), and Bruton v. United States, 389 U.S. 818, 88 S.Ct. 126, 19 L.Ed.2d 70 (1968), both involved confessions by codefendants which implicated the accused. While the confession was not actually offered in evidence in *Douglas,* the procedure followed effectively put it before the jury, which the Court ruled to be error. Whether the confession might have been admissible as a declaration against penal interest was not considered or discussed. *Bruton* assumed the inadmissibility, as against the accused, of the implicating confession of his codefendant, and centered upon the question of the effectiveness of a limiting instruction. These decisions, however, by no means require that all statements implicating another person be excluded from the category of declarations against interest. Whether a statement is in fact against interest must be determined from the circumstances of each case. Thus a statement admitting guilt and implicating another person, made while in custody, may well be motivated by a desire to curry favor with the authorities and hence fail to qualify as against interest. See the dissenting opinion of Mr. Justice White in *Bruton.* On the other hand, the same words spoken under different circumstances, e.g., to an acquaintance, would have no difficulty in qualifying. The rule does not purport to deal with questions of the right of confrontation.

The balancing of self-serving against dissenting aspects of a declaration is discussed in McCormick § 256.

For comparable provisions, see Uniform Rule 63(10); California Evidence Code § 1230; Kansas Code of Civil Procedure § 60–460(j); New Jersey Evidence Rule 63(10).

Exception (4). The general common law requirement that a declaration in this area must have been made *ante litem motam* has been dropped, as bearing more appropriately on weight than admissibility. See 5 Wigmore § 1483. Item (i)[(A)] specifically disclaims any need of firsthand knowledge respecting declarant's own personal history. In some instances it is self-evident (marriage) and in others impossible and traditionally not required (date of birth). Item (ii)[(B)] deals with declarations concerning the history of another person. As at common law, declarant is qualified if related by blood or marriage. 5 Wigmore § 1489. In addition, and contrary to the common law, declarant qualifies by virtue of intimate association with the family. *Id.,* § 1487. The requirement sometimes encountered that when the subject of the statement is the relationship between two other persons the declarant must qualify as to both is omitted. Relationship is reciprocal. *Id.,* § 1491.

For comparable provisions, see Uniform Rule 63(23), (24), (25); California Evidence Code §§ 1310, 1311; Kansas Code of Civil Procedure § 60–460(u), (v), (w); New Jersey Evidence Rules 63–23), 63(24), 63(25).

1974 Enactment

Note to Subdivision (a)(3). Rule 804(a)(3) was approved in the form submitted by the Court. However, the Committee intends no change in existing federal law under which the court may choose to disbelieve the declarant's testimony as to his lack of memory. See *United States v. Insana,* 423 F.2d 1165, 1169–1170 (2nd Cir.), cert. denied, 400 U.S. 841 (1970).

Note to Subdivision (a)(5). Rule 804(a)(5) as submitted to the Congress provided, as one type of situation in which a declarant would be deemed "unavailable", that he be "absent from the hearing and the proponent of his statement has been unable to procure his attendance by process or other reasonable means." The Committee amended the Rule to insert after the word "attendance" the parenthetical expression "(or, in the case of a hearsay exception under subdivision (b)(2), (3), or (4), his attendance or testimony)". The amendment is designed primarily to require that an attempt be made to depose a witness (as well as to seek his attendance) as a precondition to the witness being deemed unavailable. The Committee, however, recognized the propriety of an exception to this additional requirement when it is the declarant's former testimony that is sought to be admitted under subdivision (b)(1).

Note to Subdivision (b)(1). Rule 804(b)(1) as submitted by the Court allowed prior testimony of an unavailable witness to be admissible if the party against whom it is offered or a person "with motive and interest similar" to his had an opportunity to examine the witness. The Committee considered that it is generally unfair to impose upon the party against whom the hearsay evidence is being offered responsibility for the manner in which the witness was previously handled by another party. The sole exception to this, in the Committee's view, is when a party's predecessor in interest in a civil action or proceeding had an opportunity and similar motive to examine the witness. The Committee amended the Rule to reflect these policy determinations.

Note to Subdivision (b)(2). Rule 804(b)(3) as submitted by the Court (now Rule 804(b)(2) in the bill) proposed to expand the traditional scope of the dying declaration exception (i.e. a statement of the victim in a homicide case as to the cause or circumstances of his believed imminent death) to allow such statements in all criminal and civil cases. The Committee did not consider dying declarations as among the most reliable forms of hearsay. Consequently, it amended the provision to limit their admissibility in criminal cases to homicide prosecutions, where exceptional need for the evidence is present. This is existing law. At the same time, the Committee approved the expansion to civil actions and proceedings where the stakes do not involve possible imprisonment, although noting that this could lead to forum shopping in some instances.

Note to Subdivision (b)(3). Rule 804(b)(4) as submitted by the Court (now Rule 804(b)(3) in the bill) provided as follows:

Statement against interest.—A statement which was at the time of its making so far contrary to the declarant's pecuniary or proprietary interest or so far tended to subject him to civil or criminal liability or to render invalid a claim by him against another or to make him an object of hatred, ridicule, or disgrace, that a reasonable man in his position would not have made the statement unless he believed it to be true. A statement tending to exculpate the accused is not admissible unless corroborated.

The Committee determined to retain the traditional hearsay exception for statements against pecuniary or proprietary interest. However, it deemed the Court's additional references to statements tending to subject a declarant to civil liability or to render invalid a claim by him against another to be redundant as included within the scope of the reference to statements against pecuniary or proprietary interest. See *Gichner v. Antonio Triano Tile and Marble Co.,* 410 F.2d 238 (D.C.Cir.1968). Those additional references were accordingly deleted.

The Court's Rule also proposed to expand the hearsay limitation from its present federal limitation to include statements subjecting the declarant to criminal liability and statements tending to make him an object of hatred, ridicule, or disgrace. The Committee eliminated the latter category from the subdivision as lacking sufficient guarantees of reliability. See *United States v. Dovico,* 380 F.2d 325, 327 nn. 2, 4 (2nd Cir.), cert. denied, 389 U.S. 944 (1967). As for statements against penal interest, the Committee shared the view of the Court that some such statements do possess adequate assurances of reliability and should be admissible. It believed, however, as did the Court, that statements of this type tending to exculpate the accused are more suspect and so should have their admissibility conditioned upon some further provision insuring trustworthiness. The proposal in the Court Rule to add a requirement of simple corroboration was, however, deemed ineffective to accomplish this purpose since the accused's own testimony might suffice while not necessarily increasing the reliability of the hearsay statement. The Committee settled upon the language "unless corroborating circumstances clearly indicate the trustworthiness of the statement" as affording a proper standard and degree of discretion. It was contemplated that the result in such cases as *Donnelly v. United States,* 228 U.S. 243 (1912), where the circumstances plainly indicated reliability, would be changed. The Committee also added to the Rule the final sentence from the 1971 Advisory Committee draft, designed to codify the doctrine of *Bruton v. United States,* 391 U.S. 123 (1968). The Committee does not intend to affect the existing exception to the *Bruton* principle where the codefendant takes the stand and is subject to cross-examination, but believed there was no need to make specific provision for this situation in the Rule, since in that event the declarant would not be "unavailable". House Report No. 93–650.

Note to Subdivision (a)(5). Subdivision (a) of rule 804 as submitted by the Supreme Court defined the conditions under which a witness was considered to be unavailable. It was amended in the House.

The purpose of the amendment, according to the report of the House Committee on the Judiciary, is "primarily to require that an attempt be made to depose a witness (as well as to seek his attendance) as a precondition to the witness being unavailable."

Under the House amendment, before a witness is declared unavailable, a party must try to depose a witness (declarant) with respect to dying declarations, declarations against interest, and declarations of pedigree. None of these situations would seem to warrant this needless, impractical and highly restrictive complication. A good case can be made for eliminating the unavailability requirement entirely for declarations against interest cases. [Uniform rule 63(10); Kan.Stat.Anno. 60–460(j); 2A N.J.Stats.Anno. 84–63(10).]

In dying declaration cases, the declarant will usually, though not necessarily, be deceased at the time of trial. Pedigree statements which are admittedly and necessarily based largely on word of mouth are not greatly fortified by a deposition requirement.

Depositions are expensive and time-consuming. In any event, deposition procedures are available to those who wish to resort to them. Moreover, the deposition procedures of the Civil Rules and Criminal Rules are only imperfectly adapted to implementing the amendment. No purpose is served unless the deposition, if taken, may be used in evidence. Under Civil Rule (a)(3) the Criminal Rule 15(e), a deposition, though taken, may not be admissible, and under Criminal Rule 15(a) substantial obstacles exist in the way of even taking a deposition.

For these reasons, the committee deleted the House amendment.

The committee understands that the rule as to unavailability, as explained by the Advisory Committee "contains no requirement that an attempt be made to take the deposition of a declarant." In reflecting the committee's judgment, the statement is accurate insofar as it goes. Where, however, the proponent of the statement, with knowledge of the existence of the statement, fails to confront the declarant with the statement at the taking of the deposition, then the proponent should not, in fairness, be permitted to treat the declarant as "unavailable" simply because the declarant was not amenable to process compelling his attendance at trial. The committee does not consider it necessary to amend the rule to this effect because such a situation abuses, not conforms to, the rule. Fairness would preclude a person from introducing a hearsay statement on a particular issue if the person taking the deposition was aware of the issue at the time of the deposition but failed to depose the unavailable witness on that issue.

Note to Subdivision (b)(1). Former testimony.—Rule 804(b)(1) as submitted by the Court allowed prior testimony of an unavailable witness to be admissible if the party against whom it is offered or a person "with motive and interest similar" to his had an opportunity to examine the witness.

The House amended the rule to apply only to a party's predecessor in interest. Although the committee recognizes considerable merit to the rule submitted by the Supreme Court, a position which has been advocated by many scholars and judges, we have concluded that the difference between the two versions is not great and we accept the House amendment.

Note to Subdivision (b)(3). The rule defines those statements which are considered to be against interest and thus of sufficient trustworthiness to be admissible even though hearsay. With regard to the type of interest declared against, the version submitted by the Supreme Court included inter alia, statements tending to subject a declarant to civil liability or to invalidate a claim by him against another. The House struck these provisions as redundant. In view of the conflicting case law construing pecuniary or proprietary interests narrowly so as to exclude, e.g., tort cases, this deletion could be misconstrued.

Three States which have recently codified their rules of evidence have followed the Supreme Court's version of this rule, i.e., that a statement is against interest if it tends to subject a declarant to civil liability. [Nev.Rev.Stats. § 51.345; N.Mex.Stats. (1973 Supp.) § 20–4–804(4); West's Wis.Stats.Anno. (1973 Supp.) § 908.045(4).]

The committee believes that the reference to statements tending to subject a person to civil liability constitutes a desirable clarification of the scope of the rule. Therefore, we have reinstated the Supreme Court language on this matter.

The Court rule also proposed to expand the hearsay limitation from its present federal limitation to include statements subjecting the declarant to statements tending to make him an object of hatred, ridicule, or disgrace. The House eliminated the latter category from the subdivision as lacking sufficient guarantees of reliability. Although there is considerable support for the admissibility of such statements (all three of the State rules referred to supra, would admit such statements), we accept the deletion by the House.

The House amended this exception to add a sentence making inadmissible a statement or confession offered against the accused in a criminal case, made by a codefendant or other person implicating both himself and the accused. The sentence was added to codify the constitutional principle announced in *Bruton v. United States,* 391 U.S. 123 (1968). Bruton held that the admission of the extrajudicial hearsay statement of one codefendant inculpating a second codefendant violated the confrontation clause of the sixth amendment.

The committee decided to delete this provision because the basic approach of the rules is to avoid codifying, or attempting to codify, constitutional evidentiary principles, such as the fifth amendment's right against self-incrimination and, here, the sixth amendment's right of confrontation. Codification of a constitutional principle is unnecessary and, where the principle is under development, often unwise. Furthermore, the House provision does not appear to recognize the exceptions to the *Bruton* rule, e.g. where the codefendant takes the stand and is subject to cross examination; where the accused confessed, see *United States v. Mancusi,* 404 F.2d 296 (2d Cir.1968), cert. denied 397 U.S. 942 (1907); where the accused was placed at the scene of the crime, see *United States v. Zelker,* 452 F.2d 1009 (2d Cir.1971). For these reasons, the committee decided to delete this provision.

Note to Subdivision (b)(5). See Note to Paragraph (24), Notes of Committee on the Judiciary, Senate Report No. 93–1277, set out as a note under rule 803 of these rules. Senate Report No. 93–1277.

Rule 804 defines what hearsay statements are admissible in evidence if the declarant is unavailable as a witness. The Senate amendments make four changes in the rule.

Note to Subdivision (a)(5). Subsection (a) defines the term "unavailability as a witness". The House bill provides in subsection (a)(5) that the party who desires to use the statement must be unable to procure the declarant's attendance by process or other reasonable means. In the case of dying declarations, statements against interest and statements of personal or family history, the House bill requires that the proponent must also be unable to procure the declarant's *testimony* (such as by deposition or interrogatories) by process or other reasonable means. The Senate amendment eliminates this latter provision.

The Conference adopts the provision contained in the House bill.

Note to Subdivision (b)(3). The Senate amendment to subsection (b)(3) provides that a statement is against interest and not excluded by the hearsay rule when the declarant is unavailable as a witness, if the statement tends to subject a person to civil or criminal liability or renders invalid a claim by him against another. The House bill did not refer specifically to civil liability and to rendering invalid a claim against another. The Senate amendment also deletes from the House bill the provision that subsection (b)(3) does not apply to a statement or confession, made by a codefendant or another, which implicates the accused and the person who made the statement, when that statement or confession is offered against the accused in a criminal case.

The Conference adopts the Senate amendment. The Conferees intend to include within the purview of this rule, statements subjecting a person to civil liability and statements rendering claims invalid. The Conferees agree to delete the provision regarding statements by a codefendant, thereby reflecting the general approach in the Rules of Evidence to avoid attempting to codify constitutional evidentiary principles.

Note to Subdivision (b)(5). The Senate amendment adds a new subsection, (b)(6) [now (b)(5)], which makes admissible a hearsay statement not specifically covered by any of the five previous subsections, if the statement has equivalent circumstantial guarantees of trustworthiness and if the court determines that (A) the statement is offered as evidence of a material fact; (B) the statement is more probative on the point for which it is offered than any other evidence the proponent can procure through reasonable efforts; and (C) the general purposes of these rules and the interests of justice will best be served by admission of the statement into evidence.

The House bill eliminated a similar, but broader, provision because of the conviction that such a provision injected too much uncertainty into the law of evidence regarding hearsay and impaired the ability of a litigant to prepare adequately for trial.

The Conference adopts the Senate amendment with an amendment that renumbers this subsection and provides that a party intending to request the court to use a statement under this provision must notify any adverse party of this intention as well as of the particulars of the statement, including the name and address of the declarant. This notice must be given sufficiently in advance of the trial or hearing to provide any adverse party with a fair opportunity to prepare to contest the use of the statement. House Report No. 93–1597.

1987 Amendments

The amendments are technical. No substantive change is intended.

1997 Amendments

Subdivision (b)(5). The contents of Rule 803(24) and Rule 804(b)(5) have been combined and transferred to a new Rule 807. This was done to facilitate additions to Rules 803 and 804. No change in meaning is intended.

Subdivision (b)(6). Rule 804(b)(6) has been added to provide that a party forfeits the right to object on hearsay grounds to the admission of a declarant's prior statement when the party's deliberate wrongdoing or acquiescence therein procured the unavailability of the declarant as a witness. This recognizes the need for a prophylactic rule to deal with abhorrent behavior "which strikes at the heart of the system of justice itself." *United States v. Mastrangelo*, 693 F.2d 269, 273 (2d Cir.1982), *cert. denied*, 467 U.S. 1204 (1984). The wrongdoing need not consist of a criminal act. The rule applies to all parties, including the government.

Every circuit that has resolved the question has recognized the principle of forfeiture by misconduct, although the tests for determining whether there is a forfeiture have varied. *See, e.g., United States v. Aguiar*, 975 F.2d 45, 47 (2d Cir.1992); *United States v. Potamitis*, 739 F.2d 784, 789 (2d Cir.), *cert. denied*, 469 U.S. 918 (1984); *Steele v. Taylor*, 684 F.2d 1193, 1199 (6th Cir.1982), *cert. denied*, 460 U.S. 1053 (1983); United States v. Balano, 618 F.2d 624, 629 (10th Cir.1979), *cert. denied*, 449 U.S. 840 (1980); *United States v. Carlson*, 547 F.2d 1346, 1358–59 (8th Cir.), *cert. denied*, 431 U.S. 914 (1977). The foregoing cases apply a preponderance of the evidence standard. *Contra United States v. Thevis*, 665 F.2d 616, 631 (5th Cir.) (clear and convincing standard), *cert. denied*, 459 U.S. 825 (1982). The usual Rule 104(a) preponderance of the evidence standard has been adopted in light of the behavior the new Rule 804(b)(6) seeks to discourage.

GAP Report on Rule 804(b)(5). The words "Transferred to Rule 807" were substituted for "Abrogated".

GAP Report on Rule 804(b)(6). The title of the rule was changed to "Forfeiture by wrongdoing." The word "who" in line 24 was changed to "that" to indicate that the rule is potentially applicable against the government. Two sentences were added to the first paragraph of the committee note to clarify that the wrongdoing need not be criminal in nature, and to indicate the rule's potential applicability to the government. The word "forfeiture" was substituted for "waiver" in the note.

2010 Amendments

Subdivision (b)(3). Rule 804(b)(3) has been amended to provide that the corroborating circumstances requirement applies to all declarations against penal interest offered in criminal cases. A number of courts have applied the corroborating circumstances requirement to declarations against penal interest offered by the prosecution, even though the text of the Rule did not so provide. *See, e.g., United States v. Alvarez*, 584 F.2d 694, 701 (5th Cir. 1978) ("by transplanting the language governing exculpatory statements onto the analysis for admitting inculpatory hearsay, a unitary standard is derived which offers the most workable basis for applying Rule 804(b)(3)"); *United States v. Shukri*, 207 F.3d 412 (7th Cir. 2000) (requiring corroborating circumstances for against-penal-interest statements offered by the government). A unitary approach to declarations against penal interest assures both the prosecution and the accused that the Rule will not be abused and that only reliable hearsay statements will be admitted under the exception.

All other changes to the structure and wording of the Rule are intended to be stylistic only. There is no intent to change any other result in any ruling on evidence admissibility.

The amendment does not address the use of the corroborating circumstances for declarations against penal interest offered in civil cases.

In assessing whether corroborating circumstances exist, some courts have focused on the credibility of the witness who relates the hearsay statement in court. But the credibility of the witness who relates the statement is not a proper factor for the court to consider in assessing corroborating circumstances. To base admission or exclusion of a hearsay statement on the witness's credibility would usurp the jury's role of determining the credibility of testifying witnesses.

2011 Amendments

The language of Rule 804 has been amended as part of the general restyling of the Evidence Rules to make them more easily understood and to make style and terminology consistent throughout the rules. These changes are intended to be stylistic only. There is no intent to change any result in any ruling on evidence admissibility.

No style changes were made to Rule 804(b)(3), because it was already restyled in conjunction with a substantive amendment, effective December 1, 2010.

HISTORICAL NOTES

Revision Notes and Legislative Reports

1975 Acts

House Report No. 94–599, see 1975 U.S. Code Cong. and Adm. News, p. 1585.

Rule 805. Hearsay Within Hearsay

Hearsay within hearsay is not excluded by the rule against hearsay if each part of the combined statements conforms with an exception to the rule.

(Pub.L. 93–595, § 1, Jan. 2, 1975, 88 Stat. 1943; Apr. 26, 2011, eff. Dec. 1, 2011.)

ADVISORY COMMITTEE NOTES

1972 Proposed Rules

On principle it scarcely seems open to doubt that the hearsay rule should not call for exclusion of a hearsay statement which includes a further hearsay statement when both conform to the requirements of a hearsay exception. Thus a hospital record might contain an entry of the patient's age based on information furnished by his wife. The hospital record would qualify as a regular entry except that the person who furnished the information was not acting in the routine of the business. However, her statement independently qualifies as a statement of pedigree (if she is unavailable) or as a statement made for purposes of diagnosis or treatment, and hence each link in the chain falls under sufficient assurances. Or, further to illustrate, a dying declaration may incorporate a declaration against interest by another declarant. See McCormick § 290, p. 611.

2011 Amendments

The language of Rule 805 has been amended as part of the restyling of the Evidence Rules to make them more easily understood and to make style and terminology consistent throughout the rules. These changes are intended to be stylistic only. There is no intent to change any result in any ruling on evidence admissibility.

Rule 806. Attacking and Supporting the Declarant's Credibility

When a hearsay statement—or a statement described in Rule 801(d)(2)(C), (D), or (E)—has been admitted in evidence, the declarant's credibility may be attacked, and then supported, by any evidence that would be admissible for those purposes if the declarant had testified as a witness. The court may admit evidence of the declarant's inconsistent statement or conduct, regardless of when it occurred or whether the declarant had an opportunity to explain or deny it. If the party against whom the statement was admitted calls the declarant as a witness, the party may examine the declarant on the statement as if on cross-examination.

(Pub.L. 93–595, § 1, Jan. 2, 1975, 88 Stat. 1943; Mar. 2, 1987, eff. Oct. 1, 1987; Apr. 11, 1997, eff. Dec. 1, 1997; Apr. 26, 2011, eff. Dec. 1, 2011.)

ADVISORY COMMITTEE NOTES

1972 Proposed Rules

The declarant of a hearsay statement which is admitted in evidence is in effect a witness. His credibility should in fairness be subject to impeachment and support as though he had in fact testified. See Rules 608 and 609. There are however, some special aspects of the impeaching of a hearsay declarant which require consideration. These special aspects center upon impeachment by inconsistent statement, arise from factual differences which exist between the use of hearsay and an actual witness and also between various kinds of hearsay, and involve the question of applying to declarants the general rule disallowing evidence of an inconsistent statement to impeach a witness unless he is afforded an opportunity to deny or explain. See Rule 613(b).

The principal difference between using hearsay and an actual witness is that the inconsistent statement will in the case of the witness almost inevitably of necessity in the nature of things be a *prior* statement, which it is entirely possible and feasible to call to his attention, while in the case of hearsay the inconsistent statement may well be a *subsequent* one, which practically precludes calling it to the attention of the declarant. The result of insisting upon observation of this impossible requirement in the hearsay situation is to deny the opponent, already barred from cross-examination, any benefit of this important technique of impeachment. The writers favor allowing the subsequent statement. McCormick § 37, p. 69; 3 Wigmore § 1033. The cases, however, are divided. Cases allowing the impeachment include *People v. Collup,* 27 Cal.2d 829, 167 P.2d 714 (1946); *People v. Rosoto,* 58 Cal.2d 304, 23 Cal.Rptr. 779, 373 P.2d 867 (1962); *Carver v. United States,* 164 U.S. 694, 17 S.Ct. 228, 41 L.Ed. 602 (1897). *Contra, Mattox v. United States,* 156 U.S. 237, 15 S.Ct. 337, 39 L.Ed. 409 (1895); *People v. Hines,* 284 N.Y. 93, 29 N.E.2d 483 (1940). The force of *Mattox,* where the hearsay was the former testimony of a deceased witness and the denial of use of a subsequent inconsistent statement was upheld, is much diminished by *Carver,* where the hearsay was a dying declaration and denial of use of a subsequent inconsistent statement resulted in reversal. The difference in the particular brand of hearsay seems unimportant when the inconsistent statement is a *subsequent* one. True, the opponent is not totally deprived of cross-examination when the hearsay is former testimony or a deposition but he is deprived of cross-examining on the statement or along lines suggested by it. Mr. Justice Shiras, with two justices joining him, dissented vigorously in *Mattox.*

When the impeaching statement was made prior to the hearsay statement, differences in the kinds of hearsay appear which arguably may justify differences in treatment. If the hearsay consisted of a simple statement by the witness, e.g. a dying declaration or a declaration against interest, the feasibility of affording him an opportunity to deny or explain encounters the same practical impossibility as where the statement is a subsequent one, just discussed, although here the impossibility arises from the total absence of anything resembling a hearing at which the matter could be put to him. The courts by a large majority have ruled in favor of allowing the statement to be used under these circumstances. McCormick § 37, p. 69; 3 Wigmore § 1033. If, however, the hearsay consists of former testimony or a deposition, the possibility of calling the prior statement to the attention of the witness or deponent is not ruled out, since the opportunity to cross-examine was available. It might thus be concluded that with former testimony or depositions the conventional foundation should be insisted upon. Most of the cases involve depositions, and Wigmore describes them as divided. 3 Wigmore § 1031. Deposition procedures at best are cumbersome and expensive, and to require the laying of the foundation may impose an undue burden. Under the federal practice, there is no way of knowing with certainty at the time of taking a deposition whether it is merely for discovery or will ultimately end up in evidence. With respect to both former testimony and depositions the possibility exists that knowledge of the statement might not be acquired until after the time of the cross-examination. Moreover, the expanded admissibility of former testimony and depositions under Rule 804(b)(1) calls for a correspondingly expanded approach to impeachment. The rule dispenses with the requirement in all hearsay situations, which is readily administered and best calculated to lead to fair results.

Notice should be taken that Rule 26(f) of the Federal Rules of Civil Procedure, as originally submitted by the Advisory Committee, ended with the following:

"* * * and, without having first called them to the deponent's attention, may show statements contradictory thereto made at any time by the deponent."

This language did not appear in the rule as promulgated in December, 1937. See 4 Moore's Federal Practice ¶¶ 26.01[9], 26.35 (2d ed.1967). In 1951, Nebraska adopted a provision strongly resembling the one stricken from the federal rule:

"Any party may impeach any adverse deponent by self-contradiction without having laid foundation for such impeachment at the time such deposition was taken." R.S.Neb. § 25–1267.07.

For similar provisions, see Uniform Rule 65; California Evidence Code § 1202; Kansas Code of Civil Procedure § 60–462; New Jersey Evidence Rule 65.

The provision for cross-examination of a declarant upon his hearsay statement is a corollary of general principles of cross-examination. A similar provision is found in California Evidence Code § 1203.

1974 Enactment

Rule 906, as passed by the House and as proposed by the Supreme Court provides that whenever a hearsay statement is admitted, the credibility of the declarant of the statement may be attacked, and if attacked may be supported, by any evidence which would be admissible for those purposes if the declarant had testified as a witness. Rule 801 defines what is a hearsay statement. While statements by a person authorized by a party-opponent to make a statement concerning the subject, by the party-opponent's agent or by a coconspirator of a party—see rule 801(d)(2)(c), (d) and (e)—are traditionally defined as exceptions to the hearsay rule, rule 801 defines such admission by a party-opponent as statements which are not hearsay. Consequently, rule 806 by referring exclusively to the admission of hearsay statements, does not appear to allow the credibility of the declarant to be attacked when the declarant is a coconspirator, agent or authorized spokesman. The committee is of the view that such statements should open the declarant to attacks on his credibility. Indeed, the reason such statements are excluded from the operation of rule 806 is likely attributable to the drafting technique used to codify the hearsay rule, viz. some statements, instead of being referred to as exceptions to the hearsay rule, are defined as statements which are not hearsay. The phrase "or a statement defined in rule 801(d)(2)(c), (d) and (e)" is added to the rule in order to subject the declarant of such statements, like the declarant of hearsay statements, to attacks on his credibility. [The committee considered it unnecessary to include statements contained in rule 801(d)(2)(A) and (B)—the statement by the party-opponent himself or the statement of which he has manifested his adoption—because the credibility of the party-opponent is always subject to an attack on his credibility]. Senate Report No. 93–1277.

The Senate amendment permits an attack upon the credibility of the declarant of a statement if the statement is one by a person authorized by a party-opponent to make a statement concerning the subject, one by an agent of a party-opponent, or one by a coconspirator of the party-opponent, as these statements are defined in Rules 801(d)(2)(C), (D) and (E). The House bill has no such provision.

The Conference adopts the Senate amendment. The Senate amendment conforms the rule to present practice. House Report No. 93–1597.

1987 Amendments

The amendments are technical. No substantive change is intended.

1997 Amendments

The amendment is technical. No substantive change is intended.

GAP Report. Restylization changes in the rule were eliminated.

2011 Amendments

The language of Rule 806 has been amended as part of the restyling of the Evidence Rules to make them more easily understood and to make style and terminology consistent throughout the rules. These changes are intended to be stylistic only. There is no intent to change any result in any ruling on evidence admissibility.

Rule 807. Residual Exception

(a) In General. Under the following circumstances, a hearsay statement is not excluded by the rule against hearsay even if the statement is not specifically covered by a hearsay exception in Rule 803 or 804:

(1) the statement has equivalent circumstantial guarantees of trustworthiness;

(2) it is offered as evidence of a material fact;

(3) it is more probative on the point for which it is offered than any other evidence that the proponent can obtain through reasonable efforts; and

(4) admitting it will best serve the purposes of these rules and the interests of justice.

(b) Notice. The statement is admissible only if, before the trial or hearing, the proponent gives an adverse party reasonable notice of the intent to offer the statement and its particulars, including the declarant's name and address, so that the party has a fair opportunity to meet it.

(Added Apr. 11, 1997, eff. Dec. 1, 1997; Apr. 26, 2011, eff. Dec. 1, 2011.)

ADVISORY COMMITTEE NOTES

1997 Amendments

The contents of Rule 803(24) and Rule 804(b)(5) have been combined and transferred to a new Rule 807. This was done to facilitate additions to Rules 803 and 804. No change in meaning is intended.

GAP Report on Rule 807. Restylization changes in the rule were eliminated.

2011 Amendments

The language of Rule 807 has been amended as part of the restyling of the Evidence Rules to make them more easily understood and to make style and terminology consistent throughout the rules. These changes are intended to be stylistic only. There is no intent to change any result in any ruling on evidence admissibility.

ARTICLE IX. AUTHENTICATION AND IDENTIFICATION

Rule
901. Authenticating or Identifying Evidence.
902. Evidence That Is Self-Authenticating.
903. Subscribing Witness's Testimony.

Rule 901. Authenticating or Identifying Evidence

(a) In General. To satisfy the requirement of authenticating or identifying an item of evidence, the proponent must produce evidence sufficient to support a finding that the item is what the proponent claims it is.

(b) Examples. The following are examples only—not a complete list—of evidence that satisfies the requirement:

(1) Testimony of a Witness with Knowledge. Testimony that an item is what it is claimed to be.

(2) Nonexpert Opinion About Handwriting. A nonexpert's opinion that handwriting is genuine, based on a familiarity with it that was not acquired for the current litigation.

(3) Comparison by an Expert Witness or the Trier of Fact. A comparison with an authenticated specimen by an expert witness or the trier of fact.

(4) Distinctive Characteristics and the Like. The appearance, contents, substance, internal patterns, or other distinctive characteristics of the item, taken together with all the circumstances.

(5) Opinion About a Voice. An opinion identifying a person's voice—whether heard firsthand or through mechanical or electronic transmission or recording—based on hearing the voice at any time under circumstances that connect it with the alleged speaker.

(6) Evidence About a Telephone Conversation. For a telephone conversation, evidence that a call was made to the number assigned at the time to:

(A) a particular person, if circumstances, including self- identification, show that the person answering was the one called; or

(B) a particular business, if the call was made to a business and the call related to business reasonably transacted over the telephone.

(7) Evidence About Public Records. Evidence that:

(A) a document was recorded or filed in a public office as authorized by law; or

(B) a purported public record or statement is from the office where items of this kind are kept.

(8) Evidence About Ancient Documents or Data Compilations. For a document or data compilation, evidence that it:

(A) is in a condition that creates no suspicion about its authenticity;

(B) was in a place where, if authentic, it would likely be; and

(C) is at least 20 years old when offered.

(9) Evidence About a Process or System. Evidence describing a process or system and showing that it produces an accurate result.

(10) Methods Provided by a Statute or Rule. Any method of authentication or identification allowed by a federal statute or a rule prescribed by the Supreme Court.

(Pub.L. 93–595, § 1, Jan. 2, 1975, 88 Stat.1943; Apr. 26, 2011, eff. Dec. 1, 2011.)

ADVISORY COMMITTEE NOTES

1972 Proposed Rules

Note to Subdivision (a). Authentication and identification represent a special aspect of relevancy. Michael and Adler, Real Proof, 5 Vand.L.Rev. 344, 362 (1952); McCormick §§ 179, 185; Morgan, Basic Problems of Evidence 378 (1962). Thus a telephone conversation may be irrelevant because on an unrelated topic or because the speaker is not identified. The latter aspect is the one here involved. Wigmore describes the need for authentication as "an inherent logical necessity." 7 Wigmore § 2129, p. 564.

This requirement of showing authenticity or identity falls in the category of relevancy dependent upon fulfillment of a condition of fact and is governed by the procedure set forth in Rule 104(b).

The common law approach to authentication of documents has been criticized as an "attitude of agnosticism," McCormick, Cases on Evidence 388, n. 4 (3rd ed. 1956), as one which "departs sharply from men's customs in ordinary affairs," and as presenting only a slight obstacle to the introduction of forgeries in comparison to the time and expense devoted to proving genuine writings which correctly show their origin on their face, McCormick § 185, pp. 395, 396. Today, such available procedures as requests to admit and pretrial conference afford the means of eliminating much of the need for authentication or identification. Also, significant inroads upon the traditional insistence on authentication and identification have been made by accepting as at least prima facie genuine items of the kind treated in Rule 902, *infra.* However, the need for suitable methods of proof still remains, since criminal cases pose their own obstacles to the use of preliminary procedures, unforeseen contingencies may arise, and cases of genuine controversy will still occur.

Note to Subdivision (b). The treatment of authentication and identification draws largely upon the experience embodied in the common law and in statutes to furnish illustrative applications of the general principle set forth in subdivision (a). The examples are not intended as an exclusive enumeration of allowable methods but are meant to guide and suggest, leaving room for growth and development in this area of the law.

The examples relate for the most part to documents, with some attention given to voice communications and computer printouts. As Wigmore noted, no special rules have been developed for authenticating chattels. Wigmore, Code of Evidence § 2086 (3rd ed. 1942).

It should be observed that compliance with requirements of authentication or identification by no means assures admission of an item into evidence, as other bars, hearsay for example, may remain.

Example (1). Example (1) contemplates a broad spectrum ranging from testimony of a witness who was present at the signing of a document to testimony establishing narcotics as taken from an accused and accounting for custody through the period until trial, including laboratory analysis. See California Evidence Code § 1413, eyewitness to signing.

Example (2). Example (2) states conventional doctrine as to lay identification of handwriting, which recognizes that a sufficient familiarity with the handwriting of another person may be acquired by seeing him write, by exchanging correspondence, or by other means, to afford a basis for identifying it on subsequent occasions. McCormick § 189. See also California Evidence Code § 1416. Testimony based upon familiarity acquired for purposes of the litigation is reserved to the expert under the example which follows.

Example (3). The history of common law restrictions upon the technique of proving or disproving the genuineness of a disputed specimen of handwriting through comparison with a genuine specimen, by either the testimony of expert witnesses or direct viewing by the triers themselves, is detailed in 7 Wigmore §§ 1991–1994. In breaking away, the English Common Law Procedure Act of 1854, 17 and 18 Vict., c. 125, § 27, cautiously allowed expert or trier to use exemplars "proved to the satisfaction of the judge to be genuine" for purposes of comparison. The language found its way into numerous statutes in this country, e.g., California

Evidence Code §§ 1417, 1418. While explainable as a measure of prudence in the process of breaking with precedent in the handwriting situation, the reservation to the judge of the question of the genuineness of exemplars and the imposition of an unusually high standard of persuasion are at variance with the general treatment of relevancy which depends upon fulfillment of a condition of fact. Rule 104(b). No similar attitude is found in other comparison situations, e.g., ballistics comparison by jury, as in *Evans v. Commonwealth,* 230 Ky. 411, 19 S.W.2d 1091 (1929), or by experts, Annot., 26 A.L.R.2d 892, and no reason appears for its continued existence in handwriting cases. Consequently Example (3) sets no higher standard for handwriting specimens and treats all comparison situations alike, to be governed by Rule 104(b). This approach is consistent with 28 U.S.C. § 1731: "The admitted or proved handwriting of any person shall be admissible, for purposes of comparison, to determine genuineness of other handwriting attributed to such person."

Precedent supports the acceptance of visual comparison as sufficiently satisfying preliminary authentication requirements for admission in evidence. *Brandon v. Collins,* 267 F.2d 731 (2d Cir.1959); *Wausau Sulphate Fibre Co. v. Commissioner of Internal Revenue,* 61 F.2d 879 (7th Cir.1932); *Desimone v. United States,* 227 F.2d 864 (9th Cir.1955).

Example (4). The characteristics of the offered item itself, considered in the light of circumstances, afford authentication techniques in great variety. Thus a document or telephone conversation may be shown to have emanated from a particular person by virtue of its disclosing knowledge of facts known peculiarly to him; *Globe Automatic Sprinkler Co. v. Braniff,* 89 Okl. 105, 214 P. 127 (1923); California Evidence Code § 1421; similarly, a letter may be authenticated by content and circumstances indicating it was in reply to a duly authenticated one. McCormick § 192; California Evidence Code § 1420. Language patterns may indicate authenticity or its opposite. *Magnuson v. State,* 187 Wis. 122, 203 N.W. 749 (1925); Arens and Meadow, Psycholinguistics and the Confession Dilemma, 56 Colum.L.Rev. 19 (1956).

Example (5). Since aural voice identification is not a subject of expert testimony, the requisite familiarity may be acquired either before or after the particular speaking which is the subject of the identification, in this respect resembling visual identification of a person rather than identification of handwriting. Cf. Example (2), *supra, People v. Nichols,* 378 Ill. 487, 38 N.E.2d 766 (1942); *McGuire v. State,* 200 Md. 601, 92 A.2d 582 (1952); *State v. McGee,* 336 Mo. 1082, 83 S.W.2d 98 (1935).

Example (6). The cases are in agreement that a mere assertion of his identity by a person talking on the telephone is not sufficient evidence of the authenticity of the conversation and that additional evidence of his identity is required. The additional evidence need not fall in any set pattern. Thus the content of his statements or the reply technique, under Example (4), *supra*, or voice identification under Example (5), may furnish the necessary foundation. Outgoing calls made by the witness involve additional factors bearing upon authenticity. The calling of a number assigned by the telephone company reasonably supports the assumption that the listing is correct and that the number is the one reached. If the number is that of a place of business, the mass of authority allows an ensuing conversation if it relates to business reasonably transacted over the telephone, on the theory that the maintenance of the telephone connection is an invitation to do business without further identification. *Matton v. Hoover Co.,* 350 Mo. 506, 166 S.W.2d 557 (1942); *City of Pawhuska v. Crutchfield,* 147 Okl. 4, 293 P. 1095 (1930); *Zurich General Acc. & Liability Ins. Co. v. Baum,* 159 Va. 404, 165 S.E. 518 (1932). Otherwise, some additional circumstance of identification of the speaker is required. The authorities divide on the question whether the self-identifying statement of the person answering suffices. Example (6) answers in the affirmative on the assumption that usual conduct respecting telephone calls furnish adequate assurances of regularity, bearing in mind that the entire matter is open to exploration before the trier of fact. In general, see McCormick § 193; 7 Wigmore § 2155; Annot., 71 A.L.R. 5, 105 id. 326.

Example (7). Public records are regularly authenticated by proof of custody, without more. McCormick § 191; 7 Wigmore §§ 2158, 2159. The example extends the principle to include data stored in computers and similar methods, of which increasing use in the public records area may be expected. See California Evidence Code §§ 1532, 1600.

Example (8). The familiar ancient document rule of the common law is extended to include data stored electronically or by other similar means. Since the importance of appearance diminishes in this situation, the importance of custody or place where found increases correspondingly. This expansion is necessary in view of the widespread use of methods of storing data in forms other than conventional written records.

Any time period selected is bound to be arbitrary. The common law period of 30 years is here reduced to 20 years, with some shift of emphasis from the probable unavailability of witnesses to the unlikeliness of a still viable fraud after the lapse of time. The shorter period is specified in the English Evidence Act of 1938, 1 & 2 Geo. 6, c. 28, and in Oregon R.S.1963, § 41.360(34). See also the numerous statutes prescribing periods of less than 30 years in the case of recorded documents. 7 Wigmore § 2143.

The application of Example (8) is not subject to any limitation to title documents or to any requirement that possession, in the case of a title document, has been consistent with the document. See McCormick § 190.

Example (9). Example (9) is designed for situations in which the accuracy of a result is dependent upon a process or system which produces it. X rays afford a familiar instance. Among more recent developments is the computer, as to which see Transport Indemnity Co. v. Seib, 178 Neb. 253, 132 N.W.2d 871 (1965); *State v. Veres,* 7 Ariz.App. 117, 436 P.2d 629 (1968); *Merrick v. United States Rubber Co.,* 7 Ariz.App. 433, 440 P.2d 314 (1968); Freed, Computer Print–Outs as Evidence, 16 Am.Jur.Proof of Facts 273; Symposium, Law and Computers in the Mid–Sixties, ALI–ABA (1966); 37 Albany L.Rev. 61 (1967). Example (9) does not, of course, foreclose taking judicial notice of the accuracy of the process or system.

Example (10). The example makes clear that methods of authentication provided by Act of Congress and by the Rules of Civil and Criminal Procedure or by Bankruptcy Rules are not intended to be superseded. Illustrative are the provisions for authentication of official records in Civil Procedure Rule 44 and Criminal Procedure Rule 27, for authentication of records of proceedings by court reporters in 28 U.S.C. § 753(b) and Civil Procedure Rule 80(c), and for authentication of depositions in Civil Procedure Rule 30(f).

2011 Amendments

The language of Rule 901 has been amended as part of the restyling of the Evidence Rules to make them more easily understood and to make style and terminology consistent throughout the rules. These changes are intended to be stylistic only. There is no intent to change any result in any ruling on evidence admissibility.

Rule 902. Evidence That Is Self–Authenticating

The following items of evidence are self-authenticating; they require no extrinsic evidence of authenticity in order to be admitted:

(1) Domestic Public Documents That Are Sealed and Signed. A document that bears:

(A) a seal purporting to be that of the United States; any state, district, commonwealth, territory, or insular possession of the United States; the former Panama Canal Zone; the Trust Territory of the Pacific Islands; a political subdivision of any of these entities; or a department, agency, or officer of any entity named above; and

(B) a signature purporting to be an execution or attestation.

(2) Domestic Public Documents That Are Not Sealed but Are Signed and Certified. A document that bears no seal if:

(A) it bears the signature of an officer or employee of an entity named in Rule 902(1)(A); and

(B) another public officer who has a seal and official duties within that same entity certifies under seal—or its equivalent—that the signer has the official capacity and that the signature is genuine.

(3) Foreign Public Documents. A document that purports to be signed or attested by a person who is authorized by a foreign country's law to do so. The document must be accompanied by a final certification that certifies the genuineness of the signature and official position of the signer or attester—or of any foreign official whose certificate of genuineness relates to the signature or attestation or is in a chain of certificates of genuineness relating to the signature or attestation. The certification may be made by a secretary of a United States embassy or legation; by a consul general, vice consul, or consular agent of the United States; or by a diplomatic or consular official of the foreign country assigned or accredited to the United States. If all parties have been given a reasonable opportunity to investigate the document's authenticity and accuracy, the court may, for good cause, either:

(A) order that it be treated as presumptively authentic without final certification; or

(B) allow it to be evidenced by an attested summary with or without final certification.

(4) Certified Copies of Public Records. A copy of an official record—or a copy of a document that was recorded or filed in a public office as authorized by law—if the copy is certified as correct by:

(A) the custodian or another person authorized to make the certification; or

(B) a certificate that complies with Rule 902(1), (2), or (3), a federal statute, or a rule prescribed by the Supreme Court.

(5) Official Publications. A book, pamphlet, or other publication purporting to be issued by a public authority.

(6) Newspapers and Periodicals. Printed material purporting to be a newspaper or periodical.

(7) Trade Inscriptions and the Like. An inscription, sign, tag, or label purporting to have been affixed in the course of business and indicating origin, ownership, or control.

(8) Acknowledged Documents. A document accompanied by a certificate of acknowledgment that is lawfully executed by a notary public or another officer who is authorized to take acknowledgments.

(9) Commercial Paper and Related Documents. Commercial paper, a signature on it, and related documents, to the extent allowed by general commercial law.

(10) Presumptions Under a Federal Statute. A signature, document, or anything else that a federal statute declares to be presumptively or prima facie genuine or authentic.

(11) Certified Domestic Records of a Regularly Conducted Activity. The original or a copy of a domestic record that meets the requirements of Rule 803(6)(A)–(C), as shown by a certification of the custodian or another qualified person that complies with a federal statute or a rule prescribed by the Supreme Court. Before the trial or hearing, the proponent must give an adverse party reasonable written notice of the intent to offer the record—and must make the record and certification available for inspection—so that the party has a fair opportunity to challenge them.

(12) Certified Foreign Records of a Regularly Conducted Activity. In a civil case, the original or a copy of a foreign record that meets the requirements of Rule 902(11), modified as follows: the certification, rather than complying with a federal statute or Supreme Court rule, must be signed in a manner that, if falsely made, would subject the maker to a criminal penalty in the country where the certification is signed. The proponent must also meet the notice requirements of Rule 902(11).

(Pub.L. 93–595, § 1, Jan. 2, 1975, 88 Stat. 1944; Mar. 2, 1987, eff. Oct. 1, 1987; Apr. 25, 1988, eff. Nov. 1, 1988; Apr. 17, 2000, eff. Dec. 1, 2000; Apr. 26, 2011, eff. Dec. 1, 2011.)

ADVISORY COMMITTEE NOTES

1972 Proposed Rules

Case law and statutes have, over the years, developed a substantial body of instances in which authenticity is taken as sufficiently established for purposes of admissibility without extrinsic evidence to that effect, sometimes for reasons of policy but perhaps more often because practical considerations reduce the possibility of unauthenticity to a very small dimension. The present rule collects and incorporates these situations, in some instances expanding them to occupy a larger area which their underlying considerations justify. In no instance is the opposite party foreclosed from disputing authenticity.

Note to Paragraph (1). The acceptance of documents bearing a public seal and signature, most often encountered in practice in the form of acknowledgments or certificates authenticating copies of public records, is actually of broad application. Whether theoretically based in whole or in part upon judicial notice, the practical underlying considerations are that forgery is a crime and detection is fairly easy and certain. 7 Wigmore § 2161, p. 638; California Evidence Code § 1452. More than 50 provisions for judicial notice of official seals are contained in the United States Code.

Note to Paragraph (2). While statutes are found which raise a presumption of genuineness of purported official signatures in the absence of an official seal, 7 Wigmore § 2167; California Evidence Code § 1453, the greater ease of effecting a forgery under these circumstances is apparent. Hence this paragraph of the rule calls for authentication by an officer who has a seal. Notarial acts by members of the armed forces and other special situations are covered in paragraph (10).

Note to Paragraph (3). Paragraph (3) provides a method for extending the presumption of authenticity to foreign official documents by a procedure of certification. It is derived from Rule 44(a)(2) of the Rules of Civil Procedure but is broader in applying to public documents rather than being limited to public records.

Note to Paragraph (4). The common law and innumerable statutes have recognized the procedure of authenticating copies of public records by certificate. The certificate qualifies as a public document, receivable as authentic when in conformity with paragraph (1), (2), or (3). Rule 44(a) of the Rules of Civil Procedure and Rule 27 of the Rules of Criminal Procedure have provided authentication procedures of this nature for both domestic and foreign public records. It will be observed that the certification procedure here provided extends only to public records, reports, and recorded documents, all including data compilations, and does not apply to public documents generally. Hence documents provable when presented in original form under paragraphs (1), (2), or (3) may not be provable by certified copy under paragraph (4).

Note to Paragraph (5). Dispensing with preliminary proof of the genuineness of purportedly official publications, most commonly encountered in connection with statutes, court reports, rules, and regulations, has been greatly enlarged by statutes and decisions. 5 Wigmore § 1684. Paragraph (5), it will be noted, does not confer admissibility upon all official publications; it merely provides a means whereby their authenticity may be taken as established for purposes of admissibility. Rule 44(a) of the Rules of Civil Procedure has been to the same effect.

Note to Paragraph (6). The likelihood of forgery of newspapers or periodicals is slight indeed. Hence no danger is apparent in receiving them. Establishing the authenticity of the publication may, of course, leave still open questions of authority and responsibility for items therein contained. See 7 Wigmore § 2150. Cf. 39 U.S.C. § 4005(b), public advertisement prima facie evidence of agency of person named, in postal fraud order proceeding; Canadian Uniform Evidence Act, Draft of 1936, printed copy of newspaper prima facie evidence that notices or advertisements were authorized.

Note to Paragraph (7). Several factors justify dispensing with preliminary proof of genuineness of commercial and mercantile labels and the like. The risk of forgery is minimal. Trademark infringement involves serious penalties. Great efforts are devoted to inducing the public to buy in reliance on brand names, and substantial protection is given them. Hence the fairness of this treatment finds recognition in the cases. *Curtiss Candy Co. v. Johnson,* 163 Miss. 426, 141 So. 762 (1932), Baby Ruth candy bar; *Doyle v. Continental Baking Co.,* 262 Mass. 516, 160 N.E. 325 (1928), loaf of bread; *Weiner v. Mager & Throne, Inc.,* 167 Misc. 338, 3 N.Y.S.2d 918 (1938), same. And see W.Va.Code 1966, § 47–3–5, trademark on bottle prima facie evidence of ownership. *Contra, Keegan v. Green Giant Co.,* 150 Me. 283, 110 A.2d 599 (1954); *Murphy v. Campbell Soup Co.,* 62 F.2d 564 (1st Cir.1933). Cattle brands have received similar acceptance in the western states.

Rev.Code Mont.1947, § 46–606, *State v. Wolfley,* 75 Kan. 406, 89 P. 1046 (1907); Annot., 11 L.R.A.(N.S.) 87. Inscriptions on trains and vehicles are held to be prima facie evidence of ownership or control. *Pittsburgh, Ft. W. & C. Ry. v. Callaghan,* 157 Ill. 406, 41 N.E. 909 (1895); 9 Wigmore § 2510a. See also the provision of 19 U.S.C. § 1615(2) that marks, labels, brands, or stamps indicating foreign origin are prima facie evidence of foreign origin of merchandise.

Note to Paragraph (8). In virtually every state, acknowledged title documents are receivable in evidence without further proof. Statutes are collected in 5 Wigmore § 1676. If this authentication suffices for documents of the importance of those affecting titles, logic scarcely permits denying this method when other kinds of documents are involved. Instances of broadly inclusive statutes are California Evidence Code § 1451 and N.Y.CPLR 4538, McKinney's Consol.Laws 1963.

Note to Paragraph (9). Issues of the authenticity of commercial paper in federal courts will usually arise in diversity cases, will involve an element of a cause of action or defense, and with respect to presumptions and burden of proof will be controlled by *Erie Railroad Co. v. Tompkins,* 304 U.S. 64, 58 S.Ct. 817, 82 L.Ed. 1188 (1938). Rule 302, *supra.* There may, however, be questions of authenticity involving lesser segments of a case or the case may be one governed by federal common law. *Clearfield Trust Co. v. United States,* 318 U.S. 363, 63 S.Ct. 573, 87 L.Ed. 838 (1943). Cf. *United States v. Yazell,* 382 U.S. 341, 86 S.Ct. 500, 15 L.Ed.2d 404 (1966). In these situations, resort to the useful authentication provisions of the Uniform Commercial Code is provided for. While the phrasing is in terms of "general commercial law," in order to avoid the potential complications inherent in borrowing local statutes, today one would have difficulty in determining the general commercial law without referring to the Code. See *Williams v. Walker–Thomas Furniture Co.,* 121 U.S.App.D.C. 315, 350 F.2d 445 (1965). Pertinent Code provisions are sections 1–202, 3–307, and 3–510, dealing with third-party documents, signatures on negotiable instruments, protests, and statements of dishonor.

Note to Paragraph (10). The paragraph continues in effect dispensations with preliminary proof of genuineness provided in various Acts of Congress. See, for example, 10 U.S.C. § 936, signature, without seal, together with title, prima facie evidence of authenticity of acts of certain military personnel who are given notarial powers; 15 U.S.C. § 77f(a), signature on SEC registration presumed genuine; 26 U.S.C. § 6064, signature to tax return prima facie genuine.

1974 Enactment

Note to Paragraph (8). Rule 902(8) as submitted by the Court referred to certificates of acknowledgment "under the hand and seal of" a notary public or other officer authorized by law to take acknowledgments. The Committee amended the Rule to eliminate the requirement, believed to be inconsistent with the law in some States, that a notary public must affix a seal to a document acknowledged before him. As amended the Rule merely requires that the document be executed in the manner prescribed by State law.

Note to Paragraph (9). The Committee approved Rule 902(9) as submitted by the Court. With respect to the meaning of the phrase "general commercial law", the Committee intends that the Uniform Commercial Code, which has been adopted in virtually every State, will be followed generally, but that federal commercial law will apply where federal commercial paper is involved. See Clearfield Trust Co. v. United States, 318 U.S. 363 (1943). Further, in those instances in which the issues are governed by Erie R. Co. v. Tompkins, 304 U.S. 64 (1938), State law will apply irrespective of whether it is the Uniform Commercial Code. House Report No. 93–650.

1987 Amendments

The amendments are technical. No substantive change is intended.

1988 Amendments

These two sentences were inadvertently eliminated from the 1987 amendments. The amendment is technical. No substantive change is intended.

2000 Amendments

The amendment adds two new paragraphs to the rule on self-authentication. It sets forth a procedure by which parties can authenticate certain records of regularly conducted activity, other than through the testimony of a foundation witness. See the amendment to Rule 803(6). 18 U.S.C. § 3505 currently provides a means for certifying foreign records of regularly conducted activity in criminal cases, and this amendment is intended to establish a similar procedure for domestic records, and for foreign records offered in civil cases.

A declaration that satisfies 28 U.S.C. § 1746 would satisfy the declaration requirement of Rule 902(11), as would any comparable certification under oath.

The notice requirement in Rules 902(11) and (12) is intended to give the opponent of the evidence a full opportunity to test the adequacy of the foundation set forth in the declaration.

GAP Report—Proposed Amendment to Rule 902

The Committee made the following changes to the published draft of the proposed amendment to Evidence Rule 902:

1. Minor stylistic changes were made in the text, in accordance with suggestions of the Style Subcommittee of the Standing Committee on Rules of Practice and Procedure.

2. The phrase "in a manner complying with any Act of Congress or rule prescribed by the Supreme Court pursuant to statutory authority" was added to proposed Rule 902(11), to provide consistency with Evidence Rule 902(4). The Committee Note was amended to accord with this textual change.

3. Minor stylistic changes were made in the text to provide a uniform construction of the terms "declaration" and "certifying."

4. The notice provisions in the text were revised to clarify that the proponent must make both the declaration and the underlying record available for inspection.

2011 Amendments

The language of Rule 902 has been amended as part of the restyling of the Evidence Rules to make them more easily understood and to make style and terminology consistent throughout the rules. These changes are intended to be stylistic only. There is no intent to change any result in any ruling on evidence admissibility.

HISTORICAL NOTES

Termination of Trust Territory of the Pacific Islands

For termination of Trust Territory of the Pacific Islands, see note set out preceding 48 U.S.C.A. § 1681.

Rule 903. Subscribing Witness's Testimony

A subscribing witness's testimony is necessary to authenticate a writing only if required by the law of the jurisdiction that governs its validity.

(Pub.L. 93–595, § 1, Jan. 2, 1975, 88 Stat.1945; Apr. 26, 2011, eff. Dec. 1, 2011.)

ADVISORY COMMITTEE NOTES

1972 Proposed Rules

The common law required that attesting witnesses be produced or accounted for. Today the requirement has generally been abolished except with respect to documents which must be attested to be valid, e.g. wills in some states. McCormick § 188. Uniform Rule 71; California Evidence Code § 1411; Kansas Code of Civil Procedure § 60–468; New Jersey Evidence Rule 71; New York CPLR Rule 4537.

2011 Amendments

The language of Rule 903 has been amended as part of the restyling of the Evidence Rules to make them more easily understood and to make style and terminology consistent throughout the rules. These changes are intended to be stylistic only. There is no intent to change any result in any ruling on evidence admissibility.

ARTICLE X. CONTENTS OF WRITINGS, RECORDINGS, AND PHOTOGRAPHS

Rule

1001. Definitions That Apply to This Article.
1002. Requirement of the Original.
1003. Admissibility of Duplicates.
1004. Admissibility of Other Evidence of Content.
1005. Copies of Public Records to Prove Content.
1006. Summaries to Prove Content.
1007. Testimony or Statement of a Party to Prove Content.
1008. Functions of the Court and Jury.

Rule 1001. Definitions That Apply to This Article

In this article:

(a) A "writing" consists of letters, words, numbers, or their equivalent set down in any form.

(b) A "recording" consists of letters, words, numbers, or their equivalent recorded in any manner.

(c) A "photograph" means a photographic image or its equivalent stored in any form.

(d) An "original" of a writing or recording means the writing or recording itself or any counterpart intended to have the same effect by the person who executed or issued it. For electronically stored information, "original" means any printout—or other output readable by sight—if it accurately reflects the information. An "original" of a photograph includes the negative or a print from it.

(e) A "duplicate" means a counterpart produced by a mechanical, photographic, chemical, electronic, or other equivalent process or technique that accurately reproduces the original.

(Pub.L. 93–595, § 1, Jan. 2, 1975, 88 Stat. 1945; Apr. 26, 2011, eff. Dec. 1, 2011.)

ADVISORY COMMITTEE NOTES

1972 Proposed Rules

In an earlier day, when discovery and other related procedures were strictly limited, the misleading named "best evidence rule" afforded substantial guarantees against inaccuracies and fraud by its insistence upon production or original documents. The great enlargement of the scope of discovery and related procedures in recent times has measurably reduced the need for the rule. Nevertheless important areas of usefulness persist: discovery of documents outside the jurisdiction may require substantial outlay of time and money; the unanticipated document may not practically be discoverable; criminal cases have built-in limitations on discovery. Cleary and Strong, The Best Evidence Rule: An Evaluation in Context, 51 Iowa L.Rev. 825 (1966).

Note to Paragraph (1). Traditionally the rule requiring the original centered upon accumulations of data and expressions affecting legal relations set forth in words and figures. this meant that the rule was one essentially related to writings. Present day techniques have expanded methods of storing data, yet the essential form which the information ultimately assumes for usable purposes is words and figures. Hence the considerations underlying the rule dictate its expansion to include computers, photographic systems, and other modern developments.

Note to Paragraph (3). In most instances, what is an original will be self-evident and further refinement will be unnecessary. However, in some instances particularized definition is required. A carbon copy of a contract executed in duplicate becomes an original, as does a sales ticket carbon copy given to a customer. While strictly speaking the original of a photograph might be thought to be only the negative, practicality and common usage require that any print from the negative be regarded as an original. Similarly, practicality and usage confer the status of original upon any computer printout. *Transport Indemnity Co. v. Seib,* 178 Neb. 253, 132 N.W.2d 871 (1965).

Note to Paragraph (4). The definition describes "copies" produced by methods possessing an accuracy which virtually eliminates the possibility of error. Copies thus produced are given the status of originals in large measure by Rule 1003, *infra.* Copies subsequently produced manually, whether handwritten or typed, are not within the definition. It should be noted that what is an original for some purposes may be a duplicate for others. Thus a bank's microfilm record of checks cleared is the original as a record. However, a print offered as a copy of a check whose contents are in controversy is a duplicate. This result is substantially consistent with 28 U.S.C. § 1732(b). Compare 26 U.S.C. § 7513(c), giving full status as originals to photographic reproductions of tax returns and other documents, made by authority of the Secretary of the Treasury, and 44 U.S.C. § 399(a), giving original status to photographic copies in the National Archives.

1974 Enactment

Note to Paragraph (2). The Committee amended this Rule expressly to include "video tapes" in the definition of "photographs." House Report No. 93–650.

2011 Amendments

The language of Rule 1001 has been amended as part of the restyling of the Evidence Rules to make them more easily understood and to make style and terminology consistent throughout the rules. These changes are intended to be stylistic only. There is no intent to change any result in any ruling on evidence admissibility.

Rule 1002. Requirement of the Original

An original writing, recording, or photograph is required in order to prove its content unless these rules or a federal statute provides otherwise.

(Pub.L. 93–595, § 1, Jan. 2, 1975, 88 Stat. 1946; Apr. 26, 2011, eff. Dec. 1, 2011.)

ADVISORY COMMITTEE NOTES

1972 Proposed Rules

The rule is the familiar one requiring production of the original of a document to prove its contents, expanded to include writings, recordings, and photographs, as defined in Rule 1001(1) and (2), *supra*.

Application of the rule requires a resolution of the question whether contents are sought to be proved. Thus an event may be proved by nondocumentary evidence, even though a written record of it was made. If, however, the event is sought to be proved by the written record, the rule applies. For example, payment may be proved without producing the written receipt which was given. Earnings may be proved without producing books of account in which they are entered. McCormick § 198; 4 Wigmore § 1245. Nor does the rule apply to testimony that books or records have been examined and found not to contain any reference to a designated matter.

The assumption should not be made that the rule will come into operation on every occasion when use is made of a photograph in evidence. On the contrary, the rule will seldom apply to ordinary photographs. In most instances a party *wishes* to introduce the item and the question raised is the propriety of receiving it in evidence. Cases in which an offer is made of the testimony of a witness as to what he saw in a photograph or motion picture, without producing the same, are most unusual. The usual course is for a witness on the stand to identify the photograph or motion picture as a correct representation of events which he saw or of a scene with which he is familiar. In fact he adopts the picture as his testimony, or, in common parlance, uses the picture to illustrate his testimony. Under these circumstances, no effort is made to prove the contents of the picture, and the rule is inapplicable. Paradis, The Celluloid Witness, 37 U.Colo.L.Rev. 235, 249–251 (1965).

On occasion, however, situations arise in which contents are sought to be proved. Copyright, defamation, and invasion of privacy by photograph or motion picture falls in this category. Similarly as to situations in which the picture is offered as having independent probative value, e.g. automatic photograph of bank robber. See *People v. Doggett,* 83 Cal.App.2d 405, 188 P.2d 792 (1948), photograph of defendants engaged in indecent act; Mouser and Philbin, Photographic Evidence—Is There a Recognized Basis for Admissibility? 8 Hastings L.J. 310 (1957). the most commonly encountered of this latter group is of course, the X ray, with substantial authority calling for production of the original. *Daniels v. Iowa City,* 191 Iowa 811, 183 N.W. 415 (1921); *Cellamare v. Third Acc. Transit Corp.,* 273 App.Div. 260, 77 N.Y.S.2d 91 (1948); *Patrick & Tilman v. Matkin,* 154 Okl. 232, 7 P.2d 414 (1932); *Mendoza v. Rivera,* 78 P.R.R. 569 (1955).

It should be noted, however, that Rule 703, *supra*, allows an expert to give an opinion based on matters not in evidence, and the present rule must be read as being limited accordingly in its application. Hospital records which may be admitted as business records under Rule 803(6) commonly contain reports interpreting X-rays by the staff radiologist, who qualifies as an expert, and these reports need not be excluded from the records by the instant rule.

The reference to Acts of Congress is made in view of such statutory provisions as 26 U.S.C. § 7513, photographic reproductions of tax returns and documents, made by authority of the Secretary of the Treasury, treated as originals, and 44 U.S.C. § 399(a), photographic copies in National Archives treated as originals.

2011 Amendments

The language of Rule 1002 has been amended as part of the restyling of the Evidence Rules to make them more easily understood and to make style and terminology consistent throughout the rules. These changes are intended to be stylistic only. There is no intent to change any result in any ruling on evidence admissibility.

Rule 1003. Admissibility of Duplicates

A duplicate is admissible to the same extent as the original unless a genuine question is raised about the original's authenticity or the circumstances make it unfair to admit the duplicate.

(Pub.L. 93–595, § 1, Jan. 2, 1975, 88 Stat. 1946; Apr. 26, 2011, eff. Dec. 1, 2011.)

ADVISORY COMMITTEE NOTES

1972 Proposed Rules

When the only concern is with getting the words or other contents before the court with accuracy and precision, then a counterpart serves equally as well as the original, if the counterpart is the product of a method which insures accuracy and genuineness. By definition in Rule 1001(4), *supra,* a "duplicate" possesses this character.

Therefore, if no genuine issue exists as to authenticity and no other reason exists for requiring the original, a duplicate is admissible under the rule. This position finds support in the decisions, *Myrick v. United States,* 332 F.2d 279 (5th Cir.1964), no error in admitting photostatic copies of checks instead of original microfilm in absence of suggestion to trial judge that photostats were incorrect; *Johns v. United States,* 323 F.2d 421 (5th Cir.1963), not error to admit concededly accurate tape recording made from original wire recording; *Sauget v. Johnston,* 315 F.2d 816 (9th Cir.1963), not error to admit copy of agreement when opponent had original and did not on appeal claim any discrepancy. Other reasons for acquiring the original may be present when only a part of the original is reproduced and the remainder is needed for cross-examination or may disclose matters qualifying the part offered or otherwise useful to the opposing party. *United States v. Alexander,* 326 F.2d 736 (4th Cir.1964). And see *Toho Bussan Kaisha, Ltd. v. American President Lines, Ltd.,* 265 F.2d 418, 76 A.L.R.2d 1344 (2d Cir.1959).

1974 Enactment

The Committee approved this Rule in the form submitted by the Court, with the expectation that the courts would be liberal in deciding that a "genuine question is raised as to the authenticity of the original." House Report No. 93–650.

2011 Amendments

The language of Rule 1003 has been amended as part of the restyling of the Evidence Rules to make them more easily understood and to make style and terminology consistent throughout the rules. These changes are intended to be stylistic only. There is no intent to change any result in any ruling on evidence admissibility.

Rule 1004. Admissibility of Other Evidence of Content

An original is not required and other evidence of the content of a writing, recording, or photograph is admissible if:

(a) all the originals are lost or destroyed, and not by the proponent acting in bad faith;

(b) an original cannot be obtained by any available judicial process;

(c) the party against whom the original would be offered had control of the original; was at that time put on notice, by pleadings or otherwise, that the original would be a subject of proof at the trial or hearing; and fails to produce it at the trial or hearing; or

(d) the writing, recording, or photograph is not closely related to a controlling issue.

(Pub.L. 93–595, § 1, Jan. 2, 1975, 88 Stat. 1946; Mar. 2, 1987, eff. Oct. 1, 1987; Apr. 26, 2011, eff. Dec. 1, 2011.)

ADVISORY COMMITTEE NOTES

1972 Proposed Rules

Basically the rule requiring the production of the original as proof of contents has developed as a rule of preference: if failure to produce the original is satisfactorily explained, secondary evidence is admissible. The instant rule specifies the circumstances under which production of the original is excused.

The rule recognizes no "degrees" of secondary evidence. While strict logic might call for extending the principle of preference beyond simply preferring the original, the formulation of a hierarchy of preferences and a procedure for making it effective is believed to involve unwarranted complexities. Most, if not all, that would be accomplished by an extended scheme of preferences will, in any event, be achieved through the normal motivation of a party to present the most convincing evidence possible and the arguments and procedures available to his opponent if he does not. Compare McCormick § 207.

Note to Paragraph (1). Loss or destruction of the original, unless due to bad faith of the proponent, is a satisfactory explanation of nonproduction. McCormick § 201.

Note to Paragraph (2). When the original is in the possession of a third person, inability to procure it from him by resort to process or other judicial procedure is a sufficient explanation of nonproduction. Judicial procedure includes subpoena duces tecum as an incident to the taking of a deposition in another jurisdiction. No further showing is required. See McCormick § 202.

Note to Paragraph (3). A party who has an original in his control has no need for the protection of the rule if put on notice that proof of contents will be made. He can ward off secondary evidence by offering the original. The notice procedure here provided is not to be confused with orders to produce or other discovery procedures, as the purpose of the procedure under this rule is to afford the opposite party an opportunity to produce the original, not to compel him to do so. McCormick § 203.

Note to Paragraph (4). While difficult to define with precision, situations arise in which no good purpose is served by production of the original. Examples are the newspaper in an action for the price of publishing defendant's advertisement,

Foster–Holcomb Investment Co. v. Little Rock Publishing Co., 151 Ark. 449, 236 S.W. 597 (1922), and the streetcar transfer of plaintiff claiming status as a passenger, *Chicago City Ry. Co. v. Carroll,* 206 Ill. 318, 68 N.E. 1087 (1903). Numerous cases are collected in McCormick § 200, p. 412, n. 1.

1974 Enactment

Note to Paragraph (1). The Committee approved Rule 1004(1) in the form submitted to Congress. However, the Committee intends that loss or destruction of an original by another person at the instigation of the proponent should be considered as tantamount to loss or destruction in bad faith by the proponent himself. House Report No. 93–650.

1987 Amendments

The amendments are technical. No substantive change is intended.

2011 Amendments

The language of Rule 1004 has been amended as part of the restyling of the Evidence Rules to make them more easily understood and to make style and terminology consistent throughout the rules. These changes are intended to be stylistic only. There is no intent to change any result in any ruling on evidence admissibility.

Rule 1005. Copies of Public Records to Prove Content

The proponent may use a copy to prove the content of an official record—or of a document that was recorded or filed in a public office as authorized by law—if these conditions are met: the record or document is otherwise admissible; and the copy is certified as correct in accordance with Rule 902(4) or is testified to be correct by a witness who has compared it with the original. If no such copy can be obtained by reasonable diligence, then the proponent may use other evidence to prove the content.

(Pub.L. 93–595, § 1, Jan. 2, 1975, 88 Stat. 1946; Apr. 26, 2011, eff. Dec. 1, 2011.)

ADVISORY COMMITTEE NOTES

1972 Proposed Rules

Public records call for somewhat different treatment. Removing them from their usual place of keeping would be attended by serious inconvenience to the public and to the custodian. As a consequence judicial decisions and statutes commonly hold that no explanation need be given for failure to produce the original of a public record. McCormick § 204; 4 Wigmore §§ 1215–1228. This blanket dispensation from producing or accounting for the original would open the door to the introduction of every kind of secondary evidence of contents of public records were it not for the preference given certified or compared copies. Recognition of degrees of secondary evidence in this situation is an appropriate *quid pro quo* for not applying the requirement of producing the original.

The provisions of 28 U.S.C. § 1733(b) apply only to departments or agencies of the United States. The rule, however, applies to public records generally and is comparable in scope in this respect to Rule 44(a) of the Rules of Civil Procedure.

2011 Amendments

The language of Rule 1005 has been amended as part of the restyling of the Evidence Rules to make them more easily understood and to make style and terminology consistent throughout the rules. These changes are intended to be stylistic only. There is no intent to change any result in any ruling on evidence admissibility.

Rule 1006. Summaries to Prove Content

The proponent may use a summary, chart, or calculation to prove the content of voluminous writings, recordings, or photographs that cannot be conveniently examined in court. The proponent must make the originals or duplicates available for examination or copying, or both, by other parties at a reasonable time and place. And the court may order the proponent to produce them in court.

(Pub.L. 93–595, § 1, Jan. 2, 1975, 88 Stat. 1946; Apr. 26, 2011, eff. Dec. 1, 2011.)

ADVISORY COMMITTEE NOTES

1972 Proposed Rules

The admission of summaries of voluminous books, records, or documents offers the only practicable means of making their contents available to judge and jury. The rule recognizes this practice, with appropriate safeguards. 4 Wigmore § 1230.

2011 Amendments

The language of Rule 1006 has been amended as part of the restyling of the Evidence Rules to make them more easily understood and to make style and terminology consistent throughout the rules. These changes are intended to be stylistic only. There is no intent to change any result in any ruling on evidence admissibility.

Rule 1007. Testimony or Statement of a Party to Prove Content

The proponent may prove the content of a writing, recording, or photograph by the testimony, deposition, or written statement of the party against whom the evidence is offered. The proponent need not account for the original.

(Pub.L. 93–595, § 1, Jan. 2, 1975, 88 Stat. 1947; Mar. 2, 1987, eff. Oct. 1, 1987; Apr. 26, 2011, eff. Dec. 1, 2011.)

ADVISORY COMMITTEE NOTES

1972 Proposed Rules

While the parent case, *Slatterie v. Pooley,* 6 M. & W. 664, 151 Eng.Rep. 579 (Exch.1840), allows proof of contents by evidence of an oral admission by the party against whom offered, without accounting for nonproduction of the original, the risk of inaccuracy is substantial and the decision is at odds with the purpose of the rule giving preference to the original. See 4 Wigmore § 1255. The instant rule follows Professor McCormick's suggestion of limiting this use of admissions to those made in the course of giving testimony or in writing. McCormick § 208, p. 424. The limitation, of course, does not call for excluding evidence of an oral admission when nonproduction of the original has been accounted for and secondary evidence generally has become admissible. Rule 1004, supra.

A similar provision is contained in New Jersey Evidence Rule 70(1)(h).

1987 Amendments

The amendment is technical. No substantive change is intended.

2011 Amendments

The language of Rule 1007 has been amended as part of the restyling of the Evidence Rules to make them more easily understood and to make style and terminology consistent throughout the rules. These changes are intended to be stylistic only. There is no intent to change any result in any ruling on evidence admissibility.

Rule 1008. Functions of the Court and Jury

Ordinarily, the court determines whether the proponent has fulfilled the factual conditions for admitting other evidence of the content of a writing, recording, or photograph under Rule 1004 or 1005. But in a jury trial, the jury determines—in accordance with Rule 104(b)—any issue about whether:

(a) an asserted writing, recording, or photograph ever existed;

(b) another one produced at the trial or hearing is the original; or

(c) other evidence of content accurately reflects the content.

(Pub.L. 93–595, § 1, Jan. 2, 1975, 88 Stat. 1947; Apr. 26, 2011, eff. Dec. 1, 2011.)

ADVISORY COMMITTEE NOTES

1972 Proposed Rules

Most preliminary questions of fact in connection with applying the rule preferring the original as evidence of contents are for the judge, under the general principles announced in Rule 104, *supra*. Thus, the question whether the loss of the originals has been established, or of the fulfillment of other conditions specified in Rule 1004, supra, is for the judge. However, questions may arise which go beyond the mere administration of the rule preferring the original and into the merits of the controversy. For example, plaintiff offers secondary evidence of the contents of an alleged contract, after first introducing evidence of loss of the original, and defendant counters with evidence that no such contract was ever executed. If the judge decides that the contract was never executed and excludes the secondary evidence, the case is at an end without ever going to the jury on a central issue. Levin, Authentication and Content of Writings, 10 Rutgers L.Rev. 632, 644 (1956). The latter portion of the instant rule is designed to insure treatment of these situations as raising jury questions. The decision is not one for uncontrolled discretion of the jury but is subject to the control exercised generally by the judge over jury determinations. See Rule 104(b), *supra*.

For similar provisions, see Uniform Rule 70(2); Kansas Code of Civil Procedure § 60–467(b); New Jersey Evidence Rule 70(2), (3).

2011 Amendments

The language of Rule 1008 has been amended as part of the restyling of the Evidence Rules to make them more easily understood and to make style and terminology consistent throughout the rules. These changes are intended to be stylistic only. There is no intent to change any result in any ruling on evidence admissibility.

ARTICLE XI. MISCELLANEOUS RULES

Rule
1101. Applicability of the Rules.
1102. Amendments.
1103. Title.

Rule 1101. Applicability of the Rules

(a) To Courts and Judges. These rules apply to proceedings before:

- United States district courts;
- United States bankruptcy and magistrate judges;
- United States courts of appeals;
- the United States Court of Federal Claims; and
- the district courts of Guam, the Virgin Islands, and the Northern Mariana Islands.

(b) To Cases and Proceedings. These rules apply in:

- civil cases and proceedings, including bankruptcy, admiralty, and maritime cases;
- criminal cases and proceedings; and
- contempt proceedings, except those in which the court may act summarily.

(c) Rules on Privilege. The rules on privilege apply to all stages of a case or proceeding.

(d) Exceptions. These rules—except for those on privilege—do not apply to the following:

(1) the court's determination, under Rule 104(a), on a preliminary question of fact governing admissibility;

(2) grand-jury proceedings; and

(3) miscellaneous proceedings such as:

- extradition or rendition;
- issuing an arrest warrant, criminal summons, or search warrant;
- a preliminary examination in a criminal case;
- sentencing;
- granting or revoking probation or supervised release; and
- considering whether to release on bail or otherwise.

(e) Other Statutes and Rules. A federal statute or a rule prescribed by the Supreme Court may provide for admitting or excluding evidence independently from these rules.

(Pub.L. 93–595, § 1, Jan. 2, 1975, 88 Stat. 1947; Pub.L. 94–149, § 1(14), Dec. 12, 1975, 89 Stat. 806; Pub.L. 95–598, Title II, § 251, Nov. 6, 1978, 92 Stat. 2673; Pub.L. 97–164, Title I, § 142, Apr. 2, 1982, 96 Stat. 45; Mar. 2, 1987, eff. Oct. 1, 1987; Apr. 25, 1988, eff. Nov. 1, 1988; Pub.L. 100–690, Title VII, § 7075(c), Nov. 18, 1988, 102 Stat. 4405; Apr. 22, 1993, eff. Dec. 1, 1993; Apr. 26, 2011, eff. Dec. 1, 2011.)

ADVISORY COMMITTEE NOTES

1972 Proposed Rules

Note to Subdivision (a). The various enabling acts contain differences in phraseology in their descriptions of the courts over which the Supreme Court's power to make rules of practice and procedure extends. The act concerning civil actions, as amended in 1966, refers to "the district courts * * * of the United States in civil actions, including admiralty and maritime cases. * * *" 28 U.S.C. § 2072, Pub.L. 89–773, § 1, 80 Stat. 1323. The bankruptcy authorization is for rules of practice and procedure "under the Bankruptcy Act." 28 U.S.C. § 2075, Pub.L. 88–623, § 1, 78 Stat. 1001. The Bankruptcy Act in turn creates bankruptcy courts of "the United States district courts and the district courts of the Territories and possessions to which this title is or may hereafter be applicable." 11 U.S.C. §§ 1(10), 11(a). The provision as to criminal rules up to and including verdicts applies to "criminal cases and proceedings to punish for criminal contempt of court in the United States district courts, in the district courts for the districts of the Canal Zone and Virgin Islands, in the Supreme Court of Puerto Rico, and in proceedings before United States magistrates." 18 U.S.C. § 3771.

These various provisions do not in terms describe the same courts. In congressional usage the phrase "district courts of the United States," without further qualification, traditionally has included the district courts established by Congress in the states under Article III of the Constitution, which are "constitutional" courts, and has not included the territorial courts created under Article IV, Section 3, clause 2, which are "legislative" courts. *Hornbuckle v. Toombs,* 85 U.S. 648, 21 L.Ed. 966 (1873). However, any doubt as to the inclusion of the District Court for the District of Columbia in the phrase is laid at rest by the provisions of the Judicial Code constituting the judicial districts, 28 U.S.C. § 81 et seq., creating district courts therein, id. § 132, and specifically providing that the term "district court of the United States" means the court so constituted. *Id.* § 451. The District of Columbia is included. *Id.* § 88. Moreover, when these provisions were enacted, reference to the District of Columbia was deleted from the original civil rules enabling act. 28 U.S.C. § 2072. Likewise Puerto Rico is made a district, with a district court, and included in the term. *Id.* § 119. The question is simply one of the extent of the authority conferred by Congress. With respect to civil rules it seems clearly to include the district courts in the states, the District Court for the District of Columbia, and the District Court for the District of Puerto Rico.

The bankruptcy coverage is broader. The bankruptcy courts include "the United States district courts," which includes those enumerated above. Bankruptcy courts also include "the district courts of the Territories and possessions to which this title is or may hereafter be applicable." 11 U.S.C. §§ 1(10), 11(a). These courts include the district courts of Guam and the Virgin Islands. 48 U.S.C. §§ 1424(b), 1615. Professor Moore points out that whether the District Court for the District of the Canal Zone is a court of bankruptcy "is not free from doubt in view of the fact that no other statute expressly or inferentially provides for the applicability of the Bankruptcy Act in the Zone." He further observes that while there seems to be little doubt that the Zone is a territory or possession within the meaning of the Bankruptcy Act, 11 U.S.C. § 1(10), it must be noted that the appendix to the Canal Zone Code of 1934 did not list the Act among the laws of the United States applicable to the Zone. 1 Moore's Collier on Bankruptcy ¶ 1.10, pp. 67, 72, n. 25 (14th ed. 1967). The Code of 1962 confers on the district court jurisdiction of:

"(4) actions and proceedings involving laws of the United States applicable to the Canal Zone; and

"(5) other matters and proceedings wherein jurisdiction is conferred by this Code or any other law." Canal Zone Code, 1962, Title 3, § 141.

Admiralty jurisdiction is expressly conferred. *Id.* § 142. General powers are conferred on the district court, "if the course of proceeding is not specifically prescribed by this Code, by the statute, or by applicable rule of the Supreme Court of the United States * * *" *Id.* § 279. Neither these provisions nor § 1(10) of the Bankruptcy Act ("district courts of the Territories and possessions to which this title is or may hereafter be applicable") furnishes a satisfactory answer as to the status of the District Court for the District of the Canal Zone as a court of bankruptcy. However, the fact is that this court exercises no bankruptcy jurisdiction in practice.

The criminal rules enabling act specified United States district courts, district courts for the districts of the Canal Zone and the Virgin Islands, the Supreme Court of the Commonwealth of Puerto Rico, and proceedings before United States commissioners. Aside from the addition of commissioners, now magistrates, this scheme differs from the bankruptcy pattern in that it makes no mention of the District Court of Guam but by specific mention removes the Canal Zone from the doubtful list.

The further difference in including the Supreme Court of the Commonwealth of Puerto Rico seems not to be significant for present purposes, since the Supreme Court of the Commonwealth of Puerto Rico is an appellate court. The Rules of Criminal Procedure have not been made applicable to it, as being unneeded and inappropriate, Rule 54(a) of the Federal Rules of Criminal Procedure, and the same approach is indicated with respect to rules of evidence.

If one were to stop at this point and frame a rule governing the applicability of the proposed rules of evidence in terms of the authority conferred by the three enabling acts, an irregular pattern would emerge as follows:

Civil actions, including admiralty and maritime cases—district courts in the states, District of Columbia, and Puerto Rico.

Bankruptcy—same as civil actions, plus Guam and Virgin Islands.

Criminal cases—same as civil actions, plus Canal Zone and Virgin Islands (but not Guam).

This irregular pattern need not, however, be accepted. Originally the Advisory Committee on the Rules of Civil Procedure took the position that, although the phrase "district courts of the United States" did not include territorial courts, provisions in the organic laws of Puerto Rico and Hawaii would make the rules applicable to the district courts thereof, though this would not be so as to Alaska, the Virgin Islands, or the Canal Zone, whose organic acts contained no corresponding provisions. At the suggestion of the Court, however, the Advisory Committee struck from its notes a statement to the above effect. 2 Moore's Federal Practice ¶ 1.07 (2nd ed. 1967); 1 Barron and Holtzoff, Federal Practice and Procedure § 121 (Wright ed. 1960). Congress thereafter by various enactments provided that the rules and future amendments thereto should apply to the district courts of Hawaii, 53 Stat. 841 (1939), Puerto Rico, 54 Stat. 22 (1940), Alaska, 63 Stat. 445 (1949), Guam, 64 Stat. 384–390 (1950), and the Virgin Islands, 68 Stat. 497, 507 (1954). The original enabling act for rules of criminal procedure specifically mentioned the district courts of the Canal Zone and the Virgin Islands. The Commonwealth of Puerto Rico was blanketed in by creating its court a "district court of the United States" as previously described. Although Guam is not mentioned in either the enabling act or in the expanded definition of "district court of the United States," the Supreme Court in 1956 amended Rule 54(a) to state that the Rules of Criminal

Procedure are applicable in Guam. The Court took this step following the enactment of legislation by Congress in 1950 that rules theretofore or thereafter promulgated by the Court in civil cases, admiralty, criminal cases and bankruptcy should apply to the District Court of Guam, 48 U.S.C. § 1424(b), and two Ninth Circuit decisions upholding the applicability of the Rules of Criminal Procedure to Guam. *Pugh v. United States,* 212 F.2d 761 (9th Cir.1954); *Hatchett v. Guam,* 212 F.2d 767 (9th Cir.1954); Orfield, The Scope of the Federal Rules of Criminal Procedure, 38 U. of Det.L.J. 173, 187 (1960).

From this history, the reasonable conclusion is that Congressional enactment of a provision that rules and future amendments shall apply in the courts of a territory or possession is the equivalent of mention in an enabling act and that a rule on scope and applicability may properly be drafted accordingly. Therefore the pattern set by Rule 54 of the Federal Rules of Criminal Procedure is here followed.

The substitution of magistrates in lieu of commissioners is made in pursuance of the Federal Magistrates Act, P.L. 90–578, approved October 17, 1968, 82 Stat. 1107.

Note to Subdivision (b). Subdivision (b) is a combination of the language of the enabling acts, supra, with respect to the kinds of proceedings in which the making of rules is authorized. It is subject to the qualifications expressed in the subdivisions which follow.

Note to Subdivision (c). Subdivision (c) singling out the rules of privilege for special treatment, is made necessary by the limited applicability of the remaining rules.

Note to Subdivision (d). The rule is not intended as an expression as to when due process or other constitutional provisions may require an evidentiary hearing. Paragraph (1) restates, for convenience, the provisions of the second sentence of Rule 104(a), *supra.* See Advisory Committee's Note to that rule.

(2) While some states have statutory requirements that indictments be based on "legal evidence," and there is some case law to the effect that the rules of evidence apply to grand jury proceedings, 1 Wigmore § 4(5), the Supreme Court has not accepted this view. In *Costello v. United States,* 350 U.S. 359, 76 S.Ct. 406, 100 L.Ed. 397 (1965), the Court refused to allow an indictment to be attacked, for either constitutional or policy reasons, on the ground that only hearsay evidence was presented.

"It would run counter to the whole history of the grand jury institution, in which laymen conduct their inquiries unfettered by technical rules. Neither justice nor the concept of a fair trial requires such a change." *Id.* at 364. The rule as drafted does not deal with the evidence required to support an indictment.

(3) The rule exempts preliminary examinations in criminal cases. Authority as to the applicability of the rules of evidence to preliminary examinations has been meagre and conflicting. Goldstein, The State and the Accused: Balance of Advantage in Criminal Procedure, 69 Yale L.J. 1149, 1168, n. 53 (1960); Comment, Preliminary Hearings on Indictable Offenses in Philadelphia, 106 U. of Pa.L.Rev. 589, 592–593 (1958). Hearsay testimony is, however, customarily received in such examinations. Thus in a Dyer Act case, for example, an affidavit may properly be used in a preliminary examination to prove ownership of the stolen vehicle, thus saving the victim of the crime the hardship of having to travel twice to a distant district for the sole purpose of testifying as to ownership. It is believed that the extent of the applicability of the Rules of Evidence to preliminary examinations should be appropriately dealt with by the Federal Rules of Criminal Procedure which regulate those proceedings.

Extradition and rendition proceedings are governed in detail by statute. 18 U.S.C. §§ 3181–3195. They are essentially administrative in character. Traditionally the rules of evidence have not applied. 1 Wigmore § 4(6). Extradition proceedings are accepted from the operation of the Rules of Criminal Procedure. Rule 54(b)(5) of Federal Rules of Criminal Procedure.

The rules of evidence have not been regarded as applicable to sentencing or probation proceedings, where great reliance is placed upon the presentence investigation and report. Rule 32(c) of the Federal Rules of Criminal Procedure requires a presentence investigation and report in every case unless the court otherwise directs. In *Williams v. New York,* 337 U.S. 241, 69 S.Ct. 1079, 93 L.Ed. 1337 (1949), in which the judge overruled a jury recommendation of life imprisonment and imposed a death sentence, the Court said that due process does not require confrontation or cross-examination in sentencing or passing on probation, and that the judge has broad discretion as to the sources and types of information relied upon. Compare the recommendation that the substance of all derogatory information be disclosed to the defendant, in A.B.A. Project on Minimum Standards for Criminal Justice, Sentencing Alternatives and Procedures § 4.4, Tentative Draft (1967, Sobeloff, Chm.). Williams was adhered to in *Specht v. Patterson,* 386 U.S. 605, 87 S.Ct. 1209, 18 L.Ed.2d 326 (1967), but not extended to a proceeding under the Colorado Sex Offenders Act, which was said to be a new charge leading in effect to punishment, more like the recidivist statutes where opportunity must be given to be heard on the habitual criminal issue.

Warrants for arrest, criminal summonses, and search warrants are issued upon complaint or affidavit showing probable cause. Rules 4(a) and 41(c) of the Federal Rules of Criminal Procedure. The nature of the proceedings makes application of the formal rules of evidence inappropriate and impracticable.

Criminal contempts are punishable summarily if the judge certifies that he saw or heard the contempt and that it was committed in the presence of the court. Rule 42(a) of the Federal Rules of Criminal Procedure. The circumstances which preclude application of the rules of evidence in this situation are not present, however, in other cases of criminal contempt.

Proceedings with respect to release on bail or otherwise do not call for application of the rules of evidence. The governing statute specifically provides:

"Information stated in, or offered in connection with, any order entered pursuant to this section need not conform to the rules pertaining to the admissibility of evidence in a court of law." 18 U.S.C.A. § 3146(f). This provision is consistent with the type of inquiry contemplated in A.B.A. Project on Minimum Standards for Criminal Justice, Standards Relating to Pretrial Release, § 4.5(b), (c), p. 16 (1968). The references to the weight of the evidence against the accused, in Rule 46(a)(1), (c) of the Federal Rules of Criminal Procedure and in 18 U.S.C.A. § 3146(b), as a factor to be considered, clearly do not have in view evidence introduced at a hearing under the rules of evidence.

The rule does not exempt habeas corpus proceedings. The Supreme Court held in *Walker v. Johnston,* 312 U.S. 275, 61 S.Ct. 574, 85 L.Ed. 830 (1941), that the practice of disposing of matters of fact on affidavit, which prevailed in some circuits, did not "satisfy the command of the statute that the judge shall proceed 'to determine the facts of the case, by hearing the testimony and arguments.' " This view accords with the emphasis in *Townsend v. Sain,* 372 U.S. 293, 83 S.Ct. 745, 9 L.Ed.2d 770 (1963), upon trial-type proceedings, *id.* 311, 83 S.Ct. 745, with demeanor evidence as a significant factor, *id.* 322, 83 S.Ct. 745, in applications by state prisoners aggrieved by unconstitutional detentions. Hence subdivision (3) applies the rules to habeas corpus proceedings to the extent not inconsistent with the statute.

Note to Subdivision (e). In a substantial number of special proceedings, *ad hoc* evaluation has resulted in the promulgation of particularized evidentiary provisions, by Act of Congress or by rule adopted by the Supreme Court. Well adapted to the particular proceedings, though not apt candidates for inclusion in a set of general rules, they are left undisturbed. Otherwise, however, the rules of evidence are applicable to the proceedings enumerated in the subdivision.

1974 Enactment

Note to Subdivision (a). Subdivision (a) as submitted to the Congress, in stating the courts and judges to which the Rules of Evidence apply, omitted the Court of Claims and commissioners of that Court. At the request of the Court of Claims, the Committee amended the Rule to include the Court and its commissioners within the purview of the Rules.

Note to Subdivision (b). Subdivision (b) was amended merely to substitute positive law citations for those which were not. House Report No. 93–650.

1987 Amendments

Subdivision (a) is amended to delete the reference to the District Court for the District of the Canal Zone, which no longer exists, and to add the District Court for the Northern Mariana Islands. The United States bankruptcy judges are added to conform the subdivision with Rule 1101(b) and Bankruptcy Rule 9017.

1988 Amendments

The amendments are technical. No substantive change is intended.

1993 Amendments

This revision is made to conform the rule to changes in terminology made by Rule 58 of the Federal Rules of Criminal Procedure and to the changes in the title of United States magistrates made by the Judicial Improvements Act of 1990.

2011 Amendments

The language of Rule 1101 has been amended as part of the restyling of the Evidence Rules to make them more easily understood and to make style and terminology consistent throughout the rules. These changes are intended to be stylistic only. There is no intent to change any result in any ruling on evidence admissibility.

HISTORICAL NOTES

Revision Notes and Legislative Reports

1975 Acts

House Report No. 94–599, see 1975 U.S. Code Cong. and Adm. News, p. 1585.

1982 Acts

Senate Report No. 97–275, see 1982 U.S. Code Cong. and Adm. News, p. 11.

Effective and Applicability Provisions

1982 Acts

Amendment by Pub.L. 97–164 effective Oct. 1, 1982, see section 402 of Pub.L. 97–164, set out as a note under section 171 of this title.

1978 Acts

Amendment of subds. (a) and (b) of this rule by section 251 of Pub.L. 95–598 effective Oct. 1, 1979, see section 402(c) of Pub.L. 95–598, set out as a note preceding section 101 of Title 11, Bankruptcy.

Change of Name

United States magistrate appointed under section 631 of Title 28, Judiciary and Judicial Procedure, to be known as United States magistrate judge after Dec. 1, 1990, with any reference to United States magistrate or magistrate in Title 28, in any other Federal statute, etc., deemed a reference to United States magistrate judge appointed under section 631 of Title 28, see section 321 of Pub.L. 101–650, set out as a note under section 631 of Title 28.

Pending Actions

Amendments of Supreme Court to the Federal Rules of Evidence effective December 1, 1993, applicable, insofar as just and practicable, in all proceedings then pending, pursuant to the Order of April 22, 1993.

Rule 1102. Amendments

These rules may be amended as provided in 28 U.S.C. § 2072.

(Pub.L. 93–595, § 1, Jan. 2, 1975, 88 Stat.1948; Apr. 30, 1991, eff. Dec. 1, 1991; Apr. 26, 2011, eff. Dec. 1, 2011.)

ADVISORY COMMITTEE NOTES

1991 Amendments

The amendment is technical. No substantive change is intended.

2011 Amendments

The language of Rule 1102 has been amended as part of the restyling of the Evidence Rules to make them more easily understood and to make style and terminology consistent throughout the rules. These changes are intended to be stylistic only. There is no intent to change any result in any ruling on evidence admissibility.

Rule 1103. Title

These rules may be cited as the Federal Rules of Evidence.

(Pub.L. 93–595, § 1, Jan. 2, 1975, 88 Stat.1948; Apr. 26, 2011, eff. Dec. 1, 2011.)

ADVISORY COMMITTEE NOTES

2011 Amendments

The language of Rule 1103 has been amended as part of the restyling of the Evidence Rules to make them more easily understood and to make style and terminology consistent throughout the rules. These changes are intended to be stylistic only. There is no intent to change any result in any ruling on evidence admissibility.

HISTORICAL NOTES

Short Title

1978 Amendments

Pub.L. 95–540, § 1, Oct. 28, 1978, 92 Stat. 2046, provided: "That this Act [enacting rule 412 of these rules and a provision set out as a note under rule 412 of these rules] may be cited as the 'Privacy Protection for Rape Victims Act of 1978'."

TABLE OF CASES

A

A.V.I., Inc. v. Heathington, 842 S.W.2d 712 (Tex. App.—Amarillo 1992)—**Rule 406**

Aguilar v. State, 715 S.W.2d 645 (Tex. Crim. App. 1986)—**Rule 504**

Ake v. Oklahoma, 470 U.S. 68, 105 S.Ct. 1087, 84 L.Ed.2d 53 (1985)—**Rule 702**

Alamo, City of v. Casas, 960 S.W.2d 240 (Tex. App.—Corpus Christi 1997)—**Rule 403**

Alba v. State, 905 S.W.2d 581 (Tex. Crim. App. 1995)—**Rule 705**

Allen v. St. Paul Fire and Marine Ins. Co., 960 S.W.2d 909 (Tex. App.—Texarkana 1998)—**Rule 103**

Allied Chem. Co. v. DeHaven, 824 S.W.2d 257 (Tex. App.—Houston [14th Dist.] 1992)—**Rule 609**

Almendarez v. State, 153 S.W.3d 727 (Tex. App.—Dallas 2005)—**Rule 503**

America West Airlines, Inc. v. Tope, 935 S.W.2d 908 (Tex. App.—El Paso 1996)—**Rule 702**

American Bankers Ins. Co. of Florida v. Caruth, 786 S.W.2d 427 (Tex. App.—Dallas 1990)—**Rule 201**

American Motorists Ins. Co. v. Sells, 747 S.W.2d 27 (Tex. App.—Texarkana 1988)—**Rule 606**

Anderson v. State, 15 S.W.3d 177 (Tex. App.—Texarkana 2000)—**Rule 406**

Angleton v. State, 971 S.W.2d 65 (Tex. Crim. App. 1998)—**Rule 901**

Appling v. State, 904 S.W.2d 912 (Tex. App.—Corpus Christi 1995)—**Rule 806**

Arndt, In re Estate of, 187 S.W.3d 84 (Tex. App.—Beaumont 2005)—**Rule 103**

Associated Indemnity Corp. v. Dixon, 632 S.W.2d 833 (Tex. App.—Dallas 1982)—**Rule 803**

Atlantic Richfield Co. v. Misty Products, Inc., 820 S.W.2d 414 (Tex. App.—Houston [14th Dist.] 1991)—**Rule 103**

Austin v. State, 934 S.W.2d 672 (Tex. Crim. App. 1996)—**Rule 503**

Azar Nut Co. v. Caille, 720 S.W.2d 685 (Tex. App.—El Paso 1986)—**Rule 105**

B

Bagley, United States v., 473 U.S. 667, 105 S.Ct. 3375, 87 L.Ed.2d 481 (1985)—**Rule 608**

Banda v. Garcia, 41 Tex.S.Ct.J. 79, 955 S.W.2d 270 (Tex. 1997)—**Rule 103**

Bartley v. Budget Rent–A–Car Corp., 919 S.W.2d 747 (Tex. App.—Amarillo 1996)—**Rule 202**

Bass, In re, 113 S.W.3d 735 (Tex. 2003)—**Rule 507**

Bay Area Health Group, Ltd. v. McShane, 239 S.W.3d 231 (Tex. 2007)—**Rule 103**

Beall v. Ditmore, 867 S.W.2d 791 (Tex. App.—El Paso 1993)—**Rule 103**

Bean v. Baxter Health Care Corp., 965 S.W.2d 656 (Tex. App.—Houston [14th Dist.] 1998)—**Rule 403**

Beavers on Behalf of Beavers v. Northrop Worldwide Aircraft Servs., Inc., 821 S.W.2d 669 (Tex. App.—Amarillo 1991)—**Rules 103, 407, 705**

Benavides v. Cushman, Inc., 189 S.W.3d 875 (Tex. App.—Houston [1st Dist.] 2006)—**Rule 103**

Benetiz v. State, 5 S.W.3d 95 (Tex. App.—Amarillo 1999)**Rule 513**

Berger v. Lang, 976 S.W.2d 833 (Tex. App.—Houston [1st Dist.] 1998)—**Rule 501**

Bigby v. State, 892 S.W.2d 864 (Tex. Crim. App. 1994)—**Rules 602, 701**

Bingham v. State, 987 S.W.2d 54 (Tex. Crim. App. 1999)—**Rule 803**

Birchfield v. Texarkana Mem'l Hosp., 747 S.W.2d 361 (Tex. 1987)—**Rule 704**

Bird v. W.C.W., 868 S.W.2d 767 (Tex. 1994)—**Rule 402**

Bisby v. State, 907 S.W.2d 949 (Tex. App.—Fort Worth 1995)—**Rule 603**

Blue v. State, 41 S.W.3d 129 (Tex. Crim. App. 2000)—**Rule 103**

Board of Trustees of Fire and Police Retiree Health Fund v. Towers, Perrin, Forster & Crosby, Inc., 191 S.W.3d 185, 193 (Tex. App.—San Antonio 2005)—**Rule 701**

Bodin v. State, 807 S.W.2d 313 (Tex. Crim. App. 1991)—**Rule 508**

Bordman v. State, 56 S.W.3d 63 (Tex. App.—Houston [14th Dist.] 2001)—**Rule 505**

Boswell v. Brazos Elec. Power Co-op., Inc., 910 S.W.2d 593 (Tex. App.—Fort Worth 1995)—**Rules 703, 705**

Boyle v. State, 820 S.W.2d 122 (Tex. Crim. App. 1989)—**Rule 412**

Bradley v. State ex rel. White, 990 S.W.2d 245 (Tex. 1999)—**Rule 605**

Brady v. Maryland, 373 U.S. 83, 83 S.Ct. 1194, 10 L.Ed.2d 215 (1963)—**Rules 608, 612**

Branzburg v. Hayes, 408 U.S. 665, 92 S.Ct. 2646 (1972)—**Rule 501**

Bristol–Myers Squibb Co. v. Hancock, 921 S.W.2d 917 (Tex. App.—Houston [14th Dist.] 1996)—**Rule 509**

Brochner v. Thomas, 795 S.W.2d 215 (Tex. App.—Eastland 1990)—**Rule 509**

Broders v. Heise, 924 S.W.2d 148 (Tex. 1996)—**Rule 702**

Brookshire Bros., Inc. v. Lewis, 911 S.W.2d 791 (Tex. App.—Tyler 1995)—**Rule 407**

Broussard v. State, 910 S.W.2d 952 (Tex. Crim. App. 1995)—**Rule 601**

Brown v. American Transfer and Storage Co., 601 S.W.2d 931 (Tex. 1980)—**Rule 402**

Bruton v. United States, 391 U.S. 123, 88 S.Ct. 1620, 20 L.Ed.2d 476 (1968)—**Rule 803**

Buentello v. State, 826 S.W.2d 610 (Tex. Crim. App. 1992)—**Rule 606**
Bullcoming v. New Mexico, 564 U.S. ______, 131 S.Ct. 2705, 180 L.Ed.2d 610(2011)—**Rule 803**
Burks v. State, 876 S.W.2d 877 (Tex. Crim. App. 1994)—**Rule 103**
Burlington Northern Santa Fe Ry. Co. v. Gunderson, Inc., 235 S.W.3d 287(Tex. App.—Fort Worth, 2007)—**Rule 202**
Burroughs Wellcome Co. v. Crye, 907 S.W.2d 497 (Tex. 1995)—**Rules 702, 803**
Burrow v. Arce, 997 S.W.2d 229 (Tex. 1999)—**Rules 702, 703**
Butler v. Commission for Lawyer Discipline, 928 S.W.2d 659 (Tex. App.—Corpus Christi 1996)—**Rule 801**

C

Cain v. Whitlock, 741 S.W.2d 528 (Tex. App.—Houston [14th Dist.] 1987)—**Rule 601**
Campbell v. Salazar, 960 S.W.2d 719 (Tex. App.—El Paso 1997)—**Rule 1006**
Carlisle v. Philip Morris, Inc., 805 S.W.2d 498 (Tex. App.—Austin 1991)—**Rule 803**
Carmell v. Texas, 527 U.S. 1002, 119 S.Ct. 2336 (2000)—**Rule 101**
Carter v. Steere Tank Lines, Inc., 835 S.W.2d 176 (Tex. App.—Amarillo 1992)—**Rule 803**
Casey v. State, 215 S.W.3d 870 (Tex. Crim. App. 2007)—**Rules 403, 404**
Castaldo v. State, 78 S.W.3d 345 (Tex. Crim. App. 2002)—**Rule 404**
Chandler v. Chandler, 842 S.W.2d 829 (Tex. App.—El Paso 1992)—**Rule 803**
Channel Two Television Co. v. Dickerson, 725 S.W.2d 470 (Tex. App.—Houston [1st Dist.] 1987)—**Rule 501**
Chavis v. Director, State Worker's Compensation Div., 924 S.W.2d 439 (Tex. App.—Beaumont 1996)—**Rule 103**
Christus Spohn Hospital Kleberg, In re, 222 S.W.3d 434 (Tex. 2007)—**Rule 703**
City of (see name of City)
Clancy v. Zale Corp., 705 S.W.2d 820 (Tex. App.—Dallas 1986)—**Rule 606**
Clark v. Trailways, Inc., 774 S.W.2d 644 (Tex. 1989)—**Rule 103**
Clayton v. First State Bank of Gainesville, 777 S.W.2d 577 (Tex. App.—Fort Worth 1989)—**Rule 608**
Coastal Transport Co., Inc. v. Crown Central Petroleum Corp., 136 S.W.3d 227 (Tex. 2004)—**Rule 702**
Coates v. Whittington, 758 S.W.2d 749 (Tex. 1988)—**Rule 509**
Cockrell v. Republic Mortg. Ins. Co., 817 S.W.2d 106 (Tex. App.—Dallas 1991)—**Rule 803**
Cockrell v. State, 933 S.W.2d 73 (Tex. Crim. App. 1996)—**Rule 103**
Coffin v. State, 885 S.W.2d 140 (Tex. Crim. App. 1994)—**Rule 804**
Cofield v. State, 891 S.W.2d 952 (Tex. Crim. App. 1994)—**Rule 803**
Coker v. Burghardt, 833 S.W.2d 306 (Tex. App.—Dallas 1992)—**Rule 701**
Cole v. State, 839 S.W.2d 798 (Tex. Crim. App. 1990)—**Rule 803**
Coleman v. United Savs. Ass'n of Tex., 846 S.W.2d 128 (Tex. App.—Fort Worth 1993)—**Rule 803**
Collins, M.D., In re, 286 S.W.3d 911 (Tex. 2009)—**Rule 509**
Colvin v. Colvin, 291 S.W.3d 508 (Tex. App.—Tyler 2009)—**Rule 202**
Comegys v. Glassell, 839 F.Supp. 447 (E.D. Tex. 1993)—**Rule 503**
Commerce, Crowdus & Canton, Ltd. v. DKS Constr., Inc., 776 S.W.2d 615 (Tex. App.—Dallas 1989)—**Rule 103**
Commitment of Day, In re, 342 S.W.3d 193 (Tex. App.—Beaumont 2011, pet. denied)—**Rule 103**
Computer Assocs. Int'l, Inc. v. Altai, Inc., 918 S.W.2d 453 (Tex. 1994)—**Rule 507**
Continental Gen. Tire, Inc., In re, 979 S.W.2d 609 (Tex. 1998)—**Rule 507**
Cooper Tire & Rubber v. Mendez, 204 S.W.3d 797(Tex. 2006)—**Rule 702**
Crawford v. Washington, 541 U.S. 36, 124 S.Ct. 1354 (2004)—**Rule 803**
Creavin v. Moloney, 773 S.W.2d 698 (Tex. App.—Corpus Christi 1989)—**Rule 202**
Credille v. State, 925 S.W.2d 112 (Tex. App.—Houston [14th Dist.] 1996)—**Rule 107**
Crowson v. Kansas City Southern Railway Co., 11 S.W.3d 300 (Tex. App.—Eastland 1999)—**Rule 606**
Cuadros-Fernandez v. State, 316 S.W.3d 645 (Tex. App.—Dallas 2009, no pet)—**Rule 803**

D

D.O., In re, 338 S.W.3d 29, 37 (Tex. App.—Eastland 2011, no pet.)—**Rule 403**
Dallas, City of v. Donovan, 768 S.W.2d 905 (Tex. App.—Dallas 1989)—**Rule 803**
Dallas County v. Crestview Corners Car Wash, 370 S.W.3d 25 (Tex. App.—Dallas 2012)—**Rules 103, 703**
Dallas County Bail Bond Bd. v. Mason, 773 S.W.2d 586 (Tex. App.—Dallas 1989)—**Rule 609**
Dallas Morning News v. Garcia, 822 S.W.2d 675 (Tex. App.—San Antonio 1991)—**Rule 501**
Damian v. Bell Helicopter Textron, Inc., 352 S.W.3d 124 (Tex. App.—Ft. Worth 2010, no pet.)—**Rule 702**
Daubert v. Merrell Dow Pharmaceuticals, Inc., 509 U.S. 579, 113 S.Ct. 2786, 125 L.Ed.2d 469 (1993)—**Rule 702**
Daugherty v. Southern Pacific Transp. Co., 772 S.W.2d 81 (Tex. 1989)—**Rule 202**
Davidson v. Great Nat'l Life Ins. Co., 737 S.W.2d 312 (Tex. 1987)—**Rule 501**
Davis v. Washington & Indiana v. Hammon, 547 U.S. 813, 126 S.Ct. 2266 (2006)—**Rule 803**
De La Paz v. State, 273 S.W.3d 671 (Tex. Crim. App. 2008)—**Rule 803**
Delgado v. State, 235 S.W.3d 244 (Tex. Crim. App. 2007)—**Rule 105**
Delk v. State, 855 S.W.2d 700 (Tex. Crim. App. 1993)—**Rule 609**
Denison, City of v. Grisham, 716 S.W.2d 121 (Tex. App.—Dallas 1986)—**Rule 612**

DeWitt and Rearick, Inc. v. Ferguson, 699 S.W.2d 692 (Tex. App.—El Paso 1985)—**Rule 501**
Dico Tire, Inc. v. Cisneros, 953 S.W.2d 776 (Tex. App.—Corpus Christi 1997)—**Rule 702**
Direct Communications, Inc. v. Lunsford, 906 S.W.2d 537 (Tex. App.—Dallas 1995)—**Rule 103**
Director, State Employees Workers' Compensation Div., State of Tex. v. Lara, 901 S.W.2d 635 (Tex. App.—El Paso 1995)—**Rule 902**
Dixon v. State, 2 S.W.3d 263 (Tex. Crim. App. 1998)—**Rules 608, 613**
Dolcefino v. Ray, 902 S.W.2d 163 (Tex. App.—Houston [1st Dist.] 1995)—**Rule 501**
Dorado v. State, 843 S.W.2d 37 (Tex. Crim. App. 1992)—**Rule 801**
Downen v. Texas Gulf Shrimp Co., 846 S.W.2d 506 (Tex. App.—Corpus Christi 1993)—**Rule 613**
Drilex Sys., Inc. v. Flores, 1 S.W.3d 112 (Tex. 1999)—**Rule 614**
Druery v. State, 225 S.W.3d 491 (Tex. Crim. App. 2007)—**Rule 901**
Dubai Petroleum Co. v. Kazi, 12 S.W.3d 71 (Tex. 2000)—**Rule 203**
DuBose v. State, 915 S.W.2d 493 (Tex. Crim. App. 1996)—**Rule 104**
Dudley v. Humana Hosp. Corp., 817 S.W.2d 124 (Tex. App.—Houston [14th Dist.] 1991)—**Rule 403**
Dufrene v. State, 853 S.W.2d 86 (Tex. App.—Houston [14th Dist.] 1993)—**Rule 601**
Duncan v. Board of Disciplinary Appeals, 898 S.W.2d 759 (Tex. 1995)—**Rule 609**
Duncan v. State, 95 S.W.3d 669 (Tex. App.—Houston [1st Dist.] 2003)—**Rule 801**
Duncan Dev., Inc. v. Haney, 634 S.W.2d 811 (Tex. 1982)—**Rule 803**
Duncan-Hubert v. Mitchell, 310 S.W.3d 92 (Tex. App.—Dallas 2010)—**Rule 702**

E

E.F. Hutton & Co., Inc. v. Youngblood, 741 S.W.2d 363 (Tex. 1987)—**Rule 702**
E.I. du Pont de Nemours and Co., Inc., In re, 136 S.W.3d 218 (Tex. 2004)—**Rule 503**
E.I. du Pont de Nemours and Co., Inc. v. Robinson, 923 S.W.2d 549 (Tex. 1995)—**Rules 104, 702, 703, 803**
E.P. Operating Co. v. Sonora Exploration Corp., 862 S.W.2d 149 (Tex. App.—Houston [1st Dist.] 1993)—**Rule 901**
E.V.R. II Assocs., Ltd. v. Brundige, 813 S.W.2d 552 (Tex. App.—Dallas 1991)—**Rule 407**
Easley v. State, 837 S.W.2d 854 (Tex. App.—Austin 1992)—**Rule 505**
Eckmann v. Des Rosiers, 940 S.W.2d 394 (Tex. App.—Austin 1997)—**Rule 204**
Editorial Caballero S.A de C.V. v. Playboy Enterprises, Inc., 359 S.W.3d 318 (Tex. App.—Corpus Christi 2012)—**Rule 606**
Edmond v. State, 911 S.W.2d 487 (Tex. App.—Texarkana 1995)—**Rule 508**
El Centro del Barrio, Inc. v. Barlow, 894 S.W.2d 775 (Tex. App.—San Antonio 1994)—**Rules 501, 503**
Elbaor v. Smith, 845 S.W.2d 240 (Tex. 1992)—**Rule 408**
Eoff v. Hal & Charlie Peterson Foundation, 811 S.W.2d 187 (Tex. App.—San Antonio 1991)—**Rule 407**
Erazo v. State, 144 S.W.3d 487 (Tex. Crim. App. 2004)—**Rule 401**
ESIS, Inc., Servicing Contractor v. Johnson, 908 S.W.2d 554 (Tex. App.—Fort Worth 1995)—**Rule 103**
Estate of (see name of party)
Ethicon, Inc. v. Martinez, 835 S.W.2d 826 (Tex. App.—Austin 1992)—**Rule 701**
Ethington v. State, 819 S.W.2d 854 (Tex. Crim. App. 1991)—**Rule 103**
Ewing v. Ewing, 739 S.W.2d 470 (Tex. App.—Corpus Christi 1987)—**Rule 202**
Ex parte (see name of party)
Exxon Corp. v. Breezevale, Ltd., 82 S.W.3d 429 (Tex. App.—Dallas 2003)—**Rule 203**

F

Fagbemi v. State, 778 S.W.2d 119 (Tex. App.—Texarkana 1989)—**Rule 603**
Fairow v. State, 920 S.W.2d 357 (Tex. App.—Houston [1st Dist.] 1996)—**Rule 704**
Fairow v. State, 943 S.W.2d 895 (Tex. Crim. App. 1997)—**Rules 602, 701**
Felix v. Gonzalez, 87 S.W.3d 574 (Tex. App.—San Antonio 2002)—**Rule 803**
First Nat'l Bank of Amarillo v. Jarnigan, 794 S.W.2d 54 (Tex. App.—Amarillo 1990)—**Rule 201**
First Southwest Lloyds Ins. Co. v. MacDowell, 769 S.W.2d 954 (Tex. App.—Texarkana 1989)—**Rules 705, 803**
Fletcher v. State, 39 S.W.3d 274 (Tex. App.—Texarkana 2001)—**Rule 702**
Flores, Ex parte, 537 S.W.2d 458 (Tex. Crim. App. 1976)—**Rule 201**
Fontenot, In re, 13 S.W.3d 111 (Tex. App.—Fort Worth 2000)—**Rule 503**
Ford Motor Co. v. Leggat, 904 S.W.2d 643 (Tex. 1995)—**Rules 408, 501**
Ford v. State, 305 S.W.3d 530 (Tex. Crim. App. 2009)—**Rule 101**
Fort Worth Children's Hosp., In re, 100 S.W.3d 582 (Tex. App.—Fort Worth 2003)—**Rule 509**
Fort Worth, City of v. Holland, 748 S.W.2d 112 (Tex. App.—Fort Worth 1988)—**Rule 103**
Freeman v. State, 786 S.W.2d 56 (Tex. App.—Houston [1st Dist.] 1990)—**Rule 101**
Frost, In re, 998 S.W.2d 938 (Tex. App.—Waco 1999)—**Rule 507**
Frye v. United States, 293 F. 1013 (D.C. Cir. 1923)—**Rule 702**
Fullick v. City of Baytown, 820 S.W.2d 943 (Tex. App.—Houston [1st Dist.] 1991)—**Rule 902**

G

G.F.O., Matter of, 874 S.W.2d 729 (Tex. App.—Houston [1st Dist.] 1994)—**Rule 901**
G.M.P., Matter of, 909 S.W.2d 198 (Tex. App.—Houston [14th Dist.] 1995)—**Rules 404, 608**
Gabriel v. Lovewell, 164 S.W.3d 835 (Tex. App.—Texarkana 2005, no pet. h.)—**Rule 105**

Gammill v. Jack Williams Chevrolet, Inc., 972 S.W.2d 713 (Tex. 1998)—**Rule 702**
Garcia v. State, 126 S.W.3d 921 (Tex. Crim. App. 2004)—**Rule 803**
Garcia v. State, 868 S.W.2d 337 (Tex. Crim. App. 1993)—**Rule 803**
Garcia-Chapa, Matter of Estates of, 33 S.W.3d 859 (Tex. App.—Corpus Christi 2000)—**Rule 203**
Gee v. Liberty Mut. Fire Ins. Co., 765 S.W.2d 394 (Tex. 1989)—**Rules 103, 702**
Geiselman v. Cramer Fin. Group, Inc., 965 S.W.2d 532 (Tex. App.—Houston [14th Dist.] 1997)—**Rule 602**
General Elec. Co. v. Joiner, 522 U.S. 136, 118 S.Ct. 512 (1997)—**Rule 702**
General Motors Corp. v. Iracheta, 161 S.W.3d 462 (Tex. 2005)—**Rules 103, 702**
Geuder v. State, 115 S.W.3d 11 (Tex. Crim. App. 2003)—**Rule 103**
Gibbs v. State, 819 S.W.2d 821 (Tex. Crim. App. 1991)—**Rule 803**
Ginsberg v. Fifth Court of Appeals, 686 S.W.2d 105 (Tex. 1985)—**Rules 501, 503**
Glover v. State, 110 S.W.3d 549 (Tex. App.—Waco 2003)—**Rule 606**
Goff v. State, 931 S.W.2d 537 (Tex. Crim. App. 1996)—**Rule 103**
Golden v. First City Nat'l Bank in Grand Prairie, 751 S.W.2d 639 (Tex. App.—Dallas 1988)—**Rule 606**
Golden Eagle Archery, Inc. v. Jackson, 24 S.W.3d 362 (Tex. 2000)—**Rule 606**
Gonzalez v. State, 45 S.W.3d 101 (Tex. Crim. App. 2001)—**Rule 505**
Goode v. Shoukfeh, 943 S.W.2d 441 (Tex. 1997)—**Rule 612**
Graff v. Whittle, 947 S.W.2d 629 (Tex. App.—Texarkana 1997)—**Rules 201, 803**
Granada Corp. v. Honorable First Court of Appeals, 844 S.W.2d 223 (Tex. 1992)—**Rules 501, 503**
Granados v. State, 85 S.W.3d 217 (Tex. Crim. App. 2002)—**Rule 101**
Gray v. Maryland, 523 U.S. 185, 118 S.Ct. 1151, 140 L.Ed.2d 294 (1998)—**Rule 803**
Grayson v. State, 786 S.W.2d 504 (Tex. App.—Dallas 1990)—**Rule 601**
Great Global Assurance Co. v. Keltex Props., Inc., 904 S.W.2d 771 (Tex. App.—Corpus Christi 1995)—**Rule 601**
Greenberg Traurig of New York, P.C. v. Moody, 161 S.W.3d 56 (Tex. App.—Houston [14th Dist.] 2005)—**Rule 103**
GT & MC, Inc. v. Texas City Refining, Inc., 822 S.W.2d 252 (Tex. App.—Houston [1st Dist.] 1991)—**Rule 803**
GTE Southwest, Inc. v. Bruce, 998 S.W.2d 605 (Tex. 1999)—**Rule 702**
Guadalupe-Blanco River Auth. v. Kraft, 77 S.W.3d 805 (Tex. 2002)—**Rules 702, 703**.
Guevara v. Ferrar, 247 S.W.3d 662 (Tex. 2007)—**Rule 702**
Guidry v. State, 9 S.W.3d 133 (Tex. Crim. App. 1999)—**Rule 103**
Gutierrez v. Dallas Indep. Sch. Dist., 729 S.W.2d 691 (Tex. 1987)—**Rule 702**
Guyton v. Monteau, 332 S.W.3d 687 (Tex. App.—Houston [14th Dist.] 2011)—**Rule 201**
Guzman v. State, 955 S.W.2d 85 (Tex. Crim. App. 1990)—**Rule 104**

H

Hall v. State, 297 S.W.3d 294 (Tex. Crim. App 2009)—**Rule 101**
Hamal v. State, 352 S.W.3d 835 (Tex. App.—Dallas 2011, no pet.)—**Rule 702**
Hammons v. State, 239 S.W.3d 798 (Tex. Crim. App. 2007)—**Rule 801**
Handl v. Long Trusts, 757 S.W.2d 848 (Tex. App.—Texarkana 1988)—**Rule 601**
Harlandale Indep. Sch. Dist. v. Cornyn, 25 S.W.3d 328 (Tex. App.—Austin 2000)—**Rule 503**.
Harrell v. State, 884 S.W.2d 154 (Tex. Crim. App. 1994)—**Rules 104, 404**
Harris v. State, 846 S.W.2d 960 (Tex. App.—Houston [1st Dist.] 1993)—**Rule 803**
Harrison v. State, 241 S.W.3d 23 (Tex. Crim. App. 2007)—**Rule 405**
Hartman v. State, 946 S.W.2d 60 (Tex. Crim. App. 1997)—**Rule 702**
Hartman v. Trio Transp., Inc., 937 S.W.2d 575 (Tex. App.—Texarkana 1996)—**Rule 801**
Havner v. E-Z Mart Stores, Inc., 825 S.W.2d 456 (Tex. 1992)—**Rules 602, 701, 703**
Hayden v. State, 295 S.W.3d 549 (Tex. Crim. App. 2009)—**Rule 404**
Haygood v. De Escabedo, 356 S.W.3d 390 (Tex. 2011)—**Rules 402, 403**
Heidelberg v. State, 36 S.W.3d 668 (Tex. App.—Houston [14th Dist.] 2001)—**Rule 103**
Heise v. Presbyterian Hosp. of Dallas, 888 S.W.2d 264 (Tex. App.—Eastland 1994)—**Rule 702**
Henderson v. State, 962 S.W.2d 544 (Tex. Crim. App. 1997)—**Rule 503**
Hernandez v. Houston Lighting & Power Co., 795 S.W.2d 775 (Tex. App.—Houston [14th Dist.] 1990)—**Rule 201**
Hernandez v. State, 116 S.W.3d 26 (Tex. Crim. App. 2003)—**Rules 201, 702**
Hernandez v. State, 176 S.W.3d 821 (Tex. Crim. App. 2005)—**Rule 404**
Herzig v. Metropolitan Life Ins. Co., 907 S.W.2d 574 (Tex. App.—Corpus Christi 1995)—**Rule 901**
Hinojosa v. Columbia St. David's Healthcare Sys., 106 S.W.3d 380 (Tex. App.—Austin 2003)—**Rule 701**
Hinterlong, In re, 109 S.W.3d 611 (Tex. App.—Fort Worth 2003)—**Rule 402**
Holder v. Mellon Mortg. Co., 954 S.W.2d 786 (Tex. App.—Houston [14th Dist.] 1997)—**Rule 803**
Holifield v. State, 856 S.W.2d 575 (Tex. App.—Beaumont 1993)—**Rule 107**
Holland v. Lovelace, 352 S.W.3d 777 (Tex. App.—Dallas 2011, no pet)—**Rule 702**
Holmes v. State, 323 S.W.3d 163 (Tex. Crim. App. 2009)—**Rule 103**
Hooper v. Chittaluru, 2006 WL 771390 (Tex. App.—Houston [14th Dist.] 2006)(unpublished)—**Rule 103**
Hooper v. Torres, 790 S.W.2d 757 (Tex. App.—El Paso 1990)—**Rule 803**
Horizon/CMS Healthcare Corp. v. Auld, 985 S.W.2d 216 (Tex. App.—Fort Worth 1999)—**Rule 105**
Houston Exploration Company v. Wellington Underwriting Agencies, Ltd, 352 S.W.3d 462 (Tex. 2011)—**Rule 402**
Huckaby v. A.G. Perry & Son, Inc., 20 S.W.3d 194 (Tex. App.—Texarkana 2000)—**Rule 103**

Huffman v. State, 479 S.W.2d 62 (Tex. Crim. App. 1972)—**Rule 201**

Huie v. DeShazo, 922 S.W.2d 920 (Tex. 1996)—**Rule 503**

Hunter v. NCNB Texas Nat'l Bank, 857 S.W.2d 722 (Tex. App.—Houston [14th Dist.] 1993)—**Rule 601**

Hyde Corp. v. Huffines, 314 S.W.2d 763 (Tex. 1958)—**Rule 507**

I

IHS Treatment Ctr. of DeSoto, Texas, Inc. v. Mason, 143 S.W.3d 794 (Tex. 2003)—**Rule 702**

In re (see name of party)

In Interest of (see name of party)

Irving Healthcare Sys. v. Brooks, 927 S.W.2d 12 (Tex. 1996)—**Rule 501**

J

J.C., In re, 892 S.W.2d 87 (Tex. App.—El Paso 1995)—**Rule 701**

Jackson v. State, 889 S.W.2d 615 (Tex. App.—Houston [14th Dist.] 1994)—**Rule 103**

Jelinek v. Casas, 328 S.W.3d 526, 532–533 (Tex. 2010)—**Rule 701, Rule 702**

Jenkins v. State, 912 S.W.2d 793 (Tex. Crim. App. 1993)—**Rules 615, 705**

Joachim v. Chambers, 815 S.W.2d 234 (Tex. 1991)—**Rule 605**

John Paul Mitchell Sys. v. Randalls Food Mkts., Inc., 17 S.W.3d 721 (Tex. App.—Austin 2000)—**Rule 507**

Johnson v. City of Houston, 928 S.W.2d 251 (Tex. App.—Houston [14th Dist.] 1996)—**Rule 403**

Jones v. Colley, 820 S.W.2d 863 (Tex. App.—Texarkana 1991)—**Rule 106**

Jones v. Red Arrow Heavy Hauling, Inc., 816 S.W.2d 134 (Tex. App.—Beaumont 1991)—**Rule 402**

Jones v. State, 950 S.W.2d 386 (Tex. App.—Fort Worth 1997)—**Rule 803**

Jordan v. State, 928 S.W.2d 550 (Tex. Crim. App. 1996)—**Rule 702**

K

Kamel v. Kamel, 760 S.W.2d 677 (Tex. App.—Tyler 1988)—**Rule 803**

Kansas City Southern Railway Co. v. Carter, 778 S.W.2d 911 (Tex. App.—Texarkana 1989)—**Rule 801**

Keene Corp. v. Rogers, 863 S.W.2d 168 (Tex. App.—Texarkana 1993)—**Rules 202, 804, 901**

Kelly v. State, 824 S.W.2d 568 (Tex. Crim. App. 1992)—**Rule 702**

Kendall v. Whataburger, Inc., 759 S.W.2d 751 (Tex. App.—Houston [1st Dist.] 1988)—**Rule 606**

Kiefer v. Continental Airlines, Inc., 10 S.W.3d 34 (Tex. App.—Houston [14th Dist.] 1999)—**Rule 606**

Klein v. Dimock, 705 S.W.2d 408 (Tex. App.—Fort Worth 1986)—**Rule 201**

K–Mart Corp. v. Honeycutt, 24 S.W.3d 357 (Tex. 2000)—**Rule 702**

Knisley v. State, 81 S.W.3d 478 (Tex. App.—Dallas 2002)—**Rule 103**

Knops v. Knops, 763 S.W.2d 864 (Tex. App.—San Antonio 1988)—**Rule 202**

Kubin v. State, 868 S.W.2d 394 (Tex. App.—Houston [1st Dist.] 1993)—**Rule 803**

Kumho Tire Co., Ltd. v. Carmichael, 526 U.S. 137, 119 S.Ct. 1167, 143 L.Ed.2d 238 (1999)—**Rule 702**

L

L.M.W. v. State, 891 S.W.2d 754 (Tex. App.—Fort Worth 1994)—**Rule 408**

L.S., P.P., G.S. and M.S., In Interest of, 748 S.W.2d 571 (Tex. App.—Amarillo 1988)—**Rule 803**

Langdale v. Villamil, 813 S.W.2d 187 (Tex. App.—Houston [14th Dist.] 1991)—**Rule 201**

Langley v. Commission for Lawyer Discipline, 191 S.W.3d 913 (Tex. App.—Dallas 2006)—**Rule 103**

LaPointe, State v., 225 S.W.3d 513 (Tex. Crim. App. 2007)—**Rule 412**

Larson v. Cactus Util. Co., 730 S.W.2d 640 (Tex. 1987)—**Rule 105**

Larson v. Downing, 197 S.W.3d 303 (Tex. 2006)—**Rule 701**

Laub v. Pesikoff, 979 S.W.2d 686 (Tex. App.—Houston [1st Dist.] 1998)—**Rule 402**

Lawrenson v. Global Marine, Inc., 869 S.W.2d 519 (Tex. App.—Texarkana 1993)—**Rule 203**

Leaird's, Inc. v. Wrangler, Inc., 31 S.W.3d 688 (Tex. App.—Waco 2000)—**Rule 103**

Lee v. Illinois, 476 U.S. 530, 106 S.Ct. 2056, 90 L.Ed.2d 514 (1986)—**Rule 803**

Leitch v. Hornsby, 935 S.W.2d 114 (Tex. 1996)—**Rule 702**

Leviton Mfg. Co., In re, 1 S.W.3d 898 (Tex. App.—Waco 1999)—**Rule 507**

Lilly v. Virginia, 527 U.S. 116, 119 S.Ct. 1887, 144 L.Ed.2d 117 (1999)—**Rule 803**

Lipsey v. Texas Dep't of Health, 727 S.W.2d 61 (Tex. App.—Austin 1987)—**Rule 703**

Liptak v. Pensabene, 736 S.W.2d 953 (Tex. App.—Tyler 1987)—**Rule 703**

Livingston v. State, 739 S.W.2d 311 (Tex. Crim. App. 1987)—**Rule 107**

Long Distance Int'l, Inc. v. Telefonos de Mexico, 49 S.W.3d 347 (Tex. 2001)—**Rule 203**

Loper v. Andrews, 404 S.W.2d 300 (Tex. 1966)—**Rule 803**

Lopez v. State, 928 S.W.2d 528 (Tex. Crim. App. 1996)—**Rule 404**

Louder v. De Leon, 754 S.W.2d 148 (Tex. 1988)—**Rule 704**

Lowry, State v., 802 S.W.2d 669 (Tex. 1991)—**Rule 508**

LSR Jt. Venture No. 2 v. Callewart, 837 S.W.2d 693 (Tex. App.—Dallas 1992)—**Rule 403**

M

Macias v. State, 776 S.W.2d 255 (Tex. App.—San Antonio 1989)—**Rules 601, 603**

Mack Trucks, Inc. v. Tamez, 206 S.W.3d 572 (Tex. 2006)—**Rule 702**

Madden v. State, 799 S.W.2d 683 (Tex. Crim. App. 1990)—**Rule 803**
Magro v. Ragsdale Bros., Inc., 721 S.W.2d 832 (Tex. 1986)—**Rule 404**
Malone v. Foster, 956 S.W.2d 573 (Tex. App.—Dallas 1997)—**Rule 803**
Manning v. State, 773 S.W.2d 568 (Tex. Crim. App. 1989)—**Rule 503**
Marin Real Estate Partners, L.P. v. Vogt, 373 S.W.3d 57 (Tex. App.—San Antonio 2011)—**Rules 103, 702**
Maritime Overseas Corp. v. Ellis, 971 S.W.2d 402 (Tex. 1998)—**Rule 702**
Martin v. Ford, 853 S.W.2d 680 (Tex. App.—Texarkana 1993)—**Rule 402**
Martinez v. State, 98 S.W.3d 189 (Tex. Crim. App. 2003)—**Rule 103**
Massachusetts Institute of Tech., United States v., 129 F.3d 681 (1st Cir. 1997)—**Rule 501**
Massimo v. State, 144 S.W.3d 210 (Tex. App.—Fort Worth 2004)—**Rule 901**
Mathis v. State, 930 S.W.2d 203 (Tex. App.—Houston [14th Dist.] 1996)—**Rules 104, 1008**
Matter of (see name of party)
McCarty v. State, 257 S.W.3d 238 (Tex. Crim. App. 2008)—**Rule 803**
McCraw v. Maris, 828 S.W.2d 756 (Tex. 1992)—**Rules 103, 801**
McDonald v. State, 179 S.W.3d 571 (Tex. Crim. App. Nov. 23, 2005)—**Rule 404**
McDuffie v. State, 854 S.W.2d 195 (Tex. App.—Beaumont 1993)—**Rule 504**
McFarland v. State, 845 S.W.2d 824 (Tex. Crim. App. 1992)—**Rule 803**
McGary v. State, 750 S.W.2d 782 (Tex. Crim. App. 1988)—**Rule 613**
McGowan v. O'Neill, 750 S.W.2d 884 (Tex. App.—Houston [14th Dist.] 1988)—**Rule 509**
McIntyre v. Wilson, 50 S.W.3d 674 (Tex. App.—Dallas 2001)—**Rule 402**
McLellan v. Benson, 877 S.W.2d 454 (Tex. App.—Houston [1st Dist.] 1994)—**Rule 404**
Medrano v. State, 768 S.W.2d 502 (Tex. App.—El Paso 1989)—**Rule 101**
Melendez v. Exxon Corp., 998 S.W.2d 266 (Tex. App.—Houston [14th Dist.] 1999)—**Rule 103**
Melendez-Diaz v. Massachusetts, 557 U.S. 305 (2009)—**Rule 803**
Memorial Hosp.-The Woodlands v. McCown, 927 S.W.2d 1 (Tex. 1996)—**Rule 501**
Menchaca, Ex parte, 854 S.W.2d 128 (Tex. Crim. App. 1993)—**Rule 609**
Menefee v. Ohman, 323 S.W.3d 509, 514 (Tex. App.—Fort Worth 2010, no pet.)—**Rule 702**
Merck & Co., Inc. v. Garza, 347 S.W.3d 256 (Tex. 2011)—**Rule 702**
Merrell Dow Pharmaceuticals, Inc. v. Havner, 953 S.W.2d 706 (Tex. 1997)—**Rule 702**
Merrell Dow Pharmaceuticals, Inc. v. Havner, 907 S.W.2d 535 (Tex. App.—Corpus Christi 1994)—**Rule 703**
Metro Fuels v. City of Austin, 827 S.W.2d 531 (Tex. App.—Austin 1992)—**Rule 204**
Meuth v. Hartgrove, 811 S.W.2d 626 (Tex. App.—Austin 1990)—**Rule 106**
Michigan v. Bryant, 562 U.S. ____, 131 S.Ct. 1143 (2011)—**Rule 803**
Miller v. State, 36 S.W.3d 503 (Tex. Crim. App. 2001)—**Rules 401, 403**
Miller, Estate of, 243 S.W.3d 831 (Tex. App.—Dallas 2008)—**Rule 103**
Minnesota Mining & Mfg. Co. v. Atterbury, 978 S.W.2d 183 (Tex. App.—Texarkana 1998)—**Rule 702**
Missouri Pacific R.R. Co. v. Roberts, 849 S.W.2d 367 (Tex. App.—Eastland 1993)—**Rule 403**
Mitchell v. State, 931 S.W.2d 950 (Tex. Crim. App. 1996)—**Rule 104**
Montgomery v. State, 810 S.W.2d 372 (Tex. Crim. App. 1990)—**Rules 104, 403, 404**
Moore v. Grantham, 599 S.W.2d 287 (Tex. 1980)—**Rule 703**
Moore v. Polish Power, Inc., 720 S.W.2d 183 (Tex. App.—Dallas 1986)—**Rule 703**
Morrow v. H.E.B., Inc., 714 S.W.2d 297 (Tex. 1986)—**Rule 702**
Morton Int'l v. Gillespie, 39 S.W.3d 651 (Tex. App.—Texarkana 2001)—**Rule 702**
Moyer v. State, 948 S.W.2d 525 (Tex. App.—Fort Worth 1997)—**Rule 803**
Murray v. State, 864 S.W.2d 111 (Tex. App.—Texarkana 1993)—**Rule 508**
Musick v. State, 862 S.W.2d 794 (Tex. App.—El Paso 1993)—**Rule 508**

N

National County Mut. Fire Ins. Co. v. Hood, 693 S.W.2d 638 (Tex. App.—Houston [14th Dist.] 1985)—**Rule 201**
National Tank Co. v. Brotherton, 851 S.W.2d 193 (Tex. 1993)—**Rule 503**
Nelson v. State, 765 S.W.2d 401 (Tex. Crim. App. 1989)—**Rule 104**
New Braunfels Market Outlet Ctr. v. IHOP Realty Corp., 872 S.W.2d 303 (Tex. App.—Austin 1994)—**Rule 803**
Nicholson v. Wittig, 832 S.W.2d 681 (Tex. App.—Houston [1st Dist.] 1992)—**Rule 505**
Norsul Oil & Mining Ltd. v. Commercial Equipment Leasing Co., 703 S.W.2d 345 (Tex. App.—San Antonio 1985)—**Rule 801**
North Dallas Diagnostic Ctr. v. Dewberry, 900 S.W.2d 90 (Tex. App.—Dallas 1995)—**Rules 103, 104**

O

Oadra v. Stegall, 871 S.W.2d 882 (Tex. App.—Houston [14th Dist.] 1994)—**Rule 609**
Ocomen v. Rubio, 24 S.W.3d 461 (Tex. App.—Houston [1st Dist.] 2000)—**Rule 702**
Office of Public Util. Counsel v. Public Util. Comm'n of Tex., 878 S.W.2d 598 (Tex. 1994)—**Rule 204**
Ogletree v. Crates, 363 S.W.2d 431 (Tex. 1963)—**Rule 202**
Onwuteaka v. Gill, 908 S.W.2d 276 (Tex. App.—Houston [1st Dist.] 1995)—**Rule 703**
Orion Enters., Inc. v. Pope, 927 S.W.2d 654 (Tex. App.—San Antonio 1996)—**Rule 605**
Osbourn v. State, 92 S.W.3d 531 (Tex. Crim. App. 2002)—**Rules 701**
Ossorio v. Leon, 705 S.W.2d 219 (Tex. App.—San Antonio 1985)—**Rule 203**

Osteopathic Med. Ctr., In re, 16 S.W.3d 881 (Tex. App.—Fort Worth 2000)—**Rule 501**
Owens-Corning Fiberglas Corp. v. Keeton, 922 S.W.2d 658 (Tex. App.—Austin 1996)—**Rule 104**
Owens-Corning Fiberglas Corp. v. Malone, 972 S.W.2d 35 (Tex. 1998)—**Rule 105**
Owens-Corning Fiberglas Corp. v. Wasiak, 917 S.W.2d 883 (Tex. App.—Austin 1996)—**Rule 804**

P

Pacesetter Corp. v. Barrickman, 885 S.W.2d 256 (Tex. App.—Tyler 1994)—**Rules 406, 408**
Page v. State, 137 S.W.3d 75 (Tex. Crim. App. 2004)—**Rule 404**
Parrish v. Brooks, 856 S.W.2d 522 (Tex. App.—Texarkana 1993)—**Rule 601**
Parten v. Brigham, 785 S.W.2d 165 (Tex. App.—Fort Worth 1989)—**Rule 501**
Pediatrix Medical Group, Inc., v. Robinson, 352 S.W.3d 879 (Tex. App.—Dallas 2011, no pet.)—**Rule 702**
Pena v. State, 353 S.W.3d 797 (Tex. Crim. App. 2011)—**Rule 107**
Pennington v. Brock, 841 S.W.2d 127 (Tex. App.—Houston [14th Dist.] 1992)—**Rule 105**
Pennwell Corp. v. Ken Assocs., Inc., 123 S.W.3d 756 (Tex. App.—Houston [14th Dist.] 2003)—**Rule 203**
Penwell v. Barrett, 724 S.W.2d 902 (Tex. App.—San Antonio 1987)—**Rule 607**
Perkins v. State, 902 S.W.2d 88 (Tex. App.—El Paso 1995)—**Rule 801**
Perry v. New Hampshire, 565 U.S. ____, 132 S.Ct. 716 (2012)—**Rule 403**
Perry v. Texas Municipal Power Agency, 667 S.W.2d 259 (Tex. App.—Houston [1st Dist.] 1984)—**Rule 105**
Pitman v. Lightfoot, 937 S.W.2d 496 (Tex. App.—San Antonio 1996)—**Rule 402**
Pittsburgh Corning Corp. v. Caldwell, 861 S.W.2d 423 (Tex. App.—Houston [14th Dist.] 1993)—**Rule 503**
Pittsburgh Corning Corp. v. Walters, 1 S.W.3d 759 (Tex. App.—Corpus Christi 1999)—**Rules 202, 403, 704**
Pondexter v. State, 942 S.W.2d 577 (Tex. Crim. App. 1996)—**Rules 404, 615, 803**
Poole v. State, 974 S.W.2d 892 (Tex. App.—Austin 1998)—**Rule 403**
Pope v. State, 207 S.W.3d 352 (Tex. Crim. App. 2006)—**Rule 503**
Porras v. Craig, 675 S.W.2d 503 (Tex. 1984)—**Rule 701**
Porter v. Nemir, 900 S.W.2d 376 (Tex. App.—Austin 1995)—**Rules 105, 404, 609**
Powell v. State, 5 S.W.3d 369 (Tex. App.—Texarkana 1999)—**Rules 403, 404**
Powell v. State, 63 S.W.3d 435 (Tex. Crim. App. 2001)—**Rule 404**
Powers v. McDaniel, 785 S.W.2d 915 (Tex. App.—San Antonio 1990)—**Rule 601**
Prescott v. State, 744 S.W.2d 128 (Tex. Crim. App. 1988)—**Rule 609**
Puente v. State, 888 S.W.2d 521 (Tex. App.—San Antonio 1994)—**Rule 105**

R

R.K. v. Ramirez, 887 S.W.2d 836 (Tex. 1994)—**Rules 509, 510**
Rabbani v. State, 847 S.W.2d 555 (Tex. Crim. App. 1992)—**Rule 803**
Ramirez v. State, 802 S.W.2d 674 (Tex. Crim. App. 1990)—**Rule 607**
Ramsey v. Lucky Stores, Inc., 853 S.W.2d 623 (Tex. App.—Houston [1st Dist.] 1993)—**Rule 613**
Raw Hide Oil & Gas, Inc. v. Maxus Exploration Co., 766 S.W.2d 264 (Tex. App.—Amarillo 1988)—**Rule 103**
Reading and Bates Constr. Co. v. Baker Energy Resources Corp., 976 S.W.2d 702 (Tex. App.—Houston [1st Dist.] 1998)—**Rule 203**
Redman Homes, Inc. v. Ivy, 920 S.W.2d 664 (Tex. 1996)—**Rule 701**
Reece v. State, 772 S.W.2d 198 (Tex. App.—Houston [14th Dist.] 1989)—**Rule 504**
Reid Road Mun. Utility Dist. No. 2 v. Speedy Stop Food Stores, Ltd., 337 S.W.3d 846, 849–850 (Tex. 2011)—**Rule 701**
Rendleman v. Clarke, 909 S.W.2d 56 (Tex. App.—Houston [14th Dist.] 1995)—**Rule 103**
Republic Ins. Co. v. Davis, 856 S.W.2d 158 (Tex. 1993)—**Rules 501, 503**
Republic Waste Services, Ltd. v. Martinez, 335 S.W.3d 401 (Tex. App.—Houston [1st Dist.] 2011, no pet.)—**Rule 403**
Richardson v. Green, 677 S.W.2d 497 (Tex. 1984)—**Rules 103, 802, 803**
Riddle v. Unifund CCR Partners, 298 S.W.3d 780 (Tex. App.—El Paso 2009)—**Rule 803**
Rivas v. State, 275 S.W.3d 880 (Tex. Crim. App. 2009)—**Rule 613**
Roberts v. Allison, 836 S.W.2d 185 (Tex. App.—Tyler 1992)—**Rule 803**
Robinson v. Harkins & Co., 711 S.W.2d 619 (Tex. 1986)—**Rule 803**
Rodriguez v. Ed Hicks Imports, 767 S.W.2d 187 (Tex. App.—Corpus Christi 1989)—**Rule 1003**
Rodriguez v. State, 1997 WL 527843 (Tex. App.—Dallas 1997) (unpublished)—**Rule 505**
Rotella v. State, 2004 WL 1682885 (Tex. Crim. App. 2004) (unpublished)—**Rule 103**

S

S.V. v. R.V., 933 S.W.2d 1 (Tex. 1996)—**Rule 702**
Saavedra v. State, 297 S.W.3d 342 (Tex. Crim. App. 2009)—**Rule 801**
Salazar v. State, 38 S.W.3d 141 (Tex. Crim. App. 2001)—**Rule 803**
Salinas v. State, 542 S.W.2d 864 (Tex. Crim. App. 1976)—**Rule 201**
Sanchez, State v., 354 S.W.3d 476 (Tex. Crim. App. 2011)—**Rule 803**
Sanchez v. Jary, 768 S.W.2d 933 (Tex. App.—San Antonio 1989)—**Rule 706**
Sauceda v. State, 162 S.W.3d 591 (Tex. App.—Houston [14th Dist.] 2005)—**Rule 107**
Schindler Elevator Corp. v. Anderson, 78 S.W.3d 392 (Tex. App.—Houston [14th Dist.] 2001)—**Rule 103**

Schutz v. State, 957 S.W.2d 52 (Tex. Crim. App. 1997)—**Rule 702**
Sciarrilla v. Osborne, 946 S.W.2d 919 (Tex. App.—Beaumont 1997)—**Rules 103, 702**
Scurlock Oil Co. v. Smithwick, 724 S.W.2d 1 (Tex. 1986)—**Rule 408**
Seaside Indus., Inc. v. Cooper, 766 S.W.2d 566 (Tex. App.—Dallas 1989)—**Rules 703, 803**
Service Corp. Intern. v. Guerra, 348 S.W. 3d 221, 234 (Tex. 2011)—**Rule 103, Rule 404**
Service Lloyds Ins. Co. v. Martin, 855 S.W.2d 816 (Tex. App.—Dallas 1993)—**Rule 608**
Sharpe v. Safway Scaffolds Co. of Houston, Inc., 687 S.W.2d 386 (Tex. App.—Houston [14th Dist.] 1985)—**Rule 703**
Shugars v. State, 814 S.W.2d 897 (Tex. App.—Austin 1991)—**Rule 602**
Simpson v. Canales, 806 S.W.2d 802 (Tex. 1991)—**Rule 706**
Simpson v. Tennant, 871 S.W.2d 301 (Tex. App.—Houston [14th Dist.] 1994)—**Rule 505**
Sims v. Brackett, 885 S.W.2d 450 (Tex. App.—Corpus Christi 1994)—**Rule 403**
Skinner v. State, 956 S.W.2d 532 (Tex. Crim. App. 1997)—**Rules 612, 703**
Slaton v. Slaton, 987 S.W.2d 180 (Tex. App.—Houston [14th Dist.] 1999)—**Rule 803**
Smith v. Smith, 720 S.W.2d 586 (Tex. App.—Houston [1st Dist.] 1986)—**Rule 513**
Soliz v. Saenz, 779 S.W.2d 929 (Tex. App.—Corpus Christi 1989)—**Rule 606**
Solomon v. State, 49 S.W.3d 356 (Tex. Crim. App. 2001)—**Rule 701**
Sosa By and Through Grant v. Koshy, 961 S.W.2d 420 (Tex. App.—Houston [1st Dist.] 1997)—**Rule 705**
Southwest Country Enters. v. Lucky Lady Oil, 991 S.W.2d 490 (Tex. App.—Fort Worth 1999)—**Rule 103**
Southwestern Elec. Power Co. v. Martin, 844 S.W.2d 229 (Tex. App.—Texarkana 1992)—**Rule 201**
Spin Doctor Golf, Inc. v. Paymentech, L.P., 296 S.W.3d 354 (Tex. App.—Dallas 2009)—**Rule 702**
St. Paul Med. Ctr. v. Cecil, 842 S.W.2d 808 (Tex. App.—Dallas 1992)—**Rules 104, 703**
Star Houston, Inc. v. Kundak, 843 S.W.2d 294 (Tex. App.—Houston [14th Dist.] 1992)—**Rule 701**
State v. (see name of opposing party)
State Bar of Tex. v. Evans, 774 S.W.2d 656 (Tex. 1989)—**Rule 404**
State Farm Mut. Auto. Ins. Co. v. Wilborn, 835 S.W.2d 260 (Tex. App.—Houston [14th Dist.] 1992)—**Rule 408**
Steenbergen v. Ford Motor Co., 814 S.W.2d 755 (Tex. App.—Dallas 1991)—**Rules 104, 901, 1008**
Sterling v. State, 814 S.W.2d 261 (Tex. App.—Austin 1991)—**Rule 504**
Straitway Transport, Inc. v. Mundorf, 6 S.W.3d 734 (Tex. App.—Corpus Christi 1999)—**Rule 701**
Striegler, In Interest of, 915 S.W.2d 629 (Tex. App.—Amarillo 1996)—**Rule 201**
Strong v. State, 773 S.W.2d 543 (Tex. Crim. App. 1989)—**Rule 503**
Subia v. Texas Dep't of Human Servs., 750 S.W.2d 827 (Tex. App.—El Paso 1988)—**Rule 510**
Sungrowth VI, California Ltd., State v., 713 S.W.2d 175 (Tex. App.—Austin 1986)—**Rule 204**
Swidler & Berlin v. United States, 524 U.S. 399, 118 S.Ct. 2081, 141 L.Ed.2d 379 (1998)—**Rule 503**
Syndex Corp. v. Dean, 820 S.W.2d 869 (Tex. App.—Austin 1991)—**Rule 803**

T

Tarrant County v. English, 989 S.W.2d 368 (Tex. App.—Fort Worth 1998)—**Rule 408**
Taylor v. State, 268 S.W.3d 261 (Tex. Crim. App. 2008)—**Rule 803**
Taylor v. Texas Dept. Of Protective and Regulatory Services, 160 S.W.3d 641 (Tex. App.—Austin 2005)—**Rule 702**
Terrell v. State, 949 S.W.2d 49 (Tex. App.—Texarkana 1997)—**Rule 103**
Texaco, Inc. v. Pennzoil, Co., 729 S.W.2d 768 (Tex. App.—Houston [1st Dist.] 1987)—**Rules 606, 801**
Texas Commerce Bank Nat'l Ass'n v. New, 3 S.W.3d 515 (Tex. 1999)—**Rule 802**
Texas Dep't of Human Servs. v. Green, 855 S.W.2d 136 (Tex. App.—Austin 1993)—**Rule 106**
Texas Dep't of Public Safety v. Struve, 79 S.W.3d 796 (Tex. App.—Corpus Christi 2002)—**Rule 702**
Texas Dep't of Public Safety Officers Ass'n v. Denton, 897 S.W.2d 757 (Tex. 1995)—**Rules 501, 503**
Texas Employer's Ins. Ass'n v. Sauceda, 636 S.W.2d 494 (Tex. App.—San Antonio 1982)—**Rule 803**
Texas Farmers Ins. Co. v. Stem, 927 S.W.2d 76 (Tex. App.—Waco 1996)—**Rule 408**
Texon Energy Corp. v. Dow Chem. Co., 733 S.W.2d 328 (Tex. App.—Houston [14th Dist.] 1987)—**Rule 803**
Theus v. State, 845 S.W.2d 874 (Tex. Crim. App. 1992)—**Rule 609**
Thomas v. State, 837 S.W.2d 106 (Tex. Crim. App. 1992)—**Rule 402**
Thornhill v. Ronnie's I–45 Truck Stop, Inc., 944 S.W.2d 780 (Tex. App.—Beaumont 1997)—**Rule 411**
Tilton v. Marshall, 925 S.W.2d 672 (Tex. 1996)—**Rule 501**
Torres v. State, 117 S.W.3d 891 (Tex. Crim. App. 2003)—**Rule 404**
Tran v. Fiorenza, 934 S.W.2d 740 (Tex. App.—Houston [1st Dist.] 1996)—**Rule 201**
TransAmerican Natural Gas Corp. v. Powell, 811 S.W.2d 913 (Tex. 1991)—**Rule 501**
Transcontinental Ins. Co. v. Crump, 330 S.W.3d 211, 216–217 (Tex. 2010)—**Rule 702**
Traweek v. Larkin, 708 S.W.2d 942 (Tex. App.—Tyler 1986)—**Rule 201**
Tschirhart v. Tschirhart, 876 S.W.2d 507 (Tex. App.—Austin 1994)—**Rule 201**
Turner v. Montgomery, 836 S.W.2d 848 (Tex. App.—Houston [1st Dist.] 1992)—**Rule 501**
Turner v. State, 733 S.W.2d 218 (Tex. Crim. App. 1987)—**Rule 201**

U

Uniroyal Goodrich Tire Co. v. Martinez, 977 S.W.2d 328 (Tex. 1998)—**Rule 1006**
United Blood Servs. v. Longoria, 938 S.W.2d 29 (Tex. 1997)—**Rules 103, 702**
United States v. (see name of opposing party)

United States Fire Ins. Co. v. Millard, 847 S.W.2d 668 (Tex. App.—Houston [1st Dist.] 1993)—**Rule 408**
United Way of San Antonio, Inc. v. Helping Hands Lifeline Foundation, Inc., 949 S.W.2d 707 (Tex. App.—San Antonio 1997)—**Rule 602**
Upton v. State, 894 S.W.2d 426 (Tex. App.—Amarillo 1995)—**Rule 601**

V

Valle v. State, 109 S.W.3d 500 (Tex. Crim. App. 2003)—**Rule 804**
Vela, State v., 209 S.W.3d 128 (Tex. Crim. App. 2006)—**Rule 702**
Volkswagen, A.G. v. Valdez, 909 S.W.2d 900 (Tex. 1995)—**Rule 501**
Volosen v. State, 227 S.W.3d 77 (Tex. Crim. App. 2007)—**Rule 204**

W

W & G Trucking, Inc., In re, 990 S.W.2d 473 (Tex. App.—Beaumont 1999)—**Rule 503**
Wal–Mart Stores, Inc. v. Merrell, 313 S.W. 3d 837, 840 (Tex. 2010)—**Rule 702**
Waldon v. City of Longview, 855 S.W.2d 875 (Tex. App.—Tyler 1993)—**Rules 406, 801**
Wall v. State, 184 S.W.3d 730 (Tex. Crim. App. 2006)—**Rule 803**
Walter v. State, 267 S.W.3d 883 (Tex. Crim. App. 2008)—**Rule 803**
Walters v. State, 247 S.W.3d 204 (Tex. Crim. App. 2007)—**Rule 107**
Waring v. Wommack, 945 S.W.2d 889 (Tex. App.—Austin 1997)—**Rule 702**
Washington v. Crawford, 541 U.S.36, 124 S.Ct. 1354 (2004)—**Rule 803**
Washington v. State, 902 S.W.2d 649 (Tex. App.—Houston [14th Dist.] 1995)—**Rule 508**
Watts v. State, 99 S.W.3d 604 (Tex. Crim. App. 2003)—**Rule 201**
Weatherred v. State, 15 S.W.3d 540, 542 n.4 (Tex. Crim. App. 2000)—**Rule 702**
Weaver v. State, 855 S.W.2d 116 (Tex. App.—Houston [14th Dist.] 1993)—**Rule 504**
Webb v. State, 840 S.W.2d 543 (Tex. App.—Dallas 1992)—**Rule 803**
Welder v. Welder, 794 S.W.2d 420 (Tex. App.—Corpus Christi 1990)—**Rules 703, 705, 1006**
Wesbrook v. State, 29 S.W.3d 103 (Tex. Crim. App. 2000)—**Rule 105**
Westheimer v. Tennant, 831 S.W.2d 880 (Tex. App.—Houston [14th Dist.] 1992)—**Rule 501**
Wheeler, Ex parte, 203 S.W.3d 317 (Tex. Crim. App. 2006)—**Rule 411**
Whittaker v. State, 286 S.W.3d 355 (Tex. Crim. App. 2009)—**Rules 103, 105**
Whorton v. Bockting, 549 U.S. 406 (2007)—**Rule 803**
Wil-Roye Inv. Co. II v. Washington Mut. Bank, FA, 142 S.W.3d 393 (Tex. App.—El Paso 2004)—**Rule 513**
Wilford v. State, 739 S.W.2d 854 (Tex. Crim. App. 1987)—**Rule 103**
Willard v. State, 719 S.W.2d 595 (Tex. Crim. App. 1986)—**Rule 101**
Williams v. State, 790 S.W.2d 643 (Tex. Crim. App. 1990)—**Rule 801**
Williams v. State, 937 S.W.2d 479 (Tex. Crim. App. 1996)—**Rule 103**
Williams v. State, 958 S.W.2d 186 (Tex. Crim. App. 1997)—**Rule 403**
Williamson v. United States, 512 U.S. 594, 114 S.Ct. 2431, 129 L.Ed.2d 476 (1994)—**Rule 803**
Wilson v. State, 677 S.W.2d 518 (Tex. Crim. App. 1984)—**Rule 201**
Wolfe v. Wolfe, 918 S.W.2d 533 (Tex. App.—El Paso 1996)—**Rule 105**
Wood Oil Distributing Co., Inc., State v., 751 S.W.2d 863 (Tex. 1988)—**Rule 103**

Y

Yard v. DaimlerChrysler Corp., 44 S.W.3d 238 (Tex. App.—Fort Worth 2001)—**Rule 702**

Z

Zuliani v. State, 97 S.W.3d 589 (Tex. Crim. App. 2003)—**Rule 803**

INDEX

Abbreviations

Texas Rules of Evidence .... Evid Rule
Federal Rules of Evidence .... FRE

ABSENCE AND ABSENTEES
Federal Rules of Evidence, this index

ABSENCE OF MISTAKE
Character and reputation, **Evid Rules 404, 405**

ACCIDENTS
Character and reputation, **Evid Rules 404, 405**

ACCUSED
Character, evidence, **Evid Rules 404, 405**

ACKNOWLEDGED DOCUMENTS
Self authentication, **Evid Rule 902**

ACTIONS AND PROCEEDINGS
Evidence, generally, this index

ADJUDICATIVE FACTS
Judicial notice, **Evid Rule 201**

ADMINISTRATIVE LAW AND PROCEDURE
Judicial notice, **Evid Rule 204**

ADMINISTRATORS
Personal representatives. Probate Proceedings, this index

ADMISSIBILITY OF EVIDENCE
Evidence, this index

ADMISSIONS
Evidence, this index

ADOPTION OF CHILDREN
Admissibility, records, **Evid Rule 803**

AFFIDAVITS
Depositions, generally, this index
Foreign countries, judicial notice, **Evid Rule 203**
Records and recordation, authentication or identification, **Evid Rule 901 et seq.**

AGENTS AND AGENCIES
Insurance, admissibility, **Evid Rule 411**

AGGRAVATED SEXUAL ASSAULT
Victims, previous sexual conduct, **Evid Rule 412**

ALCOHOLICS AND INTOXICATED PERSONS
Communications, privileges, **Evid Rule 510**
Privileges and immunities, **Evid Rule 510**

ANCIENT DOCUMENTS
Authentication or identification, **Evid Rules 803, 901 et seq.**
Hearsay, **Evid Rule 803**

ANNUAL REPORTS
Reports, generally, this index

APPEAL AND REVIEW
Conviction of crime, impeachment, **Evid Rule 609**

APPLICATION OF RULES
Generally, **Evid Rule 101**

ARREST
Application of rules, **Evid Rule 101**
Warrants, evidence rule, application, **Evid Rule 101**

ASSOCIATIONS AND SOCIETIES
Lawyer client privilege, **Evid Rule 503**
Reports, disclosure, privilege, **Evid Rule 502**

ATTORNEYS
Definitions, privileges and immunities, **Evid Rule 503**
Privilege and immunities, **Evid Rule 503**

AUTHENTICATION
Generally, **Evid Rule 901 et seq.**

BAIL AND RECOGNIZANCES
Application of rules, **Evid Rule 101**
Evidence, application, rules, **Evid Rule 101**

BALANCING TEST
Expert witnesses, **Evid Rule 705**

BAPTISMAL CERTIFICATES
Hearsay, **Evid Rule 803**

BIAS OR PREJUDICE
Federal Rules of Evidence, this index
Insurance, witnesses, **Evid Rule 411**
Relevant evidence, exclusion, **Evid Rule 403**
Witnesses, **Evid Rule 613**

BIBLES
Hearsay, **Evid Rule 803**

BIGAMY
Privileges and immunities, husband and wife, exemptions, **Evid Rule 504**

BIRTH CERTIFICATES
Hearsay, **Evid Rule 803**

BOOKS AND PAPERS
Authentication or identification, **Evid Rule 901 et seq.**

BOUNDARIES
Hearsay, **Evid Rule 803**

BRIEFS
Foreign countries, judicial notice, **Evid Rule 203**

BUSINESS AND COMMERCE
Corporations, generally, this index
Hearsay, records, **Evid Rule 803**
Incorporation. Corporations, generally, this index
Records and recordation, authentication or identification, **Evid Rule 901 et seq.**
Routine practice, **Evid Rule 406**

CERTIFICATES AND CERTIFICATION
Hearsay, **Evid Rule 803**

CERTIFIED COPIES
Self authentication, **Evid Rule 902**

CHARACTER AND REPUTATION
Generally, **Evid Rules 404, 405**
Admissibility, **Evid Rule 803**
Federal Rules of Evidence, this index
Hearsay, **Evid Rule 803**
Sexual assault, previous sexual conduct, **Evid Rule 412**
Witnesses, **Evid Rule 608**

CHARACTERISTICS
Authentication or identification, **Evid Rule 901 et seq.**

CHEMICALLY DEPENDENT PERSONS
Privileges and immunities, communications, **Evid Rule 510**

CHILDREN AND MINORS
Husband and wife, privileges and immunities, **Evid Rule 504**
Witnesses, competency, **Evid Rule 601**

CHRISTIAN SCIENCE PRACTITIONERS
Communications, privileges and immunities, **Evid Rule 505**

CLERGY
Communications, privileges and immunities, **Evid Rule 505**
Definitions, privileges and immunities, **Evid Rule 505**

CLIENT
Definitions, attorneys, privilege, **Evid Rule 503**

COMMENTS
Privileges and immunities, **Evid Rule 513**

COMMERCE
Business and Commerce, generally, this index

COMMERCIAL PUBLICATIONS
Admissibility, **Evid Rule 803**

COMMUNICATIONS
Alcoholics and intoxicated persons, privileges, **Evid Rule 510**
Authentication, **Evid Rule 901 et seq.**
Clergy, privilege, **Evid Rule 505**
Drug addicts, privileges, **Evid Rule 510**
Optional completeness, **Evid Rule 107**
Related writings or recorded statements, **Evid Rule 106**

COMPETENCY
Witnesses, this index

COMPILATIONS
Authentication, **Evid Rule 901 et seq.**
Evidence, admissibility, **Evid Rule 1005**

COMPLETENESS
Related writings or recorded statements, **Evid Rules 106, 107**

COMPROMISE AND SETTLEMENT
Generally, **Evid Rule 408**

COMPUTERS
Duplicates, admissibility, **Evid Rule 1001 et seq.**
Originals, **Evid Rule 1001 et seq.**

CONDUCT
Character and reputation, **Evid Rules 404, 405**
Witnesses, **Evid Rule 608**

CONFESSION
Suppression, evidence rule, applicability, **Evid Rule 101**

CONFIDENTIAL OR PRIVILEGED INFORMATION
See, also, Privileges and Immunities, generally, this index
Generally, **Evid Rule 501 et seq.**
Definitions, attorneys, privilege, **Evid Rule 503**

CONFUSION
Relevant evidence, exclusion, **Evid Rule 403**

CONSISTENT STATEMENTS
Witnesses, **Evid Rule 613**

CONSTRUCTION OF RULES
Generally, **Evid Rule 102**

CONSUMERS
Subsequent remedial measures, **Evid Rule 407**

CONTEMPT
Application of rules, **Evid Rule 101**
Evidence, rules, application, **Evid Rule 101**

CONVERSATIONS
Communications, generally, this index

CONVICTIONS
Crimes and Offenses, this index

COPIES
Federal Rules of Evidence, this index

CORPORATIONS
Hearsay, records, **Evid Rule 803**
Lawyer client privilege, **Evid Rule 503**
Reports, disclosure, privilege, **Evid Rule 502**
Routine practice, **Evid Rule 406**

CORRECTIONS
Generally, **Evid Rule 103**

COURT INTERPRETERS
Witnesses, **Evid Rule 604**

COURTS
Judges, generally, this index
Jury, generally, this index

CREDIBILITY
Witnesses, this index

CRIME VICTIMS
Character and reputation, **Evid Rules 404, 405**
Exclusion, court, **Evid Rule 614**
Sexual offenses, previous sexual conduct, **Evid Rule 412**

CRIMES AND OFFENSES
See, also, Fines and Penalties, generally, this index
Convictions, hearsay, **Evid Rule 803**
Depositions, generally, this index
Evidence, generally, this index
Federal Rules of Evidence, this index
Fines and Penalties, generally, this index

CROSS EXAMINATIONS
Witnesses, this index

CUSTOMS
Admissibility, **Evid Rule 803**

DATA COMPILATION
Admissibility, **Evid Rule 1005**
Authentication, **Evid Rule 901 et seq.**

DEATH
Certificates, hearsay, **Evid Rule 803**
Witnesses, conversations, deceased, **Evid Rule 601**

DECLARANT
Definitions, hearsay, **Evid Rule 801**

DECLARATIONS
Optional completeness, **Evid Rule 107**
Related writings or recorded statements, **Evid Rule 106**

DEEDS AND CONVEYANCES
Hearsay, **Evid Rule 803**
Records and Recordation, generally, this index

DEFECTS
Notice, **Evid Rule 407**

DEFINITIONS
Words and Phrases, generally, this index

DELAY
Relevant evidence, exclusion, **Evid Rule 403**

DEPOSITIONS
Hearsay, **Evid Rule 801**
Optional completeness, **Evid Rule 107**
Related writings or recorded statements, **Evid Rule 106**

DISCLOSURE
Expert witnesses, **Evid Rule 705**
Federal Rules of Evidence, this index
Privilege and immunities, **Evid Rule 501 et seq.**

DISCRIMINATION
Insurance, witnesses, **Evid Rule 411**
Relevant evidence, exclusion, **Evid Rule 403**

DUPLICATES AND COPIES
Generally, **Evid Rule 1001 et seq.**
Definitions, records, **Evid Rule 1001**

DURESS OR COERCION
Privileges and immunities, **Evid Rule 512**

DYING DECLARATIONS
Hearsay exception, **Evid Rule 804**

ELECTIONS
Privileges and immunities, secret ballots, **Evid Rule 506**
Secret ballot, privilege, **Evid Rule 506**

EMBARRASSMENT
Witnesses, **Evid Rule 611**

EMOTIONAL CONDITION
Hearsay, **Evid Rule 803**

EMOTIONAL ILLNESS
Mental Health, generally, this index

EVIDENCE
Administrative Code, judicial notice, **Evid Rule 204**
Admissibility of evidence, **Evid Rule 401 et seq.**
Duplicates, books and paper, photography and pictures, **Evid Rule 1003**
Hearsay, **Evid Rule 801 et seq.**
Relevancy, **Evid Rule 401 et seq.**
Writings or recordings, **Evid Rule 1001 et seq.**
Admissions, parties, opponents, hearsay, **Evid Rule 801**
Alcohol abusers, communications, **Evid Rule 510**
Application of rules, **Evid Rule 101**
Authentication, **Evid Rule 901 et seq.**
Bad acts, admissibility, **Evid Rule 404**
Bail and Recognizances, this index
Basis of opinion, expert testimony, **Evid Rule 703**
Character evidence, admissibility, conduct, **Evid Rule 404**
Clergy, communications, privilege, **Evid Rule 505**
Coercion, privilege, **Evid Rule 512**
Comments, privilege, **Evid Rule 513**
Compromise and settlement, **Evid Rule 408**
Construction, rules, **Evid Rule 102**
Contents, writings, recordings and photographs, **Evid Rule 1001 et seq.**
Defect, notice, **Evid Rule 407**
Depositions, generally, this index
Disclosure, compulsion, privileged matter, **Evid Rule 512**
Drug abusers, communications, **Evid Rule 510**
Duplicate, books and papers, photography and pictures, **Evid Rule 1003**
Erroneous rulings, **Evid Rule 103**
Exceptions, hearsay, **Evid Rules 803, 804**
Experts, **Evid Rule 701 et seq.**
Federal Rules of Evidence, generally, this index
Foreign countries, judicial notice, laws, **Evid Rule 203**
Foreign states, judicial notice, laws, **Evid Rule 202**
Fundamental errors, notice, **Evid Rule 103**
Habit, admissibility, **Evid Rule 406**
Hearsay, **Evid Rule 801 et seq.**
Federal Rules of Evidence, this index
Husband and wife, privilege, **Evid Rule 504**
Identity and identification, **Evid Rule 901 et seq.**
Inference, claim of privilege, **Evid Rule 513**
Informers, identity and identification, **Evid Rule 508**
Insurance, **Evid Rule 411**
Judicial notice, **Evid Rule 201 et seq.**

EVIDENCE—Cont'd
Jury, this index
Lawyer client privilege, **Evid Rule 503**
Lay witnesses, opinion testimony, **Evid Rule 701**
Limited admissibility, **Evid Rule 105**
Medical expenses, payment, **Evid Rule 409**
Objections and exceptions, erroneous rulings, **Evid Rule 103**
Offer of proof, **Evid Rule 103**
Opinions and expert testimony, **Evid Rule 701 et seq.**
Optional completeness, **Evid Rule 107**
Ordinances, judicial notice, **Evid Rule 204**
Original documents, **Evid Rule 1002**
Parties, admission or testimony, **Evid Rule 1007**
Photography and pictures, content, evidence, **Evid Rule 1001 et seq.**
Physician patient privilege, **Evid Rule 509**
Pleas and plea discussions, **Evid Rule 410**
Political vote, privilege, **Evid Rule 506**
Preliminary questions, **Evid Rule 104**
Previous sexual conduct, **Evid Rule 412**
Privileges, **Evid Rule 501 et seq.**
Punishment, character evidence, relevancy, **Evid Rule 404**
Records and recordation, content, evidence, **Evid Rule 1001 et seq.**
Related writings or recorded statements, **Evid Rule 106**
Relevancy, **Evid Rule 401 et seq.**
Remainder, related writings or recorded statements, **Evid Rule 106**
Remedial measures, **Evid Rule 407**
Reports, organizations, disclosure, privilege, **Evid Rule 502**
Routine practice, admissibility, **Evid Rule 406**
Rulings, **Evid Rule 103**
Scope of rules, **Evid Rule 101**
Self authentication, **Evid Rule 902**
Special grounds, exclusion of relevant evidence, exclusion, **Evid Rule 403**
Subsequent remedial measures, **Evid Rule 407**
Summaries, documents, **Evid Rule 1006**
Titles, rules, **Evid Rule 101**
Trade secrets, privilege, **Evid Rule 507**
Ultimate issues, opinions, expert testimony, **Evid Rule 704**
Underlying facts or data, expert testimony, **Evid Rule 705**
Vote, privilege, **Evid Rule 506**
Waiver, privilege, **Evid Rule 511**
Witnesses, generally, this index
Writings, contents, **Evid Rule 1001 et seq.**

EXAMINATIONS AND EXAMINERS
Cross examinations. Witnesses, this index

EXCEPTIONS
Objections and Exceptions, generally, this index

EXCISED STATEMENTS
Witnesses, **Evid Rule 615**

EXCITED UTTERANCES
Hearsay, **Evid Rule 803**

EXEMPTIONS
Hearsay, **Evid Rules 803, 804**
Husband and wife, privileges, **Evid Rule 504**

EXEMPTIONS—Cont'd
Informers, identity, **Evid Rule 508**
Lawyer client privilege, **Evid Rule 503**

EXTRADITION
Application of rules, **Evid Rule 101**

FAMILY RECORDS
Hearsay, **Evid Rules 803, 804**

FEDERAL RULES OF EVIDENCE
Generally, **FRE 101 et seq.**
Absence and absentees,
Accidents, evidence of other crimes or wrongs, **FRE 404**
Hearsay rule, exception, **FRE 804**
Mistakes, evidence of other crimes or wrongs, **FRE 404**
Accidents, absence and absentees, evidence of other crimes or wrongs, **FRE 404**
Actions and proceedings,
Child molestation, similar crimes, relevancy, **FRE 415**
Sexual assault, similar crimes, relevancy, **FRE 415**
Acts of Congress, self authentication, **FRE 902**
Admiralty, application of rules, **FRE 1101**
Amendments, **FRE 1102**
Ancient documents,
Authentication, **FRE 901**
Hearsay rule, exceptions, **FRE 803**
Annulment, conviction of crime, impeachment, **FRE 609**
Appeal and review, conviction of crime, impeachment, pending appeals, **FRE 609**
Application of rules, **FRE 101, 1101**
Arrest warrants, application of rules, **FRE 1101**
Attorneys, privileges and immunities, **FRE 502**
Authentication, **FRE 901 et seq.**
Bail, application of rules, **FRE 1101**
Baptismal certificates, hearsay rule, exception, **FRE 803**
Bases of opinions, opinion and expert testimony, **FRE 703**
Best Evidence Rule, **FRE 1001 et seq.**
Bias or prejudice,
Compromise and settlement, relevancy, **FRE 408**
Exclusion, **FRE 403**
Liability insurance, relevancy, **FRE 411**
Books and papers,
Best evidence, **FRE 1001 et seq.**
Self authentication, **FRE 902**
Boundaries,
Judgments and decrees, hearsay rule, exception, **FRE 803**
Reputation, hearsay rule, exception, **FRE 803**
Burden of proof, presumptions, **FRE 301**
Capital punishment, impeachment, conviction of crime, **FRE 609**
Character and reputation,
Conviction of crime, **FRE 609**
Hearsay rule, exception, **FRE 803**
Methods of proof, **FRE 405**
Relevancy, **FRE 404**
Witnesses, **FRE 404, 608**
Children and minors,
Juvenile delinquents and dependents, impeachment, conviction of crime, **FRE 609**

FEDERAL RULES OF EVIDENCE—Cont'd
Children and minors—Cont'd
Molestation, similar crimes, relevancy, **FRE 414, 415**
Civil cases, definitions, **FRE 101**
Commercial paper, self authentication, **FRE 902**
Commercial publications, hearsay rule, exception, **FRE 803**
Compensation and salaries, court appointed experts, **FRE 706**
Competency. Witnesses, post
Compromise and settlement, relevancy, **FRE 408**
Confessions, admissibility, **FRE 104**
Confidential or privileged information. Privileges and immunities, generally, post
Confusing evidence, exclusion, **FRE 403**
Contempt, application of rules, **FRE 1101**
Conveyances, hearsay rule, exception, **FRE 803**
Copies,
Admissibility, **FRE 1003**
Best evidence, **FRE 1001 et seq.**
Public records, self authentication, **FRE 902**
Credibility,
Conviction of crime, **FRE 609**
Preliminary determinations, **FRE 104**
Crimes and offenses,
Application of rules, **FRE 1101**
Compromise and settlement, relevancy, **FRE 408**
Conviction of crime,
Judgments and decrees, hearsay rule, exception, **FRE 803**
Witnesses, credibility, **FRE 609**
Definitions, **FRE 101**
Opinion and expert testimony, ultimate issues, **FRE 704**
Cross examinations, **FRE 611**
Calling by court, **FRE 614**
Hearsay, prior statements, **FRE 806**
Impeachment, conviction of crime, **FRE 609**
Preliminary matters, **FRE 104**
Cumulative evidence, exclusion, **FRE 403**
Death penalty, impeachment, conviction of crime, **FRE 609**
Declarants, definitions, hearsay, **FRE 801**
Deeds and conveyances, hearsay rule, exception, **FRE 803**
Definitions, **FRE 101**
Attorney client privilege, **FRE 502**
Best evidence, **FRE 1001**
Child molestation, similar crimes, relevancy, **FRE 414**
Children and minors, molestation, similar crimes, relevancy, **FRE 414**
Hearsay, **FRE 801**
Sexual assault, similar crimes, relevancy, **FRE 413**
Work product protection, **FRE 502**
Direct examination, **FRE 611**
Disclosure,
Attorneys, privileges and immunities, **FRE 502**
Court appointed experts, **FRE 706**
Opinions and expert testimony, facts or data underlying expert opinion, **FRE 705**
Sex offenses, similar crimes, relevancy, **FRE 413 et seq.**
Witnesses, prior statements, **FRE 613**
Domestic public documents, self authentication, **FRE 902**

FEDERAL RULES OF EVIDENCE—Cont'd
Emotional condition then existing, hearsay rule, exception, **FRE 803**
Examinations and examiners, witnesses, **FRE 611**
Excited utterances, hearsay rule, exception, **FRE 803**
Exclusion, witnesses, **FRE 615**
Exemptions, impeachment, conviction of crime, **FRE 609**
Extradition, application of rules, **FRE 1101**
Family history,
Exception, hearsay rule, **FRE 803, 804**
Hearsay rule, exception, **FRE 803, 804**
Foreign countries, records and recordation, self authentication, **FRE 902**
Former testimony, hearsay rule, exception, **FRE 804**
Fraud,
Impeachment, conviction of crime, **FRE 609**
Pleas, relevancy, **FRE 410**
General history,
Judgments and decrees, hearsay rule, exception, **FRE 803**
Reputation, hearsay rule, exceptions, **FRE 803**
Grand jury, application of rules, **FRE 1101**
Habits, relevancy, **FRE 406**
Handwriting, authentication, **FRE 901**
Hearsay, **FRE 801 et seq.**
Admissibility, **FRE 802**
Credibility of declarant, **FRE 806**
Definitions, **FRE 801**
Exceptions,
Declarant availability immaterial, **FRE 803**
Declarant unavailable, **FRE 804**
Hearsay within hearsay, **FRE 805**
Residual exception, **FRE 807**
History,
Judgments and decrees, hearsay rule, exception, **FRE 803**
Reputation, hearsay rule, exception, **FRE 803**
Identity and identification, **FRE 901 et seq.**
Other crimes or wrongs, **FRE 404**
Imminent death, statement made under belief, hearsay rule, exception, **FRE 804**
Immunities. Privileges and immunities, generally, post
Impeachment,
Subsequent remedial measures, relevancy, **FRE 407**
Witnesses, **FRE 607 et seq.**
Indictment and information, validity, jurors, witnesses, **FRE 606**
Instructions, jury,
Judicial notice, **FRE 201**
Limited admissibility, **FRE 105**
Insurance, liability insurance, relevancy, **FRE 411**
Intent, evidence of other crimes or wrongs, **FRE 404**
Interpreters, **FRE 604**
Judges or justices, witnesses, **FRE 605**
Judgments and decrees, conviction of crime, family history, general history, boundaries, hearsay rule, exception, **FRE 803**
Judicial notice, **FRE 201**
Jury,
Competency, witnesses, **FRE 606**
Instructions,
Judicial notice, **FRE 201**
Limited admissibility, **FRE 105**
Photographs and pictures, **FRE 1008**
Preliminary determinations, **FRE 104**

FEDERAL RULES OF EVIDENCE—Cont'd
Jury—Cont'd
Records and recordation, **FRE 1008**
Rulings, **FRE 103**
Witnesses, competency, **FRE 606**
Writings, **FRE 1008**
Juvenile delinquents and dependents, impeachment, conviction of crime, **FRE 609**
Knowledge, evidence of other crimes or wrongs, **FRE 404**
Leading questions, witnesses, **FRE 611**
Learned treatises, hearsay rule, exception, **FRE 803**
Liability insurance, relevancy, **FRE 411**
Limited admissibility, instructions to jury, **FRE 105**
Lost or destroyed originals, other proof, admissibility, **FRE 1004**
Maritime cases, application of rules, **FRE 1101**
Market reports, hearsay rule, exception, **FRE 803**
Marriage certificates, hearsay rule, exception, **FRE 803**
Medical care and treatment,
Payment, relevancy, **FRE 409**
Statements, hearsay rule, exception, **FRE 803**
Mental condition then existing, hearsay rule, exception, **FRE 803**
Mistakes,
Absence and absentees, evidence of other crimes or wrongs, **FRE 404**
Rulings, **FRE 103**
Motive, evidence of other crimes or wrongs, **FRE 404**
Newspapers, self authentication, **FRE 902**
Notice,
Crimes or wrongs, **FRE 404**
Hearsay, residual exception, **FRE 807**
Impeachment, conviction of crime, **FRE 609**
Oaths and affirmations,
Interpreters, **FRE 604**
Witnesses, **FRE 603**
Offenses. Crimes and offenses, generally, ante
Opinion and expert testimony, **FRE 701 et seq.**
Bases of opinion, **FRE 703**
Character evidence, **FRE 405**
Court appointed experts, **FRE 706**
Facts or data underlying expert opinion, disclosure, **FRE 705**
Lay witnesses, **FRE 701**
Ultimate issues, **FRE 704**
Witnesses, **FRE 608**
Opportunity, evidence of other crimes or wrongs, **FRE 404**
Originals, writings, records and recordation, photography and pictures, **FRE 1001 et seq.**
Other crimes or wrongs, relevancy, **FRE 404**
Pamphlets,
Hearsay rule, exception, **FRE 803**
Self authentication, **FRE 902**
Pardons, impeachment, **FRE 609**
Parties,
Statements, hearsay, **FRE 801**
Writings, recordings, or photographs, **FRE 1007**
Admissibility, **FRE 1004**
Past sexual history or predisposition, sex offenses, victims, relevancy, **FRE 412**
Pending appeals, impeachment, conviction of crime, **FRE 609**
Periodicals,
Hearsay rule, exception, **FRE 803**
Self authentication, **FRE 902**

FEDERAL RULES OF EVIDENCE—Cont'd
Personal history,
Exception, hearsay rule, **FRE 803, 804**
Hearsay rule, exception, **FRE 803, 804**
Personal knowledge, witnesses, competency, **FRE 602**
Personal property, records and recordation, hearsay rule, exception, **FRE 803**
Photography and pictures, best evidence, **FRE 1001 et seq.**
Physical condition then existing, hearsay rule, exception, **FRE 803**
Plain errors, **FRE 103**
Plans and specifications, evidence of other crimes or wrongs, **FRE 404**
Plea of nolo contendere, relevancy, **FRE 410**
Pleas, relevancy, **FRE 410**
Preliminary examination, **FRE 104**
Facts, application of rules, **FRE 1101**
Preparation, evidence of other crimes or wrongs, **FRE 404**
Present sense impressions, hearsay rule, exception, **FRE 803**
Presumptions, **FRE 301**
State laws, **FRE 302**
Previous conviction of crime, hearsay rule, exception, **FRE 803**
Prior conviction, impeachment, conviction of crime, **FRE 609**
Prior statements,
Hearsay, **FRE 801, 806**
Witnesses, **FRE 613**
Privileges and immunities, **FRE 501**
Application of rules, **FRE 1101**
Attorneys, **FRE 502**
Preliminary determinations, **FRE 104**
Self incrimination, character and reputation, **FRE 608**
Probation, application of rules, **FRE 1101**
Procurement, witnesses, hearsay rule, exception, **FRE 804**
Property, records and recordation, hearsay rule, exception, **FRE 803**
Public offices, definitions, **FRE 101**
Purpose of rules, **FRE 102**
Rape shield, victims of crime, past sexual history or predisposition, **FRE 412**
Real estate, records and recordation, hearsay rule, exception, **FRE 803**
Recorded recollections, hearsay rule, exception, **FRE 803**
Records and recordation,
Absence of entry, hearsay rule, exception, **FRE 803**
Authentication, **FRE 901**
Best evidence, **FRE 1001 et seq.**
Copies, admissibility, **FRE 1005**
Definitions, **FRE 101**
Extrinsic evidence of contents, **FRE 1005**
Hearsay rule, exception, **FRE 803**
Offers of evidence, **FRE 103**
Self authentication, **FRE 902**
Refreshing memory, witnesses, writings, **FRE 612**
Regularly conducted activities, records and recordation,
Hearsay rule, exception, **FRE 803**
Self authentication, **FRE 902**
Rehabilitation certificates, conviction of crime, impeachment, **FRE 609**

FEDERAL RULES OF EVIDENCE—Cont'd
Related writings, **FRE 106**
Relevancy, **FRE 401 et seq.**
  Admissibility, **FRE 402**
  Character evidence, **FRE 404, 405**
  Compromise and settlement, **FRE 408**
  Conditioned on fact, preliminary determinations, **FRE 104**
  Confusing evidence, **FRE 403**
  Crimes and offenses,
    Compromise and settlement, **FRE 408**
    Other crimes or wrongs, **FRE 404**
  Cumulative evidence, **FRE 403**
  Habit, **FRE 406**
  Liability insurance, **FRE 411**
  Medical care and treatment, payment, **FRE 409**
  Pleas, **FRE 410**
  Prejudicial evidence, **FRE 403**
  Routine practices, **FRE 406**
  Sex offenses, **FRE 412 et seq.**
  Subsequent remedial measures, **FRE 407**
Religion, impeachment, **FRE 610**
Religious organizations and societies, records and recordation, hearsay rule, exception, **FRE 803**
Rendition, application of rules, **FRE 1101**
Reports, public reports, hearsay rule, exception, **FRE 803**
Rest of writings, **FRE 106**
Routine, relevancy, **FRE 406**
Rule prescribed by the Supreme Court, definitions, **FRE 101**
Rulings, **FRE 103**
Scope of rules, **FRE 101**
Searches and seizures, warrants, application of rules, **FRE 1101**
Self authentication, **FRE 902**
Self incrimination, character and reputation, **FRE 608**
Sentence and punishment, application of rules, **FRE 1101**
Settlement and compromise, relevancy, **FRE 408**
Sex offenses, **FRE 412 et seq.**
  Children and minors, molestation, similar crimes, relevancy, **FRE 414, 415**
  Civil cases, similar crimes, relevancy, **FRE 415**
  Definitions, similar crimes, relevancy, **FRE 413**
  Relevancy, **FRE 412 et seq.**
  Similar crimes, relevancy, **FRE 413 et seq.**
  Victims past sexual behavior or predisposition, relevancy, **FRE 412**
Specific instances of conduct,
  Character evidence, **FRE 405**
  Witnesses, **FRE 608**
Statements, hearsay, **FRE 801 et seq.**
Statements against interest, hearsay rule, exception, **FRE 804**
Statutes, self authentication, **FRE 902**
Subsequent remedial measures, relevancy, **FRE 407**
Summaries, writings, recordings, or photographs, admissibility, **FRE 1006**
Summons, criminal cases, application of rules, **FRE 1101**
Telecommunications, authentication, **FRE 901**
Time,
  Conviction of crime, impeachment, **FRE 609**
  Judicial notice, **FRE 201**
Trade inscriptions, self authentication, **FRE 902**

FEDERAL RULES OF EVIDENCE—Cont'd
Ultimate issues, opinion and expert testimony, **FRE 704**
Unavailable declarants wrongfully caused, **FRE 801 et seq.**
Unobtainable originals, other proof, admissibility, **FRE 1004**
Verdicts, validity, jurors, witnesses, **FRE 606**
Victims of crime,
  Character evidence, **FRE 404**
  Sex offenses, past sexual behavior or predisposition, relevancy, **FRE 412**
Vital statistics, records and recordation, hearsay rule, exception, **FRE 803**
Voices, authentication, **FRE 901**
Waiver, attorneys, privileges and immunities, **FRE 502**
Weight of evidence, preliminary determinations, **FRE 104**
Witnesses,
  Calling by court, **FRE 614**
  Character and reputation, **FRE 404, 608**
  Competency, **FRE 601 et seq.**
    Judges and justices, **FRE 605**
    Jurors, **FRE 606**
    Personal knowledge, **FRE 602**
  Conviction of crime, credibility, **FRE 609**
  Crimes and offenses,
    Conviction of crime, credibility, **FRE 609**
    Refreshing memory, writings, **FRE 612**
  Cross examinations, generally, ante
  Direct examination, **FRE 611**
  Examinations and examiners, **FRE 611**
  Exclusion, **FRE 615**
  Impeachment, **FRE 607 et seq.**
  Interrogation, **FRE 611, 614**
  Leading questions, **FRE 611**
  Oaths and affirmations, **FRE 603**
  Opinion and expert testimony, generally, ante
  Presentation, **FRE 611**
  Prior statements, **FRE 613**
  Qualifications, preliminary determinations, **FRE 104**
  Refreshing memory, writings, **FRE 612**
  Specific instances of conduct, **FRE 608**
  Writings,
    Authentication, **FRE 903**
    Refreshing memory, **FRE 612**
Work product, **FRE 502**
Writings, best evidence, **FRE 1001 et seq.**

FIDUCIARIES
Personal representatives. Probate Proceedings, this index

FILMS
Duplicates, admissibility, **Evid Rule 1001 et seq.**
  Originals, **Evid Rule 1001 et seq.**

FINES AND PENALTIES
Application of rules, **Evid Rule 101**
Character and reputation, **Evid Rules 404, 405**
Evidence,
  Character evidence, **Evid Rule 404**
  Rules, application, **Evid Rule 101**

FOREIGN COUNTRIES
Judicial notice, **Evid Rule 203**

FOREIGN COUNTRIES—Cont'd
Writings, authentication or identification, **Evid Rule 901 et seq.**

FOREIGN DOCUMENTS
Authentication or identification, **Evid Rule 901 et seq.**
Translations, **Evid Rule 1009**

FOREIGN LANGUAGES
Translations, **Evid Rule 1009**

FOREIGN STATES
Judicial notice, **Evid Rule 202**

FORMER TESTIMONY
Witnesses, **Evid Rule 804**

FORMS
Records and recordation, authentication or identification, affidavit, **Evid Rule 902**

FRAUD
Lawyer client privilege, exemption, **Evid Rule 503**

FUNDAMENTAL ERRORS
Generally, **Evid Rule 103**

GENEALOGY
Hearsay, **Evid Rule 803**

GRAND JURY
Application of rules, **Evid Rule 101**
Evidence, rules, application, **Evid Rule 101**

GUARDIAN AND WARD
Lawyer client privilege, **Evid Rule 503**

GUILTY PLEAS
Admissibility, **Evid Rule 410**

HABEAS CORPUS
Application of rules, **Evid Rule 101**
Evidence, application, rules, **Evid Rule 101**

HABIT
Generally, **Evid Rule 406**

HANDWRITING
Writings, generally, this index

HARASSMENT
Witnesses, **Evid Rule 611**

HEARING IMPAIRED PERSONS
Lawyer client privilege, **Evid Rule 503**

HEARSAY
Evidence, this index

HEARSAY WITHIN HEARSAY
Generally, **Evid Rule 805**

HOMICIDE
Character and reputation, victims, **Evid Rule 404**

HOSTILE WITNESSES
Leading questions, **Evid Rule 611**

HUNG JURY
Mistrial. Trial, this index

HUSBAND AND WIFE
Privileges and immunities, **Evid Rule 504**

IDENTITY AND IDENTIFICATION
Generally, **Evid Rule 901 et seq.**
Character and reputation, **Evid Rules 404, 405**
Informer, privilege, **Evid Rule 508**

ILLEGALITY
Evidence, suppression, **Evid Rule 101**

IMMUNITIES
Privileges and Immunities, generally, this index

IMPEACHMENT
Witnesses, this index

IMPRISONMENT
Fines and Penalties, generally, this index

INCOMPETENCY
Mental Health, generally, this index

INCONSISTENT STATEMENTS
Witnesses, **Evid Rule 613**

INDICTMENT AND INFORMATION
Jury, witness, **Evid Rule 606**

INFERENCES
Expert witnesses, **Evid Rule 703**
Privileges and immunities, **Evid Rule 513**

INFORMER
Identity and identification, privilege, **Evid Rule 508**

INSANE PERSONS
Mental Health, generally, this index

INSURANCE
Admissibility, **Evid Rule 411**
Discrimination, witnesses, **Evid Rule 411**

INTENT
Character and reputation, **Evid Rules 404, 405**

INTERPRETERS
Witnesses, this index

INTERROGATION
Witnesses, **Evid Rule 611**

IRRELEVANT EVIDENCE
Generally, **Evid Rule 402**

JUDGES
Comment, privilege, **Evid Rule 513**
Competency, witnesses, **Evid Rule 605**
Witnesses, competency, **Evid Rule 605**

JUDGMENTS AND DECREES
Admissibility, **Evid Rule 803**

JUDICIAL NOTICE
Generally, **Evid Rule 201 et seq.**
Adjudicative facts, **Evid Rule 201**
Administrative Code, **Evid Rule 204**
Foreign countries, **Evid Rule 203**
Foreign states, **Evid Rule 202**
Ordinances, city or county, **Evid Rule 204**
Texas Register, **Evid Rule 204**

JURY
Duplicates or copies, books and papers, **Evid Rule 1008**
Evidence, hearings,
Preliminary questions, **Evid Rule 104**
Rulings, **Evid Rule 103**
Federal Rules of Evidence, this index
Mistrial. Trial, this index
Objections and exceptions, witnesses, competency, **Evid Rule 606**
Original documents, **Evid Rule 1008**
Preliminary questions, **Evid Rule 104**
Privileges and immunities, comment or inference, **Evid Rule 513**
Witnesses, competence, **Evid Rule 606**

JUVENILE DELINQUENTS AND DEPENDENTS
Witnesses, impeachment, **Evid Rule 609**

KNOWLEDGE
Authentication and identification, **Evid Rule 901 et seq.**
Character and reputation, **Evid Rules 404, 405**
Witnesses, **Evid Rule 602**

LAWYER CLIENT PRIVILEGE
Generally, **Evid Rule 503**

LAY WITNESSES
Opinions and decisions, **Evid Rule 701**

LEADING QUESTIONS
Witnesses, **Evid Rule 611**

LEARNED TREATISES
Admissibility, **Evid Rule 803**

LIABILITY INSURANCE
Admissibility, **Evid Rule 411**

LIMITED ADMISSIBILITY
Generally, **Evid Rule 105**

LOST OR DESTROYED INSTRUMENTS
Duplicates, **Evid Rule 1004**

MAGAZINES
Authentication or identification, **Evid Rule 901 et seq.**
Self authentication, **Evid Rule 902**

MANUFACTURERS AND MANUFACTURING
Subsequent remedial measures, **Evid Rule 407**

MARKET REPORTS
Admissibility, **Evid Rule 803**

MARRIAGE
Hearsay, certificates and certification, **Evid Rule 803**

MATTER ASSERTED
Definitions, hearsay, **Evid Rule 801**

MEDICAL CARE AND TREATMENT
Alcoholics and intoxicated persons, communications, privileges, **Evid Rule 510**
Drug addicts, communications, privileges, **Evid Rule 510**
Expenses, self authentication, affidavits, **Evid Rule 902**

MEDICAL CARE AND TREATMENT—Cont'd
Hearsay, **Evid Rule 803**
Payment, **Evid Rule 409**

MEMORANDUMS
Hearsay, **Evid Rule 803**

MEMORY
Witnesses, refreshing, **Evid Rule 612**

MENTAL HEALTH
Hearsay, **Evid Rule 803**
Privileges and immunities, **Evid Rule 510**
Witnesses, competency, **Evid Rule 601**

MILITARY FORCES
Application of rules, **Evid Rule 101**
Evidence, rules, application, **Evid Rule 101**

MISLEADING EVIDENCE
Exclusion, **Evid Rule 403**

MISSIONS
Hearsay, **Evid Rule 801**

MISTRIAL
Trial, this index

MOTION PICTURES
Duplicates, admissibility, **Evid Rule 1001 et seq.**
Originals, **Evid Rule 1001 et seq.**

MOTIONS
Judicial notice, foreign states, **Evid Rule 202**
Witnesses, production, statements, **Evid Rule 615**

NEGLIGENCE
Insurance, admissibility, **Evid Rule 411**
Subsequent remedial measures, **Evid Rule 407**

NEGOTIABLE INSTRUMENTS
Authentication or identification, **Evid Rule 901 et seq.**
Self authentication, **Evid Rule 902**

NEWSPAPERS
Authentication or identification, **Evid Rule 901 et seq.**
Self authentication, **Evid Rule 902**

NOLO CONTENDERE PLEA
Admissibility, **Evid Rule 410**

NON COMPOS MENTIS
Mental Health, generally, this index

NOTICE
Defects, **Evid Rule 407**
Federal Rules of Evidence, this index
Judicial Notice, generally, this index
Sexual assault, previous sexual conduct, **Evid Rule 412**
Witnesses, conviction of crime, impeachment, **Evid Rule 609**

NUMBERS AND NUMBERING
Duplicates, admissibility, **Evid Rule 1001 et seq.**
Originals, **Evid Rule 1001 et seq.**

OATHS AND AFFIRMATIONS
Witnesses, this index

OBJECTIONS AND EXCEPTIONS
Erroneous rulings, **Evid Rule 103**
Evidence, this index
Husband and wife, privileges, **Evid Rule 504**
Jury, this index
Witnesses, refreshing memory, **Evid Rule 612**

OFFERS OF PROOF
Erroneous rulings, **Evid Rule 103**

OPINION AND EXPERT TESTIMONY
Witnesses, this index

OPINIONS AND DECISIONS
Character and reputation, **Evid Rule 405**
Witnesses, religion, **Evid Rule 610**

OPPORTUNITY
Character and reputation, **Evid Rules 404, 405**

OPTIONAL COMPLETENESS
Generally, **Evid Rule 107**

ORDINANCES
Judicial notice, **Evid Rule 204**

ORIGINAL
Definitions, records, **Evid Rule 1001**

ORIGINAL DOCUMENTS
Generally, **Evid Rule 1001 et seq.**

PARDONS AND REPRIEVES
Witnesses, conviction of crime, impeachment, **Evid Rule 609**

PAROLE
Application, rules, **Evid Rule 101**
Evidence, rules, application, **Evid Rule 101**

PARTIES
Depositions, generally, this index
Federal Rules of Evidence, this index

PARTNERSHIPS
Routine practice, **Evid Rule 406**

PATIENTS
Physician patient privilege, **Evid Rule 509**

PATTERNS
Authentication or identification, **Evid Rule 901 et seq.**

PAYMENT
Medical care and treatment, **Evid Rule 409**

PENALTIES
Fines and Penalties, generally, this index

PERSONAL INJURIES
Medical care and treatment, payment, **Evid Rule 409**

PERSONAL KNOWLEDGE
Witnesses, **Evid Rule 602**

PERSONAL PROPERTY
Records and Recordation, generally, this index

PERSONAL REPRESENTATIVES
Probate Proceedings, this index

PETIT JURIES
Jury, generally, this index

PHOTOCOPIES
Authentication or identification, **Evid Rule 901 et seq.**
Originals, **Evid Rule 1001 et seq.**

PHOTOGRAPHY AND PICTURES
Definitions, **Evid Rule 1001**
Originals, **Evid Rule 1001 et seq.**

PHRASES
Words and Phrases, generally, this index

PHYSICAL CONDITION
Hearsay, **Evid Rule 803**

PHYSICIAN PATIENT PRIVILEGE
Generally, **Evid Rule 509**

PHYSICIANS AND SURGEONS
Medical Care and Treatment, generally, this index
Privileges and immunities, **Evid Rule 509**
  Mental health, information, **Evid Rule 510**

PLANS AND SPECIFICATIONS
Character and reputation, **Evid Rules 404, 405**

PLEAS
Admissibility, **Evid Rule 410**

POLITICAL VOTE
Secret ballot, privilege, **Evid Rule 506**

POPULAR NAME LAWS
Rape Shield Law, **Evid Rule 412**

PORTRAITS
Family portraits, hearsay, **Evid Rule 803**

PREJUDICE
Bias or Prejudice, generally, this index

PRELIMINARY QUESTIONS
Generally, **Evid Rule 104**

PRESENT SENSE IMPRESSION
Hearsay, **Evid Rule 803**

PRESUMPTIONS
Self authentication, **Evid Rule 902**

PRETRIAL DETENTION
Application of rules, **Evid Rule 101**

PRIMA FACIE EVIDENCE
Evidence, generally, this index

PRIOR STATEMENTS
Witnesses, **Evid Rule 613**
  Hearsay, **Evid Rule 801**

PRIORITIES AND PREFERENCES
Rules, **Evid Rule 101**

PRIVILEGED COMMUNICATIONS
Witnesses, **Evid Rule 501**

PRIVILEGES AND IMMUNITIES
  Generally, **Evid Rule 501 et seq.**
Alcoholics and intoxicated persons, **Evid Rule 510**

PRIVILEGES AND IMMUNITIES—Cont'd
Application of rules, **Evid Rule 101**
Bigamy, husband and wife, exemptions, **Evid Rule 504**
Clergy, communications to, **Evid Rule 505**
Comments, **Evid Rule 513**
Drug abusers, **Evid Rule 510**
Federal Rules of Evidence, this index
Husband and wife, **Evid Rule 504**
Informers, identity and identification, **Evid Rule 508**
Lawyer client privilege, **Evid Rule 503**
Organization reports, **Evid Rule 502**
Physician patient privilege, **Evid Rule 509**
Political vote, **Evid Rule 506**
Preliminary questions, **Evid Rule 104**
Revocation or suspension, evidence rules, application, **Evid Rule 101**
Trade secrets, **Evid Rule 507**
Waiver, **Evid Rule 511**
Witnesses, **Evid Rule 501**

PROBATE PROCEEDINGS
Personal representatives, lawyer client privilege, **Evid Rule 503**
Witnesses, **Evid Rule 601**

PRODUCTION
Witnesses, statements, **Evid Rule 615**

PRODUCTS LIABILITY
Subsequent remedial measures, **Evid Rule 407**

PROOF
Evidence, generally, this index

PSYCHIATRISTS AND PSYCHIATRY
Privileges and immunities, **Evid Rule 510**

PSYCHOLOGISTS
Privileges and immunities, **Evid Rule 510**

PUBLIC RECORDS
Records and Recordation, generally, this index

PUBLICATION
Self authentication, **Evid Rule 902**

PUNISHMENT
Fines and Penalties, generally, this index

PURPOSE
Rules, **Evid Rule 102**

QUESTIONS
Preliminary questions, **Evid Rule 104**
Witnesses, leading question, **Evid Rule 611**

RAPE
Shield Law, **Evid Rule 412**
Victims, previous sexual conduct, **Evid Rule 412**

RAPE SHIELD LAW
Generally, **Evid Rule 412**

REAL ESTATE
Hearsay, **Evid Rule 803**
Records and Recordation, generally, this index

RECORDED RECOLLECTION
Hearsay, **Evid Rule 803**

RECORDS AND RECORDATION
Admissibility, evidence, **Evid Rule 1001 et seq.**
Authentication or identification, **Evid Rule 901 et seq.**
Definitions, **Evid Rule 1001**
Duplicates, admissibility, **Evid Rule 1001 et seq.**
Erroneous rulings, **Evid Rule 103**
Evidence, this index
Federal Rules of Evidence, this index
Hearsay, recollection, **Evid Rule 803**
Identification, **Evid Rule 901 et seq.**
Optional completeness, **Evid Rule 107**
Originals, **Evid Rule 1001 et seq.**
Related writings or recorded statements, **Evid Rule 106**
Self authentication, **Evid Rule 902**

REFRESHING MEMORY
Witnesses, **Evid Rule 612**

REGISTER OF TEXAS
Judicial notice, **Evid Rule 204**

RELEVANCY
Generally, **Evid Rule 401 et seq.**
Federal Rules of Evidence, this index
Preliminary questions, **Evid Rule 104**

RELEVANT EVIDENCE
Definitions, **Evid Rule 401**

RELIGION
Witnesses, **Evid Rule 610**

RELIGIOUS ORGANIZATIONS AND SOCIETIES
Hearsay, records, **Evid Rule 803**

REMEDIAL MEASURES
Subsequent measures, **Evid Rule 407**

RENDITION
Application of rules, **Evid Rule 101**

REPORTS
Audits and auditors, admissibility, **Evid Rule 706**
Authentication or identification, **Evid Rule 901 et seq.**
Evidence, this index
Hearsay, **Evid Rule 803**
Privileges and immunities, **Evid Rule 502**

REPRESENTATIVE OF THE LAWYER
Definitions, privilege, **Evid Rule 503**

REPUTATION
Character and Reputation, generally, this index

RETARDED PERSONS
Mental Health, generally, this index

ROUTINE PRACTICES
Generally, **Evid Rule 406**

SCIENTIFIC EXPERTS
Generally, **Evid Rule 702 et seq.**

SCOPE OF RULES
Limited admissibility, **Evid Rule 101**

SEALS
Self authentication, **Evid Rule 902**

SEARCHES AND SEIZURES
Second and subsequent offenses, admissibility, **Evid Rule 803**
Warrants, evidence, rules, application, **Evid Rule 101**

SECRETS AND SECRECY
Trade secrets, privileges, **Evid Rule 507**

SELF AUTHENTICATION
Generally, **Evid Rule 902**

SENTENCE AND PUNISHMENT
Fines and Penalties, generally, this index

SEX OFFENSES
Federal Rules of Evidence, this index
Victims, previous sexual conduct, **Evid Rule 412**

SMALL CLAIMS COURTS
Evidence, rules, application, **Evid Rule 101**

SOUND RECORDINGS
Duplicates, admissibility, **Evid Rule 1001 et seq.**

SPIRITUAL ADVISOR
Communications, privileges and immunities, **Evid Rule 505**

STATE HOSPITALS
Mental Health, generally, this index

STATEMENTS
Definitions,
  Hearsay, **Evid Rule 801**
  Witnesses, **Evid Rule 615**
Pleas, admissibility, **Evid Rule 410**

STATEMENTS AGAINST INTEREST
Admissibility, **Evid Rule 803**

STRICT LIABILITY
Subsequent remedial measures, **Evid Rule 407**

SUBSCRIBING WITNESS
Authentication or identification, **Evid Rule 903**

SUBSEQUENT REMEDIAL MEASURES
Generally, **Evid Rule 407**

SUMMARIES
Admissibility, **Evid Rule 1006**

SYSTEMS
Authentication or identification, **Evid Rule 901 et seq.**

TAPE AND SOUND RECORDINGS
Duplicates, admissibility, **Evid Rule 1001 et seq.**
Originals, **Evid Rule 1001 et seq.**

TECHNICAL EXPERTS
Generally, **Evid Rule 702 et seq.**

TELECOMMUNICATIONS
Authentication or identification, **Evid Rule 901 et seq.**

TESTIMONY
Evidence, generally, this index
Witnesses, generally, this index

TEXAS REGISTER
Judicial notice, **Evid Rule 204**

TIME
Witnesses, conviction of crime, impeachment, **Evid Rule 609**

TITLE TO PROPERTY
Hearsay, records, **Evid Rule 803**
Insurance, admissibility, **Evid Rule 411**

TOMBSTONES
Hearsay, **Evid Rule 803**

TRADE
Business and Commerce, generally, this index

TRADE SECRETS
Privileges and immunities, **Evid Rule 507**

TRADEMARKS AND TRADE NAMES
Self authentication, **Evid Rule 902**

TRAITS
Character and reputation, **Evid Rules 404, 405**

TRANSLATIONS
Foreign languages, documents, **Evid Rule 1009**

TREATISES
Foreign countries, judicial, **Evid Rule 203**
Hearsay, **Evid Rule 803**

TREATMENT
Medical Care and Treatment, generally, this index

TRIAL
Depositions, generally, this index
Evidence, generally, this index
Jury, generally, this index
Mistrial, witnesses, statements, production, **Evid Rule 615**
Witnesses, generally, this index

TRUSTS AND TRUSTEES
Lawyer client privilege, **Evid Rule 503**

ULTIMATE ISSUES
Expert witnesses, **Evid Rule 704**

UNAVAILABILITY
Declarant, hearsay exception, **Evid Rule 804**

URNS
Family records, hearsay, **Evid Rule 803**

VENIRE
Jury, generally, this index

VERDICTS
Witnesses, **Evid Rule 606**

VICTIMS
Crime Victims, generally, this index

VIDEO TAPES
Duplicates, admissibility, **Evid Rule 1001 et seq.**
Originals, **Evid Rule 1001 et seq.**

VITAL STATISTICS
Hearsay, **Evid Rule 803**

VOICE IDENTIFICATION
Generally, **Evid Rule 901 et seq.**

VOIR DIRE EXAMINATION
Expert witnesses, **Evid Rule 705**

VOLUNTARY DISCLOSURE
Privileges and immunities, waiver, **Evid Rule 511**

WARRANTS
Arrest, this index
Searches and Seizures, this index

WITNESSES
Generally, **Evid Rule 601 et seq.**
Appeal and review, conviction of crime, impeachment, **Evid Rule 609**
Authentication, **Evid Rule 901 et seq.**
Balancing test, expert witnesses, **Evid Rule 705**
Character and reputation, **Evid Rules 404, 405, 608**
Children and minors, competency, **Evid Rule 601**
Competency, **Evid Rule 601**
Application of rules, **Evid Rule 101**
Judges, **Evid Rule 605**
Jury, **Evid Rule 606**
Conduct, **Evid Rule 608**
Consistent statements, **Evid Rule 613**
Conviction of crime, impeachment, **Evid Rule 609**
Credibility,
Conviction of crime, **Evid Rule 609**
Hearsay, **Evid Rule 806**
Impeachment, **Evid Rule 607**
Cross examinations, **Evid Rule 611**
Character and reputation, **Evid Rule 405**
Federal Rules of Evidence, this index
Declarants, unavailable, **Evid Rule 804**
Depositions, generally, this index
Disclosure, expert witnesses, **Evid Rule 705**
Embarrassment, **Evid Rule 611**
Excised statements, **Evid Rule 615**
Exclusion, **Evid Rule 614**
Experts. Opinion and expert testimony, generally, post
Federal Rules of Evidence, this index
Former testimony, **Evid Rule 804**
Harassment, **Evid Rule 611**
Hearsay, prior statements, **Evid Rule 801**
Hostile witnesses, leading questions, **Evid Rule 611**
Identity and identification, **Evid Rule 901 et seq.**
Impeachment,
Conviction of crime, **Evid Rule 609**
Credibility, **Evid Rule 607**
Prior statements, **Evid Rule 613**
Incompetency, **Evid Rule 601**
Inconsistent statements, **Evid Rule 613**
Inferences, expert witnesses, **Evid Rule 703**
Insurance, bias or prejudice, **Evid Rule 411**
Interpreters, **Evid Rule 604**
Interrogation, **Evid Rule 611**
Judges, **Evid Rule 605**
Jury, this index
Juvenile delinquents and dependents, impeachment, **Evid Rule 609**
Knowledge,
Authentication and identification, **Evid Rule 901 et seq.**
Personal knowledge, **Evid Rule 602**
Lay witnesses, opinions, **Evid Rule 701**
Leading questions, **Evid Rule 611**

WITNESSES—Cont'd
Memory, refreshing, **Evid Rule 612**
Mental health, competency, **Evid Rule 601**
Mistrial, statements, production, **Evid Rule 615**
Motions, production, statements, **Evid Rule 615**
Notice, conviction of crime, impeachment, **Evid Rule 609**
Oaths and affirmations, **Evid Rule 603**
Opinion and expert testimony, **Evid Rule 701 et seq.**
Authentication or identification, **Evid Rule 901 et seq.**
Federal Rules of Evidence, this index
Lay witnesses, **Evid Rule 701**
Religion, **Evid Rule 610**
Personal knowledge, **Evid Rule 602**
Preliminary questions, **Evid Rule 104**
Prior statements, **Evid Rules 613, 801**
Privileges and immunities, **Evid Rule 501**
Production, statements, **Evid Rule 615**
Questions, leading questions, **Evid Rule 611**
Refreshing memory, **Evid Rule 612**
Religion, opinions and decisions, **Evid Rule 610**
Statements,
Prior statements, **Evid Rules 613, 801**
Production of, **Evid Rule 615**
Subscribing witnesses, authentication, **Evid Rule 903**
Ultimate issues, expert witnesses, **Evid Rule 704**
Voir dire, expert witnesses, **Evid Rule 705**
Writings, testimony on, **Evid Rule 1007**

WORDS AND PHRASES
Business, hearsay, **Evid Rule 803**
Clergy, privilege, **Evid Rule 505**
Client, attorneys, privilege, **Evid Rule 503**
Confidential,
Attorneys, privilege, **Evid Rule 503**
Clergyman, privilege, **Evid Rule 505**
Declarant, hearsay, **Evid Rule 801**
Duplicates,
Admissibility, **Evid Rule 1001 et seq.**
Records, **Evid Rule 1001**
Hearsay, **Evid Rule 801**
Lawyer, privilege, **Evid Rule 503**
Matter asserted, hearsay, **Evid Rule 801**
Original, records, **Evid Rule 1001 et seq.**
Photography and pictures, **Evid Rule 1001**
Recordings, **Evid Rule 1001**
Relevant evidence, **Evid Rule 401**
Representative of the lawyer, privilege, **Evid Rule 503**
Statements,
Hearsay, **Evid Rule 801**
Witnesses, **Evid Rule 615**
Unavailability as a witness, hearsay exception, **Evid Rule 804**
Writings, **Evid Rule 1001**

WORK PRODUCT
Lawyer client privilege, **Evid Rule 503**

WRITINGS
Authentication or identification, **Evid Rule 901 et seq.**
Definitions, **Evid Rule 1001**
Duplicates, admissibility, **Evid Rule 1001**
Evidence, contents, **Evid Rule 1001 et seq.**

WRITINGS—Cont'd
Identification, **Evid Rule 901 et seq.**
Optional completeness, **Evid Rule 107**
Originals, **Evid Rule 1001 et seq.**
Related writings or recorded statements, **Evid Rule 106**
Self authentication, **Evid Rule 902**
Witnesses, refreshing memory, **Evid Rule 612**

X RAYS
Duplicates, admissibility, **Evid Rule 1001 et seq.**
Originals, **Evid Rule 1001 et seq.**

†